A
WORLD
OF
VILLAGES

Books by Brian M. Schwartz

China Off the Beaten Track
A World of Villages

A WORLD

OF VILLAGES

BY BRIAN M. SCHWARTZ

Crown Publishers, Inc., New York

Published by Crown Publishers, Inc.,
225 Park Avenue South, New York, New York 10003
Manufactured in the United States of America

Crown is a trademark of Crown Publishers, Inc.
Designed by Dana Sloan
10   9   8   7   6   5   4   3   2   1
First Edition

Library of Congress Cataloging-in-Publication Data

Schwartz, Brian.
A world of villages.

Includes index.
1. Schwartz, Brian.   2. Voyages and travels—
              1952–   . I. Title.
G465.S38   1986   910.4   85-24249
              ISBN 0-517-55815-7

CONTENTS

ACKNOWLEDGMENTS

A writer writes alone. His words tumble forth from a magical inner void that is mysterious even to himself, and that no one else can enter. Nevertheless, this book might never have been written without the generous help, guidance, and support provided by a few close friends during the long years of writing. Foremost among them are my parents, Professor Bernard Schwartz and Judge Aileen H. Schwartz; my agent, Gerard McCauley; my editor, James O. Wade, who like Phidias strives for excellence even when only the gods are watching; Ann Wren; and Anne Williams. Belated thanks are also due to those whose words and deeds inspired me and helped shape my life: my grandparents; my teachers at school; my tutors at Oxford, John Simopoulos and Wilfrid Knapp; my friends and professors at Yale Law School; and Judge Irving R. Kaufman and my fellow law clerks on the U.S. Court of Appeals. Thanks also to the entire hardworking staff of Crown Publishers, especially Jane von Mehren.

But I am indebted most of all to the people of the villages I visited. They took me, a stranger, into their homes and lives without question or hesitation or grumbling about an extra mouth to feed. They made me feel welcome when I was lonely and very far from home. This is *their* book.

LIST OF MAPS

A
WORLD
OF
VILLAGES

1

AFRICA: OVERTURE

I reached Douala just before the rains. In the poorer part of town, where the pavement ended, market women sat beside the dusty road, selling huge green mangoes. I stopped outside a beer hall and ate a mango while watching the noisy drinkers inside. Beer was beyond my means. Much of my money had gone to the Central African police and I had spent most of the rest when, after four dust-filled days of waving at trucks that never stopped, I decided to pay my way to the Cameroun frontier. Cameroun is the hinge between West and Central Africa; a few days' journey west of the border, the jungles of the interior give way to the palm groves of the Atlantic coast. The night before, I had slept on a beach, but Douala offered more elegant accommodation. Less than a mile away, just beyond the suburban shantytowns, the glass-and-steel buildings of the international airport shimmered in the heat haze like a modern mirage.

I was nudged awake in the middle of the night and looked up at the neatly pressed khaki uniform of the airport guard. When he realized that I was not African, he became friendlier, but the sight of a white man forced to sleep on floors puzzled him. I told him of my journey, west through Singapore, India, Afghanistan, and on to Cairo, then south, following the Nile, then west again, through the Congo Basin, hitching across the center of the continent. It had taken me three years to reach Douala, and though I did not know it then, I had three years more to travel. As I talked, the guard stared at my muddy backpack and the patches on my jeans. "We Africans cannot understand," he said, "why you should suffer so much to see our country."

I could have told him that to sleep on the red earth of a village street was no hardship at all, if I could wake to the sound of laughter and pestles pounding corn and cassava, to the smell of the dew-damp forest, so strong, so rich with life that, when I breathed it in, it burned in my blood like malaria. Woodland, desert, rice fields, savannah—wherever I traveled, I learned new rhythms from the land; the people I met, and the friends I made, taught me even more. Such knowledge, I wanted to tell the guard, was worth any sacrifice.

But I came from a country that produced televisions and rocket ships and Cadillacs, a land where a man could earn enough to buy all his dreams, and the guard could never have grasped why I had forsaken such a paradise to seek a life he yearned to leave behind. Had I tried to tell him, he would have thought I was crazy, and might even have told me to leave the airport. So I spoke to him of excitement, romance, and adventure, things that he, a young man like me, could understand.

Perhaps I was being more truthful than I realized. I grew up before television became a national obsession, and, while other children were being enthralled by "Dragnet" or "The Untouchables," I was drawn to the gentler tales of an earlier era. I read of pirates and buried treasure, cannibal chiefs with bones through their noses, lush oases and impassable jungles, and always, the unchanging backdrop to all these dramas, the tropical sun blazing in an azure sky. In school in the early sixties, I was stuffed with more prosaic facts—the capital of Upper Volta is Ouagadougou; Liberia produces rubber, ginger, and coffee; the Congo is a constant source of trouble. But even as I devoured long lists of countries, presidents, and principal exports, through the windows of my mind I saw the fiery equatorial sun. I memorized the contours of national boundaries, but onto the map of Africa I projected the map of my dreams.

At Oxford, I studied philosophy and political theory; in law school

I trained in economics, sociology, and jurisprudence, as well as law. I read a lot, went to raucous parties, and often spent the night drinking coffee with friends and analyzing the meaning of life. But it was life in England and America that we dissected, while the rest of the world lay forgotten. The same was true of my studies: the West hogged the stage, while Eastern philosophy, African history, and Third World economics made, at most, cameo appearances. What little I learned about the southern half of the world came mostly from newspapers and was uniformly bleak. African cities were invariably described as "dusty" or "kiln-hot" or "windswept," while Asian towns were always "dirty" and "overcrowded." Tin-pot dictators paraded through the pages of the *New York Times,* and presidents-for-life were deposed every other week. Too many children were born and too many children died. The Third World seemed a wasteland of empty lives, ignorance, and starvation.

It never rained during my schooldays—or so it seems when I look back now. But the winter after graduation was unusually cold and gray. I was in New York, clerking at the U.S. Court of Appeals. It was a seven-day-a-week job, and I drank five cups of coffee to get through each day. My friends were scattered across the country. In the law firms where they worked, the rule was "up or out"; for every associate who moved up, five were thrown out. The slightest mistake—a wrong citation, too wide a tie, a scruple shown at the wrong time—could ruin a young lawyer's chances. My friends dressed with care, talked with care, and were slow to smile. For the first time in our lives, our worth was measured in dollars. The goal set before us was not acquiring knowledge but doing a job.

During those dreary months, as I read news reports about Third World cities, the very names were whisperings of magic: Surabaya was the wind in the palm trees; Kathmandu was temple bells in the clear air. After my year's clerkship had ended, I resolved to find a country where winter was a fairy tale, a story so unbelievable it would make children smile.

And so, based on a blend of facts and daydreams, I decided to go to Africa. About the real Africa, I knew almost nothing at all.

2

ACROSS AFRICA

My year at the court ended in May of 1976, but I stayed in New York until November. Again and again I postponed my departure. I found plausible reasons for each delay, but the truth was that I was afraid. Through all the adventure stories, romances, and even news reports I had read ran an undercurrent of fear: the African jungle bristled with death and danger. I remembered tales of snakes, crocodiles, murderous natives, and unspeakable diseases. Much later, after I had spent years in Africa without encountering a single headhunter or fer-de-lance, I realized that these phobias had been masking deeper, more formless terrors—a fear of the alien, the unknown. We all know what Columbus discovered—that you can sail anywhere on Earth without falling over the edge, that because the world is round you can always return to the place from which you started. But buried deep within us are pockets of doubt.

In the end, I compromised. I went to a travel agent who specialized in "adventure" tours; he gave me a handful of glossy brochures. One was for a tour of the Sahara ("a kaleidoscope of desert life that will leave an indelible impression on our minds"); another advertised "purely exploratory expeditions" to Central and East Africa. ("The people are beautiful, the women modest, and the girls saucily turned out in head feathers, beads, copper bracelets, and cowries. Out in the wilds the men and women go naked.") A third option, which seemed to combine the best of the other two, was a three-month, ten-thousand-mile camping trip from London to Kenya.

The "expedition vehicles" on that tour were old army surplus trucks. The route ran south through France and Spain to the Mediterranean. Then came a two-hour boat ride to Ceuta, a tiny Spanish enclave in the northwest corner of Africa. From there, the trucks drove south across the Sahara, passing through Morocco, Algeria, and the Republic of Niger. On the other side of the desert, after a two-day rest stop in the Nigerian town of Kano, the trucks turned east for the long and muddy ride across Central Africa. Their route led through Cameroun, the Central African Empire, and the Republic of Zaire, which, when I studied the world in high school, was called the Congo. Beyond the jungles of Zaire and the hills of Rwanda lay the East African plains, where the journey ended.

That tour left in November. Those trucks fill quickly, the travel agent said, so I paid my fare (a thousand dollars) and reserved a seat. On November 9, 1976, I flew to London. The slick, confident language of the brochures, which stressed that the tours were run by seasoned, "Africa-toughened" experts, had long since dispelled all my fears. I was slightly uneasy about having my adventure spoonfed, but I took comfort in the brochure's promise "to give members a 'real' experience of Africa."

We left London in the dead of winter and headed south. There were eighteen of us. We had all met for the first time that November day at the main entrance to Paddington Station. The truck, covered with bright blue canvas, was colder inside than out, and as the wind whipped through the canvas we huddled together and forgot we were strangers.

Once we were across the Channel, the weather was even colder but wine was cheap. We drank bottle after bottle to fight off the chill, as we burrowed under mountains of sleeping bags and sang in eighteen different keys, each of our howls louder than the wind.

There were flowers in southern Spain, and trees with glossy leaves flanked the roads. In Morocco, the markets were filled with fruits and a thousand spices, carefully sorted and heaped in huge baskets, and men in swirling robes who squatted by the produce or flitted from stall to stall.

We crossed the Algerian border, and the crowded cities gave way to the warm, open spaces of the Sahara. A fortnight before, our laundry had turned to ice on the clotheslines, and now it was summer. This accelerated, premature passage of the seasons affected us all. We felt reborn as we stripped off down jackets and heavy sweaters. We were newly, intensely alive under the fiery desert sun.

For three weeks, we saw nothing but rock, sand, and sky. One night we camped near a range of sand dunes. We ran up and down the dunes in the moonlight, not seeing where we went, not knowing up from down, free from fear of falling or rolling or breaking a leg. It seemed as if nothing could hurt us.

A few hundred miles farther south, two French-speaking Tuaregs visited our camp. They built a fire under the stars, served us sugary tea, and showed us how to tie a *chech*, the cloth headdress of the Sahara. They examined our dust-encrusted truck. This truck is our friend, we told them. This truck is your life, they replied.

In the town of Agadez, in Niger, we drank Coca-Cola in a café facing a four-hundred-year-old mosque built of mud. Darkness fell as we lingered, and from the city behind us came the sound of doors creaking open, footfalls, drumbeats, the noises of the night. I left the group to follow the drums. The moon had not yet risen, and the streets were dark but I saw light ahead. There were people holding lanterns, people dancing, raising huge clouds of dust from the unpaved road, and, in the middle of the whirling clouds, the drummers, sweat-soaked and pounding a beat that set the city throbbing. I wanted to dance through the streets with them, but I was afraid the truck might leave without me. As I walked back to the café, a string of camels glided silently by. The blue-robed riders glowed like ghosts in the starlight.

The road south of Agadez was corrugated with bumps and ridges, and by the time we reached Nigeria, the truck could go no farther. New parts had to be sent from London, the nearest source of supply. For three weeks we waited, stuck in the nightmare city of Kano. The town sprawled for miles, wide paved roads leading nowhere, flanked by rows of concrete pylons, patiently waiting for the electric wires that should have been strung years before. Beyond the concrete, wire-mesh fences guarded lawns of bare earth spotted with long-dead grass. This was the respectable part of town. On the other side of the city, beyond the racetrack, beyond the exclusive Kano Club, beyond the even more select Kano Golf Club, beyond the sky-blue dome of the Central Hotel, was the old town, where vultures feasted on heaps of garbage thrown from mud-walled houses.

It was a pity that our truck library, which contained the collected works of Arthur Hailey, did not also have a copy of *One Hundred Years of Solitude,* for some of Garcia Marquez's more hallucinatory passages might have made sense when read in such a surreal setting. In any case, it was far too hot to read. Instead we passed the time drinking iced Pimms in the lounge of the Central, loitering in the parking lot of the Kano Club, where we hoped to collar a member who would sign us in, or sitting in the dirt by the racetrack (which doubled as a campsite for tourists), lazily swapping stories as we sweated in the sun. Another truck had arrived from the north. Its owner used to lead overland tours like ours, but on this trip he had driven down alone, planning to sell the truck and find work in Kano. Black-bearded and bare-chested, with the look of an outlaw, he aroused in us a mixture of fear and fascination. He had done the India route many times and claimed to be an expert in dealing with Indians. "They're lazy bastards and you've got to be tough," he said. "To get my truck fixed, I bang the guy's head against the chassis and tell him, 'Fix it where you see the blood.' " I spent many hours in his green canvas army tent, listening to improbable tales of Afghan adventures and, in the background, the music of his only cassette, an old Moby Grape tape he had picked up in Kabul. A few days after Christmas, the Kano State Department of Transport offered him a job, and he drove off, leaving me to wonder how his approach to truck maintenance, which had had such success in India, would fare in Nigeria.

The new gear box arrived a few days later and was installed in record time. We left Kano and headed east, through parched grasslands speckled with earth-walled houses. The villages, the dying plants, the soil—everything in sight was brown, just as it had been in Kano, which was basically a desert town grown fat. But across the border in Cameroun we entered a world of green. There were plants and flowers everywhere, except on the road itself, an anomalous and fragile river of earth running through the endless vegetation. The air was filled with the scent of damp soil, fallen leaves, and hidden flowers. As we moved south, the trees became taller, the air more humid, and the road narrower, until the road seemed like a canyon hemmed in by the cliffs of the forest.

Western explorers hated the jungle. They found it gloomy and oppressive, a malevolent spirit that had to be attacked, exorcised, and hacked away. But I never saw the forest as an enemy. To me, it was a joyous celebration of life and fertility, a cathedral with vaulted roofs and windows stained a million shades of green. Still, we were not part of the forest, but alien beings who moved through it.

As in the desert, our truck was our life. When the truck broke down, we had to fix it. When it got bogged in mud, we had to dig it out. Most of our day was spent driving, and much of the rest was consumed by the tedious chores of survival. Every evening we had to unload the tents from the truck, clear the ground, pitch the tents, unload the pots and food and plastic plates, gather wood, build a fire, peel the potatoes, stew the meat, eat the food, unload the forty-four-gallon water drums from the front of the truck, wash the pans and dishes, and then load everything back. In the morning, there were tents and sleeping bags to pack and breakfast to make before we could begin another day of driving.

In the beginning, nobody had minded the work. But after Kano, things were different. Blame it, perhaps, on the heat, or the high humidity, or the wall of trees that narrowed our horizons. For whatever reason, the collective, exuberant "we" broke up, shattered into eighteen separate people.

I would have liked to leave my truckmates behind but I was chained to them, inescapably. Their habits began to annoy, nibbling away at me like the ever-present flies and mosquitoes. The others also suffered from this heightened sensitivity. I was a city boy, and a Cub Scout dropout, and had never learned how to build a fire or how to repair a stalling engine. Now, people began to notice my deficiencies, and to comment on them.

In late January 1977, we reached Lisala, a tiny port on the north bank of the Congo River in Zaire. The river was as broad and sluggish as an inland sea. East of Lisala, the land was densely populated, and each night our camp was surrounded by silent, staring villagers. We thought we saw anger in their faces, but it was fear that hardened their eyes. One morning, our driver awoke to find his tent slit open, his money gone. We posted sentries each night after that. I chose the midnight shift, and every third midnight, I sat on guard, wide-eyed and alert in the blackness of the night. Sometimes I heard drums from nearby villages, where men and women, drunk with wine and laughter, danced until dawn.

Finally, the forest ended. We left Zaire and drove through the volcanic hills of Rwanda to the East African plains. It was as if a bubble surrounding us had burst; the stale air inside was swept away by the cool breezes of the highlands. We spent two weeks in Tanzania and southern Kenya, cruising around the game parks of the Serengeti, looking for lions and stuffing ourselves with rich food and beer. By the time our journey ended in Nairobi, we were friends once more.

3

A HOSTAGE IN AMIN'S UGANDA

We reached Nairobi in late February 1977. In those days, Uganda, Kenya's neighbor to the west, was ruled by Idi Amin. He was Africa's most famous leader. South African journalists and European conservatives found in him living proof that black government leads to chaos. To the rest of us, Amin was a fairy-tale figure, part clown, part ogre. "Don't let Amin catch you," a French policeman had shouted to us as we drove through Paris on our way to Africa. But I was not afraid of that.

Several years later, after Amin had been chased out of Africa, I saw a film about him, a gory, made-in-Kenya epic that broke all box-office records when shown in Nairobi. As a curtain raiser, a tourist was arrested and shot. "You can't shoot *me*, I'm an American," his last words, made the moviegoers rock with laughter. When I left my truckmates and went to Uganda, I felt even more invulnerable than the tourist did; after all, his was only a bit part, but I was the hero of my tale.

The trip to the border town of Busia was reassuringly routine. A bored-looking civil servant had given me a Ugandan visa in Nairobi. The only requirement had been that I pay the forty-two-shilling fee with exact change. The overnight bus from Nairobi to Busia, with its streamlined curves and sagging seat cushions, reminded me of one of the city buses of my childhood, and very possibly it was. We arrived in Busia early the next morning, and I walked through the busy market and through Kenyan customs to the cluster of tin-roofed sheds that housed the Ugandan border post. That was as far as I got. The Ugandan police, without explanation, sent me back to Kenya. But there was another border crossing at Malaba, twenty-five miles north, and a driver headed that way offered me a ride. As we drove, we listened to Radio Uganda denouncing American spies and secret agents. It was obviously not a good time for Americans to go to Uganda.

At Malaba, I was welcomed by a scholarly, bespectacled immigration officer dressed in a dark suit and narrow tie. He seemed the embodiment of the Rule of Law. Mr. Rule of Law carefully stamped my passport and cheerfully accepted a one-hundred-shilling bribe. (This was unusual, though I did not know it at the time. Only once again during my six years of travel did I pay a bribe.) Within an hour, I was on a bus to Kampala.

The road passed through Tororo, through Iganga, and through Jinja, where it crossed the Nile. The land was greener, more fertile, more tropical than the mile-high plateau around Nairobi. There was even a tiny stretch of rain forest west of Jinja, used as a dumping ground for those killed by Amin's police. Just beyond the forest were the rolling hills of Kampala.

It is a very beautiful town, though this is not evident in the bombed-out center, which those who know have said is worse than Hanoi. To see Kampala in all its glory, you must go up the hill to the International Hotel, the tallest building in town. As often as not, the elevators are out of order, but the view from the roof is worth the seventeen-story climb. Around the hotel are tile-roofed houses, parks and gardens, and lush emerald hills beyond. To the north, the view of hill and field is unbroken, but if you look south, you can see Lake Victoria at the horizon. It's a lovely spot to linger, and it's high enough up to be safe from the gunfire that spatters from the streets below.

But Kampala's charm can be seen only from above. The bus from Malaba dropped me off at the bottom of the town, the huge market at the foot of the steep hill at the end of Bokassa Road. Though less than a mile from the granite-and-glass International, this muddy market belonged to another world. This division is not a Ugandan invention. Though few other towns are built split-level, as is Kampala, every city in Africa has its top and its bottom. In colonial days, the top, with its well-stocked shops, its villas and gardens, was for Europeans only. The shantytowns at the bottom were left to the natives. Even now, you will find few whites in the African town, except for tourists chasing after a bit of local color, but ever since independence the dividing line has been wealth, not race: there is a city for the rich and a city of the poor. The market where I first set foot in Kampala was a neutral zone between the two. The shantytowns started right behind it, while the business district was just up the hill.

Since then I have learned, if I have the choice, to seek out the poorer part of any town. It is less comfortable to live in, but much more lively, and the people are usually far friendlier. But in Kampala I was not given a choice. Inflation was rampant, and prices were five times what they were in Nairobi. I could have gotten a better rate of exchange on the black market, but I changed my dollars at the bank; it was worth the extra cost to stay out of trouble. At the legal rate, even the cheap hotels around the market were overpriced. After a long search down nameless alleys, I found a boardinghouse called the New Lodge. It was not very new, and it was above a butcher shop, but a bed could be had for six dollars a night.

The next day, I wandered up the hill and along Bokassa Road. Along with Kampala Road, one block over, Bokassa was one of the town's two main thoroughfares. It still is today, though it is no longer named after the Central African autocrat whom Amin admired. As soon as Amin was booted out, the street was renamed Luwum Road, after the Anglican archbishop who was murdered, some say by Amin himself, only a few days before I arrived in Kampala.

The shops along Bokassa and Kampala roads appeared forlorn, with nothing in stock except a shirt or two, or perhaps some cans of corned beef or beans. This was not the last time I saw empty shelves in Africa. I found them in Guinea, in Zaire, where big supermarkets had nothing but ketchup and paint remover, and in Ghana, where one had to leave the country to buy a bar of soap. Sometimes bare counters and boarded windows were the legacy of unchecked greed and ambition; sometimes they came when visions of socialist triumph fell apart. But the stores that lined Kampala Road had the barest shelves I ever saw—until I returned to the same shops three years later.

I walked up Bokassa and down Kampala and found only one store with something to sell: the duty-free shop, where hard cash (dollars only, please) bought hard liquor. The whiskey section was crammed with diplomats snapping up three-dollar bottles of imported gin. Next door, milk was on sale, and though I had no ration coupons, I persuaded the clerk to part with a pint. I tried to buy a newspaper also, but that day's *Voice of Uganda* was nowhere to be found.

I carried my milk uphill to the International Hotel, where I sat on a terrace overlooking the hotel's exuberant garden. A waiter brought me a glass and a newspaper. As usual, the entire front page was devoted to Amin's exploits, although, to provide an illusion of variety, some headlines referred to President-for-Life Idi Amin, others to Field Marshall Idi Amin, and the rest to His Excellency Idi Amin. Journalistic monomania was not out of place in a continent where rulers have been known to call themselves the Guide or the Redeemer, to crown themselves Emperor or to appear on television wearing angel's wings. But that day's edition of the *Voice of Uganda* was unusual, even by African standards, and I saw at once why it had sold out. The President for Life had sent a long, rambling telegram to President Jimmy Carter, who had had the effrontery to question His Excellency's respect for human rights. Uganda, replied the Field Marshal, "is more peaceful than certain parts of the United States . . . where a lot of murders are taking place." Obviously, Carter had been misinformed: "You should not be blinded by those who want to overthrow you," His Excellency cautioned. "You should therefore be like Field Marshal Amin, who is a black super power in Africa."

This madcap buffoonery was made more sinister by an announcement printed below it. All U.S. citizens in Uganda were ordered to report on Monday to the International Conference Center in Kampala, and no Americans would be allowed to leave the country until then.

I was alarmed, but less than I should have been. Kampala seemed like an ordinary African city, poorer than most but normal nonetheless. The people I met—the waiter at the International, the kindly woman who ran the New Lodge, and even passersby in the street—were prone to smile and went out of their way to welcome the visiting American. It was not, as I had expected, a city of fear. I did not know that its tranquillity was a pose, a carefully maintained illusion. People in Uganda (and everywhere else) prefer to close their eyes to monstrosities rather than admit their existence. Besides, standards of normality had slowly changed over the years. The ever present monstrosities had become an accepted part of everyday life. Kampala was a city where civil servants on their way to the office casually brushed past bloody corpses in the street, where the patrons of a café calmly sipped their tea as they watched gunfights through the window.

I saw the corpses and the shootouts on my second visit to Kampala in 1980. In Amin's time, atrocities were organized more neatly, and bodies were discreetly dumped outside the city center. They were easier to ignore although impossible to wish away. Uganda in February 1977 was in the midst of a wave of killing, as Amin's police eliminated His Excellency's enemies, the friends of his enemies, those seen talking to suspected enemies, those belonging to tribes suspected of being enemies. It is likely that Amin planned to use the Americans to divert world attention from his purges. Had I seen that day's *New York Times,* with its front-page headlines that called us hostages, I would have known the danger I was in. But the *Times,* like all newspapers and magazines printed outside Uganda, was banned.

In any case, I could not leave the country. I was trapped in Kampala, and all I could do was wait. Night had fallen while I read, and I made my way downhill to the New Lodge. The small restaurants around the market were packed with the usual nighttime crowd of *waragi* drinkers, who loudly traded boasts and stories as they belted down the home-brewed banana gin.

The next morning, I explored the African part of town. The tiny stalls in the busy market were piled high with goods. Their proprietors, like market traders throughout Africa, had mysterious sources of supply that the half-empty stores in the business district could not tap. On the far side of the sprawling market was a district of shanties and beer halls: the workingman's part of town. Music poured out of one of the drinking houses. They were playing records from Zaire. Zairean rock has repetitive riffs and driving rhythms; it is minimalist music with a boogie-woogie beat. Inside the drinking house, people were dancing. They waved to me and I joined in. The other dancers rode the rhythms with sinuous ease, while my ungainly body tried to mime their graceful undulations. Suddenly, a shout and the dancers froze. I looked up—straight into the barrel of a machine gun.

There were two of them: two guns, and two military policemen pointing them at me. The soldiers were tense, their muscles taut and ready for action. I moved toward them slowly, so they wouldn't panic and pull the trigger. Nearby was a lot, empty now, where buses were parked overnight, and a sentrybox for the watchman who guarded the buses. The tiny shelter was vacant during the daytime; the soldiers put me inside it while they debated what to do with the dangerous foreigner. They searched me, found my passport, and realized I was an American. One went back to his base to get instructions, while the other stood outside the hut. He was doubtless bored by the wait, and passed the time by whipping a boy he had caught in the lot.

The child was far more pleased than I when a car arrived and the soldier, releasing him, motioned me inside. I was taken to a long one-story stucco building which, like every jail in Uganda, had been built by the British. This one, smaller than most, was a neighborhood lockup adjoining the local police station. I was put in a cell twenty feet square; there were at least thirty men already inside. They sat on the floor and wore their trousers inside-out to prevent the outside from fraying. Obviously, they expected to be sitting there for a long time.

A policeman passed a bucket of food inside, along with plates and a ladle. One of the prisoners took it and served each of us an equal share. After we ate, another man wiped spilled food from the floor. One of the men spoke English, and told me that most of the prisoners were charged with robbery, picking pockets, and other common crimes. This surprised me. I did not know that people faced with long prison terms would care about how their trousers looked or whether their cell was clean and I expected thieves and robbers to fight over food instead of peaceably dividing it. By the end of our overland tour, I and my truckmates had begun to bicker over division (especially when Angel Whip, a sugary dessert mix, was on the menu), and I was astonished to find a cellful of criminals who were more civilized than we were.

The one English speaker was not a criminal. He was in more serious trouble. A student at Makerere University, he had spoken out

against Amin's rule. A Canadian university had awarded him a scholarship, but a few days before he was to leave Uganda, he had been
arrested. He did not expect to be released. I was lucky, he told me,
because I had been arrested by the military police. They were worse
than the ordinary police, but far kinder than Amin's personal police
force, the innocuously named but dreaded State Research Bureau. It
was easy, I learned, to tell the police forces apart: the civilian police
dressed and acted like British bobbies, the M.P.s wore khaki uniforms with red-and-white striped belts, and the State Research men
preferred to dress like pimps, in loud flowered shirts, flashy bell-bottom trousers, sunglasses, and platform heels, all imported on Air
Uganda's weekly cargo flight from London.

After eating, I was taken to another room and questioned by a
plainclothes policeman. There was a look of evil about him, a dead-
ness in his eyes that smacked of State Research, but he was, he said,
with the CID, which, as in England, is a division of the ordinary police. He sat at a big desk and, as he interrogated me, meticulously
wrote down both questions and answers. He was a serious man and
the only time he laughed out loud was when I asked him to notify the
nearest U.S. embassy of my plight. He asked me where I had traveled in Africa, and I listed the countries we had crossed in the truck,
thinking, maybe if I name a lot of places he won't think I'm a spy
sent directly to Uganda. But he could not understand why I would
visit those backward and impoverished lands if I had no ulterior motive. "Why," he asked, again and again, "would a lawyer want to
travel so much?" After an hour, he gave up, filed his report, and took
me back to my cell. I looked for the student, but he was gone.

Later that evening, the officer in charge of the police station visited me. He had just found out that a white man was being held in his
jail, and he wanted to be sure that I had been properly treated. If it
were up to him, he said, he would release me at once, but he could
not, because the army police had called in the State Research Bureau.

They came for me just before midnight. There were four men, all
carrying submachine guns and dressed like Shaft. State Research. A
white Volkswagen was waiting outside; they bundled me in, squeez-
ing themselves on either side of me. It was a tight fit, but I didn't
complain; prisoners usually were stuffed in the trunk.

We drove through dark and empty streets into a part of town that
was new to me. One road was narrower than the rest and hemmed in

by high brick walls. We stopped there, and one of them got out and walked back along the alley. I waited. The guards, unmoving and silent, waited also. The one who had gone had left his gun behind, but it was just beyond my reach. "Why have we stopped?" I asked. "What are we waiting for?" "You ask too many questions," they said.

I sat in silence after that, watching the men and the walls outside. Twenty minutes later, the missing policeman returned. He told the driver where to go; apparently, he had telephoned headquarters and had been given instructions. The men talked in a language I failed to recognize, peppered with a few Swahili phrases I didn't understand. I heard one sentence in English: "The order said, hold those trying to leave the country." Most State Research documents were written in English, but Amin's army spoke in Swahili, which meant that the State Research agents, most of whom came from the Sudanic tribes of the north, had to be fluent in four or five languages and at times used them all in the same conversation. From the one English phrase they let slip, I guessed that the bureau was keeping a special watch on Americans to prevent them from escaping from Uganda and foiling Amin's plans to use them. I had somehow aroused their suspicions and was being held either as a potential escapee or a possible spy. I was never told, then or later, why I was arrested, and these were the only clues I was ever given. We drove back along Kampala Road to our new destination, the Central Police Station.

The Central Police Station, where I was to spend most of my remaining time in Uganda, overlooks the Square, a grassy mall just off Kampala Road. The Square was a legacy of the British; its leafy trees and old, reassuringly solid buildings brought back vague recollections of my Oxford days, pleasant memories which were muted by the bars on my basement cell's window. It was a block of cells, really, three rooms and about twenty inmates. I had my own straw mat to sleep on. This was luxury compared to the crowded cell I left behind, and was infinitely better than the military jails where, during that last week in February, prisoners stayed up all night loading freshly butchered corpses into trucks. James, one of my cellmates, had just been transferred from an army prison, but I did not hear about the trucks full of battered bodies from him. He never talked about his experiences, and I did not press him, for I was hardly eager to learn about a place I might soon see for myself.

Anyway, I could never have imagined James heaving bodies onto trucks. He lent me a dogeared copy of *On the Road* and, as I reread that kinetic classic, it struck me that James had much in common with Kerouac's peripatetic buddies. He shared their driving energy and hard-edged style. We all liked him; he even managed to befriend some of the guards.

James came from Trinidad. Ours was a sort of international cell. There were Eritrean refugees, Rwandans who had asked for asylum, and other assorted Africans. Apparently, the government dealt with applications for asylum by throwing the applicants in jail. I was the only white man there—until the next evening.

We sat up late that first night, talking and making jokes to chase the fear away. Afterwards, I lay down. There was a chill in the air, and I slept on the concrete floor, using my pallet as a blanket. I fell soundly asleep, but a half-hour later I was shaken awake. Three soldiers stood over me, demanding money. I refused. One wore a uniform decorated with a pattern of spots intended to make the wearer resemble a leopard. He spoke French. I explained that my money had been counted when I entered Uganda and that if I had less when I left than when I came in, excluding money for which bank receipts could be shown, I would be arrested for trading on the black market. This was true, though arrest at the border was not one of my major worries that night. It seemed to satisfy him, and the soldiers departed. They went off to another cellblock, where they amused themselves by beating up the inmates. For them, the evening was therefore not a total loss; but my fear and the sounds of scuffles kept me awake all night.

Still, I felt wide awake the next morning, too wide awake. I was fidgety from lack of freedom, and I paced around, staring at the Square through the window bars. By standing on tiptoe, I could see the duty-free shop, open for business and already jammed, on the other side of the park. I had only been in for a day; what would it feel like if they kept me there for years?

One of the prisoners had a wife in Kampala, and that morning the guards brought him a meal that she had cooked, fresh fish from the Nile stewed in brown sauce. There were mountains of food, neatly packed in a series of metal pots. The woman had made enough for him to share with all of us, and he did, for that is the African tradition: a man's good fortune is shared, not hoarded, and no one goes hungry while another eats.

After eating, I went back to the window. Everything outside, even the garish blue façade of the duty-free, looked especially bright and beautiful then. I would have given quite a lot to walk for twenty minutes along Kampala Road, which only the day before I had found ugly and depressing. From time to time, I saw Europeans enter the duty-free shop, and toward noon one of them started to walk across the Square. In a few minutes, he would pass within ten yards of my window. No one knew I was in Uganda and my request to contact my embassy had been laughed at. The young white man walking toward me was my only chance for help. In my pocket was a bank receipt, with my name and passport number. I wrapped it around a shilling and, when he reached the window, I waved and threw out the coin. He saw me, took the packet, nodded, and walked away. He gave the receipt to a Kenya-bound traveler who took it the next day to the U.S. embassy in Nairobi. But of course I did not learn this until later.

After a few hours, the State Research men came. They spoke to the guard, and he called out my name. I waved good-bye to James and went with them to the white VW that waited outside. Once again, we drove through an unfamiliar part of town, but this time we passed villas and carefully tended gardens instead of factory walls. State Research headquarters was rumored to be in just such a suburb. Perhaps they were taking me there, or possibly to the rain forest on the Jinja road. I knew the Jinja highway was east of town. I thought we were going east but wasn't sure. Before I could work out our direction, the car turned into a driveway and parked in a garden. I tried to conceal my mounting apprehension; I would show them that Americans do not scare easily. "That is a pretty tree," I said. "It is mango tree," replied the State Research man.

It was indeed a beautiful garden. Around the massive tree, the lawn was dappled with sunshine. Though just off a busy road, the place was as drowsy and quiet as a forest clearing. They could shoot me there, under the tree, I thought, and the cars on the main road wouldn't even slow down.

A jeep drove up, and a man got out. His brown bell bottoms stamped him as State Research, and the deference he received from my guards marked him as an officer. He questioned me: Why had I come to Uganda? When had I come to Uganda? and so forth. What concerned him most, apparently, was where I had stayed in Kampala. I had succeeded in finding a hotel so obscure, so marginal, that its existence was unknown even to the police. The State Research Bureau viewed every visitor as a potential spy or invader and placed all foreigners under constant surveillance. An unknown American claiming to reside at an unknown hotel made them very nervous.

My story would be checked thoroughly, said the officer. If it proved accurate, I would be released. He left, after giving instructions to the men who had brought me. I was driven back into town, where I showed the agents the unmarked red gate behind which a flight of stairs led to the New Lodge. After that, I was returned to jail. James, the refugees, and even the police were surprised to see me again.

That evening, soldiers brought another tourist, an Italian, to our cell. He had driven from Nairobi the day before and had gone to see the old Entebbe airport, scene of the Israeli rescue mission of a few months before. That was a mistake. After the raid, Amin spent most of his days at the airport—if the Israelis came back, the Field Marshal would deal with them personally—and the runways swarmed with soldiers ready to arrest anything that moved.

The Italian was in a state of shock, numb with terror. One of his captors, an officer with a huge dagger strapped to his belt, assured me as he passed that the Army of Uganda knew how to deal with people like us. His voice dripped hate; it was not surprising that his prisoner cringed. But James had a gift for dispelling fright and providing reassurance, and he talked to the Italian until the fear had gone out of his eyes. By that time it was almost midnight. I burrowed under the straw and fell asleep.

An hour later, I was awakened by a scream. It came from another cellblock far away, but it seemed terrifyingly near and would not stop. I did not know a man could scream so loud or so long; surely no vocal cords could stand that kind of strain. I did not want to think what could cause such a shriek, and tried for a while to put it out of my mind, but the scream went on and on without even a pause for breath, and long before it ended I knew I would not sleep again that night.

I was tired the next morning but not too groggy to notice that things had changed. The guards seemed less vigilant and more re-laxed; they no longer bothered to keep themselves between me and the door to the outside. Sometime during the night, State Research had decided that I was probably not a dangerous secret agent after all. Perhaps their hands were forced by events beyond even their control. The message I had wrapped around a coin had reached the American embassy in Nairobi. There was no U.S. embassy in Kam-pala, so the Americans asked the West German ambassador to Uganda to investigate. Meanwhile, Amin's closest allies—including President Mobutu of Zaire, whose country received millions of dol-lars in U.S. aid—sent him private but urgent messages urging the release of all Americans. And, somewhere in the Indian Ocean, the aircraft carrier *Enterprise* changed its course and headed for the East African coast.

Just before noon I was driven to a police station on Parliament Road to have my photograph taken. It was a classic mug shot: I held my placard with my name and number painted on it, and I took care to grin at the camera. It was easy to smile; my escort was an ordinary copper in uniform, and the only State Research man in sight was guarding another prisoner, a robber, who was being turned over to the police because his crimes were too petty to warrant State Re-search attention. Besides, I had company: two other travelers, newly arrested, had been brought in. One man was French, the other from Chile. He had left Santiago in 1970, driving a battered two-cylinder Citröen. Now, seven years later, he and the car had reached Uganda.

The two of them posed for photographs. Afterward, we were all to be taken back to the Central Police Station, a mile away. The policemen asked us if we would like to walk. "Yes!" I shouted, but the others preferred to go by car and we were driven back to the Square.

Soon after our return, the French and Italian consuls visited the station. They took the names of their nationals, and mine as well, and offered words of reassurance. They could offer little more, but the fact that they had been permitted to visit at all meant that State Re-search was no longer involved. That evening, an even pleasanter surprise awaited: I was allowed to sleep at a hotel. The police kept my passport, of course, and I had to report back the next morning, but the night was mine. The Frenchman and the Chilean were also freed, and we ate together in a restaurant near the market. After dinner, we lingered over glasses of beer, but I left before they did. As I walked out of the restaurant, they heard a chair scrape as one of the other diners, who had come in just behind us, hurriedly followed me out. They tried to spot their own tails after that, but could not.

The next morning, back at Central Police Station, one of the guards shared his breakfast with me. As usual, it was *matoke,* the flavorless banana paste which most Ugandans, if lucky, ate every day of their lives. They were not bad people, the policemen who guarded me, only frightened, and now that State Research was out of the picture, they were friendlier and told me I had nothing to fear. The West German ambassador said this as well, when he visited the prison an hour later. He advised me to be patient and wait.

Fortunately, I did not have to wait long. It was barely noon when I, the Chilean, the Frenchman, and the Italian were taken to an upstairs office. Behind a desk sat a man in a brown suit. The suit was superbly tailored and doubtless imported; it was the finest I had seen since leaving London. Clearly here was a man of importance. He was, probably, a minister or senior bureaucrat, but not a member of Amin's inner circle of cronies; his English was too fluent and easy, his clothes too conservative for that. We were being freed, he told us. That afternoon a car would take us to the Kenyan border. He advised us to stay in our cell until then. If we wanted to go outside, he would not stop us, but if the army caught us again, there was nothing he—or anyone—could do to save us.

But I felt caged by locked doors and barred windows, and I was too restless to stay inside. I walked to the Imperial Hotel, where a few souvenir shops stayed open, waiting for tourists who never came. Ugandan banknotes, each emblazoned with a portrait of Amin in uniform, were worthless outside the country, so I spent my remaining shillings on T-shirts which bore the legend TOURISM IN UGANDA. Then, I made my way slowly back to Central Police Station. The streets swarmed with army jeeps and trucks; whenever one passed, I ducked into the nearest doorway.

Later that afternoon, a long Peugeot limousine pulled up outside the station. The driver wore a raffish straw hat and a big grin. The car was built for speed and comfort, and he was looking forward to pushing the accelerator to the floor on the road to the border.

The Italian, to everyone's surprise, decided to stay in Kampala to search for his car, which had been confiscated at the airport. The two others rode in the antiquated Citröen, and so I was the Peugeot's only passenger. My straw-hatted chauffeur was ordered, much to his disgust, to follow the other car. The tiny orange Citröen, whose dented doors were flecked with rust, and the sleek limousine trailing behind it made a strange and slow-moving cortege. Night had fallen before we reached Tororo. We were bound for Busia, the customs post at which I had been rebuffed less than a week before. As far as I knew, the border was still closed to Americans, and I feared they would turn me back or, worse, would search my bag and find the paper on which I had written the names of the cellmates I had left behind. James and the others were being held incommunicado; I planned to give their embassies news of their plight. But the driver was a police officer—and not, as I had guessed from the happy-native hat and grin, a tourist guide—and he outranked the men at the border. They waved me through and I ran across the bridge, not pausing for breath until I reached the WELCOME TO KENYA sign. I stayed a while there, looking back at Uganda through the darkness, shouting insults and swear words—until I remembered the Citröen had yet to cross.

On the Kenya side, the night bus to Nairobi was about to leave. I found a seat in back and dozed off, only to be awakened by cries and shouting. The other passengers had caught a man opening my duffel bag and rudely shoved the suspected thief off the bus. I stayed awake after that, watching the headlights slice through the darkness. A country road on a moonless night looks the same anywhere in the world: gray waves of grass under a skyful of stars, the darker blur of trees, sometimes a house with a lantern burning. But this road was special to me—it was Kenya and I was free.

✕◈✕

We arrived at Nairobi in the quiet hour before dawn. Most of the passengers sat in the bus until sunup; Nairobi, like New York, is one of the few cities in the world where it is unsafe to walk at night. I left at first light and walked to the U.S. embassy, which then was on the top floor of a downtown office building. It was barely seven o'clock, and the place was deserted except for the marine guard. He welcomed me with a steaming mug of instant coffee. He knew all about me; when he showed me the morning papers, I realized that a lot of other people had heard about me as well. The "Uganda crisis," as the

New York Times called it, was front-page news that morning and had been all week; that day's papers reported me missing in Uganda. I leafed through the latest *Newsweek,* which had a glowering Amin on the cover, and then told the marine my story. Embassy duty is an elite assignment, but the guard was nonetheless young enough to gape at me with wide-eyed admiration just because the papers had printed my name.

"A few reporters would like to meet you," said the man from the embassy. We had spent the past hour in his office, whose fluorescent lights, bright beige walls, and U.S. government-issue furniture I found strangely comforting. I had slept four hours in the past four days and was in no condition to talk to anyone, but I agreed, provided that strong coffee be supplied. And so, after a meal of fried chicken and pound cake at the embassy man's suburban ranch house, I went off to meet the press.

The embassy had rented one of the large conference rooms in the basement of the Hilton. Reporters sat shoulder to shoulder on tiny folding chairs; latecomers crowded the aisles. The only clear space was a floodlit stage in front. As soon as I reached it the cameras started to whir. They sounded like pesky flies, so much so that some of the photographs show my hands waving to shoo them away. I told my tale and then fielded questions; in all, I was on stage for over an hour, and after the conference ended reporters surrounded me. The last to leave was the correspondent from the Voice of America. He had been outshouted all evening, but there was a question he was determined to ask: "Is what happened to you typical of Africa or typical of Uganda?" I thought of the Ugandans I had met—prisoners and policemen who shared their food with me, the thirty men in the holding cell who wore their trousers inside-out—and answered, "Neither, my arrest was typical only of Amin."

My news conference was timed to make the American evening news, and my face was exhibited on TV screens coast to coast. The next morning, my picture stared from the newsstands, shocking my friends into sudden wakefulness as, groggy and shivering in the freezing dawn, they made their way to their law offices. For a few hours, I was a celebrity.

I hitchhiked to the coast of the Indian Ocean the morning after the press conference. I had not slept well; that night I was jittery and afraid, suffering the emotional hangover that often comes in the wake of danger. Surf and sunshine and palm trees are American symbols of tranquillity, and I naturally gravitated in their direction. An Englishwoman gave me a ride; she had seen my photo in the *Nairobi Standard.* Of course I pretended not to care—I knew it would be vulgar to crave notoriety, especially of such an ephemeral variety—but I was secretly pleased. That week I bought both *Time* and *Newsweek* and clipped out the articles that reported my release. For months afterward I kept them in the pocket of my jeans, ready to exhibit at the slightest excuse. I didn't think to save the clippings, I would say, but I just might have them in my pocket, I never throw anything away, and out would come the crumpled pages. The *Newsweek* story served another purpose as well. It was painful for me to tell my tale; it was far easier to let others read about it. I did not like to think how narrowly I had escaped death. Indeed, I was luckier than I knew: two French tourists, I found out years later, were taken into custody by State Research soon after my release. They were never seen again.

VISTA

4

INDIA AND
NEPAL: 1977

"India fries your brains, man. People go there, they do a lot of dope; after two, three months, they lose control." My informant was American, wore a scraggly beard and metal-rimmed glasses, and probably did a lot of dope himself. I hardly listened; I had heard the same story many times before. Instead, I watched the waves roll in from Bombay and break on the East African shore. We sat on the beach on Lamu Island, a nine-mile scimitar of sand that swept as far as the horizon. The smooth, clean curve of the sand and the scalloped, ever-surging sea, with its intricate pattern of sparkling wavelets, were a Zen rock-and-sand garden magnified a millionfold. Arabian swords, Japanese temples, and the Indian Ocean—everything on Lamu evoked not Africa but the larger land mass to the east. Traders from Arabia had settled on the island many hundreds of years before and built a town which even today is a warren of ancient walls and crumbling mansions, streets so narrow you can touch both sides at once, innumerable mosques, and groves of palm trees that sway in the breeze. It is a lazy, charming place; small wonder that I fell under its Asian spell and bought a plane ticket to India.

But every traveler I met on the island seemed determined to shatter my dreams. Some, like the American on the beach, told horror stories of brains short-circuited by drugs and an alien culture, of burnt-out tourists begging on the street. I couldn't go there, I couldn't stand the poverty, said others—mostly, it seemed, educated American women. "I can't believe how stupid Indians are," said one young lady. (Surprisingly, she, too, was educated and American.) "They can't do anything right."

"Except the thieves," her boyfriend added. "They've made robbery into a science."

"You don't believe us now," she said, "but when you get there you'll become a believer."

Facts do not travel well; the farther one is from a place, the more outrageous the rumors become. The stories that made the rounds on Lamu beach were as full of lies and exaggerations as the tales of medieval explorers. There was, though, a grain of truth behind each of them (except, I should add, for the myth of the stupid Indian). The poverty that scared Americans away is less pervasive and dehumanizing than I had imagined, and besides, the poor are mostly hidden, relegated to suburban shanties or rural villages, swept under the rug—they needn't spoil one's journey. But the poverty is there, combined, as elsewhere in Asia but in total contrast to Africa, with an inequality of wealth and status that has grafted itself onto the country's deepest traditions.

I learned these facts about the Indian economy and culture on later visits. During my first year in the East, I was aware of Asian tradition as an exotic, pervasive aura, like incense—something I could smell but could not understand. How could I have known more? In my first year I never met any Asians.

To live in Asia without knowing any Asians is not as difficult as it sounds. It must have been even easier in imperial days, when people of color were barred from first-class railway cars, but even today there are Englishmen born and bred in places like Hong Kong who state with pride that they don't know a word of the local lingo—"still sounds like monkey talk to me." Foreigners in Asia stick together: diplomats dine with other diplomats, businessmen drink with other businessmen, and travelers spend their time with other travelers.

Perhaps this is why the stories that made the rounds on Lamu were so inaccurate; the people who spoke so glibly about stupid Indians, poor Indians, thieving Indians, etc., had never had an Indian friend, had never talked to an Indian except for such conversations as "Two mutton curries with rice." "Right away, *sahib.*"

Still, as any traveler will tell you, the best thing about India is the people you meet: people from home. Every year, a million of us Westerners put on backpacks and head for the Orient. We come from all over—I have met Japanese in Kenya and Poles in Afghanistan—but most are from Britain, France, Germany, and the Commonwealth. At any given moment, a fifth of Australia and half of New Zealand are on the road, or so it seems. And all visit the same towns, stay at the same hotels, eat and drink in the same cheap cafés and bars. If you meet someone in Kathmandu, you will probably see him again in Ko Samui, in Penang, and in Kuta Beach.

It may sound as if I loathed the travelers I met, but I didn't. Some of my happiest moments were spent in their company. Still, most travelers I met carried a guidebook, sometimes two, and never went anywhere that wasn't recommended. These backpackers never called themselves "tourists," a word they used to describe the sort of people who stayed in Hiltons, went on guided tours, and afterward bored their friends with endless slide shows. But most travelers had more in common with the Hilton set than they would admit and, my first year of travel, so did I. I had three guidebooks in my pack, I followed their teachings religiously, and I met travelers from all over the world. Still, I had a good time, that first year.

✕◈✕

My flight to India was four days late. The airline put me up at the Nairobi Hilton, where I spent the days sprawled by the pool, basking in the sun and unaccustomed luxury. The pool was outdoors, set in the midst of Nairobi's stubby skyline, and Bombay and the mysteries of the Orient seemed impossibly far away. But four nights later I was at Santa Cruz airport in Bombay's suburbs. The arrival hall was hot, humid, and disappointingly modern; airports everywhere are alike.

Gandhi is supposed to have said that Delhi is not India. Neither is Bombay, which, like large cities throughout the world, is really a foreign country itself, an alien in the land of its birth. Architecturally at least, Bombay is more English than Indian though it is a beautiful city, especially at twilight, when the stolid Victorian buildings around Flora Fountain are suffused with the gold of the dying sun. Then the sky over the ocean turns to lavender and the lights along Marine Drive, the mile-long string of lights called the Queen's Necklace, come on. Now families, lonely men, beggars, and lovers promenade under the lights, or sit on the seawall watching the pounding waves. But I was looking for India, and after a few days I left.

I took the Rajdhani Express to Delhi. It was the fastest train in India, and it crossed the huge states of Maharashtra, Gujarat, and Rajasthan in under seventeen hours. I read, ate, and tried to sleep on my upholstered chair, and all the while India was just outside the window. We passed hundreds of tiny stations, where men wearing turbans and women in faded saris patiently squatted by their luggage—brass pots and cloth bundles—and watched the train speed by. I should have taken a slower train, I should have gotten off at any one of these stations, and *then* I would have seen India. But the express made no stops in these backward areas, and so I saw New Delhi instead.

I found New Delhi appalling. It had Bombay's alien rootlessness but none of its charm. The older part of town has charm, and tradition as well—bright banners draped across crowded, narrow streets, all of which lead to the huge, ornate Jama mosque—but I did not know to go there. I stayed in Connaught Place, whose dirty white colonnades and endless shopping arcades recall the sooty and unpleasant parts of London.

I met a lawyer from Colorado named Ron Margolis. He was one of those rare visitors to India who talked with Indians and learned from them. We paid a call on a family he knew. They are not very Indian, he warned me. And he was right: their ultramodern house would have been a credit to any American suburb, and their collection of Indian wall hangings and brasswork, displayed as curios, reminded me of the native artifacts that adorn the homes of retired colonial administrators. At dinner, which was eaten with knife and fork, the conversation somehow turned to the Indian use of the left hand instead of toilet paper. The topic fascinated them—one of the daughters raised it—and embarrassed them. Use of paper would be viewed as barbaric by most Indians, and use of hand would stamp them as savages in the eyes of the West. I am fairly certain they opted for paper, which is dreadfully overpriced in Delhi because only *sahibs* buy it.

I was disappointed by Ron's friends—I had wanted to see "real" Indians, not what in my youth we would have called Uncle Toms. Then I remembered an Indian of quite another sort I had met long before. I was nine, and my parents and I were driving across the country in our beige Pontiac. In South Dakota, we saw an Indian chief standing by the road. Tourists paid him a dollar, and he posed for photographs. He wore a buckskin jacket and a crown of feathers, just like on TV. Why did this sad-eyed chief suddenly spring to mind? Perhaps because I had secretly hoped to dine with his Asian equivalent, a turbaned representative of an exotic, untouched culture. I did not realize that the Dakota chief had not been a "real" Indian; he had turned himself into a tawdry Tonto. But Ron's friends, and their numerous Westernized counterparts throughout the Third World, were real people, coping as best they could with a world where values conflict and cultures collide. It would, I know now, be wrong to ignore them as unreal, or to scorn them as imitation white men or to force them to wear a crown of tribal feathers. Still, I wish they had more respect for the cultures they left behind.

I wanted to leave Delhi but I did not know where to go; my guide-book's chapter on India was woefully inadequate. There was a Nepali bus parked near my hotel. I bought a ticket and rode to Kathmandu.

Nepal is one of the poorest countries in the world, with few roads and no industry. But it straddles the trade route between India and Tibet, and so its ancient cultures are infused with a rich and heady blend of Hindu and Tibetan influences. Most Nepalis are Hindu, and profoundly religious. Nepal was never a colony; it is a monarchy; what wealth there is is highly concentrated. The combination of all these factors virtually guarantees a country that will seem exotic, even medieval, to Western eyes. And Nepal is indeed so pleasantly quaint, so wonderfully Hobbit-like, that tourism has become the country's primary source of income.

Most of the tourists were young and poor (by Western standards) and wore backpacks. In those days, you could get from Kew to Kathmandu for less than a hundred dollars, hitching across Europe in the enormous TIR trucks that carried freight to Teheran, and taking local buses from there. Many hippies came to Kathmandu that spring. They wore capes, robes, and bright baggy trousers, and they swaggered like pirates. There were several on my bus; they had wintered on the beaches of Goa and were going to Nepal to escape the summer heat. When we arrived in Kathmandu, the bus stopped at the Oriental Lodge, and all the hippies got off. Avoid the Oriental Lodge, my guidebook warned, it is patronized by freaks and hippies. I went inside, paid three rupees, the equivalent of one American quarter, and got a bed for the night. My roommates were a fat French girl who sniffled and a German boy with a cough. The next morning, I moved to a single room—eight rupees a day—and set out to explore the town.

The Oriental Lodge was on Jhochen Tole, a thoroughfare which everyone—even the official maps—called Freak Street. It was Haight-Ashbury reborn. There were cozy restaurants, with paper lanterns and posters of the Swiss Alps, where you could buy banana pancakes or yogurt shakes or buffalo burgers. Most had upstairs rooms where favored clients lazily smoked pipe after pipe of hash. Nearby was a dirty lane nicknamed Pig Alley. The infamous pie shops of Kathmandu were there, five of them, dishing out huge sugary portions of pineapple upside-down cake, chocolate tart, and lychee pie—the best baking east of Suez.

It was strange and slightly disappointing to find a hippie heaven at the back of beyond. Still, it was a pleasant place and quite innocent in those days—like Haight-Ashbury before 1967. There were remarkably few cheats and hustlers, and the only unsavory character I met was a Nepali call girl who solicited me as she relieved herself in the gutter. But the best thing about Freak Street was the square at the end of it.

Durbar Square was a vast cobbled plaza surrounded by palaces and pagodas of exquisite and alien beauty. On the Freak Street side of the square was a cluster of stone bollards on which the patrons of the Oriental Lodge were wont to roost. The rest of the square, which could have swallowed an army, was usually empty. There were three pagodas on the far side, ancient and weatherbeaten with sagging stone steps and ornate eaves propped up by timeworn wooden beams. Looking north from the top of the tallest pagoda, I could see the busy market just below, a crowded, cobbled street—the old road to Tibet—more pagodas, and hills and sky beyond. Even the sky was different here; it was lighter, a robin's-egg blue tinged with green.

I spent many, many hours on those temple steps. A first journey is like first love, or early childhood: one's perceptions, unclouded by cognition, are fresher and stronger than they will ever be again. I was ignorant then, I know, and I viewed other people (especially the Nepalis) as actors playing bit parts in my dreams. But I wish I could recapture now the innocence that came so easily then, when I sat on those steps, looking north, drunk with the strangeness of it all.

One night, a group of Italian hippies came to town. The men wore brown robes and the women wore saris and bangles. I thought: a tribe of gypsies. Carlo, their bearded leader, looked vaguely familiar and then I realized he looked like a painting of the hermit St. Jerome that once hung in my parents' bedroom. "Tomorrow we go to Pokhara," he told me. "You come too. Is good place." So I went.

Pokhara, a few hundred miles west of the capital, *was* a good place. There were little wooden hotels around a lake, with fields and pastures behind. Usually, clouds shielded the mountains, but sometimes at dawn I could see the peaks, crinkled shining sheets of rock and virgin snow hanging four miles above me.

Carlo and his tribe settled in an earth-and-thatch cottage in the hills nearby. Sometimes they came to the lake and sat in a circle passing around the conical peacepipe known as a *chillum*. It was so strong that each in turn would fall over coughing after smoking it. I visited their house once in the evening, and together we sat in awe and silence as an enormous moon rose through the blackness of the sky. I felt as if I had joined a primitive clan living in the dawn of time. Marco, one of the Italians, went inside. "He take too much morphine," Carlo told me.

Days in Pokhara were gentle and indolent. During the day I sat in the sun by the huge green lake. I went to the cafés and drank tea and buffalo milkshakes. Pokhara went to bed early, and only one café stayed open at night. One evening, I was leafing through the proprietor's collection of Tintin comics—*Tintin in the Congo, Tintin in Tibet*—when a traveler I had never seen before rushed in. "I'm dead, I'm dead," he cried. He wept and shouted and we shouted too, to tell him he was still alive. But none of us could convince him—perhaps we were not sure ourselves—and finally he walked away.

There was a tea shop at the other end of the lake where few tourists ventured, and the next morning I went there. As I sat, something that looked like a tree walked toward me. It was a farmer, scrawny but strong like all the undernourished peasants of the world, carrying a load of branches twice as big as he. They were barely worth burning, those puny twigs, but firewood is hard to come by in Nepal and he was lucky to find any at all within a day's walk of his home. I called out to the man, and he jumped with fear, then smiled. He had thought I was a ghost.

I rode back to Kathmandu on the best bus in Asia. Custom-built in Switzerland thirty years before, it had the classic, elegant curves of a vintage Rolls-Royce. Only Westerners rode that bus; the fare was five dollars, and so, like the milkshake bars and pie shops and dollar-a-day hotels that we travelers frequented, it was far beyond the means of most Nepalis. The poverty line in Nepal was fifteen cents a day, half the price of a yogurt shake. Over a third of the country fell below it. But most travelers considered the Swiss bus a bargain, and I was lucky to get a seat. My neighbor, a pretty young Frenchwoman, fell asleep as we drove, and her head settled on my shoulder, but I barely noticed. It had been cloudy the day I drove to Pokhara from Kathmandu, but the sky was clear now and the mountains shimmered in the distance. In Pokhara, the peaks, though thirty miles or more away, had seemed almost within reach, with every snowy ledge and rocky outcrop clearly visible. The range that loomed beyond the rice fields by the highway, though, was over a hundred miles to the north. Distance stripped the details away, leaving only the barest essentials: an arc of shining snow that cut across the sky, floating far above the horizon, a glittering blue white wall of energy and light. It terrified me, this vision of a cold heaven; it was beautiful, far too beautiful, and that icy fire in the sky was a burning challenge. I believed in a world of matter; safe, inert matter. But that electric blaze on the horizon was something else, something stronger and older than the material world: ice, energy, and the Void. I felt relieved when, early in the afternoon, the fog rolled in.

I did not see the mountains again that year; the season of clouds and mist had begun. In Kathmandu, the sky was overcast, the air damp and heavy. The yearly monsoons had already reached western India. Soon the rains would come to Nepal. I stayed a few more days in Kathmandu, playing with the children who were drawn to the hippie area by its funny, friendly, generous people. These street kids were one of the many features of Asian life which reminded me of Dickens's novels: bands of orphans who beg and scavenge and sleep in the streets, each boy scrupulously sharing his rags and pickings with the others. They were streetwise, of course, but not hardened, in Kathmandu at least, and I think they liked me. The oldest boy— he was twelve—taught me to joke and swear in Nepali. On my last night in town, I took the whole giggling gang of them to buy pies on Pig Alley, and the stoned and sleepy pie-shop patrons suddenly found their store invaded by laughing, swearing, screaming children.

5

FROM BURMA
TO BALI

I arrived in Rangoon on a sweltering day in June. Burma was a gentle, sleepy land of ancient temples, red-robed monks, and gold-roofed pagodas; dirt roads, horse-drawn carts, and old wheezing buses; sluggish rivers, bright green jungle, and water-logged rice fields. Men wore skirts and women smoked cigars. The official state policy was Buddhist socialism and it didn't work: there was a state-owned People's Patisserie in Rangoon, but to buy anything more substantial than pastry you had to go to the black market, whose stalls in some towns sprawled over most of the city center. The country was torpid and traditional and wanted to stay that way. Sometimes it hardly seemed a country at all, but a wedge of lazy anarchy sandwiched between Thailand and Tibet.

These were my first impressions of Burma. They were superficial, inevitably so, because I, like all travelers, was allowed to stay only a week. On my first visit I did what every other tourist did: I went to Mandalay and Pagan. Mandalay was run-down shops and dusty streets, and Pagan was vast, brooding temples on a flat, sun-baked plain. Those long-abandoned monasteries were eerily, unforgettably impressive: well worth the journey. I would have done better, though, to have wandered through towns and villages chosen at random. That was what I did on my second trip to Burma, and my view of the country, its politics and traditions, was radically altered. But that would come four years later, in 1981.

My next stop was Thailand. Bangkok, its capital, was an hour's flight from Rangoon. Rangoon is a city where nothing has changed in thirty years; most of Bangkok was built within the past twenty. It had high-rise hotels and huge shopping centers. There were eight-lane highways clogged with big shiny cars. Bangkok was the biggest, fastest, most modern city I had seen since leaving London, and I was not ready for it. I barely noticed the thousands of temples that dotted the town; I did not know that hidden behind the office buildings were backwater side streets of grassy lots and wooden houses. I fled north, to Chiang Mai.

In Bangkok, the travelers, like the town, were smoother, more sophisticated than the vagabonds I had met in Nepal. The cost of plane fare, as well as the Thai police, kept the hippies out. There were a lot of clean-cut Aussies and the like in Chiang Mai, but the place attracted a different sort of traveler as well. Chiang Mai is at the bottom edge of the Golden Triangle, the hilly, lawless region where Burma, Laos, and Thailand meet. Number 4 heroin, the area's top foreign-exchange earner, was 85 percent pure and sold at 1 percent of the New York price. My hotel on Moon Muang Road was full of well-heeled, polite junkies. Next door to me was a pudgy British mathematician. He was studying for a doctorate but now he was on vacation and he meant to enjoy it to the fullest. For twelve dollars, he had bought a bag of heroin as big as his thumb, and planned to use it up, then go back to math. "If you went to France, you'd try the wine," he said as he offered me a snort. "I don't drink," I said.

My other neighbor was an American. He had been in the country for years and claimed to be fluent in Thai. "But the people are so stupid," he complained, "they don't understand me even when I speak their language." He had just returned from two weeks in the hills near the Burmese border. This was where I wanted to go, and I asked his advice. "You won't find road signs there," he told me. "It's easy to lose your way and wander into Burma and if you do, you won't come back. A lot of heroin convoys use those trails. If you meet one, the guards might shoot you."

All this was true, and yet thousands of travelers visited the Triangle every year. Several enterprising Chiang Mai travel agencies even organized guided tours: three days for twelve dollars, everything included, safety (they assured me) totally guaranteed. I booked a place on a tour leaving the next day.

We took a bus north to Thaton, where the road ended. Beyond lay range after range of jungle-clad hills, narrow trails, and villages built of bamboo. The people who lived in these mountain villages were not Thai, and the Thais despised them. The Thais I met considered the "hill tribes" savages—dirty, primitive, and superstitious—"like in your Wild West," they said. The hill people were fiercely independent as well, and clung tenaciously to their traditions, and this intensified the Thais' hatred. Isolated and self-sufficient, the hill people kept to their hills; they grew rice, kept pigs, hunted and, on the Burmese side of the Triangle, grew poppies for opium.

I spent two days with the tour, slogging along jungle trails and fording stream after muddy stream. Rarely had I been so far from roads and the sound of cars passing. Here the noise of the highway was replaced by different rhythms, slower yet stronger: water rushing; flies buzzing; in the villages, the *thonk-thonk-thonk* of rice being pounded.

Our tour guide had little interest in the rhythms of the hills, or their people. He smoked grass all day and drank whiskey at night. The only other member of our group was an overweight Indian who puffed and panted as we walked. We slept in huge bamboo dormitories specially constructed to house visiting tour groups. On the second night I met two Australians, who were on another tour. We decided to leave our groups the next day, and continue on our own.

My guide had told me that there was a Lisu village one day's walk north, on the Burmese border. The Lisu had come from Yunnan, in China, and were part of the Yi, a fierce group of tribes who once terrorized and at times enslaved those Chinese foolhardy enough to intrude upon their mountain domain. I wanted to meet them and so, early the next morning, I and my two companions climbed the hill behind the rest house. The path, little more than a break in the fo-

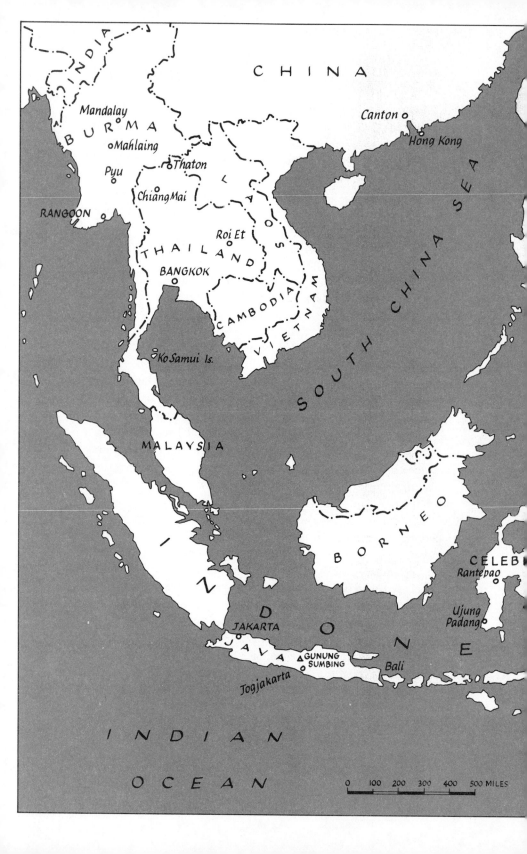

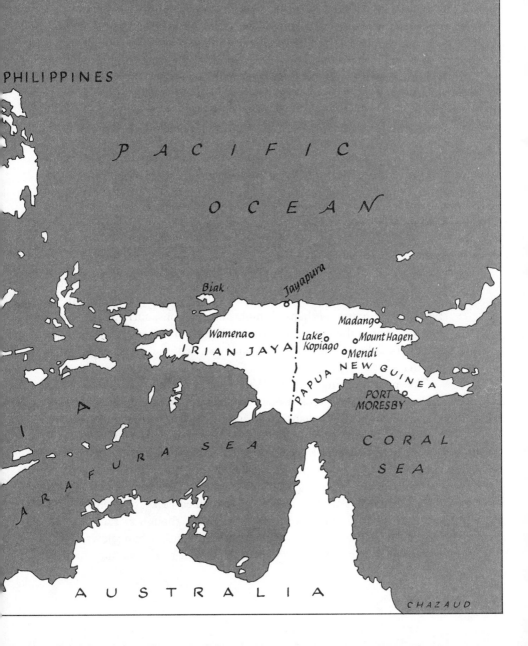

SOUTHEAST ASIA

PHILIPPINES

P A C I F I C

O C E A N

Biak

Jayapura

Madang

Wamena   Lake   Mount Hagen
Kopiago
IRIAN JAYA   Mendi

PAPUA NEW GUINEA

PORT
MORESBY

I A

A R A F U R A   S E A

C O R A L

S E A

A U S T R A L I A

CHAZAUD

liage, was not easy to follow. At one point we took a wrong turn and took the trail that led from Thailand to Burma, but we realized our mistake in time and retraced our steps.

Just before sunset we came to a clearing. We saw rickety houses built of bamboo, women in brightly colored dresses, scampering pigs and children. Just then, gunfire exploded behind us and echoed in the hills. A band of men carrying M-16 assault rifles emerged from the jungle. They were the men of the village, returned from the day's hunt, firing their rifles to shout their joy at being home again.

A man called to us from a nearby house. We went inside and he fed us rice. Rice in Asia is always polished, and so it was here—at another village I had seen an ingenious water-powered rice mill—and the bran, rich in nutrients, had been fed to the pigs or thrown away. Still, the rice was different here. It was that upland variety that grows in the mountains without irrigation and, though it had been stripped of its vitamins, it was the best rice I had ever tasted.

After eating, I went outside. It was dark by then, and the village seemed deserted. There was a light in one of the houses and I went inside. The whole village was there; the room was as densely packed as Times Square on New Year's Eve and there was the same electric aura of tense anticipation. By standing on tiptoe I could see the center of the room. There was a sick child lying there, and a shaman standing over him, waving a bagful of charms. The village had come to witness, or perhaps to aid in, this battle between life and death. It went on for hours, perhaps all night, incantations, sprinkling of ash, tying of string, the hushed crowd watching—but after a while I could barely breathe. I went outside and watched the stars shine over Burma.

The next morning we left. We walked until we reached the Kok River and there we took a boat to Chiang Rai where we spent the night. I left the Australians there and took a bus to Bangkok, a train to Surat Thani on the narrow neck of land that leads to Malaya, and a boat to Ko Samui. Ko Samui, an island ringed with beaches and filled with palm trees, pleasant villages, and waterfalls, has become the best-known watering hole in Southeast Asia, and every backpacker between Bangkok and Bali has stopped there, or soon will. In those days, the island was much less popular, though at Lam Lamai on the south coast I saw rows and rows of identical bungalows, built of shiny new wood with very quaint thatched roofs, waiting for the tourists to come. I rented a room at Tongtakien, a fishing village at the eastern end of the island, and one night the fishermen took me out with them. The boat was long and narrow, like a big canoe, and one man stood at the prow, with a lantern in one hand and a long spear held high in the other. Every few minutes he thrust the spear into the water; with every stab, he speared a fish. There was a girl from New Zealand named Sabrina staying at Tongtakien. We took the boat to the railhead together. She was lovely and I sorely wanted to travel with her, but I was too shy to ask. So she caught the train to Bangkok and I went south to Singapore.

Singapore was a city fast devouring itself, demolishing its pleasant Chinese neighborhoods of two-story stucco houses festooned with laundry, spewing up huge glassy skyscrapers in their place, and wide sterile streets adorned with posters saying $100 FINE FOR LITTERING or WORK HARD TO BUILD YOUR NATION! or (in offices) PERSONS WITH LONG HAIR WILL BE SERVED LAST. But who was I to judge? Those quaint old houses were probably noisome slums inside. After a few days spent gawking at skyscrapers while I waited for my Indonesian visa, I flew to Jakarta.

Indonesia, nation of islands. No one knows for sure how many lie within its watery borders. Perhaps three thousand, perhaps thirteen thousand. Some of the islands have scores, even hundreds, of different ethnic groups and cultures; some are barely explored. Instead of traveling around the world, I could have spent six years exploring the archipelago, sailing from island to island across the indigo sea—and perhaps I would have had as much to tell. But I stayed only three months in Indonesia, and most of that I spent in Bali.

Bali is a tiny, densely populated island just east of Java, an even more crowded island where close to a hundred million people live. There is only one large town on Bali, and I never went there. Even at this early stage of my travels, I had learned to seek out village life; most cities were places best avoided.

In the towns of Indonesia, inefficiency and corruption are a continuing scandal and a way of life. But in Bali (and throughout the archipelago) village life is organized efficiently, humanely, and more or less democratically. Bumbling bureaucracies dominate the national scene, while the villages are halfway to utopia: I saw this contrast time and again as I traveled (especially in Africa), so often that I began to wonder whether the nation-state, a legacy of colonial times, was at all appropriate for most of the world. Balinese local government is a socialist dream come to life; village councils, with one member chosen by each family, supervise land use and water rights, lend money to needy members, and regulate all aspects of daily life. But the secret of village harmony is not how the people are governed but what they share. Shared tradition, shared religion, shared culture, and countless festivals—times for happiness and sharing—bind the village together. Religion, art, work, play: sometimes it is hard to say where one leaves off and the other begins.

All this is true in Bali, and it is true throughout Asia. What makes Bali stand out, even in Asia, is the richness and profusion of its art: its paintings and its plays, and its dances, its sculpture, its puppet theater and its *gamelans,* which are orchestras of xylophones whose music shimmers like moonlight on water. But Bali's fecund, exotic culture, its gentle people, and its long sandy beaches have attracted crowds of tourists who are slowly destroying the culture and souring the kindness and turning the peaceful beaches into crowded holiday camps.

Most of the travelers stayed at Kuta Beach, a warren of cheap but pleasant hotels where the only Balinese in sight were souvenir vendors and soft-drink sellers. There were so many of them that they formed a constant procession as they shuffled between the sunbathers and the sea. And time, too, seemed to shuffle and drag its steps in Kuta, and the days slid by in a quiet and unnoticed parade. It was pleasant, but it wasn't Bali, so after two weeks I moved to Ubud.

The town of Ubud is the center of Balinese culture, and everyone there is an artist. The proprietor of my hotel played in a *gamelan* orchestra; in the house next door lived a painter; the hotel owner's massive uncle trained fighting roosters—to the Balinese, a cockfight embodies passion, myth, and drama—and every morning the birds' ecstatic chorus shattered my sleep as they welcomed the dawn.

There is a small museum in Ubud which is filled to overflowing with the paintings produced in the town. In olden days, Balinese paintings were never signed. They portrayed religious themes and communal motifs, and the name of the artist, like his thoughts, was not considered worth recording. Then the Europeans came, and taught the young Balinese to paint *their* emotions, *their* view of the cosmos, and not the village's. I spent hours in the museum, awed by their works. Magical dragons and demons and Hindu divinities sprang from the canvas. They were as richly charged with emotion as the new Expressionist art which was to sweep New York several years later; but the Expressionists of the 1980s lack—as all artists born in an age of anomie must lack—the magic and knowledge and assurance of these young Balinese.

Behind the museum the rice fields began. When I first saw this area of hills and paddies, I thought I had found the most beautiful place on earth. It was more than a landscape; every bit of it was painstakingly sculpted and lovingly tended. The paddies were steps carved into the hills, and glossy-leafed plants and trees sprang from the earthworks between the fields. The trees, the clover-covered earth, everything was green, and the rice was a green that was greener than green. You could walk for miles in any direction and see nothing but these electric-green fields, and maybe an occasional shrine or wood or duck-filled stream. Bali, along with its much larger neighbor, Java, is one of the most densely populated places on earth, and not an inch of land is wasted.

The evening before I left Ubud I went to an *arja,* a play performed by dancers—something of a cross between an opera and a ballet. The stage was outside, on a grassy hill behind the town. It was hard to find a place to sit; farmers from outlying villages had streamed into town·for the play. On the other side of the hill were rows of food stalls, lit by lanterns and run by pretty girls who spent the evening flirting with the handsomer customers. The dance itself was intricate and complex; each gesture, each turn of the head or blink of the eye or sinuous wave of the fingers had meaning. It was too subtle for me, and I left shortly after midnight. But those unlettered farmers from the hills were enthralled by the dance, discussed and evaluated each gesture, and roared with laughter at the comic parts; most probably stayed until the dance ended at dawn.

I flew from Bali to Ujung Padang, where I caught the daily plane to Jayapura. Jayapura was the back end of the archipelago; it was the capital of West Irian, the Indonesian half of the island of New Guinea. This was my real goal—all the rest was prelude.

6

NEW GUINEA: JOURNEY TO THE INTERIOR

In the days of my childhood, when I used tropical names to conjure up tropical dreams, New Guinea was the most potent name of all. It evoked visions of unmapped jungles and unknown peoples, tribes so isolated that their universe included their valley and the roof of sky above it, and nothing more. My daydreams, for once, were founded in fact: when I was young, much of central New Guinea had not yet been explored, and even today there may be uncharted pockets of forest where people live and die in blithe ignorance of the outside world. As I flew toward Jayapura I understood how the island had escaped exploration for so long. Below the plane lay an undulating carpet of green: unbroken rain forest concealing range after range of treacherously steep hills. For over an hour the jet flew over the jungle. There were no towns, no highways, nothing but that endless sea of trees; the portion of New Guinea which lies west of Jayapura is over three times the size of England but has only one hundred miles of roads. To cross the island you must fly—or walk.

Most of the hundred miles of highway were in and around Jayapura and were filled with brand-new minibuses equipped with extra-loud horns and huge speakers that blared Western rock. Raucous, jerry-built, loud and boring, Jayapura was a boom town without a boom. There was a street of stores selling knickknacks from Jakarta and Singapore; there were food stalls serving Javanese food, dishes with names like *gado-gado* and *nasi goreng;* there was even a big white mosque; it was a Javanese city transplanted across the sea. The people, too, were Javanese, almost without exception; they had left their crowded, poor island in search of fortune, and had ended up hawking mangoes or sweeping floors in a jerkwater town two thousand miles from home.

Prices were high in Jayapura. I checked into a hotel less expensive than most. It, like the rest of the town, had been slapped together as quickly and cheaply as possible. My room was windowless, but the view from outside was superb: steep green cliffs, the blue Pacific, and between them, like a scar, the tin roofs of the town.

I spent two weeks in Jayapura, loitering in shops and markets, taking minibuses to the end of the road and back, or watching the waves break on long-abandoned landing craft, relics of the days when General MacArthur made his headquarters here, rusty hulks which no one in the past thirty-five years had taken the trouble to clear away. I had applied for permission to fly inland to Wamena in the Baliem Valley where, forty years before, the first European visitors found a complex network of fields, canals, villages, and watchtowers. My application had little hope of success. A war raged around Wamena; the people of the valley were trying to drive the Indonesians out. For the New Guineans, being a part of the Republic of Indonesia meant being governed by an alien race. An Indonesian pilot, who invited me into his house one day for tea and cupcakes, told me how he had flown deep into the jungle, across the Papua New Guinea border, chasing spear-waving rebels and gunning them down.

After a fortnight's wait, my application was denied, and I caught the weekly plane to Wewak. Wewak was in the eastern half of the island, a former Australian colony which had been given independence two years before and was now known as Papua New Guinea.

In a science-fiction novel I once read, the world suddenly shattered into different eras; you could walk down the street and step into another century. Papua New Guinea was like that: some parts lived in prehistory, while others were as modern as anything between Singapore and Sydney. Many people were caught straddling the line. Mt. Hagen, where I flew after a day in Wewak, was full of men dressed in the leafy loincloth locally known as "ass-grass." Some wore sport jackets over the leaves. They had come from their villages to eat hot dogs and doughnuts, deposit money in the bank, buy beer and comic books, and go to the movies. One day, I joined them at the Hagen Cinema and saw an old James Stewart film; it was a western, part comedy and part adventure. The audience gasped with horror at the gunfights, and roared with laughter at all the corny pranks and pratfalls. Folktales and drama are important parts of New Guinea rural life, but the screen was a hundred times larger than life—every pore on James Stewart's face was visible, and his lazy smile was six feet wide. Surging waves of raw emotion stunned the villagers, some of whom might never before have seen a photograph or viewed a face that wasn't real. When they go back to their villages, I thought, they will bring the restlessness of the city with them. Never again will they be satisfied by stories told around a campfire.

I was disappointed in Mt. Hagen. In my youthful fantasies of primitive New Guinea there was no room for milkshake bars, supermarkets, or bookstores that sold souvenirs. When I first read about the area, twenty years before, Mt. Hagen had barely been settled. The place had changed and, like me, come of age; my childhood dreams were out of date. But the highlands, that central region of hills, plateaus, and snow-capped mountains, were large, and I decided to try another town. I flagged down a PMV—or public motor vehicle, one of those flatbed freight trucks which are the only means of intercity transport in Papua New Guinea—and rode to Mendi, several hours west of Hagen. Mendi was smaller; there were no soda parlors, only a few tin-roofed general stores and a tiny hot-dog stand with an awning where shivering highlanders, their ass-grass dripping, huddled during the brief squalls of rain that swept through the streets. Mendi was still what Mt. Hagen had once been: an outback town, a frontier town. It was raw, new, a little ugly and a little wild. Not so long ago there had been nothing but trees and a rushing river. Then Australians had come and chopped down the trees and cut them into logs that they used to build those stores and houses. And in the wake of the pioneers had come shopkeepers and schoolteachers and government patrol officers. And missionaries.

I saw a lot of missionaries in New Guinea, which probably has as many missionaries per square mile as any place on earth. I viewed them with mixed feelings and still do. They are dedicated and tireless and they build schools and hospitals in places no one else will go. They save lives. But they also try to save souls. I have come to believe that a person's soul is tied to the soul of his people, bound up in a fragile, complex web wherein myth and morals and tradition, one's view of the world, and one's place in it, are woven together. Touch one strand and ripples will run throughout the web. Christianity, with its teachings of sin and guilt and salvation, can tear the web to shreds. Christianity changes people. In New Guinea Christians become quieter and more mature, a shade more restrained; they walk in fear of hellfire. They grow ashamed of their backwardness. They yearn for Western clothes. The missionaries, whether intentionally or not, have served as harbingers of Western culture, agents of modernization. Some gloried in the role; the cultures they destroyed, they said, were noteworthy only for headhunting and tribal warfare, for cannibalism, and for casual murder. Perhaps these missionaries saw only what they wanted to see. In the forests west of Mendi I met people who were neither Christian nor savage.

The first missionaries I ever met were an old Australian couple who ran Mendi's only guesthouse. About them hovered an indefinable aura compounded of self-righteousness, intolerance, and sexual repression. Typical, I thought, having just read *Rain;* but these were the only missionaries I met who resembled the priggish characters so vividly described by Somerset Maugham. And even these Australians were in their way admirable; they had the strength of pioneers. They had cut down trees to bridge raging rivers. Once, the husband had been wounded in the bush—he showed me the scar—and had crawled miles to get help. I could easily imagine them facing down an army of tribesmen with their steely, determined gaze.

On the wall of the guesthouse parlor hung a map of the world, with a colored pin speared through each city where a mission was established. Late at night, when the others had gone to bed, I amused myself by sticking pins in Peking, Mecca, and Omsk. The Australians had regional maps as well, and they knew which tribes were

Christian and which were not; but they could tell me little about the culture or customs of the highlanders they hoped to convert.

I sorely needed information and advice. A vast patchwork of peoples lay around Mendi. There are 750 languages spoken in New Guinea, which means that you are never more than ten miles away from a new language, a different culture.

There was an Australian high-school teacher in Mendi who knew the area as well as anyone in town. He invited me to dinner with some of his students. As his wife opened cans of meat and vegetables and emptied them into plates, he spread a map over his rumpled bed and we clustered around it. I had come to the highlands, I told him, to see traditional village life. I avoided using such words as *primitive* or *unspoiled,* but he guessed what I was after. "Go to Lake Kopiago," he said. It was one of the last districts in the area to be brought under government control, and in the forests north of the lake, where the Hewa people lived, control was in name only. "But you won't be allowed into the Hewa area," he said. "It's the one part of the highlands I haven't seen." Until two years before, it was classified as a restricted area—closed to everyone, and left undisturbed. After independence, all the restricted regions were opened, but the Hewas' territory was, despite its new status, still unsettled and possibly dangerous. To the Huli and the Duna, the people who lived south and east of the lake, the Hewa were a secretive and cunning people, who attacked in stealth and who were best left alone. The Huli were fierce fighters themselves; the teacher passed around pictures of Huli men taken in Tari, a police post between Mendi and Kopiago. The photographs showed proud, muscular warriors wearing huge wigs adorned with flowers. It would be worth the trip to the lake to see them. In any case, I had already decided to go to Kopiago, to visit the Hewa.

Air Niugini did not fly to Kopiago, so I hitched a ride on a government plane. After an hour's flight over a jumbled and primeval landscape of cliffs, forests, and waterfalls, the tiny Cessna landed, its wheels kicking up dirt as the pilot dodged the potholes. Beyond the airstrip I could see the town: missions, a school, a police station, a scattering of zinc-roofed houses. And one patrol officer, who was hurrying to meet the plane.

In settlements like Kopiago, the patrol officer was the government. He could, if he desired, order me back on the plane, which was revving up for the return flight. Fortunately, he liked me. Though he was born near Wewak—he was one of the few civil servants who were not Australian—he knew the Kopiago area well, and as we walked toward the town I asked his advice on where to go. "You must visit the Hewa," he said. There was a police patrol leaving for the north in a few days, and I would be allowed to join them.

In later years, I realized how fortunate I had been. In most of the world, the explorer's main problem is avoiding the police. Bureaucrats and policemen view us with suspicion. Businessmen, diplomats, and missionaries are known quantities, easily classified and pigeonholed, but travelers are not. They cannot understand why we travel, and bureaucratic minds are always made uneasy by anything they cannot understand—particularly if the thing has longish hair and faded jeans.

There was an abandoned bungalow, with its roof and most of its walls intact, where I was allowed to set up camp. That evening, I was invited to dine with the patrol officer. We ate canned fish and rice, considered a sophisticated meal by the nation's elite because neither ingredient is native to New Guinea. After dinner, we sat on the veranda, drank beer, and swapped stories by lantern light. He told funny tales about the difficulties of taking censuses and holding elections in a land that had not been fully explored; the year before, a patrol had stumbled upon a previously unknown tribe of nomads who presumably were eligible to vote at the next election. I told him about the other half of the island, where elections were held at gunpoint; according to one story making the rounds, those who voted against Indonesian rule were immediately shot and their votes disallowed.

In the days that followed, I had dinner or tea or lunch with everyone in Kopiago: peanut butter sandwiches courtesy of the Methodist mission; imported sausage and pumpernickel at the home of the Catholic missionary, a quiet, studious Austrian who felt far more at ease with his highland friends than with other Europeans; tea at the Seventh-Day Adventist compound where I was treated to an exhibit of paintings depicting non-Christians and other sinners roasting in Hell; and coffee with the Kopiago police force—Geoffrey and Nicholas. When my services as town guest were not in demand, I swam in the lake, changing clothes in a shack on which someone had painted ROYAL LAKE KOPIAGO YACHT CLUB. On one trip to the lake, I passed a group of Duna walking toward town. They stopped, surrounded me, and, one by one, kissed my hand. As every highlander knows, white men have magic powers. How else could they make flashlights and motorcars and cigarettes? Perhaps this magic would rub off; it was worth a try. I was stunned. It was outrageous, being deified on a public highway; it was a scene straight out of the Phantom comic books, which were best sellers in New Guinea. The missionaries have it easy here, I thought. I could convert these men to anything I chose in ten minutes.

No one wore a watch in Kopiago; there were no trains to catch or appointments to keep. If a time for a meeting had to be specified, it was always 6 A.M. or 6 P.M.—sunrise or sunset—the two times of day everyone knew. One morning, about a week after my arrival, at 6 A.M. precisely, the police patrol left for the Hewa. Besides myself, the patrol included Geoffrey—one of the policemen—two medical officers, and a string of guides and porters. A few years before, I was told, a permanent police post had been set up in Hewa country, but after a few months spent in gloomy isolation, the policemen had run away. This abandoned post was our destination. The medics would set up a clinic and Geoffrey would show the flag, though, as his colleagues in Kopiago had told me, if a Hewa wanted to hide in the forest, there was no way the police could track him down.

At first, the trail was easy. We crossed the grasslands that surrounded the lake. The path sloped gently upward, and there were fine views of rolling hills and blue water. But then the forest began, an unbroken, unending canopy that covered the whole of the Hewas' domain. The hills were steeper here and slippery with mud, and the trail was never level. The land was beautiful, as all rain forests are, and there were a thousand places I would have liked to stop to admire a flower, or a cluster of ferns and clover, or a jumble of mossy rocks behind a waterfall. But there was no time; we were constantly climbing up or down. The ascents were tiring, and the descents were treacherous, and both took me far too long. I could barely keep up. The others were all native New Guineans, and for them the trail was as easy as walking down Broadway. They did not pant, they did not sweat, they barely noticed the clouds of mosquitoes that swarmed around us. The worst part was the bridges. Many streams watered the forest, and most were spanned with a single log. I have trouble walking on a log at the best of times, and the sight of sharp rocks ten or twenty feet below me made it even harder to keep my balance. Usually Geoffrey, who would have run across the bridge had he been alone, would have to coax me across.

We came to a deserted house just before sunset. There were many abandoned homesteads in the forest, because the Hewa are seminomadic. They build a house, clear land and farm it; in a few years, the soil is exhausted and they move on. The house that we found was in fairly good condition, and so we slept there. In the overgrown garden behind the house, there were a few sweet potatoes, which we dug up and ate. The next day, there were more hills, more mud, more bridges. Late in the afternoon, we came to a cluster of log cabins that had once been a police station.

The post was in a large clearing surrounded by forest. Its previous occupants had felt oppressed, hemmed in by the jungle, but I felt liberated. Sometimes, especially toward sunset, when the light was soft and the sky hazy, it seemed as if I and my companions were alone in a virgin world of forest and clearing and sky. The lands that lay beyond, where one could find tin roofs and law firms and city buses, seemed a phantom world, immaterial; it was, as the people of the highlands all believed, a land of ghosts and spirits too far away to be real.

Our camp was a few miles from the Lagaip, a wide and raging torrent that was the headwaters of the Strickland, one of New Guinea's largest rivers. On the far side, called North Hewa, the land was more or less unexplored and it was there that I wanted to go. Geoffrey found me a guide; he didn't know the area but neither did anyone else. We planned to build a raft and paddle across. It was dangerous—an Australian patrol officer had died trying to cross that very stretch of river, a fact which my companions delighted in reminding me of—but with luck we just might make it. I decided to leave the next day. The entire camp—even the porters—planned to accompany me to the Lagaip and watch me try to cross. It would be an exciting spectacle even for those jaded from watching too many films. I slept fitfully that night, but by morning was resigned to my adventure, and I felt bitterly disappointed when I learned that the guide had disappeared. It wasn't the river that had frightened him off, Geoffrey told me; it was the people on the other side.

The guide was never seen again, and I could not find another. I decided to explore the forest around the post instead. There were, according to one of the porters who knew the area, several houses on our side of the river a few miles upstream. Geoffrey persuaded him to take me there. The porter spoke the Hewa language and would try to induce one of the families to take me in.

We set off the next morning. My new guide was stocky and self-assured, and he swaggered along the steep and slippery path. I realized why Geoffrey and the others had found the trek from Kopiago so easy; that trail was a veritable highway compared to the one I now blundered along. For much of the way, there wasn't any path at all. Fortunately, fairly few plants blocked our way; the floor of a rain forest is too shady to support the impenetrable tangle of vegetation that is Hollywood's idea of a jungle.

It was early afternoon when we came to a clearing and saw the house. Many Hewas live in trees, building their homes on platforms thirty feet above the ground, but this house had been constructed on a scaffold that jutted out from the steep hillside. We climbed the stairs that led to the front door.

My childhood experiences, however banal they might seem if I could repeat them today, often serve as a benchmark to which few things in later life measure up. When I was six, my third-grade class had toured a museum in New York that contained huge dioramas of an Indian wigwam, a caveman's lair, and several similar curator's fantasies. As I entered the Hewa house, I felt again the thrill that had swept through me when, twenty years before, I had come face-to-face with those primitive, alien tableaux and had pressed my body against the glass in a longing to step through it. Cooking fires, smoke-blackened rafters, raffia baskets, women in grass skirts, and men with bows and arrows, and bamboo plugs through their noses—it was a daydream come alive. For almost an hour, I sat in stunned and wide-eyed silence. Then I began to notice the people around me, and I never confused them with my fantasies again.

During that first hour, the others were in a state of shock as well. They would have been no more surprised had a flying saucer landed and little green men jumped out. The porter spoke to them for several minutes—I have no idea what he said—and then he left. I was on my own.

One of the men grabbed a piglet that was playing on the floor and carried it outside, motioning for me to follow. Pigs in New Guinea are a way of life, just as cars are with us: they are capital assets, symbols of wealth and status; they are thought of with tolerant affection as fat, stupid, oinking children, and, a man on Karkar Island once told me, sometimes they die of old age because they are too loved to be eaten. But the Hewa considered my arrival so important that a little pig was killed in my honor. The head of the household, whose name, I later found out, was Iamiah, spoke—a prayer, by the sound of it—and then shot the pig with an arrow. Then a pit was dug and stones heated on a fire. The pig was cut into pieces, the pieces wrapped in leaves and put in the pit, and the hot rocks were heaped on top with dirt thrown over them.

Building a fire, roasting the rocks, and wrapping the pig were everyday tasks, and they helped the Hewa return to the normal rhythms of life which I had for a short while interrupted. I sat and watched. One of the medics had prepared a list of twenty Hewa words with their English equivalents, but I could hardly join in the conversation. Even the two-year-old, youngest of the clan, spoke far better Hewa than I. Still, within a few hours I had learned a lot about my new companions, without benefit of speech. There was Iamiah, for example. No one had to tell me that he was the head of the family. He spoke with the assurance of a man whose every word is respected. Though I liked him, I don't know why. He was vain, slightly spoiled, and a bit of a dandy. He spent much of his time preening himself, or admiring his reflection in my mirror.

Two other men lived in the house, as well as a gawky boy who hovered on the verge of manhood. Bamiah and Borobuan were brooding, silent men who passed their days staring into space as if baffled by some mystery too sad and deep for words. The boy was different. Unlike the rest, he knew a few words of pidgin, that jolly and racist lingua franca of the island much of whose vocabulary was derived from English. It was spoken throughout the country, while English was not, and though I never became fluent, I was forced to learn a few words. "The white man's wife made a mistake," for example, was translated "Meri bilong masta buggerup." Pidgin was the language of the police post, the town, and the plantation; by learning it, the boy had set his sights on the world outside the forest. Someone, perhaps a porter or a policeman, had filled his head with tales of the miracles that were everyday occurrences there: pictures that talk, boxes that fly, and so forth. I had come from this magical world, and the boy idolized me, following me everywhere. Some of his family's ways embarrassed him; he would not talk about the row of fetishes—chicken claws and other oddments tied into bundles—that hung from the rafters, and if he had spoken English he doubtless would have sighed "Primitive superstition!" and dismissed them with a shrug.

The boy had not yet learned to be ashamed of the clothes he wore; like the men, he was naked except for a belt of bark from which hung a fringe of grass. It was a most convenient mode of dress: new clothes grew everywhere, ready to be picked and worn. The women's clothes were different; they wore skirts made of a plant which had been dried and cut into strips and necklaces made of cowrie shells. There were four women—one wife for each of the men, and an older woman. Bamiah and Borobuan had, I think, married Iamiah's sisters, and the older woman, who acted like a jovial matriarch, was probably related to Iamiah as well.

At first, I thought the women had been cheated. A rope divided the house into two parts. On one side were the three men and the almost-grown boy, and in the other part, which was one-quarter the size of the men's section, were the four women and all the children. The women cut and cooked the pig, and the men got the best parts of it. Later, I found out that the women did most of the rest of the work as well: farming, cleaning, fetching water. But in their way the women were stronger. Bamiah, Borobuan, and the boy all seemed dissatisfied, unhappy in their separate ways. But the women were bold and saucy, always laughing, and forever teasing the men. I was an easy and tempting target. That first afternoon, they asked me to help them prepare the pig—implying that I was low enough in status to do women's work. When I refused, it meant that I was incapable of doing it. The women grinned for hours after that, and repeated the joke every day at dinnertime.

We ate inside the house that first evening. The sun had set by the time the meal was ready, and no one went outside after dark, though what they feared I never learned: spirits, perhaps, or possibly the neighbors.

That was, for me, the best part of the day: nightfall and the hours that followed. The big house—it was one huge room, thirty feet by twenty—was lit only by two tiny fires, and so it was a magical, shad-

owy time. The men would sit by their fire and one of them, Iamiah
or Bamiah or Borobuan, would tell a story. It would begin in a whisper, a voice as faint as the fire, but the storyteller would change his
voice to suit each character, and, without understanding a word spoken, I could tell that this person was pompous and that one a whining
coward, and that one a young boy and this one an old man barely able
to talk. The house seemed filled with players; it was hard to believe
that only one man was speaking. The women, seated by their fire at
the other end of the big room, would watch and listen, usually in silence, though one or another would sometimes interrupt the performance with a well-timed quip. When this happened, Iamiah would
grab my walking stick, rush into the women's section, and pretend to
beat the offender as all the women roared with laughter.

After a few hours, the stories would end and the house grew quiet
as the men and women, pigs, dogs, and children drifted off to sleep.
The men curled up by the fire, fitted together as snugly as a stack of
spoons, and on the other side of the house, the women did the same. I
carried my bedding in my pack—a blue plastic mat that I eventually
lost in Niger and a blanket that lasted until the Ivory Coast—and I
spread it out in the middle of the room, which was deserted except
for an occasional wandering piglet who would nuzzle me as I slept.
Several times each night, I was awakened by the men's soft voices as
they stirred, talked, and fell asleep again. They slept together, woke
together, and probably dreamed together. Sometimes I thought they
valued their dreams more highly than their waking life.

During the day the house was empty except for me. The women
tended the potato patches, most of which were far from the house,
and foraged for leaves and breadfruit, while the men went off to
hunt. Almost all of our food came from the fields. Occasionally one
of the dogs would bring in a rat or a lizard, which were surprisingly
tasty when grilled, but hardly enough to feed eight people. The
men's daily hunt served mainly as a pretext to be alone in the jungle.
Borobuan and Bamiah, I think, found some measure of peace deep in
the forest; those two lived only to hunt and to dream.

There were four or five young children in the family, and the pack
of them spent their days running wild in the forest. It wasn't all play,
though; their games helped them to learn the skills and responsibil-
ities of adulthood. Even the two-year-old was given simple tasks,

such as fetching water. He would wait until afternoon, when the men were back, and then burst into the house carrying a tiny cup of water from the spring, beaming and ready to be praised for a job well done. Still, the boys in that house were not forced to grow up too soon, and on many nights I was awakened by a squalling child, usually one of the older boys, aged nine or ten, who would not stop crying until comforted by his mother. As for the one girl, who was about seven, she spent much of her time in the fields with the women, though her chief joy was spying on me and following me around, especially when she thought I might be visiting the toilet, which was a log perched on a cliff.

All the days were alike in the forest. The house would empty at daybreak, fill again at suppertime, then would come darkness and stories and sleep—after a while I lost track of time, though I believe I stayed with Iamiah's clan a fortnight. A few memories, though, stand out like islands in a formless sea. One afternoon, as supper was slowly cooking, everyone rushed into the house and a heavy plank was pushed in front of the doorway. Iamiah loaded his bow and peered through a chink in the wall. Tribal feuds were far from unknown in New Guinea, and bands of warriors would at times mount surprise raids to kill their enemies. I suddenly realized that the house was built like a fortress; on each side were loopholes through which bows could be fired, and though the front door, now barred, was only four feet off the ground, the rest of the house, because it was built on a steep slope, was twenty feet above the hillside.

After a while, Iamiah crept outside and crawled through the undergrowth in the clearing that surrounded the house. He soon returned; it was a false alarm.

That evening, perhaps to celebrate, the men chewed betel nut. The betel palm grows throughout the tropics, in Africa and Asia as well as New Guinea. In every town in India and southeast Asia, the streets are scarred with the blood-red gobs of juice that betel-chewers leave behind. Most people consider betel nut a mild intoxicant, but those that grew in Hewa country packed a wallop found nowhere else. The men grew wilder as nut after nut was passed around. After chewing three, Bamiah stood on a narrow beam that protruded from the back of the house and, oblivious to the twenty-foot drop below his feet, yodeled chants and war cries as the other men grinned.

The men ignored me that evening, but on most nights I was an inexhaustible source of wonder and amusement. My bright orange backpack, adorned with a blazing sun embroidered in Nepal, stood in the center of the house. The Hewa were too polite, or perhaps too fearful, to open it and look inside. But the pack itself and anything left outside it was considered fair game for examination, and everyone, even Bamiah and Borobuan, spent hours staring at the strange, unfathomable objects that lay on the floor: a plastic water bottle, a roll of toilet paper, and a pair of shoes. One night, I opened a can of corned beef and divided it among us. Afterward, the empty can was passed around and admired. In the end, I gave it to Iamiah, who treasured the gift. From time to time, I saw him take out the can and, with joy on his face, smell it. How fragile their world is, I thought. The boy has already left it, and even Iamiah or Borobuan might forsake the forest they love if offered enough cans in exchange.

As the days passed, I grew restless. Too much of my life had been spent in cities, and I had become addicted to constant stimulation. The endless peace and harmony of the forest bored me. The others never found life tedious; Bamiah, Borobuan, and even the boy could sit for hours staring at the wall, and I sometimes wondered whether they were in a yogic trance or a bovine stupor. The Hewa had no expectation of change and, until recently, no desire for it: for hundreds of years, the round of daily life had remained the same, as fixed and inevitable as the sunrise. Now, of course, shiny, tempting trinkets of change—tin cans, steel axheads—had penetrated the forest and in a few years the boys who woke me at night with their bawling would leave in search of more. And if they lingered too long in the towns, they might gain a wristwatch and maybe even a radio, but they would lose the magic of the forest. If they ever went back, they would, like me, be bored to distraction, unless they took their radio along.

I thought about these things to fill the time. There was a sheet of paper in my pack, and I tore it up to make a deck of cards. I taught the boy a few simple games; he learned quickly, though he could not understand why a card with two diamonds was not the same as a card with one. Finally, I decided to leave. I said my farewells that evening. I had come prepared. I had bought a load of trinkets in Mendi and I gave them out in partial return for the family's hospitality: there were pocket knives for each of the men and boys, a tarpaulin and a blanket for the women, a bright red belt for the teenager, and a photograph of me for the girl who had followed me around. Some people believe that a camera can capture the spirit of a man, and if this is true, and I would like to think it is, then a part of my soul has remained with Iamiah's clan in that far-off forest.

Still, the people seemed strangely disappointed with what I had given them—except for the oldest woman, who promptly claimed the blanket for herself and hugged it all night. Many highland tribesmen, even those who wear wristwatches and boxer shorts, believe that white men are visitors from the spirit world. Europeans must be the ghosts of dead New Guineans, for why else would they return to New Guinea? More than likely, Iamiah and the others were expecting me to bring them instructions and messages from their ancestors, or perhaps news of a dead brother or child. They must have thought me rude and heartless for not passing on the information, not even on our last evening together, and perhaps they were also puzzled why, even after a fortnight, I still pretended not to speak their language.

The next day I left the clearing for the first time since my arrival. Borobuan went along to show me the way. Geoffrey had long since left for Kopiago, but one of the medics was still at the police post. Using him as an interpreter, I convinced Borobuan to go with me to Kopiago; I could never have found my way alone. We left at once and were joined by two Hewa teenagers I had not seen before.

When I was cooped up in the house, I had looked forward to the long walk to Kopiago. I had thought the trail would be easier the second time, but the hills were just as steep, the path was just as slippery, the bridges were just as frightening as three weeks before. The only difference was the company. The Hewa were happy walkers. The teenagers stopped to pick flowers and braid them in their hair. They sang songs. The lyrics were improvised; each man in turn would make up a verse. They sang about the fine sweet potatoes they would eat in Kopiago. Once, Borobuan found an empty cardboard cookie box on the trail; carefully, he picked it up and hung it on a tree branch for all passersby to admire.

We spent the night in an abandoned homestead. The next day, shortly after noon, we came out of the forest. We were on a hill above the plain and, for the first time in weeks, I could see the horizon, with sun and sky above and lake below. The Hewa sang louder and walked faster, and within an hour we reached the town. The head teacher saw me arrive and invited me into his house, a bright modern bungalow. Borobuan came in as well, and that was the last time I saw him. He looked smaller somehow and ill at ease, sitting on the carpet among the upholstered chairs and Formica coffee tables, and after a while he left for the forest.

7

NEW GUINEA
TO INDONESIA

During those last days with the Hewa, when I began to feel hemmed in by the jungle, I dreamed of India: the noise, the color, the crowds. I wanted to surround myself with crowds. Besides, I had never really seen India; somehow I had been sidetracked to Nepal. I would, I decided, head west toward India. But I did not leave New Guinea until December 1977, and that was a month later.

I spent a few days in Kopiago as a guest of the head teacher, wolfing down enormous quantities, much more than was polite or even reasonable, of canned fish and rice. After two weeks of eating undercooked sweet potatoes, with an insect grub or a piece of lizard sometimes added as a special treat, I thought the mackerel, which was packed in an exquisitely salty tomato sauce, was the most delicious dish ever created.

I took a plane to Tari. From there I hitchhiked to Hagen and then to Mandang on the northeast coast of New Guinea, where I caught a boat for the short ride to Karkar. Karkar was a lazy South Pacific island, full of coconut palms and little thatch houses. There were a lot of coconut plantations where men from the highlands came in search of money to spend on pigs and radios. I spent a night on one of the largest farms, drinking with the workers and sleeping on the floor of a flea-infested dormitory. I was perhaps the only white man the workers had met, except for missionaries and the Australian owner of the plantation, and they plied me with beer after beer.

The next day I hitched a ride on a jeep to Wadau village on the north coast. I had read long and detailed anthropological studies of the people of Karkar. According to the articles, they, like the highlanders, believed that Europeans came from the spirit world, and I looked forward to a welcome befitting a visiting deity. But my information was out of date. That was twenty years ago, Sibon Luang, the chief of Wadau, told me. His son, Aibob, who was home for a few days from high school in Madang, took me around the village. Wadau was a cluster of airy houses, walled with bamboo and roofed with thatch, and a photo of the village would have made an ideal postcard, to be captioned "Charm of the South Pacific." But cameras can lie: rock music blared from every hut and on clotheslines hidden behind the houses blue jeans and T-shirts flapped in the breeze. The isolation and superstition of an earlier era were things of the past, but the tradition of courtesy and welcome remained.

After Karkar, I visited Madang and Lae, where my pockets were picked as I slept at the Salvation Army hostel. From Lae I flew to Port Moresby, capital of Papua New Guinea and the largest town on the island. One morning, I collapsed on the street, and it was several hours before I was able to stagger to a hospital. I had caught malaria, probably on the walk to Kopiago, and I was forced to spend several weeks in Port Moresby. I came to hate the town. There were department stores, and any number of soda fountains, and one or two buildings tall enough to have elevators, but the town was ugly and sprawling and graceless, and something in the air reminded me of Jayapura.

In fact, Jayapura was pleasant after those weeks in Port Moresby. I flew more or less directly there, stopping only to change planes. Jayapura's markets, the tiny food stalls, and the hordes of Javanese, all of which had seemed so out of place on my first visit, were a welcome change from the Little Australia across the border. The signs in the street were written in Indonesian, people spoke and shouted and sang in Indonesian, and the air was full of the smells of Indonesia: clove cigarettes, mangoes, the pungent odor of mosquito coils. I was back in Asia again.

One morning when there was nothing better to do, I applied once again for a permit to travel to the Baliem, that fascinating, war-torn highland valley that had been off-limits since the revolt broke out. As I had expected, the army command refused permission, but at the immigration office, which I tried next, the man on duty wrote out a permit at once and stapled it into my passport. "Hanya Wamena," the permit said, only Wamena. I could visit, the man told me, the town of Wamena but not the villages around it.

The old twin-engine plane that made the daily run to Wamena was slow and low-flying and for over an hour we flew over forest and swampland that had not changed since the days when the first men landed on the island of New Guinea, migrants from harbors long since forgotten. Through the haze of the propeller, I could see a range of hills ahead. The plane swooped through a narrow gap in the hills, and we were in the valley. There were earthworks below, strange mounds and burrowings as alien and enigmatic as the canals on Mars. These were sweet potato fields. The Dani, the people of the Baliem valley, dug and piled the earth and pierced it with a sharpened stick, a technique of farming that the rest of the world had abandoned thousands of years before. A spiderweb of irrigation channels brought water to the plants. As we approached Wamena, the fields were a carpet below us. It was the most crowded terrain I had seen in New Guinea; I could walk in any direction and find a village, and that is what I decided to do. When the plane landed, I could see the tin shacks of Wamena in the distance, and I walked as fast as I could in the opposite direction, away from the town.

There was a track through the fields and I followed it. It was far easier walking than the vertical forests of the Hewa. The valley was a mile-high pocket of level savanna and, were it not for the potato patches, I could have imagined that I had never left the grasslands of East Africa. Certainly the men who stood in the fields had a limber grace and pride of bearing which I had thought was uniquely African. They were naked except for a tubular gourd that was worn like a condom and shaped like one as well, though four times the size. It was used to show virility; the longer the gourd, the higher the wearer's status in the village. Their muscular bodies gleamed with grease. Dani men were vain and would spend hours braiding their hair and painting their faces and rubbing pig fat into their skin. They were warriors, the Dani, whose chief joy and source of meaning in life was the constant raids and tribal battles, many (but not all) of which were ritual combats, as bloodless as a baseball game. The Dutch, and the Indonesians after them, tried for years to end the constant fighting, and finally succeeded. Now the men passed their days combing their hair and keeping their bodies oiled, but without a war to fight they were useless and knew it. Only the older men were content. They had fought and fought well, and their days of fighting now were over, so they could sit in the sun with their memories and dreams.

An hour after leaving the airstrip, I met a visiting missionary from Jayapura. There was a young boy with him who spoke Indonesian, and he told the boy to take me to the village of Akima, two hours' walk away. I spent the night there. Dani men slept together, apart from their wives, and so I stayed in the *honnay,* the men's house. It was made of wood and thatch, shaped like a beehive, and not much taller than I, but it had two stories. There was a fire on the ground floor and the men gathered around it. The talk, to judge from the flat, matter-of-fact tone of their voices, was of crops or politics or village scandal; those epic tales that gave wings to the Hewas' imagination were apparently unknown here. One by one as the night wore on, the men pulled themselves up through a hole in the ceiling and, after a while, I did the same. The second floor was a soft carpet of leaves and branches crowded with snoring Dani. I found a space, curled up, and slept.

I dreamed of drums and singing and when I woke just before dawn, the singing was still going on. The music came from a nearby house. Inside, a hundred people sang and swayed. There was barely room to move and the air was so stale and smoky that at first I could not breathe, yet the crowd inside had swayed and sweated through the night. They seemed tired and happy and purged somehow. I never learned whether what I had witnessed was magic, ritual, or entertainment; whether I had stumbled upon a profound and mystic rite or merely a Dani discotheque. Like most village ceremonies, it was probably all of these at once; villagers have not yet learned to divide their lives into tidy categories.

I had left my money belt in the *honnay,* and when I picked it up I realized that someone had been through it. The thief had taken a few small notes, worth a dollar in all, but had not touched the bundle of ten-thousand-rupiah notes, a denomination which was not known in the Baliem. The robber was either very foolish or very wise. In West New Guinea, work is a privilege reserved for Javanese, and if a native flashed big banknotes in Wamena, the police would know at once that he was a thief.

I left Akima then and followed a footpath until I came to Wena-bubaga. Wenabubaga was larger than Akima, and dirtier. Old men sat by the palisade that surrounded the village and, oblivious to the nimbus of flies that hovered around them, picked lice from each other's hair. I sat down with them and they ran their fingers through my hair as well; this was, I guessed, a sign of friendship and welcome.

The flies were in luck that day, and so was I. There was a pig kill, a giant feast and festival, in progress. Hundreds of Dani had flocked to Wenabubaga hoping for a taste of meat. The pig was slowly roasting in a pit near where I sat. It had been cut up, wrapped in leaves, and placed over heated stones—the same method that I had seen Iamiah's family use.

I saw other similarities as well; pig feasts like this one were popular around Mt. Hagen, and even the word for pig, *wam,* was the same in both Dani and Hewa. Several hundreds of miles of marshland and mountain and deep limestone gorges separated Wenabubaga from Kopiago, yet at some point in the prehistory of the island, intrepid and unknown travelers had brought their language, ideas, and technology from the Papua New Guinea highlands to the Baliem. Perhaps ideas traveled in stages, from neighbor to neighbor—but the Dani's nearest neighbors, the Jale, lived a week's walk away, on the other side of a range of razor-sharp cliffs.

I imagined an island crisscrossed by trails and traders, and this took my mind off the flies. Soon, the pig had been cooked, and divided, and passed around on taro-leaf plates, and greedily eaten. Most of the men licked their fingers and left, and the rest went inside the *honnay.* I followed. I had been given a huge helping of pork, tender and red, and felt sated and drowsy. I climbed through the hole in the ceiling and fell asleep.

I awoke to commotion and shouts from outside. I crawled through the low entrance to the *honnay.* Above me was a man with a gun. It had been ten months since I left Uganda, and I thought I had put the fear behind me, but it came flooding back. It's like the skull beneath the skin, I thought. Asia had been a land of smiles but now the flesh was stripped away, leaving the skeleton-grin of fear and loaded rifles.

The man, an Indonesian policeman, took me to the army post at Jiwika. The commander was a short, wiry man with a leathery face and a killer's eyes. In actual fact, most of the murderers I have met in the world have a sweet and gentle gaze, full of a sadness that can never be expelled, but this man's hard eyes, though far from gentle, would, I thought, barely blink as he gunned a man down. "You must give me ten thousand rupiahs or I will shoot you with this pistol," he said, drawing his gun and putting the barrel in my ear. I managed a grin and he laughed. It had been a joke, or maybe a test of courage. After that, there were questions: What was I doing in a Dani village in a combat zone? I took the position that the wording of my travel permit, "Only Wamena," should be construed to include the area around Wamena, and in the end the soldier accepted this line of reasoning; they had taught me well at Yale Law School.

The commander had other business to attend to, and I ate with several of the soldiers in their barracks. They had just been transferred from East Timor, scene of a bloody and festering conflict which from time to time inspires short articles in the back pages of American newspapers, with headlines of the sort, HUMAN RIGHTS GROUP ACCUSES INDONESIAN ARMY OF ATROCITIES IN TIMOR. I was now eating rice with the men charged with these atrocities. They were young and shy and friendly and most of them wore souvenir T-shirts bought in Timor.

After the meal I watched the commander at work. There were three old Dani men outside, and he was questioning them. Most Javanese look on the Dani as savages who must be clothed and civilized, but this man tried to shock them instead. He showed them photographs of a sort which I had thought unavailable in prudish Indonesia. The Dani elders stared at the closeup photos of naked women with spread legs and flesh the color of pigskin, and manfully tried to conceal their revulsion.

I spent the night at the Catholic mission in Jiwika, where I slept soundly on a bed with a quilt and a mattress. The next morning, a policeman took me back to Wamena. I must not, he told me, go outside the town except to board the plane for Jayapura. Presumably I could, if I so desired, stay in Wamena until my visa ran out. But after a visit to Wamena market, where I saw tin-roofed sheds adorned with posters of Charles Bronson, I decided to catch the next plane to Jayapura, which I had once considered the ugliest town in the world.

From Jayapura I planned to take the Pelni boat for the leisurely cruise to Jakarta, but when I arrived at the quay, I found the boat full of happy Javanese on their way home. There was a space two yards square remaining on deck; I would have to sit on that soggy piece of deck for two weeks and possibly more. A few years later, when my funds ran out and I learned to sleep on floors and pavements, I would have taken the boat, and gladly. But I had more money and less patience in those early days of my travels, and so I flew to Bali.

My plane made an overnight stop in Biak, a tiny South Pacific island a few hundred miles west of Jayapura. A Japanese airbase during World War II, Biak was the scene of a bloody, three-month battle in 1944. Few Americans have been there since then. I followed the road around the coast and saw groves of palm trees, dense green jungle, tin-roofed shanties, and dilapidated churches. It was as tropical as Karkar, but seedy; no one would ever buy a postcard of this place, or make a travel poster with those zinc shacks on it.

The next stop was Ujung Padang, the main city on the island of Celebes. On a map, the islands of Indonesia appear as a string of stepping-stones linking Asia to Australia. New Guinea is only a short hop away from Australia; and the western end of the chain, which includes Java and Bali, is geologically and culturally a part of the Asian mainland. Celebes, which is due south of the Philippines, is the center of the arc. The island looks like an amoeba about to divide; pseudopodlike peninsulas shoot out from a central area of barely explored forest. "To find aboriginal tribes," my wonderfully offbeat guidebook to the island said, "walk seven days through the forest. Watch what the monkeys eat, that's what you can eat." I wasn't adventurous enough for that, but I decided to spend a few days in Celebes anyway. I slogged through streets swamped with rainwater and got a bed at the Alaska Hotel.

The next day I took a bus up-country to Rantepao. It was an all-day ride, with beautiful views of waterlogged paddies, houses on stilts and, in the distance, a range of green mountains that were reflected in the flooded fields. The Toraja people live around Rantepao. They have become famous in recent years for their gaudy and joyous funerals. A happy funeral is possible only if religious faith is universal and unquestioned; the rites of death have become such a sordid thing in the West that the Torajas' carnivallike ceremonies attract curious tourists from all over Europe.

I went to a funeral in a village near Rantepao. I joined in the feasting and watched nine buffalo being slaughtered in sacrifice. But I liked Rantepao market much better; there were no tourists there, only farmers from the hills, and in the restaurants around the market, all the patrons—the farmers, the city folk, and I—sat in a circle, talked, teased the pretty proprietress, and drank palm wine from huge tankards made of bamboo. At one stall, I guiltily sampled curried dog and beer as I listened to tomorrow's meal barking in back; but most Indonesians consider dog an embarrassingly dirty thing to eat, and I once made a waiter in Rantepao fall on the floor and roll with laughter by asking him if he ate dog meat on the sly.

I stayed a week in Celebes and then returned to Bali. A place— like a person, perhaps—is never the same the second time around; the magic or mystery or tedium of the first visit can be remembered but never recaptured. All too often, the second visit spoils the first; the place that thrilled me once bores me now, and what I thought was love turns out to be a brief infatuation, fueled by novelty and nothing more. Sometimes, a town I detested reveals hidden charms when I return: Jayapura, Jakarta, and Bangkok were like that. But best and rarest of all is the place that, like an old friend, claims a part of me: when I go back to a place like that, it feels as if I've come home.

My return to Kuta Beach in Bali was a curious mixture of disappointment and homecoming. Perhaps it was the travelers. I liked the people I met in New Guinea, and still think of them as friends, but there were barriers between us. I never could, for example, fathom Borobuan's deep sadness, nor could he hope to understand my restlessness and need to travel. But the backpackers of Kuta Beach shared my dreams and desires; we were products of the same culture, flotsam on the same sea. And yet, we had less in common than before; in New Guinea, I saw the world beyond the tourist trail for the first time.

I stayed two weeks in Kuta. I ate pizza and apple pie and avocados stuffed with shrimp. Fleetwood Mac had just released a new LP, called *Rumours,* and the restaurants played it every night. Christmas came, and a week later it was 1978. I left for Java a few days after that. On my last day in Bali, I carried all my guidebooks to the bookstore and traded them for a dogeared copy of *Shogun.* It was a fair exchange.

Jogjakarta is a city in central Java that is known as the home of Javanese culture. It is also home to innumerable souvenir shops where the tourist can buy mass-produced paintings and batik. I went to the tourist office and asked the young clerk to suggest a place where tourists never went. "Go to Kaliangkrik," he said. "No one goes there."

I took a bus to Magelang. There were a lot of teenagers with motorbikes standing on a corner near the bus station, smoking cigarettes and trying to look like Charles Bronson. I paid one of these street cowboys to take me to Kaliangkrik on his bike. I spent the night there, and walked out of town the next morning.

I had thought that no place on earth could be more beautiful than Bali, but I was wrong. The hills around Kaliangkrik were, like central Bali, a world of infinite detail, infinite care, and infinite green. There were thousands of paddies; each had been cut, shovelful by shovelful, from the rich red earth of the hillside, and each tiny green shoot in each rice field had been carefully transplanted and watered and lovingly tended. Between the fields grew an array of plants and blossoms in bright and unusual colors. And towering over all of this was the perfect cone of Gunung Sumbing, a volcano ten thousand feet tall, as impressive as Mt. Fuji, as remote as the moon.

I spent two days at a hamlet in those hills, as a guest of a studious man who was the richest farmer in the village. In poor and over-crowded Java, this meant only that his whitewashed house had more than one room and his larder held enough rice to feed a guest. Perhaps my host was even poorer than I thought; I was not yet aware that most of the world's people would rather go hungry themselves than deny food to a stranger.

Near the village was a dirt track that led toward the mountain, and on the third morning I followed it into the foothills. The path was steep and wide and jammed with women in bright sarongs carrying baskets filled with produce to the market in Kaliangkrik. Every few miles there was a village, usually perched on a hilltop or concealed behind a hedge. They seemed to be hiding from visitors. I could hear children playing, but when the people saw me they became sullen and silent. One of the villages had huge and handsome houses built of wood and painted in bright blues and reds and yellows. The headman invited me into his house and served me tea in a room paneled with dark brown wood. Old photographs hung on the wall and a clock ticked on a low sideboard; it was a room from another time and place, a Victorian parlor perhaps, and outside I could hear chickens squawking. I wanted to spend the night—or perhaps a week or a month—in this bizarre and beautiful place, but the chief wouldn't let me stay, even though the sun was setting and I might be forced to sleep outside. Fortunately, there was another village farther on, and the chief, a tall and wiry old man, let me stay there, in a big communal sleeping room where I and about ten others sprawled on straw mats. The room also served as the village conference hall, and the headman and elders of the village talked far into the night. This was how the *kampongs* of Indonesia are governed—by discussion, consultation, and consensus, by old men talking over steaming glasses of tea. Though I appreciated the chance to watch village democracy in action, I would have preferred to sleep. After they left I dozed off, but it was a restless sleep and toward dawn it grew too cold to sleep at all. In the morning, soldiers came and took me back to Kaliangkrik. They took me to a schoolhouse, where an interpreter waited, and asked me what I was doing in the hills. I told them that the place had been recommended to me as one that tourists never visited. They laughed at that, and the interpreter told me that Kaliangkrik was a military area, off-limits to all outsiders.

The soldiers talked among themselves, scrutinized my passport, and in the end decided to let me go. Outside the schoolhouse was the road to Magelang. The soldiers stopped the first truck that passed and put me on it. The interpreter glared at me as the truck pulled away; I had spent three illicit days in a forbidden zone, *his* zone, and was getting off scot-free.

The truck took me to Magelang, where I caught the first bus to Jogjakarta, and the next morning another bus to the Buddhist ruins of Borobudur. In the days before Java was Moslem, it was Hindu, and in the days before that, eleven hundred years ago and more, it was Buddhist. That was Buddhism's greatest era: from the deserts of Afghanistan, through Kashmir and the Himalayas, Tibet, India, and Ceylon, through Southeast Asia, and into Indonesia, Buddhism reigned supreme. But then came a resurgence of Hinduism, and after that Islam swept in from the west, until today, in most of those lands, all that remains of Buddhism's days of glory are timeworn ruins rising from the jungle, like Borobudur.

Borobudur was covered with scaffolding when I arrived; it was being restored by the staunchly Moslem government of Java, which viewed it as a national monument and world-class tourist attraction. Through gaps in the bamboo frame, I could see row after row of sculptured friezes and countless statues, some staring, others headless, but most of the monument was hidden from view. When I traveled, much of my time was spent like that: peering through a fence, catching glimpses through a veil.

That evening, back in Jogjakarta, a woman came up to me in the street and offered to share my bed for a few dollars. No, I said, but she was young and pretty and I told her that as well, to soften the sting of my refusal. "No, I am ugly," she replied, and by Javanese standards perhaps she was, though she had the long-legged grace of a fashion model, and her face, though rough-hewn, was startlingly attractive. I tried to explain this to her and, because I grew to like her, I kissed her on the cheek when I left. She jumped back and screamed with alarm. "We are outside," she explained, "people are watching." Of course, the watchers knew that, behind closed doors, she was a prostitute, but a kiss in public was far worse: if she had not jumped away, it would have showed the world that she was without self-control and without shame.

I slept in Yogya that night, alone, and caught the morning train to Jakarta. The big, black, coal-burning locomotive chuffed and chugged and pulled the train through the rice fields, and I stood at an open door the whole day through, wide-eyed with wonder. No artist could paint those paddies, unless blessed with the painstaking patience of Vermeer and the bright and gaudy palette of a Fauve. And whenever the train stopped, a long line of women selling food marched through the crowded cars, gaily shouting the praises of the snacks they carried in metal pails.

I saw villages from the train, and children who ran along the tracks scavenging litter, but most of the land was devoted to fields, not houses. Java is as densely populated as anywhere on earth, but people there do not, as I had imagined they would, live shoulder to shoulder; they must eat as well as sleep. Toward evening, the villages seemed bigger and closer together, and then it was all village, no fields, with a few skyscrapers here and there. We had reached Jakarta.

I rented a room on Jalan Jaksa, a street near the center of town famous for its cheap hotels. Wisma Delima, the lodge where I stayed, had an outside garden where travelers, many wearing the hotel's striped sheets as sarongs, sat on rusty metal chairs and fed the mosquitoes. "Ignore them and let them bite," a blond and bearded American told me, "after fifteen minutes you won't feel a thing." His advice worked, and perhaps I would never have noticed the bites at all had the rest of Asia not been relatively insect-free. Few places in Asia can boast half as many flies or mosquitoes as the wilds of Connecticut, where I spent my childhood summers.

Near Jalan Jaksa I found a streetless zone of jerry-built plywood houses and crooked muddy lanes: not the poorest part of town, but a slum nonetheless. But the people who lived there kept their homes clean and painted them in bright colors: white, and sky-blue. Laughing, giggling, scampering children followed me as I walked. One family invited me inside; there were armchairs, and teacups on a tray, and, incredibly, a television, of which they were inordinately proud. Outside, a gang of kids stared through the window, watching me or perhaps the cartoons being shown on TV. The children neither knew nor cared that they were living in one of the poorest cities east of Calcutta; why should they, when there were games to play, and cartoons to watch, and a big funny white man to laugh at?

I flew from there to Singapore, that skyscraper-studded success story of a city. There's a hum of smug prosperity, and you can almost hear the GNP growing. My hair was short and I was clean and clean-shaven, so the immigration officials let me in. They gave me a one-week visa, but I did not stay that long. I went by train to Bangkok and, on January 28, took a plane to Calcutta.

Before I left Singapore, I took a bus to the harbor. One of the other passengers did not have the correct fare, and the driver shouted at him. I was horrified, and then I realized that in all my months in Indonesia, I had not heard a voice raised in anger.

8

INDIA

Calcutta was crowded—I had expected that. Like New York, it was a city with a reputation. Most Europeans look at me, a New Yorker, with either disgust or compassion, and I pictured Calcutta as they imagine Harlem: a monochrome, twilight world of rats and rubble and a million ways of dying. And so I was quite unprepared to find a vibrant, exciting place, as colorful and lively as a carnival. The whole town was on the move. The streets were jammed with trucks and carts and cows, rickshaws and motorbikes and antiquated double-decker buses and people, everywhere people: people strolling, people squatting and spitting and drinking tea; people washing at hydrants and pounding their laundry on the curb, people selling fruit and betel nuts and saris and shoeshines. They were poor, incredibly poor, the people I saw. Many lived on the sidewalks and those who earned a dollar a day considered themselves lucky. After all, with money like that, a family could be adequately fed, unlike half of India, which goes to bed hungry.

North of the city center, across the narrow bridge that spans the Hooghly River, and beyond the train station was the district known as Howrah. A never-ending stream of people, carts, and cars poured across the bridge, and Howrah Station was, like every train station in India, packed with families who had set up camp in the vast waiting hall: they slept there, cooked there, and ate there, and scattered among them were vast mounds of luggage. Whether these people were waiting for a train, or merely waiting for something to turn up, I could not tell. But on the other side of the tracks the crowds thinned out. It was one of the poorest parts of town, and few people went there unless they lived there.

One morning I walked across the tracks and spent the day in Howrah. I saw unpaved lanes with muddy puddles. I saw earth-brick shanties with tile roofs; they had been subdivided into tiny rooms. Outside one house, young men sat in a circle playing cards. They were a boisterous bunch, and I watched them grin and shout and slap the cards down.

"Ah, if only I were poor! It is the poor people here who are really happy." I heard these lines time and again in India, and the speaker was invariably rich, or at least middle-class. The cardplayers, the squatters at the station, and the rest of Calcutta's poor did not live a life of ease and bliss, but their energy surprised me. They were not ennobled by poverty but they were not broken by it either, and even the poorest had not forgotten how to smile.

There were exceptions. In an alley behind my hotel an old woman asked me for alms. She told me her story, which a passerby translated. She had worked as a seamstress all her life. Then her eyesight failed and she lost her job. Now she lived by begging; it was that or starve. Most of India's poor have friends and family, and that gives some meaning to their lives, but this old woman was alone.

After four days in Calcutta, I went to Howrah Station and took a train to Varanasi (also called Benares), four hundred miles to the west. It was an overnight ride, not long by Indian standards, but it was a journey from one world to another. Calcutta may well be India's most secular city. It is famous for its universities and free-thinking intellectuals, and socialism, as much as Hinduism, is the state religion. In Calcutta, people look to the future, either in hope or despair, but Benares looks to the past. Age-old, almost as ancient as India itself, Varanasi was well into its third millennium when Calcutta was founded. And, to a Hindu, Varanasi is the holiest spot on earth.

Except for the neighborhood just north of the river, Benares is a typical Indian town. There is a train station, big and crowded and cavernous, and outside it hundreds of bicycle rickshaws and their drivers wait for customers. Near the station is the Cantonment, once the British enclave and now the preserve of rich Indians in colonial mansions and tourists in high-rise hotels, newly built and already decaying. It is a Cantonment like any other: wide, dusty roads, dead lawns and English gardens baked brown by the sun; a place of space and silence and earth as dry as sand—in its way, a desert.

South of the Cantonment the crowds begin, and the noise—bicycle bells and mooing cows and car horns. Tired policemen, held up by uniforms starched stiff as boards, stand on traffic islands in the human sea. The buildings stand shoulder-to-shoulder now: tailor shops and cinemas and restaurants with names like Central, Kwality, and Modern. But very little is modern in downtown Varanasi. Architecturally at least, the clock seems to have stopped in 1935. There is none of the sleek, plastic sophistication of an American (or a Thai) shopping mall, and no skyscrapers either, and a McDonald's would be as out of place as a spaceship in the Baliem Valley. Supermarkets and department stores, too, are unknown, but the sidewalk itself is a bazaar. Some stalls are filled with saris and others have nothing but keys and locks. There are money changers who offer ninety-eight one-paisa coins for a one-rupee note. There are cigarette sellers and newsstands and book vendors who will sell you the latest novel by Judith Krantz, and then buy it back for half price, and sell it again as new. Scattered among the stalls are tables surrounded by benches; these are Indian fast-food shops, where, if you order tea or *lassi*—a yogurt shake—it is served in an earthenware cup, carefully shaped by hand on a potter's wheel, used only once, and thrown away. A waste of the potter's work, perhaps, but labor is cheap. Besides, the customer must be sure that his cup has never touched lips of lower caste than his. (Never *hers;* I never saw an Indian woman eat at a food stall, or even, unless chaperoned, in a restaurant.)

Downtown Varanasi—bustling, pleasantly outdated, and slightly provincial—is, strangely enough, shaped and preserved by the government's policy of modernization. To encourage home-grown industry to develop, most imports are banned and foreign investment is strictly controlled. India makes its own trucks, refrigerators, silicon microchips, designer jeans, cornflakes, and razor blades. And India builds its own buildings, and the slick, glassy creations common in Bangkok and Singapore—made with imported materials, imported capital, and imported know-how—are in short supply, even in Bombay. This is why India is not forced to depend on foreign loans, imports, and handouts. And this is why McDonald's does not sell vegetable burgers in downtown Varanasi.

Varanasi is built on the bank of the Ganges, and, closer to the river, it becomes impossible to think about industry and modernization. The buildings are older than those in the business district, and they look even older than they are. The houses are several stories high and built of stone, painted brown or sable or sky-blue, and their façades are laden with curlicues and carvings. High above the riverbank stone ramparts soar, and palaces are built, like the houses, in the ornate fashion of the Moguls, a style whose sinuous curves evoke *The Arabian Nights.* Off the main road and behind the palaces, uncharted lanes and tiny alleys barely wide enough for a man to pass run among houses, temples, and gardens. There is something magical about those side streets; I have a good sense of direction but whenever I left the main road I invariably got lost.

The Ganges floods from time to time, and so most of Varanasi/Benares is built far above the level of the river. The streets don't slope down to the water, they drop down, in cascades of stone steps. Below the steps are wide stone plazas, and then more steps, leading into the river. These are the *ghats.* They are wide and narrow, with the cliffs of the city just behind, and always crowded. Pilgrims and holy men come to the *ghats* from all over India, for Hindus believe that the water of the Ganges is sacred, and to walk into it will purify the soul.

Pilgrimages, holy men and holy waters, perilous journeys and quests for salvation. In the Western world that sort of thing died with Chaucer and Sir Gawain. Redemption, death, rebirth, curtains and voids, cycles of lives—in our society, it is unfashionable to confront the ultimate, and unscientific to seek it out. Only children believe in lucky rivers, magic waters, demons and fairies; we adults have outgrown these superstitions. Of course, all these things—or their unnameable counterparts—exist, in the rich inner landscape of our minds, but we have walled them off, labeled them terra incognita, off-limits, unreal. In India, myths and archetypes are still alive. The world of the heart and of the spirit is accepted, and is projected onto another sphere where it can be felt, and known, and named, and shared. This other world is the world of the Hindu religion.

Away from India, it is easy for me to reduce the Hindu pantheon to a symbolic shorthand for mental phenomena. It is that, but it is more. Not only do Hindu myths map the mind, but they attempt to chart the cosmos as well. The names of the goddesses and gods are names for the primordial energies that flow through the universe and bind it together. Or so it seemed as I sat on the *ghats* of Benares.

My hotel was near the main *ghat*, Dasaswamedh. By the time it reaches Benares, the Himalayan water of the Ganges has almost completed its journey to the sea. The river is old and slow and very wide. There is nothing on the far shore but sand, a few trees, and an occasional party of pilgrims. The view from my seat on the *ghat* was a vista of sand and space, water and sky. It was, in its way, as stark and unearthly as the mountains I had seen on the road to Kathmandu. At dusk, the *ghats* fell silent, except for the rustle of water on stone, but from dawn to sunset the air was filled with chanting from a nearby temple. "Sri Ram, Jai Ram, Jai Jai Ram"—the priests sang the mantra through the day, the same words endlessly repeated, slow and hypnotic as the Ganges. Sometimes they were accompanied by the drone of a harmonium; sometimes the sound of bells cut through the chant. There was a gong in the temple above the *ghat* that was supposed to ward off smallpox, and most of the pilgrims rang it. They knew the disease had been conquered, but they thought it best to take no chances.

There was a constant stream of pilgrims at Dasaswamedh. They prayed in the temples and bathed in the water and clustered in circles around learned Brahmins who sat under burlap awnings preaching or reading from three-thousand-year-old Hindu scriptures. They came from all over India, these pilgrims, from the smallest, poorest, and remotest places, and, for many, their time between the ramparts and the river was the climax of their lives. I remember the pilgrims as a blur of brown; they were too many, and too alike in their ecstasy, for their separate personalities to register.

Some men stood out in the crowd. They wore voluminous robes of coarse orange cloth. Most carried begging bowls; some held tridents made of iron. They were ascetics, holy men, perpetual pilgrims. Millions of them spend their life wandering across India. They are called *sadhus.*

We are caught, say the Hindus, in an endless and painful cycle of life, death, and reincarnation. Most Hindus are happy enough with life on earth and hope only that in their next incarnation they will earn more money. The *sadhus* are different; by poverty, pilgrimage, and meditation, they seek to escape the cycle entirely; to achieve what the Buddha called nirvana. Many of the *sadhus* I saw were quite old, and some, it was rumored, had once been millionaires, or directors of large corporations. I never found out if those stories were true, but what impressed me was that the transition from rich man to mendicant was regarded not with scorn but with admiration.

Most of the *sadhus* I saw had three white horizontal lines painted on their foreheads, but some bore a white trident on their brow. The lines showed devotion to Shiva, and the pitchfork was the sign of Vishnu. Vishnu and Shiva are the two main gods in the Hindu pantheon. Vishnu, an observer and preserver, watches over the world and from time to time assumes human form. Two of these human incarnations are themselves worshiped: Rama and Krishna. They are complex figures, especially Krishna, and the myths spun around them are fraught with symbols. Krishna, of royal birth but raised as a cowherd, grew up to be a warrior, a lover, a demon-killer and, in the end, a philosopher who preached devotion to duty.

Krishna has come to represent love as well as steadfast devotion; Shiva, who was originally a fertility god, is more remote. He personifies the energy of the cosmos and is usually portrayed, dreamy eyed and in a trance, meditating amidst snowy mountains. It is fitting that *sadhus,* who seek truth through contemplation, should worship him, and most of them are in fact Shaivites.

I watched the *sadhus* with awe and from a distance. I did not dare talk to them, and they did not care to speak with me. Some *sadhus* did seek out tourists, but those could hardly be called holy men. Some wanted handouts and one, younger than the rest, sold the best *ganja* (marijuana) in town, far stronger than the stuff stocked by the government shops. This *sadhu* pusher had a Yugoslav friend named Robbie. At least, I think that was his name, because I could understand little of what he said. He babbled a lot. He was rail-thin, unshaven, and broke. India had fried his brains.

I never felt a part of Varanasi life. As in any tourist town, the people had put up barriers between themselves and the tourists. We were fenced out; we couldn't even set foot in the temples. What else could I expect? Too many Robbies had staggered through.

Though the temples were closed to me, the Ganges was not so exclusive. As I sat alone on the *ghat*, I could share the pilgrims' excitement and fervor, and the other-worldly beauty of the river that drew them to its banks. I spent two weeks in Benares, and had it been warmer I might have stayed a lot longer. But I had grown used to the endless summer of the South Pacific, and Varanasi in February was far too cold. I went south.

There is an express train twice a week between Varanasi and Madras. It is always crowded and most of the berths are booked months in advance, but tourists got priority and I was able to get a place on the next train out.

One can learn a lot about a society by seeing how its trains run. In parts of Africa, the tracks and carriages are so creaky, it's a wonder they work at all, and as often as not they don't. Trains in China are a Maoist dream of order imposed on an anarchic people: at the stations, police push the crowds into orderly lines that break up into a formless, brawling mob when the train rolls in. Indian Railways, that still-flourishing relic of the Raj, is methodical, uses far more clerks and paper than it needs, and usually runs on time. One does not just buy a ticket; there are forms to be filled in. Name, age, sex, seat preference must be made known, and the fusty old booking clerk painstakingly copies the information into a musty old ledger. The ballpoint he uses seems out of place; surely a quill would be more appropriate. On the day of departure, printed lists are posted showing each passenger and his berth number.

Each carriage of the Ganga-Kaveri Express to Madras had a steward who kept the car clean and kept out people from the class below. First class was no longer whites-only, but the express was still rigidly hierarchical. It had four classes; mine was one up from the bottom and my carriage had tiers of wooden shelves for sleeping. There was no dining car, but the steward took food orders, which were telegraphed to the next station along the line where the meals would be waiting, neatly stacked in metal trays.

Twelve hundred miles of tracks lay between Varanasi and Madras. The train chugged through two nights and a day, and I lost count of the tin-tray teas and breakfasts and dinners. Sometimes we stopped at small country junctions where crowds of giggling children begged for coins. On the third day we reached Madras. It was sunny and pleasantly warm. Most of the hotels claimed to be full, but, after an hour's search, I found a room. "Cost will be six rupees only," said the portly clerk. "Five rupees for room plus one rupee 'presentation.' " I gave him five rupees and he didn't object.

The south was cheaper than the north. A decent room, not including presentation, was five rupees, about sixty American pennies, and two rupees would buy a mountain of rice and vegetable curry. But two rupees was the average daily wage in Tamil Nadu, the state in which Madras lay. The south was supposed to be more traditional as well as poorer, since it had remained under Hindu rule for much of the time that the north was under Moslem dominion. The cities, though, looked more modern. There were no winding alleys, no age-old houses. Instead, I saw flimsy but brightly painted concrete and stucco storefronts, some proudly emblazoned with the date of construction—1958, perhaps, or 1973.

The south was almost another country. The people were darker and more graceful and spoke a different language (in Madras, Tamil). And life was slower here, the pace was far less hectic and hurried than in the large cities of the north, which sometimes seemed to be one big jostling crowd.

A branch railway line connects Madras with Pondicherry, a hundred miles away. Pondicherry was a colony of France until 1954, and the tricolor still flies outside the French consulate, a big beige mansion by the waterfront. Nearby is a park, a statue of Joan of Arc, and the *lycée*, which sometimes holds dances for the few remaining French settlers. The Gallic veneer is thin, though charming, and most of Pondicherry appears to be, and is, a sleepy Indian town. If you walk along the beach in either direction, you will come to a tropical warren of tiny, crowded shacks, tightly packed together and shaded by palm trees: a very pretty place, but a slum nonetheless.

I checked into the Grand Hotel d'Europe on rue Suffren. My room had French windows, a big four-poster bed complete with mosquito net, and a wall thermometer whose white enamel mounting was decorated with an advertisement for Martell cognac. The hotel was aggressively Gallic, obsessively French in every detail; it was the sort of place found only in remote outposts and never in France itself.

I met a *sadhu* in Pondicherry. He was an old and gentle man who wore orange robes and a long grizzled beard, and it was hard to believe that he had been an officer in the French army and had fought in Vietnam. He was still, in his pacific way, a commander, and his quiet presence could fill the largest room. But he was tired, he told me, of the awe he inspired. As we walked by, children playing in the street would stop their games and stand at attention, unaware that all he wanted was to share their laughter.

The *sadhu* came from a rich family which owned land in a village an hour's ride away. He offered to take me there. The village was several miles off the main road, too far for him to walk, and so we hired a taxi. I put my backpack in the trunk, for I hoped to stay the night, and longer if I could.

At first I thought the village was very small. The taxi deposited us at the end of a long and bumpy dirt lane, with only six houses in sight, three on either side of the road. But the *sadhu* led me behind the houses and across a wide strip of sandy ground that obviously served as the village toilet, and I could see more houses just beyond. They were built of adobe and roofed with thatch; they were long and low and looked cool and clean. Nearby was a well and a little temple. It was separate and self-contained, this cluster of neat brown houses, almost another village. Untouchables live here, said the *sadhu.*

The origins of India's system of castes are, as Victorian travel writers love to say, shrouded in the mists of time. The Aryan conquest of India three thousand years ago probably played a part, for the light-skinned Aryans viewed the darker peoples they ruled as inferior races. Hindu notions of purity and pollution were also involved; people whose occupations entailed contact with death or human emissions were thought to be defiled, ill-omened, and taboo. Shoemakers, who flay dead cows, fishermen, who take life, and laundrymen, who touch soiled garments, were all beyond the pale. In many villages, one caste—sometimes the Brahmins but usually not—became dominant; its members were richer, wielded more power, and owned more land than the rest. The dominant group had a special stake in maintaining the caste system; to a landowner, the untouchables represented a pool of easily exploited farm labor.

The roots of caste are deep and tangled, and this is not surprising, for the segregation of untouchables in India is the oldest system of apartheid on earth. It was, until recently, also one of the harshest.

Untouchables were treated as lepers, or worse. In some parts of Tamil Nadu, they were not allowed within ninety-six paces of a Brahmin. The British, perhaps realizing that a divided nation is easier to rule, left the caste system alone. After Independence, the government did its best to help the hundred million untouchables, who are now called "Harijans," or "Children of God." Discrimination was made illegal, and the Indian constitution reserved 22 percent of all government jobs for Harijans. But in that village south of Pondicherry, the untouchables still lived apart.

Indeed each caste, each occupation had its own neighborhood. The road with six houses, which I had at first taken for the village, was the street of the merchants, and beyond it, in the opposite direction from the Harijans, stood several much larger houses, built of brick with concrete façades. They were the bastions of the dominant caste. By the beach was a settlement of fishermen, and farther inland lived the men who tapped the coconut palms. The tappers were a low caste, but not quite untouchable, and in the old days they were permitted to stand as close to a Brahmin as thirty-six paces.

Perhaps there were other compounds as well, barricaded behind hedges or hidden in the palm groves. I never explored the entire village, though I stayed a week, and it is possible that none of the villagers had either. Because I came with the *sadhu,* a young Harijan couple invited me to live with them, and I spent most of my time with my hosts. In front of their house was a tiny veranda, shaded by the thatched roof's ample eaves, and there I set up camp. I was never asked inside. They were scrupulously clean and took care, as far as I could tell, to observe every Hindu ritual. They probably feared that I, a non-Hindu, would pollute their hearth.

But they may have been too ashamed to invite me in. The house was tiny, the smallest in the compound. The woman of the house spent most of the day inside, cooking and cleaning and mending clothes. Though she did not, as some religious Hindu women do, feel obliged to hide her face from strangers, I saw very little of her. She wore an old brown sari, plain and faded but strong; it had withstood a thousand washings and was good for a thousand more. She was always busy and rarely found time to smile, though this may have been because I came at a bad time. She had just learned that the family's landlord wanted to evict them.

I was another source of anxiety. She worried about the cost of the food I ate, not knowing that I planned to leave a gift when I left. Whenever I stayed in a village, I gave my hosts a present, usually cash, and timing was always a problem. In most societies, the guest presents his gift just before departure; if I gave the money sooner, it would be a payment and not a present, but if I waited until the end, my hosts might think I was a freeloader. Fortunately, most villagers took me in out of kindness or, at worst, curiosity; they were happy to receive my money but would not have been disappointed if they didn't. But this Tamil woman was poor enough for every grain to matter.

Each evening, she gave me massive helpings of vegetables and rice. It was she who had made the decision to let me stay, and if I were not properly fed, she would have failed in her duty to her guest. On the night before I left, one of the children, who spoke English, told me that my hostess needed two rupees for food. I took the opportunity to give her my farewell present—about fifty rupees. "If only I had known," she said, "I would have served you much better. You would have had meat every day." Unlike the Brahmins, these people were not vegetarian out of choice.

Though they lived on rice and vegetables, the villagers did not seem underfed. The woman was slender but not skinny, and her husband was tall and strong. He worked in the fields. Each morning, before he left, he bathed, put on a clean shirt, and went to the Harijan temple for prayers. I did not see him again until sundown.

During the day, the sun seared the land, but the evening was a gentler time, cool and pleasant. The men would return from the fields and the women would emerge from their houses. Chairs would be carried outside. The couple I lived with would usually visit one of the other families. They seemed happiest when part of a large, loud, laughing group; for them, as for most of the world, privacy was not a value but a curse. The wife would chat with the other women and perhaps help with their cooking, and her husband would run to find his friend. The two men were complete opposites. The husband was tall and somewhat languid; his friend was wiry, very short, and bursting with nervous energy, like a leopard in a cage. He was rarely still and even when he was he seemed as if he would prefer to pace or pounce. They were hardly compatible, these two, but they were inseparable. They would talk for hours without pause and then sit in silence under the stars. Sometimes they would share a bottle of whiskey or perhaps a *ganja* cigarette. I don't think they were brothers but they could have been; in villages, friendship can be as binding and permanent a tie as blood.

Indeed, the whole village society was a web of friends and relations. People spent so much time at the houses of friends that I was never sure who lived where. Kinship and friendship provided the framework that supported their lives; it was as important to them as the ground under their feet, for without it each would be adrift and alone.

I felt from the first that I was accepted into this family of friends. The difference between cold and warm is difficult to describe but impossible to mistake, and I could feel the warmth of the people when we spoke. I spent my evenings with the tall man and the short, sharing their whiskey and listening to their conversation. Once or twice I walked toward the beach, needing to be by myself, but they would always follow.

During the day, while the men were at work, I was able to stroll around the village on my own. I awoke quite early, but the village rose even earlier, and on most mornings my sleeping mat would be surrounded by a circle of small boys, already dressed in their blue school uniforms, quietly watching me sleep. They had learned a few words of English—"Good morning!" "What is this?" We shouted the phrases together, and then they ran off to class and I headed for the tea stall.

Midway between the village and the main highway, a factory was under construction. Nearby was a rough lean-to built of raffia mats draped over bamboo poles. A screen divided the shelter in half. A barber had set up shop on one side and the other was a tiny restaurant that served tea and simple curries. I had breakfast there every day. I liked the owner and his eight-year-old son, who soon took to calling me "Uncle." He taught me several useful tricks, including how to make my hands into a swimming fish, using my thumbs as fins. Sometimes the foreman, who was quite old but still strong, came for tea. He spoke English and liked to talk about America. Once I got a shave at the barber, who scraped my face with a dull blade until I told him to stop.

I would usually walk back to the village by way of the palm groves. There was a small pond which reflected the palm trees that grew on its shores. Where the path met the water was a little house built of logs and shingles. Inside was a bar, with benches made of tree trunks, where the tappers came to drink the wine made from the sap they collected. Palm wine is sweet but strong; the tappers drank it like water. They were loud and raucous and fun to be around. I envied them their energy; I would have been asleep on my feet had I spent the morning climbing trees.

From the palm groves it was a short walk to the beach. The white sands stretched unbroken to the horizon and beyond. Next to the beach, flimsy shacks and shanties huddled together: the fishermen's quarter. I did not go there often because the fishermen were rough and sometimes hostile. There were exceptions; on one visit I found a man leaning against a beached boat, reading a book aloud. It was an English text; he was studying for the civil service examination. It was his only hope of escape.

One afternoon, on my way to the ocean, I took a wrong turn and ended up north of the merchants' street, in the area where the village notables lived. A door opened and a young man invited me in. He spoke good English; he was a civil servant in Cuddalore, the nearest city to the south. His job bored him and he had taken a day off to visit his parents. Their house was huge. Inside was a sunny courtyard with walls painted white. A stairway led to the upper floors. Over the stairs was a light bulb; this part of the village was electrified. The man was surprised to see a stranger in his village. When I told him where I lived, he looked at me with pity and horror. "They are very dirty people," he said.

By the time I left the mansion, it was too late to go to the sea. I spent most of the next day walking on the beach, following the sands north toward Pondicherry. I found another fishing village and, nearby, a pair of crude terra-cotta idols, each larger than a man. They were very old and looked prehistoric, but freshly cut flowers had been laid at their feet.

Usually, I did not venture so far afield. School let out in the early afternoon, and I tried to return to my part of the village by then. There were sure to be races and chases and games of tag, and I was allowed to join in. The young girls, most of whom did not go to school, stood in small groups, silently watching. Sometimes, I moved in their direction, and the girls ran off, laughing and screaming, but they always came back and once or twice they sneaked up behind me and tapped me on the shoulder.

After a week in the village, I grew restless. I wanted to be on the road. I missed the solitude and anonymity of travel. In the village, I was an oddity, a celebrity, on call twenty-four hours a day. Even when I slept, I was watched. But it was not easy for me to leave. My two drinking buddies begged me to stay one more day, one more week. Finally, I promised them—and myself—that I would travel around the south and then return for another week before going north. Yet I never went back, and I wish I had.

When I left the village, I walked to the main road and flagged down the first bus that passed. It took me to Cuddalore, where I caught another bus to Madurai. There was a temple in Madurai which my childhood hero Richard Halliburton, in one of his rare lapses of judgment, found so bizarre and barbaric that, he said, its very existence showed the innate superiority of Christianity.

I loved the place. I could understand that a Westerner might find it unsettling. There are the towers, for example, ten of them, each twenty stories high and almost as wide. Each is covered with a jumble of writhing statues: staring gods and leering demons, hundreds of thousands of nightmare images, and all painted in the most lurid hues of the rainbow. They are hideous, no doubt, but unearthly as well, and by battering the senses they hint at a world beyond them.

Beneath the towers sprawled the huge Meenakshi Temple. The buildings now standing are only four centuries old, but to me they seemed far older, as old as India, as old as the pharaohs. The long, dark chambers with low ceilings supported by squat, ornate columns reminded me of photographs I had seen of temples in Egypt. Back when the priests said prayers to Amon-Re in Karnak, I thought, Shiva was worshiped on this very spot by people wearing the same crude costumes—wraps made of coarse cloth—as the pilgrims I saw. In Thebes today, only bare columns remain, standing in silence at the desert's edge, but Madurai endures. And it is still a place of worship.

Like the temples of ancient Egypt, the Meenakshi was composed of concentric chambers which became darker, holier, and more mysterious as I approached the center. First was a large, well-lit hall where the men of the city came to chat, relax, and nap. Beyond was a vast and quiet courtyard with a deep pool of stagnant, sacred water. I made my way through the crowded court, past a sign, which I barely noticed, which said HINDUS ONLY, and down corridor after lengthy corridor, all dimly lit and deserted, with gray walls of rough-hewn stone. Finally I came to a chamber larger than the rest, and palpably more sacred, a shrine to Shiva. Around the central altar of this holy of holies were bronze images of the god dancing. They were perfect, these centuries-old statues; they captured the divine energy and grace that Shiva's dance is said to represent. Next to the statues was a box for offerings. A family came into the shrine, and the father gave his youngest child a coin to put in the slot. He lifted her up to reach the box, and she beamed with joy, happy to be the center of attention and proud that these magical statues would, in return for her gift, place her under their protection.

I went by train from Madurai to nearby Rameswaram, where I found another temple of sacred and labyrinthine corridors. Rameswaram is a seaport, and I took a boat to Talaimannar on Sri Lanka, the teardrop-shaped island that the British called Ceylon. From Talaimannar I went to Colombo and then to Kandy and then to Trincomalee. I loved the names of the Sri Lankan towns. There was a lilt and a music to them; they were like gentle breezes from the sea, laden with the scent of salt and spices. Colombo was big and very British, with enormous government buildings built of dirty beige stone. Kandy was a charming city built by a lake and ringed by jungly hills. It was all quite pretty and charming, but I found it too peaceful, too orderly. I missed the turbulence and chaos of Indian towns. After a day in Trincomalee, a lazy town of tin shacks and green gardens and long white beaches, I decided to go back to India. In another month it would be too hot to travel, and I wanted to see more of the north before the season of heat and rain. And the gibbous moon that hung in the sky reminded me that the Taj Mahal was best seen on the night of the full moon.

I traveled nonstop from Trincomalee to Agra, and it took five days. I traveled by bus and train to Talaimannar, where I caught the boat back to India. Then I took a slow local to Madras and another train, this one an express, across the center of the subcontinent to Agra. And all this effort was more or less in vain, because, on the night when it was full, the moon was blotted out by an eclipse.

Designed by a Persian, erected by command of the great-grandson of a Mongol invader, and built with the domes and minarets of an Arabian mosque, the Taj Mahal has nevertheless come to symbolize India to the Western world. It is as famous as the Eiffel Tower. Half the Indian restaurants outside India are named after it, and even its silhouette, subject of countless prints and plastic placemats, has become somewhat kitsch through overuse, a visual cliché. When I visit a superstar landmark like the Taj, I expect to be disappointed; a place so famous must be overrated.

But the Taj exceeds its reputation. In photographs, it seems squat and ungainly. But when I saw it, I found it perfect in shape and soaring design, and its marble shone purest white in the harsh glare of the sun. And, by the light of the not quite full moon, it hangs suspended, pale and ghostlike, in the blackness of the sky; it seems to float and shimmer, like a gossamer tapestry woven from the stuff of dreams. During my days in Agra, I returned time and again to the Taj, and hour after hour passed by unnoticed as I sat in its quiet gardens.

I stayed at a boardinghouse in the Cantonment area at the other end of Taj Road, several miles away. It was run by a fussy old lady and had once been her home, and she viewed the lodgers as something midway between guests and intruders. I used to go to the Taj by rickshaw. Shop owners paid the driver a rupee for each tourist he brought; if you agreed to take a detour to the Mall or Hastings Road and visit two shops—"No need to buy, sir!"—you could ride free. One day, I took a rickshaw to the old part of town where the streets had names like Chhipi Tola Road and Kinari Bazar.

I wore my oldest clothes that day. It was the day of the water festival, Holi, when everyone throws water on everyone else. Vendors had set up stands all over Agra, selling squeeze bottles and buckets and bright indelible dye to mix with the water. Holi is a one-day respite from laws of caste and status, and the poorest Harijan can douse Brahmins and millionaires with impunity. Most Brahmins sensibly spend the day indoors. It is a happy holiday, and there is little if any hooliganism and violence, but anyone caught outside is fair game for a soaking. I expected to be thoroughly drenched, and I was not disappointed. A gang of youths carried me on their shoulders through the winding streets of the old town, as women standing on the rooftops emptied huge buckets of icy water on our heads. I was dry by evening, and I took an overnight train to Kotah, in Rajasthan.

Until not so long ago, Rajasthan was divided into tiny kingdoms, ruled by *rajputs*. They were foreign invaders, possibly Mongols, but they became Hindu and patronized the Brahmins, who in return decreed that the new rulers were really of Indian descent, second only to the priests in caste. The warlike *rajputs* resisted Mogul dominion and, under the British, they continued to rule their autonomous princely states. The rajahs levied huge taxes and used the revenue to maintain palaces and strings of polo ponies and send their sons to Eton. The wealth and feudal glamour of the princely states captivated the English imagination but, after independence, the new Indian government was less impressed, and within two years the last of the rajahs had been pensioned off. They were allowed to keep their palaces and some, like needy aristocrats the world over, have turned them into hotels.

The city of Kotah was old but unattractive. I stayed just long enough to board a bus to Bundi, forty miles north, a town that was once the capital of one of the princely states. Bundi is one of the few towns in India not on a rail line. It is very old and quite small. Rudyard Kipling visited the town and fell in love with it; "Bundi the beautiful," he called it, but his slightly florid description is tinged with sadness because, he wrote, he "believed that he would never again see anything half so fair." That was almost a century ago, and Bundi has changed little since then. The bus station, one of the few intrusions of the modern age, is about a mile outside the city wall. Nearby is the Circuit House, an old beige bungalow built to house visiting government officials. Spare rooms are rented to the few tourists who find their way there. As I went to my room, a group of giggling policemen, still celebrating Holi, squirted a fire hose my way. I changed my clothes and walked into town.

Rajasthan is the driest part of India and, though the land around Bundi receives more rain than the desert to the west, the rolling red hills that surround the town are rocky and bare. Perhaps in reaction to the austere landscape, Rajasthanis love bright colors, and the men I saw on my way to town wore huge red turbans and white shirts still splotched with dye from the previous day's water fights. Most of the people were farmers, come to visit the crowded markets just outside the city gate.

Inside the walls, the streets were cobbled and narrow. Tiny shops lined the sidewalk, and I could hear tinkers and coppersmiths hammering away. The houses were older and plainer than the rococo confections of Benares. The walls leaned at crazy angles and apparently had been erected before the invention of the plumb line. Though brightly painted, the smooth façades were bare of ornament, but around each door were lively murals of women in saris and men on horseback.

Bundi is the sort of place where visitors stay much longer than they intend. I came for the day but spent a week. During the daytime, I explored the hilly maze of side streets within the walls, or sat in one of the outdoor cafés near the market, watching the crowds pass by. Sometimes I walked along an acacia-shaded path that went around the wall to a small lake. Women pounded laundry on the stone steps that led to the water.

By late afternoon, the farmers would leave for their villages, the dust would settle in the marketplace, and the town would grow quiet. But one evening, a noisy parade marched through the streets. It was a wedding procession, led by a band dressed in snappy blue uniforms. They blew their trombones and clarinets with volume and vigor. Just behind came the groom, who rode a horse draped in red. He looked more scared than happy, but his friends danced and shouted and clapped and sang. For them at least, the wedding was a joyous event, or perhaps an excuse for joy.

The parade went on for hours, and I returned to my room long after dark. Usually, I spent the evening at the Circuit House, where I dined in solitary splendor at a table large enough to seat the members of an entire officers' mess. The Circuit House was mostly empty, though I occasionally saw visiting officials wandering about. One was a doctor attached in some vague way to the civil service. His uncle, a poor and very distant relation of the local rajah, owned some land in the district, and the doctor gave me a letter of introduction to visit him. It was addressed "Akolia Village, near Dablana."

There was a lot north of the city gate for those buses deemed too old, rickety, or unimportant to use the main terminal. The bus to Dablana left from there. Dablana was a dusty, windswept town with a teahouse and little else. I drank tea until a bus arrived that, the driver claimed, was going to Akolia. We drove along a dirt track across a dry and barren plain. After an hour the bus stopped, and the driver pointed to the left and said "Akolia." I put on my pack and started walking. A half-hour later, I saw fields of wheat and then a village.

The doctor's uncle was a thin old man who had been dried up by the wind that blew in from the desert. He did not seem very pleased to see me, or displeased either. He fed me and gave me a place to sleep—a *charpoy*, or string bed, placed in the yard—but I spent most of my two days in Akolia in the fields.

The old *rajput*'s home stood on a hill, aloof from the rest of the village, a cluster of neat white houses several hundred yards away. There was farmland between the two, crowded with people at work. It was harvest time, and the whole village was in the fields. Women cut the wheat with sickles and bundled it into sheaves. The women wore bright saris and bangles, the wheat was gold, the hills in the distance were purple and red. The men, meanwhile, cut sugarcane, loaded it onto oxcarts, and fed it into a press powered by two oxen yoked to a long wooden bar which, as they walked, turned a wheel. The press stood in a dusty square next to the houses, and the older men squatted in the dust, watching the mill turn and drinking freshly squeezed sugar juice. A boy in a red turban walked behind the plodding oxen, goading them to move faster. He was about sixteen, and taller and stronger than most of the men. When he saw me, he grabbed my hand, put the whip in it, and pulled me to the press. He wanted me to drive the oxen. I did. Then he wanted to wear my sunglasses. That was going too far, I thought, so I refused. He snatched them and tried them on. I grabbed his turban and put it on my head. Then I took back the sunglasses. I had gained a friend and a bright red turban.

My new friend's younger brother drove an oxcart into the square and we both got in. We headed for the fields to collect more sugarcane and, on the way back, with a full cart, we balanced on top of the load. The older brother drove and, when he saw a pothole on the path, he hit the ox to make the bump more jarring. We shrieked and laughed together, and the harder the jolt the louder the laughter. The brothers had transformed a mindless, menial task into an enjoyable excursion.

After we had unloaded the cane, we sat by the press and drank sugar juice. Then the old *rajput* came into the square to collect me for lunch. My friend jumped up and stood at attention, his exuberance replaced by deference. This was his landlord, and half the harvest belonged to him.

As we crossed the fields, my host pointed, a little sadly, at a new diesel engine that the government had just installed to replace one of the three ox-driven irrigation pumps. One could not escape change, not even in Akolia. The Indian government has dug wells and erected pumps and power pylons throughout the country, and over the past twenty years harvests have doubled, although food-grain production is still half that of China. Still, I was glad that my host was opposed to progress. A few hundred miles away, in neighboring Punjab State, the landlords have discovered that, by buying tractors, they can dispense with half their workers and still farm more land than before. So tenants are evicted and farms grow larger. The landlords buy cars and televisions and the landless go off to starve in Bombay and Calcutta. If this is what the modern age has in store for India, I am not sorry that Akolia is so backward.

I left Akolia the morning after my oxcart ride. I spent the next three days riding buses, changing buses, and waiting for buses. On the third evening, I reached Jaisalmer, the remotest town in Rajasthan. It is an outpost in the western desert, built of stone the color of desert sand, and viewed from afar it appears as a city of gold. When I went closer, I found massive walls, a market full of camels whose hair had been braided in intricate designs, narrow cobbled streets, and huge mansions of yellow sandstone. Many of the houses were empty; sometimes the place seemed more like a brooding ghost than a living town. And the sun was the strongest in India, a constant reminder that here begins the vast arc of desert that sweeps through Pakistan and Persia, Arabia and Africa, not to end until Morocco, where the sand meets the sea.

After Jaisalmer, I stopped briefly in Jodhpur. Jodhpur was a pleasant town, with the usual winding streets and age-old houses, and, behind the city, a huge fort perched on a steep hill. The hotel was housed in a wing of the maharajah's enormous palace. My room cost twelve dollars per night. In all my travels, I never spent that much for lodging again—though perhaps I would have, had I found another hotel equipped with an Art Deco throne room, or an indoor swimming pool surrounded by mosaics of tropical fish.

I went from Jodhpur to Delhi, breaking my journey in Jaipur, the largest city in Rajasthan, the most famous, and, in my opinion, the ugliest. Delhi was nicer than I remembered from my first visit. I discovered the older part of town, a sprawling neighborhood of alleys and bazaars, with the largest mosque in India, the Jama Masjid, at the center. I stayed a few days there, and would have lingered longer, but the heat had begun.

Two months before, the northern plains had been unpleasantly cold, and now it was too hot. The tropics have a reputation for scorching heat and incessant rain, but much of the Third World is in fact blessed with a mild, equable climate, far more pleasant than that of London or New York. India is an exception. On an average May day in Delhi, the mercury climbs to 105 degrees.

My travel plans after Delhi were uncertain, and the weather was as much a factor as anything else. I had hoped to go through the Khyber Pass to Kabul, but when I got to the Afghan embassy, located in a steamy suburb ten miles south of my hotel, I found a sign stating NO TOURIST VISAS GIVEN. No explanation was given either, but a few days later I read in the papers that there had been a coup in Kabul. The Republic of Afghanistan had become the Democratic Republic of Afghanistan. It was April 1978 and a small group of socialists had taken over the government; though I did not know it then and neither did they, the stage was set for the Russian invasion less than two years later. I did know that tourists are not welcome in Democratic Republics, and, sweaty and discouraged, I decided to head for the hills.

In the foothills of the Himalayas, a few hundred miles north of Delhi, is the Kulu Valley. In Manali, at the head of the valley, winter's chill still lingered, and the hills around the tiny town were covered in snow. There were pine trees on the hills, and cedars, and terraced orchards full of apple blossoms, and scattered here and there were massive houses built of rough-hewn logs and plaster. The air was cold and dry and full of the smell of smoke and the promise of spring.

I took long hikes in the hills and then ate enormous helpings of fried noodles in the bazaar. There was a beggar who sat nearby, and each day as I passed I dropped a few coins in his lap. He was an old man with a beard, and his sad, limpid eyes spoke of endless suffering bravely borne. One evening, in a neighborhood that was new to me, I heard roars of laughter coming from a restaurant. Inside was the old beggar, a big bowl of barley beer beside him, entertaining a crowd of cronies and admirers with funny stories. I never went back to that part of town again, but I saw the beggar quite often in the market, his face a mask of pain and sorrow.

9

THE NORTH-WEST FRONTIER

The Kulu Valley lies on the narrow isthmus of India that joins Kashmir to the plains. Fifty miles to the east is Tibet; a hundred miles west is the Pakistan border. Here, three religions meet. Manali is a Hindu town, but the people living north and east of the valley are Tibetan Buddhists and the Pakistanis to the west are Moslem. A tiny portion of the Tibetan plateau, the Buddhist zone, spills over into India, but that area, which is called Ladakh, is snowbound until June. I might go there in the summer, I thought, but that decision could wait. I would spend the spring of 1978 in Pakistan.

Many travelers passed through Pakistan in those days, for it was the last leg of the road from Europe to India, but few cared to linger. I had heard horror stories about Pakistan as far away as Singapore, and Western women who had just come from there were jittery, nervous, and distrustful of men. But one of the travelers lent me an old issue of *National Geographic,* and there I read of another Paki-

stan, with deserts and open spaces, rugged hills and blue-eyed hill-
men, tiny valleys lost in the mountains where people spoke languages
unknown to the outside world. No one I met knew anything about
these strange, remote places, and that in itself was an irresistible incentive to go.

My first stop in Pakistan was Lahore. Most of the scare stories
told about Pakistan took place in Lahore. But Rudyard Kipling, who
a hundred years before had been a reporter for the Lahore *Civil and
Military Gazette,* wrote of the "wonderful walled city of Lahore," a
place of mystery and intrigue full of characters who lived "a life wild
as that of the Arabian Nights." In either version, Lahore promised
excitement.

I stayed in a hotel in the older part of town; the sign outside said
SINGING BATHS but there were only cold, tuneless showers. Like the
plumbing, the city did not live up to its reputation. Though crowded,
the streets seemed drab after Rajasthan, where men wore turbans
brighter than the rainbow. Here, and everywhere in Pakistan, the
men wore the *shalwar-qamiz,* a long shirt, worn with the tails hanging out, and baggy drawstring trousers of the same material. These
suits are the ancestors of our pajamas, and to Western eyes Lahore
looks like a city of sleepwalkers. It is also a city of rickety horse-
drawn carts, of tall buildings made of brick the color of rust, of street
arcades where fat men sell kebabs.

After one day in Lahore, I moved on to Rawalpindi, only to find
more red brick, more pajamas, more kebabs. At the tourist office, I
picked up an airline timetable and discovered that for ten dollars I
could fly to Gilgit.* Gilgit lay far to the north, in a quiet valley that a

---

* Though Gilgit is in Pakistan, many maps show it as part of India. Geography has
been obscured by history. Before 1947, when India (which then included present-
day Pakistan and Bangladesh) was ruled by the British, Gilgit was part of Kashmir.
An independent, princely state ruled by a rajah, Kashmir was as large as Great Britain and had borders with Afghanistan, China, and Tibet, as well as India. In 1947
British India was divided into two newly independent nations, India and Pakistan.
Both wanted Kashmir for their own. Most Kashmiris were Moslem and hoped
Kashmir would become part of Pakistan, but the rajah, a Hindu, hated Pakistan and
wished his kingdom to remain independent. Egged on by the Pakistani government,
an army of Pathan tribesmen from Pakistan's North-West Frontier invaded Kashmir and advanced toward Srinagar, the rajah's capital. Before reaching it, the
Pathans paused to loot and plunder. Meanwhile the terrified rajah signed a treaty
giving his kingdom to India, and enough Indian troops were flown in to stop the

thousand years ago was the main road to China. It is not far from the Chinese border, and close to that snowy and fabulous land where the Himalayas, the Karakorams, and the Hindu Kush meet, a region that the Pakistanis call Bam-i-Dunya, the Roof of the World. That was all I knew about Gilgit, but it was enough; even if the town were deadly dull, the flight there would surely be spectacular.

And it was. Years before, I had flown over Mont Blanc, and passengers and crew alike had stood to gape in awed silence at a vista of jagged rock and crinkled snow, a brief vision of a purer world. The flight to Gilgit passed over a hundred Mont Blancs, a white and continuous carpet of them, and some of the peaks were two miles taller than the highest Alp.

Gilgit itself was a town of muted hues: low gray houses huddled by a gray river in a valley of gray hills. And its bedbugs were the fiercest in the world.

The men of Gilgit were wiry and lean. They moved with the quiet confidence shared by all who live in a harsh land: they had survived many a cruel winter and knew they had the strength to live through many more. For six months of the year, a Canadian informed me, the temperature falls far below freezing and there is not enough wood to build a fire.

The man who told me this was a professor of linguistics from Quebec. He wore a *shalwar-qamiz* and a gaudy mustache, and walked with the assurance of a hillman. When I first saw him in the Gilgit bazaar, I took him for one of them. He was living in the Yasin Valley, a hundred miles west of Gilgit and just south of the Afghan border, and had come into town to meet his new assistant and to get supplies; there were no shops in Yasin. The language spoken in his valley, Burushaski, is not related to any other language on earth. The people who spoke it might, he thought, be the last remnants of long-

---

Pakistani advance. A few weeks later, in staunchly Moslem but still Indian-held Gilgit (where there had been periodic uprisings against the rajahs for over a hundred years) the people rose in revolt and proclaimed the region part of Pakistan. Soon afterward, the U.N. arranged a truce between the two nations. Both sides agreed to hold a plebiscite in which the Kashmiris would decide their fate, but the vote was never held. The land the Pathans occupied, together with Gilgit—a third of Kashmir in all—has been absorbed by Pakistan. The rest, including Srinagar, the fertile, densely populated Vale of Kashmir, and Ladakh, is now part of India and is known as Jammu and Kashmir State. Because the rajah turned over his state to India, many maps show all of Kashmir, even Gilgit, as part of India.

forgotten races who farmed the northern valleys before the Dards, migrants from the south, displaced them three thousand years ago. The professor spoke Burushaski fluently, but perhaps he felt lonely nonetheless, because he invited me to join him in Yasin.

Early the next morning, we met in the bazaar, where we soon found a jeep going to Yasin. Jeeps are the only means of transport in the north. They are built to hold five people but seldom carry fewer than ten, and that day's jeep to Yasin had twelve passengers, plus a full load of bulky bags and boxes with sharp corners. We were early, and there was space for us on the boxes; latecomers had to stand on the running boards.

For the first part of the journey, we followed the Gilgit River upstream into the foothills of the Hindu Kush. The gravel track, cut out of the mountainside, was barely wide enough for us to pass. Around and above us loomed the hills; no gentle rolling humpbacked hummocks these, but steep jagged scarps, black and barren, and ridges of naked rock. The earth seemed flayed, its bare bones of bedrock exposed. "It is like the moon," said the new assistant; this was his first trip outside Lahore.

The sight of those hills made us all feel small and unprotected, but the valleys were different. They were narrow oases of green, with lush fields and orchards framed by tall, slender poplar trees that waved in the wind. Around the groves were high walls of smooth, rounded stones taken from the riverbed and once or twice I saw low, flat-roofed houses built of the same egg-shaped stones.

We drove through the village of Gupis, a long, sun-dappled street of shade trees and river-stone walls. Then we crossed the Gilgit River and turned north into a canyon. The walls narrowed as we climbed to cross a pass. The gap was littered with boulders fallen from hills that looked like huge and malevolent slag heaps. Then the defile widened and I could see the valley below. It was fertile, the land that spread before us; there were trees and green meadows and fast-flowing streams.

Halfway up the long valley was a two-room rest house run by the Public Works Department of Pakistan. We reached it in the evening, ten hours after leaving Gilgit. One room was strewn with notes and language texts; it was obviously the professor's. I stayed in the other, though one night a visiting road inspector came and I had to sleep in a shed.

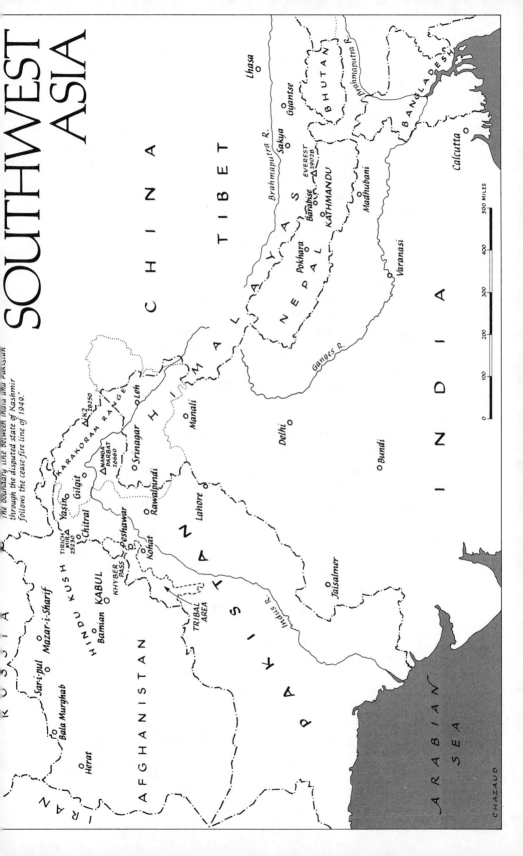

SOUTHWEST ASIA

The boundary line between India and Pakistan
through the disputed state of Kashmir
follows the cease-fire line of 1949."

RUSSIA

IRAN

AFGHANISTAN

Herat

Bala Murghab

Sar-i-pul

Mazar-i-Sharif

HINDU KUSH

Bamian

KABUL

KHYBER PASS

TRIBAL AREA

Peshawar

Kohat

TIRICH MIRA 25230

Chitral

Yasin

Gilgit

KARAKORAM RANGE

K2 28250

NANGA PARBAT 26660

Leh

Srinagar

Rawalpindi

PAKISTAN

Lahore

Indus R.

Jaisalmer

ARABIAN SEA

CHINA

TIBET

Lhasa

Brahmaputra R.

Sakya

Gyantse

HIMALAYAS

EVEREST 29028

Barabise

KATHMANDU

Pokhara

NEPAL

Manali

Delhi

Ganges R.

Varanasi

Bundi

INDIA

BHUTAN

Brahmaputra R.

BANGLADESH

Madhubani

Calcutta

0 100 200 300 400 500 MILES

CHAZAUD

At the nothern end of the valley, which is still in Pakistan but only thirty miles from the Afghan border and less than a hundred from Russia, is the Darkot Pass, the only major pass through the eastern Hindu Kush. A few months before, a jeepload of tourists had disappeared without a trace en route to Darkot, and the local government had forbidden foreigners to venture north of the rest house. The southern half of the valley was open, and so on most mornings I walked south, along the road or through the fields. Yasin was over eight thousand feet above sea level, and the morning air was chilly, but the sun was strong and warm and in the walled orchards the trees were green. Spring had come to Yasin.

The valley was sparsely settled, and most of the time I was alone, but sometimes I saw gangs of young boys roaming around, shooting slingshots, looking for mischief. They had been cooped indoors for most of the long winter, and now they ran through the fields trying to discharge the energy that coiled inside them like a tightly wound spring. Once I was given tea and salt by a gang of road workers, and once an old man invited me into his house. It looked like a crude den from the outside, with walls of roughly piled ovoid stones, but inside was a large airy room paneled with rich dark wood. There were carved chairs and benches around a central sunken hearth, where a pot of salty tea, evidently a popular refreshment, was bubbling.

During the morning, as I explored the valley, the professor and his assistant were at work. They paid local men to pronounce the same word, over and over again, into a tape recorder. The men must have thought them very strange, but they grew to think of the professor as one of their own, and in the afternoon, when I returned, I often heard him exchanging rough but friendly jests with them. "You are such a kind man," he would say to one of them. "Doubtless you beat your mother, you are so kind." And they would laugh and reply with more of the same.

Near the rest house was a small state-run clinic, and the doctor in charge sometimes stopped by to see us. He was, he told me, born in Kashgar, a large and ancient city in Sinkiang. When Mao's armies had taken the town, he had saddled his horse and ridden into the mountains, had crossed the Pamirs and the Karakorams, stopping in nomad camps along the way. At one camp, he had met a girl and fallen in love, but he had left her and ridden on. Finally, a month after leaving Kashgar, he had come down from Darkot into the green fertile valley of Yasin, and had never left.

The doctor was married now. His small son spoke perfect Burushaski and taught me a few choice phrases such as *pishkish cacamoush,* which means chicken fart. Coarse, unsubtle jests—a bearish kind of humor—were the norm here, and often I caught myself replying in kind. Humor, taste, and style vary from country to country, place to place; each people has its own distinctive blend of guilts and fears, norms and ambitions. The doctor's five-year-old son had already assimilated these complex and unspoken codes of behavior. It was as easy as breathing, and as difficult to avoid.

Like a child, I, too, absorbed the attitudes of the people around me, and as I crossed the continent from east to west, the timbre of my being changed, step by step and slowly, from Indonesian smiles to hot-blooded Afghan anger. Sometimes I wondered if there was a real, unchanging I, burning bright and constant like the sun behind a mask of drifting, transient clouds. I believe now that my real self has room enough to contain all of these things, and some have stayed with me, strange and alien splinters lodged in my soul. Like a Thai, I am ashamed to raise my voice in anger. But like an Afghan or a man of Yasin, I feel that a loud voice and righteous anger is the mark of a man.

In the evening, the surly *chowkidar,* the custodian of the rest house, who liked the professor but took pains not to show it, brought us our dinner, a stack of thick and rubbery *chapatis. Chapatis* look like pancakes and taste like bread crusts. Made from whole meal flour and baked on a griddle, they are the staple food of most of Pakistan and northern India. In Yasin, they were invariably served with a lentil sauce that succeeded in being at once bland and loathsome. Sometimes the doctor joined us and talked about his clinic. The women here are very nervous, he told us. They worry about the crops, they worry about the weather, they worry where they will get the food for the next meal. Valium was the drug he gave most often, he said, more often even than aspirin. I was surprised. I had thought that pressure and tension were Western afflictions.

On the days when the doctor was away, the tone of our conversation changed. The professor's Pakistani assistant, a brooding, dark-eyed boy, had a poet's soul, and he spoke with fervor on such topics as the virtues of melancholy. He seemed out of place in the modern age; he was kin to Donne and to Milton, though he would not have known the names. Like Milton, he would have loved to debate the respective merits of sunlight and moonlight, daytime and night. I wondered whether the men of southern Pakistan—whom I had previously seen only through the eyes of Western women—quietly pursued a tradition of courtly introspection that in the West was lost long ago.

I lingered a week in Yasin, and then took an overladen jeep to Gilgit. The flights south are often delayed by storms, sometimes for weeks at a time, but I was lucky, and, two days after saying farewell to my friends in the valley, I was in Rawalpindi, in central Pakistan. There I boarded a bus to Peshawar, capital of the North-West Frontier Province and the last city before the Afghan border.

I found a room in a hotel near the Kissa Khawani bazaar, which was crowded with tiny shops built of adobe. This part of Peshawar seemed older than Rawalpindi, and tougher. The streets were full of tall, flinty-eyed men. Some carried rifles and one wore aviator sunglasses and a huge pistol. There were no women at all.

Peshawar means "frontier town"—an appropriate name. In ancient times, the region, then called Gandhara, divided India from Persia. Later, in 327 B.C., the armies of Alexander the Great conquered the town, and, in the years after that, they were succeeded by a string of invaders, among them the Parthians, the Kishans, the Huns, the Mongols, the Moguls, the Sikhs, and the British. Peshawar was at the border of most of these empires and, from the sixteenth century onward, the region became a barrier as well, for it was settled by the Pathans, a Pakhto-speaking people from Afghanistan who are some of the fiercest warriors on earth. Though the British claimed the Pathans' land, they never could control it. Instead, they, like the Moguls before them, were forced to pay the Pathan chiefs a yearly allowance to keep the peace.

To this day, the territory remains unconquered. It has retained the name by which the British knew it: the North-West Frontier. Pakistani law does not apply inside a long and slender Vermont-size portion of the province. It is called the tribal area and this narrow strip of land may be the only truly autonomous region in the world. It is ruled by councils of Pathan chiefs and elders who follow a code of chivalry and honor called *pukhtunwali*. Its tenets are simple, and as easy to apply as the biblical eye-for-an-eye: welcome all strangers, grant refuge to all fugitives, and avenge all insults.

A strange and fascinating combination, hospitality and vengeance. I wanted to visit the people who held the modern age at bay with a few old-fashioned rifles. Foreigners are not allowed in the tribal area, except along the two main roads, but neither is the Pakistani army. If I could get past the troops that patrol the border, I thought, I would be safe, and would receive the welcome their law requires.

One morning I set out for Darra Adam Khel, a town south of Peshawar that straddled the main highway and was in consequence open to tourists. Darra lies in the tribal zone, and its busy bazaar specialized in contraband. A hundred shops sell guns, for the well-dressed Pathan never leaves home without a rifle, and gun production is the area's leading cottage industry.

I went inside one of the shops, the International Arms and Hashish Store. The owner was fat and friendly and gave me a tour of the shop. Evidently, he was used to wide-eyed Westerners who came not to buy but to stare. He showed me rifles and machine guns and tiny pistols disguised as ball-point pens and, for most backpackers doubtless the star attraction, a whole wall of shelves stacked with sheets of hash, freshly made and still pliable, and each stamped in gold with the manufacturer's logo.

Since the proprietor spoke English, I asked him about the area I wanted to visit: the Tirah, a mysterious region deep within the tribal zone, in which, it is said, no foreigner has ever been allowed to set foot. "Could I go there?" I asked, and he replied "No problem. You can go where you like." With a wave of his hand, he dismissed dangers and government regulations. Clearly, this man was a Pathan.

A road had just been built, he told me, into the Tirah. I should follow the main road south to the town of Kohat and there take a bus to a place called Kalaya, which lay within the Tirah. I followed the hashish seller's instructions and reached Kohat in time to catch the daily bus to Kalaya, which left at a time set by the whim of the driver.

The bus was soon full, and then the driver emerged from a nearby teahouse, and we set off. We took the highway that led west, toward Waziristan, but after a few miles turned into a bumpy track strewn with rocks and gravel. The land outside was brown and barren, with a few sparse tufts of grass sprouting from the stony ground, and nothing more. After an hour we came to a roadblock. I hunched down in my seat while the passengers and driver assured the soldiers that all was in order. In the end, the soldiers decided not to search the bus; they raised the barrier and let us through. I was in the tribal zone.

We stopped soon afterward to pick up passengers—all men, all armed. They sat on the roof clutching their rifles. Soon after sunset, we reached the hamlet of Kalaya, the end of the line. There was a school there, a gift from the Pakistani government, and the headmaster let me sleep in a classroom. One of the teachers was a Pathan, and we talked late into the night. I watched the flame in the lantern dance and sputter as he told me about the Tirah. Two Pathan tribes lived in the region, the Afridi and the Orakzai. The people around Kalaya were Orakzai. They were religious and fanatical. They would hate me because my hair touched my collar and my mustache grew over my upper lip. Such hirsuteness, he said, was an affront to Mohammed, and so were my faded jeans. But the Afridi were even worse, he told me. No stranger was allowed in their domain, and if they caught me, they would surely torture me. But by their law, the *pukhtunwali,* they must welcome me, I protested. That law applies only to Moslems, he said.

The next morning, I set off to try my luck with the Afridi. There are no maps of the Tirah, and I was not sure where their land lay, so I walked more or less at random, trying to avoid the road. It had been dark when I arrived in Kalaya, and I now saw the land for the first time. Its beauty surprised me; I had stumbled upon a green and gentle oasis hidden in the desert. Fields of yellow wheat rippled in the morning breeze, and in the distance there were hills, dark green and thickly forested, and meadows carpeted with long, lush grass. Here and there I could see houses, massive as castles. They had walls of baked earth the color of wheat, and when the sun lit them they glowed like burnished gold. Each house was surrounded by ramparts with, at one corner, a strong, squat tower, which resembled a medieval donjon or keep. Raids and ambushes were a part of daily life, and each family was prepared to withstand a siege.

The Afridi part of the Tirah was called the Maidan, and I asked directions from each passerby. Their answers were evasive and each contradicted the one before. Everyone knew where the Maidan was, but no one wanted me to go there. It was a disorienting experience. Distance and direction changed with each reply; my mental map of the Tirah slowly warped like a phonograph record left too long in the sun. Though only a day's ride from Peshawar, I felt as far from the known world as those nineteenth-century African explorers who spent months and even years wandering in unmapped and hostile terrain.

In the early afternoon, I came to an inn. Horses were tethered by the door. Inside, their riders squatted on the earthen floor and ate *chapatis.* They were Afridis, headed for the Maidan, but they would not take me. One of the men at the roadhouse spoke English. He gave me the usual warnings—They will torture you, they will kill you, etc.—and told me that the Afridi zone was forty miles away. I made up my mind to turn back. I could, or thought I could, face the Afridi, but a trek of forty miles with angry Pathans at the end of it was too much.

That evening, ashamed and tired, I returned to the school. I went for a short stroll around Kalaya, which, I soon discovered, was not a town or even a village; outside the school were a few earth-brick houses and nothing more. As I walked past one of the houses, a man grabbed me and pulled me inside. He jabbered at me in Pakhto as he toyed with his rifle. In desperation, I tried out my one and only Pakhto phrase— *"Dost headmaster,"* or "I am a friend of the head-master." He took me to the school, spoke to the teachers, and let me go. "He thought you were a spy," said the headmaster.

I was fortunate to escape so easily, and I decided to leave the Tirah before my luck ran out. The next day, I went by bus to Kohat and thence to Peshawar. From there I took a bus to Dir, a town far in the north of Pakistan, where vendors sold fruit ice made from snow brought from nearby mountains. I spent the night in Dir and then took a jeep still farther north through the pine forests of the Lawarai Pass, where the air was cold and thin and as exhilarating as champagne, and then down a valley to Chitral. Just beyond the crest of the pass, we stopped for tea. As we drank, an old farmer stood nearby, watching. Like most people in the hills, he wore a big shirt and baggy trousers made of homespun cloth, coarse as burlap. He was barefoot. I had a spare pair of shoes, nearly new, and I gave them to him. He knelt down and kissed my hand.

Chitral district, nestled in the fringes of the Hindu Kush, is, like Gilgit, on Pakistan's northern edge. Only a hundred miles and a range of mountains separate Chitral from Yasin, and the landscape was almost the same, though the hills here seemed less forbidding: they were rounder, smoothed by wind and time, and some were covered by green pastures or crowned with fields of grain. Though the land was softer, the people were not. On my first day in Chitral town, capital of Chitral district, the manager of my hotel brought his friends into my room, ordered tea and cakes for all, spat on my carpet, and billed me for the tea. We argued for an hour over that bill. Though I paid in the end, I won their respect by not giving in without a fight.

Fortunately, such rudeness was rare. A fair number of young backpackers made their way to Chitral, and most Chitralis, though puzzled and somewhat troubled by the vagabonds who came to their valley, tried their best to welcome them. But the younger men, in Chitral as elsewhere in Pakistan, were inflamed and disturbed by the visitors, especially the women.

Pakistani women rarely venture out of doors, and when they do, they wear a *burqa,* a shapeless shroud which covers head and body, allowing an occasional glimpse of a sandal but nothing more. Though the *burqa* is less common in Chitral than farther south, proper Chitrali ladies stay at home, and a man will rarely speak to or even see a woman not of his own family. And there is no touching, no flirting, no dating, no courtship, and few men even glimpse a woman's arm or ankle before their wedding night.

A woman who follows the rules wins the respect of men, and can even gain power over them, but a woman who doesn't is considered a whore. And the Western women who came to Chitral unknowingly broke all the rules. They talked with men, walked the streets in daylight, and a few even wore skirts and short-sleeved blouses. Doubtless they give themselves to anyone who asks, thought the Chitralis, and that thought allowed long-suppressed lust and passion to break through and explode. "When these girls come to my hotel," Zafar, the owner of an inn in a small village fifty miles north of Chitral town, told me, "I must smoke twenty joints a day, or they will drive me mad." So the men made crude advances, were spurned, and grew bitter; she does not like colored men, they thought. It was one of those nasty cultural collisions where everyone gets hurt and no one is to blame—least of all the ladies, most of whom did everything possible, short of wearing a veil, to avoid giving offense.

Zafar's hotel was long and brown and had mud walls. It looked like a stable and rooms were fifty cents a night. It fronted on a street of low, earth-brown buildings also built of mud. Behind the hotel was a wide stream whose waters, fed by barely melted mountain snow, ran fast and clear and bubbly blue. A range of brown hills loomed over the town and, twenty miles to the north but seemingly just beyond reach, a wall of rocks and ice almost five miles high touched the sky—Tirich Mir, the highest peak in the Hindu Kush. The name of this spot was Garam Chashma. It was four hours by passenger jeep from Chitral town. A jeep left Chitral every morning and after a day in Chitral I had taken the jeep.

There was a German girl named Angelika staying at Zafar's. She was nineteen, with long blond hair, and very brave and dashing. She and another girl had toured the Pathan country on horseback and had been ambushed by bandits who, as a tribute to their courage, had let them go unharmed. Angelika was quite pretty, perhaps too pretty, and disturbingly attractive. Zafar's twenty-joint solution did not appeal to me; I took long walks instead, hiking ten or fifteen miles a day in the surrounding hills. One day I met a farmer who gave me salty tea in his wood-paneled house and then took me on a short walk in the hills. There were wheat fields on the slopes, tiny plots with low stone walls around them. The hills looked like huge round hummocks, covered, like a patchwork quilt, with swathes and swatches of color. They were far steeper than they appeared, almost vertical, and the hour's hike was as frightening for me as climbing a cliff, though the young farmer happily jumped from rock to jutting rock. This was the path to his fields, and he climbed it every day of his life.

After a week in Garam Chashma, I returned to Chitral and then went on to Bumburet, a long and wooded valley where the Kalash people live. They claim descent from the army of Alexander the Great, which passed through Swat, a hundred miles south of Bumburet, on its way to India. The Kalash have their own religion, and this puts them outside the pale. In Chitral, as in most of Pakistan, religion is what matters most, more than race or nationality, and the first question a visitor is asked is "Are you Moslem?" Once, in Chitral town, I visited a teahouse in company with a Moslem traveler from Africa. A Moslem visitor has come, shouted the proprietor. Everyone within earshot came to bid him welcome, and there was free tea all round.

The Kalash are by reputation a happy people, but those I met seemed gloomy and dour. The film version of Kipling's story *The Man Who Would Be King* had just been released, and too many tourists had come to Bumburet to see the people made famous by the movie. Bumburet is on the Afghan border, and in the quiet of the evening I could hear the thump and boom of the Afghan army's heavy artillery wafting on the western wind.

Bumburet had the most flies of anywhere in Asia. After two days spent hiking in the valley, and two evenings spent lazily swatting flies and listening to the Afghan army killing Kalash, I left for Chitral, and caught the next flight to Peshawar. A few days later, I was in India. Summer had come and it was time to go to Ladakh.

10

KASHMIR, LADAKH, AND THE TRIBAL ZONE

My room in Jammu had dirty peeling walls the color of a mud-smeared, scabrous sky. It was, for the price, the best I could find, and it had taken an hour's search through strange streets to find it. The town of Jammu was a day's journey north of the closely guarded checkpoint near Lahore where I had crossed from Pakistan into India. Jammu was on the road to Srinagar, which was on the road to Ladakh. I had arrived after dark and the next day's bus to Srinagar left at 7:30 A.M.

I planned the next morning in my mind. I would wake, shower, stuff my tattered clothes in my aging knapsack, tie it closed and hope the string wouldn't tear, then carry it through dimly lit predawn streets to the bus station. It is a beautiful time, that hour before first light, as the velvet silence of the night is broken by the sounds of the city waking: the sleepy gargles of morning ablutions, tired footsteps, the swish of metal gates as shops open for the day. But I could not stop to watch and listen, because I had to find the station and get on line for tickets before they sold out. Besides, I had my pack to carry, and its weight would make me forget the beauty of the night. Sometimes, when I strapped on my backpack, I thought of another wanderer, and the corpse he carried to show that he was cursed. The largest albatross weighs eighteen pounds; my pack was twice as heavy as that, and sometimes more.

I would not sleep well that night. If I did, I would probably oversleep and miss the bus. I would doze lightly and wake up every hour or so to check the time. Before going to bed, I checked the room. Door: strong, and bolted from inside. Windows: barred, and I closed the shutters. Some thieves use fishing lines to snag wallets through open windows. Since I had the room to myself, I took off my money belt and put it under the mattress. This was luxury. Usually I wore the belt when I slept, coddling the hard lumps of my fortune under my stomach with as much tenderness and paranoia as a mother bird guarding her nest. As I drifted off to sleep, I tried to calculate how many times I had done all this, how many dingy, nameless hotels I had slept in, how many buses I had taken, how many miles I had carried my pack through alien streets that at times all looked alike in their strangeness. I fell asleep before I could finish counting.

I was weary with the world. As I expected, I slept badly. But, like the mists and vapors of the night, my mood of gloomy depression was burned off by the morning sun. North of Jammu, the land was green and hilly and, though not especially scenic, it was, like every work of nature I have seen, beautiful in its fashion.

The bus had left on time. Most Asian trains and buses—at least on major intercity lines—run on schedule, and the notion, common in the West, that Asians cannot or will not be punctual is outdated. In my travels, I saw so many stereotypes refuted that I sometimes thought that committees of bigots should be formed to keep our prejudices up to date; change in the Third World is so rapid that annual revisions might well be required.

Soon after lunch, which was a bowl heaped high with soggy bread sticks, we passed through a long tunnel cut through a mountain, and entered the Vale of Kashmir. Below us stretched an emerald plain, a carpet of rice fields. The valley was world-renowned for its beauty, and it was indeed beautiful. It *lived* on its beauty, on the tourists

drawn by its fame, and its people—at least those involved in the tourist trade—have learned to be as unctuous as gigolos. Still, I found my
first glimpse disappointing. It is slopes and contours that give rice
fields their charm, and Kashmiri paddies are as flat as Kansas.

As soon as I arrived in Srinagar, I went to the government tourist
office and rented a boat on Lake Dal, just outside town. It was a government-approved Class D houseboat and was mine for a dollar a
night. Lake Dal is famous for its houseboats, and for over a hundred
years, sophisticated travelers have thought of them as paradise afloat.
But when I think of Lake Dal, I remember the wide asphalt highway
that skirts the water; and the ugly concrete breakwater beside the
road; and beyond the wall, the lake, as crowded as a trailer park. I
remember the boats, quite gay and pretty, with striped awnings on
the sides and beach umbrellas on deck, but marred by huge, tawdry
billboards, announcing, with letters a foot high, the name of each
boat, names like *Flower Garden, Deluxe* and *New Australia.* I remember the long, narrow punts called *shikaras* which glide from boat to
boat, floating supermarkets, laden with produce; and the cries of the
boatmen who sail the *shikaras*—"Hey mister! I got flowers, I got
good hash, I got biscuits, I got toilet paper, I got morphine! What
you want, tell me, I got it!" But above all I remember the smell:
ever-present, subtly invading my memories as it pervaded every hour
spent on the lake, until, after a day or two, it was taken for granted,
barely noticed but always there. It was faint, that smell, yet fetid,
vaguely but unmistakably fecal, an effluvium which was the inevitable result of a thousand houseboats dumping raw sewage into a lake
without an outlet, and which was the sole legacy of countless generations of tourists and visitors—gentlemen in frock coats, ladies in
crinolines, dashing young sahibs in red jackets and gold braid, and,
later, beefy tourists with paunches sagging over Bermuda shorts and
cameras around their necks, and, later still, long hair and T-shirts and
dungarees, the glamour and grandeur of life on the lake decaying
with each passing decade, and the stench increasing.

My time in Kashmir was a time of sickness, and perhaps this has
colored my memories. A lot of travelers were sick that summer, and
bodily functions which are not usually mentioned after the age of ten
or eleven became the sole topic for discussion. Diagnoses and medical
advice were traded, symptoms were described with nauseating pre-
cision ("If there's blood in it, it could be amoebas") and a successful

trip to the privy was an occasion for smug self-satisfaction. I went to Pahalgham, fifty miles from Srinagar and high in the hills that ring the valley. There were alpine meadows at Pahalgham dotted with tiny white and yellow flowers, and the hills above were high and covered with tall, shaggy pines. The sickness followed me, and the smell, and the maddening conversation. Finally, in desperation, I drank a small amount of tincture of iodine, which killed whatever germs were inside me. Iodine is highly poisonous, and though I was sick countless times in the years after that, I never dared try that treatment again.

I went back to Srinagar and bought a bus ticket to Leh, eleven thousand five hundred feet above sea level and the largest town in Ladakh. Once an independent kingdom, Ladakh was conquered by the rajah of Kashmir in 1841. Along with most of the rest of Kashmir, Ladakh became part of India in 1947, but it shares a border with Tibet and its culture is not Indian but Tibetan. A few years ago, Indian Airlines began air service to Leh, which lies due east of Srinagar, but in the summer of 1978, the only way to go was by road. It is 160 miles from Srinagar to Leh by air, but 482 miles by road. The trip took two days, assuming the bus didn't fall over a cliff which, to judge from newspaper accounts, a fair number did.

For the first part of the journey, the land was green. There were paddies and then, when we reached the hills, woods and greenswards and pastures of clover. All morning the road climbed upward, curve after winding curve, and shortly after noon we crossed the first pass, Zoji La. The green stopped at Zoji La, and we passed into a realm of red and brown: Ladakh.

Ladakh is a land of space and silence and flaming mountains. Each hill has its own shape—there are pyramids and spires and concave cliffs the shape of curling waves—and many are quite complex, with a thousand crags and crinkles and peaks and pinnacles. The color of the land was soft and oddly muted, almost pastel, but surprisingly varied. The hills were covered with stripes and bands and swirls of color, and there were a thousand shades of brown. I could pick out amber and umber and ocher and rust, salmon and sable and sand, chocolate, cocoa and café au lait, beige and dun and tan, and when the sun struck the rock, I saw bronze and copper and gold. And other colors as well: red and black, mauve and violet, patches of pink and peach and flecks of orange, and peaks of steel gray and snowy white.

From the top of the pass I could see for miles, and range after range of hills and mountains lay spread below. The sky was cloudless, deep and radiant, and light poured down like a benediction. It was a strange landscape, at once disturbing and exalting, and more than a little holy.

We passed through towns with names like Drass, Kargil, and Mulbekh, across high passes and through narrow valleys, past patches of wheat and thick-walled houses, which looked like big brown boxes with tiny windows, and everything was bathed in sunlight, that clear, pure light of the high Himalayas that transformed the most mundane objects—a wooden plow, an old felt hat—into things of magic and mystery, and hinted at a hidden meaning that, especially toward twilight, seemed just beyond reach.

On the afternoon of the second day, we reached the highest point of the journey, the pass named Fotu La. From there, the road descended into the valley of the Indus, which swept through Ladakh on its way to the Arabian Sea. Just beyond the pass, a spine of rocks rose up from the valley, and on its crest I saw the stark silhouette of a monastery, built in what I later learned was the Tibetan style, with thick stone walls, flat roofs, and tiny square windows. The walls were painted white, with black squares around the windows. Strips of colored cloth, prayer flags, fluttered from the roof. Below the monastery, which was named Lamayuru, a village clung to the slopes of the crag. The houses, too, had white walls and tiny windows, and I could see people standing on the flat roofs. The bus stopped, and I could hear them shouting from rooftop to rooftop. I grabbed my pack, got off the bus, and walked to the monastery.

There was a crowd of Ladakhis, old men mostly, in the monastery, and a fat monk handed each one a portion of barley. The monasteries own much of the farmland in Ladakh, and receive their rent in grain, some of which they then distribute to the people.

The religion of Ladakh is Tibetan Buddhism, although the Gelukpa sect, which used to dominate Tibet, is poorly represented in Ladakh. Like the *sadhus* of Benares, Buddhist monks, through study, prayer, and daily meditation, seek to escape and transcend the material world. I knew little else about Tibetan Buddhism, but at some point I had read James Hilton's novel *Lost Horizon,* and I expected the lamas of Ladakh to be old and very wise, with serene, untroubled eyes and enigmatic smiles. But many of the monks I found in this clifftop eyrie were very young, no older than ten or eleven. They were still boys—small, giggling, mischievous boys. The lamaseries are powerful, and most families try to place at least one child there. Some enter the monasteries at the age of six. The older lamas were well fed and jovial. They sat in the sun, as happy as lizards on a rock, eating barley cakes as they laughed at the tourists. They seemed pleased that their remote retreat had become a "tourist attraction."

In one of the courtyards, a long shed had been built as a dormitory. I paid eight rupees to the monk in charge, just in time to get the last empty cot. My roommates were young and earnest. They were equipped with brand-new backpacks, cameras, and notebooks, and they stayed up half the night whispering in French and German, trading advice on where to find villages and monasteries not yet spoiled by the annual tourist invasion.

I spent one night at Lamayuru and the next two at Temisgang, a village a few miles north of the main road, with bright green fields and neat white Tibetan-style houses. I was the guest of a young farmer I had met on the trail to the village. His house was newly painted but it looked a thousand years old, with walls of stone as solidly built as a Crusader's castle. The ground floor was a stable, and most of the story above was taken up by the kitchen, huge and shadowy with smoke-blackened walls and wooden shelves heaped high with brass pots and spoons and kettles that gleamed dully in the dim light. I gave my host twenty rupees when I left for Leh, but he asked for more. "Pay me what you would pay a hotel," he said.

Leh is a cosmopolitan town, and has been for centuries, but the traders and caravans that once came from Kashgar and Lhasa, their yaks and ponies laden with gold and silk and spices, have been replaced by visitors from places whose names, to Ladakhi ears, are even more exotic: France, Switzerland, Australia, and even America. Leh was full of these aliens, and most of the main street was taken up by sellers of souvenirs and newly made antiques, who sat shoulder to shoulder on the pavement, their wares stacked in front of them. There were tiny restaurants with Tibetan food and menus in English, and next door to them large cafés run by Sikhs and Hindus which served such things as *samosas* and *barfi* and *paan*, a reminder that Leh is a garrison town, with forty thousand Indian soldiers guarding the Chinese border.

I was disappointed in Leh. Perhaps I had expected too much; perhaps nothing could have matched the exaltation of the ride through the mountains. And too many tourists had come to share that exaltation, and as they crowded the monasteries they saw, not the hills, or the paintings or the shining brasswork, but themselves back in Paris or Milan, murmuring "We found a curious monastery near the Tibetan border" as their friends stood silent with cocktail glasses in their hands and envy in their eyes.

I spent the last weeks of July visiting the many monasteries that dotted the valley of the Indus. I saw Hemis, the richest and largest; Alchi, nestled in red hills above a green valley; Shey, with dim halls and gilded Buddhas lit by bowls of burning butter; and Tikse, high on a hill above the valley, with walls that soar higher still, in a majestic sweep of sheer white stone that, when seen from the road a thousand feet below, seems to brush the snowy mountains that rise behind it. And each afternoon I returned to Leh, to fritter away the evening in the Tibetan noodle shop or the Indian sweet shop, or after sundown, on the rooftop of the hotel where the younger travelers stayed. Angelika was there, and Stanley, an outgoing and muscular American, pleasant to be with, whom I took for a stevedore until I learned he was a professor; and Punit, an American disciple of an Indian guru, who dressed in orange and did calisthenics in time to a recording of his master's voice.

A month passed like this. I convinced myself that the monasteries were worth the time, and indeed they were, as I learned four years later when I visited Tibet, for the lamaseries of Ladakh, even the smallest, are alive with prayer and chanting, and most of those in Tibet are in ruins. But it was not the monasteries that held me; it was the travelers. I treasure friends and friendship, and during my years in New Haven, my friends grew to be a part of me, and my feelings became real only when my friends confirmed them. But a traveler must be alone, meeting people and leaving them behind, with never enough time for friendship to form. Punit, Stanley, and especially Angelika were the closest to friends that I had, and I found it hard to leave them.

But Stanley left and then Punit and finally Angelika, and a week later so did I. Back in Srinagar, I had a week of chills and fever. Malaria again. As I lay on my mat in my Class D houseboat, I thought of Africa, in vivid memories and fever-bright dreams. I saw the endless savanna, and the elephant grass, which smells like musk and clover and glistens with dew in the chill of the dawn. My summer in Kashmir had made me aware of the pain of travel, and the tedium, and the loneliness, but now I remembered the thrill of it. Once, on a road in Zaire, I had seen a truck pass by, with a traveler standing in back, on top of the cargo. As I watched, he threw his head back and laughed, and the wind blew his hair in streamers behind him. The joy of being young, alive, and in motion; it was easy, far too easy, to forget, to let this joy and freshness fade away. Perhaps I could find it in Africa; like Ponce de Leon, I believed youth could be regained through exploration.

My fever passed, but the dream remained. I could choose Africa, or spend the winter in New York. I counted my money. I had eleven hundred dollars left, plus whatever balance, if any, remained in my account in New York. I would learn to live more cheaply; I would go as far as eleven hundred dollars would take me, overland across Asia and then south through Sudan.

The traveler's grapevine of hearsay and rumor, sometimes reliable but as often not, carried reports that Afghanistan was open. I would spend a month there, I decided, on my way west. And so in the first week of September of 1978, I left Srinagar. I traveled fast and reached Peshawar three days later.

There was an Afghan consulate at Peshawar, where I filled in an array of forms in triplicate, attached a photograph to each, and left my passport with a harried clerk, who put it in a drawer that was already overflowing with passports. When I returned a day later, a visa had been stamped in, with Arabic-looking script written in purple ink, and below it a revenue stamp and the seal of the consulate, which was quite ornate and full of curlicues and crescents. It was a tourist visa; it allowed me to stay a month inside Afghanistan.

Though the Afghan visa stamp was fancier than most, the procedure was typical. The boring paperwork, the bored officials, the heap of passports awaiting the consul's signature—I had seen it all before, in India and Indonesia and every country in between, and often as I stood on line in the visa office I wondered if the long and tiresome procedure served any purpose. But I never complained. What fun would a steeplechase be without hurdles?

Before I left Peshawar, I paid a final visit to the tribal zone of Pakistan's North-West Frontier where, a few months before, I had failed in my attempt to reach the Afridi part of the Tirah. On that trip, I had slept in a school and had not been allowed to set foot inside a Pathan house, but while in Ladakh I had conceived a plan that would allow me to spend a night with a Pathan family. A few miles south of the gun bazaars of Darra was a group of villages known as Bosti Khel which, fifty years before, had been the headquarters of a Pathan chief who became legendary for his bold and daring raids against the British. I had first read about this Pathan hero some months before, and his story intrigued me. Fifty years ago it was fairly common for Pathans to sneak alone into heavily guarded British encampments, in order to steal spare parts for their rifles. Such bravery was considered average, and a man who gained renown for his courage must have done wondrous things indeed. When I had passed through Darra on my way to the Tirah, a shopkeeper had written down the name of this leader's family. If I could track them down, I would hear the story of this Pathan Robin Hood as told by his descendants. We would talk well into the night, and they would invite me to stay until morning.

While in Leh, I had bought a *shalwar-qamiz,* and, after I picked up my Afghan visa, I put on the loose shirt and baggy brown trousers, tied my hair in a knot and stuffed it under a cap, and boarded a bus to Kohat. I asked the driver to let me off at Bosti Khel, and, when we reached a particularly desolate stretch of highway, the bus stopped. The road was built on an embankment. There was a valley below, and I could see a few fields and one or two houses, but most of the valley was out of sight, hidden behind a low knoll. I made my way down the slope toward the houses.

At the first house, which was rather small, an old man served me lemonade as he pondered what to do with me. He understood that I wanted to see Mohammed Khan, the descendant, for I had repeated his name several times, but since we had no languages in common I could not explain why. Mohammed Khan was clearly an important man in these parts, and my host, who obviously was not, hesitated to bring him an uninvited foreigner on an unknown errand. So he told me his son would take me there, and he had his son lead me out of the tribal area toward the nearest police station. I saw the station in the distance and stopped. The son, who accorded me the jovial deference given small children, foreigners, and madmen, said "Mohammed Khan" and pointed ahead with much nodding of head and rolling of eye, but I wasn't fooled. I ran back to his father's house.

His father, meanwhile, had brought in the neighbors and, after long and excited discussion, the group agreed to take me where I wanted to go. The old man picked up his rifle and slung it over his shoulder, and we set off to see the khan.

This time we walked away from the road, behind the hill and into a hidden valley. After about a mile, we came to a large and imposing dwelling, whose mud-brick walls enclosed an area larger than a city block. We went inside, through a massive gate into a courtyard several hundred feet in length surrounded by a covered portico. Various rooms adjoined this walkway; one, larger than the rest, was a gun factory, with metal vises set in the floor.

Mohammed Khan was a big man. He was burly, but not fat, bluff and hearty, with an aura of command about him, and though I stood beside him it took me a long time to realize that I was taller than he. He wanted to know why I had come. Though I spoke the name of his famous ancestor many times, he still did not understand. Perhaps I am pronouncing it wrong, I thought, and showed him the paper on which the merchant had written the name. He could not read the name, which was written in English, but he could read the letterhead, which was in both English and Pakhto: International Arms and Hashish Shop. That he could understand; I was here to buy hashish. He had none to sell, but he nonetheless bade me a grudging and provisional welcome.

There was a breach in the wall of the house and, before the interruption of my arrival, Mohammed Khan and several other men had been carrying stones to repair it. I joined them, hefting the weighty stones uphill from quarry to wall. I was taking a risk by helping, because in many parts of Asia, a host would look down on a guest who performed menial labor, but the khan liked a man who was not afraid to get his hands dirty, and from that time on I felt truly welcome. One of the children made a joke about me, and the khan gave him a resounding clout that knocked him down; this was the only time in my travels I saw a parent hit a child.

After sunset, the khan and his many henchmen and retainers sat on *charpoys* in the huge courtyard, talking softly in the cool, quiet night. Then food was brought, cooked by women, perhaps, though I never saw them. While I was eating my bread and lentil curry, a man arrived—sent for, probably, by the khan—who spoke English. I learned from him that I had come to the wrong place; the family I wanted was named "Gul" and not "Khan." Mohammed Khan apologized to me, for though he had of course heard of the hero of Bosti Khel, he could tell me very little about him. I could, he said, stay the night, and go back to Darra in the morning. I thanked him, and I was indeed grateful, because I had gotten what I really wanted.

And so I slept in the courtyard of Mohammed Khan, in a rope bed under a leafy tree. The night was warm and everyone slept outside, in beds like mine. The next day I went back to Peshawar, and the day after that I squeezed myself into a crowded Chevrolet headed for Torkham, on the Afghan border. The road wound its way through the chain of parched and hostile hills known as the Khyber Pass. In these hills, I thought, a few men could hold off an army. It was not surprising that my thoughts ran to violence; on the hilltops were massive forts manned by tough-looking Pakistani soldiers in crisply pressed fatigues and here and there were houses with round and crenelated towers built of earth. They loomed above us like huge and malevolent sand castles, shining in the harsh glare of the sun.

At the far side of the pass we came to the town of Landi Kotal. This was in the days before Landi Kotal (and Darra too, probably) became one of the world's leading producers of heroin, but the place was reputed to be a town of outlaws even then. We drove through the town, past dirty cafés crowded with hard-faced men with raptor's eyes. A few minutes later we arrived at Torkham. I could not find the Pakistani border post—one building looked like a customs shed, but it was deserted—so I walked along the road until I came to Afghanistan.

11

AFGHANISTAN

The first thing I noticed was the soldiers. There were at least five roadblocks between Torkham and Kabul, each manned by a truckload of soldiers who wore heavy, vaguely Russian greatcoats with big collars, peaked caps, and woolen trousers. Coat and trousers were Confederate gray, usually too large, invariably frayed and covered with patches. Dressed like ragamuffins, and holding antiquated rifles with sharp bayonets, the Afghan troops looked like illustrations from *Tintin in Ruritania,* or photographs of czarist troops in World War I.

Kabul is not a pretty town, but it is at its best in September, when the sun is warm but the breeze is fresh and invigorating, a hint of winter from the Russian steppes. I stayed in Shah-i-nao, the new quarter, with low modern buildings and tree-lined avenues. Most of the foreign legations could be found in that part of town, and, perhaps for that reason, Shah-i-nao was surprisingly cosmopolitan. Important-looking businessmen hurried past, dressed in dark suits and ties and astrakhan hats. Women wearing knee-length dresses and high-heeled shoes strolled from shop to shop. All of the women were beautiful, or so it seemed, for they were the only unveiled women between Rawalpindi and Teheran.

The summer of 1978 was a good one for the women of Kabul, a time for hope and dreaming. About the new government, little was known, but it was socialist and modern and anything was possible: freedom for women, schools in the villages, electricity and irrigation and maybe even tractors . . . I was optimistic at first, but then I read the papers. The press in India is Asia's freest; the *Pakistan Times,* though very pro-government, does not insult the reader's intelligence; but the newspapers of Kabul had no news at all, only articles like "The workers or Kabul Textile Factory [or cement factory or matchbox factory or whatever] unanimously pledged their resolute support to the government of the People's Party of Afghanistan under the leadership of Chairman Taraki." It was the same old story, endlessly repeated. Pictures of the new leader hung everywhere. He smiled down on the patrons of restaurants and shops; he watched, serene and unblinking, as visiting hippies smoked huge pipes of hash. In every street there were soldiers.

I spent my days in Kabul roaming through the bazaars and the curio shops on Chicken Street, lunching at the Istanbul Restaurant, where a plate of soggy spaghetti or sinister stew cost twenty afghans, or half a dollar. After a week of that, I went to Bamian, eighty miles northwest of Kabul. For much of the way, the road ran uphill. After chugging up the highest hill, the minibus broke down. So it was dark when I arrived. There was one main street of low adobe houses. Outside each building hung a kerosene lantern on a pole; the town was lit by torchlight. I found a hotel, dickered a bit out of habit over the price (forty afghans), left my bag in my mud-walled room, and walked out into the night.

I followed the line of torches to the end. There was an open space, and then a cliff. Cut into the rock was a huge standing Buddha, almost two hundred feet high. It was sculpted in the graceful style of Gandhara, and its robes seemed to ripple in the starlight. I could see another one a short distance away. When those Buddhas were carved, Bamian was a famous center of Buddhist learning, and a thousand monks lived within sight of that cliff. Sometime in the intervening fourteen hundred years, Moslems had scaled the rock and smashed the Buddha's face. After a while I realized I was not alone. There was a soldier guarding the Buddhas. Wrapped in a ragged greatcoat, he stood in silence beside the statue's feet.

When I got back to town, I heard music. I followed the sound through deserted streets, and came to a large and well-lit hall, a café probably, with the tables cleared away. Inside, a hundred men and maybe more sat in a rough and pulsing circle. In the center, a man played an instrument that looked like an Indian sitar. It was stirring music, galloping music, much faster and more melodic than Indian ragas, and more emotional too; it sang of freedom and the endless steppes. The men sat in awe as the music poured over them. They swayed and clapped and I half expected them to break into a bearish dance, like Zorba the Greek, who, I decided, should have been born an Afghan.

The next day I went west to Band-i-Amir, a chain of lakes in the midst of the great central desert. The town (also called Band-i-Amir) consisted of eight hotels, all built on the same plan—one large room where everyone slept together on a floor covered, as was every floor I saw in Afghanistan, with thick, richly woven crimson carpets. There was a stove in the middle of the room for heat and another in back for cooking. Meals were served outside on metal tables. I picked a hotel at random and checked in. "You do not have to eat in my hotel," the owner told me, "you may eat in any other hotel. But do not eat in the hotel on the left at the end of the street, because that man is my enemy." I would not like to have an Afghan for an enemy, I thought. They were the toughest people I had ever met, and I pitied any nation foolhardy enough to invade theirs. But I ate at the restaurant at the end of the street anyway. Even St. Augustine knew that forbidden fruit tastes the sweetest.

The lakes of Band-i-Amir were blue, that richest and rarest of ocean blues where the sea seems to be lit from below. Homer compared this luminous blue to the radiant color of wine; both are brilliant, both are intoxicating. I had seen such a blue only twice before—beneath the cliffs of Capri and in the ocean east of Bali—and now I found it a third time, in the middle of a desert.

One day later, back in Bamian, I went to the bus station. The clerk, who spoke English, was telling a German couple the times and fare of the buses to Kabul. "Is there a bus to Kabul?" I asked. And the man said, "No, they were stopped three months ago." But the minibuses, which looked like big station wagons, were still running. I had come in one from Kabul and I left in one bound for Pul-i-Khumri, which was on the main road north of Kabul.

The easiest and fastest way to cross Afghanistan is the southern route, south from Kabul to Kandahar and then west to Herat. The road is paved, the terrain flat and boring. Brand-new German buses made the journey to Herat in a day—a long, hot day, for the buses had sealed windows and no ventilation; they were obviously designed to endure the rigors of a Prussian winter. I decided to go by the northern road, which was shorter than the southern but took five times as long to travel. My choice was, I suppose, predictable. In grade school, I was force-fed thousands of lines of verse, and the one I vividly remember is Robert Frost's injunction to take the road less traveled by.

The road to Pul-i-Khumri followed a winding river through narrow, slate-gray gorges. At Pul-i-Khumri, I caught one of the many buses that run from Kabul to Mazar-i-Sharif. It was hot that day, and the crowded bus was stifling, but the windows could not be opened. Still, the road was paved and the ride was short.

We stopped for tea on the way. As I carried my cup back on the bus, I stumbled and splattered my neighbors with tea. There were a hundred Afghans on the bus, and they all roared and shook with laughter. I could see their turbans bobbing behind me.

There was a large square in the center of Mazar-i-Sharif with a big blue mosque nearby. The gray concrete buildings around the square housed hotels and shops. The shops sold televisions and cameras and were full of Russians on shopping sprees. This was over a year before the Russian invasion, and I never found out what business brought those Russian visitors to Mazar-i-Sharif. I guessed at the time that they were party officials on vacation; Mazar-i-Sharif was only a day's drive from Russia.

That night I watched television, beamed in from Samarkand, just across the border. There were cartoons, time signals, pictures of Moscow, and a long speech by Brezhnev. I wondered why the Russians used their precious exit visas to buy televisions. I wondered why anybody bought televisions. It was, as far as I could remember, the first time I had watched TV since leaving America.

The northern highway turned west at Mazar-i-Sharif, and passed through Balkh, a tiny village that long ago was the capital of Bactria and, a thousand years later, of Khurasan. West of Balkh was Shibarghan, and a few miles later the paved road ended. I left the main road just before Shibarghan, and went south to Sar-i-pul. A Frenchman I had met in Kabul had told me that, even if I stopped nowhere else in Afghanistan I should go there. Later, I wondered how he first found the town, for Sar-i-pul is so obscure, so reclusive a place that most maps leave it out. The road to Sar-i-pul was hardly a road at all, and the truck I took from Shibarghan simply drove across the flat sandy plain. Hours went by, and I was beginning to fear we were lost in endless desert, when, just after sunset, in that quiet pastel hour that ushers in the night, the town came into view.

Sar-i-pul stands at the confluence of two wide and muddy rivers. It is a logical spot for caravans to halt, trade, and take on water. For over two millennia, traders have passed through the region on their way to India, China, Egypt, or Rome, and so Sar-i-pul might, like Balkh, be quite old. Like most of the ancient oases along the Silk Route, Sar-i-pul has become a backwater, but it still lives by trade. There are villages and farms along the river; the farmers bring their crops to the town to barter for pots and pans and brocade and bangles in the bazaar. In the afternoon, their business done, the men gather in the crowded *chaikhanas* (teahouses) where for a penny they buy a pot of tea and endless conversation.

For me, like the villagers, the teahouses were an inexhaustible source of fascination and delight. I spent hours watching the farmers, staring at their beards and bright turbans and baggy linen trousers as they in turn stared at me. Though I could not understand their conversation, I enjoyed the shouts of surprise and barks of laughter that greeted particularly juicy morsels of gossip.

Most of the teahouses were, like every building in town, built of brown adobe bricks, but a few were outdoor affairs, like sidewalk cafés, with striped awnings above and plush red carpets underfoot. The tea came from huge bubbling samovars, and with it you could have kebabs and spicy pilaus studded with plump raisins and bunches of juicy grapes and, best of all, thick round loaves of bread, sweet and light as cake. Twice every hour, runners brought fresh bread from the bakery. At the time, I thought it the best bread in the world and, since memories, like trees or money in the bank, grow with age, I probably always will.

The only government-approved rest house in town was a dank concrete compound a half mile outside the city, and my nights there were a dreary counterpoint to my sunny days in the town. Still, I stayed four nights. On the fifth morning, I took a truck back to Shibarghan. There I rejoined the main road through Oxiana, now a dirt track, which ran through tiny Turkmen villages to Andkhoi, a bleak whitewashed town a few miles south of the Oxus River, and after that to Maimana, an ugly city built of garish pink stone.

The road got worse after Maimana. There were no buses, so I rode in the back of an antiquated flatbed truck whose engine loudly voiced its indignation whenever it was forced to climb a hill. My fellow passengers were a grizzled old man, a young soldier, a woman in that shapeless shroud-cum-veil called a *burqa,* and enough younger men to fill the truck. They refused to believe that I could not speak their language, and they shouted questions at me until the meaning sank in. We came to a hill, and the American-made engine popped and coughed. "Amerika girt girt girt!" said the grinning soldier. "America farts farts farts!"

That evening, the truck stopped in Bala Murghab. The town of Bala Murghab consisted of a tinker, a tailor shop, two stores that sold used clothes, and a government rest house that once, very long ago, had been a rough Afghan approximation of a British country house. Behind the hotel, a soft grassy bank overlooked the Murghab River. Rather than spend the next day bouncing in the truck, I stayed in Bala Murghab. The Russian border was a few miles away, so I put on my brown *shalwar-qamiz* and set off to have a look at it. I followed a muddy track across a gently rolling plain. It was close to harvest time, and the land, which was planted in cotton, was covered with fluffy, white tufts that waved in the wind. The fields stretched on without end, and I wondered whether I had perhaps crossed the frontier unawares and reached the vast steppes of Russia.

I stopped at a village to rest. The long, low earthen houses had no windows, but on the roofs were curious domes and skylights. A gaunt old man, sullen and suspicious, brought me tea. He asked if I had come from Russia. I drank the tea and went on. I heard a jeep coming from the other direction and, before I could hide, its driver saw me. A soldier got out from the passenger side, and when I saw his uniform, which was Afghan but superbly tailored, I knew I was in trouble. Only the highest-ranking officers wore uniforms that fit.

They asked for my papers, and when they saw I was American, they relaxed slightly. They had thought I was Russian and, in that last year before the invasion, the people the Afghans feared the most were their allies, the Russians.

The soldiers took me back to Bala Murghab and questioned me. I played the part of the dumb tourist, a role I had acted many times before. Then a civilian came, also apparently of high rank, since people greeted him by kissing his hand. There were more questions, but in the end the soldiers decided to send me to Herat the next day. Until then, I was not to leave the hotel.

There were four or five other travelers at the rest house that night, among them a Dutch girl who seemed sympathetic. The moon rose, and I invited her to take a stroll by the river. We sat down on the grass and for a few moments I forgot my troubles, but then the watchman happened by. He was a pudgy man with a glabrous, leering face, and he fancied the girl, or perhaps me. He told me he would call the soldiers if I didn't go back to my room, and though I seethed with rage, I saw at once that there was nothing I could do but obey. I was in enough trouble already.

The next morning, a squad of soldiers came and put me on a truck bound for Herat. The Dutch girl, who was traveling in the other direction, came to say good-bye. "Boo hoo hoo" chorused the soldiers, who pretended to be moved to tears by the sadness of seeing love frustrated.

The road to Herat was a sandy track through rough, hilly terrain. The truck had the usual complement of hot-blooded Afghans, and after a day of bumps and jostles and shouted conversation, we arrived at the town of Qala Nau, where we spent the night. I wanted to walk around the town, but when the truck stopped soldiers were waiting. They took me to the hotel and told me to stay there. The next day, after much arguing over who was sitting where, we set off for Herat. The road was somewhat better, and we reached the city by nightfall. I expected another relay of soldiers to escort me to the border, but there were none in sight when our truck pulled in, and I realized I was free.

The next morning, I went to the Iranian consulate. It was in the newer part of town, a neighborhood of wide and dusty boulevards and green, leafy trees. Then, while I waited for my visa, I explored the older part of town, just beyond the city center. It was an endless maze of muddy alleys that went nowhere, hemmed in on either side with high walls plastered with earth that the sun had baked a golden brown. A home in Herat, as in much of the Moslem world, is a very private place, and a man's garden, like his women, is hidden from strangers' prying eyes. I wandered for hours, soaking in the drowsy quiet of the side streets, watching the occasional passerby shuffle past. After a while, I realized I was completely lost. I could not even ask for directions, because when I said, "Where is Herat?" the people said, "This is Herat." Finally, I came to a street wider than most, and flagged down a bus that was passing by. The driver spoke fluent Russian and a little English and offered to take me back to the city center. I got on but something in his eyes made me suspicious and after a few blocks I jumped off. I walked in the opposite direction from the way he was taking me, and ten minutes later I came to my hotel.

Down the block from my hotel were several shops that sold used clothing. My jeans, which were my only trousers apart from my flimsy *shalwar-qamiz*, had become a mosaic of patches and what little was left of the original denim was frayed by countless washings. I bought a slightly faded pair of Levi's to replace them. Usually, the shopkeeper would knock five dollars off the price if you gave him your jeans in exchange, but mine were so worn that he gave me only half a dollar, and that grudgingly.

I lingered in Herat until my Afghan visa expired. I had come to love the Afghans and I was reluctant to leave them. They were a strong people, spirited and proud, and though they would shout at me in incomprehensible languages, and laugh long and loudly at my slightest clumsiness, and never allow me a moment's peace or respite, there was affection behind their banter, and I always felt welcome in their land.

So I spent another week in Herat. It was that golden yet poignant time that heralds the end of summer. The days were warm, the leaves had not begun to fall and their shadows still dappled the boulevards, but at night there was a nip in the air that warned of winter and the chill to come. Somehow, I and all the other travelers I met knew that it was our last summer in Afghanistan. On my final night in Herat, I sat on soft carpets in the lounge of my hotel listening to an old Beatles album owned by the proprietor while through the window I watched a line of silent men file past. They were guarded by soldiers, who were marching them through the town on their way to prison.

12

IRAN, SYRIA, AND EGYPT: 1978

It was an easy drive to the border. I left Herat at eight and got there well before noon. On the Afghan side was a large shed that was painted a dirty beige. Inside, the officer in charge sat at a rickety wooden desk. He was about eighteen but he looked younger, and he wore a faded blue U.S. Air Force uniform that was too large for him. He glanced at my passport and stamped it with a bang, and I got back in the bus and rode to Iran.

The Iranian border post was a huge concrete bunker studded with antennas. Beefy cops swaggered about, wearing well-tailored American-style police uniforms with huge leather gun belts. They tried to act like tough-talking Texas sheriffs.

Inside the building was the drug museum. Whenever the police found drugs hidden in a tourist's luggage, they packed the tourist off to jail and put his luggage in the museum. There were books with hollow insides, boxes with false bottoms, tires with pockets inside, all carefully arranged in glass cases with neatly printed labels listing the name of the tourist, the drugs found, and the date of arrest.

I filled out the entry forms and waited while the police leafed through my passport, and all the while I wished I were back in Afghanistan. I had never met a traveler who had anything good to say about Iran, and I would never have gone there at all had it not been on the way to Africa. I had to cross it but decided to do so in the shortest possible time. I raced from border to border, a thousand miles in four days—not a record, perhaps, but close. Now, of course, I wish I had stayed longer.

I reached Meshed the first evening, in time to catch the last bus to Teheran. We drove through the night across a vast and empty plain, but when I awoke the next morning I could see hills in the distance, and I knew we were approaching the Elburz Mountains. From time to time, we passed through a city, and I saw shiny modern buildings, crowds of soldiers, and, once or twice, a thick column of smoke where rioters had set a building ablaze. For the first time, I wondered whether the shah, who had seemed as durable as Darius or Xerxes, might actually be in danger. But those thoughts were fleeting, and by the time I arrived in Teheran they were long gone.

On a sooty side street near Sepah Square was a big concrete building that had once been painted white. This was the Amir Kabir Hotel. Every backpacker who passed through Teheran stayed there, and you had to have a foreign passport to get in. Otherwise, the owner told me, all the men of Teheran would come to look at the ladies. Western women had a bad time of it in Teheran, though many lived there in those days because jobs were easy to find. Many stayed at the Amir Kabir, and the hotel was usually full, but after waiting an hour, I got a bed. I chained my pack to the headboard and walked to Sepah Square.

It was twilight. The square was vast and gray and barren and the buildings around it, which housed banks and government offices, were gray too. Massive and monumental, with huge gray columns, those palaces of bureaucracy were so solid that a million rioters could not have knocked them down. Around the square, sentries in battle dress stood at attention, with rifles ready and bayonets gleaming.

Night fell, and floodlights around the square came on. They spotlit a big picture of the shah. I went back to the hotel. There was a television in the lounge, tuned to the U.S. Army channel, so I sat on a sagging sofa and watched old American sitcoms until it was time for sleep.

I had planned to leave Teheran the next day, and I bought a ticket for the afternoon bus to Tabriz, but though I waited an hour at the station the bus never came. The ticket clerk had told me the wrong departure time, so the bus company gave me a free seat on the next day's bus. They also paid for my bed at the Amir Kabir, which cost more than the bus fare.

There is a swing and a rhythm to long-distance travel, and inescapable laws of momentum and inertia come into play. I had grown used to being on the move, to sitting on buses and watching the land roll by, and I felt restless and ill at ease that last day in Teheran, for I had planned to be in Turkey by then. I spent the day walking the streets in the northern part of town. There were small but very chic boutiques that sold designer clothes, food stores stocked with sausages and ice-cold Coca-Cola, and even a Hilton Hotel. Teheran was a fast, flashy town, too modern for me, and far too American.

I got to the bus station, as usual, much too early, and so I spent my last hours in Teheran staring at the brown plastic wallpaper of the waiting room, which was designed to resemble wood. Only forty minutes more, I thought. Not long, not longer than two sides of a record. Twenty minutes. Ten. Time to board.

It was still night when I arrived in Tabriz, and by midmorning I was at the border. The two customs posts shared a single building; the entrance was in Iran and the exit was in Turkey. When I stepped outside and onto Turkish soil, I saw Mount Ararat above me, a single massive peak of stone and snow. I took a taxi into Dogubayazit and then a bus to Agri, where I spent the night. The next day I took an express bus along the shores of turquoise Lake Van, through Bitlis and Diyarbakir, to a tiny town just beyond that had gray stone walls, an old castle, and a river. I slept there, rose early, and got the first bus going west. I wanted to leave Turkey as soon as I could, for I did not feel welcome there. Time and again, when I took a seat on a bus, the man next to me would move away. Sometimes, in the small, rough towns of the east, where the men wore second-hand suits and stubbly beards, I was greeted with shouts of "Amerika Kapitalist! You no good." These were the only words of English the people knew. I met with constant, implacable hostility and I blamed myself, as is my wont. After all, I thought, my clothes are old and my hair is too long. If I spent more time in the country, got off the main roads, things might improve. All this is true. But the fact remains that Turkey is the only country in the world where I was ever made to feel unwelcome.

I got off the bus at Gaziantep, which is near the Syrian border, and spent an hour trying to find out how to get to Syria. Nobody knew. I boarded another bus and went on, west to Iskenderun where I saw the Mediterranean, gray and leaden in the dawn. I followed the coast south to Antioch, where I took a taxi to the Syrian border. The jovial guards leafed through my passport, filled a page with green and brown stamps, and helped me find a ride to Aleppo.

Aleppo was a large but pleasant city with surprising touches of elegance—legacies, perhaps, of the two decades of French rule that ended in 1941. There was a big park in the center of town with massive wrought-iron gates, lawns, fountains, and formal gardens. Around the park stood graceful townhouses with French windows and carved limestone façades. Not far from the park was the older part of town, a tangle of cobbled lanes and covered markets and ancient houses dominated by a massive citadel—legacy of four centuries of Turkish rule—perched high on a hill. I found a barber shop near the fort and had my hair cut short. The barber, a rough and brawny man, was delighted with his assignment. He tugged at my locks and cut them off with savage glee.

After Aleppo, I stopped at Hama. The friendly young owner of the hotel where I stayed took me to meet all his buddies and proudly showed me a photograph of his older brother, who was a soldier stationed at the Israeli border. My host planned to enlist and join him there, and I hope he did, because a few years later a rebellion arose in Hama, and the Syrian army attacked the town and laid a good part of it to waste.

My next stop was Damascus. In those days, the roads across the Sinai were closed, and my plan was to go as far as I could by land and then fly to Cairo. But the airfare from Damascus to Cairo was as low as it would be from anywhere else, so I decided to make Damascus my last stop in Asia. It seemed larger than Aleppo, and more modern, with a lot of tall glassy buildings in the northern end of town. I stayed in the southern part of the city, which was older, cheaper, and more attractive. I shared a tiny room with two fat and grumpy Turks who were on their way to Mecca. They did not welcome me, but they did not shun me either. I was glad my hair was short.

Damascus is landlocked and far from the sea, but the light and lazy pace of life reminded me of the Mediterranean. Young men with carefully blow-dried hair strolled along the streets; they wore tailored army uniforms with shaped waists and bell-bottom trousers. These jaunty soldiers seemed familiar. I knew I had seen their like before, other men with faces and clothes and swaggers like theirs. Then I remembered; it was many years before and only a few miles away, on Dizengoff Street in Tel Aviv.

I flew into Cairo on a hot and muggy night in late October. I cleared customs and took a bus into town, and it was nearing midnight when the bus dropped me off at Tahrir Square. I had grown used to towns that shut down early and rose at dawn, places where streets are dark at midnight, and deserted except for skulking dogs and a few stragglers trudging home to bed. But Tahrir Square pulsed with life and the streets around it were jammed. From the elevated walkway that went around the huge plaza, the carpet of cars looked like rivers of molten light, white and red. It was an invigorating sight, but by the time I found a hotel I was too tired to go out again.

Cairo was even more crowded by day than by night. Its population, which was two million thirty years before, when most of the streets and sewers were laid down, had since grown to ten. In America, prisons far less overcrowded have been shut down by court order. Still, Cairo has its charm. The Nile, fast and wide, though narrower than I expected, cuts through the city, and along its eastern bank runs Corniche Road. Here the buildings—posh hotels, mostly—are wide and white and modern, with rows of balconies overlooking the water, but as you go inland, the buildings become older: ten-story Art Deco apartment palaces with scalloped façades along Talaat Harb Street, slightly plainer ones around Ataba Square with, nearby, a grandiose and decaying opera house that opened the same year as the Suez Canal, and then, farther east, domes and minarets and ancient citadels, all built of massive blocks of stone the color of Nile mud, and, finally, between the mosques and monuments and at the city's borders, those narrow, nameless streets and nondescript houses where most of Cairo lives.

I spent a week wandering through Cairo and I am sure I missed most of it. The place was just too big and there were too many distractions. One of the hallmarks of a civilized city, I think, is a supply of public places to sit and linger. Cafés are ideal, and Cairo was blessed with an abundance. They had cane chairs and marble tables, both inside and on the sidewalk, and really good coffee. I spent hours at those outside tables, drinking tiny cups of sweet, thick coffee and watching the multitudes of Cairo pass before me.

It is five hundred miles from Cairo to Aswan, at the other end of Egypt; the train follows the Nile all the way. I left Cairo in the morning and sat back and watched the land. On the left was the river, and along it were fields of brilliant green, dotted with houses. To the right was a red and rocky wasteland. Egypt is desert, for the most part, and its people owe their lives to the river, which carries the rain of Central Africa to water the Egyptian sands. And, by providing an assured and fairly steady supply of water and silt, by allowing the growth of a concentrated population (which the desert protected against invasions by outsiders), and by requiring the people to band together to build irrigation channels, the Nile gave birth to one of the world's earliest civilizations.

The day wore on, and the train moved south without stopping, always within sight of the river, always at the desert's edge. The Nile made Egypt's growth possible, but it also sets its limits. Though Egypt is almost twice as large as France, the Nile waters a strip of land that is roughly the size of Belgium. But the population, perhaps as low as two million in Pharaonic times and twelve million in 1900, is forty-five million today. Forty-three million live on that narrow swathe of green by the banks and delta of the Nile. With two million people, the land produced a steady surplus of food, enough to feed Pharaohs and painters and pyramid builders. Civilization could flourish. With forty-three million people on the same land, survival becomes a struggle. A series of dams and reservoirs, constructed over the past century, allows three harvests a year instead of one, but with this important exception the land is tilled and watered as it was in the days of the Pharaohs. I saw plows and sleds drawn by buffalo, and near the river I could see *shadufs,* long levers with buckets at the end, which the farmers use to raise water to the fields. The lush, green blades of newly sprouted wheat waved and shimmered in the noonday sun; the most modern machinery could not have coaxed more from the land. Here and there I saw clusters of houses. They were flat-roofed, rectangular, and built of sun-baked earth, and they resembled a model of a farmer's house I had seen in a Cairo museum. But the model, which once adorned an Eleventh Dynasty tomb, was four thousand years old.

I got off the train at Luxor, four hundred miles south of Cairo. Luxor is a tiny and somnolent town of horse carts and stucco houses built near the site of ancient Thebes. The next morning, I walked to the ruins of the Temple of Karnak, where I saw stark colonnades like bare bleached bones. I felt like an ant exploring the beached skeleton of a whale. Then I took the train to Aswan, at the edge of Egypt. Beyond, on the other side of Lake Nasser, lay the Sudan.

13

THE SUDAN

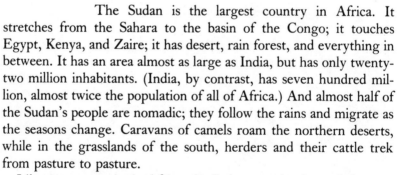

The Sudan is the largest country in Africa. It stretches from the Sahara to the basin of the Congo; it touches Egypt, Kenya, and Zaire; it has desert, rain forest, and everything in between. It has an area almost as large as India, but has only twenty-two million inhabitants. (India, by contrast, has seven hundred million, almost twice the population of all of Africa.) And almost half of the Sudan's people are nomadic; they follow the rains and migrate as the seasons change. Caravans of camels roam the northern deserts, while in the grasslands of the south, herders and their cattle trek from pasture to pasture.

Like most countries in Africa, the Sudan owes its size and shape to historical accident. Its boundaries were defined by colonial conquests, and the conquerors gave little thought to achieving ethnic balance. In many nations, this policy has worked fairly well. Colonial divisions often coincided with ethnic borders, and most Africans I met had as much of a sense of national identity as the average resident of New York, which, like the countries of Africa, is a place where many tribes live together. But some boundaries appear expressly designed to incite bloodshed, and foremost among these rank the sprawling confines of the Sudan.

From the Egyptian border to Khartoum and a few hundred miles beyond, the people are Arabs; they are of mainly Semitic descent, they speak Arabic, and they are devoutly Moslem. But somewhere between the sleepy Nile port of Kosti and the even more somnolent river town of Malakal runs an invisible frontier. Those who cross it leave the Arab world behind and enter black Africa, a rugged land of swamps and jungles and papyrus thickets. Though certain tomb paintings at Luxor suggest that some brave Egyptians ventured into the area 3,000 years ago, virtually the only outsiders to visit the south between that time and the last century were bands of Arabs in search of slaves. Their raids depopulated the region, and even today vast tracts of fertile land lie fallow for lack of farmers.

In 1820, Egypt conquered northern Sudan, and fifty years later, Egyptian armies, commanded by Samuel Baker and later by Charles Gordon, annexed the south. From 1899 on, the south, along with the rest of the Sudan, was ruled jointly by England and Egypt, which for most of that period was itself governed by England. This strange arrangement was called the Anglo-Egyptian Condominium, an appropriate name for a government set up along the lines of a holding company. It came to an end in 1956, when the Sudan became independent. Then the trouble began.

The northerners and southerners were as different from each other as any two peoples could be, and to make matters worse, the Arabs, who controlled the government, viewed the Africans as naked, pagan savages. The new government refused to grant the southerners autonomy, and replaced Christian mission schools with Arabic teachers. The result was a long and bloody civil war in which perhaps a half million people died. Fighting was bitter, with no holds barred. One of the army's favorite ploys was to surround a church and kill everyone inside. When they found a mosque, the rebels did the same. The war continued until 1972. In 1983, long after I had left the region, fighting began again. Some people say the war had never really ended.

The very first project the British undertook in Sudan, begun even before Kitchener had reached Khartoum, was the building of a railway linking the Sudan with Egypt. That rail line, completed in 1899 and still more or less in working order, runs from Wadi Halfa to

Khartoum. Between Aswan in Egypt and Wadi Halfa in the Sudan is a very long lake, a vast reservoir created by the Aswan High Dam. On the map it looks like a fat, sluggish snake. Twice a week, a ferry sailed down the lake to Wadi Halfa. When the boat ran on time, the crossing took two days.

I got to Aswan on a Tuesday and the boat left on Thursday. There were two other travelers waiting for the boat, an English woman and a red-haired Australian, who had an Oxford accent. They spent Tuesday night swapping horror stories about the boat, and most of Wednesday buying enormous jerrycans which they filled with drinking water. Visions of shipwreck, memories of Gericault's *Raft of the Medusa,* flashed in my mind, and I bought a plastic can and two tins of beef to stave off starvation.

Early Thursday morning I lugged my pack and can of water to the lake and boarded a bobbing barge that, I hoped, would take me to the boat, which was presumably anchored offshore. Time went by and more and more people crowded on board, and I realized that this *was* the boat, and what I took for a cute canopy was a second deck with a few first-class cabins hidden in the center. So I jostled my neighbors and carved out a space on deck and sat there for two days, reading *Lord Jim* as I listened to the drums of jubilant pilgrims on their way to Mecca, until we came to the far shore. The boat was on time.

I ran through the streets of Wadi Halfa, which was a desert town built of earth and corrugated iron. Corrugated metal is apparently one of the country's chief imports, and I passed through town after town filled with shops built of metal sheets, never shiny but always rusty or covered with peeling paint. The train station, though, was solid Colonial brick. I bought a fourth-class ticket and boarded the train.

Fourth-class carriages had no windows but they did have benches, and for the first part of the ride I managed to get a seat, squeezed between two fat Arabs. The train left Wadi Halfa on time, but after twenty miles the engine broke down, and we spent the night stalled in the desert. I stayed in my seat, afraid that if I got off, the train might leave without me. The Sahara was no place, as Paul Theroux would say, to be duffilled.

Twelve hours later a new locomotive arrived from Wadi Halfa. The engine coughed and sputtered but the trainmen coaxed it to life and we headed south. Somewhere north of Atbara, I lost my seat, and for the rest of the ride I squatted in the corridor. There were many stops, each one maddeningly long, but the only way to get off was to squeeze through a ventilator shaft and drop seven feet to the ground. Going down was easy, but getting back was not. I tried it once at Atbara and got stuck. I dangled between train and platform until my former seatmates hoisted me inside.

Three days after leaving Wadi Halfa, the train pulled into Khartoum station. It was two days late. I longed for a bath and a soft bed, and so did the other travelers on the train, even though they had had the sense to ride third class. We prowled the streets of Khartoum together in search of a room but after three days on the train we looked like a pack of vagabonds, and hotel after hotel turned us away. Finally, at the Hotel Royal, I sneaked back after the others had gone. "I'm not with them," I said. "Well, I do have one place," the owner replied.

It was a bed in a room of four, a vast high-ceilinged hall with windows on all sides. The Royal had been a mansion, and might once have been quite elegant. But that was long ago and now the grandest thing about it was the name. Most of the tenants were Eritrean refugees who had been there for years and had no place else to go. They supported themselves by forging documents and doing other odd jobs.

Khartoum was a disappointment. I had expected another Cairo but found another Kano instead. Khartoum is a city of dust and asphalt, wide tarry roads with garish streetlamps and ugly gas stations, sandy side streets with high blank walls on either side behind which lie gardens perhaps, or maybe more dust. And it is a city of constant, chronic shortages; you might have to walk miles for a glass of tea, because none of the teahouses could get sugar and in sweet-toothed Sudan when a teahouse runs out of sugar it closes. It is a city where, as a result of the shortages, the favorite word is *mafi*, which means "there is none," or "we're out of it," most often spoken with a drawl and a smug smile.

After *mafi*, the best-loved words and phrases are *insh'allah, bukra,* and *malish,* which translate as God willing, tomorrow, and it doesn't matter. These three words summarize the outlook of the people, an easygoing, fatalistic approach to life which has been known to drive visiting European businessmen to drink and distraction, but which

could, if adopted in moderation by these same businessmen, help
them to live longer and enjoy life more.

A spate of bureaucratic *bukras* kept me in Khartoum for three
weeks. I arrived on the first day of a five-day holiday, and many
shops, most restaurants and all offices stayed closed until the end of
the week. When they reopened, I took my passport to the Zaire embassy and reclaimed it three days later, with one of the few remaining
blank pages now filled with a Zairois visa. The stamp was emblazoned with a snarling leopard's head, a crossed brace of spears, and
the motto "Justice, Peace, and Work"; not the most appropriate slogan perhaps for Zaire's official seal, but counterbalanced by the leopard, which is the only animal as rare and elusive as a Zaire visa, which
had been denied me in Teheran, in Damascus, and in Cairo. After
that, I made the round of embassies and *bureaux:* the Central African
Empire's legation for a new visa, since the one I had gotten in Cairo
had expired before I reached Khartoum; the British embassy for a
Kenya visa, in case I decided to go that way; the Ministry of the Interior for permission to visit the south; the American embassy to have
more pages glued into my now-full passport; and back to the Interior
Ministry for a visa extension because my original visa gave me a
month in the Sudan and this had already been taken up by paperwork.

Each of these applications took several days to come through, and,
while I waited, as a sort of busman's holiday, I amused myself by ap-
plying for a refund on my ticket from Wadi Halfa. Students were allowed to ride half price, and I had paid the full fare. I had lost my
ticket on the train and my student card months before, so I borrowed
someone else's third-class stub and took it to the Youth Ministry on
Nile Avenue. There, the clerk examined my ticket and my New
York Public Library card and wrote me a letter of authorization, in
duplicate, which I picked up the next day. I took it across town to the
railway station, where I spent several hours shuttling from office to
office before being told that I must write a refund petition in triplicate; each copy would require the signature of a different official. Office hours are short in the Sudan, and lunch breaks are long, so it
took another day and a half before I cornered the three train bosses
and got their written approval, and it was late afternoon on the second, or perhaps the third day, when a sleepy clerk opened an ancient
safe and gave me the three pounds I was owed. In those days, vast

development projects were afoot all over Sudan—an enormous sugar mill to be erected here, a cement mill to be built there, and somewhere else a thousand square miles of wilderness to be irrigated and planted with cotton. As I sat in the gritty and decaying station waiting for various officials to get back from second breakfast or first lunch or whatever other meal they invented to get away from work, I wondered how, if it took so much time and effort for the Sudanese government to part with four dollars, it could ever coordinate the vast flow of imports, machinery, supplies, and expertise needed for any one of these grandiose schemes. I could not see how officials who could not distinguish between a library pass and a student card could prevent the polite, soft-spoken negotiators sent by large Western corporations from quietly stealing the *galabiehs* off their backs.

Sometimes, as a pleasant contrast to my bureaucratic battles, I walked along Nile Avenue. With rambling old mansions on one side and the river on the other and, above, the thick, leafy crowns of century-old banyan trees, Nile Avenue is about the nicest city street you'll find between Cairo and Nairobi. On other days, I followed the railroad tracks to the youth hostel to meet other travelers. Most of the talk was about the south, and the dangers of travel there. I heard that all trains south had been halted; I heard that all the borders had been closed; I heard stories about tourists stranded for weeks in towns that had no food, or marooned on riverboats that got lost in endless papyrus swamps, tourists who died on trucks, tourists who died on boats. All, or at least most, of these stories were fables like the "tall tales" the backwoodsmen used to swap a hundred years ago in the days when travel in America was as much of an adventure as crossing the Sudan.

All over Africa, hearsay and rumor, most of it wholly without foundation, spreads like fire on a dry savanna. But I did not know that then, and I was grateful for the prolonged paper chase that filled my days, because it gave me a reason to postpone my departure into the unknown. Khartoum was depressingly tawdry, but it had the Hilton, the Sudan Club, and the U.S. embassy (where I saw the original version of *King Kong*), and I clung to these familiar trappings like a child to its mother. But my money was running out and I had only five hundred dollars left, so I bought a ticket for the weekly train to Wau. This time I went second class. Second class had reserved seats and cost twelve pounds, or about thirteen dollars. (The Sudanese pound was then worth a little more than a dollar; "Our money is stronger than yours," people told me with pride.)

Wau, the southern railhead of Sudan Railways, is close to the center of the continent; on the same latitude, but far to the west, lie Cameroun, Nigeria, Ghana, and Sierra Leone. It is another world from Khartoum, but it is only six hundred miles away, though the rail line between the two towns, which zigs and zags like a fickle dragon, is about nine hundred miles in length. The Khartoum-Wau express was supposed to make the run in five days, but it had been known to arrive a week late, or even more. ("It is such a long way!" people replied when I complained about these delays.) Second class seemed expensive to me, and took hours in line to reserve, but it was worth the extra time and money to avoid standing for five days. And, as I later saw, on the southern line even standing inside is a luxury; latecomers had to climb on top of the train and cling to the curving, sunbaked roof.

At first the train ran more or less on time. We reached the tin sheds of Kosti after twenty hours, and the metal shacks of Er Rahad about fifteen hours later. A few people left the train, but many more got on, and the corridor of my car was full of squatters. Still, I had a bit of bench to myself, and the old wood-paneled compartment was not unattractive, though the first-class cars put it to shame. They were lovingly crafted at the turn of the century with ornately carved mahogany scrollwork. There was even a dining car which did not run out of food until the second day, which was when the locomotive broke down. It was a shiny new American diesel; either Sudan Railways had been sold a dud or they had neglected some small but vital procedure such as lubricating the bearings.

We were in a region of red rock and scrub somewhere east of Babanusa. The train had stopped near a village, a cluster of houses that looked like heaps of twigs. Some of the villagers came to stare. One of the men in my compartment wanted to buy a sheep, and they directed him to one of the houses. Eager to stretch my cramped legs, I went along. He and the shepherd could not agree on a price, though they haggled for the better part of an hour, but before we left, the shepherd, a white-haired old man in a dirty *galabieh*, brought us an enormous meal of meat and millet. There was so much food that it filled the washbasin in which it was presented. He and his family may go hungry, a man on the train told me, but that is better than the shame of allowing a guest to leave without having eaten. Fortunately, I learned this after I had eaten my fill; otherwise, I might have refused the food and hurt my host even more.

Later that afternoon, a new locomotive arrived from Er Rahad. I never thought a man could sleep sitting up, but after two nights on the train, I found it remarkably easy, and I dozed all the way to Babanusa.

Babanusa was a junction town. The bright green diesel continued west to Nyala, and I waited in the shade of a corrugated iron shed while my carriage was coupled to another locomotive, this one an old coal-burner of the sort used in the American West when cowboys rode the range. On level ground, the engine was capable of speeds faster than a man could walk, but it did not have enough power to climb even the gentlest slope. The engineer had doubtless faced this problem many times before and when we came to a grade he moved the train forward and back, forward and back, until he had built up enough momentum to make the climb. But a few hours after leaving Babanusa we came to a slope that was just too steep, so the train stopped while a second locomotive was sent from the junction. This second engine stayed with us for the rest of the drive, and thanks to its added power, our average speed on this last leg of the journey exceeded six miles an hour.

Sometime during the night, we crossed that invisible line, dividing northern from southern Sudan. The sun slipped beneath the edge of the western desert and rose again over a harsh, raw land of elephant grass and thorn trees. The grass was damp with dew, and I recognized the smell: Africa. The train stopped to take on water, and I got out and walked along the tracks in the freshness of the dawn. I looked in the third-class carriages. The passengers, too, had changed. The men were tall and dark. They carried spears and wore gowns of white cotton. Their ears were pierced and decorated with pink plastic hoops or bangles with red flashing stones, and their foreheads were adorned with tribal scars in geometric design. They stood on the platform in groups of two or three, perfectly erect, and looked about them with the lazy self-assurance of an aristocrat surveying his domain. They stared at me with amusement and wide-eyed wonder. I was an oddity to them, a man with bleached skin, dressed in tubes of cloth. And I stared back, for they were the first Dinka I had ever seen; the Dinka were the largest tribe in the southern Sudan, and one of the least Westernized in Africa.

Later that morning, we stopped for two hours at a tiny, nameless siding. The only building in sight was a grass hut like the one the Big Bad Wolf blew down. Two old men squatted in the dust, playing a board game, moving pebbles around a plank incised with squares. A young man, naked except for a belt and a spear, stood beside them and watched the game. He was a Jur, a tribe distantly related to the Dinkas. Nearby, two women exchanged greetings. They held hands, and then each woman sang, in a high-pitched melodic voice, welcoming and praising the other.

The sun beat down, and for a while I daydreamed about a New York subway car, full of commuters, suddenly arriving at this station. Would the passengers be afraid? Or delighted? Or worried they would be late for work? In the end I decided that most would not notice anything amiss; they would keep their noses buried in the *Times* until the train went underground again. Perhaps my fantasies were hunger pangs; there was no food at these southern stations.

The engine coughed and chugged and we started off. By now, the cars were full to overflowing, and so were the roofs, and a special detachment of railway police rode with the train. Their job was to club passengers who tried to board when we stopped to water the engine. Just after sunset we reached Aweil and a few hours later—and 120 hours after leaving Khartoum—the train slid into Wau Station.

Wau (pronounced "Wow!") did not live up to its name. There was a large Catholic mission, built in Victorian Gothic style, a few streets of brick bungalows, several small shops run by Arabs far from home, and three or four restaurants, one of which sold custard. There was also a youth hostel; my first few days in Wau were spent in its garden. I was tired and sick, barely able to walk. My eyes turned yellow. But I was lucky; within a week I could hike around the town and a week after that I was well enough to travel.

A few minutes' walk outside town, by the grassy banks of the Jur River, was the market, a warren crowded with stalls whose wickerwork walls were black with smoke. Most of the soot was produced by the blacksmith, who hammered scrap iron into spears as his apprentice pumped the bellows to heat the forge. The art of mining and smelting iron was developed two thousand years ago, at Meroe, north of present-day Khartoum, and rapidly spread south from there. This blacksmith probably knew how to make iron ore into ingots, but found it far easier to forge plowshares into spears.

The other side of Wau, away from the river, was on the edge of the grasslands. Close to town, the land was crisscrossed with paths and dotted with houses. There were people outside most of the houses, women in skirts and men in gym shorts, both sexes bare to the waist. I waved as I passed, and most people waved back, but one man called out in English for me to join him. He came, he told me, from Abyei, several hundred miles away and about as far north as you can go before the desert. The land there was dry and barren, and he had decided to take his family south. For months he, his wife and child had wandered across the savanna, searching for a place to settle. There was much land to be had, but they were selective; they didn't want to pick the first good site they came to, when there might be even better farmland a few days' walk away. So they pressed on, reached the banks of the Jur River, and followed it south. Finally, near Wau, either because the land was the best they had seen, or because they were tired of constant travel, they staked a claim, built a house, and settled down. The husband was employed part-time by one of the Arab merchants in Wau and, when he wasn't working in town, he tilled his fields. But it was evening now, and he was resting. He was about my age or younger; but he was a homesteader, a pioneer, following a way of life which I had believed was quintessentially American and long extinct. In America, the frontier closed in 1890, but it is still open in the Sudan.

By this time I had been in Wau almost a fortnight and I wanted to move on. Someone told me that there was a cluster of Dinka settlements around a town named Gogrial, sixty miles to the north. All I knew about the Dinka at this point was that, unlike many African peoples, they clung proudly and tenaciously to their traditional way of life. Some of the Dinka I later met owned a thousand head of cattle, enough, if sold, to finance a move to Khartoum or even New York, but leaving their homeland was unthinkable to them, though the mere mention of a big city brings a light of desire to most Africans' eyes.

I had already seen Dinka youths on the train, and had admired their Pathan-like pride and regal bearing, so I decided to go to Gogrial. In the southern Sudan, you can't travel anywhere without police permission, and my travel permit was only for the main road to Juba, so my first stop was the police station. I was directed to an office in back, where a group of men were studying a list of all foreigners then in Wau. They went down the list name by name, discussing each visitor and what was known about him. They seemed to know a lot about everyone. I waited silently, hoping to hear what they said about me, but when they saw me, they stopped talking and hid the list. It is a sad fact of life in many African nations that the only efficiently run organization is the secret police. The men in the office were agents of State Security, an organization so secret that most visitors are unaware of its existence, unless they violate the travel regulations.

It took a day to get the permit for Gogrial, two days after that to find a truck going that way, and half a day to drive there. Gogrial had one street of weatherbeaten stone storefronts and, behind the shops, an agglomeration of earthen huts packed as closely together as possible. There were no hotels or places to eat, and it was lucky I met "Chinese." He was a Dinka, my age or a little younger, tall and husky, and his friends at school called him Chinese because, they said, he was as solid as the Great Wall of China. He spoke English, so we talked a while, and then he gave me a tour of the town. On the main street, we passed by a pockmarked wall about which one of his friends later said, referring to the years of war between north and south, "The soldiers killed men here." He showed me his house: one round room with smooth earth walls; inside, two beds with iron frames. He invited me to stay. His brother, who slept in the second bed, would double up with him, and I would have a bed to myself. "The guest must take the best we have," he said. "That is our custom."

Darkness fell, and we lay in our beds, I stretched on mine, they squeezed onto theirs, and talked long into the night. They told me about initiation, the rite of passage by which a boy becomes a man. It is a great ceremony, undergone by many youths on the same day, a fearsome test of courage. First, they told me, the initiate's front lower teeth are pulled out, and then his forehead is gashed seven times with a red-hot spear, and during all this the boy must show no pain, for if he does, he will be considered a coward for the rest of his life. But if he suffers bravely, he becomes, immediately and irrevocably, a man, a full-fledged Dinka, and the scars display his courage for all to see. And the women? I asked. They are initiated too, he replied, in the same fashion.

Most of the men are in the cattle camp now, Chinese said. In the season between the rains, he explained, when all the land around the village has been grazed, the cattle are taken to the lush green fields close to the Nile. There they stay until the rains come, and the young men and women who take them sleep outside, behind a thorn-bush stockade, a group of youths alone on the endless, treeless plains. Chinese, I think, wanted to go to the camp, but had to attend school instead. He spoke of camp life with longing. "It is an easy life," he said, "a free life, and at night men and girls sit together under the vast starry bowl of a sky, and the young men sing songs to their beloved."

Years later, I read some of the songs in translation, in a book by Francis Deng, himself a Dinka. Dinka songs are subtle, cryptic, and richly allusive, and elusive as well, with metaphors which shift in meaning from one line to the next. I couldn't understand them. They reminded me of the British administrator who wrote a book about the Murle, a reclusive tribe (which I visited two years later) who live far to the east of the Nile, in which he said that certain aspects of Murle philosophy were too complex and subtle for him to grasp, since he had studied it for only ten years.

There was a Dinka village three miles north of town, and early the next morning Chinese took me there. The land was flat and brown. That year's crop of millet had been harvested, and in the fields only stubble remained. In the early morning sun, millet stalks, earth walls, thatched roofs, and bare trees all took on a rich, warm glow which made me think of honey, polished pine, amber: pleasant, mellow memories. We passed an old woman on the path. She smiled when she saw me, and spoke at length. My friend translated: "She welcomes you to our land. She thanks you for traveling so far to visit our land." Though she had no idea why I had come, she bade me welcome.

A bit farther on, we saw the wooden framework of a half-completed house, and a large and somewhat boisterous group of people shouting and singing as they plastered the walls with mud. When a man builds a house, Chinese told me, his neighbors will help him, but in return he must feed them and give them beer.

By now we had reached the outskirts of the village, and we soon came to the compound where the village chief lived. In theory at least, a Dinka chief has authority rather than power; he is a spiritual leader and not a tyrant. Still, this chief was the richest man in the village, and his house amazed me. It was round and surprisingly large, with a soaring beehive roof thirty feet high, and its clean and simple design was pleasing to the eye. The walls were so smooth and white that I was sure they were concrete, but Chinese assured me that the house was made of earth, wood, and dry grass, and nothing more.

We entered the house through a low door and sat down. The inside was cool and clean. An old woman came through the door with a big bowl of food. She knelt down and crawled toward me, put the food in front of me, and crawled backward out the door. "She is the senior wife of the chief," Chinese told me between mouthfuls of stew. And as we ate he told me about his uncle, who was the chief of the entire region and who had fifty wives, far more than his father, who had only seven.

Later, the senior wife returned and knelt before us. We thanked her for the meal, and my friend told her that I wanted to spend the night in her village. She told us that we must ask the chief, who had gone to Gogrial but would return that afternoon. So we waited in drowsy silence, happy to be out of the midday sun.

Time passed. The air grew cooler. I sat outside and watched a young girl milking a cow. The cow was large and had sharp, menacing horns. Most of the cattle were at the camp, but a few cows had been left behind to provide milk for the villagers. A pity, for I wanted to see the oxen, which were supposed to have horns three feet long. The oxen are strong yet tame—the Dinka ideal of a civilized man—and the Dinka youths identify with them. Each boy takes a calf as his "personality ox." After initiation, he takes the name of this ox as his own; by assuming the name of a full-grown bull, he tells the world he has become a man. The young man spends hours grooming his ox, currying its coat, tying tassels to its horns, and composing songs in its honor, paeans and hymns of praise which he sings as he parades through the cattle camp, his gaily caparisoned ox beside him. He compares his ox to a lion or a fierce storm, his bellow to thunder, and he warns the elephant to beware. And all the while the young man is really praising himself, proclaiming his own virility and power, for the bull's strength is also his own.

In the afternoon, a group of boys, sons of the chief's many wives, came into the house and stood around me, their eyes wide and staring. They were, Chinese told me, soon to be initiated, and looked forward to the ceremony with a mixture of fear and excitement. After it was over, they would be pampered and fussed over until the wounds healed and then—best treat of all—would be allowed to go to the cattle camp. I told them that I would answer questions about my country, and there was silence until one boy asked, and Chinese translated, Do you have cattle in America?

The boys left, and then the chief came. He was an old man, tall and dignified despite his plaid shirt and trousers. His senior wife—the one who had crawled before us—had told him not to let me stay. She was afraid; who could say what a white man, a total alien, might not do when the moon rose? The chief decided that I could sleep there only if Chinese stayed too, to watch over me. But Chinese had to be in school the next morning, and so I had to leave. And, when I got back to town, I was met by a policeman, who warned me not to visit the villages again; it was against the law.

That evening, instead of sitting around a village campfire, as I had hoped to do, I propped myself against the counter of one of the shops, drinking beer and talking with Chinese's classmates. I apologized for not speaking the Dinka language. That pleased them because, one said, their teachers had told them that Dinka was not a language but a mere dialect. Africa is a dark continent, one of the students told me, but you Europeans have brought a little light.

What could I answer? Some schools taught learning, but theirs had taught forgetting, and these students, unlike Chinese, were well on their way to forgetting their past, forgetting their pride. And, though I admired much of what I saw in Dinkaland, I respected the people's pride and quiet dignity most of all. According to Francis Deng, dignity is the thing the Dinkas hold dearest. To the Dinkas, he says, dignity connotes many things, among them politeness, hospitality, self-restraint, grace, elegance and kindness, and none of these many facets of humanity was lacking in the people I met in Gogrial.

The next morning, I was back in Wau, staying at the Catholic mission. It had been founded by Italians many years before and was now staffed by Dinkas with names like Gregorio and Antonio. I shared a room with an Englishman named Jackson whom I had met in Khartoum. He was an ascetic, a self-proclaimed Buddhist, with blazing eyes and the beard of a prophet. He liked to talk, and what he had to say was usually worth listening to. He had a passion for logic, truth, and knowledge, and he reminded me of those stormy intellectuals who figured so prominently in the Russian novels that were his favorite reading. Hidden behind all the logic and the dialectic fog, rigidly suppressed but never totally concealed, was kindness and a sense of humor.

A few days later, I left Wau and Jackson and headed south. Aside from the short trip to Gogrial, this was my first African truck ride, and it was not as bad as I had feared. The truck was filled with sacks of grain, and I sat on top of the load, fifteen feet above the ground. My perch was precarious and hard on the haunches, but it was far cheaper than an inside seat and, though I felt every bump, there were compensations. There was a wind in my face and I could see for miles, and there were no bars or window frames to clutter the horizon.

That first day we got as far as Tambura, a desolate place with a police post and one or two shops with nothing to sell. I slept on a concrete patio outside the police station. After Tambura, the road continued south until Source Yubo, a pleasant village washed by the soft light that filtered through the leafy mango trees that grew everywhere. The brightly painted shops had French names, for Source Yubo was on the border of the Central African Empire. We took the main highway east from Source Yubo; like every other road in the southern Sudan, it was a rutted dirt track. A few hours later, we bounced into Nzara.

Nzara was an ugly scar of a town, a place of smokestacks, concrete, and cotton mills. This was once the site of the Nzara Scheme, a British attempt to turn tribesmen into cotton pickers and factory workers. It was a blot on the countryside, but happily a very small blot, and a few minutes' walk in any direction lay the rolling plains of Azandeland, a timeless landscape of tall grass and thorn trees and little thatched houses.

The Azande empire was created two centuries ago by a people called the Ambomu who swept into Sudan from their homeland a short distance to the west, carving out for themselves a vast territory several hundred miles wide. They assimilated the tribes who lived in the area, and this ethnic amalgam became known as the Azande. Azandeland became a Central African Sparta, divided into districts ruled by governors directly responsible to the king; the men of each

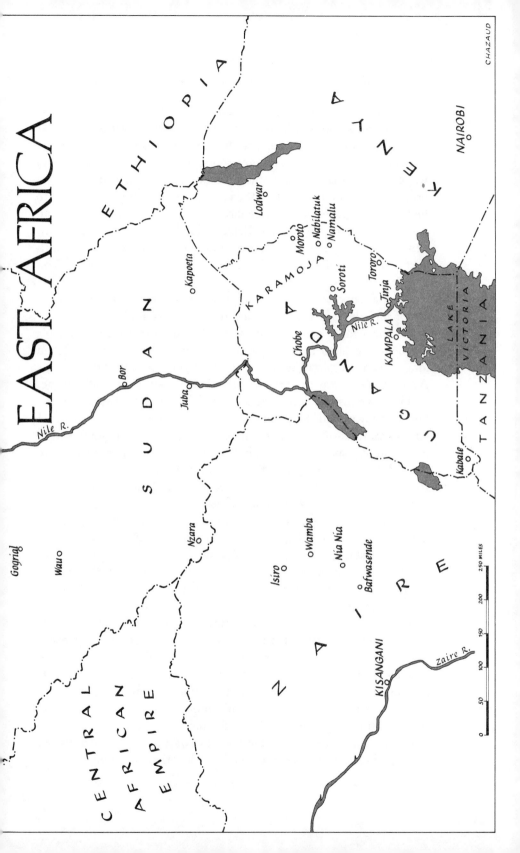

EAST AFRICA

ETHIOPIA

SUDAN

KENYA

NAIROBI

Lodwar

Kapoeta

Bor

Juba

Nile R.

Gogrial

Wau

Nzara

CENTRAL
AFRICAN
EMPIRE

ZAIRE

Isiro

Wamba

Nia Nia

Bafwasende

KISANGANI

Zaire R.

KARAMOJA

Moroto
Nabilatuk
Namalu

Soroti

Tororo

Chobe

Nile R.

Tinja

KAMPALA

UGANDA

Kabale

LAKE
VICTORIA

TANZANIA

0   50   100   150   200   250 MILES

CHAZAUD

district were organized into companies that could be ready for battle at a moment's notice. The government of this warrior nation was far more centralized, absolute, and hierarchical than is the norm in Africa; there were kings and governors, nobles and commoners, and when one commanded, the other obeyed. The Azande empire lasted until the beginning of this century, when, having the misfortune to find itself caught between three far larger empires, it was conquered, and split up between Britain, Belgium, and France. After independence, the conquerors left but Azandeland remained divided, with part lying in the Sudan, part in Zaire, and part in the Central African Empire.

I met a schoolteacher in Nzara, and I asked him to write me a letter of introduction which I could use in an Azande village to persuade the people to take me in. He warmed to his task, and his eloquent appeal to the villagers filled a large sheet of paper. I had long been an admirer, he wrote, of the Azande people and all things Azande, and it was my lifelong ambition to visit an Azande village.

The sawmills and cotton fields of the old Nzara scheme lay to the north of town, and the main road ran from west to east, so when I left Nzara the next morning, I followed a narrow track going south. The land was sparsely settled, but what few houses there were were freshly thatched and painted and spotlessly clean, with the yard in front carefully raked and swept. Some of the houses had gardens, with flowers planted in ornamental designs.

It was a cool, sunny morning, a perfect time for walking, and I hiked several hours longer than I had planned. Then I saw a tiny footpath east of the road, a foot-wide swathe of cleared ground snaking across the savanna. The end of the path lay out of sight beyond the horizon, so I followed it, to see where it might lead. As I walked, the path became fainter and harder to find, and after an hour it disappeared entirely. I looked behind me and there was no path in sight; I looked down and saw mud up to my ankles. A warthog, a large and hairy wild pig, rushed past me, its tail held aloft like a flagpole. Like any pig, warthogs love to wallow; animal trails had crossed the footpath in several places and at one of these intersections I had taken the wrong fork and followed a hog path into a swamp. Once again, the road less traveled by had made all the difference.

I slogged my way out of the bog, and by that time I had lost all sense of direction. I decided to choose a direction at random and follow it. I would reach the road within an hour if I chose correctly, but if I walked the wrong way, the nearest road was a hundred miles away with nothing but wilderness in between. There was smoke on the horizon and I went toward it, though as likely as not, I was walking into a forest fire.

After a while, I saw a small white house in the distance, surrounded by smoldering grass. The fields had been set ablaze to clear them for planting and my decision to follow the fire, though stupid, had been correct. In the years that followed, my sense of direction improved greatly, but what I learned that day was even more important: never leave the road unless you know where you are going. I never forgot this rule, and quite often even obeyed it.

The sun had gone down by the time I reached the cottage. I heard a soft murmur of voices; in the yard outside the house sat an old man and his wife, resting after a day in the fields as their evening meal cooked over a fire. The woman was tired, and she leaned her head on her husband's shoulder. They were doubtless astonished to see a mud-smeared white stranger emerge from the bush, but out of politeness they showed no surprise. They shared their porridge with me, and gave me a blanket and a cowhide mat to sleep on.

The next morning, the man led me along a narrow path through a tangled jungle of head-high grass. Most Africans live in compact villages, for they fear loneliness more than they value privacy; but the Azande prefer to live far apart, and it was ten minutes before we came to the farmer's nearest—and newest—neighbor, a heavyset man in a loincloth. He was busily thatching the roof of his newly built house, but when he saw me he jumped down from the rafters and followed us, glad of any excuse to stop work.

A short time later, the three of us arrived at the compound of the chief. A man in a threadbare khaki uniform lounged outside; he was the chief's personal policeman. My host spoke to him, and there was deference in the old man's voice and a trace of fear in his eyes. The policeman went away, hurried back, and motioned for me to follow. He led me to the chief, who sat on a raised platform under a thatched canopy.

The chief was thoroughly modern. He wore Western clothes—a white shirt and gray trousers—and he greeted me in passable English. The Sudanese government had made him an assistant district officer, but the foundations of his authority were far deeper and older than that: he was a noble and heir to the old Azande governors. His ancestors' commands had been obeyed without question, and so were his. The chief read my letter, and I think it pleased him, for he read it aloud to everyone he met that day, even his policeman, but the old farmer never got to hear it, because he was only a commoner. I made sure that the chief learned of his kindness to me, and I think that he and his neighbor shared in the feast served that afternoon. The chief's dais was furnished with wooden chairs and a table, and the chief and I sat together as the meal was prepared. Then two men carried in a huge platter, several feet in diameter, heaped high with meat and porridge. It seemed enough for ten men, or maybe twenty, and I hoped my host would not take offense if I left most of it over.

All the peoples I met in my travels had a code of politeness and etiquette, but the rules differed from place to place. In some cultures, the guest must take the food and finish it; in others, such as Afghanistan, he must refuse it until his host begs him to eat; and in others, such as China, he should leave some over, to show that his hunger has been satisfied. But the Azande customs were new to me; I had never been presented with a meal so large that two men were needed to carry it, and I complimented my host on his generosity. "We will eat," he told me, "and what we leave my family will eat, and what they leave my servants will eat," and as he said this he carefully picked the choicest cubes of meat out of the porridge, and I did the same. I wanted to leave some beef for my farmer friend, but it would never have gotten past the chief's wives.

After we ate, the chief read my letter again and told me that I was the first white man to visit his village in twenty years. I knew that every year several hundred backpackers passed through Nzara, only ten miles away, on their way to Kenya. In Africa, as in Asia, most travelers never leave the main tourist trail. I have since met many people who want to go overland to East Africa, and most of them ask if Kenya is worth the long journey. No, I reply, but the journey is worth the journey.

Because I was the first European since independence to visit the chief's domain, I was treated with as much pomp and deference as an ambassador plenipotentiary. The weekly market was held the next day, and that morning, after a night spent in a hut in the chief's compound, the chief took me to the crowded fairground. There were many men at the market, and even more women, all wearing their most colorful dresses. The chief's policeman rang a gong, and the assembly fell silent. The chief gave a speech in the short staccato gunbursts of the Azande language in which, he told me later, he introduced me as his personal guest and asked everyone present to accord me a welcome befitting a friend of the chief. After that, the women crowded around me to heap fruit at my feet.

That night, I stayed at the house of one of the chief's nephews, a studious young public health worker who had gone to school in Juba. He found village life backward and boring and was glad of the chance to talk about the world outside.

I left early the next morning for the long walk back to Nzara. Jackson was in town. He had hitchhiked from Wau and had a rough time of it. He had not known to sit toward the front of the truck and, seated in the very back, had been bounced around like a squash ball until the truck overturned north of Tambura. He had spent the night in the bush, unable to sleep and hearing a leopard in every whisper of the wind.

A third traveler had arrived with him, a tall Swiss named René who was ruggedly handsome and knew it. We are each the center of our own universe, but René expected to be the center of everyone else's as well. I tolerated René because of the company he kept. He spent his days in the Azande settlements on the fringes of town, drinking home-brewed beer with the people or serenading them with his guitar. The villagers worked hard all day on their farms, but in the evening they drank a lot and laughed a lot. I remembered my host the chief, who was a conscientious ruler and a kindly one, but far too serious and a little too pompous, and I decided that commoners have more fun.

In those days, the only intercity bus in the southern Sudan was the converted pickup truck which ran between Nzara and nearby Yambio. After a day in Nzara, I took the bus. I had planned to go on to Yei, two hundred miles farther east. From there, according to my Michelin map, a road led to the Zaire border post at Aba. I had met several travelers in Khartoum who had been refused entry at Aba, though their visas had been as valid as mine, but I hoped I would be luckier than they. And I was, for the bus driver told me that there was a road, not marked on any map, running south from Yambio into Zaire.

Yambio was a pleasant town of old whitewashed houses and a

market whose tin-walled stalls sold bread and beans and halvah from Khartoum. Most African towns, even the poorest, are full of cheer and color, with blaring music, bustling bars and markets, and crowds of people all dressed in their Sunday best; but about the towns in the southern Sudan hung an almost palpable pall of gloom and desolation. Yambio, with its halvah and its fragrant mango trees, was the best of the lot, so I decided to wait for a ride to Zaire.

Three days passed. I kept watch on the customs house, and slept on the sidewalk just outside it, knowing that any vehicle bound for Zaire would have to stop there, but none did. I whiled away the afternoons watching a team of Filipino workers put up a huge television transmitter. They swung from the hundred-yard-high antenna with the insouciance of trained acrobats. They provided the entire town with unforgettable entertainment, but I wondered whether this was the best use to which government funds could be put in a town with no running water or sewage system. And the electricity supply was too unreliable to allow the operation of TV sets. Then I realized that the aerial could also be used by the army as a radiotelephone link to Khartoum. In the Sudan, as everywhere in Africa, the first concern of the government is to consolidate its own control.

On the third day, I got an exit permit from the police. My Sudan visa was about to expire, and if I couldn't find a ride I would have to walk. That evening, my last in the Sudan, I watched young boys, as nimble as the Filipinos, climb a tall tree in search of honey. They carried blazing branches in their mouths to distract the bees while they raided their nest. When I got back to the customs house, there was a truck parked outside.

14

ZAIRE: VILLAGES AND PYGMIES

Early the next morning, the truck left the Sudan and headed for Zaire, formerly known as the Belgian Congo. The driver, a well-dressed and reassuringly portly Zairois businessman, was returning to his home in Isiro and let me ride in back. The rear of the small blue pickup was empty except for a large drum of gasoline, a tangle of rubber tubing, a brace of pheasants in a wicker cage, and the driver's assistant, who sat on the fuel drum as he chain-smoked a pack of foul Zairois cigarettes.

After an hour, we came to a mud hut with a yardful of clucking chickens and the forest-green flag of Zaire fluttering on a pole. This was the border post. A young soldier took my passport and scrutinized it. He seemed puzzled. At first I thought he could not read but, like every border guard I encountered in Africa, he was literate, and fluent in several languages; the boorish customs officer who holds passports upside-down, a stock character in the sort of African novels sold at airports, does not exist in real life. But this soldier had never in his life seen a passport, or a visa, and did not even know what they were. At this most remote of border crossings, no one used either. A letter from the police was all most travelers carried, so I showed the guard my Sudanese travel permit with its exit stamp, and based on that he let me in. He refused to stamp my passport—that is for ambassadors, he said—but he wrote me a letter, in French, stating that on the fifth of January, 1979, I had lawfully entered Zaire.

A few miles beyond the border, we paid a visit to the local Azande chieftain. He proudly showed us his new house, which was big and round and painted a bright pink. The midday sun sent waves of heat bouncing off the tin roof and the garish concrete walls; a mud hut would have been far cooler. Evidently, the chief preferred prestige to comfort, and the shiny roof and flashy walls were like billboards proclaiming his wealth and status. Indeed, this was the only village house I ever saw in Zaire or southern Sudan that was not built of earth, wood, and thatch.

The town of Isiro, of course, had many brick buildings: big, sprawling colonial mansions with spacious verandas and thick walls that were slowly but visibly decaying, eroded by heat and rain and years of neglect. There was a whole street of these crumbling villas, most now housing the offices of various trading corporations, and when we arrived in Isiro the driver took me there, to meet a European family who lived in one of the larger houses.

They welcomed me with a platter of sliced ham and a cold bottle of beer, and after months of bread and beans and rubbery porridge it took all my self-control not to bolt down the ham in a few greedy gulps. What impressed me most, though, even more than the big white refrigerator, was the bright fluorescent lights. In Wau, the electricity had worked, on the average, one night a week, and most of the other towns had no power at all. Part of the problem was that the generators, ancient and ill-maintained, kept breaking down, but even more serious was the lack of fuel. Oil was in short supply throughout the world in early 1979, but the poor countries were hit harder than the rich, and Central Africa hardest of all. In the Central African Empire, where gasoline cost four dollars a gallon, hospitals closed down when their generators ran out of fuel. In Zaire, if you calculated at the legal rate of exchange, gas sold for four dollars a quart, and was available only on the black market. Since almost all freight in Zaire was transported by truck, it was not only rich motorists who felt the pinch; every farmer who sold a sack of coffee beans, every villager who bought a box of matches or a bar of soap suffered. Still, the Zairois somehow kept their generators running, though in all but the largest cities the lights were on only twelve hours a day.

At some point during my second plateful of ham and third bottle of beer, I mentioned that I had no local money, only American travelers checks. As a favor to me, my hosts changed a fifty-dollar check, for which they gave me two hundred zaires. I would have gotten only about forty-five zaires at the bank, so I profited by the deal and so, strangely enough, did Zaire. My dollars would be used to buy needed imports, such as spare parts for the family's trucks, but dollars put in the bank would, as likely as not, find their way into certain high officials' pockets. My hosts, I later learned, profited too, since other money changers would have given me two hundred seventy-five zaires for my check, and gladly. No one wanted to hoard the currency of a country where prices doubled every ten months.

Isiro was really two towns built side by side: a city of brick, for the rich and the white, and a city of mud, a sprawling overgrown village where everyone else lived. All towns in Africa are divided in similar fashion, as I had first learned in Kampala, but the Zairois even have names for the two zones: *la ville* and *la cité*. I had gorged myself that first night in the *ville*, but I slept in the *cité*, in a mud-walled hotel near the market. As in Kampala, I found the *cité* far more exciting. The stores in the *ville* were empty, but the *cité*'s huge outdoor market had row after row of crudely hewn planks resting on trestles, on which were displayed palm oil, papayas, bananas, homemade soap, dried fish and tinned fish, rice and beans. Around the perimeter were shops, restaurants, and bars, most built of earth and thatch. I liked the record stores best of all; they had huge loudspeakers mounted outside to blare their wares, and the nonstop music and the syncopated, swirling beat and the lively crowds of people come to shop, stroll, or loiter transformed the dusty market square into a constant carnival, as sunny, gay, and endless as the Zairian summer.

In the evening, the whole *cité* and most of the *ville* headed for the bars, where an ice-cold twenty-five-ounce bottle of beer—real, frothy golden beer and not the millet mash popular in the Sudan— cost one zaire. There was a bar near my hotel where they played records from sunset to closing time, no Western sounds or reggae or even Nigerian high-life, but Zairois music exclusively and without a pause, and Zaire music, as I learned that night, is the happiest music on earth; if you can listen to it and still be sad, your case is hopeless. People sat at tables drinking beer as they swayed to the music. The women would open the bottles with their teeth, drink some, and hand the rest to their men. There was a thin man with a hat at my table who talked to me at length and loudly about *la condition humaine*. "You and I, white and black, we are all people," he said.

These sentiments seemed obvious to me, though on a far higher plane than the previous night's talk of commerce and canned hams and rates of exchange, but they were a novelty in that part of the world. As in the southern Sudan, the first outsiders to visit the area were Arabs in search of slaves, and their repeated raids depopulated the region and terrorized the survivors. In the late 1870s, Henry Stanley, whose meeting with Livingstone at Ujiji had already made him famous, explored the entire Congo basin, hacking his way through the jungle from Zanzibar to the Atlantic coast. He, unlike the Arabs, regarded the blacks as potentially human. "However incorrigibly fierce in temper, detestable in their disposition, and bestial in habits these wild tribes may be today," he wrote in 1890, "there is not one of them which does not contain germs [i.e., the rudiments of humanity] and by whose means at some future date civilisation may spread, and with it those manifold blessings inseparable from it." In this passage, which epitomized not only Stanley's sentiments but those of his entire generation, Stanley is describing a group of tribes that include the Azande. Had he met the naked, spear-carrying Dinka, he doubtless would have found them equally fierce and bestial. Stanley often appears predisposed to think the worst of the people he met, and on several occasions he reportedly mistook welcome committees for warriors, and shot them down.

Though a stout believer in the superiority of European civilization, Stanley, like most of the great explorers of that era, could not abide it for very long, and scarcely a year after leaving Central Africa, he returned. He had been hired by a private corporation owned by King Leopold of Belgium to mold the vast territory around the Congo River into a single colony. This he did, and by the time Stanley left in 1884, the corporation had carved out a million-square-mile preserve which it named the Congo Free State. For the next twenty-four years, the largest colony in Africa was the private possession of one man, Leopold II.

The Congo Free State proved so profitable to its owner that France and Germany emulated his system, and leased all their Central African colonies to various European corporations. These corporations presented their African subjects with a very one-sided view of the manifold blessings of Western civilization. Thousands of villagers were dragged off to work on the slave-labor battalions that built the roads and railways, and crushing taxes, payable in rubber or ivory, were imposed on all who remained. Platoons of soldiers collected the taxes, and those who could not pay were shot on the spot. Often, entire villages were wiped out. The company that ruled the Congo was the most brutal of the lot. A young sailor named Joseph Conrad visited the Congo in 1890; a decade later, in an attempt, perhaps, to exorcise his memories of the horrors he had seen, he wrote *Heart of Darkness.*

The fierce and bestial behavior of the corporations provoked such scandal in Europe that the Belgian government took control of the Congo in 1908, although in French Equatorial Africa, the rule of the corporations continued until 1930. A Belgian government commission which investigated the Congo Free State concluded that its population had been *reduced by half* during the reign of King Leopold's corporation.

After 1908, the lot of the Congolese improved, and the Belgian Congo soon had as many primary schools and hospitals as anywhere in Africa. The Belgians called their system of government paternalistic, and they did indeed think of the Africans as children. There were many elementary schools but few high schools and no universities whatever; three hundred thousand Congolese worked as houseboys but relatively few Africans held positions more responsible than that. Throughout the colony, flogging was a routine punishment for petty offenses; the whip was thought to be the only thing the lazy, shiftless natives would obey.

When I entered Zaire, almost twenty years had passed since independence and over seventy had gone by since the demise of the Congo Free State. And yet, as I traveled south from Isiro, there were moments when it seemed that those far-off days refused to die, that they had, by their very horror, shoved the intervening years aside and thrust themselves into the present. Off the main highways, the miasma of fear and panic was so strong I could almost smell it. I liked to walk along the narrow side roads that led through the jungle and sometimes, when I stopped to rest at a village, the people thought I had come to kill them. I was alone and unarmed, but since I was white I was obviously powerful enough to slaughter the whole village. I would catch them and eat them. I would wait until nightfall and devour them in the dark. I would suck out their souls like a vampire and feast on them in the moonlight. Still, when the villagers overcame their terror, they proved as hospitable as any people on earth.

After leaving Isiro, I took a truck to Wamba, a tiny town a hundred-odd miles to the south along the muddy track that, according to my Michelin map, was a major highway. Michelin makes the most accurate road maps around, and the most artistic as well. The deserts are colored a barren shade of tan that makes you think of endless tracts of sunbaked sand, with wells and oases marked by refreshing dots of blue. The forests are shown as big blobs of green the color of glossy leaves dripping with rain. The map of Sudan rated only a few tiny green speckles, but a vast sea of green covered most of Zaire. Somewhere between Pawa and Vube, a few hours out of Isiro and long before Wamba, I entered the green.

Before the Belgians came, settlements were scattered throughout the forest, or at least on its fringes, but in the early years of Belgian rule, the villagers in this part of the Congo were relocated, sometimes forcibly, along the main roads, in order to put them within reach of the tax collector. As a result, all the land within twenty or thirty miles of the road had at some point been cleared and cultivated, and I soon realized that I could not reach the true rain forest without walking.

But even by the roadside, the land was fertile, impossibly fertile. According to the textbooks, most of the nutrients in a rain forest are in the trees, which continuously fertilize the soil as their leaves and branches fall. Cut down the trees, plant crops, and after five years the soil will be ruined. And, in the past three decades half of Africa's forests have disappeared, their trees mowed down by loggers with diesel saws, their land turned into plantations and the soil soon sucked dry, and all so that, far to the north, office workers can drink instant coffee in paper cups.

But not in Zaire. On either side of the road, the truck was dwarfed by a thick and soaring tangle of bushes, young trees, and leafy creepers that sprang from soil which should by all rights have been barren. The plants' leaves were a dark, shiny green, almost black, as if they were glutted with sap and chlorophyll. Here, in the heart of Africa, the land was so fecund, the forest so strong, that it could defy the laws of science and withstand the assault of man. I could feel its power, and smell it, and even breathe it in, for the air was damp and heavy and laden with the heady perfume of flowers and decay. It was a slow and quiet power, lazy as a buzzing bee yet irresistible as a sea in flood; it was mysterious, primeval, and richly feminine; it was the force of life and generation. Of the inhabitants of the region, some fear it and others worship it but none are left unmoved.

The world of the forest seems timeless, but in fact much has changed. The people who farm the land at the forest's edge—including the Mabudo, the tribe I later visited in a village east of Wamba—are relatively recent arrivals. Their ancestors migrated from the grasslands of West Africa about a thousand years ago. Before then, the forest lay empty, except for its original inhabitants, the people whom the Mabudo and the rest of the newly arrived farmers called the Mbuti and who were, centuries before, known to the ancient Greeks—who learned about them from the reports of still more ancient Egyptian explorers—as the Pygmies. The Pygmies are racially distinct from their farming neighbors—and from everyone else, except possibly the Bushmen of the Kalahari Desert—and farmers and Pygmies also differ in ways far more important than race. The farmers live outside the forest; they carve out clearings for their farms and villages; and some of them seem to regard the forest as an enemy, one that must be kept at bay if their crops, and they themselves, are to survive. But the Pygmies make their home in the forest; they live by hunting its game and gathering its fruits. The forest is their life, and without it they would die.

I had, some years before, read *The Forest People,* a book written by Colin Turnbull, an anthropologist who had lived with the Pygmies and had come to regard them as his closest friends. He described their hunts, their dances, their songs and jokes and legends, their young men's courtships and their children's games, and by the end of the book I felt that they had become my friends as well. One particularly vivid episode stayed in my memory. Late one night, Turnbull found his friend Kenge alone in a forest clearing, with a flower in his hair, dancing, his body dappled with moonlight. "Why are you dancing alone?" Turnbull asked, and Kenge replied, "I am dancing with the forest, dancing with the moon."

Turnbull first met the Mbuti at Epulu, a zoological research station about a hundred miles southeast of Wamba. Epulu had changed in the twenty years since Turnbull left. Now it lay on the main overland route through Zaire. I had passed through it two years before, on my way from London to Nairobi with a truckload of sweaty pioneers, and so had hundreds of other truckloads, and most of them had stopped at Epulu and paid the resident Pygmies to pose for photos. If I wanted to find the proud, independent hunters Turnbull describes, I would have to look elsewhere. But where? The forty thousand Mbuti are scattered over forty thousand square miles of densest jungle. Before leaving Isiro, I had spent several days as the guest of two Peace Corps teachers in their big, airy bungalow in the *cité*; I borrowed their copy of Turnbull's book and searched it for clues.

Just before Turnbull left the Congo, he and Kenge visited other parts of the forest, hoping to find other Pygmy bands. The search was fruitless, he said, until "some miles east of Wamba, we left the car and followed a track through the forest. At the end of a full day, we arrived at a series of old established villages of the Mabudo tribe." And nearby, they found a Pygmy camp.

According to my Michelin map, there was nothing east of Wamba: no roads, no trails, only the unbroken green of forest. But one of the traders in the *ville* had a map of the Wamba region as large as my map of East Africa, and that map showed a narrow track running east from Wamba. And so, when I arrived in Wamba, I spent the night there, and the next morning, instead of trying to find a ride south to Kisangani, I started walking east.

On either side of the road, thickets of half-tamed lawn grass surrounded gray and moldy mansions of stucco and tile. They looked deserted, abandoned to the jungle, but outside one of them a truck was parked, and the driver offered me a ride. Thirty miles or so east of Wamba was a small coffee plantation, and during the harvest season trucks were sent to collect the newly picked beans. Had I come at any other time of year, I would have had to walk.

The truck's only other passenger was a thin man in a white raincoat. He was, as luck would have it, the government official responsible for overseeing that region. Foreigners were not permitted there, he told me; I could go to his village, about ten miles away, but no farther. But, by the time we reached his house a few hours later, he had decided that I could go as far as the truck would take me. I was very likely the first tourist to venture into his domain, and the official simply did not know whether to welcome me or throw me out. Or perhaps he realized who would have to feed me if he forced me to stay with him. So I stayed on the truck. The road got narrower as the day wore on, and the surrounding jungle seemed thicker. We stopped, at one point, to repair a log bridge that the truck before had broken, and as we waited people came from the forest and jumped on the truck. They were lithe and strong and very short; they dressed in loincloths and they smelled like the forest. They were the Pygmies, the Mbuti I thought I might never find. Though they had no need of transport, they rode with us for the thrill of it, and they whooped and shouted like city kids on a roller coaster.

The sun was going down, and the Mbuti had long since jumped off the truck, when we reached Mboma, a village of Mabudo farmers at the end of the road. There were houses on either side, spread out in the Azande fashion with considerable space between them. The Mabudo houses were as spruce and neat as any in Azandeland, but the design was different. They were gable-roofed and rectangular, like European cottages, and I assumed they were small-scale imitations of the mansions the Belgians had built, until I saw etchings of similar dwellings in Stanley's journals. Then I realized that the Congolese had probably discovered the design on their own, long before the Europeans came, by that mysterious collective process of adaptation and invention which enables villagers to lead a rich, full life and even a comfortable one and still live in perfect harmony with the land, without exhausting its fruits or depleting its soil. The Zairois houses, like those in the Sudan, were cool and airy and easy to sweep clean, and they could be built in a few days from the most easy to find materials imaginable—earth, trees, and water. They were far more pleasant to live in than houses built from expensive, imported tin and concrete, and I found the earth and thatch much more attractive as well. Alas, in much of Africa, people prefer the imported look—and so, incidentally, do the fleas.

The truck stopped beside a cluster of houses where the chief of the village lived. As a rule, village headmen in Africa have a distinguished air about them. Their authority is based on respect, so chiefs quickly learn to *look* like chiefs. This one was no exception. Tall and thin, his head shaven, Chief Indumbe spoke softly and slowly, with the assurance of a man whose pronouncements are never interrupted. He welcomed me and assigned me a house next to his where I could stay as long as I liked. For the next fortnight, that little white cottage was my home. And, though I had come in search of Pygmies, I spent almost all of that fortnight with the farmers.

The chief and I had no language in common, but one of his nephews, a stocky boy of eighteen named Philippe, had gone through the third grade of primary school and spoke French fluently. Philippe willingly served as my translator. Three years of schooling had left him torn between two worlds. Though he never had any desire to leave his village for the city, he spent all his spare time with me, eager to hear my stories about apartment houses, airplanes, and other strange and wondrous things. Machines fascinated him. He wanted to know how a truck engine worked, which countries manufactured them, and the names of the manufacturers. I could not answer most of his questions, and he was amazed that I did not know or care about my own country's achievements. Indeed I had taken such things as cars and engines for granted, but Philippe's endless questions made me see the products of Western technology through his eyes, as intricate, ingenious marvels which should be admired and respected and viewed with awe.

Philippe knew far more about his world than I about mine. He knew how to clear the land, what seeds to plant and when to plant them, how to care for the budding shoots and how to harvest them. He could forage in the forest around the village; he knew what plants could be eaten, which stems made the best twine, which leaves could be used for medicine. Some leaves had an abrasive surface which, like sandpaper, could polish wood; other leaves were absorbent and made excellent toilet paper; and one leaf when boiled exuded a sap that made a strong glue. Philippe could find any of these plants within minutes. If he needed roofing thatch, he could shinny up a palm tree and gather its leaves and, while he was there, tap it for wine. He could, with nothing more than an ax and a spade, put up a house. He showed me a fine new cottage he had built in only three weeks, entirely by himself. Everyone in the village could do all these things, even the youngest of the headman's sons, who was ten. You could have dumped any one of them, alone and naked, into the jungle and he would have survived. I could not, and I knew it. I felt as dependent and helpless as the smallest child.

Philippe, unlike most of the other Mabudo farmers, loved to hunt as well as to farm, and he could stalk and track game through even the densest jungle. Two miles eat of Mboma, he told me, the virgin forest began. There were tiny Mabudo farming villages hidden in its midst, and Pygmy hunting camps as well. I wanted him to take me there, but the chief was, for some reason unknown to me, afraid to let me enter the forest, and he refused me permission to go. I stayed on, hoping he would change his mind.

I did not mind the wait, for Mboma was a delightful place to be stranded. This surprised me; in *The Forest People*—though not in his other books—Turnbull portrays the village tribes as hostile, fearful, narrow-minded, and bound by superstition. Everything I saw contradicted this description.

The small white houses of the headman's compound formed a semicircle, surrounded by a larger circle of tall, leafy trees with spreading branches. Opposite the arc of houses was a big shed made of smoke-blackened poles; this was the kitchen. The courtyard between the kitchen and the houses was the focal point of the compound. The headman's wife spent most of her time there, sitting just outside the kitchen door. She was almost always working; most of her work consisted of such tasks as sifting rice and shelling nuts. Such work is, she believed, best performed slowly, and in the company of at least two or three friends, and with plenty of talk and laughter. Much of the chief's work, meanwhile, involved drinking large amounts of palm wine with *his* friends. The headmen in these areas rule by persuasion and consent rather than force, and it is during drinking sessions that village policy is debated; the discussions are forthright and, if anyone's feelings are hurt, he can blame it on the wine.

Sometimes, usually in the evening, Chief Indumbe would eat with me, on a wooden table set up in the courtyard. Philippe had explained the Mabudo code of etiquette, so the chief would not think I was a barbarian; I should, he told me, sit up straight, and eat with my right hand only, silently, and without showing too much greed. This last was difficult, for the food was the best I ate in Africa: plump chickens cooked in pungent sauce; small, silvery fish; eggs fried in the rich red oil squeezed from the fruit of the palm tree. (Palm oil has many uses; the homemade lamp that lit our table burned palm oil instead of kerosene.) One day's dinner was fried patties, surprisingly tasty, made of minced ants and vegetables. That meal was never repeated. African army ants are like Texas fire ants injected with growth hormones. They are, as Celia Coplestone learned in Kinkanja, easy to find but painful to catch.

During my first week in Mboma, the moon was waxing, and after twilight the courtyard was bathed in silver light. Any evening in any village is a time of peace and relaxation, for all work ends at sundown, but, in Africa, moonlit nights are special. People stay up late; they sit outside and talk, and sometimes one of them will bring out a drum, and then they dance.

In Mboma, it was usually one of the headman's two sons who played the drum, while I, the other son, and a few assorted friends and cousins jumped and swayed to the beat. The boys were hardly professional drummers but nobody minded. The older, also named Indumbe, asked me why I could not drum and sing, and I told them that I never needed to. I explained that in America the best players in the country made records and anyone anywhere anytime could put on the record and listen to the finest drummers in the nation. But this idea did not appeal to Indumbe; he preferred to make music on his own.

When the moon went down, the dancing ended, and everyone went to bed. My house was furnished with a traditional-style bed with a wooden frame and bamboo slats. "We do not sleep on the ground like animals," Philippe had proudly said when he first showed me my cottage. But the cot was hard and far too small for me, so I spread my blanket on the floor. Since I had the house to myself, nobody could spread the word that I slept like an animal.

Usually, I woke soon after sunrise, but most of the men had already gone to work in the fields or perhaps were talking business over a gourd of wine. Chief Indumbe's daughter brought me breakfast; she was sixteen and always wore her best and brightest dresses when I was around. Sometimes the chief's old uncle would sit with the women near the kitchen and slowly but skillfully weave a basket. He used osiers (thin, pliable strips of wood) of two colors, which he wove into complex patterns. I asked him his name, but he refused to tell me. If I knew his name, I would have power over him; I could use his name in my magic.

There was another relative of the chief who sometimes came around in the daytime. He was, in Western terms, severely retarded, and he could barely speak. The headman would sometimes talk with him anyway, repeating the same simple phrase over and over until the young man understood it. He spent much of his time hunting in the nearby jungle, and he could stalk his prey without a sound. Next to Philippe, he was the best hunter in the village, and almost every morning he would bring his kill to the kitchen, and present it to the headman's wife with a grin that seemed to cover his face. In America, I thought, he (and perhaps the aged uncle) would be locked up and hidden away.

After breakfast, I sat in the courtyard on a deck chair, a comfortable, locally made wooden copy of that aluminum stalwart of the American patio. The Mabudo were quick to adopt any Western innovations that would improve their life; hidden behind the trees was a big wooden latrine, with a stack of leaves always on hand for use as toilet paper. This was a welcome change from the Sudan, where many towns do not have any privies at all, but there were other Western intrusions into village life whose effects were more ambiguous. There was a small coffee plantation about a mile away where Mabudo men and boys and even a few Mbuti picked beans for one zaire a day. I asked Philippe why people who can grow or forage or make everything they need would work all day under the burning sun to earn twenty cents. To buy salt, he told me. And soap. And trousers.

The other Western outpost in Mboma was a thatched shelter furnished with a blackboard and six rows of benches. This was the school. It was fairly near the chief's compound, and so I passed it quite often. Sometimes I saw the students marching along the road behind their teacher, practicing army drills in rigid military formation. When the teacher wasn't looking, the children preferred to walk in little giggling bunches. I would pretend to chase them and then run away, and the whole whooping pack of them would run after me, until we all fell down laughing. But this was possible only after the teacher had gone for the day, for he would have punished any child who laughed in class.

One day, with the instructor's permission, I sat in on a third-grade class. This was the highest grade in the school and, fortunately for me, all classes at that level were conducted in French. It was an anatomy lesson: the parts of the leg. There was a crude drawing of a leg on the blackboard, and the teacher pointed to, and named, the different parts, and as he recited them—*le pied, le genou,* etc.—all the students shouted in unison *"Voici le pied!" "Voici le genou!"* It seemed to me that only an illusion of knowledge was being conveyed. Names, it is true, have their own power, but one does not learn anything about a foot or a knee by learning what the French call it. What was really being taught, though covertly, was this: wisdom comes through memorization and is measured by one's ability to regurgitate in unison. And the anatomy lesson also taught the students that, in order to understand something, one must analyze it, break it up into parts. Much of Mabudo life—its morals and myths and traditions—operates on an intuitive level and could never withstand such intellectual scrutiny, but the system works and people are satisfied—except for the graduates. Most of them work on the plantations.

I visited the school and the plantation only rarely. Sometimes, I hiked along the road, once as far as the next village, several miles away. But most of my time was spent sitting on a deck chair in the courtyard, letting the sunlight and the peace and the silence wash over me. The women, meanwhile, calmly and leisurely shelled beans or watched the pots on the fire. Life moved slowly here; it was not something to be hurried through. I forced myself to slow down too, though at first I feared boredom and desolation. But I found instead that, as I relaxed, my senses sharpened and the world around me became richer and more vivid.

A short walk from my deck chair was a stream. The woods around it, nourished by its waters, were rank, luxuriant jungle. The place was a strange and heady mixture of the sacred and the profane. There were tall and stately trees as massive as the pillars in the nave of a cathedral, and their spreading boughs formed a soaring vault high above. Their leaves delicately filtered the sun like a million-mullioned stained-glass skylight. The trunks of these ancient trees had, over the centuries, been draped with parasitic plants and creepers, and their branches dripped with moss. Beneath the taller trees grew smaller trees and below them were ferns and under those was the forest floor, itself a miniature forest covered with little dark green plants and tree roots like gnarled brown fingers and, between the living roots and plants, a layer of fallen leaves, brown and musty and slowly turning into mulch.

Sometimes, when I wanted a change of scene from the courtyard, I walked to the woods, and sat on the damp and spongy floor. I found that tiny forest richly, flamboyantly sensual and after a while I could feel the floodtide of its life surge around me. Though the glade was close to the village, few people came there. I could sit for hours in deep and drowsy silence, punctuated occasionally by the slow and rhythmic *thok* of someone chopping wood in the village. Once I heard from far away the loud, melodic calls of Pygmies, and for a brief confused moment, I thought the forest had burst into song.

There were two Pygmy camps just outside the village, and both were a few minutes' walk from Chief Indumbe's compound. Pygmies live in little igloo-shaped shelters made of twigs and *mongongo* leaves. A family can build a house in an hour, and, if they desired, they could easily shift their camp every night. But, according to Philippe, most of the Pygmies in the region spent at least half the year camped near Mboma. They would present the villagers with meat and berries from the forest, and run little errands for them, and the villagers came to think of their Pygmies as slaves. "They are to us what we were to the Belgians," said Philippe, who should have known better.

The Pygmies, of course, did know better. If they tired of playing servant, they could always disappear into the forest, where the big, clumsy villagers could never catch them. But the Mbuti profit from their subservience. The farmers give them vegetables, salt, cloth, cooking pots, and metal for axes, knives, and arrowheads. This vaguely feudal relationship between Pygmies and farmers is not new; Turnbull described it, and so, seventy years before, did Stanley. Both believed that the "slaves" got the better of the bargain. Still, luxuries such as salt can, when readily available, easily become necessities, and the Mbuti had apparently become more closely tied to the villagers than ever before. When Turnbull visited the Mabudo villages twenty years earlier, he found only a few visiting Pygmies, and now there were two large encampments.

One of the camps was in a little glade fairly near the chief's compound, and I went there quite often. In the clearing, seven little shelters stood in a circle. The huts were old and ill-maintained. The *mongongo* leaves, which had not been changed in months, had turned dry and brittle in the sun. The first time I visited the clearing, the

Pygmies were away and the huts stood empty and forlorn. They made me think of shantytowns and refugee camps. But whenever the Mbuti were around, their camp's tumble-down disorder seemed more cheerful than shabby.

Living with the Pygmies, Turnbull wrote, was like living in a monastery, for they transformed the world around them into a sacred temple. And all the Mbuti I met were indeed imbued with a deep and quiet contentment that reminded me of the holy men I had seen in Benares. But, unlike the staid and solemn *sadhus*, the Pygmies found life funny. They were prone to fits of giggles and, even at the most serious moments, seemed always on the verge of a smile, as if their lips trembled from the effort of holding the laughter in. They used humor as the Mabudo elders used palm wine, to forestall discord and dissent, to laugh quarrels away before they could disrupt the harmony of the camp, and it worked so well that no chiefs or headmen were needed. Besides, the Mbuti regarded their village settlement as a sort of holiday camp. They spent their time singing chants, clapping their elbows and dancing to the rhythm, telling stories, and adorning their faces with a paint made from gardenias. A few smoked *bangi*—their name for marijuana—in yard-long pipes made from plant stems, but nobody drank wine; there was no need.

I danced with them sometimes, and learned to clap my elbows, and once or twice—but no more—they even allowed me to sing. The songs they liked best were fifties rock-and-roll, those venerable golden oldies that were filled with words like bum-bum-bumbee-dum-dum or shoobee-doobee-doo. But my presence in their camp always seemed to make the Mbuti slightly nervous, and so I did not visit them as often as I might have liked. Occasionally, small groups of men would leave the camp to hunt in the jungle. As I sat by the stream or in the chief's courtyard, I could hear them pass along the paths that led to the forest. Songs and shouts and giggles came through the trees mixed with the rattle of the wooden bells that hung on their hunting dogs' collars. I longed to follow the hunters. I tried once, but they brought me back to the village. I stayed clear of the jungle after that until, on my tenth day in Mboma, Chief Indumbe finally gave me permission to enter the forest, and Philippe agreed to be my guide.

Early the next morning, Philippe and I left the village and walked to the Pygmy camp, behind which Philippe showed me a path so narrow and overgrown that, though I had been on the lookout for trails to explore each time I visited the Pygmies, it had escaped my attention. We followed the path past fields and huts and into the forest, and as we walked I noticed that Philippe's face was much paler than before. "My friends told me that you will kill me in the forest," Philippe said, "but I don't believe them." His friends did not know why I would want to murder my guide—perhaps I would use certain of his vital organs in magic rituals, or possibly I would eat him whole—but whatever my motive it seemed to them the logical thing to expect. Everyone knew, after all, that all white men were cannibals. And, though Philippe claimed not to believe a word of it, his sickly gray face, which if not for its pigment, would have matched the white cotton dress shirt he wore, suggested otherwise. But after we entered the forest he relaxed, for it soon became obvious that without him I would be completely lost.

Outside the forest, the path was clearly marked, but once inside it disappeared under a carpet of fallen leaves. The sun, too, disappeared, screened out by the trees, and so I lost all idea of direction. But Philippe always knew where he was and where we were headed. No matter how much our route curved and twisted, he always knew in what direction our destination lay, and he could also, as he proudly showed me, point toward Mboma, through the wall of vegetation that surrounded us.

Perhaps my sense of direction would have been better had I not been distracted by the beauty of the forest. If I had had the time, I would have stopped to admire every square foot of it, for every inch of the miles and miles I saw was as rich and teeming with life as the tiny grove I used to frequent in Mboma. And the trees were thicker and older and taller, and their branches, festooned with moss and creepers, arced across the sky like flying buttresses, supporting a translucent roof of leaves several hundred feet above. This canopy shaded the land below, but it was not completely unbroken; there were gaps between the leaves through which I could see bits of sky, and once we came to a rocky clearing walled in by the forest. As I watched, a troupe of monkeys ran across the treetops, leaping from tree to tree and swinging from branch to branch.

The monkeys chattered as they crashed through the branches; each and every sound stood out in the forest, even though the jungle was rarely silent. Hidden animals plowed their way along hidden

paths, birds cheeped and squawked and warbled, flies buzzed lazily
by. But it was not only the noisy abundance of forest life that impressed me, it was the variety. In the colder, drier parts of the world,
survival is difficult, and a few well-adapted species dominate. But the
rain forest is so hospitable to life that just about any creature conceivable can carve out a niche for itself. So many species of plant life
grow in Zaire's forests that one-fifth of them are, it is estimated, unknown to Western science.

Though Philippe, too, loved the forest, he was often oblivious to
its beauty. He was far too practical a sort ever to try to dance with
the moon. But he knew the language of the forest and delighted in
reading its signs. He could look at a footprint or even a lump of
dung, and know what animal made it, and how long ago. Sometimes,
he stopped and sniffed the air. "A deer was here," he said at one
point, when our way crossed a narrow track, "not five minutes ago. I
can still smell him. I could find him, even now. If only I had my
bow!" And he quivered with excitement, like a hound who found the
fox's den.

Later, as we walked, I asked him if it was right to kill animals for
sport. It would be wrong, he replied, but we do not hunt for sport
alone. We kill to live; we could not survive on bananas.

Toward midday, we came to a clearing where two black cabins
stood in the midst of banana trees and *bangi* plants. Two men lived in
those huts, Philippe told me, two old recluses who, though villagers
born in Mboma, preferred to live alone in the forest. A big man in a
loincloth bade us a dour welcome, and we went inside one of the
cabins and sat down. Unfortunately, Philippe sat on a poisoned arrow
which someone had carelessly left on the bench. The arrow poisons
of Central Africa are invariably fatal and there is no antidote, so all
we could do was wait and see if the toxin had entered Philippe's
bloodstream. Our host made a gruff apology, and Philippe smiled and
tried to treat the matter lightly, but I saw that once again his face had
turned pale. Time passed, quite slowly, and Philippe did not collapse.
After a while it became apparent that the arrow had not cut deeply
enough to poison him. We stayed a while longer, for Philippe to re-
cover from his fright, and then we left the surly hermits and continued through the forest.

A man could, according to Philippe, cross the forest in seven days,
and emerge from the jungle somewhere near Epulu, where Turnbull

did his field work. Though neither of us wanted to go that far, the terrain was flat and far easier than I, remembering the Hewa country in New Guinea, had expected. There was a Mabudo village in the forest where we had planned to spend the night, but we reached it in midafternoon. We decided to go on to another farming village, which lay a few hours farther east.

In the green twilight of the forest, we lost track of time, but it must have been approaching five in the afternoon when Philippe stopped in front of a huge kapok tree around whose base thin buttresslike projections sprouted. Nearby was a wooden rack on which hung a small wood hammer, for this tree was the village bell. Forest etiquette required visitors to ring it, so Philippe took the hammer and hit one of the flanges, which gave a loud and satisfying thump. And, having announced our arrival, we continued down the path and into the nearby village.

It was a small settlement; only one family of farmers lived there. The head of the family was a thin and tired old man with a gentle, limpid gaze. He wore a plaid flannel shirt whose colors had, over the years, faded and run together to form a soft gray, broken here and there by a few bands of plaid. Many years before, when the Belgians still ruled the land, he had lived in Stanleyville, where he worked in the office of a Belgian trading concern. After twenty years as a clerk, he quit his job, and took his family into the forest. Whether he had, as a child, been raised in a village on this spot, or whether he had, like the pioneer I had met in Wau, built his homestead on virgin land, I never knew for certain, though Philippe at one point told me that there had once been a village on this site, which had been wiped out in some unspecified but dreadful calamity. But, in either version, he had forsaken the city for the cloister of the forest, and that impressed me. All too often, the movement is in the opposite direction.

There were two children in the village, a boy, five years old, and a girl of six or seven. Neither had ever been outside the forest. They were happy children, and very active; both had the same strange expression of gentle contentment as the old man, the look of a seer seared by holy fire. Perhaps their faces seemed unearthly to me because they were so innocent. They reminded me of Hansel and Gretel, who were also babes in the woods, and who, like these children of the forest, possessed hidden reserves of strength and cunning.

An old woman brought Philippe and me our dinner. She was tall, big-boned, strong and solid, and her skin was as tough and wrinkled as elephant hide. A few hours later I found her sobbing in the kitchen, and though I tried to help her, she was sad beyond comfort. Philippe later told me that she had just received news that one of her sons had died.

The village received few visitors, and the old man was glad of our company, so we spent two nights with him. I had a small hut to myself, and Philippe warned me not to leave it until morning. "If you go outside at night," he explained, "the Balese might eat you." The Balese were a tribe who, according to Turnbull, had "a not very savory reputation for cannibalism, witchcraft, and sorcery." They lived just east of the Mabudo, and we were near the border of their domain. I assumed he was joking, so I replied that I was not afraid of a few Balese. "You will be, when they catch you," he muttered.

On our third day in the forest, Philippe and I left the old homesteader and his family and headed back toward Mboma. We soon reached the Mabudo village we had bypassed two days before, and we decided to stop there for the night. So we gave the village tree a clout and walked into the clearing that surrounded the settlement. It was a much larger village than the one-family hamlet of the night before. The clearing, which covered several acres, was a lush tangle of manioc and banana plants, planted by the villagers but now half wild. Hidden in their midst were several large sprawling houses; we followed an overgrown path to one of them and went inside.

We stepped into a large room whose walls were hung with pots and baskets and whose ceiling was black with smoke. Shafts of light came through chinks in the thatch and spotlit cones of swirling smoke, leaving the rest of the room in shadow. A woman stirred a pot that was bubbling over a fire. Philippe spoke to her, and to her husband, and then told me we were welcome to stay. "If you came here alone," he said, "they would think you came to attack them, and they would kill you."

The villagers were, like many in Zaire, afraid of whites and fearful of the unknown, but they had a special reason to be suspicious of strangers, and I saw it in back of the house. A fire burned under a pot full of overripe bananas, and the stream from the pot went up a long V-shaped bamboo pipe where it cooled and condensed into liquid alcohol that slowly dripped into a waiting bottle. These people were moonshiners as well as farmers.

Yet they were friendly, and they gave us meat and rice and foul-tasting whiskey. The meal was cooked by the woman I had seen crouched by the fire, and was served by her uncommonly pretty daughter. Philippe and I shared a room that night, but in the small hours of the morning, he crept outside. Heedless of any lurking Balese, he had gone to visit the daughter. A few days before, I had given him a small gift of money, and the next morning he told me that he had presented it to the girl. If you sleep with a woman and don't give her money, he explained, she will think that you value her cheaply. But now, thanks to your gift to me, the girl likes me and I can visit her again.

Philippe and I shared a breakfast of fried bananas and, soon after, left our hosts, crossed the clearing, and went back into the forest. In four days in the forest, we had not seen any Pygmies. Sensing my disappointment, Philippe had questioned the villagers, and they had told him that there was a Pygmy camp in the area. They gave us only the vaguest of directions and of course there were no paths we could follow, only an unbroken carpet of leaves and moss, knobby roots and clover. But Philippe thought he could find the camp, and a few hours later we did. The Mbuti-Pygmies had bivouacked in a small clearing. The two Pygmy camps at Mboma—the only other camps I had ever seen—had also been in clearings, but they had been hot and dusty, sunbaked strips of land. This camp, encircled by a surging wave of trees, was cool and shady and washed by the soft green light of the forest. High above, branches from the tallest trees formed a roof over the camp; that and the shade and the sea-green sunbeams created the fairy-tale illusion of a magic cavern under the sea—though not, of course, for Philippe, who had probably never even seen a lake.

It was early afternoon and the camp was almost deserted. The men were hunting in the forest, and most of the women were out as well, probably foraging for nuts and mushrooms or perhaps looking for vines from which they would make twine or fresh *mongongo* leaves to repair their little houses. Only a few women remained, to watch the children who were playing near the huts. They recognized Philippe; this Mbuti band was related to those who lived around Mboma. But this group apparently had much less contact with the outside world than those I had encountered before. The Pygmies at the village of Mboma had seemed vaguely uneasy in my presence, but these forest Pygmies were terrified at the sight of a pale-skinned man. All but one of the children ran into the forest and, had Philippe not been with me, the women would have fled as well. Even so, if I walked within ten feet of one of them, she would back off, and quickly. The one boy who remained did not jump back when I approached. This pleased me until I realized that he did not move at all. I raised his arm and when I let go, the arm stayed up. I pushed it down and then, with a scream, the boy came out of his trance and bounded off to the forest.

The sun was slipping unseen below the horizon when the rest of the band returned. The tallest of them was almost half a yard shorter than I, but I did not notice that until much later. All I could think of then was their joyful, limber grace, the way they bounded from the forest like dancers prancing onstage. By this time, most of the children had come back as well, but two of them chose to sleep in the jungle; they were more frightened of me than of the beasts who stalk in the night. The returning hunters who, after all, were men and had to live up to their role, tried to show no fear of me—but if I approached within ten feet, they would move away. Still, they let us spend the night with them, and they gave Philippe and me a hut of our own.

The eight huts were built in a circle, and as darkness fell the women built fires outside each hut. Each family sat around its hearth, but the camp was small enough for everyone to see and hear everyone else, so that conversations were shared by all, and there was much calling from fire to fire. Philippe and I sat in front of our shelter, in sight and hearing of all the fires but not close enough to frighten our hosts. We could not understand what was said because, though the Pygmies could speak Kibudo, Philippe's native language, he did not know theirs. But whatever was said, it must have been quite amusing, for the Pygmies were free with their laughter. Much of it seemed to be good-natured teasing and witty repartee, of the sort you might hear between old friends each of whom is sure of the other's affection. Everyone in camp, of course, listened in to these exchanges, and chuckled at each sally and quick retort. I giggled too, though I did not understand, because the language was designed for humor; it was saucy and vaguely musical, like a bullfrog trying to sound like a xylophone.

The women, if anything, said more than the men, but as they talked, they skinned and cut and cooked the deer the men had brought from the forest. They had metal saucepans into which they poured palm oil and then threw chunks of meat. Soon the meat was ready and the family next to us called Philippe over and gave some to him. It was rich, savory venison, but so tough that my gums ached for hours afterward. I understood then why the Pygmies filed their teeth into jack-o'-lantern points. As we ate, the women prepared another meal, which was served an hour after the first.

By the end of that second dinner, the Mbuti at the nearest fire trusted me enough to let me get within a yard of them and, when I did, I saw a sick old man in their midst. Another man smeared a paste made from plants on his chest, and then cut his skin with an arrowhead—presumably one that had not been poisoned—to inject the medicine into his bloodstream. It looked like primitive quackery. But, though Western medicines have long, impressive names and come in glossy capsules, at least half of them—penicillin being the most famous example—are derived or originally came from plants and other organic matter, most of which come from the temperate zone. The Mbuti live in a region far richer in plant life than ours, with many species as yet undiscovered, and it is not impossible that they have found miracle drugs unknown to Western science.

The patient was sick and weary, but he seemed to be a wise man, and his companions cared for him with gentle respect. He let me approach without protesting, sensing perhaps that I meant no harm. I asked Philippe to tell him that I had come to love his forest, for its beauty and its teeming life. The man said nothing as Philippe translated, but from his smile I think he understood. And he let me sit beside him as long as I liked.

As the night wore on, the camp grew quiet, but the forest around us slowly came alive. The wall of trees became an echoing wall of sound: the incessant chirp and chirr of vast choirs of crickets; the crash and rustle of animals passing; the shriek, roar, and howl of predator and prey. At one point, a loud and bloodthirsty series of banshee screeches split the night. Philippe told me it was made by a big and hairy animal that prowled by night, made its home in trees and slothfully passed its day hanging upside-down from branches. But there are no sloths in Africa, and I wondered what unknown and

monstrous creature was screaming in the jungle. And I also wondered how the two children—who never did come back—were making out in the forest.

The Pygmies crawled into their houses and went to sleep; Philippe
and I did the same. Ours was a snug and cozy shelter, a leafy dome
three feet high, with a cushion of leaves to sleep on, and I was soon
asleep. I was awakened by shouts a few hours later. Philippe warned
me to stay inside, but I ran barefoot out of the hut and soon wished I
hadn't. Through the camp flowed a glistening river of army ants.
The Mbuti always keep a few embers burning, for they actually do
not know how to start a fire. The men were using these glowing
coals to divert the path of the marching ants away from the camp.
But I was still half asleep, and before I took in the situation I stepped
into the stream—and, wide awake, I very quickly stepped out again.
I scraped the biting ants off my legs, told Philippe that, as usual, he
had been right, and went back to sleep.

When I woke again, it was morning, and the men were preparing
for the hunt. After a hurried breakfast, they slung their nets over
their shoulders and went off into the jungle. A pack of hunting dogs
loped after them, their wooden bells rattling. Philippe and I ran behind the dogs. Only rarely do the Mbuti allow a villager to sleep in
their camp, and even rarer is the farmer who is permitted to join the
hunt, but Philippe was not a common villager. He was a good hunter
and he respected the forest, and the Mbuti liked him. He was, they
thought, almost as good as a Pygmy, and so, when Philippe asked the
band if we could follow, they let us tag along.

It was not easy going. The Pygmies dashed up hills and across
streams, through thickets and tangles of branches. They were incredibly fit and limber, and I felt clumsy beside them, and much too big
as well. Because I respected the Pygmies, I had never really noticed
that they were shorter than I, but now I did, and I envied their stature. They happily ran under branches that hit me in the chest; four
foot six was a good height to be in the forest.

Fortunately, the site for that day's hunt was only a mile from camp.
We soon reached it and, deftly and in silence, the Pygmies unrolled
their nets and began to prepare for the chase. For the Mbuti, hunting, like almost everything they do, is a team effort. Even the games
their children play have no winners and losers, because competition,
like conflict and disorder, is abhorrent to them. The Pygmies' sense

of community discouraged innovation and enterprise as well as greed, and this sometimes seemed alien to me, but their viewpoint is not unique. Throughout Africa and especially in the countryside, cooperation is the norm; I had, two months before, seen Dinkas helping their neighbor build his house, and in the years that followed I was to see many other examples of this communal spirit: herders tending each other's cattle, hungry villagers sharing their food with those even hungrier, city folk supporting poor and distant relatives, farmers plowing one another's land. But net hunting, far more than herding or tilling the fields, demands from the hunters complete cooperation and trust.

The Mbuti's nets reminded me of tennis nets. They were four feet high and perhaps a hundred feet long, and made of strong twine woven into a fine mesh. As I watched, the men strung their nets, with the bottom touching the ground and the top looped over twigs and branches. Each man knew, from long experience, where to set up his net, and each tied his net to those of his neighbors, so that in the end the nets formed an unbroken circle a thousand feet in circumference, trapping any animals who were inside.

After the nets were strung, the men regrouped near where Philippe and I stood. Philippe joined them, and I wanted to as well, for the hunt was about to begin. But the Pygmies would not have me with them and refused to hunt at all until I was safely out of the way. If I joined them, I would only be a hindrance, and, besides, the climax of the chase would be fraught with danger. They told me to climb a tree, so I hoisted myself onto an overhanging bough. As I perched there, the men, followed by their dogs, stepped over the nets and entered the circle. I lost sight of them after that, but I heard loud shouts and elbow claps as they began to drive the game toward the edge of the circle. The animal would run into the net, where the Pygmies would attack it. And, as likely as not, it would turn and attack *them*, for even an antelope can be vicious when cornered. Sometimes, the Pygmies reached the net to find, not a deer, but an enraged boar or leopard waiting to turn on its hunters.

The shouting stopped, and there was a brief moment of silence. Then more shouts and a scuffle. I heard grunts and blows and barking. More silence after that. I jumped from the tree and slowly skirted the net until I found Philippe and the Pygmies. They stood in an excited, happy circle around a small antelope which lay limply on the ground, its eyes misted over. They carried the deer back to camp, where it was divided among the seven or eight families which comprised the band. Philippe and I got a share as well, which we fried in palm oil and ate on the spot. And then, my gums throbbing, we left the Pygmies and set off for Mboma. We passed a Mabudo man along the trail. He was carrying a load of cooking pots to the Mbuti camp. In exchange for them he hoped to rent the Pygmies for a day. They would hunt on his behalf, turning over the day's bag to him. And the Pygmies would get iron pans from the far-off city without having to leave their beloved forest.

Going back to Mboma was like going home. The children saw us as soon as we reached the outskirts of the village, and they rushed off to tell the chief. When we got to the compound, a smiling Chief Indumbe and his entire family were waiting to greet us. The chief seemed relieved that we had both returned. His daughter ran around the courtyard chasing a squawking hen, and after a while returned carrying a big platter of stewed chicken which she set before us. She had sacrificed one of her few remaining fowl to show me I was welcome.

The next day was my last in Mboma. I spent it lazily, sitting in the yard, warmed by the gentle sun. Philippe, young Indumbe and the others their age probably envied me, because the next morning I would set off for the city. But, though I could walk away from their lives, I could not walk away from my own. I was free to sample their life and leave them, but I was not able to be one of them, to remake myself in their image. My mind had already been filled by a lifetime spent in cities, and twenty years of school. I had, of course, chosen to travel, and that was a choice that Philippe would, most likely, never have; even if he worked for twenty years, he could not earn enough money to leave Zaire. Most Americans do earn enough, but I saw very few on the road; lack of money is not the only thing that inhibits a man.

Besides, few of the villagers wanted to leave. Life was good in Mboma. There was land aplenty, and palm wine, and dancing under the moon. There was no need or pressure to please the boss, or snag a promotion, or get ahead. I thought of my friends back home. None of them was satisfied with his work, and indeed our economy is structured so that the vast majority of occupations involve mindless drudgery and paper-shuffling. These jobs must be filled; there must be salesmen and clerks and typists or our economy, fine but finely tuned producing machine that it is, will grind to a halt. So only a tiny fraction of us can be free; for the rest, freedom is limited to evenings and weekends.

Perhaps, as I sat in the Mboma sun, my memories of home were too bleak and somber. If I were in New York, I could walk to the nearest public library and immerse myself in a world of learning and a flood of information that no one from Mboma would ever encounter. Still, village life could be surprisingly rich and varied. Young Indumbe, for example, could continue his drumming and perhaps become a skilled musician; he could become a sculptor, if he had the talent, and carve masks and statues; or a carpenter, or basket weaver or hunter or craftsman; or a storyteller and maker of myths; or a thinker and wise man, whose words would one day command respect in the council of elders. And whatever path he chose, his peers would encourage him, for there was always a need for chairs and baskets, myths and music, and wise counsel.

That evening, I said good-bye to chief Indumbe and his family, and to his old uncle, who still would not tell me his name. I went to bed early, and the last thing I heard was young Indumbe drumming.

15

ACROSS THE
CONGO BASIN

The coffee harvest was over, and the last truck had left Mboma days before. Early the next morning, I shouldered my knapsack and started walking west. For the first ten miles, Philippe walked with me. We took turns carrying the pack. At noon, we came to a larger village where I might find a ride. Philippe left me there, and for the first time in a fortnight I was alone. A woman from one of the houses brought a chair for me; she could not allow a stranger to stand. I sat on her veranda until a truck came and took me to Wamba.

The town of Wamba had a hotel, a mud hut that someone had partitioned into tiny cells. For three zaires—about sixty cents—I rented a cubicle. There was a gang of children playing outside, and they clustered around me. "You are Mbuti!" I told them, and they said "Oooooh!" and writhed with excitement. Then I went to sleep. In the wee hours of the morning, the man in the cell next door turned on his radio and blasted me with sound. In Wamba, radios were far more popular than drums.

Long before, as far back as Cairo and maybe even earlier, I had decided to head for West Africa. The best way of getting there from Wamba was via Kisangani. Formerly named Stanleyville, Kisangani is a large city on the Zaire River. I could catch a riverboat west from there.

I spent the next day looking for a free ride to Kisangani. I had felt rich in Mboma and had made a generous gift to Chief Indumbe. Now, back on the main road, I realized I was poor. I counted my money: about three hundred dollars. Not very much, but I was slowly learning the African art of living well on very little.

There was a bar in Wamba where the truckers went, and that evening I stopped by the bar to try to find a ride. There was a tall, thin man at one of the tables. He had dark brown eyes, light brown skin, curly black hair that fell in ringlets; he said his father was Belgian. He owned a pickup truck and made his money hauling freight. He was also a mechanic and he was on his way to a back-country plantation to fix a coffee roaster that had broken down. That would take a day or two, and then he would drive to Kisangani. If I didn't mind a few days at the coffee farm, I could come along.

And so the next morning, the mechanic, his assistant, and I got into the truck, which was American-made, quite old, and smaller than a station wagon. We drove south, through Nia Nia, where the road forked, one track going southwest to Kisangani and the other to the far-off Ugandan border, and beyond that to Kenya and the sea. I tried to imagine the endless blue of the ocean that lay at road's end. It had been months since I had seen a horizon; there were always trees in the way. But we took the Kisangani road and after an hour we turned onto a side road leading west. That evening, we reached the plantation. The main house, big and sturdy, had been built by the Belgians long ago. Now the owners were Zairois, and they welcomed us. I had a room to myself that night; it had pale green walls, a cot, a kerosene lantern, and nothing else.

The next morning the sun streamed through my window and I awoke to sunbeams and the beat of a drum. It was, the mechanic told me, a talking drum, calling the coffee pickers to work. Many of Zaire's languages are tonal and the drummers, by mimicking the tone patterns of the words, can send complex messages across the jungle.

I went to breakfast with the mechanic, whose name was Denis; Christian names are illegal in Zaire, but it seemed as if everyone I met was named after a saint. As we ate, the owner of the plantation sat down to talk. He paid his workers, he said, one and a half zaires a day and, even at that low wage, he could barely break even. The market was uncertain. Machines kept breaking down.

I spent the day walking. I followed the road for miles. It was my last long walk in the forests of Zaire, and I exulted in the warmth and the dampness and the sight and smell of the life that grew all around me. After three hours, I came to a village of little white houses. The people stared at me, sullen and suspicious. Rather than leaving them that way, I stopped to talk. I told them that I was staying at the plantation and, having nothing better to do, was passing the day hiking. Those who spoke French translated my words for the rest, and as I talked, the villagers relaxed. I was not a demon after all, only a man. "You were afraid of me, weren't you?" I asked and, shamefaced, they nodded their heads.

One of the men told me that there were no other villages nearby, nothing but jungle, so I started to walk back toward the plantation. At the edge of the village, I turned around to wave good-bye and, as I watched, a band of Pygmies came out of the forest. They had brought meat to trade with the villagers, but when they saw me they ran off down the road. I thought of Gulliver's first voyage, and I lay down on the dusty track to show I meant no harm. And, a few minutes later, the Pygmies reappeared and, quite slowly, tiptoed toward me. They came within thirty feet, stood there a while, wide-eyed, and then trotted off to the village. I left them then, and got back to the plantation in time for supper.

The menu was rice and stewed manioc leaves, and the topic of conversation was the Mbuti. I told Denis about the hunt I had witnessed a few days before, and he replied that he had seen things far more amazing. Often, he told me, as he was driving at full speed, Pygmies would emerge from the bushes and gallop beside the truck, running faster than a leopard. And this was, he assured me, the truth. He had seen it with his own eyes, he said, pointing to them. Could any man move that fast? I wondered. Later, after listening to more of Denis's stories, I realized that he was too inventive to let himself be confined by the bounds of reality. I wouldn't call him a liar, but he liked to please, he liked the sight of wonder in my eyes, and he romanticized the Pygmies in the hope that some of their glamour would attach to him.

By the next morning, Denis had decided that the coffee mill was beyond repair. It needed new bearings which, like most spare parts for most machines, were not available in Zaire. Soon after, we left the plantation and drove east until we reached the main road, where we turned south. It was two hundred miles to Kisangani and we took three days to cover them. Denis's Pygmy story was, I realized, not so incredible after all; a band of Pygmies or anyone else could easily have run beside us. If they had fallen behind, they would have caught up when we stopped for water, which we were forced to do every ten minutes; the radiator was riddled with what looked like bullet holes. And after we filled the tank, we had to push the truck until it started.

Fortunately, the truck was small and there were five of us to shove it: Denis, his assistant and I, and a man and a woman from the plantation who were making an excursion to the city—the man short, thin, and unmemorable; the woman big and muscular, with her hair done up in foot-long spikes, which stuck out like antennae. This space-invader hair style was quite popular in Zaire. So were big burly bodies. The women were strong and proud of it. The day before, at the plantation, I had seen a woman carrying a huge drum of water as heavy as a man. I had offered to help her and had, quite unknowingly, insulted her instead, called her femininity into question by implying she could not lift it on her own.

Some of the villages along the main road had set up roadside restaurants and mud-hut motels, and we stopped at the first one we came to after sundown. There was warm, frothy beer in the café and I offered to split the cost of a bottle with Denis, but he gave me a glass instead. "I couldn't sell a friend a beer," he said. So we drank, and Denis spun a few yarns for us, and then we went off to sleep. I had met these people only a few days ago, but that evening it seemed as if I had known them far longer. Truck trips in Zaire are like that, I thought, remembering my first Congo crossing. In the moist, rich air of the forest, even friendships grow faster; some bloom and others fester, but there is always change, fruition, and decay.

The next day it rained. I sat in the uncovered back of the pickup with the woman and the driver's helper and let the water stream over me. The wet season was beginning and in a few months all of Central Africa would turn into marshland, all but impassable. I was in a race with the weather and I hoped I would reach Douala before the rains. Even now, the rutted dirt highway soon dissolved into mud. Our truck bogged down more than once, and all of us had to push it, the mud slurping under our feet. Finally, Denis decided to stop and wait out the storm. There was a big-wheeled freight truck stuck nearby, and I crawled under it to get out of the rain.

The rain let up and we moved on. We passed through Bafwa-sende, Bafwabalinga, and Bafwaboli, all tiny villages smaller than their names, but Bafwasende had a few stucco-fronted cafés, which still resembled neat and tidy Flemish inns. One bore a sign, all but obliterated over the years, that said something like CLUB-ROUTIÈRE DU CONGO. "The Belgians looked after these roads," Denis said, repeating perhaps what his father had told him. "Twenty years ago you could drive to Stanleyville in a day." It wasn't Belgian sweat that built these roads, I thought.

Still, from all appearances, the highway, like the Club-Routière office, had been left to rot ever since the Belgians departed. Every vehicle carried steel cables, and at some of the muddiest patches, each truck would tow the one behind it. At one steep and slippery hill, a bulldozer waited to give arriving trucks a pull. Cars and buses could not ride those roads, so trucks were the only transport around. Each time we stopped at a village, people surrounded us, hoping for a ride. Whenever Denis was out of earshot, the assistant told the villagers to talk to me, I was the owner of the truck. By then, my clothes were frayed and muddy and my face was red from dust; it was obvious from the dirt that my seat was in the back. Even so, no one ever questioned the assistant's story; I was white so I must be the boss.

We picked up riders here and there, whenever they could pay for transport, so new faces joined our group, stayed a while, then left when they reached their destination. One very tall, hawk-faced man from Rwanda got on at one of the Bafwas and stayed with us until Kisangani. He, I, and the assistant were sitting in back on the third day when we rounded a curve and saw a paved strip of highway before us. We cheered. Ten miles to go. Denis stopped the car at the nearest stream and the passengers got out, bathed, then changed into city clothes. The driver's assistant put on crimson trousers and natty white shoes. We drove on and, a few miles from town, the truck broke down, this time for good. Denis walked into town to get a taxi and the rest of us waited. After an hour, a car stopped and the driver, a Belgian who worked in the city, offered me a ride. I was eager to get to Kisangani so I took it, and sat in back with the man's wife and daughter. "These African drivers are very unreliable," the Belgian said. "You could have been there all night." I was silent but I felt as if I'd betrayed a friend.

Kisangani lies halfway between Cairo and Capetown, between the Indian Ocean and the Atlantic. It is, more or less, the center of Africa and, at the center of the center, just behind the main market and a few blocks west of the river, is the Olympia Hotel. It is owned by Greeks and patronized mostly by Europeans, and the Belgians left me there. "This is a good place for you to stay," they told me.

The first person I met in Kisangani was a Texan. Her name was Betty, and she strolled over as I was sitting in the hotel garden. Her wardrobe appeared designed and manufactured by Neiman-Marcus, and so, for that matter, did she. She was thin as a mannequin, her flaming red hair carefully coiffed, not a strand out of place. She probably doesn't perspire, I thought.

My opinion of her changed when I found out her story. She had, somehow, made her way from Texas to Bangui, in the Central African Empire. There, she told me, she and two friends she had met on the road bought a pirogue—a hollowed-out log—and sailed down the Ubangi, a tributary of the Congo, hoping to reach the Atlantic. They paddled for three months, buying supplies at villages along the way, dragging the boat on shore each night. One evening they were robbed, and every night without fail the mosquitoes found them. Unfortunately, they didn't trouble themselves about such formalities as visas. One day, when they landed in Congo-Brazzaville, Zaire's Marxist neighbor, they were arrested, their canoe confiscated, they themselves deported to Zaire. All this had taken place the year before and she had spent the intervening months traveling alone around Zaire.

Betty offered to share her room with me. There were two beds and my half of the rent would be five zaires a day. "Don't worry," she said, "I'm only looking for a roommate, nothing more." I hid my disappointment and replied, "So am I."

Still, I was happy with what I got: a bed with clean linen, a mattress and springs, the first proper bed I'd slept in since the Hotel

Royal, Khartoum. And outside the hotel were other wonders—street-lamps that worked, buildings three stories tall, a *patisserie* that served French bread and coffee. After my weeks in the forest, Kisangani seemed to me an alien, but strangely familiar world. One of Denis's Pygmy stories involved a band of Mbuti who were sent to Stanley-ville, panicked, ran off, and were never seen again. I liked the city but late at night, as I walked the asphalt streets, blocks and blocks of ghostly mansions whose concrete walls glowed pale and phosphores-cent, I could understand their terror.

On most nights, I stayed inside. Our room at the Olympia was a reassuring island of bright lights and beige walls beyond which, in any direction, were two or three miles of pavement, glass, and con-crete, and then the vast expanse of the forest, unbroken for hundreds of miles. After the bars shut down for the night, the city was quiet, as eerily silent as a derelict ship on a black and endless river. We talked then, Betty and I, and she told me tales of sorcery, magic, and mur-der: a man in Lisala had killed two tourists and eaten their hearts; a jealous woman somewhere in Kasai had put poison in Betty's drink but she, by an accident so timely as to appear providential, had knocked it over; beware of women with long fingernails; beware of love potions—a woman can mix the secretions of her body with vari-ous plants from the jungle and use this philter to enslave any man she chooses. I mentioned these tales to the European traders who could be found in the courtyard each afternoon without fail, sitting around tables with cloths of starched white linen, on which were spread meals that cost more than my room's rent for a week. The "pil-grims" did not scoff at Betty's stories as I expected and possibly hoped they would. "Who knows what plants can be found in the jungle," said one. And another told me that the longer you stay in Africa, the easier it is to believe stories like these. And that week the Kisangani newspaper carried a front-page dispatch from Monrovia, where a police chief and several politicans were on trial for killing a well-known rock singer. They had murdered him and then eaten him, believing that by devouring his body they would devour his soul as well, thus gaining enough magic to win the next election. Liberia was thousands of miles away, but the account of the trial combined with Betty's stories and the other Europeans' acceptance of them to produce a sense of brooding, almost palpable evil, and in my mind echoed the cry once whispered by another Congo pilgrim: "The horror! The horror!" But, a few miles up the road, the villagers, the Mbuti, and even Philippe had the same dread of me. I discussed this with the traders, and their reaction was, "They're all cannibals out there, so of course they think the same of us." Of course. But how to explain, in that case, the thoughts and fears of the *traders?* And, if I had to choose who cast the first stone, I felt much more of a kinship with Philippe and Chief Indumbe than with the traders, whose names and faces I did not bother to remember.

If you stayed at the Olympia long enough, you would meet every expatriate in town; teachers, traders, travelers all stopped by. One of them was a short-haired, stocky American named Mike, who worked in the Peace Corps. He invited me to stay with him; he had, he explained, plenty of room to spare. The American consulate in Kisangani had recently been closed down; as the senior worker remaining (and perhaps because he looked clean-cut and consular), Mike had been assigned the consul's house. So Betty and I moved out to the rambling mansion that had once housed a consulate.

Mike had at one point worked in Kasai; the walls were covered with masks from that province. They were magical, superbly crafted, distorted faces. He shared the house with a Peace Corps teacher named Chip, who wore a bright green shirt on which he had printed the word for white man in various African languages. The Zairois had never let him forget that he was of an alien race, and he had finally decided to flaunt the fact. From the first evening, Betty took up with Chip. She had told me that all she wanted from me was someone to share the rent, and I had, perhaps foolishly, taken her at her word. I could not help noticing, with mixed pride and regret, that Chip looked a lot like me.

The consul's house had thick walls and strong shutters. Mercenaries, riots, rebels, and warlords; the American consulate had seen them all, during the turbulent years after independence, and survived them all, only to succumb to bureaucratic budget trimmers back in Washington. Now, the nearest consulate was in Bukavu. But the memories remained and so did the shutters. One day, several suspected white mercenaries were arrested in Goma, near the Rwandan border, and that afternoon, Chip saw a Red Beret, a member of an elite—and much-feared—army unit, near the post office in the center of town. Two chance events, probably unrelated—but that night we stayed inside and locked the shutters as Mike tried to raise Bukavu on the radio. There was no answer from the consulate, only static, and then the lights dimmed; something was wrong at the power station. I half expected to hear the crackle of far-off rifles, to see commandos in red berets emerge from the hedge, come to round up suspected mercenaries. But nothing broke the silence of the night, and the bright and sunny day that followed made our fears seem foolish.

I spent another week with Mike and Chip, two weeks in all in Kisangani. It was a brief and pleasant interlude from poverty and travel. The talk of Kisangani was magic, murder, danger, and fear, but the town itself was tranquil, even somnolent, and quite pretty to look at. There were plenty of palm trees and a big, lazy river, and no city with a river, lake, or seafront can be wholly lacking in beauty.

Once a week, a boat left Kisangani for the capital, Kinshasa, a thousand miles down the mighty Congo River. After my week with the Peace Corps, I took the boat as far as the town of Lisala, from where I would hitchhike to the border post at Zongo, four hundred miles away. The boat trip took two days. In an act of wanton extravagance, I paid ten dollars for a cabin, but I spent most of the journey standing on the highest deck, looking out over the vast expanse of water. As best as I could judge, the river was about a mile wide at this point, and there was always a fringe of trees at the horizon. For hour after hour, all I saw was jungle and muddy water. The whole world was hushed and primeval, the earth on the third day of creation. Every so often, we passed a village, and the young men paddled out in canoes to see the boat and perhaps sell bags of manioc to the traders who set up shop in second class.

On the second day, we stopped in Bumba, and then Lisala, where I got off. I found a bed at the Catholic mission near the wharf and spent the next day looking for a ride to Zongo. A truck picked me up that evening, and I rode all night on a bed of cartons. I didn't get much sleep, because the truck, which was taking supplies to shops along the way, stopped every few hours to unload.

Early the next morning, I was dropped off at a nameless junction. I sat by the road and waited for a truck to pass. Toward noon, a soldier in a red beret strolled by. He, too, was hoping for a ride. He had food and whiskey and he shared them with me as we waited together. Late in the afternoon, a truck came by and we flagged it down. Another night ride. This truck, unlike most of them, was covered, so the Red Beret and I squeezed between the cargo and the green canvas roof. There were other passengers on the truck, nestled among the cartons and burlap sacks, and they teased the Red Beret, called him "little soldier," but it was done without malice and he didn't mind.

It rained that night, high winds followed by a heavy downpour, and I was glad for the canvas canopy. A few minutes past midnight, the truck stopped. The storm had uprooted hundreds of trees, and the highway was a tangle of trunks and branches. We all got out, and we cleared the road in the rain by the light of the headlights. It took an hour to clear a hundred yards and, since I assumed the rest of the way would also be blocked, I thought we would be on that road for a long time to come. But not long afterward we reached the end of the obstruction and the road was clear all the way to Zongo.

When we got to Zongo, I rented a dollar room at the nearest hotel and fell asleep. That evening, I walked to the banks of the Ubangi and watched the glittering lights of Bangui reflected in the water. Bangui, the capital of the Central African Empire, was on the other side of the river, only a short boat ride away. The next day, the second day of March 1979, I took the boat. I looked forward to Bangui's beer and neon, and it was not until later that I realized I had left Zaire. I had been there two months that seemed like forever.

16

THE ROAD WEST: CENTRAL AFRICAN EMPIRE, CAMEROUN AND NIGERIA

A short walk from the ferry boat and within sight of the water, in the center of a triangle formed by the expensive Rock Hotel, the exclusive Bangui Rock Club, and the palace of His Imperial Majesty, the Emperor Bokassa I, was a muddy, overgrown lot where travelers too poor to rent a hotel room were allowed to set up camp. I had been to Bangui before, with the overland truck, from distant London back in 1977, so I knew where to go. I headed straight for the lot. Sixty travelers, more than I had seen in all the months since leaving Khartoum, were camped there. There were two big overland trucks and a few VW campers. The night we had closed the shutters in Kisangani, Zaire had closed its borders. The mercenaries arrested in Goma had entered the country as tourists, so now no more tourists were admitted. The only other route to East and Southern Africa passed through the Sudan, but the Sudanese consul panicked at the sight of sixty applicants in one day and stopped issuing visas. All the overlanders were stuck in Bangui, bogged down in the weedy eyesore of a campground with its panoramic view of the river and beyond, lush and inviting, the rolling green hills of Zaire.

I decided, on my first day in town, that Bangui was the prettiest place in Africa. Perhaps my judgment was still distorted from the weeks I had spent in Khartoum, Wau, and Nzara. Still, Bangui undeniably has charm. Its avenues are shaded by huge trees, glossy-leaved mangoes and scarlet-flowered flamboyants, in such profusion that most of Bangui, seen from the opposite, Zairois bank of the river, appears to be a forest. Behind the campground, in the direction of the Grande Corniche, you can find shady, quiet streets of colonial mansions, their grand old stone façades cracked and worn and covered with moss. Or, if you follow Avenue du Général de Gaulle along the river, past the huge complex that houses the French embassy— the true seat of government, some say—and turn right at the market, you will come to the center of town, where chic boutiques sell designer dresses and supermarkets are stocked with fresh shrimp from Douala and bread flown in from France.

When I first saw the supermarkets, I was too awestruck by the variety of goods—the greatest I had come across since Teheran—and too stunned by the astronomical prices to wonder why one of Africa's poorest nations spent its earnings on pâté and champagne, or to calculate how many hours the hospital generators could have run on the fuel used to ship the shrimps in from the coast. For me, as for most of the emperor's subjects, shopping was a spectator sport. The currency was, as in most of France's former colonies, the CFA franc, which is supported by the Bank of France and pegged at fifty to one French franc—against which, in those bygone days, the dollar was dropping daily. I had 150 dollars, enough to buy ten nights at the cheapest hotel or ten kilos of shrimp. So I stayed at the campground, ate huge thirty-five-cent sandwiches at the market, and drank beer at the Rock Hotel.

Sometimes, as I sat in the Rock Hotel's outdoor café, which was on a breezy terrace high above the wide and muddy river, I wondered whether impoverished Africans in Paris were encouraged to camp outside the Ritz Hotel and make free use of its bars and bathrooms, or to stroll into the Jockey Club and chat with its members. Perhaps, if one of those great African empires of the Middle Ages had made a colony of France in the same way the Moors had swept up from the Sahara and annexed Spain, then a black face in France would evoke the same respect and deference that white skin is accorded in Central Africa. Mine not to reason why, I decided, and I continued to drink at the Rock, swim at the Bangui Rock Club, and sleep in the mud.

Almost all of the people at the campground were on overland truck tours, but some were loners like me. One was Michael, a Canadian ex-hockey player who was as poor as I was, a dubious distinction, but one that drew us together. We spent our evenings exchanging complaints over bottles of cheap local beer, but we never talked or even thought of leaving Africa.

I was hot-blooded in those days, and I think I was surprised even then by the energy that flowed within me. I slept very little, but I was never tired; I ate bread and little else but never felt the need for more. Perhaps I had learned, like the forests around me, to suck my strength from the sun and the soil. There was a discotheque in the hotel where the dancing was fast and frenzied. It was very chic and crowded, with no cover charge, and one hot Saturday night I went there and danced without a break until dawn.

A few hundred feet upriver from the Rock was another hotel, the Safari, where the beer was cold and the bar was quiet, with a good view of the river. It was a pleasant place to drink, and one night Mike and I drank a little more than we should have. Unfortunately, that was the night the emperor came to town.

Jean-Bedel Bokassa, the self-crowned emperor of the Central African Empire, did not visit Bangui often in those days. He was, very likely, afraid to set foot in his own capital. In January, two months before, there had been demonstrations in the streets, which his troops had dispersed by shooting the demonstrators. Europeans resident in Bangui told me that hundreds of demonstrators had died that day, and the figure would have been higher had Bangui's doctors obeyed Bokassa's orders not to treat the wounded. Everyone expected more riots. No one could say which side the army, who had not been paid for months, would take. Bokassa I prudently kept to his palace in the country and his suburban villa where, it was said, the soldiers who overthrew him a few months later found freezers full of half-devoured corpses. But, on that muggy night in March, a banquet was held at the Safari to welcome a group of European bankers who had come to negotiate a loan to the bankrupt empire. The banks of Europe and America have, in recent years, lent far too many billions to countries that have little hope of repaying them, but even the most amiable banker would hesitate to invest in a ruler whose tenure was so uncertain that he feared to leave his own palace. And so, as Mike and I downed our third bottle of beer at the Safari bar, and the barman, in our honor, played for the third time a cassette of rock music that sounded like an Indian war dance, the emperor arrived next door. He came in a limousine which, instead of a license plate, had a bronze bas-relief of a blazing sun, and he marched across a red carpet as soldiers of his elite Imperial Guard played a fanfare on their bugles.

Mike and I emerged from the bar an hour later. We had missed the chance to greet the emperor, but the carpet was still there, and the guardsmen, and the shiny brass bugles. The sight of the horns gave my fuddled brain an idea; I would borrow one and try to play it. So I grabbed the nearest horn and, much to my surprise, the Imperial Guardsman took me to the nearest jail. It was an army barracks on Avenue de Gaulle, and I had passed the place every day on my way into town. The low green shed that housed the troops had piqued my curiosity because it was guarded by sentries who did not allow anyone to walk past it; all pedestrians had to use the other side of the avenue. Now, the same soldiers who had not allowed me in would not let me out.

That night, I slept on the floor of the commander's office. The commander slept on his desk. He wanted me to pay a fine of forty dollars; that was almost half my total funds so I refused. By the next morning, I had bargained him down to fifteen. I could have left then, but, perhaps quixotically, I demanded an official receipt. I would pay a fine, but not a bribe. This angered him, but in the end I was given a receipt and released. I had gotten off lightly, all things considered, and the night I had spent in the barracks was the one night it rained.

The Central African Empire has many tribes and many regions, each with its own customs and peculiarities, but as is true throughout Africa, the most startling contrast is between city and village. The residents of Bangui have much more in common with the people of Abidjan, Douala, and Dakar than with the villagers whose mud huts lie twenty miles outside town. Bangui is like a separate nation and, quite appropriately, your passport is stamped when you cross the city limits. By this time, I wanted to leave Bangui and return to the simpler world of the countryside. But before I could, there was the usual paperwork to be done. I got a visa for Nigeria and was refused one for Cameroun. A glance at my map confirmed that I could not get to West Africa without crossing Cameroun, so I decided to go to the border and see if I could get across. My Central African visa had run out; I could not stay in Bangui any longer. Visa extensions were available, but useless; they were good for a week and took a week to get, so by the time you got the extension, it would already have expired.

On my last night in Bangui, one of the many thieves who infested the campground stole Mike's money as he slept. I gave him all I could spare, which wasn't much, and left. I took a bus to the police checkpoint called PK 12, twelve kilometers west of town, where passports were stamped and the tarmac ended. Mike had told me that it was almost impossible to find free lifts west of Bangui, but within an hour I had a ride to Yaloké, 130 miles away.

Yaloké was a trucker's town: a row of weatherbeaten concrete storefronts along the highway and a garishly painted bar. The beer hall, which had its own generator, had the only bright lights and loud music for miles around. Yaloké straddled the main road to the west, and scores of trucks passed through every day on their way to Baboua, Bozoum, and Garoua-Boulai. Most of the drivers stopped to visit the shops and stayed to drink at the bar. It was a hitchhiker's dream, this endless stream of traffic, but it took me two days to get a ride. The drivers wanted money, a lot of it; if I was too poor to pay they didn't care if I stayed in Yaloké forever. Why should they help a stranger? I longed for Zaire, where I had never been refused a ride.

In Teheran I had been nervous and impatient when I had to wait an hour for a bus; trains and buses always left at the appointed hour. But in Yaloké I might as well have thrown my watch away, for Africa ran on a different time. And, after my months in Zaire, so did I, and spending two days by the side of the road didn't bother me at all. At night, I slept on one of the shops' verandas. Nobody minded, and nobody touched my pack, which I left there during the day, chained to a case of beer. Behind the shops was a large market where

I went to eat; twenty francs bought a bowl of *bouillie,* a flavorless but filling blend of starch and hot water. Like most African markets, this one was a happy, lively, colorful place, always crowded, and I suspected that many of the people who strolled from stall to stall didn't want to buy at all, but only to exchange light talk and banter with the sellers, who were always ready to oblige them.

On my second night in Yaloké, there was an eclipse of the moon. The full moon shone a dim and ominous shade of copper, and as it was slowly devoured by the earth's shadow, a sullen silence fell over the town. As I stood in the road, a young man, a high-school student, came to talk. He was nervous and wanted to be reassured. He had learned in school about suns and planets and moons in orbit; his teacher had, using two oranges and a candle, demonstrated how eclipses are caused. But his family told him that what we were watching was spirits eating the moon, that it might disappear forever. Now he did not know which to believe—the wisdom of his teacher or the wisdom of his tribe. Later, when the moon grew once more to fullness, he breathed a sigh of relief.

Late in the afternoon of the third day, I got a ride in a flatbed truck. We drove fast and I stood in back, ecstatic, leaning into the fierce whipping wind. But the truck stopped at a village twenty miles up the road, and there I stayed for two days more. It was a village like any other: a double row of earthen cabins, the road running in between. There was a sad-eyed woman who let me sleep in her living room. Many years ago, she said, she had been the wife of a French planter, and I reminded her of him.

It was a pleasant place to stay. From about four o'clock onward, the villagers' chief occupation was getting drunk on home-brewed whiskey and dancing to music on the radio. During the day, I sat by the highway, but few trucks stopped and those that did wanted cash on the line. An overland truck, full of white faces and headed for the cul-de-sac of Bangui, zoomed past without slowing down. An old man from the village saw this, and was astounded. "Why didn't they stop?" he asked me. "They are your brothers." I told him they were going in the wrong direction. "They should have stopped anyway," he told me, "to see if they could help you." In Africa, where everybody helps those in need, people of the same tribe have a special duty toward one another. The villager could not believe that a truck full of whites, my tribe, would be so uncivilized as to ignore a fellow-tribes-man who was stranded in a strange land. The old farmer went off muttering, so indignant that his head shook from side to side.

After two nights in the village, I decided to buy a ride. I had left Bangui five days before, and unless I paid my way it might take months to reach the border. The next driver to stop wanted twenty dollars to take me to Bouar, the last large town before the border, but settled for fifteen. I had him let me off at the huge French army base five miles out of town. Several Peace Corps workers lived near the base; I had met them in Bangui and they invited me to visit them in Bouar. They bade me welcome and we talked for hours. I mentioned the eclipse and they told me that, in Bouar, the people had collected pots, jars, oil drums, sheets of tin, anything that would make a noise. When the eclipse began, they banged them with all their might, hoping the din would drive off the evil spirits and rescue the moon. And, to their great joy, the people saw their efforts were not in vain; within an hour, the moon shone again.

That night I slept between clean sheets in a huge double bed. My hosts were apologetic about the accommodation, since we shared a communal bath, but it was luxury to me. The next morning, I woke early and walked through the town. There was a control post in Bouar where passports were checked. My visa was, of course, expired, but, as I hoped, the post was closed at that early hour. So I simply walked past it. On the other side of Bouar, beyond the last houses of town, a boy stood by the road selling *bouillie.* I drank a bowl, steaming hot, and waited for a lift. After a while, a truck came by and gave me a ride to Garoua-Boulai. That lift cost another two thousand francs, but it took me to the border.

In those days, travelers were sometimes let into Cameroun without a visa, but only if they could show a respectable amount of cash, to prove they weren't paupers. Five hundred dollars was usually considered respectable enough, but one hundred wasn't. I hoped to talk my way across; I was good at talking. Leaving the empire with a long-expired visa was another problem but one that, like so many of the difficulties I encountered in Africa, seemed to solve itself. The Central African border guards didn't bother to look at my passport; they assumed it had been examined back in Bouar.

The truck left me between the borders and, as I walked toward the Cameroun border post, I passed a ragtag collection of storefronts—a shopping mall, Yaloké-style. There was a white Volkswagen minibus parked outside, and a long-haired suntanned man beside it, trying to blow up a tire. His name was Fritz, and the one inside the truck was called Utsi. They had driven down from Germany and were now driving back, though if they could get a good price for the car, they would sell it and hitchhike the rest of the way. "Come in," they said, "we'll take you across the border."

The Cameroun border post was manned by an old soldier dressed in crumpled khaki. The officer in charge, he told us, was forced to attend an important festival—out drinking, I guessed—and we should go to Bertoua, the nearest large town, and clear customs there. We drove through the night and by the next morning we were halfway across the country. In Yaoundé, Cameroun's hilly capital, we went to the immigration office, which was near the intersection of Avenue de Gaulle and Avenue Foch. Fritz and Utsi lent me all their money in case I had to show my funds; they had one hundred fifty dollars between them. The clerk at Immigration stamped my passport on the spot; Yaoundé was at the center of Cameroun, so it was far easier to let me stay than to throw me out.

We drove on, taking the road to Douala, but turning south at Edéa. Much of the road was paved, but it was pocked with treacherous, jagged potholes. Night fell as we drove, my second night on what was supposed to be a five-mile ride to the Cameroun border. At some point all three of us reached the unspoken decision that we would stay together until Douala. We could have made it there within a few hours, but instead we drove to Kribi where, for the first time since Ceylon, I saw the ocean. From Kribi, the sands stretched south unbroken. That night, we camped on the beach. I lay on the sand and listened to the surf rolling in to pound the shoreline.

Seven miles south of Kribi was a place called Grand Batanga. Betty, who had stayed there before her months on the Ubangi, had marked it on my map. Fritz and Utsi liked the sound of it, so we drove there the next morning and stayed a week. We built huge bonfires, cooked horrible meals, swam in the sea, slept on the sand. The car had a tape player, and we played it loud, drank beer, and danced. There were houses near the beach, a whole village built of driftwood, and the people tolerated us but kept their distance. They had seen many, many tourists before us. I sensed this same aloofness all along the West African coast. For five hundred years now, the flotsam of Europe has washed ashore on that Atlantic Ocean coast: slave traders, freebooters, colonizers, invaders. At some point during those long years, the hospitality of the coastal peoples was exhausted, and gave way to stoic, sullen resignation. But go a mile inland, and you'll find nothing but kindness and smiles.

When we left Grand Batanga, we headed north to Douala, the largest city in Cameroun. Fritz and Utsi left me there, and drove off toward their home, which lay far to the north, across sand and sea. They had a hundred dollars to get them there. I had less than that, so I slept at the airport, which lay just the other side of the slums and shanties that ringed the town.

Though my money belt was nearly empty, I had a bank account in New York which, I calculated, was probably still in the black. There were four or five cities in Africa to which I could have cash sent, and Douala was one of them. I walked to the Cam Voyages office on Avenue de la Liberté, presented my passport and a long-expired credit card, and persuaded them to cash a check for five hundred dollars. I didn't think it would work, it shouldn't have worked, but it did. I was rich; I could travel; I could stay in Africa. To celebrate, I had a beer in one of the smart sidewalk cafés that lined the avenue. It cost three dollars, which was not much less than what I'd spent in a week at Grand Batanga, and I didn't mind. The day was bright and sunny. The rains, which dump 150 inches of water on Douala each year— six times what London gets—had not yet come.

I continued my celebration in Victoria, a fishing town an hour's drive west of Douala. The black volcanic beach was fringed with clapboard shacks and tiny tin-roofed cafés. They spoke English in Victoria; Cameroun, a German possession until the First World War was, like all spoils of war, divided between the victors, and Victoria lay in the part the British got. Cameroun is a crazy quilt of ethnic divisions, but perhaps the most serious postindependence conflict is not between hostile tribes or rival religions, but between the former British and French zones. The Francophones control the government, and the English-speaking people, who are a minority, complain of being shortchanged; the British sector, they say, receives far less government aid than it should. A few months before, a Peace Corps worker told me, a French-speaking governor had been heckled when he gave a speech at a town in the English zone. The next day, a truckload of gendarmes visited the town and beat up residents at random. All of which goes to show that Africans are not inextricably bound to tribal loyalties; their horizons may be broadened to include more modern sources of strife.

After two days on the beach, I took a train to Yaoundé and a bus to Bafoussam. It was late when the bus let me off at the town's market, long since closed for the night, and I slept on a bench under the star-spangled sky. I had stayed in a hotel in Victoria, but I didn't want to pick up bad habits; I had five hundred dollars but might not be able to get any more. A loudspeaker woke me early the next morning, and I staggered off the bench and listened to the news, broadcast in French from Douala. Tanzanian troops were nearing Kampala, the announcer said. President for Life Idi Amin's term of office had come to a sudden end.

From Bafoussam, it was an easy drive to Bamenda and then to Dschang. The air was cool and the land was green and hilly. This was the heart of Cameroun's Bamiléké plateau, a region of tiny kingdoms whose rulers claim descent from dynasties founded eight centuries ago. Robert Brain, an Australian anthropologist, had lived in Fontem, one of the smallest and most remote of these principalities, and described its people's proud traditions in a book I had read in Singapore. Fontem was twenty miles from Dschang, along a little-used and very rugged side road that was, I later heard, made by a priest and a bulldozer many years before. From the look of it, it hadn't been regraded since. I spent several hours in Dschang market looking for a ride to Fontem. Finally, I found a truck going there, but the driver wouldn't take me. In the end, he relented and, after several hours spent driving up steep, slippery hills, I reached Fontem at dusk.

Fontem was not the pristine, undiscovered kingdom I had imagined. Perhaps it had changed since Brain had left. There was a big concrete schoolhouse, and a brand-new police post staffed with polite but officious gendarmes. Outside of town, the enormous earthen houses were much as Brain described them, but each and every one of them sported a shiny new roof of corrugated tin. Brain's book focuses on friendship, but the only friend I made in Fontem was an American, a Peace Corps worker from somewhere in the Midwest. He had been stationed in Fontem for three years and I was the first traveler to pass through, so he insisted I stay with him. The next day, he showed me around his hilly domain; there was one stretch where the road was level for a hundred yards, and he had named it Kansas.

That night we went to a loud and lively dance at the schoolhouse, and the next morning he took me to meet the king, whose official and euphonious title was the Fon of Fontem. The Fon lived in a wooden palace with black-and-white mock-Tudor siding. In the main hall, a grandfather clock slowly ticked the hours; behind the palace was a yard where the royal pigs happily devoured the royal garbage. We waited in the main foyer, beside a table covered with ledgers and accounts. The Fon was the richest man in Fontem, and the most powerful as well. He had his own army of servants and retainers, but his influence rested primarily on his wealth, his traditional authority, and his ability to intrigue. His guards were no match for the well-armed gendarmes at the post in town, who represented a far stronger—though much younger—power than his: the government of Cameroun.

We were not kept waiting long. The Fon of Fontem, an old man, bald, who wore flowing robes and a striped skullcap, entered the palace to greet us. I did not know whether Fons shook commoners' hands, so I waited until he held out his. Afterward, my Peace Corps friend told me I had acted correctly; the Fon would have been insulted had I thrust my hand forward.

That afternoon, I found a place on a truck bound for Mamfé which, like Fontem, was in Cameroun's English-speaking zone. I spent the night at the home of two Peace Corps men who were friends of the one in Fontem. They introduced me to the district commissioner. We sat in his tiny bungalow and discussed American history. He was young, well-educated, idealistic and intelligent, and he probably considered the Fon, whose kingdom comprised a tiny part of his district, a relic of the Middle Ages.

I had vague plans of going north from Mamfé, to visit a village two days' walk from the main road where, according to my Peace Corps informant, the people had recently devoured a missionary and had also—and this was the intriguing part of the tale—eaten his eyeglasses. But I never found out if this story was true, because I decided to go straight to Nigeria. One of my hosts gave me a ride to the truck stop on his motorbike; "I never could ride one of these before I came here," he called back to me as we zoomed down a hill.

I took a truck to Ekok, cleared Cameroun customs, and walked across the border to Mfum, the Nigerian post a half mile away, where the police added two new stamps to my already overflowing passport, both dated 3 April 1979. From there I got a ride to Ikom. At Ikom, there was a bus about to leave, so I got on board. It took me to Calabar, a large town on the coast.

Calabar was a squalid place, very sooty and unpleasantly crowded. The town may have had redeeming features but I didn't stay long enough to find them. The cheapest lodging around was fifteen dollars a night and that was a room not much larger than the lumpy bed in the center. I went to the police station, and talked the man at the desk into letting me sleep in the yard. It was noisy, but free, and the safest spot in town.

The next morning, I left Calabar as soon as I could. I took a passenger van to Enugu. A passenger van is a cross between a taxi and a freight truck. This hardy hybrid is found throughout Africa, except in Sudan and Zaire, where the roads are not good enough. It goes by many names: Ghanaians call it a "mammy wagon," because most of its passengers are matrons on their way to market; in Kenya, it's named a *matatu* and in Sierra Leone a *poda poda;* and throughout French West Africa, it is known as a *taxi-brousse,* or bush taxi. But, whatever name its vehicles go by, a taxi park always looks the same: a dusty, crowded lot, filled with panel trucks that look like small delivery vans and perhaps a few station wagons. Behind each van, the driver and his grease-covered assistant stand and shout the destination. Passengers mill about. They pay the drivers to cram them in the back of the truck. Usually, the vans have seats or benches. Most of the time, there are windows, but sometimes not.

When the truck is completely full, the driver shoves a few more passengers in. Then he leaves. There is no fixed departure time. Sometimes it takes all day to fill a truck. If the driver swears that there are only five more places left, the taxi is probably empty. The vans will also take freight, baggage, anything that is paid for. Once, in Ghana, I rode with a smelly, squirming cow that all but filled the truck. In Nigeria, some of the larger trucks have open backs, wooden benches and, proudly painted over the cab, inspirational apocalyptic mottoes, such as MAN PROPOSES, GOD DISPOSES, and JESUS WEPT, and GOD'S VERDICT, NO APPEAL.

Enugu lay at the heart of the land that once seceded from Nigeria and, calling itself Biafra, remained independent until the Nigerian army starved it into submission. By then, three years had passed and a million people had lost their lives. The people of this eastern region, the Ibo, have a reputation for hard work, industry, and independence. Before the British came, a time when most of West Africa was divided into centralized kingdoms, each Ibo village was autonomous.

By driving from Calabar inland to Enugu, I hoped to see the land and people in between; usually, African villages are built by the roadside and, by riding the roads, you can catch a succession of rapid-fire glimpses of rural life. But the Nigerian highways were paved and two lanes wide and I could see nothing but road and cars, with an occasional view of empty land. I might as well have been crossing New Jersey on Interstate 95. And Enugu, when I got there, seemed like the sort of town that was so spread out it would take ten minutes to get from one building to the next.

I made my way to the train station and found that the twice-weekly train to Kano, in the far north of Nigeria, was about to arrive. I hurriedly bought a third-class ticket, which was half the price of the cheapest bus. Then I stood on the concrete platform and waited for the train. The man next to me had been waiting for several days because the train, which started farther south at Port Harcourt, was usually full by the time it got to Enugu. The train arrived a few minutes later; its powerful diesel seemed to glide into the station, its gleaming streamlined sides reminding me of the rippling muscles of a powerful racehorse. Inside the third-class carriage was a seething mass of wall-to-wall people. I was forewarned; I took a running jump, landed in the middle of the mass, and crawled through it until I found a tiny space in the aisle. The people in the seats, quite friendly, shared their food with me and let me sit on their armrest.

In the middle of the second night, we reached Kano. I was exhausted and fell asleep on a bench in the station. This was my second visit to Kano. Two years before, I and my truckmates had been marooned there for three weeks, camped in the garden of parched weeds that surrounded the racecourse. I wanted to stay a few days in Kano this time, if only to see if the place was as dreadful in April of 1979 as I remembered it being in December of 1976. Besides, I traveled through Africa to learn about its people, and I did not want to rush through Nigeria, the country where one out of five Africans lived. And so, when morning came, I made my way to Sabon Gari, a busy part of town full of beer halls, eating houses, and, I hoped, cheap hotels.

Sabon Gari means "strangers' town," and is the neighborhood where immigrants from southern Nigeria live. They are truly strangers here, aliens in their own country, for the Ibo and Yoruba from the south have more in common with the people of southern Ghana and Cameroun than with their countrymen in the north. When British troops marched into Kano in 1903, and for almost a thousand years before, the area the British named Northern Nigeria was divided into tiny feudal principalities each ruled by an emir. In the fourteenth century, the Hausa, the main ethnic group, converted to Islam, and Kano, which was the terminus of the main caravan route across the Sahara, became a center of Moslem culture.

In the first decade of the nineteenth century, the Fulani, a nomadic, pastoral people whose origin is unknown but whose relatively light skin suggests a partly Berber ancestry, swept in from the Sahara and conquered the Hausa states which, however, retained their autonomy under the rigidly Moslem Fulani overlords and, to some extent, under their successors, the British. Northern and southern Nigeria were united into one colony in 1914, but, in religion, culture, and outlook, north and south remained two separate worlds. The only culture the two had in common was British, but in sophisticated, Westernized Nigeria, this forms a stronger bond than one might imagine.

In the late 1970s, Nigeria, one of the world's largest oil producers, was relatively rich. Glutted with oil revenues that seemed endless, its people, both northerners and southerners, had a sense of boundless optimism, of unlimited growth and potential that, twenty years before, was considered quintessentially American. It was a country in a hurry, a country on the move, and perhaps that was why its cities were so ugly, so sloppily built, and its drivers so reckless that its highways were among the least safe on the continent. And perhaps the abundance of easy money also accounted for something of far greater importance to me that morning: hotel prices were the highest in Africa. In Nigeria, 1 percent of the people controlled 75 percent of the country's wealth, and they were the 1 percent who travel and stay in hotels.

The third hotel I tried had an outside terrace built of planks, like a scaffold, with metal chairs and tables scattered about for the comfort of the clientele. I sat down. At the next table, a man sat alone drinking a beer, and we got to talking. I needed someone to complain to.

He wore a white shirt and tie. Above the collar, which was loosened, was a round and glossy face. He was smiling and self-assured: a man with connections, a man in control. He spoke fluent English and, but for the slightest of accents, he could have passed for a black American.

When he found out I had no lodging, he invited me to his house, and I spent three days with him, his wife, and two small boys. Their home was tiny. I slept in the living room, which was quite small, painted dark red, and dominated by a sofa upholstered in black plastic and an enormous television.

My host was, as far as I know, a northerner and a Moslem, though I had first met him in the strangers' quarter, over a glass of beer. He was, I think, a businessman, a president, or perhaps vice president of one of the numerous companies, partnerships, and corporations that sprang up like toadstools from Nigeria's oil-rich soil. But he might have held a post in one of the country's many obscure but powerful bureaucracies and state-owned enterprises. I never found out for certain, and perhaps it doesn't matter. I do know that he was a member in good standing both of the Kano Club and of the even more exclusive establishment next door, the Kano Golf Club, because we spent a long and lazy afternoon shuttling between the two.

At the Golf Club, we sat at the bar, under an awning designed to resemble a thatched roof. Two of my host's friends joined us. Like him, they were fairly young, quite well educated, very articulate and beginning to run to fat. They read *Time* and *Newsweek* regularly, they told me, though there was much in them that they found displeasing. They saw the newsmagazines' style of reporting as a subtle form of slander. Their country's ethnic conflicts, for example, were invariably portrayed as "tribal hostilities," a phrase that evokes images of naked, spear-waving warriors. But when various ethnic groups slaughtered one another in Northern Ireland and the Middle East, the word *tribal* was never used. Why, one of them asked me, are Israelis, Scotch-Irish, and French Canadians never referred to as "tribesmen?"

I could not answer. These technocrats in starched collars seemed as far removed from the world of tribe and tradition as a fifth- or sixth-generation American from his ancestral village in Sicily or Poland. I later realized that there was one thing that my host and the "primitive" villagers of Central Africa had in common, and that was a willingness to share all they had with a stranger. But I never told him that, because what lay behind his friends' anger at *Time*'s reporting was their belief, probably justified, that the white tourists and businessmen who flocked to Kano viewed them as savages in suits.

Kano was a far nicer city the second time around. I remembered the older part of town as a nightmarish warren of mud hovels separated by malodorous mounds of refuse. Now, two years later, the garbage was still there, and the vultures, but it was the houses that caught my attention. They were massive, cubical buildings, with thick walls, ornate doorways, and flat roofs decorated with strange, hornlike projections. The roofs, like the walls, were built of earth and not, as in Central Africa, of waterproof thatch, for this was a parched, sunbaked land, in climate as well as distance as close to Algeria as to Lagos or Douala. The air was dry, the walls of the old city were brown and golden, and the hot desert wind known as the *harmattan* had dusted the streets with the sand of the Sahara. I thought of Agadez, and the drummers, and camels gliding through the night. I remembered the dunes, the endless sea of sand, and the sky, a vast and velvet sweep of white-hot stars. I headed north.

17

NOMADS

I took a van to Katsina, near the Niger border. Katsina, an old and somnolent city, as ancient as Kano and once, like Kano, a center of trade and culture, is now a backwater town on a side road to the Sahara. I spent a few hours wandering through silent streets of those strange and majestic horned houses that I had first seen in Kano. A band of small boys with nothing better to do followed a few steps behind, giggling, gibbering, staring, making faces. That afternoon I got a ride that took me north, across the border, and left me in Maradi, the first large town inside the Republic of Niger. Niger and Nigeria: the two countries' names sound alike, but the former French colony of Niger—landlocked, sparsely populated, and prone to drought and famine—has little in common with its rich southern neighbor except a name and a border. Most of Niger is desert.

I slept in the town's car park and when I woke up I found a bush taxi bound for Tahoua. Tahoua, which would have been considered little more than a village in Nigeria, was one of the largest towns in Niger. It lay about a hundred miles north of the highway that ran along the southern border, connecting Maradi with the capital. The road from Tahoua to Agadez was being paved, and any traffic between the desert and the capital ran through Tahoua. By going there, I hoped to catch a whiff of the desert, a taste of Saharan sand. At that point, I had no plans at all to go farther north.

It was the hottest, driest part of the year. Along the southern highway, there were villages, dusty fields, hints of green, but we left the highway at Birni n' Konni and turned north, and after that there was no green at all, or houses either, just red rock and sun-seared soil. Every so often I saw groups of men, standing in the midst of this arid nothingness or walking across it. They wore coarse black kaftans, stained with sweat and sand, and huge conical hats trimmed with leather. Perhaps they were farmers, and if they were, I didn't envy them. Farming here was like betting with the devil. Year after year, these men would wager their lives that the rains would come on time.

That night, when we arrived, I slept at the taxi park and spent the next day wandering around the jumble of mud and dirt and tin that was Tahoua. In the evening, I went back to the car park. It was late and the lot was deserted, except for two men and a boy, who squatted in a circle as though they were around a campfire in the desert. Their robes glowed in the starlight, and their long swords were silhouetted in black against the shining cloth. I knew at a glance that they had come from the north, and that their robes would, in daylight, be as bright and rich a blue as if they had been woven from bits of sun and sky. They were Tuaregs.

The Tuaregs are the Bedouins of the southern Sahara. They are nomads, fiercely Moslem, proud and warlike. Their society is rigidly hierarchical. There are nobles and vassals, craftsmen and slaves. Except for the slaves and the artisans, most of them are Caucasians, though their skin is blue rather than white, permanently stained by the dye in their robes and in the veils which the men—but not the women—wear. In temperament as well as appearance, they have a lot in common with the Afghans and the Pathans.

I watched the Tuaregs and after a while I joined them. The boy spoke French. The two men, his father and grandfather (who, I surmised, were nobles), had brought him to Tahoua, where he would go to school. Though he tried to hide his feelings, I could see he was sad and nervous. The town was as foreign to him as it was to me; in a few days, he would be sitting in class while his brothers raced camels across the plains. As we spoke, the boy's father and grandfather sat in silence, watching. They did not understand French; in their day, no Tuareg would have set foot inside a schoolhouse—or a town either, if he could help it. But times had changed; the sons of their slaves and vassals had gone to school, and many now held high government positions. The Tuareg had learned that, in Africa today, to be uneducated is to be powerless. And so they compromised, sacrificed one son to the alien ways of the city so the other sons and, they hoped, future generations could remain free in the desert.

The boy and I talked for a few minutes; then he spoke with his father, and then again to me. His father and grandfather were returning home that evening, he told me, and I was invited to join them. "They are rich men," the boy added, "masters of the desert, and they eat meat whenever they like." And into my mind came a picture of a house, a rich man's house, built of cool stone and stucco, large and white and rambling, with verandas and courtyards and gardens. We would arrive in the evening and servants would greet us, set up couches under the stars, and bring us huge platters of roast lamb to eat as we reclined. It was a foolish fantasy, a poor man's dream, born of too many nights spent in parking lots. "Tell your father I will go with him," I said.

There was another reason why I eagerly accepted the invitation. In James Wellard's book *The Great Sahara,* which had inspired many high-school daydreams when I read it years before, the author states that the Tuaregs' style of life and culture, unchanged for a millennium, is doomed and fast disappearing. If I did not act at once, I might never get another chance.

We sat for a while longer. The boy's father let me hold his sword but the grandfather, outraged that an outsider should toy with the symbol of the family's strength, made me give it back. Then the young student hugged his father and left us, and we three walked into the desert.

Or so it seemed. Actually, I later realized, we walked beside the roadbed of the main route to Agadez until we reached a junction. We waited until a truck came, flagged it down, and climbed aboard. The rear end of the truck was closed, so we had to scale the sides, and the grandfather proved more agile than I. It was cold, and I wrapped myself in my blanket. I dozed off.

When I awoke, the road was no longer paved. It was barely a road at all. We had at some point left the main Agadez highway—which in those days was paved only thirty miles beyond Tahoua—and taken a side track which, I saw when I looked at my map, ran due north to the desert town of Tchin Tabaraden.

We stopped for a few hours at a place called Kao. I climbed down from the truck and slept on the sand, next to a thorn bush. Around me, the houses and thatched-roof granaries of the village seemed to float in the moonlight. These ghostly storage bins, full of millet, marked the northern limit of arable land. Beyond Kao, only nomads could survive.

Soon it was dawn, and the rising sun painted the earthen houses a pale and gentle shade of rose. The driver awoke and we drove north. There was nothing in sight but dead grass and sand. We followed the tracks other trucks had made. In the early afternoon, when we were about midway between Kao and Tchin Tabaraden, the truck stopped and my companions got off. To me, every stretch of desert looked the same, but they had recognized their home.

There was a man waiting with two donkeys. We loaded our baggage, including my orange pack, on their backs and the grandfather hoisted himself on top. The father and I walked behind, across sand and crumbly soil. The landscape was gently rolling, like waves fossilized in sand. Here and there were clumps and tussocks of moribund grass, and every so often I saw a stunted thorn bush. Then we mounted the crest of one of the wavelets and I saw their home.

It was at the bottom of a gently sloping bowl and so gradual was the slope of the sides that when one looked out from the bottom one had the illusion of being on a flat and endless plain. But I did not notice this until later; what I saw first was the house. It was ten feet wide, five feet high, and made of grass dried golden by the sun. It looked like a toy haystack—or perhaps a grass-covered igloo—and was home to three generations: the boy's sisters and brothers, his father and mother, and his old grandfather. These people were nomads. In a few weeks, after the rains came, they would abandon these huts and take their camels north, up near the Algerian border, to camp on the plains west of Agadez. What need had they of stone mansions?

Perhaps I would have been disappointed had I first seen the house in the noonday glare, but the sun was going down by the time we reached the encampment. We unloaded the donkeys and the boy's father, whose name, I had learned by then, was Issri, brought me a calabash filled with camel's milk. By then it was twilight, and I sat outside, under the deep blue bowl of sky. I drank the milk. It was so fresh it still retained the warmth of the camel.

Beside me sat the grandfather. Though his face was round and almost fleshy, it always seemed stern, ascetic, and disapproving. Perhaps that was because he did not like me. He was very devout and probably merciless; he obeyed to the letter every tenet of Islam and he expected everyone else to do the same. Alone among the men, he wore robes of somber black, and this heightened the impression of a man whose zealotry set him apart from his fellows. But now, silhouetted against the darkening sky as he gazed toward the illusory infinity of the horizon, the old man reminded me of something far older than Islam, of herdsmen named Abraham, Lot, and Isaac who probably lived and possibly thought very much as he did. I wished I had a Bible, to read the sparse and majestic words of Genesis as the last light left the sky.

The old man knelt and touched his forehead to the ground as he recited his evening prayers. Then the stars came out. The heavens always are closer and brighter and more alive in the desert, and so they were here. At last, I understood the Tuaregs' fierce pride and why the boy had boasted. We were alone, or so it seemed, in the vastness of the Sahara, and even the stars above were ours.

I slept outside that first night, beneath the cold, swirling canopy of stars, but toward morning I felt chilled and crawled indoors. Everyone woke at dawn, and two of the boys ran off to round up the camels which, though hobbled to prevent them from straying, always managed to hop away during the night. Camels and donkeys were the only animals I ever saw near the camp, though the family probably owned goats and sheep, and possibly cattle as well. The herds were grazed elsewhere, watched over by the children or perhaps by slaves I never saw. Though I stayed at the camp for a fortnight, I never tried to find them; the midday sun, white-hot and malevolent, was the strongest I have ever encountered. It cut like a knife and between ten and three I could barely walk a hundred feet without fainting.

The children weren't bothered by the sun. There were two boys and a girl, all between ten and fourteen. The girl was the youngest. They did all the work around camp: chasing camels, herding the unseen sheep and cattle, fetching water from the well. They seemed to think of their life and the chores that filled it as one big, endlessly amusing game. Their energy was boundless and when there was no work to do they rode around on donkeys, chased lizards, tried to spy on me when I crept behind the scraggly bush that served as a toilet.

One afternoon, they loaded leather waterbags onto their donkeys. They were going to the well, which was two miles away. One of the donkeys was riderless, so they called for me to join them. I mounted the donkey and the children rode off but my mount wouldn't budge. I shouted and prodded and still the beast didn't move. There was a placid, mulish look in its eye that angered me. Fuming, I jumped off, intending to shout at the animal, or perhaps clout it. As soon as I hit the ground, the donkey happily galloped off to join its fellows. The children, who by this time were laughing so hard they almost fell off themselves, left me and ran off to the well, and I returned to the camp, where Issri and his father—who, as nobles, never did manual labor—were drinking tea.

They spent the whole day like that, sitting in their house of grass, their legs crossed, making tea over an open fire. Brewing tea was, for them, a ceremony, a form of art and social communion, and a lazily pleasant way to pass the day. They used a sooty old kettle to heat the water, a clean ceramic teapot in which to steep the tea, and a metal box to store the precious sugar. The tea was green, and they drank it very sweet. Issri brewed the tea and carefully poured it into tiny glasses, serving first his father and then me. If there were any guests present, he served them first, and unless they were related to him, he wore his veil, a long blue winding scarf, for a Tuareg man is considered disgraced if he shows his face to a stranger.

Occasionally, when outsiders were present, Issri's wife would hold a corner of her black cape in front of her face as a veil. She smiled at me from behind the cloth to tell me that, though she knew these rules were foolish, she put up with them for the sake of the men, who were silly enough to take them seriously.

On one of these occasions, when the hut was full of blue-robed men who had come to drink Issri's tea, a large hairy spider walked into the center of the gathering. The men, doubtless grinning under their veils, all pointed to me; I should deal with it. I scooped up the spider, whose body seemed as large as a golf ball, and threw it outside, for I didn't want to kill it. The spider came running back like a faithful dog. Again I tossed it out, and again it bounded in. By then, the men were shaking with ill-suppressed laughter. After a few more repetitions, one of them mashed the stubborn spider with the kettle.

Issri's hut was crowded from dawn to dusk, but there was another house of straw that was always empty. A woman lived there, alone. Hers was the only shelter within sight of Issri's, so, though she never visited Issri, I assumed the two were related. But why she lived by herself I never found out. She may have been widowed, or divorced, and, since Tuareg women are allowed not only to leave their mates but also to keep part of the communal property, she was probably, in either case, quite well off. But, despite her wealth, she was always cloaked in sadness. It was loneliness, perhaps, and something more: the sweet, pervasive melancholy of love unrequited.

Among the Tuareg, such lovesickness is not uncommon. They have a long tradition of romance, chivalry, and courtly love. Courts of love, informal tribunals, debate questions of romantic etiquette, and women customarily devote much time and effort to composing love poems. It was easy for me to spin fantasies around her, but I never learned the facts and, since nobody spoke any language other than Tamacheq, there was no one I could ask. The children visited her house quite often. No matter what mischief they had done, no matter how angry at them the other adults were, they knew they could find a refuge there. Her house was crowded with mats and chests and calabashes, and they would sit quietly among them, and so would I. She would give us milk and tell us stories, and once I saw her wash and braid the girl's long black hair.

And so the days passed, filled with children's games and stories and endless cups of tea. Every so often, when the waterbags were empty, the children rode to the well, and on one of those trips I went with them. This time, I took care to stay on my donkey. Long before we reached the well, I could see the billowing cloud of dust raised by the herds of impatient sheep and cows and camels who milled about, waiting to drink. The water was pulled up the hundred-foot shaft in leather buckets attached to a rope. The herdsmen would haul up a bucket and dump it in a trough. It was a long and drawn-out process, tiring for the workers and far too slow to satisfy the thirsty animals.

We sat in the sand beneath a spindly acacia, watching the crowds as we waited our turn. The herdsmen were a varied lot. There were

Tuaregs and Bouzou and Fulani. The Bouzou were blacks, descendants of slaves captured by Tuareg raiders. The Tuareg have always owned slaves but, by 1979, most of the Saharan countries, including Niger (where I now was), had outlawed slavery, so, at least in theory, all the Bouzou were now free. The Fulani, who have always been their own master, and have no respect for anyone who is not, kept apart from the Bouzou; the men had somewhat lighter skin than the Bouzou and wore short leather skirts, raggedy black cloaks, and black headcloths or strange pointed hats trimmed with red leather. They were of the same people who, a hundred fifty years before, had conquered Kano, but since that time most of the Fulani—perhaps four-fifths—had settled down, built houses, and become sedentary. Those at the well were among the few who remained nomads.

When our turn came, we filled our bags and rode away. Soon we were out of earshot of the bleats and bellows of the herds at the well, and the land was wrapped in silence, a vast and awesome stillness like the world waiting for the creation. Perfectly silent, yet filled with throbbing sound—like the sound, perhaps, of one hand clapping. It awed me and it troubled the children, and as soon as we got back to camp they set off to hunt lizards.

A little green chameleon scurried across the sand twenty yards away. The sharp-eyed children spotted it and pelted it with stones. The lizard, wounded, thrashed about and then lay still, gasping. The children, ecstatic, surrounded it, their eyes scanning the ground in search of larger rocks. I chased them away, hoping to save the creature's life. I was angry by then and I pursued them through the camp, around the little houses. All the adults came out to watch me run, but the only one who could understand my rage was the woman who lived alone.

I was hot and sweaty by that time, and I took a cupful of water and went off to wash. The Tuareg, being strict Moslems, washed their hands, face, and feet five times a day, and the boys teased me because each morning I bathed only once. They called me *Kafir*, which meant infidel; this was the only Tamacheq word I understood. One day, I grabbed the nearest boy, rolled up his sleeve, and pointed out the line between the hand cleaned five times daily and the arm never washed at all. They understood, and never mentioned bathing again, but they continued to call me *Kafir*, because they didn't know my name.

And, despite all this, I could sense that the children liked me. They continually ragged and teased one another, and it was a sign of their acceptance that they treated me the same.

By then it was twilight, and the sky was washed with pale pastel, purple and blue. Two camels came over the horizon. Slowly and silently, they moved toward our camp; they seemed to swim through the shimmering air. A blue-robed rider dismounted, ran to Issri, and embraced him. A woman got down from the other camel, and a boy of sixteen, who had walked behind, unloaded a bundle of poles from the camel's back. Within a few minutes, the new arrivals had hammered in the thick wooden poles, covered them with a tent of red leather, fanned a fire to life, and started to brew tea.

I visited the tent quite often in the days that followed. It soon took on the cluttered, lived-in look of a long-established homestead. The man gave me tea and showed me how to write in Tifinagh, the ancient Tuareg script that may be the only alphabet indigenous to Africa. It was a strange, boxy writing, full of squares and corners. His wife was gentle and frail; most of the housework was done by a stout old black woman. She cooked the food and built the fires; she talked and ate with the others; she was almost a member of the family; but she was a slave.

One afternoon, a few days after the newcomers arrived, Issri and I went out walking. We took a route I had not explored before and, a few minutes after leaving our encampment, we came to another, with three straw houses and an oblong courtyard bordered with stones. The place was full of men with incredibly fierce eyes. They gave us tea and then they sat in a circle and glared at me. They kept their veils in place, so all I could see of them was those blazing, hostile eyes. Most of the nineteenth-century Saharan explorers who did not die of disease were murdered by Tuaregs, and I sensed that some of these men would have liked to add me to the score. Then the men, their swords clanking, went to pray in the courtyard, which was a makeshift mosque aligned toward Mecca. I joined them and bowed eastward but I refused to touch my head to the ground, and this angered them even more. Shortly afterward, Issri took me back to our camp.

The next day, Issri told me that he was going to Tchin Tabaraden. By gesture and pantomime, he made me understand that there was a camel race that day in which he was entered. It was strange, I thought, how much can be said without words. The Tuaregs and I rarely even used sign language; by then, we knew each other's thoughts too well to need it. But on this occasion, I thought I had misunderstood, because we did not ride camels into town. We walked to the road and hitchhiked instead. Issri clung tenaciously to Tuareg traditions but gladly accepted the incursions of the modern age when they saved him several hours of hard riding.

If you took a mud-walled oasis town from southern Algeria, stripped away all the greenery and palm trees, added a few tin roofs and brick houses, and sprayed red dust over everything, you would have Tchin Tabaraden. It was not a pretty town, but it was a lively one that morning, because the chief was in town. The Tuareg, too headstrong ever to have formed a single nation, are divided into eight large federations, each headed by a supreme chief. That day, the paramount chief of the Iullemmeden, one of the biggest of these groups, had come to Tchin Tabaraden. I saw him on the outskirts, where the houses met the desert. A tall, proud man, he dressed in rich blue brocade and wore his veil tightly fastened. I didn't dare approach him, but he greeted Issri, whom he seemed to know quite well. I did exchange a few words in French with one of his sons, a darkly handsome prince who reminded me of Rudolph Valentino. His eyes had long lashes and were rimmed with black. There was a French relief worker with him, a blond and stocky man who wore a large gold star of David on his hairy chest. The prince and the Frenchman talked about card games and horse races. To judge from their conversation, the prince had a passion for gambling, though the talk of wagers could equally well have been a standing joke between old friends. The Frenchman had been in and around Tchin Tabaraden for quite a while, drilling wells in the desert north of town.

Issri left me with him, and not long afterward a procession of camels marched toward us. The race was about to begin. There were about thirty camels, and when they lined up at the starting line I saw that Issri was one of the riders. The chief gave a signal and they galloped off into the desert. In less than a minute, they were out of sight. According to the Frenchman, the course was about ten miles. We waited, scanning the horizon, for the starting point was also the finish line. Far sooner than I expected, the camels came into view. It was a furious finish, with frenzied riders whipping their straining mounts, and I saw with pride that Issri came in second.

After the race, Issri wanted to go home. He found a truck leaving for Tahoua that would pass near his camp. But I had taken my pack with me that morning, unsure why we were going to the city, not knowing if I would or could return to Issri's encampment. I had left the knapsack with an Arab merchant who had closed up shop and gone to see the races. Now my pack was safely locked away but I could not get it. There was a shop next door, a mud-plastered room the size of a closet with trade goods stacked on wall shelves and sacks of dried fruit and millet heaped on the floor. In the midst of this clutter squatted the storekeeper. Using him as interpreter, Issri told me that he had to leave that evening and I could follow the next morning. I could take any truck bound for Tahoua; I should tell the driver to stop at the well. It was easy, Issri said.

I spent the night at the house of a young, French-speaking Tuareg. He, his wife, and I sat outside, in the cool night air of the courtyard, and talked of courts of love. Early the next morning, I picked up my bag and found a southbound truck which, a few hours later, dropped me off at the well. Easy. I set off across the sand in a vague, northwesterly direction, which I was sure would take me to Issri's camp. But it didn't. After an hour, I came to a long valley I had never seen and I realized I was lost.

At first, I barely noticed, for the valley was a fascinating place to be lost in. In the dry time before the rains, the Tuareg and other nomads who, for much of the year, graze their flocks far to the north drive their herds south, into territory shared by other peoples, less wide-ranging, who also use these lands as a winter pasture. The area in which I was now wandering was near one of the few waterholes that flowed all year round and so it was quite crowded, dotted with Tuareg, Bouzou, and Fulani who normally lived hundreds of miles apart. Of course, crowded is a relative term in the Sahara, but this little valley, which had some scant tussocks of grass and a shallow well with a few drops of water remaining, was full of herdsmen, mostly Bouzou, and their flocks. One of them, an old man, and from his clothes quite a poor one, came to me with a bowl of milk. I drank. I had no idea when or where I would eat again.

After a time, I saw a man in a cone-shaped hat climbing a steep hill on the other side of the valley. He probably knows where he is going, I thought, and so I followed him. On the other side of the hill was empty land, with not a living thing in sight. The man slowly plodded across the waste, and I trailed behind him; I had no choice. Late in the afternoon we came to a grassy plain that appeared to be a dried-up lake or marsh. There was a Tuareg camp beside it. I went to the closest hut, and found two men inside, one old, the other young, apparently father and son. They welcomed me, fed me, and let me stay the night. They had no idea why I was adrift in the desert and, unless they have since spoken to Issri, it is probably still a mystery to them. All they knew was that I was lost and in need of shelter, and that was enough. The son managed to shock me, though. When darkness fell and the stars came out, he brought a suitcase-sized tape player out of the little grass hut and shattered the still of the night with wailing music.

The next day I tried a new direction, and again crossed a fairly flat landscape of brown grass and red sand. Once or twice I saw a herds-man, wandering aimlessly across the plain. I wandered after them. One direction was as good as another. The sun rose, reached its blazing zenith, and seemed to stay there. It was a hot day, and even the sky was too bright to look at. In the early afternoon, I came to an encampment.

I had seen many camps by then, but this one seemed different, and slightly alien. There was one grass house, but it was far smaller than the usual, and very crudely built. Outside was a flimsy platform, evidently for storage, piled with reed mats and calabashes. The camp was surrounded by a low fence made from thorny branches. It must be a Fulani camp, I thought, and when I glanced at the hut I knew my hunch was right. A woman sat inside, framed by the huge door-way, calmly looking out. She had light brown skin and fine, narrow features. Around her waist was wrapped a strip of coarse black cloth. She wore no other clothing, but her proud, thin face was framed by fourteen shiny earrings, each one a brass hoop several inches in diam-eter. Her ears were each pierced in seven places to hold them. When she moved, they rustled softly, like Chinese wind chimes.

I sat outside and waited. The woman came out and began to pound the grain for the evening meal. She used a wooden mortar and a pestle as tall as she was. It was a timeless scene; it reminded me of the Dinka village I wanted to stay at but never did. I decided to spend the night, if they would let me.

Then the men came back to camp. There were two of them, both quite big and even taller than I, and they were not pleased to see me.

They let me sit a while but made it plain that I could not stay for long, and that they would, if necessary, throw me over the wall. The Fulani, like all African peoples, have a strict code of hospitality, decency, and etiquette, and indeed the Niger Fulani call themselves the Wodaabe, the people of the taboo, a name that some say refers to their code of social conduct. Perhaps I had somehow offended this code, or perhaps the Wodaabe, like everyone else, occasionally fall far short of their own standards. The thought of a big white stranger gobbling up their porridge was too much for them to bear. But I did not want to sleep outside the palisade; if they had taken the trouble to build a fence of brambles, there must be something unpleasant that lurked outside it. So I offered to buy my food and lodging. I gave the men a thousand francs and, grudgingly, they allowed me to stay.

When I left their camp the next morning, one of the men pointed across the sand. I walked in that direction, and after a few hours I saw tire tracks, and then the well, and then Issri, who was on his way to the waterhole. Strangely, I was happier to see him than to find the road. Issri rarely, if ever, visited the well; perhaps he had gone to look for me. We walked back to his camp and when we got near the little grass houses, the children rushed out and ran around us, screaming, shouting, shoving one another aside in their excitement.

I stayed a few more days at the encampment, and then it was time to leave. I gave Issri as much money as I could spare, to pay for my keep, and then I handed out little presents from my pack; to the woman who lived alone, I gave my sewing kit, which I had carried from New York, but which she could use far more deftly than I. I wanted to leave a part of myself with these people, and this was the best I could do. In the afternoon, Issri walked with me to the double line of tire tracks that marked the road. For part of the way, the children ran behind us. Issri left me at the roadside and walked away, across the rolling plain. Soon, he had gone beyond the horizon and I was alone. A truck came by an hour later, but it was full and didn't stop. Night fell, and I waited, immersed in that throbbing desert silence that seems to whisper like the wind. Obviously, Issri had known a truck would come—there was one each day—but he had never expected it to pass me by. I might be there all night. I sat and waited and watched the road and as I watched, a light came over the horizon. Slowly, the light grew brighter, lighting up the sky like fire on the plain, and still the silence was unbroken. After a time, I could see the twin beams of headlights far away and as the truck drew nearer I heard the hum of its engine. I had learned by then to tell the size of a truck by the sound its motor made, and the deep throaty roar betokened a full-size freight truck. There would be room. I stood in the road. The driver, astonished to see a white man rise up from the sand, slammed on the brakes. I got on. The back of the truck was nearly empty, so I stretched out. I was soon asleep, and as I slept the truck drove south, toward the desert's edge and the towns and trees that lay beyond.

✕◈✕

There were trees in Niamey, the capital of Niger. Niamey was over four hundred miles southwest of Issri's camp, and it took twenty-four hours of hard driving to get there. The truck dropped me off on the outskirts, near the large market, a quiet and not unattractive neighborhood of dirt-walled houses and dusty roads. The night air was cool and refreshing, and most of the populace slept outside. Lying on straw mats and swaddled in sheets, the sleepers filled the sidewalks. I fell asleep beside them, and the next day I booked a place on a van bound for Ouagadougou, the capital of Burkina Faso or, as it was then known, Upper Volta.

Just beyond Niamey is the Niger River, wide and lazy, spanned by the graceful arc of the Kennedy Bridge. On the other side of the bridge is a police post. The guards stopped the van and took me off it; foreigners needed an exit permit to leave the city. So I ran a mile to the cavernous and eerily silent building on Avenue de Gaulle that housed the Sureté, and then back to the van, because I had forgotten to take my photograph along, and then back to de Gaulle Avenue, where I filled in a form, fastened the photo on top, and in return got a new set of stamps, which filled a space in the front of the passport which is supposed to be left blank. And all this time the van waited for me on the bridge, the passengers unconcerned about the long delay, and I realized that the Africans' easygoing attitude toward time sprang from selflessness and not from self-indulgence.

It was an all-day, all-night drive, twenty-four hours riding on roads that made the van rattle like a jackhammer. And then there were the roadblocks, far too many, where identity cards were checked and re-checked. At one point in Upper Volta, we passengers stood in line, passports ready, as the policeman swaggered down the line like a general reviewing a parade. Many African governments cannot feed their people, but they all know how to control them.

It was dark by the time we reached Ouagadougou, dark even before we came to the murky and shadow-filled Bois de Boulogne, the vast park on the edge of town where most of the capital's trees can be found. The town, like the park, was ill-lit and silent. The car dropped me at the market, and I walked south, along Avenue Yennenga, past the unpainted concrete minaret of a large mosque, past blocks of little houses and shops shut up for the night. The buildings were low and flat-roofed and in the dim, uncertain light cast by the street-lamps, they could easily be taken for the mud-walled houses of a village.

At the Restaurant Rialle, they let me sleep in the courtyard for four hundred francs a night, about two dollars. I passed through Ouagadougou several times in the months that followed, and each time the owner tried to raise the price. He enjoyed bargaining with me and, besides, he thought all white men were rich. And, from his perspective, he was correct. Semidesert, overcrowded, and disease-ridden, Upper Volta is one of the poorest countries on earth. Its people live, on average, thirty-three years. Per capita income hovered around one hundred dollars per year, and I, with five hundred dollars in my pocket, was a rich man.

Knowing those statistics, I expected to find a grim town. And, also knowing that Ouagadougou, like Kano, is one of Africa's oldest cities, capital of a nation four centuries older than mine, I would not have been surprised to find another Kano, sprawling and chaotic. But, instead of that, I found myself in another Isiro or Yaloké—a bustling, good-natured, lazy market town with a few modern office buildings and hotels tacked on at the northern end, far from the real center of town, which was the enormous plaza that held the open-air market. It was several blocks wide, that plaza, and every bit of it so crowded you had to squeeze your way through, past stalls which sold used books and magazines, imported cigarettes by the stick, preworn American clothing—mostly old workshirts with logos like AL'S GA-RAGE—knives and brushes and nail clippers, antiques both new and old, spices, patent medicines, and Ghanaian money at discount rates.

Just south of the market was a cart park. Young men rented push-carts for one hundred francs a day and hauled freight for a few francs a load; on a good day they broke even. South of that was the mosque, an anomaly perhaps, since Upper Volta is the only country in the region to have resisted the spread of Islam. Well over half the population follow their traditional tribal beliefs. In the west, near the town of Bobo-Dioulasso, the people sculpt masks—stark, impressive, some as high as a man, and painted with geometric designs—to use in religious ceremonies. After Ouagadougou, I decided, I would visit those people, who were called the Bobos. The head office of one of the banks was decorated with a billboard-size map showing where each of Upper Volta's 160 tribes lived. I dropped by the bank every day—planning, dreaming, studying that fantastically complex map, trying to learn it by heart. But it was another week before I left the capital. I had applied for a Ghanaian visa, and the clerk at the embassy (a small house across from the head office of Upper Volta's National Lottery) told me to come back in a week, it might be ready by then. Ghanaian embassies in other capitals provided same-day service, but they required tourists to change thirty dollars per day into worthless Ghanaian money. A two-week visa would cost four hundred twenty dollars.

Far better, I thought, to wait in Ouagadougou, where I could fritter away the days browsing in the market and the nights at the cinema. It cost twenty cents to get in, and the theater was always packed. One night, I saw *Grease,* and the next evening *Baara,* an African film made in Mali, about a young man from the village who sets off, hopeful and excited, for the capital (which looked a lot like Ouagadougou), and ends up carrying bags for rich ladies at the market. "I knew it would be hard," he says, "but I did not think it would be this hard."

Near the cinema was an outdoor beer garden, and one night I nursed a bottle of ice-cold beer as I watched the sprawling canopy of stars. One of the stars started to move, and then another, zipping across the sky, stopping, and, after a few seconds' pause, resuming their dizzy flight. The beer was weak, and no airplane could move like that. I wondered if spacemen ever came to Ouagadougou and, if they did, what they thought of life on earth.

Markets and movies and bars. That was my week in Ouagadougou. In the morning, when the sun hit the courtyard and I awoke, I would tote a pail of water into the privy for my daily shower and, ablutions completed, would breakfast at a sidewalk stall. You can find these makeshift cafés in every West African city. They have wooden benches on either side of a long table thrown together from planks and sawhorses and covered with a bright and gaudy plastic tablecloth. In Ouagadougou, as in most French-speaking towns, the tables were heaped with long loaves of freshly baked French bread, miniature mountains of sweet butter flown in from France, and big jars of Nescafé. One morning, I had a piece of crust left over, and I threw it into the gutter. A man about my age, who was walking by, dived after the bread and bolted it down. I left Ouagadougou soon after that.

Once again I studied the huge ethnic map and picked out a village in Bobo territory. The name of the village was Nanou. To get there, I took a bush taxi to a place called Ouahabou, a hundred miles west of Ouagadougou. Ouahabou was little more than a cluster of earthen houses built around a mud-walled mosque. The mosque was stark and simple in design, chalky gray like the soil from which it seemed to spring. Its mud minarets were devoid of ornament; the French troops who annexed Upper Volta in the 1890s probably thought it primitive, while their grandchildren might well consider it daringly modern.

Nanou was seven miles northwest of Ouahabou. A farmer pointed out the way, and I followed a well-worn path across soil that crumbled like sand. Ouahabou, on the same latitude as Kano and four degrees south of Tchin-Tabaraden, was midway between the desert and the forests of the coast, and beyond the fields that surrounded the village the plain was dotted with trees. Most were of the prickly variety, with more thorns than greenery, though a few had thick trunks and leafy branches. But the summer rains were short, not enough to support a full-fledged forest, so the trees were widely spaced, with one every five or ten yards; it looked like carefully planned parkland.

In the late afternoon, about the time when I began to worry that I had taken the wrong path, I arrived in Nanou. The village was built on a gentle hummock, and first sight of it made me think of a sand castle perched on a hill. When I got closer, I saw that Nanou was not one but many castles, a labyrinth of castles jumbled together, their earthen ramparts separated by narrow alleyways. I went through a doorway and into one of the castles. Inside was a large courtyard, surrounded by a mud-brick wall ten feet high. Around the periphery were little cubical sheds and houses that leaned against the outer wall. Smoke came from one, which was obviously the kitchen. The other

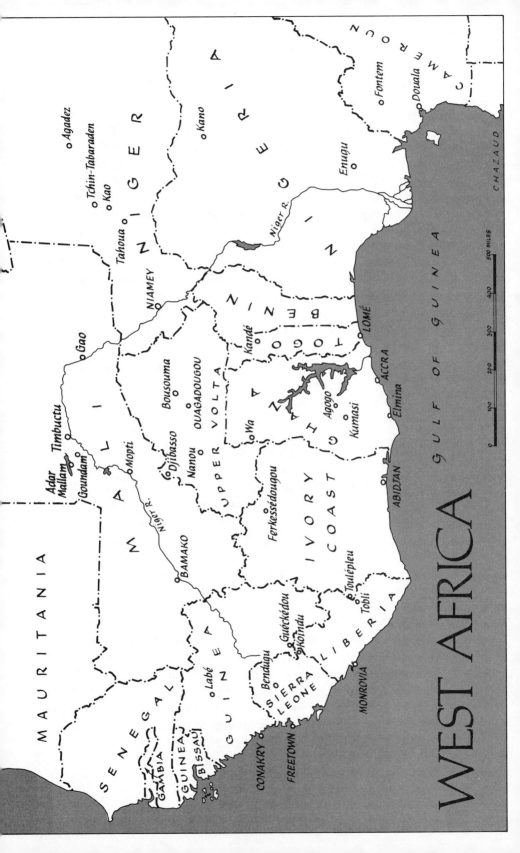

WEST AFRICA

MAURITANIA

SENEGAL

GAMBIA

GUINEA-BISSAU

GUINEA

SIERRA
LEONE

LIBERIA

MALI

IVORY COAST

UPPER VOLTA

GHANA

TOGO

BENIN

NIGER

NIGERIA

CAMEROUN

GULF OF GUINEA

CHAZAUD

Agadez
Tchin-Tabaraden
Kao
Tahoua
NIAMEY
Gao
Timbuctu
Adar
Mallam
Goundam
Mopti
Djibasso
Nanou
Bousouma
OUAGADOUGOU
Wa
Kandé
Agogo
Kumasi
Elmina
ACCRA
LOMÉ
ABIDJAN
Ferkessédougou
BAMAKO
Labé
CONAKRY
FREETOWN
Bendugu
Guéckédou
Koindu
Toblí
Toulépleu
MONROVIA
Kano
Enugu
Fontem
Douala

Niger R.

Niger R.

0   100   200   300   400   500 MILES

buildings, I surmised, were probably bedrooms and storerooms. Near the kitchen, a woman pounded grain in a big mortar; a man sat half asleep in the shade; chickens and children scampered about. The activity in the courtyard was a scene familiar to me: the somnolent bustle of village life. The wall, the barrier each family in Nanou erected between it and the others, was not. Most Africans would consider such a barricade distinctly antisocial; it is only in America that good fences make good neighbors.

Though I had invaded their fortress uninvited, the people made me welcome. Speaking in French, I asked them to take me to the chief of the village, for it is the headman's responsibility to provide lodging to strangers, but the man in the courtyard, who was the head of the family, insisted that I stay with him. He gave one of the children some money, and the boy ran off and returned with two bottles of beer. A woman carried out a chair for me, and I and the man sat and drank. The man downed his drink with gusto, to encourage me, to make me believe that he drank bottled beer all the time, which he probably didn't, since the cost of those bottles was a day's wage in Ouagadougou. When the beer ran out, my host took me to meet the chief. He was a tall man who wore a long white gown, a skullcap, and big sunglasses. He received me on the roof of his two-story mud house. In this village, he told me, there are Moslems and there are Christians. "Your host, who is a good man, is a Christian, and I am a Moslem," he said as he poured lemonade into a glass; his religion evidently forbade him to serve his guests beer. He explained that, while the Moslems believed in one God, the Christians had many gods and danced with masks. I realized later that they were, in fact, not Christians at all, but animists, followers of traditional beliefs. The chief had referred to them as Christians in the hope of pleasing me and perhaps impressing me with his village's progressive outlook. To him, all white men were missionaries. And when I asked him to let me see the masks, he refused. My host later told me that many masks had been stolen from neighboring villages for sale to American and European collectors. It would never occur to the chief that a Westerner would find beauty in their primitive artwork, but white men had been known to steal. Still, the chief gave me permission to stay in Nanou, as the guest of the man who had brought me to him. Then he took his leave of us and, the audience ended, my host led me back to his compound.

A part of the yard had been screened off and a chair and table had been set up behind the screens. While I had been with the chief, the women had killed one of their chickens, stewed it in a red, hot sauce, and put it on the table to await my return. The whole chicken was mine, to devour in privacy. The screens would prevent me from being distracted by the staring, hungry children, who ate meat perhaps once a year. The chicken was delicious and I could easily have eaten it all, but I gave most of the meat to the children, who ate it very slowly, in order to prolong their pleasure. After dinner, I asked my host if the people of Nanou were Bobos. No, he replied, they were Ko, an ethnic group I had never heard of before. And, with typical African politeness, he added "But we are very much like the Bobos." Much later, I learned that the Ko were a part of the Gourounsi people, a completely different tribe from the Bobos. But my host perceived that I expected him to be a Bobo, and he didn't want to disappoint me.

During that day and those that followed, the neighbors came calling, each suddenly needing, or so they said, to borrow a cup of beer or millet, though everyone knew the real reason for their visit was to catch a glimpse of me. Like many African peoples, the Ko exchange long and intricate greetings when they meet, so the first few minutes of each visit were taken up by the ritual of salutation and response: *Ko? Ko. Ma? Ma.* I didn't know the language, so all the greetings sounded the same to me, although in some tribes what is said varies with the time of day and is often quite poetic, praising the freshness of the morning or the fire of the noonday sun. My host's five-year-old daughter, whose name, to my ears, sounded like Natalie, listened to these greetings with rapt attention and, when she was alone, would practice them. *Ko? Ko. Ma? Ma.* She would take both parts, using different voices for host and visitor. I thought she was parodying the elders and I laughed, and was surprised when she ran away and sulked. But for her, the greeting ceremony was not a game; she was learning how to be an adult. She had already learned quite a lot. She was, at the age of five, a little flirt, who would alternately sulk and simper to get her way.

Like Natalie, the boys spent their days studying the complex rules of adulthood. They, or some obliging adult, had carved crude little masks of wood, and gangs of boys would put on the masks and practice the ritual dance. All the boys enjoyed these practice sessions, which gave them an excuse to run through the village and terrify the younger children. The adults themselves, with nothing left to practice, passed the time playing Parcheesi or drinking beer. My host was expert in the board game and his brother excelled in drinking the home-made millet brew. I slept in the brother's room, on a bamboo platform covered by a blanket, and one evening he took the place over for an all-night drinking party, which was attended by several loud men and giggling ladies. Toward midnight, they moved the party outside to let me sleep.

One morning, a week after I arrived in Nanou, the masks came out from hiding. For the Ko, their masks are magic and embody the spirits that guide the village. They are kept in secret storehouses and are displayed only on the rarest of occasions: during a festival that takes place once every three years and after the death of a chief or other person of distinction. And, the day before, one of the village elders had died.

Nanou was crowded that morning. People had come from other villages, some quite far away, to see the masks. I first caught sight of them as they paraded through the streets of the village. The masks were made of wood, and painted in red and white and black. They perched on top of the dancers' heads, and each had a long train of raffia fiber that completely covered the man who wore it. Hidden by the raffia, the dancers looked like hairy snowballs. But the effect was more frightening than comical. Groups of giggling children followed the dancers, but if the masks turned in their direction, the children scattered and ran—and so did the adults.

I could see at once that the masks were works of art and, like all great religious art, they made the invisible visible; they gave the immaterial terrifying form. Some were in the shape of fantastic animals: antelopes, perhaps, or wolves with gaping jaws or maybe birds of prey—I could not say for certain, for the sculptor had distorted their faces beyond recognition. Some were like no creature ever seen by man: flat boards with black holes for eyes and covered with strange and sinister designs. They were as perplexing and enigmatic as nature itself must seem to a people whose life depends on the vagaries of the summer rains; they represented dark, mysterious forces that were beyond good and evil and beyond the ken of man.

Outside the village was a patch of open ground. The masks would dance there. A canopy had been set up, with chairs for the chief, a few distinguished visitors, and for me, the only foreigner present. Everyone else stood. Next to me, though standing, was a man of about my age. He had come from the nearest town, where he worked for the railroads. Were the dancers spirits, I asked him, or people? There are people under the masks, he replied, men from the village. After all, the masks are only bits of wood. But sometimes spirits from the bush come in disguise to join the dance. So a wise man keeps his distance from the dancers; you can never tell if the thing you see dancing is your neighbor or a demon.

And then, one by one, the dancers pranced into the square, and leapt and bounded and worked themselves into a frenzy. They were in a state of trance by then—otherwise, the heat would have overcome them—and those of them who were not bush spirits probably thought they were. Finally, the biggest, most terrifying mask of all ran in, jumping and gyrating and waving its arms. A woman from the village followed the masks onto the field. She was quite old and obviously very drunk. Keeping behind the mask so it could not see her, and cackling with glee, she parodied every movement the dancer made.

I left Nanou a few days later. It was the middle of May and the fields around Ouahabou were deserted but in a few weeks, the spirits willing, the rains would come and planting would begin. So would the season of hard work, which would last until harvest. I walked to the main road, which passed just south of Ouahabou, and hitched a ride to Pa, from where a side road ran south to Ghana. Pa was a crossroads and nothing more, not even a village, but enterprising farmers from nearby settlements had set up outdoor benches and tables and turned the barren junction into a truck stop where drivers could buy a bowl of stew or a bottle of beer. The tables were crowded with loud, happy drivers, all of whom were heading to Ouagadougou. There was another, far more popular border crossing a hundred miles east which was reachable by paved road from the capital; no one, it seemed, used the bumpy dirt track from Pa. Night fell as I waited, and kerosene lamps were lit at each of the many tables, which were still crowded with drivers. I spread my blanket between the tables and stretched out, watching the flickering lamplight ripple on the drivers' faces and dissolve in the surrounding darkness.

18

GHANA: 1979

Early the next morning, I got a ride as far as the border. It took several hours to cover the eighty miles, including a lunch stop at the tin-roof town of Dano. At the border post at Ouessa, the officers wore snappy khaki uniforms and tried to swagger like Parisian gendarmes; on the Ghana side, at a town called Hamale, the policemen had old-fashioned navy-blue tunics that made them look like small-town English constables. The jackets were quite worn but carefully pressed, and the heavy silver buttons shone. I took a crowded van to the town of Wa where women in bright print dresses pounded grain outside mud-walled houses with tin roofs. They used six-foot-long pestles and three, four, or even five women would use the same big mortar. They synchronized their pounding to sound like drumbeats; *slap slap SLAP slap slap,* they never missed a beat, and once in a while one of the women would show off by tossing the pestle in the air, clapping her hands, catching the stick, and pounding it in the mortar, and all without breaking the rhythm.

I had heard that there was a palace in Wa, once the residence of the local chief, and the next morning I tried to find it. Near the edge of town, I saw a mud-walled and whitewashed structure with large saw-toothed buttresses. It housed municipal offices. I convinced myself that that was the palace, walked back into town, and took a "mammy wagon" south to Kumasi.

It was a long drive, well over three hundred miles, and as the day wore on the air grew moist and the landscape greener until, late in the afternoon, we crossed the Black Volta River and entered the forest zone. In densely populated southern Ghana, woodland gave way long ago to farmland, and the densest jungle was scruffy compared to any roadside in Zaire. But the vegetation seemed wanton and luxuriant to me after the dry Sahara, and when I first sighted the green, and breathed in its strangely seductive scent, I felt as refreshed as if I'd glimpsed the deep blue ocean after many years spent inland.

The sun was setting when we finally reached the vast bowl, ringed by hills, that was Kumasi. The city, Ghana's second largest, filled the valley and spilled over onto the hillsides. The first hill we came to was covered with Victorian Gothic buildings, complete with red stone façades and lancet arches, which would have been at home on, say, Banbury Road in northern Oxford but seemed out of place in tropical Africa. On a hill across the valley I saw the twin steeples of what must have been a huge church, and everywhere I looked were architectural remnants, Gothic fossils of the fifty-year English occupation. But of the city that covered these hills before the British arrived, there was nothing left at all. And yet, the first Europeans to visit Kumasi, in 1817, found a sprawling city of forty thousand people, with clean streets, tidy houses, and thriving markets. The city was a center of commerce and trade, and had been since 1700, when the people of the area, who had been divided into several tiny chiefdoms, united to form the Ashanti kingdom, which soon became the dominant power in the region. As often happens in Africa, the sacred is intertwined with the profane: the king who ruled from Kumasi derived his wealth and power from his share of the trade in ivory, kola nuts, and, above all, gold, but his subjects obeyed him because they believed that he was the representative of their ancestors' spirits and, as such, a demigod who ruled by divine right. This assertion of God-given authority strengthened the king's power but, at the same time, limited it. Although a large and efficient civil service evolved which enabled the king to supervise and control his sizable empire, any king who acted despotically or without consulting the council of elders would be deemed to have abused the trust of the ancestors and would be dethroned. Unfortunately, the last two kings to be turned out of office in this fashion lost their thrones because they advocated compromise with the British, who had emerged as the main trading power on the coast. The British were outraged by the Ashanti practice of slavery and human sacrifice and, perhaps even more, by the Ashantis' desire to control the profitable coastal trade. Rivalry led to armed conflict; the British occupied Kumasi three times and finally, in 1902, annexed it. They razed the king's palace with its forty-foot-high reception halls and the old mud-brick city and built in its place churches and law courts and jails.

I liked Kumasi. I liked the English buildings. Old, worn, and eccentrically carved, they survived, like sturdy, weatherbeaten immigrants who maintain old traditions in a strange land. I liked the wide swathe of green—rank, untamed vegetation—that grew around the old railway line that cut the town in half. I liked the way people walked as if moving to a reggae beat. Reggae was the rage in Kumasi, and often, as I walked along the streets, I heard it coming from unseen radios. It mixed well with the blue skies and the unbroken stream of sunshine that poured down on the city every day of the year. I liked the market best of all. It covered most of the flat land that formed the city center, and it was the biggest market I had ever seen. Most small-town bazaars have one or maybe two tin-roofed halls but Kumasi had row after row of big shiny shelters, and all the space in them and between was filled by traders—ten thousand of them—sitting shoulder to shoulder in front of heaps of bananas, cassavas, and yams, or smaller, neatly arranged piles of tomatoes, peppers, or eggs. All of the sellers were women. They wore bright and gaudy dresses of printed cloth with kerchiefs to match; in Ghana, the market women are a small but powerful clique of entrepreneurs who, it is widely rumored, pay the farmers far too little and charge consumers way too much. Still, the Kumasi market was always crowded, so packed with customers that if any newcomers had tried to enter they would have had to stack themselves into piles like the plantains or the yams. Kumasi's shops, by contrast, were somnolent, half empty, their shelves nearly bare. The market was the only part of Ghana's economy that worked at all.

If a nation's economy can be compared to a building, then Ghana's reminded me of some bombed-out fields of rubble I once saw in East

Berlin. It was as bad as any in Africa, and I never understood why. Ghana is rich in land and natural resources, and human resources as well; after all, the Ashanti kingdom lived by trade. It is true that Kwame Nkrumah, the energetic idealist who led Ghana to independence, turned into a despot who jailed his opponents and spent billions of dollars on such prestige projects as a fifteen-million-dollar conference hall, a twenty-mile, nine-million-dollar superhighway to a seventeen-million-dollar harbor, one of the continent's largest airlines and its most powerful radio transmitter (which used to come in loud and clear and incomprehensible in New York). Nkrumah also dipped into the country's coffers to erect a huge statue of himself which was torn down when he was overthrown in 1966. But many African leaders behave like that. It is true that the succession of army and civilian governments that followed did their best to bleed the country dry, but the one who stole perhaps the most, General Acheampong, was rumored to have embezzled and sent overseas only one hundred million dollars, while in other countries, such as Zaire, the leader's personal fortune is thirty times that. Most Ghanaians blamed the mess they were in on rampant, almost universal corruption. Market women, taxi drivers, and everyone else ignored government price controls; much of the cocoa crop was smuggled out of the country and, when the government sold what remained to European producers, half of the dollars received simply vanished. In the hospitals, patients died because the medication that would have saved them had been stolen for sale on the black market.

But whatever the cause of Ghana's ills, the symptoms were apparent. Prices were high and doubled every year. To find such luxuries as soap and toothpaste, you had to go to Togo. On the thriving black market, dollars bought four times as much Ghanaian money as in the bank. A schoolteacher earned a dollar a day, a laborer half that, which is enough to buy a bunch of bananas at the market. How did people survive, I wondered. The lucky ones had relatives in the countryside. In other, more prosperous African countries, the city folk are all but bankrupted by an endless procession of poor and distant relations from their village, by third cousins of uncles twice removed whom they had never laid eyes on before they started to draw a salary; but obligations run both ways and, in Ghana, the villagers sent their crops to their city relations.

And the workers with no rural connections? One evening, I got to talking with a distinguished-looking man dressed in white shirt and starched collar. He was selling oranges outside a movie theater. During the day, he told me in fluent English, he worked as a civil servant. His salary was too low for his family to live on, and this was the only way he could find to augment it. But there were a hundred vendors outside the theater that night, most more aggressive than he, so, though he might have made a few cents profit, he more likely lost what he paid for the fruit.

"Cheerio," the civil servant called after me as I left. He seemed very British then, like the churches and the old red-brick buildings. But the longer I stayed in Ghana, the less English it seemed. The civility and politeness of the people, which I at first assumed had come from the British, were instead the legacy of a far older tradition which fifty years of British rule had not destroyed or even changed but only briefly interrupted. One day I sought directions from a worker who was busily digging up the street. "Excuse me, can you tell me the way to Black Star Square?" I asked, and the man was offended. He expected me to go through the long Ashanti ritual of greeting, to ask about his health, his crops, his family. He assumed that I, a civilized man, would greet my fellow whites in the proper way but had addressed him discourteously because he was black— and he told me so. I explained that our customs were different, amazed that no one had noticed that during the five hundred years since the first European sailors landed on the shores of the land they called the Gold Coast. Those early slavers, I surmised, didn't say please.

The ditchdigger spoke good English and had probably been to school, but, as I discovered in a Kumasi bookstore, even the textbooks taught Ashanti etiquette. The reader was reminded to eat with the right hand only, never to offer a gift with the left hand and— most important of all—always to show respect for parents, chiefs, and elders. The Ashanti chiefs and subchiefs still retained much influence and power and some, more attuned to the *zeitgeist* than the rest, had become millionaires. The fetish priests were also quite important, and their doings were regularly reported in the Accra papers. Many Ghanaians, even today, heed the wishes of their gods and ancestors. The spirits' commands, as reported by the priests, quite often coincide with the priests' own interests.

Besides the book of Ashanti manners, the shop stocked Ashanti folk tales and a book of more modern stories that pitted a wily fetish priest against a group of bumbling, greedy businessmen from Britain. There were also a number of sociological studies of Akan villages. A note at the end of one of these monographs said that the field research was done in Agogo. I had planned to travel straight to Accra, but I saw from my map that Agogo was only twenty miles off the main Kumasi-Accra highway, so I made up my mind to go to Agogo instead.

Agogo proved to be more of a village than a town. Most of its people lived by farming and not by trade; they grew the food they needed in the fields that lay just beyond their houses. I reached Agogo a few hours after leaving Kumasi, and an hour later I had walked through it and into the fields. I followed a dirt track until I got tired, and then sat down to rest. In a nearby field, a farmer was planting yams. He built a little mound of earth around each tuber, carefully patting the soil into shape with his hands; the plow was unknown here. When he saw me watching, the farmer invited me to take a turn, and I did, scooping up earth to build a tiny hillock that immediately fell apart. This pleased the farmer no end; since I was white, I was obviously a man of wealth and education but in that one thing he was more skilled than I. He decided it was time for refreshment, and his wife brought us a gourd of palm wine. He gave me some and drank the rest, but before he did he splashed a few drops on the ground, a libation for the spirits who, just like people, build up a powerful thirst on a hot summer's day.

The farmer lived in Agogo, but had built a little hut of wattle and daub beside his fields. He and his family slept there during the planting season, which was just beginning, and during the months that followed, when the crops needed to be guarded against crows and other hungry birds and beasts. I spent the night with him and his wife, and the next morning he walked with me to the nearest village and took me to the house of the chief.

It was a large compound of mud-walled houses. Like those in Zaire, they had peaked roofs made of thatch and were built around a courtyard. In the court, a group of old men sat on low stools arranged in a circle. This was the village's council of elders, who had met to discuss the death of one of the men of the village. A funeral had to be arranged, and the man's land disposed of. The Ashanti, like most African peoples, do not believe that a person can *own* land. The

land is there for the benefit of all—the living, the dead, and those yet
to be born—and cannot be parceled up or traded away. Instead, the
chief or the village council assigns each family a plot ample enough to
support it and, when a man dies, the land he tilled reverts to the village. By and large, Africa is not divided, the way many Asian countries are, into landlords and landless—except in places (Kenya, for
example) where colonial governments introduced the concept of
freehold tenure. In the traditional African village, a state of rough
equality prevails; there are no serfs, no sharecroppers, no vast yawning gulf between rich and poor. I have heard people say that Africans
are capitalists by nature, and perhaps at a national level free enterprise has proved the most successful economic policy, but in the village they are socialists by nature as well.

When I walked in on them, the council was lazily debating the
important issue of who should get the land. Cups of palm wine passed
from hand to hand, and the ground was liberally sprinkled with liba-
tions poured for the dead man and any other ghosts that might happen to be present. After a while, the meeting broke up and the
headman took charge of me. He was old, short, and wizened, but still
spry and wiry. He was dressed, as befits a chief, in the traditional
Ashanti robes, which are worn over one shoulder like a toga. Many
people, in Agogo and even in Kumasi, wore the Ashanti toga, but the
headman had a strip of *kente* cloth sewn into his. *Kente* is a cotton
cloth patterned with geometric designs of such intricacy that it is
hard to believe the fabric is woven entirely by hand.

The chief poured me a drink and we talked for a while, and then
he took me on a tour of the fields. From a small leafy tree he pulled a
fruit the size of a small papaya. He split it in half, pulled out a seed,
and told me to taste it. It tasted like chocolate, and it was. The seeds
from the fruit that I saw on the cocoa tree would be chopped,
roasted, mixed with fat, sugar, and milk, and wrapped in shiny foil
and would end up, perhaps, in Des Moines or Chicago, sold to children who thought they grew that way, wrapped in tinsel like the fruit
of a Christmas tree. And Ghana's economic destiny (assuming that
some fraction of the crop was legally sold and the proceeds not stolen) would hinge in part upon the whims and buying habits of choco-
late-eating schoolchildren.

The Cocoa Marketing Board had a little office nearby, the only
building in the village that was built of cement, where the farmers

brought bags of beans to sell to the government agent. That evening, I, the chief, and the agent had dinner together. It was *fufu*, pounded yams, Ghana's national dish. The yams are beaten into a paste that has the taste and consistency of mashed potatoes mixed with glue. The proper way of eating it is to take a piece with the right hand, mold it into a ball, push a hole partway through the ball, and dip the ball into the stew that is always served alongside, thus using the hole like a spoon to scoop up the gravy. As with any strange cuisine, I ate it at first out of necessity, then habit, then desire, and as I grew to like it it became associated in my mind with the place I first tried it so that, in later years, if I tasted it or even saw a photograph, a dusty trunk in the attic of my mind would be opened, and forgotten memories of Ghana would come tumbling out.

Hoping for a ride on a cocoa truck, I told the chief and the agent that I planned to leave the next day. "That is Wednesday," said the agent, "and the road is closed." It developed that one day a week was set aside for spirits to use the road—after all, ghosts have to go from one place to another—and during that day, everyone kept clear of the path, frightened of what they might meet. I was not keen to meet an Ashanti spirit, so I stayed an extra day.

Early Thursday morning, I rode into Agogo on the back of a Cocoa Board tractor, which was hauling sacks of beans to town. There was a woman in Agogo who took in boarders, and I rented a room for ten cedi. That evening, I went to a party at the house of two Canadian teachers; they had joined CUSO, their country's equivalent of the Peace Corps, and had spent the past year in Agogo. The party was a big event and Peace Corps workers came from as far away as Accra. In theory, Peace Corps volunteers stationed in Ghana received the same salary in dollars as other volunteers, but they were paid in *cedi* at a ridiculously low exchange rate yielding only a few hundred cedi a month. So they lived as poorly as a New Yorker would on a thousand dollars a year. Most were quite thin, and it was rumored that one or two had been shipped home because of malnutrition. For them, parties and celebrations were rare and special occasions, to be savored to the full, which is what we did on that long and wild night.

I woke up the next morning and wished I hadn't. I was bleary-eyed and seasick and the bed was spinning and I was still half asleep when I heard a voice that claimed to have taken over the country. That woke me up in a hurry; what I had heard was my landlady's radio. I got dressed and ran over to the CUSO house. By that time, a new announcer had come on; this one said that the rebels who had attempted to overthrow the government had been roundly defeated. Don't worry, the teachers' Ghanaian friends told us, the fighting is over and the government has won. They believed whatever they heard on the radio, which is why, in any African coup, the soldiers' first objective is to capture the radio station. Music came over the airwaves, and I surmised that there was fighting around Broadcasting House, that bands of soldiers were taking over the microphone, making speeches, and then putting on long-playing records as other groups tried to chase them out. Accra was 150 miles away, but if I left right away I might get to see the tail end of the fighting. Even now, in 1979, despite my years of travel, I had never seen a gun fired in anger and was still too innocent to be frightened; two years had elapsed since my visit to Uganda, and I had begun to believe again in my own immortality.

I found a car that took me to Konongo, a gold-mining town on the main road. All I saw of Konongo was a street of shops with big verandas. I waited on one of the porches until, an hour later, a pickup truck stopped and gave me a ride to Accra. As we approached the capital, our way was blocked by crowds of laughing, happy people who had spilled out of their houses and taken over the streets. There was a loud and constant rattle of gunfire, but nobody bothered to duck. Their nonchalance amazed me, until somebody told me that what I heard was jubilant soldiers firing their rifles into the air. The fighting was over and the rebels had won.

At the YMCA on Castle Road, which is usually full to overflowing, there had been several hurried departures that afternoon, and I had no trouble getting a room. Everyone who had a radio had it on that afternoon, so I heard the announcement, made late in the day, of the new government's composition. An Armed Forces Revolutionary Council had been established, and the names and ranks of its members were read over the air. All were soldiers; there were privates, corporals, and sergeants; but no one ranked higher than lieutenant. Africa has witnessed scores of coups and military takeovers—this was Ghana's fourth in fourteen years—but this was something new: a rising from the ranks. Western news reports described the new leaders as idealistic but bitter young men, disillusioned by years of corruption; this was a coup born of bitterness and frustration. The enlisted men, like everyone else in Ghana, were paid almost nothing, and as they sold oranges on the street to survive, those who were stationed near Accra could watch their generals cruising past in expensive limousines.

The generals had ruled Ghana since 1972. They had scheduled elections for later that month and promised to hand over power to the winners provided they received immunity from prosecution. They had ruined the country and were going to get off scot-free and then the civilians would get their turn to plunder what was left; so thought many enlisted men and younger officers, and a few weeks before, one of them, Jerry Rawlings, led a short-lived coup attempt on May 15. Rawlings, an air force lieutenant, was only a few years older than I, but he had already achieved renown as one of the country's most daring pilots, and in the weeks that followed he became more famous still. The newspapers reported that he had wanted to impose an "Ethiopian solution" on Ghana, and quoted him as stating that "a bloodbath is needed to clean up the country." The government expected that these news reports would discredit the would-be *putschist*, but to their horror, the articles turned him into a folk hero. Rawlings became a symbol of hope and change, but no one knew very much about the man himself. Perhaps he was a messiah, perhaps a megalomaniac, perhaps simply a man who wanted his own Mercedes-Benz. Whatever he was, he had just been made head of the Armed Forces Revolutionary Council.

Later that night, I walked down Kojo Thompson Road toward the center of town. I had heard rumors of widespread looting and burning and soldiers going berserk. The Europeans I met at the Y warned me that the downtown area was no place for a white man that night, but the streets seemed quiet enough. The crowds had thinned since afternoon; most people had gone indoors at eight, when the curfew began. As I neared Market Street, I slowed down, trying to look black and insignificant. Perhaps I was looking for trouble that night, but if so I didn't find it. There were no scenes of gore and carnage, and no one noticed me. Everyone was busy watching the small bands of soldiers who were leisurely, almost placidly, emptying the shops around Makola Market. I watched soldiers tossing mattresses from a second-story window to their comrades below; some people would sleep better because of the revolution. Then I walked back to my room where I, too, thanks to the decline and fall of the cedi, slept on a mattress, one of the few I'd seen since coming to Africa.

This was my introduction to Accra. Often, in Africa, I spent far too much time in places I didn't like, and Accra, where I stayed two weeks in all, was one. Accra should have been a beautiful town. It has the sea. East of town is a big white seventeenth-century Danish castle surrounded by palm trees. It is near a beach where fishermen park their canoes. Jamestown, the neighborhood west of the old post office, is the sort of place you'd expect to see on a postcard sent from Jamaica: pleasantly dilapidated and gaily painted two-story houses, shops, and bars. But there is also a city center, filled with massive monoliths that house government offices, big empty supermarkets, a few scruffy parks, and a lot of asphalt in between. And then there were the blocks and blocks of houses that lay between Castle Road and the downtown district; with their green lawns and high, strong fences, they seemed a cruel and ugly parody of an American suburb.

On my first morning in Accra, I walked down Castle Road and south into town, where I wandered around the maze of barren high-rises around Black Star Square. I was looking for the Immigration Office, which I finally found in a four-story shoebox built of red stone and glass. My visa had expired a week before, and I needed an extension. To get it, the clerk told me, I would be required to change thirty dollars per day into Ghanaian money. He was young, the Immigration man, and a very flashy dresser, who liked his clothes skin-tight and expensive. Delicately, subtly, I opened negotiations. I had already changed that much money and more, I said, but had lost the receipts to prove it, and to spare myself the trouble of going back to the bank for a new receipt I would be willing to pay an additional fee of, say, five dollars. All this took several hours but in the end I got an extension, good for twenty-one days. And this was the only time in my two and a half years in Africa that I was forced to pay an "additional fee."

After concluding my business at Immigration, I walked along Kinbu Road and down Liberty Avenue to the taxi park near the market. The shooting had long since stopped, but some looting was still going on. Near the car park, I stopped to watch a squad of soldiers emptying a liquor store. A large crowd had gathered, hoping for a share of the booty. The sergeant commanding the squad saw me, called me over, and asked for identification. I kept my passport and money together, and as I pulled the passport out, a thick wad of dollars came with it and fluttered to the ground. A year's army wages lay on the pavement, and I was sure that the sergeant would demand a very large additional fee for letting me go. But he pretended not to notice, and I gathered up the bills as he checked my newly extended visa. Satisfied, he returned the passport and waved me away and went back to looting the shop.

I'd been given three more weeks in Ghana and I frittered them away. I left Accra and went straight to Elmina, a small town by the sea graced by two stunning castles. One was a huge white Portuguese fort built in 1482 and the other, high on a hill, was Dutch, erected in the seventeenth century, a period in which slave traders from Britain, Denmark, and the Netherlands built slave pens and citadels up and down the coast. The Dutch castle, Fort St. Jago, had been turned into a hotel, and for a dollar I rented a large airy room that overlooked the water far below. Inside the fort, latticed windows surrounded a cobbled courtyard, like a square in Amsterdam, and I persuaded myself that the traders themselves had lived there, and had imprisoned their stock in trade elsewhere, perhaps in the thick-walled, windowless Portuguese castle by the water.

Elmina is a pretty town. There are palm groves by the ocean and you can sit in the shade and watch the sunlight sparkle on the water. The people were not unpleasant to me, but not very hospitable either; those castles cast long shadows. Europeans had stayed at Elmina longer than anywhere else in Africa and for three hundred years one of their main occupations had been catching and buying slaves. Even now, a legacy of bitterness remained, and I made no friends in Elmina. I joined the public library at Cape Coast, took out as many trashy novels as I could carry, and sat in my room, a hundred feet above the town, reading, breathing the salty breezes that blew in from the sea. A room of my own, that was a rare luxury in Africa, and the mental muscles that clench when exposed to public view needed those weeks of privacy to relax and grow tender.

Meanwhile, in Accra, the revolution continued. The radio announced that a "house-cleaning operation" was planned, and hundreds of army officers and civilians faced trial by "people's courts" for corruption. The radio read out lists of fugitives who were ordered to turn themselves in, and the newspapers published photographs of rows of stakes put up in Accra and Kumasi that could be used by six firing squads at once. These pictures worried me, since I had two hundred dollars or so worth of cedis in my money belt, enough perhaps to make me a major black marketeer; I had bought them before the coup, when the black market was no more corrupt than the banks. Some of the newspapers ran editorials against the people's courts, but most supported them; less drastic means of ending corruption had been tried and tried again, they reasoned, and all had failed.

The army also mounted a drive to enforce price controls. Market women were arrested and a few were caned in public, and for the first time in years food prices came down—though stocks soon sold out and shortages followed. Accra's prostitutes, the newspapers reported, agreed to lower their fee from five cedis to two.

By this time, from all I could tell, Rawlings had become Ghana's most popular leader since Nkrumah. Frenzied, cheering mobs greeted his every public appearance. The workers supported him; suddenly, their wages bought more instead of less. The students believed in him. If he had run for president in a free election, he would have won in a landslide. Rawlings promised to hold free elections and to hand over power to the winner within three months, but few believed him. Idi Amin had made the same pledge in 1971, and so had every other soldier who took power at gunpoint, but none of them kept his word.

I spent the last week of June in Accra, getting visas to Mali, Togo, and the Ivory Coast. The hunt for visas shaped my itinerary, made it look like a corkscrew. I had had to go to Upper Volta to get a visa for Ghana, which was the nearest country where I could get a visa for Mali. Mali is Upper Volta's neighbor, but the two countries fought a war a few years back and neither maintains an embassy in the other's capital.

On my third day in Accra, I read in the papers that three former heads of state, Generals Acheampong, Akuffo, and Afrifa, had, along with six other top officials, faced a firing squad on Labadi Beach. Many countries, including the United States, protested these executions, and the generals who governed Nigeria—who had a very personal interest in not allowing that sort of thing to happen—cut off Ghana's supply of gasoline and threatened to keep it off if anyone else were shot. No one was.

Not long after, free elections were held. Rawlings did not run, and

Hilla Limann, candidate of the People's National Party, the successor to Nkrumah's Convention People's Party, won the presidency. Rawlings stepped down in September, a week ahead of schedule. Businessmen, released from jail, went back to business as usual. Prices began to rise and the rate of inflation soon topped 100 percent.

The new government tried to discredit Rawlings, and forced him out of the army, but he remained as popular as ever and, when I returned briefly to Accra in 1980, street vendors around Black Star Square did a brisk trade in Rawlings T-shirts, emblazoned with the pilot's photograph and the legend STAND UP FOR YOUR RIGHTS! Two years later, as the national debt climbed above two billion dollars and the shops remained empty, Rawlings, with the support of the army, ousted the PNP and took command of the country once again. This time he made no promises. But I heard of these events from afar, for I left Ghana in late June of 1979, as soon as my visas came through, and before the heady, invigorating atmosphere of Rawlings's revolution began to turn stale and sour.

19

FROM TOGO TO TIMBUCTU

Few things are as pleasant as coming into Lomé after leaving Accra. It's an easy drive to the Ghana-Togo frontier, and Lomé, the Togolese capital, is only a mile beyond, so I walked from the border into town along the beachfront road. It was night by then, and though I couldn't see the water I could hear the steady pounding of the surf and the sighing of the wind in the palm trees. It was a lazy, tranquil sound, an auditory cliché perhaps, but calm and soothing nonetheless.

All of Lomé seemed calm and soothing to me, a quiet, sun-washed city where nothing moved faster than the surf on the sea. The beach was wide and sandy, the beer was cheap and good, the town was full of little shops with more goods than shelf space and the surplus, cartons full of such luxuries as tinned sardines and toothpaste, was stacked in sloppy heaps behind the counter. People came over from Accra to buy soap and shampoo.

Much of Ghana's black-market trade is reputed to pass through

Lomé, and many of the Mercedes limousines I saw in town probably had been paid for with Ghanaian cocoa. But there is no black market for Togolese money. As throughout French West Africa, the local money is backed by the Bank of France. It is freely convertible into French francs, which is why the shops in Lomé were so abundantly stocked with French goods. Togo and her French-speaking neighbors export cash crops throughout the world and convert the dollars they receive into CFA francs, which they use to buy French soap, silk, and pâté; France is thus the greatest beneficiary of her own generosity. Much of Lomé's placid prosperity is an illusion; you can buy anything there, if you have the money but, in a country whose per capita income is no greater than the Sudan's, few people do. Still, the Togolese villager who sells a cow at the market can buy something with the money he gets. Ghanaians can't.

All talk of money aside, Lomé was far prettier than Accra. Accra had its tall, futuristic, already decaying office buildings around Black Star Square; Lomé had an old Gothic cathedral, with a colorful market in the plaza just beyond the church steps. Accra had the YMCA, concrete barracks surrounded by barbed wire, and Lomé had the Hôtel de la Plage. It was, as its name suggests, by the beach, with a sidewalk café in front and a long white bungalow behind. I shared a room with three vacationing Peace Corps teachers, who tipped me off to the Fourth of July party at the embassy. It was a barbecue, held on the big lawn behind the consulate, with games and music and hot dogs that were made in the U.S.A. Half the Peace Corps from Ghana were there; everyone knew everyone else; I, as usual, was an outsider, tolerated, lucky to be let in. I listened to groups of friends talking and felt the same faint embarrassment I suffer when I overhear, on a train perhaps, an intimate conversation between people, strangers to me, who neither know nor care that I am in earshot.

I stayed a few more days in Lomé to get a visa for Upper Volta and the morning after I picked up my passport, I carried my pack to the big and dirty truck park that lay on the outskirts of town, sandwiched between the Boulevard of the Republic and Commerce Street. I went to Kpalimé, a town in the Togo Mountains, because mountains are rare in West Africa and I had seen nothing but flatlands since Cameroun. Kpalimé was a disappointment; the peaks of the Togo Mountains are, on average, two thousand feet above sea level. After a night at a deserted castle (built by a French lawyer thirty years before), I went on to Atakpamé. There I rejoined the main highway which, like sliver-shaped Togo, runs from south to north. I got a ride on a van and got off at Kandé, an overgrown village three hundred miles north of Lomé.

Somewhere east of Kandé, in the rolling hills that straddle the Togo-Benin border, lived the tribe called the Tamberma. I had read several monographs about the Tamberma, and the little I learned about them was enough to make me seek them out. They were said to be a proud and warlike people, vaguely related to the Lobi of Upper Volta who, armed only with poisoned arrows, had held off the French army for five years. The Tamberma were the last people in West Africa to go naked. (Virtually all Africans wore some sort of clothing long before the Europeans came, and many West African peoples wove elegant cotton robes and dresses.) And they built strange, multistoried mud houses whose architecture and floor plan were designed to replicate in miniature their view of the universe. Visiting a people like that, I thought, would be like walking into a story written by Borges.

There was a Frenchman named Jean whom I had met in Lomé, seen again in Kpalimé, and now saw yet again in Kandé. I had told him glowing tales of the Tamberma and he had decided to join me. I was not sorry to find him there; I had not looked forward to walking into the bush alone.

Near the Catholic mission in Kandé a dirt track began that lazily meandered east, across a green and rolling plain. Jean and I followed it, walking briskly for four or five hours until we came to a range of low hummocks with a narrow trail, a six-inch-wide ribbon of cleared earth, running across them. I have never been able to resist the call of a narrow path whose end lies out of sight. Neither could Jean, so we followed it. After a time, it petered out and for a while we were lost in the hills, but then we came to the other side and saw a wide and fertile valley spread below us.

The houses of Nanou in Upper Volta, with their earthen ramparts and breastworks, had been an impressive sight, reminding me of castles on a hill. But the Tamberma houses that dotted the valley below put the Ko earthworks to shame. They, too, were castles, but tall and graceful châteaux. Their smooth, curving, earthen walls rose for several stories, and had cylindrical towers crowned with conical thatch roofs. Jean and I walked to the nearest; outside it, on a wooden platform shaded by a canopy of palm leaves, sat a man. He was old, with skin as shriveled as if it had been stewed, or dried in the sun like a raisin. An animal hide was wrapped around his waist and on his chest he wore an amulet made of tooth and bone. He sat cross-legged, eerily still, and impassive, and he showed no surprise when he saw us come down from the hills. I was beginning to wonder if all the Tamberma were like him when two more men arrived. They walked slowly; they had put in a full day in the fields and looked forward to a quiet evening, with a filling meal and perhaps a gourd of millet beer. They wore bathing suits; the government viewed the Tamberma's nudity as a national disgrace, and so the men were forced to wear trunks or jogging shorts as a concession to civilization. The younger of the two farmers, a solidly built youth of seventeen, spoke French, and invited us into his house where, he told us, we were welcome—as were all visitors—to spend the night.

It was dark by then, so we followed him through the large door into a vast and cavernous chamber, which was unlit but, judging from the grunts and snuffles that greeted us, occupied by animals as well as people. We went up a long, spiral staircase, and out onto the roof. High above the darkened valley, the roof was cool and quiet. We stayed there until it was time to sleep. We shared a bedroom in one of the turrets. The little round tower had a circular opening in its side, like a hole in a slice of Swiss cheese. I squeezed headfirst through the hole to find myself dangling over a round, sunken chamber. I backed out, turned around, and lowered my feet to the floor. Jean came in after. There were two straw mats, and we each took one and went to sleep.

Jean left the next morning, as soon as he possibly could. He snapped a few photos and then he was gone. The men, meanwhile, were eating breakfast in the courtyard that surrounded the house, and I joined them. They sat beside a low platform on top of which were five or six conical mounds of baked clay. They looked like yard-high obelisks, mud monuments in miniature. These, the boy who spoke French explained, were the fetishes, magical objects of great power. Each of the cones was responsible for protecting one member of the family. I noticed reddish stains and splotches on some of the mounds; otherwise, they looked quite innocuous, and some of the men used them as backrests, which seemed to me to smack of disrespect. Or perhaps not; a computer programmer might prop an ashtray or a coffee cup on top of his terminal, confident that the machine will not resent being put to so lowly a use. The Tamberma, I realized, have the same sort of faith in their fetishes as we do in our computers.

The men seemed in no hurry to finish their meal, but eventually they did, and then they picked up their hoes and headed for the fields. The boy, who had by then appointed himself as my guide, stayed with me. He took me on a tour of the neighboring châteaux, which lasted most of the day. At the first house, the nearest to ours, a woman made a speech of welcome, invited us up to the roof, and served us a large plate of stew. We ate, thanked our hostess, and left, and then my guide led me up a hill, through a grove of trees, and to a second castle, where the châtelaine made a speech of welcome, invited us in, and gave us a meal. I ate a few mouthfuls out of politeness, and the boy finished the rest. By the time we reached the third house, I realized what was happening: Tamberma etiquette required that all strangers who visit a house be welcomed with a hearty meal, and my guide was using this custom to get the biggest feast of his life. Besides, he wanted to be seen with me, to show me off, for of all the houses in the valley I had chosen his to stay in, and of all the people I had selected him to be my guide.

We returned to our house late in the afternoon, and I saw to my horror that we were just in time for dinner. In the large shadowy ground-floor hall, which served as both kitchen and stables, a big kettle was bubbling, watched over by an old woman. Her hair was white but she was still spry and able to work and, like most of the women, while in the privacy of her home she wore a leather loincloth and nothing else, except for a smooth white stone. The stone, highly polished, was the size and shape of my thumb and was worn through a hole drilled through her lower lip. It moved when she talked and looked like a goatee.

Soon dinner was ready, and I took just enough to avoid giving insult, but the boy helped himself to as much as he could and bolted it down. We sat on the roof for an hour or so, and then I crawled into bed.

When I came downstairs the next morning, the family was making a fetish. The wizened, half-naked old wizard who was the first Tamberma I met was in charge. A mound of mud was made with a small hollow scooped in it, a chicken was beheaded and its blood poured into the depression, along with other, more exotic ingredients that I couldn't identify, and then more earth was dumped over the hollow and the mound shaped into a cone like the others. It was only a foot high, the smallest of the fetishes, perhaps because it was assigned to protect a small boy, an easier task than watching over a full-grown man.

After breakfast, the men marched off to work, and this time I joined them. The month before the rains was the time of planting, the hardest work in the yearly cycle. The ground had to be broken to receive the seed, and the plow had not yet been invented. Short hoes were used, metal blades attached to a foot-long wooden handle, and to cut a furrow a man would squat down, hack at the soil, leap backward like a frog, and strike the ground again; the series of ragged incisions would form a trough of turned soil ready to be planted. It was backbreaking, agonizing work, but the Tamberma turned it into a festival, a joyous occasion. Many people worked on the same plot of land, for farming was done communally with each family helping to till the fields of their neighbors. There was a friendly rivalry among the men, and they would work side by side, each trying to be the first to finish his furrow. The winner would award himself a swig of beer, but so would the losers, and throughout the day women would arrive with jugs of beer, and would stay to see who plowed the fastest. There would be contest after contest, match and rematch, with beer and laughter in between, and slowly and unnoticed the work would get done.

The women did not help with the plowing; their work came later. The Tamberma, like many African peoples, used magic, myth, and symbol to decide which sex did what. Their concept of sex roles derived from their view of the universe. The men would cut the soil, a ravishment of sorts, but, since fertility and procreation are feminine powers, it is a woman who plants the seed. For a man to do that, they believe, would be as foolish as for a man to try to get himself pregnant.

It is out of fashion in America (though not in Europe) to derive a society from its myths. Most of us cynically suspect that the process works the other way round, that an explanation of social arrangements based on magic is—as with caste in India—usually a mask, a cover-up of exploitation. But anyone who tarries long in the tropics learns, as Claude Lévi-Strauss did in South America and Gregory

Bateson in New Guinea, that sign, myth, and symbol have a life of their own. And, in this instance at least, it was the men, not the women, who got stuck with the harder job. Sometimes, the society's myths give the women added power. Among the Baoulé, who are related to the Ashanti, a woman mistreated by her husband can use her power of fecundity to curse him, and he will die unless he appeases her.

And so, when the plowing was done, a woman came from the house to plant the seed. She stood proud and erect as she marched between the furrows, dropping seeds on the earth with the calm, measured dignity of a priestess. The ceremonial robe she wore for the occasion had, long ago, been a tatty housecoat in America, but I didn't tell her that, and perhaps if I had the knowledge would have added to the gown's attraction. Earlier that day, my guide had boasted that after the planting was done he would take me to an American meal.

And he did. He led me across the fields, over the hills, and into another valley. On the way, I saw a little grass hut that looked both familiar and out of place. "Fulani," said the boy, and I saw an old tan-skinned man leading a pair of cows. I had seen Fulani many times before; I had spent a night near a hut like that when lost in the desert in Niger. The Fulani are a far-flung tribe, and their members can be found in almost every country between Senegal and the Sudan. Many Fulani live near farmers; after the harvest, their herds crop the stubble and leave droppings that nourish the soil. Fulani and farmers thus live in more or less perfect symbiosis, though both would be shocked at the suggestion that they use the precious cattle to draw a plow.

We greeted the Fulani and went on, and after a while came to a tin-roofed building, a schoolhouse perhaps, where a group of men and boys were heating a pot of flour and water. It was corn flour and came in a white sack that proclaimed it a gift of the people of the United States of America. This is what you eat in America, isn't it, the boy asked, and I said that it was, even though the people of the United States would probably have used it to feed hogs and cattle. (A logical assumption, since each year American cattle devour enough grain to feed the combined populations of North America and Africa.)

The men prepared the corn in Tamberma fashion, making a paste

that they ate like Ghanaian *fufu,* with a vegetable stew. Native Togolese millet tasted much better, but the men ate the American corn
with the same excitement that drives Americans to consume slices of
raw fish at a sushi bar.

Another evening, another night in the turret, and then I left the
Tamberma. I hiked back to Kandé and got a lift with an oil tanker
that was carrying gasoline to Ouagadougou. It was a big, new truck
and we drove quickly, passing through Sansanné-Mango and Da-
pango without even slowing down, and then inexplicably the driver
stopped for several hours at Bittou, the first village in Upper Volta, a
windswept warren of wood huts and white sandy soil. I sat on a bench
outside a shack that passed for a café. There were a lot of Fulani in
Bittou, women with big hoop earrings who sat beside calabashes of
fresh milk and yogurt, which they sold by the dipper. It was the smell
of the milk that made me realize I had left the forest zone behind.
There are always certain subtle smells that pervade my memory of a
place, and the slightly rancid odor of milk, of people who live on
milk, and of clothing spotted with spilled milk is, for me at least, inextricably linked to the Sahel, that land of nomads and far horizons
that lies just south of the Sahara. The Fulani women at Bittou had
probably come from there, from the arid plains of Liptako a few hundred miles to the north, from waterholes with names like Gorom-
Gorom and Tin-Akof and others too small to have a name. The sight
and smell of the nomads fired my imagination, and so did a man I met
at the café. Young, educated, fluent in French, he told me tales of
sacred, hidden villages four days' walk from the nearest road. I told
him I had stayed in many places more remote than that, but his
stories affected me more than I let on. It was the myth of the untouched village, as much perhaps as anything, that drove me to wander.

Night came, and we left Bittou and drove north. After an hour,
the driver pulled off the road and stopped. I could see the dim shapes
of houses and storage tanks in the starlight. A man with a rubber
hose came out of one of the houses, connected the truck to the tank,
and siphoned off a few gallons. Then he paid the driver. The driver
stuffed the bills in his pocket, and I doubted that his employer would
ever see them. After all, a few gallons would never be missed. Many
Togolese live by smuggling and covert trade (mostly with Ghana)
and have learned to keep it within bounds.

Arriving in Ouagadougou, I went back to the Restaurant Rialle. "Oh, you again!" said the owner, who tried, without success, to raise the rent. Familiar places, reassuring places, places that hold no surprises often entice me to linger, but after two nights in Ouagadougou, I found a ride in the right direction and took it. It was market day at Djibasso, a tiny town near the Malian border, and the other passengers of the van I rode in were traders who would buy cheaply in the countryside food that they could sell dearly in the city. At the market, they told me, I could easily find a truck to take me to Mali.

I am still not sure what route we took to Djibasso. Some of the roads were too small and ill-maintained to be on any map and the driver, like most in Upper Volta, would take long detours through the bush, along tracks that weren't really roads at all, to avoid the many police checkpoints. We passed, I think, quite near Koudougou and Dédougou and by the time we reached Djibasso the market was in full swing. It was a varied crowd, for people had come from every direction to buy, sell, and trade milk and grain, fish and salt, cattle and kola nuts, medicine and textiles. There were Bobos, Bozos, and Bouzous, Bambara and Bamana, Dogon and Dioula, a few Fulani and, I think, one or two Hausa as well. I whispered the names to myself as I moved through the crowd; for me, even the names of the tribes were, and always will be, exotic, as richly evocative as the scent of incense or myrrh, and so were the clothes the people wore: conical hats, blue-and-white homespun caftans, and, for the women, wraps and dresses made of bright cloth printed with intricate designs, with earth hues predominating—brown, green, amber, gold.

The fair at Djibasso was old and established. Traders and buyers had assembled on that spot one day each week for as long as anyone could remember—centuries perhaps, even millennia—for the region which today is known as the Republic of Mali (whose borders lay ten miles to the west) has been a center of trans-Saharan trade since the days when Berber caravans crossed the Sahara carrying gold and ivory to Carthage. Recent excavations show that the trading city of Jenné, just west of Djibasso, was founded before the birth of Christ. The rulers of this region levied high taxes on this trade, and they and their people prospered. From this wealth, vast empires arose. Ghana, which controlled much of the western Sahel (but did not include the territory which today bears its name), first became a nation in the fifth or sixth century A.D. As its power grew, so did its fame, and by the eleventh century chroniclers in Spain and Sicily described the fabulous wealth and lavish pomp of the Ghanaian court.

Soon after, Ghana declined, shaken by war and invasion, and a new empire arose. It was founded by the Malinké, a prosperous tribe which had, in the fourteenth century, organized guilds of traders called Dioula. These merchants traveled throughout West Africa, founding trading stations that later grew into towns and cities, including many of the *dougous* that grace the African map, for *dougou* is the Dioula word for town.

The work of the Dioula and of the Malinké armies created a state that stretched from the Atlantic coast of what is now Senegal to the edge of present-day Nigeria. Architects and scholars were brought in from Arabia, and great cities were built of brick and stone: Niani, Jenné, and Timbuctu. Universities were founded, and schools of theology, for the emperor converted to Islam. In the early fourteenth century, the emperor, Mansa Musa, accompanied by a large retinue of courtiers, civil servants, and scholars, made a pilgrimage to Mecca which became legendary for its lavishness. Every Friday, the emperor built a mosque in whatever town he happened to be and in Cairo, where many Fridays were spent, the party spent so much as to cause an inflation. While the Egyptians were struck with the emperor's perhaps excessive prodigality, those Arabs who crossed the Sahara to Mali—and there were many, for scholars from every corner of the Moslem world came to study at the great university of Timbuctu—were even more impressed with the tolerance, courtesy, and learning of the people. Writing in 1526, the Arab chronicler known in the West as Leo Africanus observed that Mali had "great abundance of corne, flesh and cotton. Heere are many artificers and merchants in all places; and yet the king honourably entertaineth all strangers. The inhabitants are rich, and have plentie of wares. Heere are great store of temples, priests and professours. . . . The people of this region excell all other Negroes in witte, civilitie and industry. . . ."

The emperor of Mali, like the village chiefs in Zaire and Ghana, maintained order, not so much by force (though there was an army and a civil service) as by moral suasion and the respect he commanded. Today, four centuries after the collapse of Songhai, the empire that, a century before, had put an end to Mansa Musa's kingdom, the nation called Mali is one of the world's poorest, instead of richest, but the proud tradition of courtesy, hospitality, and uprightness remains.

I spent all that day at the Djibasso fair, watching the swirls of people and produce and searching for a ride. I slept in the car park, and the next morning a truck took me to Mopti. A few miles out of Djibasso, we crossed into Mali, on a road so infrequently used that my passport was never checked. "Hello, Mali!" I sang as we bounced along the dirt track that, thirty miles farther on, joined the paved highway.

In Mopti, I rented a few square feet of floor space at a seedy café that billed itself as the Hotel Bar Mali. Outside the hotel was a big empty plaza where school kids came to kick a soccer ball around. Beyond that was the river, the Niger. Its banks, which were paved with dusty flagstones, were littered with beached boats, straw shacks, and miscellaneous debris and crowded from dawn to dusk with strollers, sailors, fish dealers, who squatted beside heaps of sun-dried river fish, and a handful of vegetable sellers, who offered soggy tomatoes and mealy-looking onions. Despite the crowds and the clutter, there was an open feel to the place, a sense of space and panorama, caused by the wide river and the sandy flats beyond. It was now July and the Niger was several months away from high water. By November, it would overflow its banks and flood the vast plains north of Mopti, an area far larger than England. The river, one of the world's longest, was wide and impressive even at its ebb.

I should have spent more time in Mopti and explored the ancient, somnolent towns and pretty villages around it, such as Jenné and the Bandiagara plateau. But, like every traveler in the world, I wanted to go to Timbuctu.

Timbuctu, that great and fabled city on the desert's edge, was, until 1100, only a well on a sandy plain. But, in the twelfth century, the merchants of Jenné began using the place as a relay station for trans-Saharan trade and, because of its ideal location, the village soon became a thriving city, with vaulting mosques and houses built of stone and a university that attracted scholars from all over. In the fifteenth century, the kingdom of the Songhai, with its capital at Gao, east of Timbuctu, displaced Mali as the region's leading power. The Songhai Empire soon became as large, as rich and as great as Mali had been and Timbuctu, as perhaps the leading city of that empire (though often an independent, secession-minded one), prospered. Its population was said to have reached a million, which would, if true, have made it one of the largest cities in the world. Leo Africanus found the inhabitants "exceeding rich" and "of a gentle and chereful disposition," and saw many "doctors, judges, priests and other learned men, that are bountifully maintained at the kings cost and charges."

But, in early 1591, the Songhai Empire came to a sudden end, and with it the golden age of Timbuctu. The King of Morocco, hearing of the wealth of Songhai, determined to conquer it, and sent an army of four thousand men, mostly European mercenaries, across the Sahara. Most of the men died in the desert, but the remnant, well-disciplined and armed with guns, roundly defeated the entire Songhai army. It was one of those battles that are portents of things to come, that not only change the course of history but are the forerunners of similar but far greater changes. A band of ragged, half-starved Europeans conquered the largest, most powerful African empire in history. They couldn't hold it for long, but what they destroyed was never rebuilt, and when, in 1893, French troops—the inevitable successors to the first European invaders three centuries before—captured Timbuctu, they found six thousand people living amidst the ghosts and ruins of a town that once held a million.

Little had changed since then. Timbuctu was still quite small and very remote. Later in the summer, a pair of antiquated steamboats, built in the 1920s, would sail from Mopti to Kabara, the port of Timbuctu, on to Gao and back again. The river was still too low for the riverboats, but I found a pirogue going to Goundam, a port two hundred miles north of Mopti and only sixty miles short of Timbuctu.

A pirogue is a dugout canoe. Such boats are an ancient form of transport; Leo Africanus described them. The one I took was wooden—though whether it was made from a single hollowed log I don't know—very large, and had a canopy and an outboard motor. There were fifty-odd passengers, and we sat in two rows, shoulder to shoulder. The crew consisted of a very large woman who did the cooking, building a fire in the middle of the boat, and a small, wiry Fulani man who ran the engine. He had a puckered and puckish face, very expressive and always full of fun, and, in his free moments, entertained us with expert pantomimes; he did a superb job of imitating people talking on the telephone, though he had probably never used one in his life.

For three days, we followed the river. Soon after leaving Mopti, we entered the inland delta, a vast labyrinth of lakes, channels, and tributary streams. At times the river seemed as wide as a lake. I had expected the same sort of lush greenery that graces the shores of the Nile, but here the banks were barren, and when I think of the Niger today, I think of sun, white sand, and water.

We could not navigate safely at night, so each afternoon we beached the boat and slept ashore. The first night, we stayed just outside a village with large mud houses and leafy trees, but, like the trees, houses became rarer after that, so the other nights were spent on deserted stretches of riverbank. There were still settlements, and we saw them from time to time, collections of tall, cubical mud-brick houses that rose from the riverbank and were mirrored in the water. Sometimes I caught a glimpse of long-robed figures walking between the houses. Occasionally we passed a fishing camp, usually on an island or sandbar. The camps were marked by rickety wooden frames put up to dry the catch and straw huts for the people. The fishermen were a separate tribe, known as the Bozos.

Late on the second day, we stopped at Niafounké, the largest town of the delta. There were heaps of garbage by the dock, including gnawed limbs with furry paws still attached. I walked into town to the market, where I bought a two-pound bag of fresh dates and ate them all without getting sick. Then I sat on the wharf, staring at the garbage and hoping the boat would leave, which after a time it did. Diré, the port for Goundam, was fifty miles downriver, and we reached it the next day.

Goundam was brown. It had buildings of stone, buildings of brick, and buildings of mud, but they were all the same shade of brown, a dark umber that matched well with the lighter ocher of the sand-strewn streets and the arid plains beyond the edge of town. There was a market on the outskirts, an octagonal concrete hall, once white but now brown and dingy, where a few traders dozed in the shade. It was a drowsy town, and the streets were usually silent. On the main avenue, children sold milk and yogurt; they sat quietly beside their big brown calabashes, not even bothering to look up when potential customers walked past. Once I saw a band of Tuaregs leading their camels toward the market; the men were leaner than Issri's clan, and their robes, which were old and somewhat frayed and dirty, were not the usual blue, but apple green, white, brown—whatever color they could get. This part of Mali had been hard hit by the long and ruinous drought of the early 1970s, and, from the look of them, these Tuaregs were still feeling the pinch.

There was a Tuareg boy in town whom I often saw in the street. An orphan, and half crazy, he was followed everywhere by gangs of children who teased him and would not leave him alone. "Tell them I an a white man," he begged me, in French, hoping that that would give him some claim to superiority. "No, no," they shouted, "you're black like us."

One day I heard about a weekly market that was held at Adar Mallam, a village that lay fifty or so miles northwest of Goundam, quite near Lake Faguibine. One of the traders who had a shop in Goundam drove there every week; he would often find good, inexpensive hides or leatherwork at the market and, even if not, he could usually make a profit by taking passengers, who paid fifteen hundred Mali francs each way.

The next time the merchant took his jeep to Adar Mallam, I went along. The road was appalling, and at times nonexistent. We left before noon and it was long after dark when we arrived at a row of poles that the traders at tomorrow's market would use to erect their booths. There were no houses in sight, no people, nothing but these half-built stalls. The merchant lit a fire and cooked dinner. He gave me a bowl but made me eat apart. "Since you are not a Moslem," he explained, "doubtless you have touched pork in your life, and so you cannot eat with us." I ate alone, wrapped myself in the blanket I had bought in New Guinea, and slept.

Soon it was daybreak, and the rising sun suffused both sky and land with pale violet and rose. Beyond the palisade of poles I saw a few adobe houses: long, low boxes with flat roofs. This was Adar Mallam. Its residents, like villagers the world over, rose early. I could see the smoke of cooking fires against the lightening sky. The merchant took me to meet the headman of the village. The trader spoke French, but the chief didn't, so the trader translated. I asked for his permission to stay in Adar Mallam as his guest until the next market day. "Does he need special food," the headman asked, "or can he eat what we eat?" "I can eat any kind of food," I replied. "Then he is welcome to stay," said the chief.

And so the matter was settled. I thanked the chief and the trader, and we sat together, drank sweet tea, and waited for the market to begin. The first sellers had already begun to arrive, and within an hour the trickle of people had become a stream. They came from all directions, from the desert, from the scrubland, from the settlements by the lake. They rode on donkeys or camels or came on foot. They converged at the gently sloping plain behind the palisade, tethered their animals, unloaded their goods, and sat down beside them.

I strolled through the crowd, past men in blue robes and men in black smocks and men in leather skirts, men who wore turbans and men in conical hats adorned with leather; past bags filled with millet and brown bars of sugar and heaps of dried fish and gourds full of milk; past rows of donkeys, goats, camels, and sheep; past Tuaregs and Bouzous and Bozos and Fulani and people whose tribe I did not even try to guess; past a surfeit of strange, exotic sounds, smells and sights, with me, the only Westerner and the only person in Western dress, the strangest and most alien of all.

Many of the people I saw reminded me of my days with Issri, and I wished he were there. He was, at that moment, probably a thousand miles east of me, but Adar Mallam was at roughly the same latitude as Tchin Tabaraden, so the people were similar, and so was their way of life. They were nomads. But the headman, his family, and the other people of Adar Mallam were different. The lake provided water for irrigation, and so they were farmers. The villagers were Songhai, and their ancestors had perhaps helped create the empire that had dazzled the world five centuries before. In those days, Lake Faguibine lay at the western edge of the empire, a week's journey from Timbuctu, and the sophisticated, devoutly Moslem city dwellers most likely considered the villages around the lake primitive, half-pagan places. And Adar Mallam probably looked then much as it does now.

In outward appearance at least, the men had not changed much either. Leo Africanus describes the people of the Niger as "clad in blacke or blew cotton, wherewith they cover their heads also," and the headman, when he came to meet me that afternoon after the market, wore a long black kaftan, with a turban to match. His face was wide, with high cheekbones. We walked back to his compound, where my supper was waiting.

During my week at Adar Mallam, I was served breakfast and supper, and the meal never varied. Twice a day, one of the women brought a big metal bowl to a screened-off part of the yard, where I could eat in privacy. In the dish was a big golden mound of pounded millet, with a depression in the center that held a helping of sauce. It reminded me of a mashed potato castle filled with gravy. The millet paste was tasteless, the sauce was green and viscid, and the portion I was given weighed several pounds, but I left very little over. I did not want to offend my hosts, for whom meals like that were not a monotony but a luxury; they would consider it a blessing to eat that same meal every day of their lives.

The Songhai were farmers in a harsh and barren land. The lake provided a less erratic source of water than the rains, but even that was not reliable. During the long drought several years before, half the lake had dried up, and it had never regained its normal size. Much of the farmland, perhaps half, was now useless; too far from the lake to be irrigated, it had reverted to desert. The people whose land had not been affected gave half of their fields to the farmers who had lost theirs. The merchant from Goundam, who had told me about the lake, brought up the division of the land almost as an afterthought. For him, this surprisingly generous act was no more than one would expect from one's fellow man and hardly worth mention.

Decency was taken for granted, but the grain was not. After the harvest, the batonlike spikes were carefully gathered, dried, and stored. To prepare flour, the women pounded the spikes, and each morning, for several hours, I could hear the rhythmic pound-pound-pound of the heavy wooden pestle hitting the mortar. The powder was then put in a flat basket and tossed in the air, for the wind to blow away the chaff. The remaining flour was mixed with water, which had to be fetched from a far-off well. Most of the women's day was given over to these chores: flailing and fetching and winnowing and threshing—tasks so outmoded in the Western world that their names have a biblical ring to our ears. But, like the Tamberma men at planting time, the ebullient Songhai women turned drudgery into festivity. Women rarely pounded the grain alone. Two women sometimes shared the same mortar or, more often, used separate mortars but stayed within earshot of each other to chat, banter, and monitor each other's progress. Companionship did not make the work any less tiring, but it did make it easier to bear. And so did the well.

I spent most of my day in the courtyard of the headman's house, and I noticed that the women—his wife and eldest daughter—spent a lot of time at the well. They would leave their mortars and go off carrying a leather bucket, and then return an hour later with the pail full. One day I followed them. I saw a big crowd of women, most of them laughing; that was the well. It was a place for drawing water, but it was also the women's clubhouse, an excuse for them to come together, rest, and gossip without any men to interfere. In any case, the men were rarely around during the day. They went to plow the far-off fields, or so they said. Perhaps they had a clubhouse of their own.

The younger children didn't, and when they weren't helping with household tasks, they used to roam around the village in small bands. They had very little space to wander because just beyond the houses the desert began. Sometimes I joined them; if not, they would find me. One day they took me to a nearby house where an old man sat in the courtyard weaving cotton cloth with an intricate pattern of black-and-white squares and stripes. He used a narrow wooden loom, hand powered, and coiled the excess yarn around his foot.

The children were usually left alone to do as they liked, but there were limits. Once I saw the headman scolding his younger son, who was six or seven. I don't know what the boy had done; perhaps he had shown disrespect for an adult, or possibly he had been given food and had not shared it with his siblings. Both of these would be considered serious offenses. As punishment, he had to perform ten deep knee bends. Africans never hit their children.

Sometimes, during the day, I gave the children candy. It was Ramadan, the month of fasting, but no one observed it. The women wore wraps of red-and-yellow cloth as well as black and their faces were never covered. The Songhai were Moslems, but their traditions and behavior seemed far more African than Islamic.

I had been in Adar Mallam a little less than a week when a jeep arrived from Goundam. I decided to take it back when it returned to town. As best I could, since we had no language in common, I thanked the headman and said my good-byes. After paying the driver of the jeep, making the customary gift to the chief, and buying a big bag of candy for his children, I would, I calculated, have about seventy dollars remaining, which would have to last me at least as far as the coast. I should perhaps have turned back at Goundam, but instead I spent an additional five dollars to ride to Timbuctu.

The road to Timbuctu passed inland, through sandy groves of widely spaced thorn trees. The jeep let me off at the driver's house, which was big and brown, with mud-plastered walls as thick as a fortress and, in front, a heavy wooden door studded with spikes. Most of the buildings in Timbuctu were like that.

It was not a lively town, Timbuctu. It was wrapped in memories and silence, like a mausoleum. On the larger streets, people shuffled past; the narrow alleyways were mostly deserted. The walls of the houses had no windows. It was a ghost town, a town for ghosts.

Inside one of the old houses near the Dyinguereber Mosque was a small restaurant. The brown mud walls were unpainted, the low ceiling was held up by sagging wooden beams, the heavy wooden furniture was painted black. Whatever light there was came in through the narrow doorway. The proprietor, Baba Cisse, was an old, old man. He was hunched and frail, but he still did most of the work around the place. Baba was, I guessed, about eighty, and he might have been born before the French came, in the days when the Tuaregs were the masters of Timbuctu. He could tell me more tales than Scheherazade, I thought, and so, after I had rented a mat in the small dormitory in back of the restaurant, I asked him, "Have things changed much since you were young?" "Oh, how they've changed!" he replied. "How?" I asked. His eyes lit up. "The prices," he said. "Things were so cheap when I was young. You could buy a full meal for less than the cost of one tomato today."

I left my pack at Baba's, walked to the police station to register (as I was required to do in each town in Mali), and kept on walking. The houses became newer and more widely spaced. There were vacant lots filled with tents and grass houses. I heard songs and drumbeats from behind a concrete wall. I went through a gate and joined a party of singing, shouting, swaying Tuaregs. The women danced and beat on tambourines. It was probably a wedding. I stayed for a while, then continued down the road. A few minutes later, I met a Belgian and we got to talking. Blond and strong and bearded, he worked on a series of irrigation projects in the surrounding desert. He lived in Timbuctu, he told me, and left once a year to go to Bamako, Mali's capital. This year, he would fly home to Europe from Bamako for a long-delayed vacation. He was leaving the next day, in a convoy of three jeeps, all of which were overloaded, but if I came to the project office tomorrow morning, he would try to squeeze me in. I hoped he could. I did not have enough money to pay my way south, and vehicles were so rare that this might be the only free ride that year.

I went to the Belgian's office early the next morning, and waited in the yard as the jeeps were loaded. By ten, much loading remained to be done, but I saw that there would be room for me. We left at noon and drove east. The roads that traversed the inland delta between Goundam and Mopti had flooded, so we had to skirt the delta. That meant going all the way to Gao, 263 miles to the east, crossing the Niger, and then returning west. It was, in all, a thousand miles to Bamako, and much of the road was as bad as any I'd seen.

That first day, we drove through sand and scrub with, once we got past Bamba, occasional glimpses of the Niger. Late that night, we reached Gao. The Belgian and the other two drivers got rooms at the Hotel Atlantide; I caught a few hours' sleep in the hotel parking lot, atop one of the jeeps. I woke up early, and had time to explore the town. Near the hotel was a lively market, surrounded by streets of busy shops and brightly painted cafés. Unlike Timbuctu, Gao is still an important entrepot; the old Songhai capital has become a major truck stop on a main route between Algiers and the West African coast. I got back to the hotel by midmorning; there was just time for coffee before we left.

In the brief desert twilight, we stopped at Hombori: a shop, a small market, and clusters of thatch-roof houses nestled among tall rock outcrops. The road beyond was reputed to be quite beautiful, but we drove it at night. The road dipped and climbed, dipped and climbed as it wound its way through the range of hills and rock formations that lay west of Hombori. The moon came out, silhouetting massive cliffs and slender spires towering over us.

All night we drove across that mysterious moonlit land. By sunrise we had reached the flat plains around the Niger, and, a few hours after that, Mopti, where the paved road begins. There were four hundred miles more to cover, but the road was good. In the afternoon, we stopped in Ségou, and drank black coffee in a pleasantly seedy café-bar by the river, and by the time we got to Bamako it was night once again. We drove through the sleepy suburb of Badalabougou, across the bridge over the Niger, and through the darkened streets of what seemed a large city.

I discovered the next day that Bamako, which had appeared so cosmopolitan by night, was barely a city at all. It was, or so it seemed, a colonial town gone to seed. There were streets and streets of rambling bungalows floundering in flowers, drowning in hibiscus and bougainvillaea. In the center of town, more decaying buildings, small shops and bars with hand-painted signs, an enormous market housed in a big orange hall built like one of the old Saharan mosques.

In the decade after independence, Mali's leaders dreamed grand socialist dreams, set up huge state-owned corporations to run the country, embarked on such ambitious projects as a Russian-built cement factory that would turn out fifty thousand tons a year. But the overblown bureaucracies and corporations didn't work, and today only their names remain, harsh Soviet-style acronyms like SOMIEX (the peanut trading corporation) and SMERT (the tourist agency, which I avoided). The cement factory now produced, at last report, five tons a year. The first president of Mali was a descendant of Mansa Musa, who had supervised what was then the biggest, most efficient civil service west of Suez, and it was sad and puzzling that the great emperor's successors could not keep a cement plant running efficiently.

Almost by accident, Bamako was a very pretty town. The government, had it the money, would surely have uprooted the shade trees and creepers, demolished the old colonial mansions, and built filling stations and high-rise hotels in their place. I spent three nights in Bamako and would have stayed longer, but I had to get to Abidjan before my money ran out. Abidjan, capital of the Ivory Coast, is possibly the most modern city in West Africa and one of the few to have an American Express office. I did not have enough money for bus fare; I would have to hitch.

Early in the morning, I walked out of Bamako and flagged down a truck. It took me five miles and left me just beyond Bamako Airport, with seven hundred more miles to go. I got a string of short-distance rides after that, with a lot of waiting in between, and spent the night by the side of the road somewhere near Bougouni. The next day, I got a hundred-mile lift and then nothing until, just before sunset, a car stopped. The driver was on his way to visit a sorcerer in a village forty miles down the road. He had been driving all day just to consult with the magician, and he would drive back that night. He would have to leave me there, he said, quite apologetically; evidently, he thought a European would be appalled at the prospect of a night in a mud hut.

The sorcerer lived just off the main road, in a compound of little round houses that was all but hidden by exuberant thick-trunked trees and drooping banana leaves. If I walked fifty feet from the compound I could see the highway, but, closer to the houses, the vista of trees and flowers gave me the illusion of being deep in the womb of a silent forest.

The wizard was a very old man. Among the Senufo, the people of the region, it is not easy to become a sorcerer. Cosmology, mythology, the intricate science of magic and divination must all be learned. This vast body of knowledge, called *Poro,* is all kept secret, never written down, but transmitted orally from master to carefully selected pupil. It might take twenty years, I had heard, to become a master.

We met the wizard inside his house. A portion of the floor was covered with sand. He drew a grid in the sand, scattered a handful of pebbles over it, studied the pattern for a few long minutes, and then told his visitor what the future had in store. He offered to tell my fortune as well, but I preferred not to know and politely declined.

The man who had brought me left, to return to his home a hundred miles away. Though he knew I was destitute, too poor to leave him a gift, the magician let me stay. He did not share any of his secrets with me that night, and he did not behave at all like a sorcerer. There was no aura of power or mystery shining around him; he seemed to be nothing more than a kindly old man. A woman brought me an overgenerous portion of *fufu* and stew. Later, she led me to another hut where a bed of woven mats awaited me. I woke up early and prepared to leave, and when I was ready the wizard walked out on the highway and stopped a truck. It was a hundred-mile ride and the driver let me sit in the cab. Perhaps the old man had magic in him after all.

An hour later, the truck reached the border. We left Mali and entered the Ivory Coast. The road, which had been paved since Bamako, suddenly became a bumpy, bone-jarring track. We passed through a large town named Ouangolodougou and, thirty miles farther on, an even larger town called Ferkessédougou, where the driver let me off. I changed a traveler's check at the local bank—I had spent my last cash in Bamako—and walked along the town's main (and only) street. I stopped on the outskirts and waited for a ride. It was a very long wait. In the end, I paid two thousand francs to a truck driver who promised to take me to Abidjan. A few miles beyond town, a wide, well-graded paved road began.

The Ivorian road system is like a river, with a network of narrow dirt tracks pouring into wide, smooth-flowing highways, all of which converge and empty into the main expressway which disgorges its motley flotsam into Abidjan, the city by the sea. My truck followed the flow of the highway through Niakaramandougou, the last of the *dougous,* through Katiola, to Bouaké, where we spent what remained of the night in an enormous asphalt parking lot surrounded by cafés and noisy bars. The next day, just outside Bouaké, the police stopped us. The truck was overloaded, or so they said, and the driver had to return to town and unload. He let me off, gave me a partial refund, and not long after that a car stopped and took me all the way to Abidjan. I was two weeks out of Timbuctu by then, and less than three years out of New York, and I felt as if I had been traveling all my life.

20

LIBERIA AND
SIERRA LEONE

At first, Abidjan seemed like paradise. It was set in the midst of lagoon, beach, and forest, and it gleamed from afar like a vast jewel above the waters. The sun flashed on the glass and steel of its towers and, at night, its skyline was a vision of twinkling lights and slender spires. Alluring, beckoning, making promises no place could fulfill—that is how most people first see Abidjan. Young men with hopes and dreams come from all over Africa. Some travel for months, some come on foot, and their first glimpse of the city never disappoints. Disappointment comes later.

I, too, had traveled for many months, sometimes on foot, and the route I had taken had allowed me to taste, not once but many times, the gentle life of the village. I should have hated Abidjan. Instead, I spent my first days gawking. The city was charged with a strange, frenetic energy; it was as if the tall, metal-sheathed office towers acted as psychic lightning rods.

Most of the office towers were under thirty stories, but they were beautifully designed, no two alike, with graceful swooping slopes and curves instead of rigid right angles. Some had marble atria; one had alabaster walls and plate-glass doors with elephant tusks for handles. Scattered among the skyscrapers were sidewalk cafés with colored awnings, spotless linen, and deferential waiters in bow ties and monkey jackets; chic boutiques with designer dresses and five-hundred-dollar shoes; Italian restaurants, Vietnamese restaurants, Russian restaurants, and, of course, French restaurants; *patisseries,* florists, toy stores, and five or six enormous supermarkets which devoted entire aisles to displays of pâtés and cheeses flown in from France. There was a full supply of French wines and champagnes and steaks flown in from Argentina. There were sections for pets as well, with imported dog food (two dollars a can) and cute bone-shaped rubber toys. . . . Somehow, the inventory reads like an indictment, though of whom or what I could not say.

While in Abidjan, I started, almost inadvertently, to use such outmoded terms as "French West Africa" and even "French colonies" to refer to the Ivory Coast and her French-speaking neighbors. I found more Frenchmen in Abidjan than I had seen in all the rest of Africa. There were fifty thousand of them living in the Ivory Coast, five times as many as there had been at independence. The housewives who bought the Camembert and the dog food were French. The clerks who served them were often French. The women who worked in the florist's, the salesmen at the boutique, the concierges at the hotel, all were French. At police headquarters, where I went to extend my visa, several of the senior officers were French. At other ministries, virtually the entire staff, except for the minister, was French. Four-fifths of all jobs requiring a university degree were filled by Frenchmen. Those tall towers, built with French capital, held for the most part the offices of the French banks and trading corporations that dominate the Ivorian economy. And their investment is protected by a garrison of six hundred French soldiers.

Abidjan made me think. I had come to hate colonialism, and it was easy to dismiss the Ivorian leader, President Houphouet-Boigny, as an Uncle Tom. But his policies have transformed an impoverished colony (per capita annual income seventy dollars) with a one-crop economy into one of Africa's richest nations, with a diversified agricultural base and a per capita annual income of twelve hundred dollars. Vast plantations produce sugar, palm oil, coffee, and cocoa.

The workers on these farms come from all over West Africa, but chiefly from Upper Volta. There is not enough arable land in Upper Volta to support its population, and it is the money its workers earn in the Ivory Coast that keeps Upper Volta alive. And, in Abidjan, while many of the top jobs are held by Frenchmen, most of the work is done by Africans. The Africans get much lower wages than the French, but the salaries are high enough to attract job seekers from all over Africa, and the population of Abidjan now exceeds one million.

Most of the young men who flock to Abidjan are not fleeing starvation. They plan to work for a season or two and then go back, carrying new clothes, some extra cash, and maybe a radio. But Abidjan is addictive, and people stay longer than they intend. And when they finally return home, they often find their villages are much smaller than they remembered, and the settlement that was once the center of their world now appears primitive, boring, and stagnant.

The center of Abidjan is called the Plateau. The high-rise towers, the elegant shops, the lavish supermarkets are, almost without exception, there. The rich have their villas in Cocody, and the almost-rich and merely middle-class live in Marcory. The workers live across the lagoon in Treichville, where the buildings are made of concrete, stucco, and tin. So did I. I had cashed a check for five hundred dollars at American Express, which made me rich by Treichville's standards but dirt-poor by Cocody's.

I was not a spendthrift, that first time in Abidjan, but I lived well. I ate in little Treichville bistros with rickety chairs and chipped china and boxes of Uncle Ben's Instant Rice displayed like trophies in the window. I drank beer in bars with ceiling fans, metal seats, and a radio to entertain the patrons. Sometimes I had coffee in the sidewalk café of the Hotel du Parc on the Plateau. The pink tablecloths were never wrinkled, and the linen, the heavy silverware, and the bone china made me feel clean and coddled and even chic. I met a young Ivorian there one afternoon. His stylish, well-cut sport jacket marked him as a man of taste and means; his fluent French suggested a university education, perhaps in France. I told him about the old Senufo sorcerer and I asked him if he believed in that sort of thing. "It is not a question of belief," he said. "Here in Africa, magic is not a superstition but a fact that can be observed. I have seen it." Once, in the northwest, near the Mali border, he had seen a wizard throw an ax thirty feet in the air and then jump on top of the ax and ride it.

Was he lying? I don't think so, but he may have been. Perhaps, like my old friend Denis in Zaire, he wanted to please or impress me and would not let the truth stand in his way. Possibly, living in a city designed, engineered, and run by Europeans, he wanted me to believe that Africans, too, could work miracles.

But he was not the only person to speak of magic. From time to time I heard whisperings of strange and sinister happenings—of men who turned into animals, of fetish cults, of human sacrifice. "You white men have your science," I was told more than once in the weeks that followed, "but magic is our science."

I met a French couple who had driven from Upper Volta into Ghana. Their car had broken down between Po and the border. They were stuck by the side of the road all night and, though many cars drove past, no one would stop to help them. Finally, just after dawn, a truck gave them a lift to the nearest police station. The gendarme in charge told them, or so they told me, that the spot where they had spent the night was a favorite haunt of headhunters. Headhunting had gone commercial. "Businessmen" would drive up from the coast, find a lonely stretch of road in Upper Volta, and wait. There were villages along the road, and eventually someone was bound to walk past. They would ambush him, cut off his head, and move on. The heads would be sold hundreds of miles away, in the Ivory Coast. The gendarme showed the two French travelers photographs of headhunters and of bags of confiscated heads.

Was the gendarme telling a tall tale to a credulous couple? Or was I the one whose leg was being gently tugged? Perhaps. But I heard other stories as well. There were volumes and volumes of them in the bookstores, which were very understanding to those who browsed but did not buy. I read about fetish cults in Nzérékoré and strange moonlit ceremonies on the beach at Sassandra. Both of those towns are near the Liberian border, and the books agreed that the most powerful magic of all could be found in Liberia. That was where, a few months before, a group of politicians had gone on trial for cannibalism and ritual murder.

It took me a week to get a Liberian visa. The embassy told me two days, but when I went back to collect my passport, it was returned unstamped; there was no space, the clerk told me, to stamp the visa. My passport by then was full of extensions, pages pasted in, pages that fell out when you opened it, perhaps a hundred pages of stamps in all, and though there was one blank page at the back of one of the paste-in extensions, it was not surprising that the embassy had not been able to find it.

The American embassy glued a set of new pages into my passport, which enabled me to get a Liberian visa, and left room for a visitor's pass for Sierra Leone. Both countries were reputed to have large regions without roads, and it was the alluring vision of a narrow trail through dense, damp jungle, with an isolated village at the end of it, that drove me west. I was interested in voodoo, but villages intrigued me more.

I went to the Gare Routière, the bus and taxi station north of the Plateau, and found a passenger van going to Toulépleu, a dot on the map near the Liberian border. The van lingered all day in the lot, as vans are wont to do, and did not leave until sunset. Just beyond the city, the forest closed in. On either side of the narrow road, the faint starlight traced the dark silhouette of the jungle, a blackness so dense it stood out against the black night sky.

In the middle of the night, we came to a roadblock, where a portly, middle-aged policeman began a laborious search of the rooftop luggage rack. He told the driver that the search would take several hours but could be made much shorter for a small fee. The driver refused, and the policeman kept us for over two hours, searching, meticulously examining every item, and all the while muttering, "I have eight children in school. How can I support them on my miserable salary? I have an aged mother I must look after," and so on, until another unfortunate van arrived at the checkpoint and he let us go.

There were more roadblocks the next day. Many farmers, the driver told me, tried to smuggle their crops, especially coffee beans, into Liberia, where they fetched far higher prices than in the Ivory Coast. Farmers got about sixty cents for a pound of beans in the Ivory Coast, and seventy-seven cents across the border. We were only a day's drive from the mansions of Cocody, but if what the driver told me, and other people confirmed, was correct, the villagers were receiving less money for their labors than were the farmers of economically stagnant Liberia.

Late in the evening, we arrived in Toulépleu. I spent the night at a wretched hut that claimed to be a hotel, and the next morning shared a taxi to the border, and then another to the Liberian town of Tobli. There was a police station at Tobli and little else. On the wall of the police post, as in every official building in Liberia, hung a 1979 calendar decorated with photographs of the hanging of the eight politicians convicted of ritual murder. Beneath the grisly Desolation Row snapshots was printed the legend, IF YOU KILL, THE LAW WILL KILL YOU, a statement by President Tolbert, who was himself soon to be murdered by a disaffected soldier, Sgt. (now President) Samuel Doe. Another placard carried a more enigmatic presidential platitude, TOTAL INVOLVEMENT FOR HIGHER HEIGHTS.

Outside the police post was the main road to Monrovia. I waited by the narrow dirt track, and was joined by a teacher on his way west. He was stationed at Zia Town, fifty miles away, and had taken the day off to visit his parents. His village was several miles from the nearest road, and he invited me to join him. As we waited for a ride, I asked the teacher about fetish cults and magic. "There are some religions in Liberia," he replied, "that you should not talk about." I prudently kept off the subject after that, and that was the last I heard of Liberian voodoo.

A slat-sided truck carrying women home from market picked us up and let us off ten miles down the road. Two of the women got off with us. There were no houses in sight, only forest and a narrow trail running south. The four of us took that trail, and followed it through the jungle. The women were laden with bulky, cloth-wrapped parcels, but we made good time nonetheless. I, too, had my pack to carry, and I was not sorry when, after about an hour, I saw a clearing through the trees. There was a neat little house in the center, and the teacher led me inside. The interior was cool and quiet, and on the earthen walls hung faded sepia photographs of the teacher's ancestors and relations. The old daguerreotypes, their heavy wooden frames burnished by the setting sun, gave the room a strangely antebellum ambiance. I had expected to find such things in Liberia, a country founded by freed American slaves and, in 1979, still run by their descendants, who rigidly preserved the norms and trappings of the culture that had enslaved their forefathers. But I did not think that American influence had penetrated the forest.

I met the teacher's mother, whose house it was, and then the teacher took me to the main part of the village, a larger clearing a few minutes' walk away. There he introduced me to the chief and then left to visit his mother. He must have walked back to the road soon after that, because I did not see him again.

The village was a double row of houses, eight in all. Those men and women who were not at work in the fields sat in their houses or just outside them, but the children, of which there were many, sprawled and rolled in the dirt or chased each other all over the clearing. The chief led me around the village and the children, terrified at the sight of me, scattered screaming at my approach. Many African mothers trick their children into obedience with gruesome stories whose endings were usually, "If you don't behave, the white man will get you." Perhaps the children who ran away mistook me for a bogeyman come to carry them off, or perhaps they were terrified by my pale-skinned hairy face, so unlike any they had ever seen. To most Africans, white men look uncannily apelike, and the youngsters might have thought I was a huge monkey from the bush. Whatever the cause of their fear, the children, after a time, turned it into a game. I would pretend to chase them; they would pretend to run away. By the end of the evening, they came within a foot of me, and the next day they followed me everywhere and would not leave me alone.

The children's terror was a sign of the village's remoteness; few if any white men had passed this way before. But I soon discovered that the village was less isolated than it seemed. Most of the houses had shiny tin roofs, which had been carried through the jungle piece by piece. Just as the vision of untouched villages and thatched cottages had lured me into the forest, so had those tempting pieces of tin enticed the villagers out, to sell their crops, to work in the towns, to load tons of metal onto their backs and haul it along narrow, slippery trails.

"When will they build a road here?" several of the villagers asked me. The stillness of the forest was infinitely precious to me, but they craved the music of trucks whizzing by. And so might I, if I had to carry a hundredweight of tin.

A heap of roofing, just carted in, was lying at the edge of the clearing, and nearby I saw two men plastering a final coat of mud on newly made earthen walls. The walls were built around a framework of wooden beams that would eventually support the metal roof now lying disassembled. Why only two men, I asked the chief. I had seen houses built before, and usually the entire village, or a substantial part of it, turns out to help. These men come from Tapeta, the chief explained. (Tapeta was the nearest large town.) We hire them to build our houses. Instead of rounding up the neighbors, someone who wanted a house erected would pay to have it done. It was less fun than a house-raising party, and required a lot more effort in the end, since the laborers had to be paid (about thirty dollars each), and the villagers had to find work to earn the money to pay them. But the chief was not displeased. He beamed at the workers. He puffed out his chest. He pulled out his pipe and smoked it. He was proud of his villagers. They knew enough to call in professionals when they wanted a job done.

It was growing dark by then, and the workers quit for the night. I ate the evening meal by firelight, in one of the houses. Two women, fat and placid, sat by the fire and watched me eat. One held a baby in her lap. The little child, rail-thin, was shrunken and wizened, like an old man or a fetus. I was no doctor but I knew the child was dying. And, as likely as not, he would die of something that a few shots of penicillin or vitamins would have cured.

After a while, the headman joined me. I asked him how he came to be chief. Was he born a chief, or chosen? In Liberia, he replied, the villages elect their chiefs just like America. Our conversation trailed off after that; soon the chief left and I sat and stared at the fire, mesmerized by the dancing flames. The logs popped and crackled, but outside it was quiet, and I assumed the village was settling down for the night. I went outside. The moon had risen, and the clearing shimmered in its cold and brilliant light. I saw a group of people sitting outside, and when I got closer I realized that the entire village had gathered. A woman got up and spoke for quite a while in a loud, angry voice. When she had finished and sat down, a second woman launched into a tirade, jabbing her finger at the first woman to show who was the cause of it.

I found the chief and asked him what was going on. There was bad feeling between two houses, he told me. (I had guessed that much already.) Each family accused the other of stealing money. Both families knew that the quarrel could not be allowed to drag on forever, since they had to live and work together, and this meeting had been called to settle it. Both sides would talk, all night if need be, with the whole village as witness, judge, and chorus. In the end, a solution would emerge.

But it did not take all night. One of the women had owed money to the other. She claimed she had repaid the debt; the other said she hadn't. She had given the money to a child to deliver to her creditor, and it soon became apparent that the boy had kept the money for himself. Had this happened in a town, the police would have been called in and the case gone to court. That would have taken months, but the village palaver had discovered the truth within two hours. The two women were once again the best of friends, and to seal and celebrate their friendship and drown all memory of their quarrel, they brought bottles of whiskey from their houses, and piles of very large tin cups, and poured out cupfuls for everyone present. Soon we were all more than a little tipsy, and the meeting that had begun in anger ended in raucous laughter.

By the time I went to bed that night, the village seemed a far better place than it had a few hours before. I stayed another day. The people, tired from the night before, were unusually quiet and sub-dued, except for the children, who had gotten used to me by now and were more boisterous than ever. That evening, a soldier came to the village to visit his relatives. He left the next morning, and I left with him, for the trail had too many forks and turnings for me to go alone. Before he left, the soldier gave a few dollars to his relations; it was, he told me, the custom for a guest to leave some money for his host. I had always followed this practice, and it cheered me to see that others did as well.

As always, the trek to the highway seemed to take less time than the walk away from the road. The path and the destination were both familiar the second time around. Besides, the soldier was a fast walker. In his olive-drab fatigues with corporal's stripes on the sleeves, his peaked cap, his jungle boots, and his dark glasses, he looked like a GI. When we got to the main road, we sat together on a fence waiting for a car to pick us up. He got a ride going east and left me. A few minutes after that a passenger van came from the east. I got on. Twelve hours later, I was in Monrovia.

Monrovia, the capital of Liberia, reminds most visitors of small-town America, makes them think of a slightly dowdy and down-at-heel county seat: Main Street, Yoknapatawpha County. Perhaps be-cause I had heard about it so often, I found the resemblance less striking than I had expected. Still, there were many small surprises. The street signs and the license plates looked American, and the money *was* American. Liberia does not print its own banknotes, but uses U.S. dollars instead. One evening, through the windows of the old frame house across the street from the YMCA where I stayed, I saw a group of old men in white tie and tails returning, I guessed, from a lodge meeting or Masonic banquet. Africa was as alien to the freed slaves and their descendants as it was to the British, and both dressed for dinner in the jungle.

Liberia's long and tawdry history reads like *Animal Farm.* It was settled in 1822 by freed slaves from America. Those freed slaves and their descendants caught and kept slaves, using forced labor to farm huge plantations. In the 1930s, some became slave traders, exporting slaves to Fernando Po. Though this practice ended over forty years ago, and the indigenous, tribal Liberians, who make up 97 percent of the population, were even given the vote, there was only one party to vote for and virtually the entire government was related to the president, an Americo-Liberian, by blood or marriage. At the time of my visit, the original settlers' descendants were very clearly the masters.

I did not tarry long in Monrovia. A day was more than enough to see the churches, mansions, and rundown shopping arcades that lined Broad Street. That evening, I considered seeing a double bill at the Roxy Cinema, but the line was too long. I walked to Gurley Street, which is famous for its honky-tonk bars, and passed the evening drinking dollar beers in a saloon decorated with cardboard Stetsons and phony horseshoes and waist-high swinging doors.

The next day I walked to Water Street, where I found a van that took me to the Sierra Leone border. The man on duty at the Sierra Leone side spent an hour examining my pack and every item in it. "We must protect ourselves against mercenaries," he muttered. Finally, satisfied that I presented no threat to the nation, he stamped my passport.

I got a ride to Kenema, a rich town in the diamond country. Kenema was full of showy, expensive-looking houses, most built by Lebanese diamond traders. The owner of the van that brought me, an African, was not as rich as the Lebanese, but he was hardly poor. He invited me to spend the night at his house. It was built of brick and glass and concrete and was so new that the shiny white paint on the living room walls had barely dried. Most of the family had not yet moved in. They were awed by the place and preferred to live in a little shack in the back garden.

I slept in a bed that night, and boarded a bus the next morning for the long ride to Freetown. I had a mild attack of chills and fever on the bus, and the other passengers could not understand why I first wanted the window closed, and then wide open. They did not realize I was sick but, as a white man, I was expected to have strange and sudden whims, so they shut and opened the window as I directed. I had almost recovered by the time we got to Freetown, and I staggered through the streets to the City Hotel.

The City is probably the most famous hotel in West Africa. If there's a better-known hotel, I haven't heard of it. Graham Greene used it as a setting for his novel *The Heart of the Matter*. The book is about a weak man with a strong conscience, floundering through his life; all of his joy and purpose have been long since leached away by the endless rains of the tropics, leaving only duty behind. It is a gloomy, depressing story and its author needed a gloomy, depressing place to set it. He took the City, renamed it the Bedford, left its layout and location more or less intact, but transformed it somehow into an establishment that a reader would go to great lengths to avoid. That was almost forty years before, but Freddy, the owner, who was there then and was still there in 1979, has never forgiven him. Not for driving business away—the downstairs bar is nearly always full—but for drinking there, accepting Freddy's hospitality, and then making his hotel a byword for seediness. Probably what irked him most is a character named Harris who organized cockroach hunts in the bedrooms. (A point for every confirmed kill, but only half a point if the corpus delecti falls down the drain.)

Freddy, who must have been quite old when I saw him but didn't look it, was a kindhearted Swiss, though he struck many visitors as taciturn and dour, because he wasn't quick to make friends and because people usually made the mistake of asking him about Graham Greene. He'd far rather talk about Jerry Rawlings, who had just come to power in Ghana. Rawlings's father, who is Scottish, lived in Freetown for several years and was a regular at the City's bar. This must have been many years ago, since Freddy remembered Rawlings as a nice young lad in short trousers.

By the next day, I was well again. I had planned to go up-country as soon as I recovered, but I didn't. My travel plans had, over the years, become less and less rigid, more and more African in their flexibility. Each day I decided to leave tomorrow. Travel, though always enjoyable, is hard work, and I needed a vacation. I am not sure why I picked Freetown, though. Perhaps it was the beach, or the hamburgers at Big Boy's. More likely, it was the room. The City Hotel was a big, rambling affair built about 1925. It had a wide central staircase and wood paneling everywhere, and my room was spacious, light, airy, and clean. It had just been painted a jarring shade of purple, but I soon got used to that. The room was a refuge, a retreat, a place I could call my own.

Near my room and facing the road was a wide veranda that ran the length of the hotel. The opening scene of Graham Greene's novel, which takes place in the early 1940s, is set on this balcony; it was evidently a popular meeting place in those days, and it still is today. Greene describes it as full of cynical civil servants, shipping clerks, and red-faced merchants, but the expatriates have long since headed home (or to newer hotels), and the Peace Corps has taken over. There are over two hundred Peace Corps volunteers in Sierra Leone.

Night after night I sat on the balcony, drank bottles of beer with the volunteers, and, like the others, flicked the caps into the street. I listened to the talk and sometimes joined in. The faces changed every night; the people worked up-country for the most part, and came to Freetown only one or two days a month, if that. The faces changed, but the talk was the same. Like every group or fraternity, the volunteers had created common rites and rituals, gripes and gossip, all of which strengthened the bond between them and reminded me that once again I was an outsider. After a while, after I had learned their language, most of the volunteers accepted me as one of them, which was more than I had hoped for and perhaps more than I deserved, since most of them worked very hard and I did not, by their standards, work at all.

The ones who worked the hardest were the agriculture people, the "aggies." They spent their days sloshing through rice paddies, up to their knees in muck. Rice is one of the staple crops in Sierra Leone, and most of it is grown, and has been from time immemorial, on unirrigated land. Traditional methods of agriculture, which often strike Western observers as primitive beyond belief, are in reality the product of thousands of years of evolution and experiment and are often far more efficient than they appear. Sometimes, especially in East

Asia, they represent the optimal use of land and labor. In Sierra Leone, they do not. Without irrigation, the fields produce enough—barely—to keep the people alive, but the population is steadily growing. Irrigation, as I had seen it practiced in the emerald fields of Bali, could increase the yield many times over. Sierra Leone, after all, has twelve times as much land as Bali, much of it fertile, and only twice the population.

So the aggies preached irrigation. They didn't want to turn the villagers into Chinese; they planned on a smaller scale, hoping to get one or two fields watered, or perhaps to set up a fish pond. The villagers' diet is sorely lacking in protein, which fish can provide. A pond—basically a big hole with water in it—can be stocked with species of fish which thrive on a diet of rice bran, which the villagers traditionally discard when they polish the rice.

Irrigation and fish ponds, they sounded like great ideas to me, and the aggies, too, were fired with enthusiasm as they described them. But the farmers reacted with polite but sullen skepticism. So might a Tamberma sorcerer be greeted in Missouri if he tried to convince a group of wheat farmers to build fetishes in their fields. The villagers stood to gain extra rice if the experiment worked, but they faced starvation if it didn't. Why not stick with the old ways, they thought. They don't work very well, but at least we *know* they work. Villagers are inherently conservative and fearful of change, and a volunteer would sometimes serve out his tenure without a single pond being dug or paddy watered.

The people won't change, an aggie told me one evening, not for fifty, not for a hundred years. He was wrong. Villagers do change their ways, but slowly. (Sometimes, when I saw the young men in the shantytowns outside Abidjan, I thought, not slowly enough.) Like those farmers in Missouri, they like to be shown. The hardest part is getting the first farmer to dig a pond or irrigate a field. That first man's reputation is bound to suffer. If he fails, he will be laughed at for years to come, and if he succeeds, does better than his fellows, they will view him with envy and suspicion. They may even accuse him of witchcraft. But eventually, first one, then another, then the whole village will adopt the new technique. All this may take five or ten years—more, if the chief is hostile—but Peace Corps volunteers serve only two. The first volunteer in a village may spend his entire term laying the groundwork for his successor.

There are other problems for the volunteers to cope with. The water pumps they send us, one told me, must be cleaned and oiled every three months. As often as not, this means that the working life of a pump is three months. Overhauls are postponed, badly done, neglected, and the pump breaks down. Sometimes the oil never even reaches the pump; someone sells it on the black market. This story reminded me of the many drivers I had seen in Africa who drove too fast in the wrong gear, or continually ran their jeeps in four-wheel drive, either of which practices will wreck the engine. (It was, I noticed, only government drivers who did this; a man would never harm his own truck.) It did not surprise me that many volunteers preferred to teach English in one of the larger towns. A few lucky ones were assigned to Freetown.

African capitals are required to have a showcase street of modern office buildings. In Freetown, this was Siaka Stevens Street, named after the president. There was some new building going on when I was there, and more was planned, because the Organization of African Unity was due to hold its 1980 conference in Freetown. Millions and millions of dollars were to be spent sprucing up the city to impress the delegates. The money would have to come from somewhere, and some of the volunteers were worried that budget cuts would force their schools to close. Up to then, Freetown, one of the world's best natural harbors, had managed to have other countries pay for its facelifts. The Israelis built the Parliament house, the Chinese contributed a football stadium, and the North Koreans built the city hall and, it was rumored, helped train the president's secret police. This elite police force was not very popular and when I was in Freetown the newspapers announced that, in response to criticism, the force would be renamed. This satisfied the critics, or so the papers said.

Despite the concerted efforts of the Koreans, Israelis, and Chinese, most of Freetown remains as delightfully shabby as when, a half century before, the young Graham Greene caught his first glimpse of the city, tin roofs floating in mist. Greene hated the place on first sight, and so did the explorer Sir Richard Burton, who visited the town seventy years earlier. Both found Freetown far too British, too tame, too corrupted by the civilization they were fleeing. Both of them had a peculiar loathing for Africans who wore Western dress, and Freetown affected them the same way. But fifty years had passed since Greene's arrival, five decades of damp and mold and rain, and by the end of those years Africa had reclaimed Freetown as her own. Now the city was one of the most pleasant, most African of capitals, with street after street of tumble-down two-story wood houses and bands of children playing in between. All of the houses were painted brown, with latticed windows and old-fashioned shutters half off their hinges. All of the women were fat and majestic, and sailed through the streets in bright and billowing dresses. Every sidewalk was a market, and every day was market day.

At the Sierra Leone Women's Movement Restaurant on Charlotte Street, or the 1049 Chophouse in a tiny wooden shack one block over, you could get a huge plate of rice or *fufu* for half a leone (about fifty cents); 1049 was crowded at lunchtime and you had to wait on line to sit down. As you ate, you could hear the same thump-thump-thump as you heard in the villages; in the yard behind the Chophouse, the women were pounding cassava. Then, over to Kissy Street for another look at the markets. The sun would set, and for a few golden moments the rows of wooden houses would be transfigured by its beams. The streets would grow quiet, and it would be time to go back to the City, and pitch bottle caps into the dark.

I was happy in Freetown and I could have stayed there forever. But one day, one of the aggies told me about Lake Sonfon. He had never been there and knew very little about it, only that there was thick jungle, remote villages, and miles and miles of trails. That afternoon, I visited the Survey and Lands Department, where I examined a huge map that all but filled the tiny office. I could go by road as far as a place called Bendugu, beyond which I would have to walk. A web of dotted lines, which indicated footpaths, radiated out from Bendugu toward the lake, and a scattering of dots suggested that there were many settlements in between.

One morning a few days later, I took a bus from Freetown to Makeni, a large town about a hundred miles inland. The road was good, a well-paved highway, and I reached Makeni in time to make the daily *poda poda* to Bendugu. (*Poda poda* is the Krio name for a passenger van; Krio, Sierra Leone's lingua franca, bears a vague resemblance to New Guinea pidgin English and many of its words are just as euphonious.) The *poda poda* was a battle-scarred veteran. Its wooden sides were cracked and splintered, and the cab, which had once been painted white, was splattered with mud. At a junction a few miles outside Makeni, we left the main highway, which ran east to the diamond mines at Sefadu, and headed north. From then on, the road was appalling: muddy, unpaved, pocked, and cratered, with hills so steep the old van could barely climb them. We stopped for an hour at a village called Nukikoro. The arrival of the car from Makeni was the big event of the day, and a crowd of children raced out of the houses and clustered around me. That day, I was the main attraction. One of the youngest children, barely more than a toddler, determinedly pushed his way to the front. He was pudgy, and ungainly, with a big distended belly. He did not look well at all; it was not healthy fat; malnutrition or worms had blown him up like a balloon. *Paddy,* I called to him, you're my *paddy!* He beamed at that. *Paddy* means friend in Krio and I, a man rich enough to take a car to Makeni, had picked him as a friend. And, in a sense I had. The other, healthy faces I saw in Nukikoro are just a blur to me now, but I carry his with me forever.

We reached Bendugu at dusk. Bendugu, the end of the road, had a shop, a few tin-roofed houses, and two Peace Corps volunteers, Neil and Shirley. Shirley had gone to Freetown, so there was room for me at the Peace Corps bungalow. There was a little plaza outside the shop where women from the village sold eggs and oranges. Neil and I sat in the square for much of the evening, drinking beer we bought in the shop. Passersby stopped to chat; Neil knew everyone in town, and I surmised that it would be easy for me to find a guide. And it was; the word went around that the newcomer wanted to hire someone who knew the way to the lake, and early the next morning a boy of sixteen showed up at the house. Boys on the verge of manhood are often either shy or brash; he was the sort of adolescent who blustered. He knew all the trails; he would show me everything. As he talked, he chomped a piece of sugar cane, peeling off the bark with big strong teeth, chewing the pulp and spitting it out. He did not seem like the ideal companion, but he spoke some English and seemed to know the way. There was, he said, a very nice village a full day's walk away. He knew the local language and when we got there he would ask the chief to let me stay. It sounded ideal. I did not want to go as far as the lake, since the land around it was marshy, and dotted with patches of quicksand.

Early the next morning, we left for the village. Tall elephant grass, still damp and musky with dew, grew on either side of the narrow path, so, not five minutes' walk from the store where I had bought beer the night before, we could no longer see any trace of the town. The forest had swallowed us.

There were twists and turnings and forks in the path, but these did not slow us down. My guide, just as he had boasted, knew all the trails. The day before, at the bungalow, he had seemed cocksure but gawky, young, and a little pathetic as he munched his sugar cane and stared at the armchairs and foam-rubber beds. But now, out of sight of "civilization," he came into his own. Stocky, strong, bare chested, with a round face and deep-set eyes, he seemed to grow in size and power the farther we got from town, like a bush Antaeus returning to his native element. After an hour, he seemed positively sinister. He had been silent until then, brooding, but now he sidled up beside me and spoke, in his strange guttural accent: "I know men who fly through the night. I know men who can change into animals. This is the forest, and many things happen."

I felt helpless in the forest, and had no wish to see any of those things, so I ignored him and concentrated on the land. Through gaps in the grass, I saw rice fields with humpbacked hills beyond, rolling green waves in a vast and verdant sea. Every field had a tall wooden tower where boys sat, armed with slings and pebbles to chase the birds away. Usually, two or three boys kept watch together, and then the job became an outing, an excuse for gangs of boys to play, gossip, and hunt lizards far from adult eyes. As I walked, I could hear laughter from the towers. We stopped at one, and climbed the rickety ladder to a small platform where two boys were having a picnic. They shared their lunch—a freshly caught lizard—with us, and showed me how to shoot a sling. They were experts; they would twirl the sling like a lasso and crack it like a whip, and the stone would fly across the field; they obviously devoted much of their time on the tower to practicing their shot.

The fields and scaffolds meant that a village was near at hand and, not long after, the path widened into a circular clearing where five or six houses stood. It looked, I thought, exactly as a village should: round cottages with drooping roofs of thatch and old earthen walls, cracked and peeling like the dry sunbaked ground from which they seemed to spring. But it was not quite noon, and there was another village several miles beyond, and I decided to press on, reasoning that the second village, farther from the highway, would be even more cut off from the outside world. Each of the houses had a little, half-moon-shaped veranda shaded by shaggy thatch, and my guide and I sat on one of these balconies for a short rest. An old, bent man hobbled over with a calabash of water, and we drank. There was no one else about. The village was quiet, lulled to sleep by the heat of the midday sun, and after a half-hour or so we left it, and took the path that led deeper into the forest. More hills, more fields, more lookout towers, more talk of men who could enter the bodies of leopards, or talk with snakes, or fly through the night, and, toward the end of the day, the second village.

We came out of the forest and into a clearing, and the first thing I saw was a huge concrete bungalow. It had bright blue walls and a tin roof that gleamed proudly in the sun. It seemed to me like a scar in the forest; it would not have been worse if all the hills around the clearing had been flayed by strip mines. That was my reaction, but I soon noticed that the villagers paid no attention to the concrete intruder. The owner was never there—probably, he was someone who had left the village, struck it rich in Freetown, and had this big, empty house carried into the forest to impress his former peers—and the life of the village flowed around the mansion as a river swirls around a rock that blocks it. The villagers may have wanted a house like that, they may have been far more vulnerable to envy and greed than I realized, but they were too polite and far too proud to show it.

These people were Koranko, an offshoot of the Malinké; they were related by language, culture, and perhaps by blood to the emperors of ancient Mali, to Mansa Musa, who had dazzled the world with his wealth. The villagers were well aware of their ancestry, and the chief, a tall man well into middle age, stood perfectly straight and moved with regal bearing, as though his tatty, threadbare robe were cloaked by the mantle of proud tradition.

The chief was the first person I met in the village. He knew no English, so my guide spoke with him on my behalf, and explained that I hoped to spend a few days as his guest. The chief agreed and bade me welcome and my guide, after promising to return for me in three days, disappeared into the forest.

One of the younger men, who had a small hut of his own behind the larger house of his parents, gave the hut to me and went to stay with relations. His parents looked after me, and I spent most of my time in their house, but that first evening I ate with the chief. His house was one of the smallest in the village, and was furnished with a few straw mats and little else; wealth and power, in the village, at least, did not go hand in hand. The meal was lavish; it centered on stewed chicken and rice. He invited me again the next day, and again we ate together, from the same bowl, and, as he had the night before, he ate slowly, and with much ceremony (it would be bad manners, when eating from a common plate, to eat faster than one's guest)—but this time the meal was plain rice sprinkled with salt and pepper, and I realized that last night's dinner represented a very great sacrifice on his part.

I saw the chief only at night. He, along with the rest of the men, worked in the fields until dusk, and the children, though they had to help with household tasks in the morning, left for their towers as soon as they possibly could. During the day, the village was very quiet. The sun beat down fiercely, and the courtyard between the houses was all but deserted. Each house had a cool, shady veranda, all of which were in earshot of one another, and these porches were the focal point of daily life. The young man's hut did not have a porch, so I used to visit his parents. I sat on their veranda, and read or daydreamed or watched the women who crowded the porch, lazily swapping gossip in drowsy murmurs. Their hands were always busy—carding yarn, perhaps, or sifting rice—and their eyes were always on me. White men did not pass that way often, and the chance to observe one at close hand might not come again.

At first there was a confusion. Some of the people assumed that, like every other white man they had heard of, I must have come to dig fish ponds or to plant rice. Word of my presence spread, and one old man came from a village several hours' walk away to ask me to dig a pond there. The aggies' work, it appeared, had had far greater impact than they knew. I tried my best to explain that I was not with the Peace Corps—"*Me no Pis Koh,*" I said, in my best Krio. The chief and most of the village understood, but I don't think I managed to convince everyone, and one or two people might still tell the tale, if prompted, of the lazy Peace Corps worker who did nothing at all but read and sleep and eat their food.

And I *was* lazy. The second day I scarcely stirred from the veranda. I lay on a mat in the shade and read *Ivanhoe.* The slow and sonorous cadence of the book hinted that life was simpler then, that knowledge and self-assurance were far easier to come by when it was written. People were in less of a hurry; they had more time. Those halcyon, bygone days, true, were already bygone when Sir Walter Scott wrote—in 1820, William Blake's satanic mills were rising everywhere and life was rapidly changing—but, in the Koranko village, twenty miles from the nearest clock, the world of *Ivanhoe* seemed more real than Freetown.

Since time was so casually observed in the countryside, I never expected my guide to return when he said he would, and I feared, and at times hoped, that he would never show up at all. But he appeared exactly when he promised, on the morning of the third day, emerging quite suddenly from the jungle with a half-eaten stick of sugar cane. I said my good-byes quickly, because I hated partings and my time in Africa was filled with them; friendships that could have flourished were uprooted daily, or never made. I gave my usual gift of money to the headman. It would not repay his kindness, but it would replace the food I had consumed. The chief thanked me gravely. He was too proud to show his pleasure at my gift, too dignified even to smile, but he could not stop his eyes from glowing.

Though we walked quickly, it was evening when we reached Bendugu. The next morning, I rode the battered old *poda poda* to Makeni. When we stopped at Nukukoro, the little boy, my *paddy,* was waiting, and when he saw that I still remembered him even after a whole week had gone by, his eyes shone as brightly as the chief's the day before.

That evening I was back in Freetown. A few days later, I made a brief journey to the coastal villages just outside the city, settlements which had been founded, like Monrovia in Liberia, and like Freetown itself, by freed slaves and were still inhabited by their descendants. The area around Freetown was one of Britain's first African possessions, under English rule since 1808, while the rest of Sierra Leone did not come under British dominion until almost a century later. The coastal towns have names like Hastings, Kent, and Waterloo. I went to York, where a grassy street ran between rows of old wooden houses and overgrown, long-neglected gardens. Eyes watched me from behind shuttered windows, but the villagers kept to themselves and I never saw them. Near the beach was a concrete palace. Huge, new and ugly, built to resemble an enormous bunker, it was one of President Stevens's many mansions. The place was deserted; on the top floor, one of the rooms was open and I spent that night and the next on the president's red Naugahyde sofa. Nobody cared; nobody bothered; there were no chicken feasts or even words of welcome, and I left for Freetown two days later without having eaten.

I stayed in Freetown after that, making day trips to nearby points of interest: to Lumley Beach to bake in the sun; to Big Boy's Café, near Victoria Park, for hamburgers and milkshakes; to an embassy party to load up on vodka and shrimp salad. It was a decadent, self-indulgent existence, with little of the flamboyance or glamour that makes decadence so attractive to behold. But it was easy, so very easy, and it was just too much effort to jam myself into a van, to deal with drivers and hustlers and beggars and police, to spend my days among strangers and the next night God knows where.

I finally left Freetown in late October. My money was running out and my visa was about to expire. I took a *poda poda* to Koindu, a full day's ride east of Freetown. From there I planned to take the northern route across Liberia back to Abidjan, where I would cash another check. I had forty dollars left, and it might even have been enough, had I not let myself be diverted.

It happened at Koindu. Koindu is a small town with a very big market. It is known as the Three Country Market because it is held near the spot where Guinea, Liberia, and Sierra Leone meet, and villagers from both neighboring countries slip across the border to shop there. I had to have my passport stamped at Koindu before I could leave Sierra Leone, but the policeman in charge of immigration had gone to the market. I found him there. He had his seal with him and he glanced at my passport and stamped it. The market was closing for the night; the traders were packing their goods and going home. They waved to the policeman as they passed him. This was his job, to stroll around the market, watching for strangers, keeping a vague eye out for smugglers. It was not a bad life; he was middle-aged, friendly, had a paunch.

We talked. I said I was going to Liberia and he told me that I could, if I wanted, go to Guinea. I could, he assured me, get a visa at the border. Why not? I thought. Guinea was one of the world's most hermetic countries. Tourists were never admitted in those days (1979), and if I could get in it would be a unique opportunity. It was also a shorter, more direct route to Abidjan.

There was a *poda poda* just leaving for the border, so I got on board. It was mostly empty. The road ran between fields of tall, dried-up elephant grass and ended at a riverbank. On the other side of the river, behind a screen of trees, was Guinea. There was no bridge, not even a ferry, only a few dugout canoes which were owned by the revolutionary committee of a village on the Guinea side. The head of the revolutionary committee stood by the boats selling tickets. I paid a leone and boarded one of the canoes. The rowers dipped their oars and the canoe glided across the black and sluggish waters toward the Guinea shore.

21

THE PEOPLE'S REVOLUTIONARY REPUBLIC OF GUINEA

I was surrounded by children from the moment I stepped on shore. They stared at me with frantic desperation, as if trying to garner a lifetime of memories, and the soldiers in the little hut by the bank could not clear them away. The nearest Peace Corps volunteer lived five miles away in Koindu, and a major Liberian highway, used by hundreds of Peace Corps volunteers a year, was even closer, but these children had obviously never seen a white man in their lives. For as long as those youngsters could remember, the citizens of the People's Revolutionary Republic of Guinea had lived in militant isolation.

The adults were too polite to stare. Besides, they had seen Europeans before; until 1958, Guinea was a French colony. But in that year, the French, realizing that the sun was about to set on their empire, held a plebiscite in all their African territories. The voters were asked to choose between complete independence and continued association with France. The French expected to win the vote, thus converting French West Africa into a French Commonwealth dominated, of course, by France. All went according to plan, except in Guinea, where 97 percent of the voters opted for independence. The French president, Charles de Gaulle, visited Guinea to meet with Sékou Touré, a young trade-union leader who had emerged as Guinea's most prominent politician. De Gaulle hoped to win Touré over with the same heady blend of hauteur and charm that had entranced Africans from Dakar to Bangui. Touré, who was in his own way as forceful a leader as de Gaulle, publicly told the Frenchman to go home. "We prefer poverty with liberty," he proclaimed, "to riches in slavery"; Touré had always been a superb orator.

De Gaulle did not suffer humiliation lightly. He returned to France and so, on his orders, did all four thousand French administrators, teachers, and technicians. They took everything they could carry and smashed or burned much of the rest: government records, medicines and hospital equipment, trucks and even telephones. French aid and investment were cut off, and de Gaulle did his best to get other European countries to do the same. Guinea had indeed won complete independence.

I had already visited the countries which had chosen riches in slavery. They had indeed prospered, their capital cities had impressive skylines, but some of the people had prospered far more than others, and many of those were French. Countries like the Ivory Coast were more dependent than independent; if the French pulled out as they had in Guinea, their economy would collapse like a punctured balloon. But in Guinea, dignity and idealism were valued more highly than commerce.

I knew that the Ivory Coast's gross national product was perhaps ten times Guinea's, but much of this wealth went to enrich the wealthy, and I wanted to see which country did more for the common man—for his pocket and for his pride. I also knew that the Ivory Coast had no political prisoners whereas many of Touré's critics had disappeared without trace. Those of his opponents who fled the country, and there were perhaps two million Guineans who did, reported that it had become a police state. To them, it seemed that Guinea had, in the end, chosen poverty and slavery.

The first soldiers I met in Guinea were young and friendly and eager to please. I sat down with them in the tiny wood-and-wicker shelter that served as the border post, and I talked to them about dignity, independence, and Touré's famous speech. "I want so much to see your country," I said. "Please excuse my coming to you without a visa." The soldiers listened, stamped my passport, and welcomed me to Guinea. Their trust in me was total, their minds were devoid of all trace of suspicion, and in them I saw for the first time what I was to encounter again and again in Guinea, and much later in China—the strange and touching innocence of a people cut off from the modern age.

After clearing immigration, I went through customs. The customs inspector, tall, thin, and quite young, wore thick glasses, a navy-blue uniform, and a tin badge with the emblem of the customs service, a cornucopia overflowing with fruit and flowers. "Do you know what 'customs' means?" he asked me. "It means—please forgive me—it means I must look at your luggage." I gave him permission and showed him how to open my pack and, quite shyly, he examined a few items. I was beginning to like Guinea.

Outside the customs shed was an ancient truck. It must have been one of the first motor vehicles brought to Guinea; it must have terrified the villagers in those days, made them wonder what strange monster had been loosed in their land. Now, forty years later, it should have been retired to a museum. Instead, it was jammed with passengers, so full that it was only through the courtesy of prior arrivals, who gave me a seat on top, that I did not have to stand on the running board while clinging to the side.

The truck coughed and wheezed and pulled out of the square; it seemed as surly as an ill-tempered camel. A few minutes later, it stopped, and the driver came out to collect the fare. We were bound for Guéckédou, the first town inside Guinea, which was only twenty miles away, but the fare was 175 syli (pronounced "silly"), about nine dollars at the legal rate. I did not have that much Guinean currency, and I was beginning to wonder whether I could pay in dollars when the driver saw me. He could not take my money, he said; it would be poor hospitality to force a guest to pay for transport. So I rode for nothing. The track was hilly, slippery, covered with stones; I had never seen so bad a road. Hours passed, night fell, and we had barely gone ten miles. Then the road leveled out, though only briefly, and as we drove across that flat stretch of land the engine burst into flames. I grabbed my pack and jumped off and the other passengers, who took the fire far more casually than I, slowly gathered their belongings together and clambered down the sides. The flames died down after a time and the truck did not explode, as I had feared it would. But it obviously could go no farther.

I and the other passengers spent the night at a nearby village. The people vied for the honor of putting me up. An old man was the first to see me, and he invited me into his hut. Then the headman happened by, and decided that the hut was not good enough for the village's first foreign visitor, so he took me to his home. It was a fine house, quite large, and built of earth and thatch in the traditional manner. The chief sat on a stool smoking a long wooden pipe. I looked forward to spending the night with him, but an hour later an even more important personage came by to claim me. He was younger than the chief, but was nonetheless middle-aged. He was stout, his white shirt was freshly pressed, and his horn-rimmed glasses made him look like a clerk or a minister. He was a Party activist and, as he reminded the chief, a member of the area's PRL, or Local Revolutionary Power, the governing body of the communes into which all Guinean villages were organized. The chief, with some reluctance, gave me up to the Party man.

The PRL man lived in a big house with whitewashed walls, screens in the windows, and a radio. I slept in a bed that night, probably his; I think that he slept on a mat in the parlor but he was, of course, too polite to let me know. The next morning, my host's eldest son walked with me to the road. He was on his way to school. In many African countries, school fees are so high that many families cannot afford to educate their children, but in Guinea, the boy told me, education is free and universal. He showed me his notebook. He was studying dialectical materialism that term, and the book was filled with definitions of thesis, antithesis, and synthesis, all copied, probably from dictation, in a neat, careful hand. We passed through the village on our way to the road; it was a village like any other, quite attractive and colorful, with round thatched huts clustered into compounds. I heard laughter from the yards, and I was soon surrounded by gangs of staring children, many on their way to school. I wondered how the strident maxims of dialectical materialism could fit into such a setting.

Late in the morning, a truck came by, and took me to Guéckédou. I had to get my passport stamped again, so I went to the police station, which was opposite an army barracks whose wall was covered with a huge portrait of Fidel Castro. The chief of customs, who had custody of the necessary rubber stamp, was not there, so one of the policemen took me to the chief's home. The regional head of immigration was sitting on a stool in his back yard. Next to him, his wife was pouring rice into an iron pot, and two or three chickens ran over, in the hope that a grain would drop. I showed him my passport, and he leafed through the pages, asked me a few questions, found a blank page and stamped it.

It was evening by then. I rented a room for one hundred syli, left my pack, and went into town. Vendors had set up tables all along the main road. There were hundreds of them, each lit by flickering candles. Some sold snacks—fried beans, peanuts, boiled eggs, bananas—while other tables were covered with clothes. I saw kaftans with beautiful embroidered borders. Much of the needlework was done by hand, and was far finer than the embroidery I had seen in other countries, which was all done by machine. The candles lit the traders' faces from below, turning them to bronze, and the whole town was beautiful to me then. Everything seemed less hurried and more relaxed than in Sierra Leone, as if the clocks ran to a different, slower time. In fact, Guéckédou looked a lot like the towns across the border, but everything I saw was suffused with my excitement at being in a forbidden land.

I had planned to go east from Guéckédou, following the Liberian border until I got to the Ivory Coast. Later on, I wished I had. But the next morning, still under Guinea's spell, I decided to see as much of the country as I could. Though I had less than forty dollars, I could get one hundred syli for one dollar, and prices were far lower than I expected. A white Peugeot station wagon took me to Kissidougou, a large town sixty miles north of Guéckédou. When I got there, I decided to go on. Kissidougou was a major crossroads, and within an hour I had found a van going to Mamou. Mamou was on the other side of Guinea, and as far away as Freetown, but it lay just south of the Fouta Djalon, a rugged, fertile highland that was reputed to be the most beautiful spot in West Africa. The road to Mamou was excellent, and the journey was fast and uneventful. Just north of Faranah we crossed a small stream spanned by a concrete bridge—the Niger.

I got to Mamou in time to catch the last car to Labé. Labé was in the heart of the highlands, and the road must have been quite beautiful, but it was night by then, and the fresh, cool air was the only hint I got that we had reached the high plateau.

When we got to Labé, the main hotel was full. The driver and all the passengers, who had gone with me to make sure I was properly housed, discussed where to take me. One of the women knew of a small boardinghouse on the outskirts, so we drove there, but it, too, was full. "Find the chief of police," one of the passengers proposed. "He will be able to help." In most African countries, a citizen with a problem will go to great lengths to avoid the chief of police, but things were, apparently, different here. All the passengers agreed that seeing the chief was an excellent idea; my problem was as good as solved. I thought it was a horrible idea, but of course I couldn't say so without making my new friends very suspicious. So we all went to find the chief, who was at his home eating dinner. As I had feared, he immediately asked to see my visa. I showed him the entry stamp and the endorsement the chief in Guéckédou had affixed, but he decided that was not enough. He kept my passport. I would, he said, have to stay in Labé until the matter was cleared up. But he did find me accommodation.

Just outside the town was the Syli Lodge, a government guest house that was the closest thing Labé had to a luxury hotel. It was more of a motel, actually, with rows of round concrete chalets built to look like traditional huts. The police chief drove me there, and I was given one of the larger chalets. I did not have to pay, he said. I was a guest of the government. He would see me the next morning.

The only other occupant of the guest house was Russian. He spoke little English and lost all interest in me when he learned I didn't play chess. A chessboard was his only comfort in an alien land he probably hated but could not leave. He was the only Russian I saw in Guinea, though a few years before I might have seen many more. After the West cut off aid and investment, Touré turned to the Russians. Surely, he thought, they would help a fellow-traveler. In due course, shipments of aid arrived. Russian boats brought snowplows, toilet seats, teachers and technicians (like the one I met) who spoke only Russian. All this must have seemed like a cruel joke to the Guineans. Much of the aid took the form of loans which Guinea was forced to repay. By the time of my visit, Touré had become disillusioned with the Soviets and was seeking better relations with the West.

Early the next morning, the chief of police drove up to my chalet and took me to a restaurant in town for breakfast. We ate fried liver served on glass plates. I was curious about the PRLs, the village-level collectives, and I asked the chief what they did. "They own tractors," he said. The only tractors I had seen in Guinea were just outside Labé. There was a huge lot filled with row after row of long-abandoned tractors, so I asked the chief about them. "They are waiting for repairs," he replied.

I detected a certain lack of revolutionary fervor. I had expected to hear either a reasoned analysis of the economics of collective farming or else an unreasoned, intemperate but vigorous polemic about the superiority of Marxist ways. Instead, I found the last thing I expected, a barely concealed apathy. In all of Guinea, I found no one who was willing to talk about politics. The subject didn't make them uneasy; it bored them.

The chief drove me back to the lodge. I would have to go to Conakry, the capital, he told me. One of his men would escort me. We would go by plane, and I would wait in Labé until the next plane arrived. Air Guinea, the national airline, had no fixed schedule. Each evening, the Voice of the Revolution, Guinea's radio station, announced where the planes would fly the next day.

It was three days until a plane came to Labé. I was allowed the run of the city until then. Labé was one of the largest cities in Guinea. There was one short street of two-story stucco buildings, built by the French and covered with the patina of age and neglect. One or two housed restaurants that half-heartedly kept running, with mismatched cutlery and chipped china. The other buildings seemed deserted. Apart from them, and a very large market, all there was to Labé was a scattering of tin-roofed shacks. Labé had been left to rot. This did not mean that all of Guinea was stagnant. In Africa, when the towns prosper, the countryside usually suffers. Still, Labé was a boring place to be stranded.

At least I did not have to pay for anything. The policemen got to know me, and whenever one of them saw me in town he would ask, "Have you eaten?" Whether I said yes or no, he would take me to the nearest restaurant and buy me a meal. He could not take the chance that a guest might be hungry.

Finally, the plane arrived. I, the chief, and the young lieutenant who was to accompany me drove to the airport in the Air Guinea truck, which was crowded with passengers. The plane looked as old and battered as the truck that had caught fire near Guéckédou. It had once been a cargo plane, or possibly a troop transport, in Russia. The inside reminded me of a *poda poda*. On either side, metal benches ran the length of the vast interior. I and the other passengers squeezed onto the benches, which were like low shelves, and the luggage was stacked on the floor, between the two benches. On top of the baggage were a few late-arriving passengers and a flock of goats. The goats were understandably nervous and baaed and milled about. I was nervous too. The propellers turned, and the plane shivered, lumbered down the runway, and took off.

It was a beautiful flight. The plane flew so low and so slowly that I felt like a hovering cloud. A thousand feet below me, the landscape drifted slowly by: rolling hills, flat plateaus, sheer cliffs, and deep valleys, all colored a rich, dark green. Once or twice I saw clusters of round huts; with their brown, bushy thatch they looked more like trees than houses. Then the land dropped in a staircase of precipices, down and down to the coastal plain. Soon after that, we landed at Conakry.

The main arrivals building at Conakry Airport was a shed with walls the color of mud. The lieutenant and I found a taxi just outside. The road into town was decorated with red metal billboards painted with revolutionary slogans. Little else had changed, it seemed, since the French had left. I saw vast sprawling suburbs of tin-roofed shacks, big colonial mansions, and boulevards lined with mango trees, but no modern buildings at all. It looked run-down and shabby compared to Abidjan or even Freetown. Still, Conakry's shantytowns looked a lot like Abidjan's, the only difference being that on a clear day the residents of the latter can see skyscrapers in the distance.

Conakry could have had a backdrop of skyscrapers on a par with Freetown if not Abidjan, but the government preferred to spend the money on doctors, teachers, and tractors. The meeting of the Organization of African Unity, in preparation for which Sierra Leone had squandered much of her budget, was originally scheduled for Conakry, but Touré declined the honor of being chairman. It would, he thought, be a waste of the country's money, and so Conakry remained the only capital in Africa without a luxury hotel. No wonder journalists hated it.

The lieutenant deposited me at a large police station where I was to spend the night. He would come for me the next morning, he said, and take me to meet the foreign minister. Then he left, and I walked into town as far as the market. The market was crowded; business was good. I watched from the fringes, where boys sold Coca-Cola smuggled in from Freetown. Nearby was the huge state-owned Nafyaya department store, its garish maroon interior all but empty. Later, back at the station, I found a vacant office and fell asleep.

When the lieutenant returned the next morning, his blue uniform was crisply pressed, and I was embarrassed more than ever by my worn khaki shirt and my jeans, torn and frayed despite my best attempts to mend them. Those were not the right clothes to wear when meeting one of the most powerful men in Guinea—the six-man cabinet was the equivalent of the Russian Politburo—but they were the only clothes I had.

In the heart of Conakry, near the presidential palace, was a complex of tall government buildings. The lieutenant and I walked past a sentry post, through a doorway, and up a spiral staircase to a small anteroom just outside the foreign minister's office. The minister had not yet arrived, so we sat and waited. There were several Guineans waiting as well, one a woman in an elaborately pleated dress and matching headscarf. "Any citizen," the lieutenant told me, "has the right to consult the minister." He sat impassively, staring at the ugly green walls, not at all excited or nervous at the coming meeting, but I was glad when, after several hours, we were told that the minister would not receive any visitors that day.

Behind the office building where we had spent the morning was a low, inconspicuous barracks that housed the headquarters of the Police de l'Etat, the state police. The lieutenant took me there and left me. He had to get back to Labé. I was sorry to see him go.

More waiting. I saw a copy of an Abidjan newspaper on a table, so I picked it up and started to read it. A policeman angrily snatched the paper away. All publications were banned in Guinea, except of course for *Horoya*, the Party daily, so the copy of *Fraternité-Matin* I had so innocently been reading was a classified document. This confirmed what I had already guessed, that I was in the headquarters of the secret police.

Sometime later, I was led to another office and questioned. I was alone in the white-walled room for a few minutes in the middle of the interrogation and I saw a letter on a desk. It was from the police chief in Labé. I had, he wrote, shown a suspiciously strong interest in politics and was obviously not what I claimed to be, a simple tourist.

I was interrogated for over an hour, but I had been questioned so many times during my travels that I managed to guess most of the questions and plan replies long before they were asked. Though I was indeed a simple tourist, my back-door entry sounded extremely sinister; why, they asked, didn't I go to the Guinean embassy instead?

They typed up my answers and gave me the statement to sign. I noticed that they had changed some of my answers to strengthen my case. "I wanted to learn about the PRLs" became "I wanted to see the tourist attractions of the beautiful Fouta Djalon." I had won their confidence. I signed.

After that I was taken to see the head of the state police. He was quite young and had a slight stammer. "I see from your statement you have no money," he said. "Here is two hundred syli so you can eat." I took his money, reasoning that he was responsible for my prolonged stay in Conakry. Then I was driven by car to the nearest jail.

It was a small compound right on Avenue de la République, the main street of Conakry, and you could pass it a thousand times and never guess what was inside. Those prisoners who were allowed to sit in the courtyard could peer through the crack between the two gates and catch glimpses of the busy street outside. There was a veranda just behind the courtyard, with a desk where the policeman on duty sat. When I first arrived, I was taken to the desk, and the policeman pointed toward a half-open door behind him. I could see a row of dank, crowded cells through the door and I hesitated. "No, go on in, it's really very nice inside," said the policeman. The traditional African politeness seemed so out of place that I was tempted to laugh. I later learned that cell number 4, which I saw through the door, was the most luxurious in the compound but, fortunately for me, the policeman decided that a foreign "guest" deserved better, so he let me stay in the office, where I slept on a detective's desk.

I had the room to myself, but the door was never locked, so I spent most of my time in the yard. I was never alone. The few inmates who, like me, were allowed the run of the yard, spent every minute they could there, watching the policeman on duty, listening to music coming from a nearby building, staring at the outside world through the crack between the gates, doing any one of a thousand little tricks to fight off boredom. Every passing hour was a victory.

One of the prisoners was a middle-aged man who had been a civil servant. He was a Malinké; he came from Kankan, near the Mali border. He was a friend of Camara Laye, Guinea's leading author. His charming, wistful recollections of childhood, written in France and published as *The African Child*, are so powerfully written that by the time I had finished the book I felt as if I had visited his village myself. The clerk felt the same way. "We Malinké love that book," he said, "because it reminds us of our own childhood." "All of it?" I asked, thinking of some passages near the beginning in which the boy's father is given supernatural powers. He is visited by spirits, and with their guidance he foretells the future. I had taken those passages as metaphors for the magic and mystery which the young child projects upon the world, and for the awe in which he holds his father. I told all this to the clerk. "No," he said, "those are accurate descriptions. Such things are quite common; we have all seen them." But he did not elaborate.

One of our most reliable diversions was the policeman on duty. Most were friendly but even those who were gruff had a lot of business to attend to, and we could watch them. The telephone rang often. "Ready for Revolution," the officer would say when he picked it up; this was how one answered the phone in Conakry. From time to time, prisoners were brought in. One, a teenager, was charged with stealing the life savings of a crippled merchant from his hotel room and spending it all on a few wild nights of drinking. Those inmates who saw him brought in were outraged when they heard this story, but the thief was cool and cocky; it was not his first brush with the law.

They put him in cell number 1, a concrete bunker barely large enough to hold its ten inmates. It had a hot tin roof and no ventilation at all except for a tiny crack under the metal door. When he was taken out the next day, the youth's self-assurance had left him; he begged to sign a confession. That did not help him, for he had not been put in that airless oven to make him confess. All the prisoners, except for a lucky few, were treated that way; aside from number 4, all the cells were alike. And they, like everything else in Conakry, had been built by the French.

There were no meals served in the prison, so each day the inmates' relatives brought them food. The prisoners in the courtyard shared their meals with each other and always gave a generous portion to me. They would not let anyone, even a stranger, go hungry. One day, as we were eating, an old man arrived with a loaf of bread. He had brought it for a man who had stolen his radio. The thief had just been caught, but he had no friends or relatives to bring him food, so the old man, his victim, felt obliged to feed him. He came every afternoon after that, a long loaf of bread under his arm, his face set in the frown of one who does his duty but does not enjoy it.

Several days passed, without any word when, or if, I would be released. Once the head of the state police showed up at midnight. "They never sleep," the former civil servant whispered. "The state police are always working." But the chief had come on other business; he said nothing to me, except to ask if I had eaten.

Sometimes, especially at night, I was frightened. Do not go near the Guinea border, a guidebook to Africa advised. If you stray across it you may be locked up for years. If the Guineans decided to lock me up for years, there was nothing to stop them.

It turned out to be a matter, not of years, but of days. I was driven one morning back to state police headquarters, where Dorothy Painter, the American consul, was waiting for me. The state police had just informed the embassy that an American was being held, and she had rushed over immediately. Mrs. Painter was obviously a skilled negotiator, and when she left a few hours later I went with her. I was not allowed to leave the city, but at least I was no longer caged.

"I couldn't have done this a year ago," Mrs. Painter told me. During the past year, Touré had decided to end Guinea's isolation. He had visited the United States a few months before, and relations between the two countries (and also with France) were now much warmer than before. But I was the first tourist the embassy people had seen. The embassy, which was where Mrs. Painter took me, was stark and modern. Other legations, as well as a brand-new PLO office, stood nearby, each surrounded by a wall half-covered with bushes. This quiet diplomatic enclave of concrete and marble was a world apart from the peeling stucco storefronts of Avenue de la République. Inside the embassy, bright fluorescent light bounced off white walls. I don't remember much else about the building—probably, like most American legations, it was modeled on one of two designs: shoebox, or shoebox-on-stilts—but I found the walls and light strangely comforting.

That night I slept in an embassy apartment. Like the embassy itself, it was well lit (with flashlights on hand for the power failures that plagued the city), reassuringly modern, and my most luxurious accommodation since the Nairobi Hilton. But I could not stand to be inside any room for long, so I spent the whole next day walking. I went the length of Avenue de la République, past the Air Guinea office, the bank, the jail, and a traffic circle with a plaster Eiffel Tower in the middle, and out along the road to the airport. Beyond the city center, for as far as I could see, stretched a sprawl of whitewashed huts and small family compounds closely packed together. In a small patch of open ground outside one of the houses, an old Fulani man prepared to sacrifice a sheep. It was a Moslem feast day, and the man's children ran around the square, excited by the holiday and the lavish banquet that the women had already begun to cook.

I walked back into town, through the market, and around the square at the end of the main avenue. Near the plaza was the Syliphone recording studios, one of Conakry's few modern buildings. Inside the large, government-subsidized studios, Guinean musicians fused traditional and modern rhythms to weave haunting, complex tapestries of sound. Some played the cora, a Malinké instrument that has as many strings as a sitar. Once, on the radio, I heard a cora recital and mistook it for a harpsichord sonata.

A short walk from the square was the embassy. There was still no word on when I could leave Conakry. My money had almost run out by then, but Mrs. Painter gave me twenty dollars out of her own pocket in return for my check, which would take months to clear.

I took my money down to the market, planning to buy dinner. I stopped at a bookstore I passed along the way. The shelves were empty and covered with dust. There were a few volumes of Touré's collected works on a table and, apart from that, nothing at all. I leafed through the fattest of the volumes. It was a long and tedious catalogue of the conspiracies, plots, and machinations that Touré had thwarted during his long tenure. Empty bookstores, foreign newspapers banned, a secret police that worked around the clock, airless overcrowded prisons hidden between the banks and airlines on the main avenue—often in Conakry I felt subtle hints of menace, which were made all the more noticeable by the contrast afforded by the rest of the country. Or perhaps I had been led to expect too much, and secretly hoped that policemen would stop me in the street and buy me dinner, as they had in Labé. Food was expensive in Conakry.

The few restaurants I could find wanted several hundred syli for a meal. Every city I had visited up to then had street stalls or dingy cafés where a filthy but filling meal could be had for half a dollar, and I had gotten used to the luxury of having others cook my meals. Now, even if I could live on a dollar a day, I would be bankrupt in a month.

Four or five young men passed by, all talking at once, a group of friends on their way to a bar. I stopped them and asked them where I could buy food cheaply. They must have guessed I was too poor to eat, because each of them, without even glancing at the others, reached into his pocket and pulled out a handful of ten-syli notes to give me. Though I refused their money, it wasn't easy, and in the end I had to run away.

Finally, I bought bread and fruit at the market. Even that cost too much, but since my room was free I could pay more for food. The next day I lost the apartment. Mrs. Painter's superiors had found out that a tourist was using an apartment reserved for embassy personnel. Mrs. Painter had gone out of her way to help me, and her kindness had landed her in trouble. She succeeded in persuading the embassy staff to let me stay if I paid but, at twenty-five dollars a night, I could not. They would have taken my check, but I was far from certain that any money remained in my account.

I now had to find lodging as well as food. Near the market were lodges where rooms went for three dollars a night, but you had to show your passport to register and mine was still being held by the state police. I went back to the police station where I had spent my first night in the capital, and asked if I could sleep there, but I was turned away.

The station was on the outskirts, and as I was walking back to town I passed a large barrackslike building. Its appearance was so forbidding that it had to be either a school or a prison; since the gates were open, I guessed it was a school. There was a shack to the side of the main building outside which a middle-aged man and his two teenage sons sat stoking a fire. The older man was, he told me, the headmaster. I asked him if I could sleep in one of the classrooms. I'll be out each morning before classes start, I promised. No, he said, I would be his guest, use his bedroom, and share the meal that was simmering on the fire.

He and I ate together, but I never slept in his bedroom, because two policemen came that evening and took me away. The man's eldest son had reported me to the police. It was, it seemed, against the law to have a foreigner as a guest, and so I spent the night locked inside the same police station that had refused to admit me a few hours before.

An hour later, the headmaster came to the station and insisted on seeing me even though he must have known that in so doing he would himself attract police suspicion. He was ashamed, he told me, of what his son had done, and he asked me to forgive him. He gave me a loaf of bread and told me not to be afraid.

I spent that day and the next inside the station. It was a huge place, with two stories connected by a shaky wooden staircase and a large barracks in back where the policemen and their families lived. When I wanted to wash, I had to wait in line with women doing laundry. Finally, I was released and my passport was returned.

It would, I decided, be prudent to stay in a hotel, but all the lodges I knew were full. Then I remembered the young and cocky thief who had robbed a crippled merchant. The burglary had been done in a hotel near the market, and I remembered the proprietor, who had come to the station as a witness. He had saluted the policemen with a loud "Ready for Revolution," his forehead glistening with sweat, and the whole time he had been there his eyes had darted around as if looking for a way to escape. I found his lodge without much difficulty. He remembered me and gave me a room—as it happened, the room adjoining the unlucky merchant's—for three hundred syli.

It was several more days before I could leave Conakry. The state police had no wish to detain me further; in fact, they wanted to be rid of me as soon as possible. But things had to be done according to established police procedure, and that took time. A uniformed policeman would be needed to escort me to the Sierra Leone border, and forms had to be filled out to get a policeman from one of the uniformed branches, and then more forms were needed to authorize the payment of the policeman's bus fare to and from the border, which was about a hundred syli. I would have to pay my own bus fare.

I had liked Conakry at first, liked its drowsy sun-dappled side streets, shaded by big mango trees, liked the grand old colonial mansions and stucco storefronts and busy markets; but all these bored me now, perhaps because I was not there by choice, and I wanted nothing more than to leave.

Finally, the day of departure came. Mrs. Painter insisted on lending me two hundred syli in case I ran short. The young policeman who was my escort was happy at what he regarded as a day's outing. We went to the taxi park and took the first van to the border town of Pamelap, eighty miles away. The road was good and a few hours later I was back in Sierra Leone.

22

DOWN AND OUT
IN ABIDJAN

Hamburgers and Coca-Cola, murder movies at the Odeon, rich men's Mercedes cruising down Siaka Stevens Street—features of Freetown life stood out that a few weeks before I had barely noticed. I had seen them in Douala, in Nairobi, and in Abidjan, in so many other places that I had in time come to accept them as inevitable features of African city life, not worth further curiosity or attention. I had accepted them in the way one learns to accept a dull but constant noise and tune it out of one's hearing. But I had just come from Conakry, and so I noticed them now.

I could not afford to linger. I had thirty dollars to get me to Abidjan in the Ivory Coast. I was reasonably confident that I could cash a check within a day once I got there; I had done it two months before in only a few hours; and the chance that there was not enough money in my account to cover the check was too depressing to consider. But Abidjan was a thousand miles away.

My journey got off to a bad start. Sensing I was desperate to leave, the Freetown *poda poda* drivers raised their prices. After two days of hard bargaining, I gave up the fight and paid seven dollars for a ride to Koindu. Koindu, my jumping-off point for Guinea a few weeks before, was also on the Liberian border. On the other side of Liberia was the Ivory Coast.

It was an all-night ride along bumpy dirt roads. The truck was fully loaded, with only a space the size of a coffin remaining. I and the other passengers squeezed into that space, our shoulders hunched to avoid the wooden roof, and spent the night with our heads between our knees. The next morning, in Koindu, I walked across the border and into Liberia and stopped the first van passing.

The road passed through Kolahun and Zorzor, following the route Graham Greene had taken forty years before, threading his way along narrow footpaths with a train of twenty porters behind him. That trek, so vividly described by Greene in *Journey Without Maps*, had taken over a month, but since the coming of the highway a car can cover the distance in a day. The peaceful villages Greene learned to love have given way to shops and roadside restaurants. Most of these were built by people from the coast, of red brick with gabled roofs and handpainted wooden signs. Northern Liberia had finally entered the nineteenth century.

I rode all that day and the next, changing from van to van. Town after town slipped by, and between them a lush green landscape bisected by the narrow slash of red earth that was the road, but it could all have been a blur of gray for all I noticed. I was hungry. You could not eat in Liberia for under a dollar, so I did not eat at all after the first morning, when a kind-hearted driver shared his meal with me. The kindness I had come to take for granted in Guinea was far rarer here. Late on the second day, I arrived in Sanniquellie, the last large town before the Ivory Coast. I ate there and rested, and in the morning I found a ride to Danané.

Danané, a town fifty miles from Sanniquellie, was just inside the Ivory Coast. It was a jumble of stucco and tin with enough leafy trees and greenery to make it seem inviting when viewed from afar. Abidjan was almost as far away as Freetown, and I would not have enough money to get there unless I hitchhiked the rest of the way.

A few months before, a Dutch traveler had given me advice on hitching. "You can't stay in the towns," he said. "You must walk out along the road, and walk and walk until you get a ride. Let the drivers see you're the kind of guy who makes an effort." He was the sort of person who believes that willpower is always the answer, that effort is always rewarded. I had more willpower than cash at that moment, so I decided to try his system. I got a ride to Man, the next town, without any problem, and I had the driver let me off a mile outside town. I started walking toward Abidjan, hoping to impress any passing drivers with my resolution. I was afraid that I would have to walk most of the way, and I kept an eye out for a village to sleep in, but the first car to pass screeched to a halt. "I could not leave a white man in the bush," the driver said. The system worked—at least in the Ivory Coast.

That ride took me as far as Yamoussoukro, a tiny village which the president, who was born there, has turned into a small but thriving city, with luxury hotels, modern buildings, and a huge presidential palace. I got off before we reached the town and, with the car that had brought me still in sight on the asphalt horizon, got another lift which took me through Yamoussoukro and straight to Abidjan. I got off in Treichville, the workers' quarter that lay just south of the gleaming skyscrapers of the district called the Plateau.

There was a Catholic church on Twenty-first Street that ran a relief shelter for the poor and homeless. For a dollar a day you could sleep on a bunk, or you could sleep on the floor for nothing. The bunks had thin foam mattresses that stank of the sweat of those who had been there before, making one wonder what had happened to those numberless others—had they landed a job and moved upward, or had they shuffled off to find a flophouse even worse than this? I staked out a spot on the floor. It was damp and dirty so I slept in my clothes. I'll be rich tomorrow, I thought.

But the next morning, when the American Express agency on the Plateau cabled the head office, they were told not to accept my check without a valid American Express card. I would have to apply for a new card. My application would be processed and the card mailed from Paris, and this might take several months. I agreed, and told the clerk to send off the application, wondering as I did so how long my five dollars would last in a city where prices were higher than in New York.

Five dollars was a thousand francs. I would limit myself to a hundred francs, or fifty cents, a day. This would give me ten days to find more money.

I settled into a routine of waiting. I slept on the floor at the shelter; that cost me nothing. When I got up, I waited in line for a shower and, after that, washed my clothes, using a bar of soap since I had no detergent, wringing them dry and putting them on. Wash and wear. Then I went around the corner for coffee. This was my one luxury; it cost forty francs. The café was run by a Moslem named Mamadou who came, I think, from Senegal or Mali. There were two small rooms filled with tables, and two long tables outside on the sidewalk. The long tables were the most popular; everyone sat shoulder to shoulder and since most of the clientele came from the shelter everyone knew one another.

The coffee came in a big glass bowl and was loaded with sugar and creamy condensed milk. Most of these men had next to nothing, but they told me that as long as they had enough money left for one meal a day, they would drink coffee in the morning; they would go without a second meal rather than give up their Nescafé. Mamadou left the jar on the table, and when he wasn't looking you could load your bowl with enough coffee powder to fend off hunger until dark.

I tried to find work at the supermarkets and boutiques on the Plateau. I thought it would be easy, but every store turned me away. Under the law, only Ivory Coast citizens could be hired—or so the owner said. "What about all the Frenchmen? What about you?" I asked. They were, it seemed, hired in France under a special contract; that was allowed. Now if I were to go to Paris, I would be welcome to apply. At each shop, the same scene was repeated, and after a few days I gave up.

I continued to visit the supermarkets; how else could I have filled those endless days? I looked on them as food museums, with tasteful displays and free admission; I never allowed myself to think what it would be like to buy those pâtés, eat that cheese. Sometimes I watched the clerks bustling along the aisles or preening themselves behind the register. They wore neat brown uniforms, always freshly pressed as if to flaunt their success. They had a steady job and I envied them. The clerks were kind to me, though, kinder at times than they were to their rich clientele. One of the stores gave out free aperitifs each afternoon, a thimbleful to each customer, but the clerks always had a huge tumbler for me. The drink was loaded with sugar and they knew I was hungry.

People left the Plateau when evening came. The shops closed and the managers went home to Cocody and the clerks to Treichville. I left too, usually before five, because the bridges over the lagoon that separated Treichville from the Plateau were unsafe after dark. At night, the Plateau slumbered, but night was when Treichville came alive. Even the narrowest of the side streets, which were barely lit at all, were so crowded that, though I could see only vague shapes and dark shadows when I walked there, I could feel the body heat of the many people milling around me, and smell the dust raised by their tramping feet. And on the larger avenues, the street vendors lit candles to show their wares, and the row of flames flickered like a line of votive lamps along an endless nave.

Each evening, I bought a bowl of rice—my one meal of the day—from one of the vendors. Then I returned to the shelter. Closed during the day, it opened at seven each evening, and it was always crowded. You had to wait several days to get a bed. There were people from almost every country in West Africa, and even a few Somali refugees. They had been lured by the wealth of the glittering city, by its mansions and Mercedes, though they all would have been content with far less, content to be a busboy, or a clerk at a checkout counter, with a crisply pressed uniform and a salary to send home to their relatives with perhaps a few francs left over for beers and a movie on Sunday. They would have worked hard, but work was denied them. Though tales of Abidjan's fabulous salaries (as high as two dollars a day) had spread throughout the continent, the storytellers all forgot to mention that only Ivorian citizens were eligible to be hired. The immigrants, unable to work but too ashamed to return home failures, stayed on. Some had been at the shelter for years.

How did they live? I never did find out. I asked a few people, but their answers were evasive. The occasional gift would come from fellow countrymen who had prospered, and a few odd jobs would come their way. There were rumors that some of the men at the shelter had joined the gangs of robbers who preyed on people crossing the bridge.

The people at the shelter slept very little. Their energy was boundless. At almost any hour, you could find little groups of friends sitting in the courtyard outside the dormitories. They would discuss plans and politics, past and future, life in other countries and life on other planets. Everything excited them; there was always something to talk about; they were never at a loss for words. In the dormitories, large halls with lurid green walls, the lights were left on until very late. Some of the men, the less gregarious, would sprawl on their bunks, reading perhaps, or wrapped in their dreams. One or two would be trying to sleep, their blankets (if they had them) over their heads. People would drift in from the yard and shake their friends awake. Others would join them, and soon there would be six or eight people squeezed onto the same bunk, sitting cross-legged or with their feet hanging over the side, happily chatting without a pause until stopped in the end by shouts of "Shhhh! We want to sleep!"

Late nights and endless conversation, and in the morning the communal breakfasts at Mamadou's long outside tables—it was like being in college again, and after a while I felt again some of the buoyancy of those days, the openness and exuberance, and above all the capacity for feeling intensely—things so easy to take for granted and so easy to lose. I soon came to feel affection for the shelter, whose grimy green walls had at first inspired only despair.

Often in the evening, I could hear music coming from a tiny restaurant next door. They always played the same record, an album called *Kaya* by Bob Marley—strange music, fast and rhythmic with a touch of sadness; wistful music, haunting and bittersweet. Sometimes I went outside and into the street to listen. Others would join me and we stood together in the dark. We all loved those songs.

A week passed, and my money was almost gone. I cut out morning coffee and began to give more than passing scrutiny to the garbage cans on the Plateau. All had been picked clean. The people at the shelter knew my problem. One bought me coffee; another gave me doughnuts. Others gave advice. "Go to your embassy," one man said. "They will make you a millionaire." He was short but muscular and usually went around bare-chested; had he been born a few thousand miles to the west he would now be snapping towels at a fraternity house.

I had been toying with the idea of asking the embassy for help, though I was not keen to face those clean-cut consular types in my threadbare jeans; I did not like to ask for handouts. But, with less than a hundred francs remaining, a visit to the embassy was my only hope of a meal.

The U.S. embassy in Abidjan was an unusually large and well-appointed shoebox on Jesse Owens Street, a two-block lane in the northern part of the Plateau. The consular official was fresh out of law school. I was his first case and he was eager to do a good job. He wore a gray pinstripe suit; I had sewn some of the larger holes in my trousers but they were beginning to tear again. We stared at each other as if into a mirror of roads not taken.

When he heard my story, he authorized a loan of fifty dollars. I had to fill in a long application form headed "Emergency Subsistence Loan for Destitute U.S. Citizen," which he countersigned and took to the paymaster. As collateral, the embassy kept my passport. Come back if you need more, the consul said. He was amazed that I had survived so long on so little.

I left the embassy and went shopping. I bought a pair of brand-new jeans, a box of detergent, and a packet of blue powder, quite popular in Abidjan, that stops denim from fading. I wanted the world to know that I could afford to wear new, unfaded jeans. A supermarket had a sale on overripe Brie, so I bought a dollar's worth and took it to the Hotel du Parc café. I ordered a plate and a knife and when they came I ate the cheese quite slowly.

"You should share your money with me," said the bare-chested man back at the shelter. "Going to the embassy was my idea." I didn't share, of course, nor did he expect me to.

I moved into a bunk and once again took coffee in the morning, sometimes with a crisp slice of bread. Aside from that, my new-found wealth changed my life very little. I tramped around the Plateau in the daytime and spent the nights in conversation.

In the bunks next to mine were several men from Cameroun. The people at the shelter tended to divide themselves by nationality and the Camerouns were the largest and most cohesive of the groups. The Ivory Coast requires a passport to enter, and it is not easy to get a passport in Cameroun, so most of the men were there illegally. Over a thousand miles lie between Cameroun and Abidjan, and five borders that had to be crossed without proper papers. Two of the Camerouns had had no money for transport; they had come on foot. One of them told me he had traveled for the better part of a year, working in villages along the way. They were an elite, those Camerouns; only the toughest and most courageous youths would dare set out on that long journey. It was no wonder that the shelter was so reminiscent of college. In America, people with that drive and determination would be in college. But in Abidjan, the only place open to them was the shelter. From time to time, the police came, checked passports, and took all the Camerouns they caught off to jail.

"Stay away from those Cameroun men," Peter Johnson warned me. "They'll rob you one of these days." Peter had the English-speaker's instinctive distrust of someone who spoke French. Peter was from Liberia. Short, lithe, a dapper dresser with a penchant for button-down collars, he looked and talked like a streetwise American. He had left Liberia several years before. He had quarreled with his father, who had put a death curse on him. The curse was evidently not powerful enough to reach him in Abidjan, so in Abidjan he had stayed, not daring to go home even for a visit. He had been at the shelter for three years, which was longer than anyone else, though some of the Cameroun men he hated had arrived not long after.

Another week went by. By now I was fully a part of the world of the shelter. I hated the poverty; there were a thousand things I would have liked to do and buy. Sometimes I wanted to see a movie, or have a beer, or take a bus back home from the Plateau, and at these times I felt hemmed in by pickets of prohibitions that a handful of dollars could have swept away. At other times, I felt truly free. I had always feared poverty, the shelter, the gutter—now I was there and though it was bad it was not half as bad as I had imagined. I could survive it. This simple bit of knowledge was, I realized, something precious and rare, and I wished I could share it with those men and women in America—and there were, I was sure, many—who waste their lives doing work they hate, fawning on bosses they secretly despise, building ramparts that turn into prisons and, in the end, tombs—and all to avoid leading, to insure themselves against the smallest possibility of ever being forced to lead, a life that was really not worse than theirs.

And then, just when I was fully settled in, I heard rumors that the shelter was going to close. A few whispers at first, vague mumblings nobody believed, but soon no one was talking of anything else. The men who worked part time mopping floors in exchange for free board suddenly found themselves the center of attention; they were insiders, people in the know. Then the rumors became fact. For reasons we were never told, the church had decided to close the shelter. In order that justice be seen to be done even when it was not, we were all allowed to state our case. "What will we do, where will we go?" I asked. "All these people will have to live in the streets. They will be lucky to find a carton to sleep on." The young French priest listened politely, wearing a benign, compassionate expression, thanked us and left.

A few tense days passed, and then the announcement. The shelter was closing and in a few more days, we would all have to leave. There was a small exception made for the Somalis, who, because they were refugees, were allowed to stay on. ("Get your embassy to write in a letter that you are a refugee from the U.S.A.," the bare-chested man advised me.)

During the days that followed, life returned more or less to normal. People talked and laughed and gossiped as eagerly as before, chatted about everything and anything except the fact that very soon we would all be without a home. If no one mentioned it, we all believed, it would never happen. But, secretly, everyone made plans. Then, one evening, we found the dormitory doors were locked. Later, after all the priests had gone, the floor-moppers opened the doors and let us use the beds, telling us to be gone by sunrise. The following night, the same thing happened, but that was the last time the new, clandestine shelter operated. The next morning, the gates were locked forever.

I met Peter Johnson at Mamadou's. "I've found a place," he told me. "Why not join me?" One of his friends, he explained, a fellow-Liberian, was the custodian of a church in the suburbs. We could sleep there seven nights a week, but we would have to stay away on Sunday morning, because that was when the minister came, and the minister would not be pleased to learn that his church had been turned into a boardinghouse.

The church was in Vridi, and that was many miles away, so we took a bus. It took us south, past the port, and rows of cranes and winches, through the industrial zone, and smoke and noise and the enormous silvery storage tanks of the refinery hovering on the horizon: strange, terrifying fetishes of an alien culture. On the southern fringe of the factory zone was an enormous sprawl of shanties. It had no name, this place where tens of thousands lived, but Peter and I called it Vridi because it lay between Vridi Beach and the Vridi Canal, and Vridi sounded a cut above Industrial Zone. It was there, in this nameless, forgotten quarter that was the poorest part of Abidjan, that our church lay.

Vridi, our new home, was a place of sandy paths and palm trees.

The paths were narrow and twisting, hemmed in on both sides by high fences. Behind the fences were yards and gardens and small, neat houses. Fences and houses alike were built of rough, weather-beaten planking that smacked of the sea and reminded me of New England. I realized much later that the timber came from crates and packing cases and was indeed flotsam of a sort. Most of the houses were painted green; a few were painted white. A lot of time and work had gone into those houses. Treichville was several steps up the ladder from Vridi, so most of the people in Vridi, unlike Treichville, were fresh from the countryside, and they still had the villager's pride in clean, attractive surroundings.

Vridi was, in many ways, really a big village. Sometimes, where two footpaths met, they widened, and brightly dressed women would sit at those crossroads, selling fruit or home-baked biscuits, chatting with anyone who cared to stop. There were shops too, along the paths, and tiny cafés and bars, all built of crate wood. The smaller shops were little more than booths. They lined the wider paths and made them look like fairgrounds.

Far from those main pathways, and hidden among the houses, was a church. Ours. It was made of the usual planking and painted white inside and out. It was long and low, ten yards square with a ceiling I could almost touch. Inside were rows of rough wooden chairs, a simple lectern, a cross on the wall. Everything was spotless, even the floor, which was where I slept. Peter had his own room, a small lean-to with a foam mattress; it had been the custodian's bedroom.

Near the church was a well where I got water for washing. It was easy to stay clean, but other needs were more of a problem. There were no latrines at all in Vridi. Most of the people walked to the western edge of the settlement, where there was a huge heap of boulders thrown up during the digging of the Vridi Canal. They scrambled over the rocks and down the other side. There, the stones were close enough to the canal to be washed clean at high tide. It was a pretty spot; you could see the blue-green sea, and the large white liners passing through the canal on their way to harbor. But the boulders were rough and jagged and some were several feet high, so as often as not, after washing at the well I walked to the highway, past the huge refinery and on to Vridi Beach two miles beyond. There, the lavishly built hotels boasted gleaming public bathrooms, huge porcelain shrines each larger than the church where I slept.

Sometimes I spent the day at the beach, and watched the sea and the swaying palms and the pallid young Frenchwomen who cavorted in skimpy bikinis. On other days, I took the number 18 bus to the Plateau. The fare was eighty francs each way, forty cents, so I did not do that often. Once or twice I sneaked on board. That was risky; one in every ten buses was stopped by the police, and ticketless riders had to pay a thousand-franc fine. Those who did not pay were taken off to jail. A night in jail was no joke, Peter told me. "I had to stand up all night," he said. "There was no room to lie down and the floor was too dirty even to sit on." And, one night a year later, seventy people, all immigrants whose papers were not in order, were stuffed into an overcrowded cell at the Abidjan police station; they were dead by morning.

One day, the bus I was riding stopped at a checkpoint just south of the port. The fifty-dollar Emergency Subsistence Loan had run out, and I was on my way to the embassy to ask for more. I had neither ticket nor money nor passport. "Contact the American embassy," I told the policeman. Perhaps he thought I was a diplomat, because he let me go.

At the embassy, the young consular officer, still sympathetic, and amazed that the first loan had lasted me a month, lent me fifty dollars more, so I returned to Vridi with enough money to pay my fare.

A few days later, two French girls, teenagers, gave me a lift back from the beach. They were visiting relatives in Abidjan; it was their first trip outside France. They were quick to laugh, to gasp, to stare; everything excited them. I showed them my church and took them to my favorite drinking place. It was a big white house hidden among the other houses. Inside was a bright and cheerful room, with wooden tables covered by red-and-white checkered cloths. We sat and drank beer; the proprietor put a record on; we were the only customers. Then we strolled along the labyrinth of paths, past the fences and the palm trees and the market women at the crossroads. "If we had to live like this," one of the girls told me, "we'd go home."

That night there was a fire. There was a main street a few hundred yards north of the church; like the other avenues, it was a midway of carny booths, all closely packed together. A lamp was knocked over; the booth, a tailor's shop, burst into flames. Eruptions of sparks shot across the inky sky and soon the neighboring stalls were ablaze. I could hear sirens far away, but the fire engines never arrived; they were too wide for the paths. I thought all of Vridi would burn that night, but the crowd pulled down the shops on either side of the flaming booths, and the fire could not spread. After a time, it died out. I revisited the place the next day to see the smoldering ruins. But the tailor had swept the ashes away, and, with the help of friends, was busy rebuilding his shop. The walls were almost completed.

More days passed. Empty days, perhaps, because nothing really happened, but I never felt bored or restless or desired more than I had. One day in late December, I went back to the Plateau. Christmas was coming, and all the shops were hung with ribbons, wreaths, and streamers, with big window displays of presents that must be bought. One shop had cowboy costumes in children's sizes, only a hundred dollars complete with plastic six-guns. I went to American Express. My card had arrived.

I had spent much of my waiting time, especially during the first weeks at the shelter, fashioning daydreams around the green plastic rectangle I now held in my hand. Many of those fantasies were set in Kenya and the Sudan, on wild and endless plains covered with dew-damp grass and thorn trees. Three years of travel had not curbed my tendency to clothe far-off places in a mantle of mystery and excitement, or dissuaded me from the idea that I would find perfect happiness if only I could find the perfect setting. A perfect setting was one that matched my dreams.

I had planned to leave Abidjan the day I got the card. I had never dreamed I would want to linger, but Vridi had, almost without my realizing, become a home to me, and leaving was far harder than I had imagined. So I stayed on in the church. Finally, a few days after Christmas, I boarded a train for Ouagadougou. There, I would get a visa for Ghana. In Ghana, I would buy a ticket for Nairobi. Air tickets were slightly cheaper in Ghana even though they had to be paid for in dollars at the legal rate of exchange. I would save over a hundred dollars by flying from Accra.

The train reached Ouagadougou in the middle of the night. I slept on the floor of the station with a hundred other passengers around me. We all woke with the sun and trudged into town. I went to the Restaurant Rialle; I was only half awake but I had been there so many times before that I could have found it in my sleep.

I left my pack at the Rialle and went to the Ghanaian embassy.

Give us your passport, they told me, and come back in a few days. The government of Ghana had changed twice since my last visit, but the embassy was the same; I'd be lucky if I got my visa in a week. I decided to go up-country.

I went to the Geographic Institute (which I had discovered quite by chance on my last visit) and studied large-scale maps of the area north of Ouagadougou. On a map of the region around Kaya, a town sixty miles to the northeast, I found what I was seeking: the broken line of a trail running through a field of circles, which stood for houses. The next morning, I took a *taxi-brousse* to Kaya.

Outside the city was the savanna, the belt of brown grass and thorn that girdles the continent. It was in much the same landscape that my East African fantasies were set. There were villages everywhere. This section of Upper Volta, the most crowded part of the entire savanna, was the heartland of the Mossi people.

In the fourteenth century, when the empire of Mali was at its height, the Mossi were divided into four kingdoms, each small but powerful enough to resist Malian incursions and even, in 1333, to sack Timbuctu. In time, Mali disappeared from the map, but the Mossi kings and their successors continued to govern until, in 1896, their states were conquered by the French. Kings, courtiers, ministers, and bureaucrats brought seven centuries of stability to the land, but there was a price. The Mossi population grew far beyond the arid land's ability to support it. The area I planned to visit would, I surmised, be overcrowded and shockingly poor.

The trail ran west from a village named Bousouma. Bousouma was a small market, a scattering of houses, a policeman in khaki standing by the road. The van left me there, and I walked along the main road until I found the trail.

It was a fine, clear morning. The air was cool and I walked farther than I intended. I had meant to stop at the first village I found; instead, I went as far as the third, which was the last settlement marked on the map. It was the smallest of the villages: three or four clusters of sunbaked huts the color of sand, surrounded by sunbaked, sandy fields. The harvest was over, the fields were bare, and their naked dusty earth was the same shade as the houses. I stopped outside one of the huts. A man saw me and ran off to find the chief.

The chief of the village was building a house when he heard the news that a stranger had arrived. He came at once, his long white robe flecked with mud. He was squat and short, with a round jowly face. His hair and beard were shiny white, but despite his age and rank, which would have allowed him to spend his days lounging in the shade, he preferred to work. Someone brought a cowhide and spread it on the ground, and we sat down. The chief was nervous. Perhaps I had come from the government; perhaps I had come to change his village. One of the younger men spoke some words of French, and using him as interpreter I told the chief that all I wanted was a few nights' lodging.

"Of course," said the chief. "You will be my guest." He seemed relieved. He went back to his building. I went along and he explained, using words I could not understand and gestures that I did, how a house was built. That afternoon, he was making bricks. He filled a rectangular wooden box with mud, packed the mud tightly and then dumped it out and left it in the sun. The mud retained the shape of the mold and would dry into a brick. The chief could make several bricks a minute.

I left him and sat down near one of the houses. I was soon surrounded by staring, excited children. They frisked and wriggled and could not keep still. They ran around the houses, chased each other through the stacks of drying millet, and came back, wide-eyed, to me. Life was an endless game to them, an adventure. It had not worn them down like rocks in a river; they had not seen its sadness.

Then another visitor arrived and the children left me to flock around him. He was an old man dressed in black, a trader, probably Malinké, tramping the back roads from village to village with his wares on his back. He put down his pack, a big bag of black leather, opened it, and spread his goods on the ground. There were leaves and roots and strange heaps of powder—spices, perhaps, or herbal medicines. After a while, some of the village women came over, pushed the children aside, and examined the merchandise.

I think the trader was not altogether pleased to see me among the crowd. He was one of the village's few links with the outside world and he probably enjoyed being the center of attention. Today he had to share the limelight, and he did not stay long. He sold a few powders, packed up his bag, and walked off, following perhaps the same dusty trail his ancestors had taken five centuries before, carrying wares from Jenné and far-off Timbuctu.

Evening came, and the chief stopped work. We ate together and then he, I, and two elders sat outside under the stars. It was a quiet time. The three old men talked in low, hushed voices and most of the time they didn't talk at all. They had no need to talk; it was enough to sit together; they had known each other all their lives.

I woke early the next morning, but the village had risen even earlier. Through the wall of the hut, I could hear shouts, running feet, snatches of conversation. The village, so torpid the day before, had suddenly come alive; the adults were as excited as the children. When I went outside, I saw a crowd gathered in the neighboring compound, filling the courtyard between the houses. I walked over and joined the throng, and then I noticed that I was the only man among them. Most of the women had formed a tight, milling ring in the center of the yard, and the circle slowly revolved as the women clapped and stamped and sang. They sang loudly and more or less in harmony; joyous songs, from the sound of them, chants they had obviously sung many times before. Some of the women knew the songs better than others. When one of them remembered a line the rest had forgotten she would sing it especially loudly to celebrate her private triumph.

By standing on tiptoe, I could see inside the circle. Three little girls stood in the middle, dust swirling around them. The dancers towered over them; the frenzied crowd, the loud ululations, the wall of flesh that pressed around them must have terrified the children, but they bravely did their best not to show it.

When I saw the children, I guessed what was going on. Later that morning, those three girls would be circumcised. I had heard about these ceremonies. An old woman would cut off their clitorises with a sharp knife, a razor blade, a bit of glass. (The stories varied.) Those tales never failed to make me wince, and now I was watching the real thing. It was, I thought, hardly the proper occasion for rejoicing. But the dancers were exuberant, their sweaty faces radiant with joy. For them, the ceremony was not a mutilation but an affirmation of womanhood, and they leapt and danced to celebrate the creation of three new women.

As the morning wore on, more women joined the throng, and the ring of dancers was soon surrounded by an outer circle of spectators. A few men slunk along the periphery of the crowd, but whenever one of the women saw them, she would chase them away. This was a woman's ceremony, and they did not want any man to intrude. (Except for me. For some reason, my presence was ignored.) The women's anger made some of the younger men even more determined, and toward midday, a few of them hid behind the wall of the compound, carrying a tape deck to record the songs. Pleased with themselves for having outwitted the women, the young men burst into fits of giggles. The dancers heard the laughter and the trespassers were ignominiously routed. Soon afterward, the dancing stopped and the three initiates were pushed inside a small hut, where the old woman awaited them. I walked away.

After the ceremony, the village grew quiet. When night came, the children lit a fire, feeding it with millet stalks and brambles. The flames leapt and crackled and lit the night; shadows danced on glowing walls. Some of the older boys began to chant the Koran. They read from long wooden paddles which I saw to my surprise, since very few Mossi are Moslem, were covered with Arabic script. The chief and his two friends sat on low stools quite close to the fire. They seemed to be dozing, but each time a boy misread a verse, one of the elders called out a correction. The younger boys, meanwhile, tended the fire, stoking it until the fuel ran out. After a time, the fire died down, and a few of the most daring boys jumped over the flames, which were still several feet high. The night seemed cool after the heat of the fire, and soon everyone left for their warm huts and bed.

That was the last night of 1979. The new decade found me sound asleep on a cowhide mat in an earthen hut in a village where no one but I noticed its arrival. Perhaps the others knew but did not celebrate. What joy they had derived from old traditions; what good had a new year ever brought them?

I woke at sunrise, said my good-byes, and hiked back to the road. I went back to Ouagadougou, picked up my passport, and got a ride to the Ghana border. A few days later I was in Accra and a week after that I boarded a plane for Kenya.

Smoothly, almost serenely, the huge plane glided across the continent. It took less than two hours to cross West Africa, and shortly after that lunch was served. At about the time I ate the last of the curry, we passed more or less directly over Mboma. Five miles below me, Chief Indumbe's wife was preparing the evening meal. The chief himself was probably off somewhere drinking palm wine. The Pygmies were coming home from the hunt, and there was a good chance that Denis was not too far away, on some muddy road south of Wamba trying to coax his ancient truck to go another mile. Perhaps they looked up and saw me passing, as far-off and unreal as a ghost in the wind.

23

DOWNTOWN NAIROBI

Kenya time was several hours ahead of the west coast, so it was dark when the big jet landed. This was the third time I had passed through Nairobi's airport, and each time it had grown larger, more streamlined, more antiseptic. Many years before, my father and I arrived in Nairobi after an all-day flight across the desert. Our battered old DC-6 had flown so low that Saharan sand came through the air vents and whirled through the plane. It was night when we landed, a sultry African night, and the sky seemed as smooth as black velvet. I, my father, and the other passengers waited on the tarmac as gangs of men threw our luggage on groaning hand-carts, dragged the carts toward us, and dumped our bags on the ground. The warm night, the porters' sweating faces, the primitive method of unloading the plane—it was my first time in Africa and I was not disappointed.

Now, thirteen years later, it was night again, and I waited in the huge, gleaming arrival hall as conveyor belts carried bags and cases from the plane and paraded them around the room. My pack was as easy to spot as a tramp at the Ritz. I snatched it off the quickly moving belt and followed the signs to customs. The signs were all in English; I could have been in London or New York. At the customs counter, policemen searched suitcases, questioned passengers, stamped passports. The men were brisk and efficient; they saw more tourists in a day than most African airports dealt with in a year.

I took a bus into town and got off at the Iqbal, a hotel on Latema Road. Most of central Nairobi had been completely transformed since I had first seen it; a town of brick and stucco had become a city of glass and steel. Even in the three years since my last visit, the bulldozers had been at work. At the New Stanley Hotel, the musty old bar, with its shiny brass taps and dark wood paneling, had given way to a new coffee shop with bright Formica tables. A few blocks away, scaffolding marked the site of the new U.S. embassy. Soon the staff would abandon the cramped suite of offices where, on my first morning of freedom three years before, I had drunk scalding instant coffee with a young marine.

But Latema Road had not changed at all; it had been the same in 1977, and in 1967, and from the look of it very little had altered since the days when oxcarts rumbled down Delamere Avenue and Africans were required to wear their pass cards on chains around their necks. Most of the houses along Latema Road had been built under British rule, with slate roofs and dormer windows, and there was still something very English about them. But Latema Road never did belong to the England of the early settlers, flamboyantly aristocratic men like Lord Delamere. Theirs was an England of champagne and green meadows, of house parties and women in long summer dresses. The stolid little houses of Latema Road evoke instead another, bleaker Britain, a land of transport caffs and fish-and-chip shops and hard-faced young men in black leather jackets; not the England of the center, of Mayfair and Bond Street and golden college spires, but the England of the fringes, of bedsitters, coal mines, and the dole. The three-story row houses along Latema Road hold cheap hotels, pinball arcades, dingy cafés, and bars. The most popular bar has a floor-to-ceiling grille to protect the barman, who shoves drinks through a slot above the counter. That bar is open all night but after dark the rest of the road is dimly lit and deserted, and people who have to walk along it quicken their steps. It is a tough and grimy street and if you stay there for any length of time, as I did, you will find its dirt under your nails and its grit lodged in your soul.

Latema Road is only a few blocks long, barely worth mention. It is just one block away from the posh New Stanley Hotel, and is probably unknown to most of the well-fed businessmen who congregate around the laminated coffee tables that have replaced the well-worn oak of the old bar. Some of the junior clerks from nearby offices take their lunch at the Iqbal: low ceilings, long tables, concrete walls like an airplane hangar, crowded, every chair filled but each diner alone, staring into space as he shovels down his lamb stew and rice. (Goat meat, one shilling extra.) They do not linger; a quick cup, perhaps, of sweet and milky tea, and then back to the office. All Latema Road has to offer them is a cheap and filling meal.

But, just as an insignificant pustule may presage a serious disease, so Latema Road, short and easily overlooked, is worth attention because it is symptomatic of more widespread malaise. Latema Road runs into River Road, and River Road, a long bazaar of shops, tea halls, and bars, is the center of a large neighborhood that corresponds to Treichville in Abidjan. Treichville, though, was animated day and night, so brimming with life that you would sometimes see white businessmen and tourists, pallid and out of place as a potted geranium in a rain forest, walking along its bustling streets come to wonder at, and hopefully imbibe, the strange vital energy that pulsed around them. River Road was deserted after dark, except for the night watchmen who dozed on the sidewalk, using their ax handles and billy clubs as headrests. By day the street was crowded enough, its cheerless, windowless shops filled with grim-faced shoppers, but it was hardly a pleasant place to stroll.

I remember those crowds, bulging against the mesh fences put up to separate people from cars, spilling across the sidewalk and leaving no room to pass; I remember the crowds but no faces stand out. In Abidjan, in the rest of Africa, I had met people, talked, made friends easily, without any conscious thought or effort. To travel through Africa without meeting any Africans would be as hard to do as wading across a stream without getting wet. But Nairobi was different. There were many streams, not one, and I moved, as was expected, among people like myself: travelers, transients, and tourists. I met a few Asians, and sometimes I would stop and talk with the River Road shopkeepers' sons, who congregated along Latema Road after school. Their families had lived in Kenya for generations, and I had seen more of India than had most of them. They were Indians nonetheless, and their shy fumbling adolescent humor and talk of women seemed out of place in Africa, more suited to Bombay or Lahore. But I had almost no contact with Africans; I felt separated from them by barriers as rigid and hard to breach as the wire fences along River Road.

I blamed myself, sometimes, for my isolation; I had become, I thought, like the many backpackers who made their way along Asia's tourist trails, sticking together as closely as turkeys on a tree. At other times, and with equal justice, I laid the blame on the weather. Kenya is cursed with the world's best climate, with an almost unbroken succession of crisp chill mornings and glorious sunny days, with every day as joyously perfect as those rare and golden days of English summer, days so full of wonder they take your breath away. North of Nairobi, under the blue and endless summer sky, are rolling hills and highlands, green and fertile.

A rich land and an ideal climate; it was inevitable that white settlers would be attracted. At first the area was remote and little-known, but in 1895 the British government decided to build a railway connecting its newly acquired colony of Uganda with the Indian Ocean port of Mombasa. It was a daring, almost foolhardy project, but over the next eight years the thin line of track advanced, across desert, through uncharted marshes, snaking its way down steep escarpments. Many of the men who built it succumbed to strange plagues and a surprising number were eaten by lions. The line never reached Uganda, but it opened up the highlands, and a railway supply depot built on a deserted plain named Nairobi soon became a thriving township. The colonial government encouraged whites to immigrate, hoping that they would grow enough crops for export to make the railway pay.

Settlers came, a thin trickle at first and then a flood of thousands which poured into the highlands. They found a land that seemed deserted; some of it was the territory of the Masai and other nomads, and much of the rest, which might in normal times have been dotted with the hillside gardens of the Kikuyu tribe, lay empty because the Kikuyu had been decimated by two years of drought and plague. The colonial government reserved this supposedly empty land for European farmers; it was now illegal for Africans to trespass upon it. Blacks in Kenya, like Indians in America, were restricted to reservations. Years passed, and the African population grew, but the overcrowded reserves did not. Some of the reserves, the *New York Times* reported in 1953, had a population of 630 per square mile, a density unheard of elsewhere in Africa. The land the men could have tilled to feed their families was all owned by Europeans, much of it used to grow coffee and tea. Even if they had the money to buy a plot of land, they were, because they were black, barred by law from doing so.

Africans were, of course, welcome to buy their food from the whites (at very high prices); one reason the reserves were kept so small was to force them to do just that. Kenya was governed from Whitehall, but the white settlers strongly influenced London's policies, and since the average farm was four square miles, the farmers' paramount concern was to obtain a cheap supply of African labor. The Kikuyus were happy in their villages, and saw no need to work. Why should they? They were men in their villages, but when they worked for Europeans they became "boys."

One possible solution, used by the French in the Ivory Coast and elsewhere until the 1940s, was compulsory labor, chain gangs. Men were forced, in effect, to work at gunpoint. Though forced labor was used to some extent in Kenya before World War I, the British preferred to use subtler, more "civilized" forms of coercion. Every African family had to pay a yearly tax. Africans were forbidden to grow coffee, the major cash crop, so the only way they could raise the money was to work on a European farm. All jobs were given for at least a six-month term, and it was illegal for an African to quit work before the end of the term. Since all Africans had to carry pass cards, any runaways could easily be tracked down. Three-quarters of what the Africans received in wages (about sixpence a day) went to pay taxes, and the government used the revenue to build roads and schools for the settlers, and to subsidize their farms, which were, at least some evidence suggests, less efficient than the small African plots on the reserves.

The Kikuyu are a clever people, quick to adapt; when Dr. Louis Leakey, the anthropologist, tried to introduce a popular Kikuyu board game into Britain, English companies turned down his proposal because the game was "too complicated for the British mind." Though more than half of all Kikuyu men worked on European farms, many aspired to better things. Quite a few finished high school and went on to university in England. But, no matter how many degrees they earned, no matter how fluent their English, or how bright and eager their smile, they were still Africans, barred from hotels, nightclubs, and restaurants, banned (until 1944) from Kenya's legislature, totally excluded from white society. (The *New York Times* reported in 1954 that a foreign journalist was met with horrified stares when he dined with a black in one of the few integrated restaurants.) In French West Africa, educated, able blacks won acceptance by their rulers, but not in Kenya. At the same time that Leopold Senghor, the future president of Senegal, moved among the rarefied Proustian circles of the Parisian aristocracy and Felix Houphouet-Boigny, future president of the Ivory Coast, was elected to the French parliament, Jomo Kenyatta, who later became president of Kenya, languished in a British jail, serving a seven-year sentence for membership (never proved) in a proscribed political organization.

The organization was, of course, the Mau Mau, bands of Kikuyu guerrillas who fought to rid Kenya of the whites who ruled it. They murdered about thirty white settlers and the British, by the time the fighting was over, killed over ten thousand of them. To the whites, the Mau Mau were outlaws, savages. The guerrillas, it is true, did use terror as a tactic, but their main mistake was being born too soon; had they fought a decade or two later, they would have been viewed by much of the world as freedom fighters.

In 1956, the year the Mau Mau were defeated, not a single African colony had gained independence. A decade later, almost all had; Kenya became independent in 1963. History had won what the Mau Mau could not. Most of the white settlers left, their lands bought by the government and distributed among half a million Africans, some of whom, especially those close to Kenyatta, became large landowners themselves. The white highlands are known today as the highlands, and, in Nairobi, streets named after famous settlers were renamed after Mau Mau generals.

It is easy to change a name, but old names are still remembered; ghosts and memories are a long time dying. Perhaps this is why whites and blacks in Kenya stayed apart. The Africans I met seemed not so much hostile as indifferent; they would not show interest in me because they did not expect me to show any in them. And, as so often happens, expectations, like prophesies, are self-fulfilling.

Away from River Road, history is easier to forget. A few blocks west of the Iqbal, the office towers begin. The center of Nairobi is as skyscraper-studded as Abidjan and, though not nearly so elegant, is perhaps even more modern. With a little imagination, but not much, those so inclined could pretend they weren't in Africa at all. The inside of the Hilton was a lot like the Hilton in Beverly Hills, though the Nairobi branch appeared more modern and better designed, and both hotels catered to the same sort of crowd. Tourism was Kenya's biggest industry, and the Hilton, the Inter-Continental, and scores of other high-rise palaces did their brave best to turn Nairobi into an inland Miami Beach.

And there were other, subtler ways in which Nairobi was depressingly modern. The cinemas showed first-run films from Hollywood, and each movie was preceded by a half-hour of advertisements. Many of them were locally made, and showed Kenyan women discussing the merits of Omo washing powder or preparing freeze-dried vegetables and then serving them, the whole family smiling and the children shouting for more. My favorite was the commercial for Raymond's blankets. A man visits his fiancée's family to give them the bride price; in most Kenyan tribes, brides are not given freely, but must be paid for. The man has brought a cow, several goats, and a heap of blankets. All goes well until the mother of the bride notices that the blankets are not Raymond's but another brand. She and her husband's other wives chase the luckless fiancé from the village, shouting "Ni nataka Raymond's," "I want Raymond's." But the man saves the day; he buys a stack of Raymond's blankets in a nearby shop, and returns in triumph.

Much of Nairobi does indeed wash with Omo and go to sleep on Raymond's. Even in smaller towns and villages, women buy sacks of *posho,* commercially milled flour. The pound and thump of the pestle, which in most of Africa is the background music to village life, is seldom heard in the highlands.

Kenya's economic boom deserves admiration. The country, unlike most of Africa, has no mineral resources at all, and most of its land, perhaps as much as nine-tenths, is too arid to farm. The economy, as in the Ivory Coast, is fueled by foreign investment, but in Kenya the multinationals are not given free rein. Most of the jobs that Frenchmen do in Abidjan are filled by Kenyans in Nairobi; foreigners are not allowed to work in Kenya unless no African can fill their position. Exchange regulations prevent foreign corporations from taking more hard currency out of the country than they brought in. (At least until 1975, these exchange restrictions were a Swiss cheese of loopholes.) Imports, too, are restricted, to encourage the development of local industry, and tariffs are high. American blue jeans cost sixty dollars a pair and, just before I left Kenya, further imports were banned. But price controls kept the price of staple foodstuffs down.

In the center of town, it was easy to believe in the government's benevolence and foresight; at the outskirts, one's faith was shaken. Pumwani to the east and Mathare Valley far to the west are grim shantytowns where Nairobi's workers live. I visited Pumwani, once in 1967 and once in 1980, and, though I never went to Mathare because it was ten miles out of town, whenever I passed through the western suburbs I saw the valley's men trudging along the roads in a long and ragged procession, going to work or looking for work and walking twenty miles a day to save the bus fare. A dollar a day was the standard wage when I was in Kenya; the people who worked at the big hotels made two or three times that, but a hotel room cost almost as much as in America, where wages were twenty times higher. Profits were high for foreign companies in Kenya.

The government's economic policies were carefully planned and painstakingly administered, and this fact made Nairobi even more depressing. When I hurried along Latema Road, I was perhaps seeing what the future had in store for the rest of Africa: slums, advertisements, high-rise hotels, and ugly, unsafe streets. After a fortnight of future shock, I went to the train station, an old building to the south of town that sprawled in a state of happy dilapidation; it was the center of the railway system and, like the eye of a storm, seemed strangely unaffected by the changes the railway had wrought all around it.

The train to Mombasa runs at night; I woke the next morning to a vision of palm trees and sky, all flooded by the warm, clear light of the Kenya coast, a benison of sunlight that sparkled like wavelets on the ocean. I had gone third class and had barely slept, but I did not feel tired. I felt cleansed by the sun and the salty sea air, as if my denims, still embedded with the grime and soot of Latema Road, had been miraculously transformed into white and shining linen.

I took a bus to Malindi, and then another bus north to Lamu. After Malindi, a port a hundred miles north of Mombasa, the road became dirt, and the land dry, dusty, and deserted. There were clumps of straggly palm trees, a few forlorn villages and nomad camps, and very little else. This was the other Kenya: the vast stretches of semidesert, the roving nomads, the blazing sun. We crossed the Tana River on a ferry that was little more than a raft and a rope, all the passengers pulling on the rope to tug the craft across. Just beyond the sluggish river was Garsen, a double row of white, sun-blasted storefronts. We stopped for lunch. The town was crowded with Somalis, lithe, graceful men and women who roam the thousand miles of barren land between Malindi and the horn. The road curved far inland, but toward sunset we reached the sea and boarded a launch for the short passage to the island of Lamu. The tiny boat chugged along a narrow strait bordered on both sides by mangrove swamps. We rounded a corner, and there was the town, the thick stucco columns of the ancient, half-abandoned mansions spectral and insubstantial in the starlight. Then one of the sailors cut the engine, and there was silence, broken only by the lapping of the sea against stone pilings, and the occasional braying of the donkeys which roam Lamu's streets at night.

I think that Lamu is enchanted. It was all too easy to fall under its spell; people came for the day and stayed for the season and when they finally left the island did so as reluctantly as the sad and weeping sailors whom Ulysses dragged away from lotus land. Lamu, cut off from the rest of the country by a hundred miles of desert, was as remote and self-contained, as far removed from everyday life, as a dream. No part of Kenya should be allowed to live in the thirteenth century, said an angry government minister after a trip to the island. (Hardheaded, a pragmatic politician, he was immune to Lamu's charm.) But the people in Lamu ignored the rumblings from far-off Nairobi, and did nothing to close the gap of centuries that separate the traffic-clogged, skyscraper-strewn avenues of the capital from the winding, sleepy streets of Lamu town, streets too narrow to hold a car, which didn't really matter, since all motor vehicles were banned from the island, except for two land-rovers that no one ever used.

To be scrupulously accurate, Lamu did not really live in the thirteenth century, though one or two of the town's mosques were founded at about that time, but in the eighteenth, the island's golden age, when rich sheiks and merchants whiled away their days composing poetry in the lush gardens of the palaces they had caused to be erected. Lamu was old by then; the nearby town of Manda, now deserted, was a flourishing settlement by the year 900. Over the centuries Lamu's inhabitants, immigrants from the Arabian peninsula, coastal Africans, and their descendants, evolved their own distinctive culture, which was neither Arab nor African but a fusion of the two. It was called Swahili. During the 1700s, Lamu, then an independent republic, was a thriving entrepot. Her only rival was the neighboring kingdom of Pate. In the early nineteenth century, the citizens of Lamu, who had just fought a war with Pate and feared another, made an alliance with the Sultan of Oman. Lamu's new ally promptly invaded both islands and annexed them. After that, Lamu's fortunes went into long and lazy decline, and the ships that had once stopped at Lamu now called at the newer and larger port of Zanzibar.

I found a room at the northern end of town, in the district named Kitendetini, which means "By the Small Date-Palm." All of Lamu's neighborhoods have names, some quite fanciful, but there were many palm trees in that part of the island, in the courtyards of the houses, and in the *shambas,* the small farms that lay behind the town. As I sat in the inner courtyard of the house, warmed by the sun that shimmered on white walls and purple bougainvillaea, I could hear the rustle of palm leaves in the wind, which swept in from the sea without a pause. Sometimes, when the heat died down toward sunset, I climbed a ladder to the flat rooftop. I could see the palms from there, graceful swaying trunks with ragged green haloes, and the old stone houses, with their tall, smooth, windowless walls of graying mortar and coral. Behind the austere façades were lavish interiors, cool airy rooms decorated with ornate plasterwork, lush gardens with trickling fountains, but all of this inner wealth was hidden from view, and was all the more tantalizing for that. The hotel was on the main street of town, the Usita wa Mui, but that avenue was barely five feet wide, and I often heard women's voices from the houses across the street. Sometimes I heard laughter and I am certain that I was being watched. As the sun set, the muezzeins would chant the call to prayer. The clocks at each mosque—nineteenth-century American wall clocks, for the most part—varied. First one mosque would start the chant, and then another would join in, and another, and another, and another, for there are twenty-two mosques in Lamu town. *Allaaaaahu akbar! Allaaaaahu akbar!* The muezzeins' voices, deep-throated and melodious in their exaltation, would roll in from all directions and drift across the town, and all the chants would blend together, merging with the palms and the surf and the laughter and the bugle from the fort, and all becoming, in the end, a part of the never-ending wind.

Toward the end of February, the town got very crowded. Dhows, those sleek lateen-rigged ships of the Arabian Sea, arrived daily from other islands. They sailed around the harbor before landing, pennants flying from the mast, the passengers singing and beating tambourines. It was the time of the Maulidi, a week-long celebration of Mohammed's birthday. People come from as far away as Mecca, and for one frenetic week a year Lamu regains its eighteenth-century cosmopolitan stature. Processions of singing, white-robed men marched through the streets, and each evening all the men gathered for prayers, which were sung in the mosques to the beat of tom-toms and tambourines. The chanting, sweet and melodic, went on for hours, and the men sat and swayed and sweated as they sang, for the mosques were hot and very crowded. The drummers drummed to the point of exhaustion, but they never slowed their beat.

The birthday fell on a Thursday, and starting on Tuesday there was dancing each evening in the square outside the Riyadha Mosque, a huge Arabian confection of green domes and white walls that stood on the edge of town. Enormous drums pounded and everyone danced. Old men, wearing sunglasses and holding umbrellas, stood in a line doing the minimalist dance called the Goma; they stood perfectly rigid, slowly swaying their heads, their arms and their umbrellas in time to the drums. Younger men danced the Kirumbizi, a bizarre and dangerous dance in which two men slash at each other with broomsticks, each dodging the other's stick in time to the drums. I tried the dance only once, which was enough to set my heart pounding with excitement and relief.

The final evening, Thursday, came as an anticlimax. There was more dancing in the square and chanting in the mosque, but the dancing broke up early and a *sherif* from one of the mosques gave an impassioned sermon that went on for hours. I sneaked away long before it was over, and as I groped my way along sloping starlit streets back toward the harbor, I could hear the *sherif*'s strident voice booming in the distance. The air was still and sticky. That night was the hinge between the seasons; the four-month season of wind was over and the season of damp and rain was about to begin. It was time to go.

I left the island a few days later, crossed the narrow neck of sea in one of the tiny wooden motorboats which the local people call *mta-boti*, and took a bus to Malindi. Somewhere in the hinterland between Witu and Garsen, a troop of baboons loped across the road. The other passengers looked at me, a white man, and then at the baboons, which, like me, had straight brown hair, and shook with barely suppressed giggles.

I spent the night at Malindi. The youth hostel was almost full and I had to sleep on the roof. Malindi lay in the path of a total eclipse of the sun that was scheduled to take place the next morning. Vendors roamed through town, selling "Eclipse '80" T-shirts; Malindi, once, like Lamu, a sleepy Swahili port, has become a big-time tourist resort. Tourism has flayed the town, scarred it with wide, busy highways, streets of souvenir shops, French restaurants and pizza parlors and serried rows of huge hotels, and has turned a town as pleasant to live in as Lamu into a place one wants to hurry through. A fog of bitterness hung over the town, rancid and ugly as stale sweat, so thick and cloying it made me want to hold my breath. Constant exposure to that fog hardened the faces of the prostitutes and curio sellers who patrolled the beach. They knew that their clients spent as much for a fancy French meal as they earned in a month.

The eclipse began without fanfare, and far more slowly than I had expected. There was no sudden darkness; at first, I could see nothing more than a tiny nick in the rim of the sun. Over the next hour, the nick grew larger; it was curved, like a bite mark, and its shape made it seem as if a large and lazy monster was slowly chomping away at the sun the way a child might nibble a big round cookie. The eclipse was visible, at least in part, throughout Africa; in Yaloké, where I had seen such panic the year before during a partial eclipse of the moon, it would be almost total. Most of Africa would have no warning of the eclipse, and the next hour would be a time of madness and hysteria. Even in cocksure, sophisticated Malindi, the people grew noticeably edgy as the time of totality neared.

I went down to the beach a few minutes before the climax. During the first hour, the sun, though partially eaten away, was as bright as ever, but then it grew rapidly darker. As the sudden, unnatural twilight deepened, the beach became chilly and quiet, and a wind swept in from the sea. A thin veil of cirrus clouds scudded across the sky, but the sun was clearly visible behind. I had been watching through an old piece of film I had gotten at a camera shop, but now I risked a glance at the naked sun. A spot at the edge flashed and sparkled like a diamond, and then the sun was gone, except for the flaming halo of the corona. I had expected total darkness, but there was some light, a sickly, lurid light that made the sand shine like the pale belly of a shark seen through the water. An uneasy hush fell; people spoke in whispers, if at all. *Allaaahu akbar!* The call of the mosque cut through the silence, not the usual chant, but a special prayer for the sun's safe return.

Then, like a sliver of liquid fire, a splinter of sun emerged from hiding, and in good time the sun regained its wholeness. I left Malindi that afternoon, in time to take the night train to Nairobi.

As soon as I reached Nairobi, I began making preparations to leave it. Nairobi's tall towers awakened the latent Daniel Boone in me and made me yearn for the wilds. Daniel Boone went west whenever things got too civilized; I went north, to the Sudan.

24

RETURN TO SUDAN

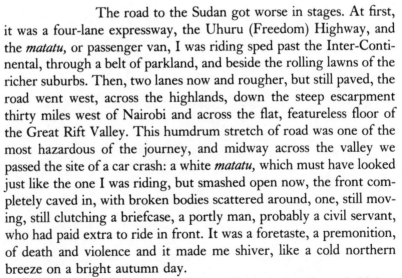

The road to the Sudan got worse in stages. At first, it was a four-lane expressway, the Uhuru (Freedom) Highway, and the *matatu,* or passenger van, I was riding sped past the Inter-Continental, through a belt of parkland, and beside the rolling lawns of the richer suburbs. Then, two lanes now and rougher, but still paved, the road went west, across the highlands, down the steep escarpment thirty miles west of Nairobi and across the flat, featureless floor of the Great Rift Valley. This humdrum stretch of road was one of the most hazardous of the journey, and midway across the valley we passed the site of a car crash: a white *matatu,* which must have looked just like the one I was riding, but smashed open now, the front completely caved in, with broken bodies scattered around, one, still moving, still clutching a briefcase, a portly man, probably a civil servant, who had paid extra to ride in front. It was a foretaste, a premonition, of death and violence and it made me shiver, like a cold northern breeze on a bright autumn day.

Then we were up, and out of the valley, passing through Naivasha, Gilgil, and Nakuru, neat little highland towns with shops and houses all brightly painted, and on to Eldoret. Until then, we had followed the main highway, but at Eldoret the two roads parted company. The main road continued west to Uganda and the road to the Sudan turned north. A few miles beyond Kitale, a town just north of Eldoret, and 250 miles from Nairobi, the paving ended. I spent the night at Kitale, a town whose ugly disarray reminded me of an auto graveyard, and in the morning took another *matatu* north.

Kitale was at the edge of the fertile land which had been the white highlands. Just beyond town, the terrain changed. The road, now a rough dirt track, wound through a stark, rugged land of sand and brush, high hills and steep escarpments. The arid soil was a strange shade of red, and the hills shone purple in the distance. The van, bumped and jarred by potholes and stones, broke down halfway, and there was a long stop while the driver patched the engine together, so it was dark when we reached Lodwar, the largest town in the north.

Except for a bar that served the last cold beer in Kenya (and in the Sudan you are lucky to find any beer at all), Lodwar had gone to bed long before I arrived. When I woke the next morning, all the shops were open. The streets were crowded with Turkana nomads who had come in from the desert, some to shop but most to look around, watch the trucks passing through, and spend the day on a shady veranda. The men wore ragged red cloaks—definitely *not* Raymond's—over their shoulders and mud and feathers in their hair. Some sported fighting bracelets, heavy metal bangles with wicked, razor-sharp edges.

It took me a day to find a ride, and I was lucky to get one at all. Terrible as the track from Kitale had been, the road north of Lodwar was far worse. It was not really a road at all, just a path trucks took across the flat, empty wasteland that was Kenya's northern frontier. There was a road from Kampala to Juba in the southern Sudan that was paved almost all the way, and the trucks that hauled freight to Juba from Mombasa, the closest port, used the Ugandan road. Only five or six trucks a year went via Lodwar. But, during the war with Tanzania a year before, the Kampala road had been closed, and all traffic into the Sudan had been diverted through Lodwar. "The road was so bad," the driver told me as we bumped across a rocky plain, "it took us a month to get to Juba." Outside the cab, an expanse of sunbaked land as white as salt glared in the sun. Over the past few months, the driver explained, part of the road had been graded, and the trip now took only a few days.

The road did not seem graded to me, and the land was deserted. Once I saw a tin shack, bravely painted green, with a few Turkana men outside: a shop. I would have liked to meet the owner, who was probably from India, to see how he had been shaped by the long years of solitude. Had he learned from the desert wind, or been eroded? But we drove on without stopping.

We spent the night parked near the police post at Lokichoggio, a compound of Nissen huts where my passport was stamped. From there to the border was fifty miles of barren sand, with quite a few riverbeds, dried up but still spongy, that had to be crossed. One of these gullies was the border, but the driver wasn't sure which.

Gradually, the terrain changed. There were parched, thorny bushes, and even a few spindly trees. This was the land of the To-posa, one of the Sudan's remotest and most reclusive tribes, and a people about whom I knew nothing except that they were reputed to be warlike. (Later, I found out that they are closely related to their traditional enemies, the Turkana and the Karamojong.)

Late in the afternoon we saw a Toposa village, a cluster of huts surrounded by a thorn stockade. The huts were round, with thatched roofs and walls of golden earth. The thatch was neatly tied in tapered rows, like shingles, and between the huts were the granaries, which looked like miniature houses perched on stilts. The village was quiet; nothing moved; not a soul was in sight. Perhaps it was the long drive, the days spent crossing empty land with the patience of a pilgrim, but that village seemed perfect to me then, a remote, untouched island in a sea of sand, a Platonic ideal of Africa captured and transfixed by the rays of the setting sun. I told the driver, "I'll get off here."

He looked at me to see if I was joking, and then he stopped, the brakes squealing. The village had seemed deserted, but at the sound of the brakes people poured out of the houses and ran to the truck. In less than a minute, there were a hundred Toposa thronged around us, all of them women, and all wearing beads and leather loincloths and nothing else. I grabbed my pack and stepped down from the cab into the crowd. The driver waited a few minutes in case I changed my mind, and then started his engine. The truck sped off and was soon gone from view.

A hundred women, and of course none of them spoke a word of

English or Swahili or Arabic. How could I explain to them why the truck had stopped and let me off? I could barely understand it; how could they? I tried a few gestures: I (pointing at myself) sleep (hands folded like a pillow, head on hands) here (pointing down). That was hardly an explanation, but the women accepted it, realizing I could give no other. They went back to their houses. A young girl showed me an empty hut where I could sleep; a dry, shriveled cowskin, stiff as a board, would be my mattress. Good, I said, and waited, quite content, watching the earthen houses blaze in the setting sun.

In the soft light of dusk, the men returned to the village. They wore burlap cloaks over their shoulders, the sort of rough and ragged garments favored by the producers of movies with B.C. in the title, except that the Toposa cloaks reached only to the waist. The nether parts were insouciantly left to flap in the breeze, but the shoulders were carefully hidden. Later, I found out why. A Toposa male is considered little more than a boy until he has killed someone of another tribe. When he does, he becomes a man worthy of respect, and in celebration his shoulder is marked with a special tattoo—the left shoulder if his victim was a man; the right, if he has murdered a woman. A well-bred man always conceals his tattoo, though everyone knows who has one and who hasn't. Happily, I did not realize this then; it would have played havoc with my peace of mind to know that every village youth saw me as an easy ticket to manhood.

And yet the village was peaceful, incredibly peaceful. It was night by now, and I sat outside my house in the starlight. A few men from the neighboring houses sat nearby, for this was the village courtyard. The air was cool, and someone lit a fire. The men gathered around the flames. Some sprawled on the ground and others propped themselves up against a nearby wall. They had been out all day with the herds and they were tired. One or two talked in low lazy voices, discussing, I surmised, crops and cows and the weather, like farmers the world over. One old man pulled out a long pipe, stuffed it with tobacco, and puffed away, noisily sucking in the smoke and expelling it in loud contented sighs. The rest of the men were silent, and so was I. The starlight, the people around me, and the stillness of the night combined to fill me with an intense yet languorous contentment; a sort of happiness I had felt before in fleeting, evanescent childhood dreams and which in waking, grown-up life can be recaptured only in small, remote places under the vast and spangled dome of night.

Many of the men around me, especially the older ones among them, shared this serenity, and it was, for them, something communal, something to be shared, something that bound them together. Their lives may have been poor and short and (worst of all from a Western standpoint) unvaried, but at least they had that.

I slept soundly that night, like a villager, and woke at dawn. A few women were sitting outside the hut when I emerged and when they saw me they led me, tugging at my sleeve, to a dusty clearing just beyond the houses. In the center of the clearing lay the carcass of a cow. A young Toposa warrior, stark naked and spattered with gore, straddled the body, hacking the meat with his spear. The man's eyes gleamed; even the onlookers seemed strangely excited; perhaps it was the smell of freshly spilled blood. I felt nervous without knowing why. Someone handed me a chunk of meat. The smell of slightly singed beef reminded me that, except for a few spoons of porridge a dour-faced woman had given me the night before, I had not eaten in almost two days. I ate hungrily and quite fast, and it was well that I did, because as I was chewing the last bit of gristle a man came into the clearing and walked over to where I sat. He wore a uniform, khaki shirt, and trousers, and was obviously not a villager. "I arrest you," he said.

On my last visit to the Sudan a year before, the police had prevented me from visiting the Dinka villages around the town of Gogrial even though I had both a travel permit for the region and a special police pass to visit Gogrial. This time, I had no permit at all so, after some ineffectual protest, I took my pack and followed the soldier to the road. We sat by the track, waiting for a ride to Kapoeta, the nearest town and the nearest police station. "These people are like animals," said the policeman. "How can you live with them?" He was a Toposa himself, but he had gone to school.

A jeep driven by a Dutch geologist took me to Kapoeta. He was surprised that I had dared to spend the night with the Toposa. "You were lucky the policeman found you," he said. Kapoeta was a windswept square of sand surrounded by sad and sagging buildings of weatherbeaten brick. Some, now blotched and tan, had once been painted white, but most no one had ever bothered to paint at all. The square was deserted, as still and silent as a ghost town. I had forgotten how bleak and desolate these Sudanese towns could be, but at the sight of Kapoeta, I remembered, and wondered why I had ever wanted to return.

A policeman came out of one of the moldering buildings, and the geologist left me with him. Inside the station, the local state security agent let me go, telling me not to leave town until he had seen me again. I had vague plans of doing a short trek around Toposaland, and I spent the evening getting directions from people who knew the area. But the next morning, the agent told me that I would have to go straight to Juba. Since I did not have a travel permit, I was not allowed to stop along the way. I could get a permit in Juba and was then welcome, he assured me, to return to Kapoeta. The security man neither hoped nor expected to see me again but in the manner of most Sudanese he was unfailingly polite. He put me on a truck to Torit, a town halfway to Juba, and instructed the driver not to charge me any fare.

Within an hour, I had left Toposaland behind and entered the hilly, rock-strewn territory of the Lotuko. Women stood by the side of the road, some pounding grain into flour, others simply watching the trucks pass by, but all wore skirts instead of loincloths. At Torit, I boarded a bus for Juba. There had been no bus service in the southern Sudan a year before, but when Amin was deposed his henchmen had fled to the Sudan by the busload. The Sudanese had kept the buses. The road, though far better than the tracks farther east, had not been made with buses in mind, and as the bus bumped along first one tire blew, and then another. As he changed the second flat, the driver announced that he had no more spares, so if another tire went, we could all walk. After that, I tensed up at each bump or jar or rattle. The third tire blew toward evening, and all the passengers cheered. When I got off, I saw why. I could see lights in the distance; it was only a few miles to town. I put on my pack and started walking.

If you included its sprawling mud hut suburbs, Juba was larger than some cities, but Juba was nonetheless more a village than a town. It was the capital of Sudan's theoretically autonomous Southern Region, an area larger than most African countries, and it was totally lacking in Western comforts and amenities. Therein lay its charm.

Juba, unlike Kapoeta, was a lively place, in its slow, seedy way, but

I found Juba as cut off as Lamu from the modern world. It was still a frontier town. The electricity worked sporadically, the toilets were pits in the ground, and the drinking water came straight from the Nile. Nature had not yet been tamed, and life had an element of uncertainty, even danger. And that, too, was a part of Juba's charm.

It was the driest part of the year and the road to Khartoum, closed for nine months of the year, was now open. North of Juba was a wild and rugged land, and only a few hours from town, I was told, I could find naked men and untouched villages. Clothing, at least according to Genesis, is the first sign of sin and civilization, and I was, as always, fascinated by the idea of people who did without it. I decided to hitchhike north, not all the way to Khartoum, but only as far as Kongor, a village a few hundred miles downriver. I had wanted to return to the Dinkas ever since leaving Gogrial, and Kongor was in Dinka territory. After a few days there, I would head south again, and return to Nairobi by the paved road through Uganda. It took a day to get a travel permit, and I left the morning after.

The road was good for the first hundred miles. It was dirt, of course, but had been recently graded, and the truck drove quickly. I sat in back, on top of the load, and I saw round, thatched houses, fields of stalks and stubble, the leavings of the harvest, and, as promised, naked men working the land, preparing to plant next year's crop of millet. After a few hours, we reached the truck's destination, the riverside town of Bor. It was the usual Sudanese scattering of thatch and tin, but the tin-roofed shops and cafés were filled with tribesmen in swim trunks (the police did not allow naked men in town) and they made Bor a lively place to be—far more interesting, I thought, than Wau. You can't judge a town by its name, I decided.

I slept at the police station, and the next morning I found another truck and continued north. A few miles outside Bor, the good road ended. The track narrowed and at the same time the horizon broadened. South of Bor, the land had been a tangle of trees and undergrowth; the fields I had seen had been hacked from the forest. Now, a grassy, rolling prairie spread before me. Here and there were clusters of big earth houses, with vaulted roofs as tall as churches. I was in Dinkaland again.

In the afternoon, the truck turned off the road, drove through what seemed like a wall of shrubbery, and parked in the midst of a glade surrounded by green, leafy trees. The driver, an Arab from

Khartoum, had spent much of his life hauling freight along this road, and he knew its hidden secrets. He spread a large white cloth in the shade of a tree and reclined upon it as his assistant cooked a stew over a fire. When the meal was ready, the driver invited me to join him. The embroidered cloth we sat on, the big communal bowl from which we took our food, and the white-robed driver, who lazily reclined even as he ate, all seemed like a bit of Arabia transplanted and set in the midst of the southern wilds.

It was a long and leisurely meal, and then we were back on the road. This portion of Sudan's highway system was a ten-foot-wide porridge of stones and mud. We drove as fast as the road would allow, and that was ten miles an hour and sometimes less, so it was midnight by the time we got to Kongor. A small circle of fires showed where other trucks were parked. The driver ran off to join the other drivers, all of whom he knew, and I curled up under the truck. The night was cool, but I had a new blanket, bought in Nairobi, which I was, much later, to abandon in a Tokyo *ryokan*. It kept me warm.

I woke at sunup and saw Kongor: a cluster of round mud huts, two larger, square buildings, also mud, which housed (as I could have guessed) a school and a police post, a few gawky, curious Dinka schoolboys who came to stare at the passing strangers. They looked at the trucks and dreamed of far-off, exciting places like Khartoum—or perhaps the dreamy look I saw in their eyes was simply a desire to be free of classes and join their older brothers at the cattle camps. It was the dry season, and most of the people were at the camps, grazing their herds near the Nile and sleeping under the stars. Kongor was all but deserted. Whenever a Dinka talked about those camps, his eyes shone with a longing to be there. I, too, wanted to go but I felt tired after the long day driving and the short cold night. I would have to walk twenty miles without trail or guide and hope there was a camp at the end of it. Even if I managed to find the camp I would probably be picked up by state security. There was a truck about to leave for Bor and in a moment of discouragement I got on it. Besides, there was another sort of camp I wanted to visit.

The Dutch contractors who were slowly widening and regrading the road lived in a camp outside Bor, which was as far as the work had got. The truck I was riding reached the camp in the early afternoon. I got off and, as I had hoped, was immediately invited to share a huge lunch of meat and vegetables washed down with the only ice-cold Heineken beer in the Sudan.

If you want to see cattle camps, one of the men told me as I left, there are some quite near here. There was a Dutch anthropologist living in Bor who could give me more information.

That same afternoon, I visited the anthropologist. The camps are about a mile from here, he told me. We were seated in the living room of his house, a large concrete-and-tin bungalow a mile outside town. Through the windows I could see several other houses, most of which seemed deserted. This was the site of an overly ambitious irrigation scheme, which was abandoned long before any crops were planted. But water still ran along disused channels, and grass, well-watered, grew in abundance on land intended for millet and cotton.

Near these artificial grasslands were the camps. The herders camped there, the anthropologist explained, were not Dinkas but Murles. The Murle are a little-known tribe who roam the trackless wastes near the Ethiopian border. They are, most people would say, far more "primitive" than the Dinka or even the Toposa, but the one person to have made an exhaustive study of their culture, a British administrator and amateur ethnologist, concluded after ten years that certain aspects of their philosophy were too complex for him to understand. The Murle usually keep to themselves, and rarely leave their territory, but drought had dried their grasslands and so the Murle had driven their herds west in search of fodder. All the land was dry and barren until they came to the irrigated land near Bor, and there they stayed. They had been there for more than a month and would stay until the rains began.

That path just beyond the house will take you to the camps, the anthropologist concluded. We had talked for over an hour and the sun was low in the sky. I put on my pack and followed the track he had shown me. The sun sank even lower and as the light faded the parched grass around the track took on a delicate purplish hue. It was African twilight, that rare and beautiful time which travel books assure us does not exist at all. The path was wide and quite crowded. Herds of skinny cattle lumbered slowly past. The men, their workday over, were driving their cows and oxen back to the corral. Plumes of smoke hung in the air; there were camps all around me now, and as they passed them the herdsmen on the path shouted greetings to their friends inside. I saw a small hut to the left of the path and went toward it; I wanted to find shelter before night fell. A teenage youth, naked like all the men I had seen, came out of the hut. Using the pantomime that had worked so well with the Toposa, I asked his permission to spend the night. He replied with a charade of chasing me away. I left and went on. At the next hut I came to, the same scene was repeated. The people could not understand why I was there and they were afraid. I was worried also, because it was already too dark for me to find my way back to Bor. Then, as the last light was leaving the sky, I came to a full-sized cattle camp.

It was a large oval enclosure, several hundred feet at its widest, completely surrounded, except for a narrow gate, by a wall of thorns. Inside was a shuffling, wall-to-wall carpet of cattle. Their horns, long and sinuous lyres, were silhouetted against the darkening sky. A few oxen stamped and bellowed but most, exhausted from a long day in the heat, were quiet except for a few contented snorts as they rubbed against their neighbors, and bedded down for the night. Around the perimeter of the enclosure were five or six small shelters, straw-walled igloos which reminded me of Tuareg encampments. I pushed my way through the cattle to the nearest of the huts. There were two teenagers inside, both boys, but the older had some of the assurance of manhood. He was not pleased when I asked him to let me stay, but he didn't chase me away. He brought me a gourd of milk and another, larger bowl of porridge. I finished both. Milk was rare, he told me. There was not enough grass and most of the cows were not giving milk. He told me all of this with gestures, for we had no language in common.

There was a fire outside the hut and we sat beside it. Two other herders came over to talk. One of the men wore pink plastic earrings and both of their naked bodies were covered with an intricate pattern of decorative scars. Murle men are slaves to fashion and spend long and painful months carving pretty designs on their chests, backs and bellies. Most men preferred geometric patterns, usually concentric circles of tiny dots, but once in Bor I saw a man with palm trees incised on his chest. The two men who now sat beside me were older than the one who had given me food but were nonetheless quite young and probably not yet married. They took great pains to appear manly and attractive to the ladies.

By now the cows were lying down, and I could see across the yard. A crowd was gathered on the other side and I walked toward them.

Men and women, awestruck and silent, sat in a circle. In the center of the circle, a woman danced. She was very old and thin as a wraith but there was magic in her frenzied dance. Her whirling arms and legs were blurs, they moved so fast, and her writhing body was a pale and shimmering shadow against the moon. Someone beat a drum but she moved to her own, faster rhythms. There was something elemental in her dance; its grace and surging power mimicked the wind and the rain. Quite likely this was in fact a dance for rain, an attempt to call forth a tempest to flood the sunbaked soil. As I watched, her dancing became even faster and more furious. I watched in fascination but not for long, because one of the men saw me and led me away, back to the hut where I was staying. An outsider's presence might taint the spell.

That night I slept badly. The hut was crowded and my two roommates coughed all night. TB is endemic among the Murle; the cows carry it and the people catch it. The Murle's birth rate is abnormally low and the tribe is dying out.

I woke at dawn. It was cold and the cows, eager to graze, were already stirring. The two youths went outside and lit a fire. The cattle, as implacable and insistent as babies, were beginning to bellow, and it would soon be time to drive them to pasture. The men sat by the fire, savoring the few quiet moments before the long workday began. I sat with them, and when they left with the herds I went back to Bor.

I took a truck to Juba and from there a bus to Nimule, a small town in the jungle-clad hills by the Ugandan border. From there, I got a ride in the back of a long, empty flatbed truck. It let me off in Atiak, the first town inside Uganda. There was a border post in Atiak, and the army officer in charge asked to see my visa, seemed on the verge of sending me back to Sudan when I told him I didn't have one, but finally let me through, telling me to report to immigration in Kampala. The paved road began at Atiak, and it was an easy ride to Gulu, the largest town in the north, where I spent the night.

The hotel I stayed at was three rooms in the back of somebody's house. There was a café in front, and two teenage girls worked as waitresses in the café and doubled as chambermaids at the hotel. That evening, one of them passed me a note scrawled in pencil. "I like you and want to stay with you in your room," it said. But this was the first room I had had to myself since leaving Kenya, and I did not want to share it, so I locked the door and went to sleep. I left early the next morning, just as the bus to Kampala, which had already left the station, was driving past the door. I waved, it stopped, and I got on.

It was 6 A.M. but that was the last bus of the day. No one wanted to get to Kampala after sunset. Curfew did not start until ten but strange things happened after dark and by seven o'clock the streets were eerily quiet and totally deserted. Nightclubs and discotheques did a booming business, but they opened just after lunch and closed at 6 P.M. Ugandans, it seemed, could adapt to anything.

That was Kampala in early 1980: a blend of hope and despair, freedom and anarchy. Amin had gone, and the terror was over. The press was perhaps the freest in Africa and, for a few giddy months after the demise of State Research, there was no secret police at all. Now the country could rebuild itself, or so everyone said; there was so much optimistic talk of reconstruction, and if things went less smoothly than expected, there was always an easy solution: blame Amin. Blame Amin for rising prices, for shootings in the street. So all the politicians blamed Amin, but blaming Amin did not put bread on people's tables.

The economy was in a tailspin and by the time of my visit, most workers were not earning enough to eat. The average wage was between two and five hundred shillings a month, the same as in Kenya, but Ugandan prices were almost ten times as high as Kenyan. The real value of the Ugandan shilling had plummeted, and that meant that many workers were paid two dollars a month, twenty-four dollars a year, and how they survived I could not begin to guess.

"Why is the cost of living so expensive?" asked a character in Uganda's most popular cartoon strip. "Because," came the reply, "the cost of dying is so cheap." And it was. People were killed for a watch or for a dollar or for nothing at all.

I spent three days in Kampala. I stayed at a hotel called the Tourist Lodge, sleeping on the roof because the rooms were full. Once, and once only, I went out at night. I passed through dark and silent streets of lifeless, unlit buildings. The city seemed abandoned, ancient, a place out of time. An Angkor or Pompeii for future generations. I hurried along, tempted to linger but too afraid, and didn't relax until I reached my rooftop. I sat by the parapet and listened to shootouts in the streets below.

On the fourth day I caught a bus to Kabalega Falls National Park, just south of Gulu and reputed to be one of the finest game reserves in the world. The bus dropped me at the entrance to the park, which was marked by a sign, a bench, and a mound of mortar shells abandoned by Amin's fleeing army. After a short wait, I got a ride to the lodge. Chobe Safari Lodge had once been quite luxurious, and the tourists who filled it paid thirty dollars a day for their bed and their view of the Nile and the rolling grassy veld beyond. That was ten years before and the hotel, like most buildings in Uganda, was scarred by a decade of looting, shooting, and neglect. Rooms cost four dollars now and the hotel was mostly empty. The next day I found out why. There was no game.

Poaching is a problem throughout Africa and will remain one so long as ivory and rhinoceros horn fetch astronomical prices, no questions asked. Hong Kong and China do a brisk trade in ivory carvings and, in Yemen, a dagger with a bit of rhino horn in the handle is considered the ultimate status symbol and sells for five hundred dollars. For a poacher, the rewards are great and the risk of detection in the understaffed parks is small. Bands of bandits, armed with machine guns, ravage the parks and the results are visible. I lost count of the rhino I saw on my first trip to Kenya in 1967, and elephants were even more common. They were almost a nuisance; they stood in the road and blocked traffic. But when I toured the same parks little more than a decade later, I saw one small herd of elephant and no rhino at all, and I was not surprised to learn that Kenya had 75 percent fewer elephant and rhino in 1980 than ten years before.

In Uganda, where most of the army, it would seem, slaughtered game for fun and profit, 95 percent of the country's elephant and rhino have been killed since 1970. At Kabalega, the situation was even worse. In 1972 there were twelve thousand elephants in the park, some of whom became virtually tame and were given names like Katie and Nelly by the wardens. Now there are at most two hundred, all in a remote corner of the park fifty miles from Chobe. On my first afternoon at Chobe, I met Iain Douglas-Hamilton, a lanky, energetic British pilot and conservationist who was doing an aerial survey of the park. He had just returned from his morning flight, on which he had spotted the bullet-riddled bodies of what had been the last herd of elephant in the area.

And so I saw no elephant at Chobe. I spent the next few days roaming the hills near the lodge in search of game, and I did see three giraffe one morning. Their necks rose like periscopes above the thorn trees, their heads turned in unison to look at me, and then they loped off with that incredible bounding grace that all animals, even elephants and lumbering rhino, seem to share when there are no fences around them.

Chobe was pleasant. There was the river to look at, and the vast and rolling plains to wander. But one week there was enough. After that I went west. A two-day bus ride brought me to Kabale, a tiny town in the remote upland region where Uganda, Rwanda, and Zaire meet. That far-off corner of Uganda is a strange and beautiful land of whalebacked hills, lakes, and volcanoes, panoramic vistas everywhere, cool nights and misty mornings. The soil is volcanic, a rich black earth that is as fertile as anywhere in Africa, and the humped hills and narrow valleys are covered with a patchwork of bright green fields. Well-worn paths zig and zag their way up and down the hills and from one hill to another. The paths are always crowded with people going to their fields or visiting neighbors and herds of cattle on their way to pasture. The cows wore bells, and their tinkling ring made me think of Kathmandu, which, too, is blessed with crisp air and green hills and the sound of many bells.

I stayed a week. Each day I followed a new path through the hills. Once I got as far as Lake Bunyoni, eight miles southwest of town. The fjordlike lake, sinuous and serpentine, was broken up by islands and fingerlike peninsulas, all of them covered with cropland right up to the waterline. Another morning, I walked by a farmhouse where a lively party was in progress. The revelers called me over and treated me to a calabash of home-brewed beer.

Then my week was over, and I took a bus to Kampala and another to Tororo and the border. The road to Tororo passed through forest and farms and abandoned plantations, through the rundown town of Jinja, where a bridge spanned the Nile at its source, then through other, smaller towns which were no more than a double row of whitewashed houses and perhaps a café where drivers could stop and drink milky tea from plastic mugs. It was a lush green lowland, that part of Uganda, in foliage as well as location midway between the drier Kenya highlands and the jungles of Zaire. I studied the landscape carefully, for I knew of no reason why I should ever pass that way again. But in the months that followed I was in fact to cover that hundred-mile stretch of road eight times more.

That was to happen in July. I spent the rest of April, May, and most of June on the white and endless sands of the Kenya coast. It was the rainy season, but there was no rain. It was a balmy, golden time, and the weather was perfect enough to be remembered for years to come, as was, for example, that warm and halcyon summer in Europe, the summer of 1914.

25

THE
FAMINE:
CONVOYS TO
KARAMOJA

Away from the coast, those cloudless, barren skies spelled disaster. For the second year in a row, the rains had failed to come, and from the north of Ethiopia to southern Mozambique millions of people faced starvation. In the arid corner of Uganda called Karamoja, people were already dying. Many tried to flee and died walking, so many that their bodies blocked traffic on the highways and at a place named Namalu the missionaries had to use tractors to push corpses from the roads.

It was several months before the outside world learned that Karamoja was starving. Late in June, a Kenyan reporter visited the area, and what he saw and wrote and photographed was horrifying enough to become front-page news. I was back in Nairobi by then, and I saw the photos the day they were published. Shriveled babies, all skin and bone with old men's faces. I had seen these faces many times before, in photographs from Biafra, the Sahel, Ethiopia, Bangladesh, and they had always seemed the same. But they looked different now. I had stayed in villages throughout Africa, had eaten the people's food and played with their children. Village children were without exception frisky and full of life, a joy to be with. The old and withered children in the photos, I realized, had been like that before the food ran out. If they were given food they would live again but if not they would die.

Once it appears in print, the news of disaster spreads quickly, and in its June 30 issue, *Time* magazine carried a long article with the headline "A Harvest of Despair: The world's hungriest continent reels under a new famine." An American free-lance correspondent had a copy of *Time,* and lent it to me when we ran into each other in the New Stanley's outdoor café. A few sentences near the end caught my eye. "Karamoja," wrote the chief of *Time*'s Nairobi bureau, "has turned into a surrealistic terror, as heavily armed marauders led by remnants of the fallen dictator's army swoop down on villages . . . [and] kill every man, woman and child in sight. After almost a dozen relief workers were murdered, CARE and other agencies considered suspending their operations. . . . In late May, Tanzanian soldiers barged into the Catholic hospital in Abim, dragged away five patients, including a six-year-old boy, and shot them to death outside the hospital gate. A week later Ugandan troops invaded the hospital and killed five staff members." "That place is a real combat zone," said the correspondent, who had been a copter pilot in Vietnam.

There could not be more than fifty or a hundred relief workers in Karamoja, I reckoned, and in less than a month a dozen had died. The risks were obviously high, but the gains, I decided, far greater. Each worker, by putting one life (his own) in danger, could save thousands.

That afternoon I went to the OXFAM office on Muindi Mbingu Street. The woman in charge was on the telephone to Kampala when I walked in. I asked if I could volunteer to help in Karamoja, and she passed the phone to me. The man at the other end was Francesco Strippoli, a senior United Nations official stationed in Kampala. "You can't imagine how bad it is in Karamoja," he told me. "I'll do any work," I said, "without pay, and I'll pay all my own expenses, but I have no training in medicine or anything else." "We need help desperately," he responded. "Come whenever you can."

It took me several days to get a Ugandan visa, and I delayed my departure several days more. I was frightened and wished to postpone the ordeal I knew awaited me. Finally, on July 12, I boarded a bus for the border.

I was delayed at Busia, where a Ugandan army officer insisted that I needed two visas, and not one, to enter. The same thing had happened three years before, and I did now what I had done then: I hitched a ride to the more lenient border post at Malaba. All this took several hours, and by the time I got to Kampala it was almost dark. Curfew time. I hurried to the Tourist Lodge and fell asleep on the roof.

Early the next morning, I went to the United Nations office building on Parliament Avenue. The elevator was working that day. I took it to the top floor and walked down a bare, unpainted hallway to the offices of the Food and Agriculture Organization. Mr. Strippoli was the regional head of the FAO. He was a busy man, and I waited all that day as he and his staff tried to find a job for me and do a dozen other things at the same time. The day seemed endless. I sat and stared out the window at the soft green hills that ring the city. Shadows on the street below moved from west to east and I began to wonder why I had come.

Come back tomorrow, they told me at five and I went back to the Tourist Lodge. That evening I had dinner with some of the U.N. staff I had met that day. It was a small, informal party, a sort of celebration. One of the men had been transferred. He was flying out in the morning and that night he was all songs and laughter. Wine flowed freely, but it wasn't the alcohol that elated him, it was the thought of leaving Uganda. His next job, he told me, was in Kabul. There was a war going on in Afghanistan, he said, but it was on the whole a lot more tranquil than Kampala.

When I showed up at the FAO office the next morning, they told me that I could work for the United Nations Children's Fund, UNICEF. The UNICEF offices were on the other side of town, out beyond Bat Valley, an aptly named part of town where the trees, seen from afar, seem to have leather leaves. It was afternoon by the time I found the office.

The first man I met at UNICEF was Brendan O'Brien, the deputy head of the office. He was from Ireland, bearded, intense, and committed to his work. I think he was pleased by the idea that someone would volunteer to work in Uganda. My first job, he told me, would be at a warehouse outside town.

We drove there the next morning. The warehouse was on the grounds of a Catholic mission ten miles west of Kampala. It was inconveniently far from town, but it was the closest building they could find that was reasonably secure from robbers. We drove past a sentry and through a gate in a high concrete wall, and parked outside a huge tin-roofed hangar. A watchman unlocked a heavy steel door and I went inside. The interior was chaotic.

During the past week, planeloads of food and medical supplies had arrived from Europe. The medicines had been loaded into trucks and dumped at the warehouse, where they lay in a jumbled heap on the floor because no one had the time to sort through them. That would be my job. I, along with two of the UNICEF staff, would bring order to this Augean warehouse, inventorying the goods and sorting them into piles. When I first saw the warehouse, I thought the work would take weeks, but we had the job done in three days.

But that was not the end of my work at the storage depot. Mr. O'Brien explained why the next morning. In any famine, the first to die are the children. They need special care and attention, and children's feeding centers were being set up throughout Karamoja. They would be staffed by doctors and nurses sent by private charities in Britain and France, and UNICEF would provide the supplies. The centers would offer both food and medical care, and so the medicines we had sorted had to be sorted again, for shipment to Karamoja. Each center would be sent a medical kit containing large quantities of thirty-six different medicines, two tons in all. Five centers were about to open, so five kits had to be prepared at once.

By the next afternoon, the kits were ready, five piles of crates and parcels, with several hundred boxes in each pile, and each box marked with contents and destination. That was the easy part; the difficult job was getting the kits to their destination. They would have to be loaded into trucks and sent overland, and Karamoja was far away. It lay in northeast Uganda, bounded to the east by Kenya and to the north by the Sudan. The route followed the road to Kenya as far as Tororo, where it curved north and then northwest to the town of Soroti. Between Kampala and Soroti were eight army roadblocks where all trucks were stopped and inspected. The soldiers who ran the roadblocks had a reputation for being volatile, totally unpredictable. They might shout at you, arrest you, maybe even shoot you, or simply welcome you and wave you through. Most vehicles were passed after a brief inspection, but army pay was low and a truckload of medicine was worth a lot.

At Soroti, the road turned east and entered the ten thousand square miles of barren land known as Karamoja. Moroto, the main settlement in the region, was a day's drive from Soroti, and much of Karamoja even farther, and the whole area was the domain of bandits, *Time*'s "heavily armed marauders."

Little was known about the bandits. There were several bands of them, each with about two hundred men, but who they were was a mystery, the subject of much speculation. Some people thought they were composed of Karamojong men who had left their villages. Cattle raiding is, these people pointed out, a traditional pastime of the Karamojong. But one U.N. worker, who had seen photographs of the remains of women tortured by the bandits, believed that the bands were organized and run by Amin's soldiers; the Karamojong, she said, would never behave so brutally on their own.

Everyone agreed that the bands were well-armed. Amin's army had abandoned fifteen thousand AK 47 assault rifles in their Moroto camp, and the bandits had simply walked into the deserted barracks and helped themselves. (The AK 47, designed by Kalashnikov and made in Russia, is the best army rifle ever designed; in some parts of the world, a single rifle will fetch two thousand dollars.)

Getting goods from Kampala to Karamoja was, at that point, the relief effort's biggest problem. Convoys were sent out and never seen again. The drivers could not always be trusted. Often, they would sell the cargo, or simply panic and abandon it, and then return to Kampala and claim the goods had been safely delivered. Someone was needed to go along with the kits and make sure they reached their destinations. Because of the unsettled conditions in the area, UNICEF workers were not allowed to go to Karamoja. But that did not apply to me since I had never been formally hired, and it was decided that when the medical kits were sent I would ride shotgun.

When the kits had been assembled, I went to the UNHCR office, a large compound on a tree-lined side street near Kampala Road. The staff of the United Nations High Commission for Refugees were in charge of organizing truck convoys to Karamoja. Since the famine did not involve refugees, the High Commission needn't have given any help at all, but the staff volunteered for the job. At the office, crowds of refugees blocked all the hallways; the UNHCR staff was doing two jobs at once, and the lights burned late at the compound.

I hoped to get a truck that day, but trucks were scarce in those early days of the famine. It would be a long wait. More trucks had been sent from Kenya, but these needed Ugandan license plates and the men at the license bureau had delayed the applications. A few dollars paid to the right people would have gotten the licenses delivered in a day, but it is U.N. policy never to pay a bribe. Bribery escalates. Some weeks later, the officials in question, realizing they would not profit by delay, issued the permits, but I was in Karamoja by then.

In the end, Brendan O'Brien hired two trucks at a price I thought extortionate until I learned that the owners were also the drivers. We loaded the kits, and each kit filled a truck. One kit would be left in Moroto, and the other would go to Namalu, south of Moroto, in the center of the region hardest hit by famine. I would go with the trucks to Namalu and back to Kampala, and a senior official from one of the relief agencies setting up the feeding centers would accompany me as far as Moroto.

We left Kampala early the next morning. Brendan O'Brien saw us off. He had brought a letter, typed in English and Swahili on impressively headed stationery. These trucks, the letter declared, were on official business for the United Nations. Below the text were numerous stamps and seals; the letter was designed to awe the average Ugandan soldier and get us through the roadblocks. It did its job well, and by evening we reached Soroti after passing all eight roadblocks without even being asked for cigarettes. We spent the night at Soroti and left for Moroto the next morning.

The road was paved as far as Soroti, though so full of potholes that you could tell drunk drivers (it was said) because only they drove in a straight line. But the paving ended at Soroti, and so did the green. Karamoja bordered on Turkanaland and on the Toposas' domain. Moroto was not that far from Lodwar and the land around it was just as barren. It was flat and arid and the earth was dusty red. Here and there, tussocks of grass were scattered, but they were parched and dying. We drove all the way to Moroto without meeting a soul.

It was a grim landscape and my companion, the man from the relief agency, spent the time talking, in order perhaps to avoid looking out the window. "Things have got better," he said."We haven't seen any bodies on the road so far. Last week I saw four." He was one of the first outsiders to reach the area, and he had come to hate it, and hate the rest of Uganda even more for ignoring the Karamojong. I liked the Ugandans I had met and said so. Listen to this, he said, and told me about a morning several weeks ago, something that had happened to one of his colleagues and not to him but which still burned in his brain. The colleague, who was named Kevin O'Dockerty, had been driving south toward Namalu, and with him was a nurse from Kampala, a competent, highly trained professional. There was a body blocking the road, and O'Dockerty stopped the jeep, examined it, and found that the man was alive. He could be saved, but only if fed immediately, through a tube. The jeep was stocked with feeding tubes and bottles of glucose solution, but O'Dockerty couldn't find them. "Have you seen the tubes?" he asked the nurse. "The man will die without them." "No," she said, "we must have forgotten to take them." O'Dockerty remembered loading the tubes; he pretended to stumble, knocked over the nurse's handbag, and the tubes fell out. She had stolen them to sell in Kampala, and chose to let the man die rather than give them up. The tubes were worth less than a dollar; the cost of dying was indeed cheap in Uganda.

That evening, in Moroto, a British nurse told me another story; all the relief workers had their stories, and told them often, as if by the telling they could be expunged, rewritten. Her tale was shorter. She was driving an ambulance. It was stopped by soldiers. They pulled her out, unloaded the dying people onto the road, loaded the vehicle with beer, and drove off. The beer was urgently needed at their barracks.

We had reached Moroto late in the afternoon and had spent the few remaining hours of daylight unloading one of the two medical kits and stacking it in a cramped and cluttered storeroom. The store was at the mission, the only safe place in town. There were Catholic missions throughout Karamoja and for the first months of famine the missionaries had been the only Europeans in the area. It was they who stored and distributed the relief food sent from Kampala. They were tireless and fearless and their work saved many lives. I am not quick to admire the work of missionaries, but these were admirable men.

After the kit was loaded, I sat in the mission courtyard watching the darkening sky. The relief worker who had driven with me from Kampala found me there. He had something important to tell me and he wasted no time on preambles. "The road to Namalu isn't safe," he warned me, and he went on to describe in detail the hazards I would face: bandits, impassable riverbeds, hostile villagers. "Don't risk it," he concluded. "Leave the kit here. I am going north tomorrow, to visit our new feeding center, and I'll take the kit with me. They need the medicine as much as Namalu."

The man who told me this had done more years of relief work than I had days, so I had to respect his advice. But, as the only UNICEF man on a UNICEF convoy, I outranked him. It was my decision, and my responsibility. I sat and thought for hours, and in the end it was clear what I should do. I had been told to take the kit to Namalu; from all I had heard, the need was greatest at Namalu; and I had the uncomfortable suspicion that the relief worker was exaggerating the dangers of the southern road in order to get the medicine for his agency.

The next morning, I told the relief worker that I had decided to go to Namalu. He was surprised and slightly angry that I had disregarded his advice, and he spent much of the time before my departure in a last effort to change my mind.

As soon as the trucks were ready, we drove off, I and the two Ugandan drivers, and somehow we found the road to Namalu. The drivers were earning their wages that day; they had heard what the relief man said and it would not have surprised me if they had refused to go beyond Moroto. The track was rugged, sandy, and all but deserted, and we saw no sign of life at all until, after driving for what seemed like hours, we found a man lying in the road. He was Ugandan and fairly well-dressed, and perhaps that was why the bandits had attacked him. They had shot him and left him for dead. That had been the day before, he later told us, and we were the first truck to stop. We put him in back of one of the trucks, where he could lie flat, and drove on. There was supposed to be a mission at a place called Nabilatuk and if they had a nurse or doctor I would leave him there.

Finding the mission was easy. The compound of chapels, halls, and modest houses had the first buildings we had seen since leaving Moroto. A nun ran out to greet us; she was the only person in sight. I told her we were bound for Namalu and she seemed disappointed. "Don't you have food for us?" she asked. "The last shipment was a month ago, and we ran out last week. People are starving, people are dying. Every day, hundreds come and we have nothing to give them." "But the place is deserted," I objected. "It is Sunday," she replied. "We do not distribute food on the Sabbath."

There was a nurse at the mission, so we left the wounded man in her care, and then we drove on. We had to reach the relative safety of Namalu before nightfall. We drove as fast as we could but the trucks were wheezy old relics and the road was dreadful. There were four *wadis* between Nabilatuk and Namalu, each a large expanse of damp, slushy sand, the road stopping on one bank and resuming again on the other. The third and widest was a notorious truck trap, and midway across it one of the trucks got stuck in the sand. We shoveled sand, pushed from the rear, tried to tow one truck with the other, but the bogged-down truck would not budge. We would have to unload the truck, carry the two-ton kit box by box across the sand, and hope the truck, now two tons lighter, could be freed. So we began to lug the crates across the river. There were a lot of boxes and only three of us, and the task seemed endless.

As we worked, people emerged from the bushes. There was a village nearby, Lolachat, and the villagers had heard the trucks' straining engines and come to investigate. One man seemed to be the leader, and we offered him money to help us haul the boxes. At once, a long and eager line of people formed. Each took a box, carried it across, and returned for more. Children carried small cardboard cartons, and one old woman lifted a huge wooden crate onto her head and proudly marched across the *wadi*. In minutes, the truck was empty.

Without its cargo the truck started easily. It took time to reload it, but we were more than halfway to Namalu and by the time the sun set we had reached our destination. At the mission, I met a French doctor who had arrived a few days before to set up the feeding center. "I've had nothing to work with before you came," he said. "Now I can really do something."

The drivers and I slept at the mission, and that evening I met Father Mengenstat for the first time. He was short and slight, seemingly frail but in fact indefatigable. Since the first days of the famine, he had managed the relief effort in Namalu single-handed. He had taken a census and used it to apportion his scanty supply of food between the villages. When the first relief shipments came, he had taken the food to the villages himself, driving a battered old jeep that only he, it seemed, could coax to start. "The people were so hungry," he said, "they ate all the food at once and we could not stop them." They ate handfuls of hard, uncooked corn. One woman drank a quart of oil and died. "These people face famine often," he said, "and there is a drought every few years, but this time is the worst ever." Like the Karamojong, Father Mengenstat had seen starvation before; he was Ethiopian. He was the only black missionary I met in Karamoja; all the others were European.

The next day I saw starvation for the first time. There was a second mission a mile or so down the road which had the only secure warehouse in the area, so the doctor and I took the kits there. We drove through a gate and into a courtyard. People, mostly women and children, filled the yard, and some of the women had built fires for cooking. The head of the mission, a red-faced, kind-hearted bear of a man named Father Fortunato, had, without consulting anyone, even the bishop, turned his entire mission into a feeding center. He never turned anyone away but now the yard was full and the food was running out.

Most of the women in the yard had been fed for several days and looked thin but healthy. The children, despite the food, did not. Skeletons shrouded in wrinkled skin, they were the photographs come alive. Most of them could walk, or at least stand upright, but some were too weak and had to be carried. One of the boys was older than the rest—by my guess, twelve or thirteen. He was in the last stages of starvation. After the flesh of the body wastes away, when the ribs stand out like cables and the arms become thin pathetic twigs you can put your fingers around, after the belly shrivels or (sometimes) fills up with wind like a hideous balloon, then and only then does the face cave in. Cheeks become sunken, eye sockets turn into holes, and the face, until then human, turns into a death's head, a skull. And that is not the worst of it. Until this last and ghastly stage, the children, if they are wearing clothes (which Karamojong children do not) seem almost normal. They walk and play and even laugh. But when the face collapses, so does the spirit, and the living skeleton that had been a boy stared at me with sad, world-weary, accusing eyes. The blame in his gaze was worse than the sadness, and afterward I persuaded myself that I had imagined it. Guilt projected, nothing more.

By now it was time to leave. "I wish I could work here with you, and not in Kampala," I said to the French doctor. He was middle-aged and sympathetic and I had told him the same thing the night before. He went into the mission and, as I had hoped but not expected, wrote a letter asking Mr. O'Brien to assign me to Namalu.

A little-used road led from Namalu south to Mbale, a town near Tororo on the main road to Kampala. It was notoriously unsafe and most drivers preferred to go to Namalu by way of Soroti and Moroto, which took two days longer. I did not care to spend two more days in Karamoja so I decided to use the southern road and the drivers agreed.

The road was good and we met no bandits. By nightfall we had reached Jinja and the next morning we were in Kampala. I gave Mr. O'Brien the French doctor's letter and a report on the journey I had written at the hotel in Jinja. I had feared he would not approve of my decision to go to Namalu despite the advice of an experienced relief worker, but Mr. O'Brien was pleased that I had stood up to the man. I had been right.

I left UNICEF and ran back to UNHCR to pass on the message from the nun at Nabilatuk. I spoke to the man in charge of convoys, and he was appalled. His records showed that three food shipments had been sent to Nabilatuk that month, but from what the nun had told me none of them had reached their destination. Food would be sent, the man promised, on the very next convoy to leave. "When will that be?" I asked. I had a personal interest as well, because Mr. O'Brien had given me permission to go back to Namalu. "As soon as we can get the trucks," the UNHCR man said. The Ugandan licenses were still being delayed, so new trucks, with Kenya plates and Kenyan drivers, were being sent from Nairobi.

And so I waited, stuck in Kampala. I was impatient to be in Namalu, and the city was more depressing than ever. In the morning, workers hurried along Kampala Road, barely glancing at the sprawled bodies of people killed the night before. I saw one corpse with a face that sagged like an abandoned rubber mask. Gently, I turned the body over and found the back of the head was gone. In that year, Kampala's murder rate was a hundred times New York's.

Finally, the convoy was ready. There were five trucks and a jeep. Kenyans drove the trucks; a Frenchman working for UNHCR took the wheel of the jeep. I rode in the jeep, along with a young Belgian couple. They had come to Uganda as tourists. Some of the relief agencies in Uganda were so desperately short of workers that their people were buttonholing travelers in the street and asking them to volunteer. The Belgians had agreed and were, like me, headed for Namalu. The only other passengers were an escort of three soldiers.

At first, the journey was uneventful. We got through all the road-blocks, spent the night at Soroti, and the next morning drove across the wide and empty plains of Karamoja. We stopped for the night at Moroto and the day after headed south to Nabilatuk. We came to a part of the road that had tall grass on either side. The track was suddenly crowded with people. When they saw us, they jumped for cover. That's odd, said the driver. Then we saw men around us and shots rang out. I had never been shot at before and the shock of it was like an electric current. I was riding in front, next to the driver, and we slumped low in our seats and drove on. For one awful second we thought the engine had been hit and would stall. A few seconds later, we reached a larger group of men. By that time, I was thinking more clearly, and I stuck my arm through the window to show them we were white. The bandits rarely harmed Europeans, or so it was rumored; they supported the relief effort because it helped feed the wives and children they had abandoned when they joined the gangs. (We did not stop to think that, since sections of different clans and subtribes often fight one another, we might be feeding the bandits' enemies.)

For whatever reason, the shooting stopped, and the driver put on the brakes and got out. I opened the door and joined him. We had to show the bandits that we were not hostile and not afraid. The men surrounded us. Some carried rifles but most had only spears. A few were dressed in well-worn khaki, many were naked, and one man, one of those who proudly clutched a rifle, was wearing a green shirt and nothing else at all. We shook hands with those warriors who were closest and the driver tried to tell them not to molest the trucks behind us; we were carrying food to their wives and children. I don't think they understood, except for the Swahili word for food. When they heard that word, they all cheered.

We got back in the jeep. I thought we should stay with the bandits until the trucks arrived to make sure they got through, and I told the driver so, but he started the jeep and we drove away. I was not in charge of the convoy this time; he was, and it was his decision. He decided not to risk our lives, and I was secretly relieved though I tried not to show it.

We stopped at the top of a hill and waited for the trucks to catch up. We waited a long time and there was no sign of them, only a still, hot noonday silence which, though quite usual on the African savanna, seemed sinister to us then. Then the trucks came, all five of them, driving fast and spewing dust behind them. They braked when they neared us, and we could see the jagged stars the bandits' bullets had punched in the windshields. All five trucks had been hit, and most of the shots formed a cluster on the right side of the windshield—right where the driver's head should be. Some of the drivers had been wounded, two badly, but all of them were amazed and grateful to be alive. Later, when we found the time to examine the trucks, we noticed that the windshields, though webbed with cracks, had not broken. They had, incredibly, stopped the bullets. A few of the shots had hit the sides of the trucks, and it was these few bullets that had wounded the drivers. None of the soldiers had been scratched. "They hit the floor before we even knew we were being shot at," one of the drivers told me. They had obviously had much combat experience, and learned from it.

We waited on the hill until we were sure the bandits had gone, and then we drove back to Moroto, the trucks right behind us. Moroto had the only hospital in Karamoja, and we left our wounded and set off for Nabilatuk. At first, the UNHCR man had wanted to return to Kampala, but Nabilatuk needed food so urgently that in the end he decided to risk the journey. The drivers agreed at once. The sight of starving children in Moroto had made them forget their narrow escape a few hours before.

We made good time after leaving Moroto, and it was midafternoon when we arrived at Nabilatuk. It was Friday and the grounds of the mission, empty the Sunday before, were crowded with waiting Karamojong. We parked near the warehouse and the people surrounded us. They knew our trucks held food inside.

The nuns unlocked the doors to the empty warehouse and we began to unload our sacks of corn and sugar. Hundreds of people pressed around us. They would not let us pass. Most of them were nearly naked, and I could see their ribs like barrel staves, their spindly legs, their panic-stricken faces. If we gave the grain to them, there would be a free-for-all and only the strongest would get fed. Finally, we pushed a path through them to the warehouse. They had not the strength to resist. After that, the drivers, the Frenchman, and I took turns carrying the sacks and holding the people back. Each sack weighed a hundred kilos and I barely had the strength to carry them the hundred feet to the warehouse. Some of the people rushed forward to grab some corn and they, too, had to be gently carried away. But they were much lighter. After the truck had been emptied, a few children jumped on board, and frantically ate the mud and dirt that coated the floor of the trucks. They had seen a few grains of sugar spill, but all they got was dust and sand.

The Kenyan drivers were skilled as well as courageous, and they guided their huge trucks across the treacherous sands of Lolachat without a single mishap. By sunset, we had reached Namalu. That evening, we sat around a table in the cool and quiet parlor of the mission and, by the dim light of a hurricane lamp, debated what to do. The UNHCR man wanted to return to Kampala and persuade the U.N. to halt the relief convoys until the Ugandan government did something to protect them. He talked of protest, confronting the authorities; he was in his early thirties so he had, I calculated, been in college in 1968, the year the students of Paris manned the barricades and fought policemen in the streets. I, of course, wanted to stay in Namalu, and so did Denis, the French doctor who had asked for my assistance. But there were three other doctors there. They had arrived the day before and they voted to go back to Kampala. Father Mengenstat advised me to go as well. Unless something were done to secure the convoys, he reminded me, shipments would stop and the Karamojong would have no food at all. "You'll be back at Namalu in a week," the UNHCR man promised me, and so I agreed to go along.

Before we left the next morning, Denis took me to see the feeding center where I would work when I returned. The center had opened a day or two before in a dusty yard outside a concrete building, now gutted and empty, that had once been a dispensary. Denis was a veteran relief worker; he had run feeding centers in Biafra and many places since. He had set up this center himself with nothing but a large pot, a ladle, and a ball of twine. He used the kettle to heat the food, the spoon to dish it out, and the twine to rope off a rectangle where the children would sit. The center was a mile and a half from the mission, and as we walked Denis described how it worked. He had managed to convince the people who had manned the dispensary to work with him, and all three of them were, he said, first-rate. They had some medical training and they knew the area well.

My first sight of the center was a big shade tree and children playing. The children ran down to meet us and formed a giggling ring around the doctor. They were the lucky ones, only slightly malnourished. The next thing I saw was a body lying in the sun. Four people had died that day; three had been children so their bodies had been flung into the bushes but this one had been a man in his prime. Though pitifully thin, he was still too heavy to move. His eyes were wide and staring. The doctor was visibly shaken; he had never seen grown men starve to death, not even in Biafra.

Then I met Florence. She was in her thirties, thin but strong, quick to anger but equally quick to smile. She greeted us and asked for news. She spoke English fluently, but with a slight accent. She's from Jamaica, I decided, or maybe Kampala. Before Amin's time and even during, those Ugandans who could afford it sent their children to study in the States. Later I learned that she was Karamojong and had never been outside Karamoja.

We stayed only a few minutes. The trucks were, we knew, about to leave. Florence promised to keep the center running until we returned. It will only be for a few days, we assured her, but we were nonetheless worried and reluctant to go. The center was unprotected; there wasn't even a lock on the door. Soldiers and even bandits think twice before molesting a European, but to them Florence would be just another Karamojong.

Denis and I rode together in one of the trucks. He spent much of the ride giving me detailed instructions on how to run the center. Malnourished children need special food and special treatment; their shriveled stomachs cannot digest the food that healthy children eat. Denis gave me a tattered sheet of recipes. Crudely printed, it bore the seal of the Biafran health department. "Keep it," he said. "You might have to go back alone."

Denis was from Réunion Island, a speck of France in the middle of the Indian Ocean. He was shocked by what he had seen in Namalu and he planned now to fly back to his island, hold meetings, round up volunteers and contributions, and then, perhaps in September, return to Uganda. Besides, he had his own patients to look after. Denis had a practice in Saint-Denis, capital of Réunion and, like all the French doctors who came to Karamoja, had donated his time and paid his own airfare and expenses.

The long trip back to Kampala passed without incident. We decided not to risk the shortcut to Mbale, so we went via Moroto and Soroti. At Moroto, we stopped at the hospital to visit the two injured drivers, both of whom were well on the road to recovery. We stayed at the Mt. Moroto Hotel, a tourist hotel with, of course, no tourists, which served three-course meals in the midst of the famine. I spent the evening with Denis and with one of the other French doctors, who had worked in Vietnam. She had felt safer there than here, she told me. The Vietcong would not have harmed relief workers, she maintained, but she was not so sure about the Ugandans.

We spent the next night in Tororo. The two Belgian tourists left us there and headed for the nearby Kenya border. They had had enough, they said; they had volunteered to help but not to be shot at. Our convoy reached Kampala the morning after. We left the trucks at UNHCR, and there they stayed, parked outside the compound, their starred and shot-up windshields attracting curious glances from passersby. The U.N. did indeed decide to stop the convoys until such time as things were safer, and for the next month, no U.N. trucks ran at all.

And so I was stuck in Kampala yet again. The days that followed were not unpleasant. The doctors and I were the guests of the French embassy. The attaché who put us up had a large house and an excellent cook. The house was modern and everything worked. There was even a washing machine. It didn't seem like Kampala at all.

After a day or two of loitering in luxury, I yearned to return to Karamoja. I was needed there, and saving lives seemed more important than a boycott. The French doctors felt the same way, and so did the five French nurses who had flown in from Paris the day the convoy was attacked. There were endless debates and discussions. Some of the volunteers wanted to hire a jeep and drive back to Namalu. I had come to Uganda on my own, so I did not feel bound by the U.N. boycott or by the French doctors' decisions. After five days in Kampala I packed my bag and left. I would take a bus to Tororo and hitchhike from there. I didn't know if any trucks still ran in Karamoja but I would get to Namalu, I decided, even if I had to walk.

26

THE FAMINE: LIFE IN NAMALU

And so began my third journey to Namalu, and though I had expected it to be the most difficult, the trip—though not the days that followed—proved to be the easiest, pleasantest, and least eventful. I went by bus as far as Soroti, and the bus had sagging seats and was full to overflowing. After weeks of riding in convoys, a tense job at the best of times, I welcomed the warm press of slow, good-natured bodies that is the normal accompaniment of travel in Africa.

In Soroti, I got a ride on a truck bound, for reasons I could not begin to guess, for Moroto. I was the only passenger. I did not expect to find any transport beyond Moroto; trucks are owned by businessmen, and there was no profit to be made in Namalu, nothing to buy or sell in a town too poor to feed itself. I could, I calculated, walk there from Moroto in two days, spending the night at Nabilatuk. But I never made the trek; someone in Moroto told me that the mission's jeeps still occasionally ran to Namalu and the next day when I stopped by the mission there was a jeep about to leave. I got on board and a few hours later I was back in Namalu.

It was evening by then, too late to stop by the feeding center, but as soon as I woke the next morning I ran to the old dispensary. Florence was there already, standing in the center of the roped-off yard. She had built a fire and was stirring a kettle that held the morning meal. Next to her was a very tall, thin man who was measuring milk powder with a plastic cup. That was Andrew, another of the dispensary staff. Together they had kept the center going.

The sun had barely risen but already children were arriving. There was no space for sleeping at the center, except for a few of the most disabled who used the floor of the old dispensary, so the rest of the children spent the night elsewhere. For many, that was not easy, because the region hardest hit by drought was the land around Lolachat, twenty miles north of Namalu. But still the children came, some from as far away as Nabilatuk, and camped in nearby villages or empty fields. One young woman came from Lolachat; too weak to walk, she had crawled much of the way with her baby on her back. Some children were brought by parents; others made their way alone. There were many children, hundreds, far too many for us to feed and there were new arrivals every day. We could take only a few and had to send the rest away. Someone had to choose.

That was my first job, and one that haunts me still. Twenty or thirty children came each morning and stood before me in a group. For them, my decision meant life or death and I could see this in their eyes. At the beginning, I had no scales, so I judged by sight, tried to pick the children with the thinnest arms, the most skeletal torsos. Each day I chose five or ten or twenty and tried to forget what would happen to the rest. Each child I accepted got a card with his name written on it. The card had to be shown at mealtimes, and most of the children fastened theirs to bits of wood or twine, and carried it with them always, like a magic talisman.

The center was meant to feed a hundred, but within a week almost four hundred cards had been issued. Four hundred children need over a ton of food a week; U.N. shipments had stopped and I was constantly worried that our food would run out. Father Fortunato's warehouse held several tons of corn and flour, but the children needed something more nutritious and easier to digest. Fortunately, we had a fairly ample supply of powdered milk, vegetable oil, biscuits, and a protein-enriched flour called Protiblend. The recipe we used was simple, and we soon knew it by heart. Take one gallon oil, four gallons milk powder (or six gallons Protiblend) and twenty-four gallons boiling water. Mix well and serve. Serves four hundred.

We did this three times a day, heating the water in a large kettle over an open fire in the middle of the rope enclosure. The children sat outside the rope, staring. Then, the children eager now, and watching our every move, we ladled the liquid into plastic bowls, along with two biscuits. When that was done, we served the children and watched them eat. That was the important part, the watching. "You must watch the mothers all the time, or they'll steal their children's food." All the relief workers I had met told me that, but I did not believe them. Now I saw it was true. I saw big, heavy women snatch the bowls from their starving children and bolt the liquid down. When they were caught they laughed, and they became indignant if reprimanded. I was horrified.

In my very first month in Africa, I had seen an old Sudanese shepherd give up his dinner to feed his guests; in the years after that, I had stayed in huts and shanties, met poor farmers and jobless teenagers and criminals in jail, and all of them were decent people who gave willingly and freely; when I thought of Africa, I thought, as often as not, of politeness, sharing, and cooperation.

But the Karamojong were different. Organized according to age, with close bonds of friendship between people of the same age-group, the Karamojong have weaker ties than other tribes between parent and child, and whatever bonds there may once have been had melted away along with people's fat and flesh, had been forgotten in the horror of starvation.

The Karamojong used to tell the story of a woman who stole a sack, thinking there was food inside. She ran off to eat her meal in secret, so as not to have to share it, but when she opened the bag she found, not food, but a fierce animal that jumped out and killed her. This story was rarely heard during the famine. Perhaps it is told again now. Perhaps people today tell the legend of the woman who drank a quart of oil all at once and died.

Malnutrition is selective; that's how the textbooks describe what happens when traditions break down. In Namalu, selective malnutrition meant skeletal babies with chubby brothers, and shamefully fat mothers whose children starved to death. The mothers were not always to blame; many tried to feed their offspring but the children were too sick or weak to digest the food. Children stole as well. Older boys from Namalu, who were relatively well fed, hid in the bushes around the dispensary, hoping to grab a biscuit from a younger child. One of the children was blind, and he was their favorite target. But the children whom we fed rarely, if ever, stole food from others. There was one little girl who wouldn't put on weight no matter how much food we gave her. I kept an eye on her, and so did Florence, and one day she noticed that the girl had a parcel, something wrapped in cloth. We opened it and found a metal bowl with that day's meal inside. The girl had been starving herself to feed her brothers, who were quite well fed already.

But that happened in September, when we had the leisure to watch and worry over a single hungry child. Not even sharp-eyed Florence would have noticed her during our first and most horrible week at the center, when all the children seemed to get thinner and more of them arrived each day. Each morning I found the tiny, wasted bodies of those who had died the night before. Since most of the children slept quite far from the center, many more would simply not turn up, disappear, and I would never know if they were dead or alive. Some, too weak to walk by themselves, died at home because their mothers got bored with bringing them, day after day, to be fed.

The children at the center were easy prey for all the bewildering variety of diseases that infest that part of the world, and in their weakened state they were liable to die of even the mildest of infections. I had plenty of medicine, two tons of it, but little idea what to do with it. Fortunately, three nurses came the day after I did; they had, like me, decided to ignore the U.N. boycott and had hired a jeep in Kampala. Patrick, Veronica, and Eric, the three nurses, who were French despite their names, set up a feeding center of their own, at a spot four miles south of the dispensary. Amaler, the place they selected, was a scattering of barracks and bungalows which were, as far as I know, the only things the British built in southern Karamoja. Amaler had been a prison. It had been abandoned long ago, left to the depredations of time and bandits, but the main prison cellblock and many of the outbuildings were still in fairly good condition. Patrick and the others chose a red-and-white concrete building which they later learned had been the prison wardens' canteen. The long, low hall (where prison guards had once, in all probability, happily downed mugs of Ugandan gin) could, they calculated, hold a hundred children and their mothers. Their center complemented mine; it took the worst cases and provided round-the-clock care and six meals a day.

On August 7, another jeep arrived in Namalu, with six French doctors crammed inside. They decided to join the three nurses at Amaler, but one of them, a blond Alsatian from Réunion, managed to get hold of a motorbike and visited my center daily. He examined the children, prescribed medicines, and, on the one or two occasions when he came by jeep, took as many of the thinnest children as he could back to Amaler.

But still the children died, despite the food, despite the medicine, died, as often as not, of diseases that baffled the doctors, of illnesses unknown in France or even much of Africa, or of sicknesses not seen in Europe since the Middle Ages. They died of diarrhea, which drained the body fluids and left the skin dry and wrinkled like a raisin, they died of coughs and colds and measles, and some (most frightening of all) died suddenly, collapsing for no apparent reason, happily playing one moment and dead the next. None of the doctors knew what caused these sudden attacks, and I worried that we were faced with a mystery illness that might soon be epidemic. Later, we learned the cause from a relief worker who was passing through Namalu: anemia, a simple deficiency of iron, easily detected and easily cured. Easily, at least in theory, because the one thing the otherwise comprehensive UNICEF kits lacked was iron injections. The doctors had brought ampules of their own, but only twenty, and were faced with the grim decision of who should get them.

Day after day, even as I cared for the dying, more children came and I had to choose among them. "They'll have to be strict at Namalu," Brendan O'Brien had told me. "They may even have to set the limit at 70 percent." Malnutrition was usually expressed in numbers, as a percent; 70 percent meant a child whose weight was seven-tenths that of a normal child of his height and age. In most of Karamoja, children of 80 percent and under were eligible for special feeding, but I had to be tougher or our food would run out. I took only the most desperate cases, because I knew that a 70 percent child was very thin indeed. Later I learned that I had been too strict, had turned away children whose weight was under 65 percent of normal.

One morning—it was, I think, my third day at the center—we

found an old man behind the dispensary. He was thin and very sick, too weak to walk or even crawl. Someone must have carried him there and left him, sprawled in the dusty yard next to the latrines. "We must help him," said Florence, and I admitted him to the center. In times of famine, the very old, like the very young, are the first to starve, and within a few days I had given cards to a dozen elders. They sat apart from the children at mealtimes, forming their own circle without a rope; between meals, they lay in the dust and dreamed. "If not for you," one of them told me, "we would have left this earth."

Many of the relief workers I later met criticized me for feeding the aged with supplies donated by UNICEF, part of whose very name means Children's Fund. (The staff of UNICEF itself, despite the name, sided with me. They wanted to save whatever lives they could.) Children's feeding centers should feed children, the critics said, and not waste food on old men. "Old men are important too," I replied, "for they are the ones who remember, and if they die the myths and traditions and culture of the Karamojong die with them."

I was living at the mission then, in those first days when the old men came, and I spent my evenings in the cool, quiet parlor, which was full of knickknacks and lace and porcelain figurines. Father Peter, the kindly old Italian priest, had brought these decorations with him from Rome; he had been in Namalu for more than twenty years, and kept the bric-a-brac to remind him of his home. Father Mengenstat was much younger, and had come to Karamoja much later, but he knew as much about the region as did Father Peter. He showed me a copy of a short thesis on the Karamojong which he had written while he was at university in Ethiopia. Much of the monograph was devoted to the Karamojong belief in a single deity, Akuj, which made the people, he thought, particularly sympathetic to Christianity; even as a student, he had wanted to be a missionary. The rest of the thesis described the Karamojong way of life. The people grew corn and raised cattle. They farmed out of necessity, but a man's cattle were the joy of his life. A man might own a hundred head of cattle but he would know every one by name, and he would name his own male children after the bravest of the bulls. As he drove his herds to pasture, he would sing to them, loud, joyous songs of celebration. Karamojong songs are always happy, which is perhaps why I had never heard anyone singing.

The Karamojong live in villages but during the dry season the cattle must be driven in search of pasture and for those months the young men become nomadic. The men are grouped according to age. Each man belongs to an age-set and a generation-set as well. The men of each age-set pass together through the three stages of Karamojong life, from child to warrior to elder, and it is the warriors who roam the land during the dry season, grazing their own cattle and organizing raids on other tribes' herds. The warriors live up to their name, for the Karamojong, like their close relatives the Toposa, do not respect a warrior whose shoulder is unmarked. But the warriors all defer to the elders, whose word is law. They are too old to fight, but their very age commands respect.

It made sad reading, this thesis; it was written but a few years before but the life it described seemed gone forever. Elders had once been respected, not left to die outside the latrines. Cattle were rarely killed, but when they were the elders had been entitled to receive the choicest bits of meat. But now there were no cattle at all, for every single one had died in the drought or else been stolen, and without their cattle the Karamojong were like people whose souls have gone away.

The days passed, and at first they all seemed the same, just as all the people seemed the same, the children a great mass of skeletal bodies to be fed, and the mothers another, fatter mass, the enemy, ready to steal the children's food if I even blinked. And then one day Florence said to me, with a great smile, "These children are getting fat," and I looked around and saw that it was true. Gradually, too slowly for me to notice, sunken death's-head faces had put on flesh and become young again. Wasted bodies swelled with muscle and even fat. Staring, apathetic children became lively again, and fun to be with. Between meals they chased each other around the yard or staged make-believe hunting expeditions in the tall grass behind the center. Sometimes, when they ran past me, I shouted out encouragement or greeting; by now I knew everyone by name.

I came to know most of the mothers as well. I knew which ones were troublemakers, and when I caught them stealing the children's food I shook my fists in their faces and shouted insults in their native language, a constant stream of them, more varied and creative, I pride myself, than any heretofore heard in Karamoja. One of the mothers, who was fatter than all the others, I named Ananganang which, roughly translated, meant "fat greedy monster" and which was how the Karamojong had referred to Idi Amin.

The Ananganang was an unrepentant food filcher, but her new name pleased her—or perhaps it was the honor of being singled out for special attention—and she began helping us with such tasks as stacking plates or putting up the rope in the morning. Later her son got sick and I sent the pair of them to the French nurses at Amaler. At Patrick's center, the patients' mothers were given two meals a day, so I never expected to see Ananganang again but one morning a few days later I arrived at the dispensary to find her at her usual place at a corner of the rope. She had been fed at Amaler, she said, but she had not liked it there. She had more fun with us.

I don't know if any of the mothers understood why the sight of food stolen from dying babies upset me so. Florence and Andrew, who were as outraged as I, tried to explain, and as time went on most of the mothers gave up stealing. Perhaps they realized that Florence, who had the eagle eyes of a grade-school teacher, was more than a match for them. The biscuits were tempting and easy to grab, so Florence broke them up and soaked them with milk. Our milk left a trace of oil on the lips of those who drank it, so Florence could tell at a glance if a mother had taken her child's food. The mothers must have thought she had magic powers. But the Karamojong are a clever, determined people, and they would not let Florence outwit them without a fight unless they had other reasons. Perhaps the mothers came to like us and gave up stealing for our sake.

"The mothers have given you a name," Florence told me. "They call you Apaloyelel." I didn't know if this was good or bad, so I wrote down the name and that night I asked Father Mengenstat. "Oh, they do you honor!" he said. "They have given you a cattle name." All Karamojong men take, as one of their names, the name of their favorite ox, and by naming me after an ox, the Karamojong had made me one of them. Apaloyelel meant a bull with a mottled blue hide. "Like your blue jeans," said the father.

The children, too, learned to call me Apaloyelel, which sounded less foreign to their ears than my other name, although to many Apaloyelel must have seemed almost as strange. It was a warrior's name, a cattle name, but most of the children had never seen a warriors' initiation ceremony and the youngest had never seen a cow. The only times they had known were hard times, and the only cultural institutions they remembered were feeding centers. In normal times, children and old men both stayed in the village when the warriors grazed the herds, and so they would spend much time together, as they did now. The elders used to pass the time by telling stories, and the children would listen and learn; that is how a tribe's traditions are passed on. But the old men at the center dozed, while the children played. One afternoon, after we had stacked the plates from the midday meal, I asked the old men to tell us stories. Andrew sat beside me to translate, and the children stopped their games and sat in a circle around us. An old woman saw a sack, one began, and went on to tell how she stole it, thinking there was food inside, and found a wild beast instead. Another elder had a tale about a frog who managed to live by tricking much larger animals into giving him their food. More tales followed, most of them about hungry old women and sacks of corn, all about food, and all (except the frog story) stressing the virtues of sharing. Selfish people—always old women, it seemed, for it was men who told the stories—were always punished for their greed. The old men had between them an amazingly large repertoire of these tales, but whether all Karamojong legends are concerned with food and famine or whether there were other, happier myths which the old men found, in present circumstances, too depressing to recall, I never learned, for after that afternoon they never told stories again.

The next day, I tried to organize another storytelling session but the old men were less than enthusiastic. They wanted salt, they complained, and sugar, and clothes. I heard a jeep passing and I used that as an excuse to leave them. The jeep stopped and a young French nurse got out. She was, she said, from a charity named Hôpital sans Frontières. There was a truck behind her that carried a fully equipped mobile hospital. "Where can we set it up?" she asked, so I told her how to get to Amaler.

There were nine French medics at Amaler already, and the arrival of the hospital brought several more. I had been sleeping at the mission, which was two and a half miles closer to the center than was Amaler, but a few days later I, too, moved to Amaler. The fathers were running low on food and I could sense that their welcome was far less enthusiastic than it had been.

Just outside the prison were several abandoned bungalows that had once been the homes of guards and wardens. Some had been taken over by squatters but a few were empty. One of these was in fairly good condition, and the French had laid claim to it and set up house inside, complete with camp beds and chairs and Coleman lamps. The old canteen, which Patrick and his colleagues had turned into a children's feeding center, was separated from the house by a large grassy field which could usually be crossed safely even at night. The main prison building, even closer to the house, had been turned into a hospital. All the doctors worked there, leaving the three overworked nurses to run the canteen. My center closed by sunset, to allow staff and children to return home in the relative safety of daylight, so I was usually home in time to serve the 7:00 P.M. meal at the Amaler center. The place was run like a high-tech assembly line; each child sat at an assigned place, marked with chalk on the floor, and was served a measured amount of food determined by his weight (twenty-five milliliters of liquid per kilogram); after the meal I examined the plates and, in a special notebook, recorded how much each child had eaten.

It was not a pleasant place, this center; most of the children I never knew by name and I could understand why the Ananganang had run away. But, except for the new arrivals, all the children were healthy and fat. Some of the mothers recognized me, and a few of the names in the notebook were familiar, and I realized that some of the chubby babies I saw at Amaler had been among the hopeless cases that the blond Alsatian doctor had culled from my center at Namalu.

Most of the children I had transferred to Amaler had died, but I was amazed that any had survived. A few days later, Andrew and Florence happened to be in Amaler, and I took them to see the canteen. The next day, we started intensive feeding at Namalu. We chose thirty-five of the thinnest children and gave them five meals a day. They were fed on a slight rise of ground a few hundred feet from the main rope enclosure. Florence said she would hire a few men to build some huts nearby; that way, the children could sleep at the center and not depend on their mothers to take them each day.

Our new system meant more work for all of us, but the one who worked the hardest was a boy named Komol Lowot. He was a cripple, abandoned by his parents, and someone had carried him to the center a week or so before. He had been horribly thin then, his arms as withered as his stunted, useless legs, but he was beginning to get his strength back, and when we started intensive feeding he spent his day dragging himself up and down the hill between the two feeding places. That way he got eight meals a day. The sight of him, waiting for his seventh meal, trying to blend in with the three-meal-a-day crowd and not be noticed, made us laugh with delight; he was like one of the old legends, those tales of crafty frogs and greedy people, come to life. We gave him as much food as he wanted, and within a few weeks he was stronger and fatter than he had ever been in his life. All of us liked Komol Lowot, but I don't think he ever knew what joy he gave us. He never laughed or smiled the way the other children did, but at least he was well fed, and that meant a lot in Karamoja.

All this happened toward the end of August 1980, which was about the time that Monique came. Tall, short-haired and wiry, Monique had endless reserves of energy. The year before, she had run a feeding center in Somalia and she now decided to run ours. I had met her in Kampala and had liked her then, but one morning she turned up unannounced at the dispensary, gathered Florence and her colleagues together, and told them to choose one of their number to be chief of staff. She was setting up a chain of command. I had been stacking the dishes for the morning meal and I saw the group of them talking and ran over in time to catch the end of it. Florence and the others were downcast but trying not to show it. One reason they had worked so well together was that all of them were equal. Florence could be bossy in her way, and she probably would have emerged as leader. Andrew and Joseph, the other two staff members, knew this, and they would not have enjoyed working for a woman. And Florence would not have wanted to be subordinate to either of them.

Monique worked at the center until the middle of September. A chief of staff was never chosen and the issue of who was in command smoldered and was never resolved. Because of her experience, I deferred to her decisions unless I was convinced she was wrong and the staff agreed. And she, once she had made up her mind, would never change it. But she was a trained nurse and a capable one, and not afraid of hard work, and the center benefited by her presence. Under her direction, we started weighing every child once a week, something we should have done long before. We found fifty-five children whose weight was under 70 percent of normal, and of them nine were under 60 percent. Five days later, we weighed the thinnest children again and many of them had gained 10 percent. One boy had put on almost seven pounds; he was a new arrival, from a village somewhere in the barren wastes west of Nabilatuk. He was in his early teens, almost a warrior. He, his sister, and his grandmother had come on foot, and then on hands and knees, all of them so wasted by the time they reached us that a stiff breeze would have blown them away. All of them recovered quickly, and the grandmother, though her hands had been ruined by leprosy, cared for the two children and found time to help other mothers with theirs. She would have made a good nurse. I tried to help her in return, and gave her a Dapsone tablet every day that I remembered, but I knew it was futile; she would have to take the pills for four years or the leprosy would come back, and we didn't have a four-year supply. She understood this, I think, but she took the few pills I gave her anyway. Why not? They did no harm.

By the end of August, the first hut had been completed. The men Florence hired had done nothing, and after a fortnight we decided to hire others to replace them. The men were angry, and I and they exchanged bitter words and even threats (with Florence translating), but in the end we chased them away. "Now I'll find people who'll work instead of talk," said Florence, and she picked out ten of the mothers, including of course the Ananganang, and had a quiet talk with them. The women worked furiously that day and the next, and by the morning after the house was completed and the mothers, proud and beaming, lined up to receive their promised pay: two pounds of corn and two dried fish apiece.

All the children in intensive feeding were allowed to stay in the hut, because otherwise they might not come to the center at all. Many mothers let their children starve rather than waste the day taking them to the center, and before the hut was built many children came for a few days and then disappeared. Most I forgot, but a few I remembered. One was Ilukol Locap. He had come to the center that first week in August, and even then had been thinner than the rest. He was tougher than most and gained weight quickly, but after a week his mother stopped bringing him. I thought he was gone forever and tried to forget him. A few weeks later, Father Mengenstat took some of the doctors to see a typical Karamojong village, and I went along. It was several miles' walk away. When we got there, I went inside a typical house, and there was Ilukol Locap, as thin as ever. I found the mother and had Father Mengenstat tell her that we had all come to look for the boy. If she didn't bring him to the center, I said, she would be in serious trouble. She stared at the six doctors and then at me, and she brought Ilukol to us the next morning. A few days later, the hut was built, and Ilukol moved in. I think his mother was glad to be rid of him.

With the huts built and the center running smoothly, we decided to reopen the old dispensary. The French doctors had brought several tons of medicine, and they gave us as much of it as we could carry. Monique, Florence, Joseph, and Andrew took turns diagnosing the patients, bandaging wounds, and doling out medicine to the hundred or so patients who showed up each morning. They took their pills away in little parcels, and I sometimes wondered if they ever used them. Some Karamojong thought that there was no point in taking more than one dose of anything; if a drug didn't work at once, it wouldn't work at all. Others swallowed as much medicine as they could get their hands on. They got pills from us in the morning and went to the hospital at Amaler in the afternoon. Twice the dose, they thought, is twice as good for you.

Most of the patients suffered from disease, and some from simple hunger, but each morning also brought last night's wounded—people who had been shot or stabbed or hit by shrapnel and who limped or crawled or were carried in for treatment. A few were casualties of bandit raids, but most of the people had been hurt by the soldiers who had been sent to protect them.

After our ill-fated convoy was attacked on the road to Namalu, the U.N. did everything in its power to prod the Ugandan government into making the area more secure. The Ugandans sent the army in, and a company of fifty soldiers came to Namalu. They set up camp at Amaler, near our house and right next to the old prison, which was now a hospital. "Now we can provide perfect protection," boasted the smiling lieutenant who commanded the company. He visited our house several times during the company's first week at Amaler, and he was always grinning, always sweaty, always drunk. He insisted we call him by his first name, which was David. Why was he so friendly at first? Perhaps he was trying to do his job, which was to protect the relief workers. Or, more likely, he guessed that the French would have good whiskey on hand. Possibly he had at one time been lorded over by Europeans and wanted to show that he could mix with us as an equal. Perhaps. I never found out and after a time I didn't care.

But I went out of my way to be friendly to him, and whenever he came by I poured him a drink. After a time, David grew convinced that I was one of the leaders of the relief contingent. This irritated the relief workers, most of whom looked down on me because I wasn't a doctor and wasn't even French.

While David busied himself socializing with what he regarded as Namalu's elite, bands of his men roamed the area, robbing men, raping women, beating up anyone in sight. At night, when the local populace prudently retreated behind closed doors and there was thus no one on the road to molest, the soldiers amused themselves by firing their rifles into the air, or at anything on the ground that moved. An AK 47 shoots with a brutal bang, much louder than I would have believed possible and loud enough to make me jump even when I heard it from a distance. As soon as the sun set the shooting began, whole series of shots as magazines were emptied, interspersed with the hollow muffled *crump!* of the mortars that the soldiers set off as a special treat. It wouldn't have been so disturbing if we could have been sure the men were firing into the air, but the men were drunk enough to see a bandit in every shadow.

I learned this firsthand one night. The children at the Amaler feeding center were always given a late snack of milk and biscuits, and that night I had served it. It was after ten when I finished, completely dark outside, but I knew my way back to the house and I walked back by feel and instinct. And then shooting began, louder than the crack of thunder, and I hit the deck and crawled toward the house on my belly. There was shooting on both sides of me, and strange red sparks that arced over me like laser beams. I wriggled to the house, just as I'd seen it done in the movies, but the shots were never so loud in the films, and the movie soldiers were never scared and shaking the way that I was. There was a bottle of Scotch in the house (David was right), and I poured a stiff dose and drank it down. I wondered what caused the sparks; months later, I read about tracer bullets in a war novel and realized what they must have been.

There was shooting for most of the night, as there was every night, and the next morning, as they did every morning, the soldiers went out on the road looking for victims. The French had hired people from Namalu to work as porters and cleaners and nurses' aides, but on most mornings they didn't show up because they were afraid of the soldiers. Florence, Joseph, and Andrew also lived in Namalu and had to walk almost as far each morning but they never missed a day's work. In theory, I had to walk the farthest, four miles each way, but I almost always managed to get a ride. One afternoon, Monique got one of the other nurses to pick us up in a jeep. Halfway to Amaler, David tried to flag us down. "You should stop," I said, but Monique, who was driving, didn't even slow down. When we got to Amaler, David was there waiting; he must have had his own jeep. He and two of his men grabbed Monique and hauled her out of the jeep. "It was my decision," I said. "I told Monique not to stop." "I know that is not true," said David. "You are my friend and would have stopped." But he let Monique go and then he left. Monique never thanked me; she was worried, perhaps, that David might have believed me when I said I was in charge.

But that was not the worst thing that happened with me, Monique, and the soldiers. The worst thing happened a few days later. Once again it was afternoon and once again Monique had gotten hold of a jeep. We had stopped at the Amaler feeding center, because Patrick had promised to let us have a few sacks of milk to take to Namalu. Patrick wasn't there but one of his Ugandan staff was, so I went in with him to get the milk. I heard shouts coming from outside. The Ugandan went out to see what was going on and then rushed back to get me. "Come quick," he said, "the soldiers are taking one of our patients away. They are going to kill him." I ran back outside. There was a man on the ground, an old man with a wounded leg, and standing over him was a man with a knife. The younger man, a soldier, was trying to drag the old man away but the elder's white-haired wife, sobbing and screaming, was doing her best to stop him. She grabbed him, clutched on to his uniform and would not let go, so the soldier stabbed her arm and she fell back. In order to deal with the woman, the soldier had let go of the man, and that was when I stepped between them. Then I turned to face the soldier. He was big and tall, far taller than I had realized and there was murder in his eyes. They burned with the desire to cut me to pieces, but I was a relief worker, a European, and, unlike the Karamojong, I could not be killed with impunity. If the soldier even touched me, he would face a court martial. (Or so I told myself.)

We stood like that for several minutes, frozen and unmoving. "What shall we do?" I called to Monique. "Get the old man in the car and drive him to the prison," she suggested. The soldier, too, meanwhile, was deciding what to do. His face was distorted with emotion as rage competed with fear and for a few moments I was sure his anger would win out. Perhaps in time it would have, but Monique and I didn't give him any time. She helped me block the soldier as we carried the old man to the jeep, threw him in, and jumped in after. The motor was running, so we slammed the doors and roared off, leaving the soldier in a cloud of dust. I looked back and could see him running—not after us but back to the barracks to get his gun.

The front of the prison was built like a fortress, with high concrete walls and a steel gate that looked thick enough to stop a tank. Monique and I stood behind the gate, half deafened by the rifle fire that came from the other side. We had barely had time to drive the jeep through the gate and slam it before the soldier came, bringing not only his gun but his buddies. We lay on the floor and hoped the bullets would not pierce the gate. Then the shooting stopped. I peeped through a window and saw the soldiers walking around to the side of the prison. Though the front of the jail was a high and impressive wall, the back and sides were nothing but a low wire fence. Perhaps the money had run out during the jail's construction. I had hoped the soldiers didn't know about the fence, but of course they did. Now they were standing outside it. I left the gatehouse and walked out to talk to them.

I was shivering with fear and hoping the soldiers did not notice. I had to show them that I was not afraid. We stood on opposite sides of the fence and talked. I don't remember what was said. They were all angry, even David, but at least they were shouting instead of shooting.

Then Christian, the head of the hospital, ran out. Christian, an ex-soldier himself, was built like a bull and looked as if he ate nails for breakfast. He had spent much of his life in Africa, long enough to learn the value of tact and diplomacy. He invited David into the hospital and, one hour and half a bottle of Scotch later, the problem was forgotten and David and he were once again the best of friends.

I could hear Christian and David talking as I stood outside the gatehouse. Christian's voice was as deep and full of gravel as John Wayne's. A man like that, I knew, would approve of what I had done, and I secretly hoped for his praise. But when I saw him he was livid. My conduct put the entire hospital in jeopardy, he said. I should have let the soldier take the man. Better that one life be lost than to risk all. "If you let them kill one man today," I said, "they will want five tomorrow." I remembered reading about Abim, where soldiers dragged off five patients and killed them. There had been similar incidents, they had told me at UNICEF, throughout the entire region.

The doctors, without exception, took Christian's side. Monique saw which way the wind was blowing and kept silent; she never told anyone that she had been with me, leaving me to take the blame alone. "I respect your reasons," I told the doctors, "but they sound like the words of cowards." The French never forgave me. Brendan O'Brien of UNICEF approved of what I had done, but I didn't see him until October. The only people in Namalu who thought I had done right were those whose opinion I most respected: Florence, Joseph, Andrew, and Father Mengenstat, and most likely the old man whose life I saved—though he fled the region as soon as he could walk and I never saw him again.

Time proved me right, though the French never admitted it. The soldiers never molested our patients again, and, unless they themselves needed medical attention, they never set foot in either feeding center after that day.

✖◈✖

It is days like that one that I remember, but most of the days slipped by unnoticed, though they, too, left their hidden scars upon me. The children got slowly fatter. A few died. A few new ones came. The BBC nightly news, which came in loud and clear from London, and which a month before had carried daily bulletins about the famine, the raiders, and Namalu, rarely mentioned Karamoja any more. The big news was the upcoming Ugandan elections. There were many parties competing, and of them the one called the Uganda People's Congress was expected to win, not because it had, as its name implied, the support of the people but because it had the support of the current government, which would count the votes. The UPC—which did indeed win the elections a few months later—was headed by Milton Obote, who had ruled the country until 1971. The night he was ousted, the streets of Kampala were filled with dances and impromptu celebrations. The politicians, like everyone else in

Uganda, ignored the Karamojong, whom they thought of, if at all, as savages. But one UPC candidate, remembering that even savages have votes, took a squad of soldiers to Moroto, raided a U.N. warehouse, and when a crowd gathered, distributed the contents as UPC food.

Most of the candidates running in Karamoja found it easier to distribute slogans instead of food. They were catchy little jingles and I sometimes heard the children at the center reciting them. "Corn! UPC! Meat! UPC! Fish! UPC!" They did not know what UPC was, but anything with meat in it had to be good.

The UPC candidate for southern Karamoja was a tall, soft-spoken Karamojong who lived in Namalu. His name was Johnny Akol. He visited me at my center the day I arrived in Karamoja. "You've already met one of my uncles," he told me. The uncle turned out to be the wounded man I had rescued in July just north of Nabilatuk. I got on well with him and I made every effort to be friendly because in a few months he would very likely be an M.P. One night in late August, some of the soldiers, for reasons unknown, threw a few grenades into his house. The next morning I found him, badly wounded, at my dispensary. I stopped a passing jeep and took him to Christian's hospital at Amaler.

Though Johnny Akol recovered, and is probably an M.P. by now, most of the hospital's patients did not. Most of the people who were carried to the hospital were barely alive; nothing could save them. Before coming to Uganda, Christian had worked on the Cambodian border. There, he told me, only one patient in a hundred had died. In Amaler the figure was probably nine in ten; the hospital had become a home for the dying. For the doctors, the strain was impossibly great. The Karamojong dread dead bodies and will not touch them, and so the doctors, in addition to their other duties, had to bury the dead. Even as they worked to save the living, they had to listen to the keens and wails of the mothers whose children had just died. I helped out at the hospital—both burying and nursing—in whatever spare time I had and, like the Ananganang, I was always glad to get back to Namalu.

It was hard to believe, especially when you saw the burial parties go by and heard the shrieks and sobs and screams that formed incessant background, which after a time became breathed rather than heard, like the monotone chirp of crickets in happier, rain-blessed places; it was hard to believe, but this hospital at Amaler was probably the best in Uganda. And lives *were* saved; I was there when they brought in a child, unconscious, who looked like a sack of bones, and I helped hold the hoses as they gave her oxygen and intravenous food, and I saw her open her eyes and smile and make funny faces at us, just like a little girl, which she was. Patients came from as far away as Mbale, which wasn't even in Karamoja, and a young German doctor from Amudat, east of Moroto, visited us to borrow medicine. Amudat is fairly near Kenya, and, the doctor told us, there was famine in Kenya as well. Starving Kenyans, too weak to stand, had crawled across the border to Amudat. There were no feeding centers in Kenya because the Kenyan government refused to accept foreign aid, refused even to admit that there was a famine. They did not want to spoil the country's image.

The doctor left the next day, and soon after that more visitors arrived: a jeepload of U.N. personnel, including Mr. Strippoli himself. That night, the soldiers provided their usual entertainment, and Mr. Strippoli, who drove out at night to inspect the road, saw bands of drunken, raucous soldiers staggering back to barracks. The rest of the visitors stayed inside and didn't see the soldiers, but all of them heard the roar of mortars and machine guns which the doctors referred to as "our nightly serenade." Many of the U.N. famine specialists shuttled between Uganda and Cambodia that year, and all of the visitors who had been in Phnom Penh jumped for cover when they heard the mortars.

Mr. Strippoli left for Moroto the next day. He promised to report what he had seen to the Ugandan government, and a few days later, David and his men left Namalu. I hoped they would leave the army as well, but the next day I heard they had been transferred to Amudat, and I felt sorry for the young doctor I had met a week before.

We spent one night without any soldiers to guard us, a peaceful, quiet night, and then a new company arrived. David's replacement was a lieutenant named Patrick. Patrick was born in Uganda but trained in Tanzania, and I was never sure which army he belonged to—Uganda's or Tanzania's. Most of the Tanzanian troops who had routed Amin were still in Uganda one year later. They had stayed to help the new Ugandan government and (some said) to control it. The Tanzanian soldiers were more disciplined than the Ugandans, though the differences were often subtle. The Tanzanians would, it was said, kill a man for a watch or a radio but not for sport, as the Ugandans did.

The men in Patrick's company were Ugandan but there were three Tanzanian noncoms to watch over them. The nightly shooting stopped, and the road to Amaler was once again reasonably safe to walk on. The raiders, during the first days of September, stayed north of Moroto, and the U.N. food trucks had started running again.

With the trucks, more medics arrived. All the doctors donated their time and paid their passage, as Denis had done, and most could stay no longer than a month. As for the nurses, their airfare was paid and they received a small allowance to cover expenses, so they could stay slightly longer. They were hired under two-month contracts, and most left at the end of their term, their strength sapped and spirits shattered. By mid-September, the only people left who had been there from the beginning were the three tireless nurses who ran the Amaler feeding center; most of the rest were newcomers. Many of the new arrivals seemed disappointed; things weren't nearly as bad as they had expected. Talking to them made me notice how much things had changed in a month. There were four hundred children at my center in early August, and only a hundred now. Of those hundred, only nine weighed under 70 percent of normal (as against fifty-five a month before), and most of the nine would have been turned away six weeks before as too healthy to feed.

And the other three hundred, the children who had been there a month before and were gone today? The weakest had died, the strongest were fat, and the rest were alive. Alive for how long? They, like the rest of Karamoja, were being kept alive by U.N. food, for there had been no harvest that year. In Namalu, the bags of corn and dried fish brought by the U.N. convoys were still being distributed by Father Mengenstat, though the nuns at Nabilatuk,who let their flock starve on the Sabbath, had handed over their warehouse keys to two young Australians sent by the World Food Program, another U.N. agency. They had been hired on two-year contracts; the WFP expected to be in Karamoja for a long time to come. Next year's harvest would probably be scanty; with soldiers, drought, and raiders still as menacing as ever, most of the people would not bother to plant. It was easier to sit and wait for the relief trucks to arrive. The WFP, as well as Mr. Strippoli's FAO, planned to implement food-for-work programs, giving food only to families who tilled their fields. Many of the U.N. people wanted to turn the Karamojong into farmers; the tribe's affection for cattle, the relief workers thought, was a luxury they must learn to do without. Some proposed food-for-school programs as well; educate the Karamojong, let them go to the cities and find jobs.

Sometimes, the power we relief workers wielded in Karamoja amazed me. We had the power of life and death; we could decide who was fed and who was not. And, with the invention of food-for-work, the tribe's traditions, too, came within our grasp; we could determine the fate and shape of a people's culture. But what was the choice? If not for us, the entire tribe would be dead, people as well as culture, and there would not be a single man, woman, or child alive in northeast Uganda.

"What good is it?" Christian sometimes asked, usually late in the evening when the day's work was done and there was time to feel depressed. "As soon as we leave, as soon as the U.N. leaves, these people will die anyway." "If we hadn't come," I usually answered, "they would be dead already. Even a few extra months of life is a blessing. Three months times four hundred children equals a hundred years. We have made, you, I, and the rest of us, a hundred years of life. Few people have ever done that much. Don't worry about tomorrow."

And, at the feeding center, life continued. Things got done, though we didn't plan ahead, but lived from day to day. The second hut was completed. Ilukol Locap, who still slept at the center, was sleek and glossy-skinned, and Komol Lowot was positively fat. We were starting to record weights in excess of normal. Most of the children spent the day running around the yard and playing in the tall grass beyond the dispensary. One day Ilukol came to me with a dead rat; he had caught it in the grass. The Karamojong have a craving for meat and, though the center now served one meal a day of dried fish and flour, that was not the same. It had been many months since Ilukol had tasted meat, and at that moment his chief desire in life was to eat that rat. Instead, he gave it to me. "That is probably the first gift he has given in his life," said Florence.

The thought of eating a rat no longer made me squeamish; I had been on the road too long for that. But I think I would have eaten that rat even if I found it the most loathsome thing on earth.

Florence roasted it for me and it was delicious. It looked and tasted like chicken, soft and tender, and when I ate it Ilukol's sacrifice meant all the more.

Things were going so well at the feeding center that I took to spending one or two afternoons a week helping the doctors at the hospital. Most of them had come to feel that it was wasteful to use a dozen doctors to treat fifty patients when, outside, thousands were dying. Famine and disease formed a vicious cycle in Karamoja; hunger sapped people's strength and made them vulnerable to disease, which weakened them still more and magnified the effects of malnutrition. And so the doctors adopted a new approach to break the cycle: preventive medicine in the field. They divided the region into five zones, each with its own consultation point. A team of doctors would visit each point once a week, with a different medicine each time: Thiabendazole, which kills stomach parasites, one day, measles vaccine the next. The people of the zone would be told the schedule in advance, and when the team came all those assembled at the consultation points would be given the medicine *du jour*.

It was a simple program and it worked. I went along to help dole out the pills and round up the children for shots. We drove to the consultation points on roads that had been hacked from the bush a few weeks before. Father Mengenstat had started a food-for-work program of his own, giving extra food to villages that helped on the roads. The new roads made it possible to deliver food to each zone; before their construction, all relief food had been distributed at points along the main road, and those too weak to walk there didn't get fed. Our consultation points were also food distribution points, and perhaps that was why hundreds of people waited at each point we visited. Vaccinating children was something the doctors were used to doing, and each of them could inoculate a hundred squirming, bawling patients in less than an hour. The diseases we immunized them against were among the leading killers of Third World children, and that hour's work probably saved more lives than the hospital did in a week. If simple, effective programs like that were implemented throughout Africa (which UNICEF is now trying to do), millions of children could be saved from dying.

The hospital, of course, stayed open. The doctors ran it and the vaccination program simultaneously, which meant that the hospital was often shorthanded. Once a week I took the night shift, which meant sitting in darkness for half the night on the concrete porch that ran along the cellblock, listening for trouble, and checking each ward twice an hour. The sky was starless; I sat on the unlit veranda, drifting in the black void of sky. Time seemed to slow down, move more sedately, but the nights passed.

Sometimes at night I heard shooting from the barracks; the new soldiers, sullen and bored after a fortnight in Karamoja, had taken to drinking, looting, and firing their guns. Once again drunken soldiers roamed the roads, and one night a band of them shot up a house in Namalu; later, they claimed that it had been occupied by raiders. It hadn't, but a young girl had been inside and now she was dead.

A few nights later, I and some of the doctors were eating dinner when firing broke out. We all jumped clear of the windows and crouched behind a wall. "I'll put a stop to this," I said, and ran out toward the barracks; one of the newly arrived doctors was young and pretty and I wanted to impress her. I thought it would be easy; I envisaged happy, drunken soldiers shooting into the air and myself calmly ordering them to stop. It might even have worked. But the barracks seemed deserted when I got there, and the night was as quiet as death. Happy drunks are noisy drunks and I began to feel uneasy. The land around the barracks was covered with elephant grass, and all around me I heard the quiet snick of rifles cocking. I knew the Swahili words for friend and white man and I shouted them both, hoping the soldiers knew Swahili, hoping the magic words would work. They did. Heads popped up from the grass, and then men. The men took me to Patrick, who saw I was shaking and gave me a drink. He went out on a tour of inspection and soon came back. All quiet now, he reported. Apparently, he told me, one of his men had been cleaning his rifle and accidentally set it off. Other soldiers heard the shots and thought the raiders were attacking; they fired at the first soldier who, thinking they were bandits, fired at them. I had arrived just in time to prevent the entire camp from shooting one another to pieces. It was perfect slapstick, unbelievable and hilarious, but the bullets were real.

Christian and the doctors were furious at me; if I had been shot the whole hospital would have been in jeopardy. They thought I had acted stupidly, and when I thought back on what I had done I tended to agree with them. But the next time we heard gunshots from the army camp, it was Christian who, with a satisfied scowl on his face, went to the barracks and ordered the men to stop.

The soldiers' trigger-happy panic was not groundless; during the last week of September, the raiders returned to Namalu. Lone homesteads were attacked within a mile of the dispensary, and one night we heard a rumor that the bandits planned to attack Amaler. All of the French spent that night huddled together inside the thick-walled cells of the former prison. I stayed at the house. I knew no one would sleep a wink at the prison, and I needed the rest to be able to work the next day. The house was blissfully quiet that night, and the attack never came. But a few days later, the bandits raided a village a few miles to the north named Alamacar and left between ten and thirty dead.

That raid may have been some strange form of retaliation for what the soldiers had done a week before. Monique and I had been at the dispensary when we heard the rumble of a motorbike coming from the north. We knew it was Father Fortunato, the feisty priest who lived down the road from Father Mengenstat; no one else would dare ride a motorcycle on that road. The bike stopped; the father's face, always ruddy, was even redder; he was stunned and angry. He had driven down from Nabilatuk, he gasped when he had caught his breath. He had seen smoke at Lolachat, and when he got closer he had seen the soldiers. They were going from hut to hut, setting the village on fire and killing everyone they could find. The officer in charge saw the priest and barked out an order. The shooting stopped and the officer waved the father through. After he had passed, Father Fortunato heard the shooting begin again. He could not guess how many people died there; many more, probably, than at Alamacar, and some of them, very likely, were among those who had helped me carry medicines across the dried-up river where my truck was trapped.

Patrick's men were not involved in the massacre at Lolachat; Father Fortunato had never seen the men before and thought they were probably from the militia. The militia, which was the Ugandan equivalent of our national guard, had as bad a reputation as the army. The villagers who farmed the fertile lands west of Karamoja feared an influx of starving Karamojong refugees, and the militia took it upon themselves to prevent this. They set up roadblocks along the routes out of Karamoja. Trucks were stopped, all passengers hauled out, and anyone who looked like a Karamojong was killed on the spot. Fortunately, the militia were barred from the two roads that led to Soroti and to Mbale, so I never saw the checkpoints, but I met someone who did. One of the British relief workers had decided to take a shortcut. His driver's assistant, a boy of fifteen, was a Karamojong— or perhaps he just looked like one—and when they came to the roadblock a militiaman pulled the boy out and shot him. He fired again and again and when the magazine ran out he changed it and kept on shooting. When the second clip was empty, the soldiers waved the truck through.

It was mid-September when Lolachat was wiped off the map. A few days later, Monique and two other nurses left for Nabilatuk and opened a feeding center there. That was something I had wanted to do but never found the time. After she left, my days were even fuller; I ran the center in Namalu, helped at the hospital, and on most days served one of the meals at the feeding center at Amaler. Patrick, the French nurse, and his two colleagues, who had founded the Amaler center, still ran it, and Patrick found time to organize a residence hall for children whose parents had died in the famine. He was proud of those orphans; he gave them food each day and they all shared it and, infinitely less important than the sharing but also a source of pride to Patrick, they learned to wear clothes and sing "Frère Jacques." ("Cultural pollution," I said to Patrick, and then realized I had hurt him.) But Patrick and the others had to be back in France by the end of September; they had been admitted to medical school. Patrick spent his last week fretting over the fate of his center and the children in it and trying to convince the people at the hospital to take charge of the feedings. But they were full-fledged doctors and not mere nurses, and they told Patrick that the function of doctors is to provide medical aid; serving meals, in other words, was beneath them. (Denis, who held a far broader view of a doctor's duties, was still in Réunion.) Even the hospital was in jeopardy; the program of preventive medicine had been completed and many of the doctors, seeing the improvements made during the past month, thought the famine was over. The heads of two of the charities involved came to Namalu from Paris to decide whether to pull out.

At this point, a *deus ex machina* arrived in the shape of a jeepload of Irish relief workers. The news of the probable French departure had reached Kampala, and they were the vanguard of a team that would take over children's feeding in southern Karamoja.

Patrick, happy, left two days later, as a choir of orphans sang "Alouette." By then, the first group had been joined by a new batch, four nurses from Ireland and one from Illinois. In all my time in Karamoja, she was the only American I saw, apart from a priest from upstate New York, who came to Namalu for a brief visit and ended up spending a fortnight there, helping Father Mengenstat distribute maize. The new arrivals ran the Amaler center and made plans to increase its capacity. Three of the nurses went to Nabilatuk to take over Monique's center. Monique returned to Namalu and left for France a few days later.

A month in Karamoja inflicts as many shocks and scars as a year in any normal place. Monique was exhausted when she left, and so was Patrick, and so, by then, was I. Every day had been etched with a latticework of fears and flares of emotion as vivid as tracer trails. I suffered from bouts of exhaustion and fever and had collapsed several times while working at the center. I had been in Namalu longer than anyone else on the team and I would have left in mid-September but there was no one to relieve me. I wanted to be sure the children would be fed when I left. Now relief had arrived and I could leave. Christian was planning to drive to Nairobi at the beginning of October. I would go with him as far as Mbale and get a bus to Kampala from there.

A few of the mothers found out I was leaving, and soon the whole center knew. "I want to go with you," said one of the women, a wizened old grandmother. I explained (Florence translating) how cold it was in America; she'd turn to ice in her flimsy goatskin, I said, but that didn't deter her. "You can be my secretary," I said, "if you learn to type." I had no plans of taking up any profession where typing was needed, but that seemed as good an answer as any. Florence explained what "typing" meant. The old woman, of course, hadn't seen a typewriter in her life (or a paved road or a radio or a building higher than one story) but she was dauntless. "I can type," she announced, balling her hands into fists and banging them against an imaginary keyboard.

That night Christian told me he would leave on October 2. That was less than a week away. Good-byes and partings always sadden me, and these promised to be unbearable. I remembered what villagers do to make happy times from sad, and I decided to turn my leaving into a festival. I gave Florence some money and told her to buy as much meat as she could. The few people in Karamoja who still owned cattle were very eager to sell them, and on the first morning in October Florence came to work carrying thirty pounds of meat. I had persuaded the French to donate a bag of salt and I passed it around to be admired. The people prized salt the way Venetians once valued spices, and many had never seen a bag like that.

All of the children, their mothers and sisters and brothers, and most of the rest of Namalu were there that day. I had let the word get around that everyone who came would be fed. They all watched intently as we prepared the meat. We cut it into chunks and simmered it in a stew. The cutting and cooking took all morning. While Florence and Andrew stirred the stew and banked the fire, Joseph and I climbed the hill to the two huts. A few of the old men I had admitted a month before still slept at the center. There was one who was even older than the rest. His name was Longok Lopeiyon and he was a warrior before the British came. I wanted to talk to him before I left. Joseph, the only one of the three assistants who was not Karamojong, nevertheless spoke the language fluently; he would interpret.

Longok Lopeiyon was sitting just outside the hut, warming himself in the sun. I asked his permission to talk about the old days, and he said I could. "Was it a good life then?" I asked him. He thought a bit, then spoke slowly, as if every word mattered. "It was not very good, but it was good," he said. "It was a hard life; sometimes, between the rains, we had to drive the cattle thirty, even forty miles every day." "And the raiding, was that fun?" I asked. (Some of my reading had given me the idea that the Karamojong viewed it as a sort of manly sport, like football.) "No, not fun," he answered at once, without pause for thought. "When you are running away and a man with a spear is chasing you, it's not a game. If he catches you, you die."

It didn't sound like a good life so far—forty-mile marches, being chased at spearpoint—but even when he described the raiding there was a soft, tender fondness in the old man's voice; he liked the life more than he let on. "Sometimes," he said, "a man would take his favorite ox and lead him around the camp. He would sing, and other men would join him, each with his best ox behind him. Soon the whole camp would be parading. We had many cattle in those days, almost more than you could count; all of our oxen were fat and glossy, and the ones the men paraded were the best and fattest of them all. The women would come out of their houses to watch. If a woman liked a man and wanted him to know it, she would put a wreath of flowers around his ox. And then we danced, danced for joy at the beauty of it all, leapt and danced and shouted until exhaustion made us stop."

The old man and I talked a while longer, about his surprise, a half-century before, when he met a British soldier, the first white man he had ever seen, and the first trousers. I asked him another question; there were hundreds more I wanted to ask, for this old man was my only link to an age long vanished, and his frail and fragile voice made the joys and sweat of fifty years before come vividly alive. "I am tired now," said Longok Lopeiyon. "I must go and rest." And he dragged himself inside the empty hut.

Joseph and I went back down the hill and pushed our way through the throng to where the stew was cooking. By now the meal was ready to serve. The children who lived in the huts sat down inside the rope, and I served them first. Komol Lowot got a big, meaty bone and I saved a hefty chunk for Ilukol Locap. Then I served the rest: children, old men, mothers, strangers I had never seen before, the hangers-on from Namalu who had spent their days cadging and stealing other children's food and who had been caught so often that I knew them almost as well as the needy children I fed, there was enough meat for everybody. I gave the last of the people the last bit of meat, and then I realized I had forgotten to take any for myself, so I never found out if I had put in too much salt.

I saw all the old men whispering together as they ate, and after everyone had finished the whole group of elders formed a line and marched up to me. "They want to say a blessing," Florence explained, "to keep you safe from harm." The Karamojong believe that even one elder has the power to doom a man by cursing him; assuming the elders' power to bring good fortune was equally great, the blessing of twelve of them would be a treasure indeed. I sat down and they stood above me and blessed me with their hands and chanted in deep, melodic voices. And when their chanting finished someone started clapping and the women, who were standing, started jumping up and down. All the mothers pressed around me, still jumping and I jumped with them. They sang as they leapt, and they leapt higher and higher, jumping for the sheer joy of it, their arms held high, reaching to catch the sun. Squat and spring, bend and leap, up and down and up; I used all my strength and jumped as high as I could, for in a Karamojong dance there is no holding back. Sweat drained from me; the jumping seemed to drive the poisons out and I felt weaker but purer. The dance went on. All the mothers and most of the children had joined in by now, and somehow I found the strength to keep on jumping. As I danced the women took my arms and when I looked down there were bracelets on them, brass bracelets, the mark of the Karamojong warrior. The Dinkas scar their foreheads at initiation to show manhood and belonging, but the Karamojong, instead of scarring, put on bracelets and never take them off. I never took off mine. One, newly made, broke the next day, but the other, thicker, better made, and far older, has stayed on my wrist ever since.

We kept on dancing and then it was evening, time to leave. I'll be back, I promised, and I meant it; Denis had made the same promise and probably meant it too. But I never went back. I spent my last night in Karamoja at Amaler and the next morning Christian and I took the southern road straight to Mbale. Halfway to Mbale we came to a small stream and a wooden bridge. Christian said it was the border of Karamoja. We crossed over the bridge and into another district. We drove on in silence and after an hour we reached the paved highway. We followed it through green hills and fertile cornfields and soon we were in Mbale.

Mbale was probably the richest town in Uganda and life seemed almost normal. There were shops with things to sell, restaurants where food was served, and even a movie house. I was warned not to go out at night, but at least in the daytime there wasn't a soldier in sight. And outside town the land was lush and fertile, the soil so rich you could just drop in seeds and watch them grow. It was hard to believe that Mbale and Namalu were both in the same country, or even on the same planet.

I stayed in the Mount Elgon Hotel, which was a big, rambling mansion in the hills outside of town. It had once been a grand old hotel and though the place had gone to seed touches of elegance remained: parquet floors and chandeliers. My room had such unfamiliar luxuries as beds and running water. There was a window overlooking the garden and a writing table beside it, and I spent most of the next two days there, composing my report to Brendan O'Brien. It was the first writing I had done in four years, apart from postcards and customs forms, and it was not an easy job, for I could not write about those months without reliving the pain. The report was thirteen pages long and was quite objective, even clinical, in tone. I told how a feeding center was run, what medicines we used most, how much food was needed in a week. I wrote about children but didn't mention Ilukol Locap; I discussed the behavior of mothers without naming the Ananganang.

I wrote most of the report in Mbale. I finished the last section, on the "problem of security," in a café in Kampala and, as I wrote about soldiers and raiders and guns, two men shot it out with pistols in the street outside. The people in the café joked and laughed and sipped their tea as they watched the gunfight through the window.

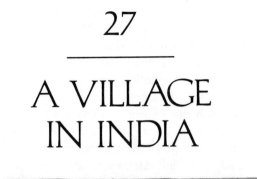

27

A VILLAGE
IN INDIA

Halfway between the Ganges and the Himalayas, near the northern edge of the vast and fertile plain that stretches across the subcontinent of India, is a village named Nagda. Nagda is a two-mile hike from the nearest road; if you had a fast car waiting where the trail from the village joins the highway, you would be only a day's drive away from Lumbini, where the Buddha was born, or Sarnath, where he preached, or Kushinagar, where he died. Or from Patalipura, which two thousand years ago was one of the greatest cities on earth; or from Benares (Varanasi) which, as any Hindu will tell you, is the holiest spot in the world. Much closer to Nagda (though no one is sure exactly where) is the birthplace of Sita, who became the wife of Rama, the incarnation of the god Vishnu. Or so the people say, for this is a part of India so rich in history and tradition that facts and legends intertwine.

Nagda is old, perhaps as old as India, but nobody great or famous was ever born there, and the village is not on any map. I came upon it quite by chance. That was in April 1981, which in India as well as Africa is the dry time before the rains. I had arrived in India a month before. During the previous five months I had been exhausted, shell-shocked, and drained of emotion, unable to face another spell in Karamoja and unwilling to admit it. In January, back in Nairobi, I met two of the Irish nurses from CONCERN; there were ten of them now, they told me, living in Namalu and running the center there. The children will be all right without me, I thought. I wanted to go far, far away and I left Africa soon after. A plane to Addis, another plane to Sana. A week in Yemen and then a flight to Bombay, and by train to Delhi, to Benares, and then to Muzaffarpur, a big town in the state of Bihar where the rail line ended.

Bihar fascinated me; it is reputed to be, and perhaps is, the poorest, most backward state in the nation, but a thousand years ago and more it was the center of India, famous for culture and learning. Bihar, in Sanskrit, means monastery, and in those days, monastery also meant university. Bihar's three great universities attracted students from all over Asia. But those universities were destroyed by Moslem invaders in the twelfth century (about the time that the first colleges in Europe were founded), and after that Bihar became a cultural backwater instead of vanguard.

I had learned by then that places known as backward are those where tradition is best preserved; to find the soul of a country, you must travel its back roads, seek out its remotest places. And, most important, you must visit its villages. Africa had taught me this, and I wanted to apply the lesson to India.

In Bombay, I had bought the most detailed map of Bihar I could find. It was not a very good map, but it did have a sentence or two, printed on back, about each of the larger towns. About a place called Madhubani, there was this: "It is a center of Mithila learning and tradition." Madhubani was not mentioned in any guidebook I had ever seen; if I had had a more detailed source of reference in my backpack (the *Encyclopaedia Britannica*, for instance), I would have learned that Mithila was a large and well-planned city which disappeared from the map about 400 B.C. but which gave its name to the region around Madhubani. The district was (says the *Britannica*) "long noted for its conservatism and the learning of its Brahmans." I did not know that then, but the one sentence, enigmatic but alluring, combined with the fact that no book I could find mentioned the town, was enough.

Madhubani was too small to be served by long-distance bus lines, so I took a bus from Muzaffarpur to Darbhanga, a larger town in the same region. It took me an hour to find a hotel; few people, evidently, wished to spend the night there. It was nonetheless a pleasant town, with a main square built of red sandstone; nearby, a wall made of the same red stone, fifteen feet high with sawtooth crenellations, surrounded the extensive grounds of the local rajah's palace. It must have been a mile long, that wall; I followed it round, looking in vain for a breach to peer through. The wall led me out of town and into open country, past rice fields and shady trees, and I left the wall and walked through the fields toward a red speck I had seen on the horizon. When I got closer I found a group of tiny temples, deserted and half in ruins. They, too, were built of sandstone, with frail and delicate Mogul domes, so graceful they seemed to float, to hover just above the earth instead of resting on it. Later, back in town, I tried to find out who had built those temples and when, but no one knew.

The next day, I found a ride to Madhubani. It was a disappointment: one long street of shops and little art or culture apparent. But I hadn't planned to stay in the town, but rather use it as a jumping-off point to visit nearby villages. Whatever Mithila learning and tradition was, I expected to find it there.

I had prepared a letter and had it translated into Hindi. "I am an admirer of India and a lover of Hindu culture," it began, "and it has been my lifelong ambition to visit a Hindu village." These phrases were borrowed from the letter to the Azande that I had used with such success in the southern Sudan, but there was more than a little truth in them. During my time in Africa, I sometimes thought about India, and it was always with the feeling that, though I had been there twice already, there was something vague, something ineffable, something essential I had missed.

I walked to the bus stop, a dusty, crowded lot near the edge of town. There were three buses waiting, all nearly full. I picked one at random and got on; there was no space inside so I rode on the roof. People climbed up behind me, and, when no more could squeeze on, the driver, who had been squatting in the shade, got up, strolled over, and started the bus.

In a few minutes we had left the town behind. I tried to guess which way the bus was heading but wasn't quite sure. The driver had turned in to a side road that wasn't on my map. So much the better, I thought. There were rice fields on either side of us, dry and stubbly at this time of year, and from time to time I saw houses huddled together, villages. I found fault with each of them. Too small. Too large. Too close to town. In Africa, I had found my villages by walking. I had never stopped a bus at random and now I was afraid. I dreaded the moment when I would get off and the bus would pull away. Or, even worse, the driver might make trouble, ask me (in Bihari) why I wanted to stop, or simply refuse and drive on. So I sat and waited and squinted into the wind. An hour passed, and then I saw a white, almost alkaline, stretch of land with a rutted cart track running across it. Perfect. I banged on the roof. The bus stopped and I climbed down. It drove off but I didn't notice. I was already dreaming of what lay at the end of the track.

My first sight of Nagda was a row of mud-walled houses and an old man reading. He had a page of *sutras* in his hand and was reading the sacred verses aloud to a group of small boys who sat at his feet. Then he looked up and saw me. I walked over and greeted him, and then I gave him my letter. He squinted at it and began to read.

The last part of the note explained that I would pay five rupees a day for expenses; I put it in because I remembered the woman in the faded sari. Three years before, in a village near Pondicherry, she had taken me in and fed me for a week and probably worried the whole time about the amount of food I was eating.

But money was not a polite thing to mention and I feared the old man would take offense. The old man read slowly. He neither frowned nor smiled. I was sure he would turn me away, tell me to go back home. The village in southern India had welcomed me, but the people I stayed with had been untouchables and anyone of higher status would risk losing it by having me, a non-Hindu, as their guest. In India, as in Karamoja, the old pass on their knowledge by telling stories, and there was one tale I had heard many times. A man goes on a pilgrimage, falls sick, and, starving, accepts food from a kindly stranger. When he returns home, he is shunned by everyone, even his own family, because the food that had saved his life might have been given him by someone of lower caste than he. The man in the story eventually regained his caste after long and costly rites of purification, but he was a *vaishya*, a trader. The man who now held my letter wore a piece of string looped around his shoulder, and that tatty bit of thread meant that he was a Brahmin, the highest caste of all.

And then he spoke. His English was far from fluent, which was not surprising, since it was obviously his fourth language; the letter was in Hindi, the scriptures Sanskrit, and his native language was Bihari. "You may stay," he said, "you are welcome. But you are a guest and we cannot take money. Bela Babu is coming," he added. "Wait for him."

Soon after that, the man they called Bela Babu arrived; one of the children must have gone to fetch him the moment I came into view. Bela Babu was the oldest man in the village. He was tall and thin and stood very straight, but he used a heavy wooden staff to support himself. He was crippled, and it seemed to me when I first saw him that he could hardly walk at all. He told me later that he walked several miles a day, dragging himself along behind his staff. "I can go as far as anyone," he said. "It just takes longer."

Bela spoke to the man who had welcomed me, and then to me. "Come," he said, "you will stay with me." And he limped off at a speed that surprised me. I followed him to his house, which was small but built of brick. We sat outside, on the veranda facing the path. A wizened old man dressed in black passed by. When he saw me, he stopped and squatted on the lowest of the steps leading to the veranda. Mesmerized, it seemed, he stayed and stared for quite a while. "Who is he?" I asked Bela. "Why doesn't he come up the steps and stay on the veranda?" Bela seemed amused at that. "He is a *chamar*," Bela said. The *chamars*, or leatherworkers, were untouchables. There are perhaps two thousand castes in India, and most villages have six or ten or twenty or more, but I was slowly beginning to realize that Nagda, unlike any village I had ever heard or even read about, was made up of only two: Brahmins and untouchables.

"We will go to see Hari Chander," Bela announced, and led me behind his house through a labyrinth of paths and alleys. The village was evidently far larger than I had expected. We passed open yards with earthen houses and wickerwork fences behind which I could hear the soft shuffling of cows.

"Hari Chander is the richest man in Nagda," Bela said, and then I saw his house. It was perhaps twenty yards in length but it seemed much larger, perhaps because of what Bela had just told me, or perhaps because of its design. It was built in a squared-off U around a veranda. The porch was covered and the roof was supported by squat, massive pillars. The columns were bright red, but the yard-thick walls, which were made of concrete, had been left unpainted. It was not pretty, this dank bunker of a mini-mansion, but it was monumental. When I met him, Hari Chander told me that he had paid ten thousand rupees (about twelve hundred dollars) to have it erected. How much would it cost in America, he asked. I told him twelve thousand dollars, and he was pleased, because a hundred thousand rupees was a fortune so large as to be almost beyond belief.

Hari Chander was indeed the richest man in Nagda, but that was the only time I ever heard him mention money. Perhaps he, like I, was nervous at our first meeting. He was dressed in white that day, as always. He was quite handsome, with short gray hair, large brown eyes at once liquid and alert, and a face unmarked by time. His English was broken and halting, but he always managed to get across whatever he wanted to say. We talked a lot in the days that followed, because he prevailed on Bela to let me stay with him. Bela, who loved to talk but lived alone, would have wanted me as a guest, but the old man was far from rich. He was too proud to take my money and could not afford to be responsible for feeding me. "One day I will prepare dinner for you," he told me when he left. "I am very good at cooking."

And so was Hari Chander's wife or mother or whoever it was who prepared the meals that three times a day were set before me, beginning that evening after sunset. I never went inside the mansion, except to visit Hari Chander's study, a square room in the left-hand wing with a desk and a wooden armchair, and, except for that study, the inside was the women's domain. The women of Nagda kept themselves in *purdah*, and so I never saw them, save as shadowy presences glimpsed through half-open doors. Whether they ruled the house or were its prisoners I cannot say; we and they lived in separate worlds.

The nights were warm and I was happy to sleep outside, on the veranda, to be awakened by the rising sun. As I sat on the hassock where I had slept, Hari Chander's son Ganesh, sleepy-eyed and yawning, came out of the house carrying a shiny brass jug of water. "To wash your eyes and mouth," he said, and so I did. Then I went off to fertilize the fields behind the house, and when I came back there was tea waiting. I drank, put on bathing trunks, and followed Ganesh to the tank.

The tank was a large pond, much bigger than a football field and perfectly square. At some time in the far distant past, the villagers had dug the tank out of earth and rock, but in the centuries since then nature had claimed it for its own. The gently sloping dike that formed its shore was covered with grass and even the stone staircase that led down to the water had been smoothed by time and flecked by moss and lichen. Water purifies, and Hindus are required by their religion to bathe at least once a day, so the steps of the *ghat* were usually crowded. Men would come and stay for hours, washing and talking and sitting in the sun. The water was dark and very cold and I liked to jump in all at once to make the shock even greater. I swam a few hundred feet out to the middle of the tank and looked back at the *ghat*, much smaller now, framed by grass and bushes. The women had their own *ghat*, hidden by a screen of trees, and sometimes I would hear, far-off and faint, the echoes of their laughter.

That was morning in Nagda; it was always the same, and there was comfort in this sameness. It was the ritual invocation that ushered in the day, and linked it to the uncounted parade of days that had gone before. But each afternoon was different; there were always surprises. Afternoon was the time for walks and excursions, for feasts and festivals on occasion, and above all, for visits. Upwards of three thousand people lived in the cluster of settlements that was Nagda, and Hari Chander knew every one of them, though he might not have admitted to knowing the *chamars*. He had more cousins and uncles and friends than I could count. One, whom he took me to meet on my second day in Nagda, was the village scholar, a fat and dour old man who spoke English, French, and German and perhaps ten languages besides. He had written several books, which were proudly displayed on a bookshelf above his desk. He had been a professor but he was retired now, returned to his village, but his desk was covered with open books and half-completed manuscripts. He had not stopped writing.

Another of Hari Chander's friends (a cousin, I think) had vacant eyes and an amiable smile. He spent his days eating the green paste called *bhang*, which is made from marijuana leaves and is legal in Bihar. On most days, a group of men gathered in a house next door to sit on the veranda and talk about politics, and once or twice Hari and I joined them. And then there were two old men who lived in a house by the fish pond. A low palisade ran around their yard; through it, I could see the pond and a sandy shore beyond. It was not a large expanse of water, but it was as bright and blue as the sea.

When Hari Chander went calling, I always went with him, but sometimes he would leave late or come back early and I would have a few minutes on my own. Sometimes I went to the village temple, a tiny shrine, always locked, with a wide veranda. The veranda and the yard outside it was a popular meeting place. In the late morning, an elderly man who lived nearby set up a stove and sold tea, and the men of Nagda would come to the square to share tea and gossip. The tea stall closed early, and by late afternoon the square was usually deserted, but I sometimes found Ganesh there, with his friends, sitting in the shadow cast by the temple. One afternoon someone brought a harmonium, which looks like an accordion and sounds like a church organ, and Ganesh played it and sang, with all his friends joining in. They sang traditional Indian mantras, their voices deep but lilting. "Hare Krishna, Hare Krishna, Krishna Krishna, Hare Hare." I had heard that song before, on the streets of New York, but it seemed to have a lot more meaning here.

Often, instead of walking to the temple, I stayed on Hari Chander's veranda, pretending to read as I watched the life around me. In the afternoon, the yard of sunbaked earth just below the patio was used for threshing. A cow would be tethered to a pole in the center, and a tall, thin man dressed in black would drive her round and round in a circle, crushing the grain that was spread in a golden carpet underfoot. The man was a hired hand, a *chamar*, as were all the men who tilled the fields, because Brahmins are not allowed to do manual labor. The workers were paid four rupees a day, about half a dollar. They came to the veranda in the afternoon to collect their wages. Sometimes they were paid in grain. Hari Chander's father, who was white-haired and short but built like a wrestler, sat like a stolid Buddha, with a pair of scales and a heap of rice. The *chamars* waited their turn on the veranda; they were allowed to squat or sit on the floor but not on the chairs. Sometimes, in the afternoon, one or two would squat on the veranda steps and watch me. If the crops failed, if there was no work and these men were starving, I asked one of the Brahmins, would you give them food? No, he answered.

Like the women, the untouchables were invisible. We never visited their part of the village, but sometimes we passed near it on our way to the road. The *chamars'* ancestors had converted to Islam, which has no castes, and I could see their mosque, which was decorated with plaster carvings and inscriptions in Arabic. Once I saw colored lights outside one of the houses. There was a happy crowd inside; I could hear singing and music; someone was getting married.

A glimpse of the party, a few snatches of Hindi film songs, and then we were through the village on our way to the road. Hari walked quickly; we were going to the market. It was a mile or so down the highway and took place once a week in a vacant plot of ground behind a row of tea shops. By the time we got there, the empty lot had been turned into a patchwork of vegetables. The lot was very crowded, but most of the people, like Hari, had come to talk and not to buy. In India, as in West Africa, the weekly market is a social occasion.

I recognized many of Hari's friends; even the old professor was there, examining heads of lettuce. He bought some lettuce and a melon; perhaps he, too, had come to gossip, but he didn't want to admit it. Hari greeted him and then took me to have lunch at one of the tea stalls. We sat inside, well back from the road; a small boy brought us tea. He was eight years old or maybe younger, and I asked Hari about him. He was, Hari said, an orphan; he slept in the shop and was paid two rupees (twenty-five cents) a day. We ate, Hari paid the bill, and then we left. No one ever tips in India, but I gave the boy a two-rupee note when Hari wasn't looking.

On our way back to Nagda, we passed a burning pyre. It was just outside the village. Someone had died. There was no nearby river, so his ashes would be scattered in the fields where his crops had grown. The pyre was a rough heap of logs and untrimmed branches. We stopped for a few moments; Hari had known the man.

The next night it rained. There was thunder and lightning and I had to move my bed next to the wall of the house. In the middle of the night someone ran up and pounded on the door. He spoke to Hari and then both of them ran off into the rain. One of Hari's friends had just died, I found out later, and he had been cremated that very night. I wondered how they started the fire in the storm.

Three days after that, Hari and his father and his son Ganesh left the house and came back an hour later with their heads shaved. Ganesh was embarrassed; if someone had said hello to him, Ganesh would have thought he was making fun of his smooth scalp. "Any man who has witnessed a funeral," Hari explained as Ganesh sulked nearby, "must shave his head within three days. That is our custom." Hari and I walked over to the temple square. Two barbers had set up shop there and a long line of men waited to have their heads shaved. Since I had not been to the funeral, Hari told me, I could keep my hair. For days after that, I worried that someone would remember that I had stopped at that other funeral the day of the market.

By shaving their hair, the Brahmins purged themselves of the pollution of death. Indians, like Karamojong, consider dead bodies unclean and unlucky, and most Hindus leave the task of cremation to a caste called the *doms*, who are considered the lowest of the untouchables. But in Nagda, the Brahmins cremated their own. "Why don't you leave it to the *doms?*" I asked Ganesh. "We will not let *doms* enter our village," he answered. "We will not let them touch us even after death."

The two funerals I saw were sad and somber occasions but they did not leave a cloud of gloom behind them. Those who died, the people knew, would soon be born again. Grief was shaved away along with hair, and life went on. One of the men who lived in the house by the fish pond announced that his child was getting married. Parents arranged their children's marriages long beforehand. There were intricate negotiations between the families over such issues as dowry and, even more important, a visit to the astrologer to be sure the bride and groom were compatible. Matchmakers and astrologers love gossip as much as anyone, so the old man's announcement probably did not come as a surprise. The village's main interest seemed to be the feasts that would be given. The next day, Hari told me, there would be a feast for all the children of Nagda, and, the day after that, for all the men, including me. "Curd and rice!" said Bela Babu, when he passed our house on his daily walk to the temple. "There will be curd and rice!"

The children's party took place at lunchtime, in a grassy plot under a banyan tree. Ganesh and his friends were there sitting under the tree; they were far too old to be fed but they came to watch and sing and play the harmonium. Plates of pastry and buckets of curry and heaps of saffron-colored rice had been set up under the tree. The old man wanted to start serving, but the children were too excited; they milled about and would not settle down. Hari had told me that all the village children would be there, and though there were a hundred boys and girls playing in the yard I had expected more. All the children meant all the Brahmin children, Ganesh explained.

Since Brahmins will not eat together with someone of another caste, I wondered whether I would be invited to join the men's feast the next day. Bela and Hari both talked about nothing else. Curd and rice! Curd and rice and sugar! As much as you like! By now I sorely wanted to go.

Hari and I left for the feast around noon the next day. All the paths were crowded and for the last hundred yards we had to squeeze our way through the throng. We barely got in the gate. Inside, in the vast yard behind the fence, the men of Nagda sat in rows; between the rows, banana-leaf tablecloths formed stripes of green. The yard was far bigger than I remembered, but all of it was used that day. The father stood near the gate; he gave an almost imperceptible nod when we entered, to let Hari know that I could join them.

Platters of rice, buckets of curd—yogurt, really, white and creamy—and bowls of powdered sugar were placed before us. We served ourselves, heaping rice and yogurt onto the banana leaves that served as plates. Sugar was a luxury in Nagda, and yogurt a special treat; those rich Brahmins were, by American standards, incredibly poor. We all ate more than we should, and for a long time after that I grew sick at the thought of curd and rice.

After curd and rice came the actors and after that the fair and somewhere in between was dirt and mud. Each new day brought another festival, a new excuse for celebration, most of them, unlike the weddings, observed by the entire village. Had I, I wondered, chanced to come on the one week when everything happened? Or was life in Nagda as eventful as this throughout the year?

The actors came as a surprise even to Hari. They just showed up one day, one of the many troupes of players, magicians, and troubadours who wander through the Indian countryside, putting on shows and passing the hat. But these actors had passed through Nagda before, and the village had liked them. They built a stage in an empty field, and by evening the field was full of people waiting. Most of Nagda was there, and people from nearby villages as well. The stage was lit by lanterns; the rest of the field, by now, lay in darkness. Then the play began. The actors' robes were rich and gaudy; tinsel shimmered in the lamplight. The actors themselves were fond of loud, resounding declamations, sobs of anguish, pleas of passion. It was easy to pick out the villain; he stomped on stage with a fearsome scowl. I could not follow the plot beyond that, and I soon grew bored. The rest of the audience sat in rapt, spellbound silence. For them, and especially, I think, for the children, the show was magic, the tawdry tinsel glistened like gold, and the hanging lanterns framed a window on a new, exciting world which for a few short hours was more real to them than the houses of Nagda, which shone softly in the starlight behind the stage.

I left the play early, walked back alone through silent, deserted pathways, and went to sleep. The next morning, instead of bathing in the tank, I changed into my oldest T-shirt. I had been warned what to expect; it was the day for dirt and mud.

It was celebrated once a year, this festival of mud, and there may well have been some arcane religious explanation behind it, but if there was no one knew it; what the people did know was that it was noisy and dirty and a lot of fun. "Dirt and mud!" said Bela Babu. "Dirt and mud!" And he stared at me through his spectacles to see if his new slogan thrilled me as much as curd and rice. It did, and that morning I walked to the temple to share the fun.

Ganesh was there, and so were most of his friends and many young men I had never seen before. Whooping and laughing, they pelted each other, not only with dirt and mud, but straw and dust and clay, and a few of the naughtiest had cow pies in reserve. One or two had brought ten-gallon tin pails filled with filth to dump on unsuspecting passersby. The man who ran the tea stall walked past and received a bucket, most of which he scooped up and threw back, but there were very few unsuspecting passersby that morning. Anyone who did not want to join the mud fight stayed indoors. A few women walked past, and some paused a few seconds to watch, but no one dared throw anything in their direction. I asked why. "It is not done," said Ganesh.

As a guest, I would have enjoyed the same status of exemption from defilement, but I cast the first mudball and by the time the morning was over I was as dirty as the rest of them. By noon, all the mud was used up and all the pails were empty, and we were all laughing too hard to stand up, so the fight was adjourned by common consent. I changed into a swimsuit and jumped in the tank.

"Dirt and mud," said Bela when he saw me. I had changed my

clothes of course, but word of my exploits had reached him. It was evening; he had invited me to dinner and had spent the whole day preparing it. He had made eight different curries, only a tiny amount of each, and he served all of them together in shiny metal bowls on a tray. The eight bowls were arranged in a circle, with rice in the center. As he had said, Bela was very good at cooking.

Bela did not eat with me. Perhaps it would pollute him to eat with someone not a Brahmin. More likely, I decided, there was not enough food for both of us to eat so lavishly; he would eat later and more simply. As I ate, he talked. He had traveled, he said, not as much as I but he had been to Benares and that was the holiest place on earth. He had been there last winter and stayed a month and every morning he had spent the hour before dawn immersed in the waters of the holy Ganges.

Nights are freezing in Benares at that time of year, and I tried to imagine Bela dragging himself through streets enveloped in cold and darkness, guiding himself by the few dim streetlamps, tiny islands of light swimming in the predawn mist, and then down and down the rime-slippery steps and into the icy water, no light at all there, only cold and pain and blackness, and the only sound his own voice praying. And then the dawn, and the pale, enormous winter sun would rise above the waters. It would be like watching the world created. I could string the images together, but I couldn't fully imagine the glory or the pain.

I had finished eating and Bela took my plate away. He was wearing a white *dhoti* and that and his round glasses made him look like Gandhi, but taller. I wished he could have told me what he had felt at Benares. But perhaps his silence told me, and the peace and stillness that surrounded him when he sat down. I spoke to him about my travels, we talked a while longer, and then I left. I knew Bela must be tired, because he always rose before the sun. As I walked back to Hari's house and my veranda, I could see Bela's lantern still burning. He was saying his evening prayers.

The next morning, Hari took me to a fair at a nearby village. It was an hour's walk away and we got there close to noon. The fairgrounds were a grassy meadow behind the houses. A midway of booths had been set up; some sold food and others offered entertainment. There were jugglers, magicians, and musicians and the space outside their booths was so crowded we had to push our way through. We stopped for cakes and tea and then went on. Beyond the booths, in a large fenced-off enclosure, was a wooden platform shaded by a cloth canopy, like a marquee with the sides rolled up. This was the center of the fair, and its reason for existence; all the rest, all the food and performers and even the crowds, were side-shows, incidental. Hari spoke to the people guarding the platform and then led me over the fence and onto the stage. A ring of Brahmins, bare-chested under robes of saffron, sat around a fire. The flames came from a deep pit under the platform. The priests tossed handfuls of rice into the pit; the rice popped and hissed as the flames devoured it. The priests chanted as they hurled the rice, filling the air with a low crackling drone of words that sounded like the oldest language known to man. I could not see the bottom of the pit and the flames seemed to shoot up from the center of the earth. A tiny cog in the cosmos, this throwing of rice, but if it weren't done who knew what wheels might stop?

The vision left me as we left the enclosure. From the other side of the fence, the ritual seemed dull. The noise of the midway drowned out the prayers. I hoped for a chance to watch the entertainers, but Hari hurried past their booths without even stopping. "Now you will meet a holy man," he said.

The holy man lived in a small tent which he had set up near the fairgrounds. Hari's cryptic statement had conjured up an image that looked a lot like Bela Babu, but when the holy man emerged from his tent I saw a young man dressed in black. His hair was black and short and his beard was neatly trimmed. He and Hari spoke, and then he talked with me. I don't remember what was said; all I could think of was the waves of power that rippled in his voice and surged from his dark, staring eyes. After we left I told Hari that I didn't like him. Hari didn't like him either, he said. "He is not a good man. But he is my friend," he added. "And a holy man."

One or two of Hari's many friends had told him they were going to the fair, so he and I strolled around the grounds once again, hoping to spot someone he knew. We didn't, and after another cup of tea we set off for Nagda. We had come to the fair along the road, but we walked back through the fields. That was slightly shorter than the highway, but took more time. The path was a ribbon of dusty earth that threaded its way between the paddies. At first we could hear the sounds of the fair—holy prayers and snatches of song and shouts and barks of laughter all blended into a formless babble—but as we walked farther into the fields all that was swallowed up by silence. Sometimes, in the flat, harsh plains of India, the silence of the countryside seems to hum with meaning, and so it did then. Briefly, I thought of Africa: the grass, the dew, the perfumed forests. The land in Africa is rich with the smell and promise of life, and the stark Indian flatlands are equally eloquent, but they hint at something beyond life, or above it. Perhaps that is the one difference between the stately and ancient civilization of India and the equally old and dignified cultures of Africa: Africa believes in the spirit world, and the wise man tries to live in harmony with it, but only in India does it seem possible to merge with it and be a part of it. It is the difference between the green, rich forest and those barren fields of earth, parched and cracked and waiting for the rain.

Then I realized that the fields around me, though dry now, were paddies, like those in Java, with smooth flat centers and shallow dikes all lovingly sculpted by careful hands. Generation after generation had worked here, and over the years, with the patience and persistence of ants, they had slowly remade the land. Generation after generation, and as I walked across the fields that were their handiwork I felt far closer to them, those long-dead nameless people, than to the present-day populations of cities like Delhi or Bombay. If their ghosts still watched over the land they had created, they found it little changed. Very little. A little less civilized perhaps, a bit more hurried, but basically the same. There were still fairs and plays and scholars, as there were a thousand years before, and if the Buddha passed through Nagda (which he might have done, on his way to southern Bihar and enlightenment), he would have seen the same vista that spread before me now: well-kept fields, a few palm and pipal trees, wooden plows and swayback cows and earthen houses in the distance.

Time is circular, Indians believe, and all progress an illusion. In recent decades, change has come to India—land reform acts have been passed and to some extent implemented, factories have been built, villages electrified—but in Nagda time still moves in Hindu fashion. Harvest follows rain follows planting follows harvest. Feasts and festivals, pilgrimages and processions punctuate the sequence of seasons. Thus has it always been, thus will it always be. There are clocks in Delhi; in Nagda, none. There time rolls on, as slow and steady and serene as the Ganges, whose waters are ever changing but always look the same.

It was late now; we could see the village. The sun was going down and the light was soft and unearthly. The long, low earthen houses were firm brown brushstrokes against a pastel sky. Then the sun touched the distant walls and for a fleeting moment I had the delusion to which all travelers aspire: I had escaped to another planet, or possibly another century, and was irrevocably cut off from the world I had left behind.

The moment passed, as all such moments do. The same sun that set on Nagda was rising now over New York. It had taken me almost five years to get from one to the other, and if the nature of things, the laws of nature, seem to have changed along the way, it was only because village ways were older, and life was far less cluttered. No great cosmic insight that, only a glimpse at a happy way of life.

28

NEPAL, THAILAND AND BURMA, REVISITED

"Stay with us," said Hari. "Stay, and I will give you land." I could, I thought, I could stay forever, build a house, and never go back. But that vision, like the other, began to fade even before it became fully real. There are no clocks in Nagda, but I would always hear clocks ticking; my mind, like the life I had left behind, was too cluttered, noisy, filled with echoes from every place I had ever been. I could never be an Indian.

I left a few days later. Hari walked with me to the highway. He insisted on carrying my heavy pack and he waited with me until my bus came. I sat in back and waved good-bye through the dust-spattered rear window. For a few moments I saw Hari, standing by the roadside watching me drive away. Then the bus went around a curve and I was alone again.

The nearest city to Nagda—closest, that is, in terms of distance but not of time needed to get there and certainly not in terms of cultural affinity—is the capital of Nepal, Kathmandu. I went the fastest way possible, which was a combination of bus, van, and rickshaw, and it took me three days to get there.

Kathmandu had changed; the magic had gone out of it in the four years I'd been gone. The Oriental Lodge had closed, and so had the Original Pleasure Room, and all the hippies had left or cut their hair. Durbar Square, the three temples, the whole old city beyond, was the same as before; perhaps it was I who had changed.

I booked a flight to Bangkok. There were five days before it left, not enough for a long trek, but enough for something. I took a bus to a place named Barabise, the last town on the road to Tibet. Most of Nepal is Hindu, and almost all of the few Buddhists live hundreds of miles from the highway, but east of Barabise were a few Buddhist villages and even a small monastery named Dolangsa.

Barabise was a bazaar town. Hundreds of shops, stalls, and tea-houses lined its one long street. I walked from one end of town to the other and finally found a path going east. After a mile, it ended at a cliff.

There were stairs cut into the cliff, and I started to climb. The climb was so long that I lost count of the times I decided to give up. The steps went on and on and somewhere between earth and sky I reached the top. I saw fields and trees and neat, trim cottages with thatched roofs and bright red walls. I found a trail and followed it. There were more houses, then a large village where the trail petered out. From then on it was guesswork.

I walked a long time without seeing any houses at all, and as the sun climbed the air turned damp and swampy. Toward midday I came to a house. It was large and half-timbered, the sturdy masonry covered with a rough, whitewashed plaster, the crossbeams stout and black, the roof thatched; it was the sort of house that inspires medieval daydreams. I went inside.

The house was full of people, most of them drinking, most of them laughing, all of them trying to talk at once. An old woman, her face all grins and wrinkles, handed me a frothy mug of beer. I was thirsty and I drank; then I was tired, and I rested. After a time the revels died down. A man got up and three boys followed, and everybody else trailed after them. On a low knoll outside the house was a long-dead, leafless tree. The man climbed the hill, tied a white cloth around the tree, and chanted a long incantation. One by one, the boys did the same. These people weren't Buddhist, to judge from their manner of praying, or Hindu either. Who were they, and what rite had I witnessed? I did not know and never was to learn. But I had shared their beer and celebration, and they had touched my life, if only briefly, and that mattered more than names and explanations.

The ceremony ended and I walked on. A few more hours, a few more hills and valleys, and then I came to Budipa. The village was nothing more than a row of tall stone houses, hardly enough of them to be worth naming, perched on a knoll with a river below and rugged green hills all around. The people were distinctly unfriendly, though they grudgingly sold me a package of biscuits and found me a place to sleep.

I left at sunrise. Beyond Budipa was a series of streams to be forded and then a range of brown and rounded hills. The path made a long sweeping curve after that, up a valley, across a bridge over a rushing stream, and then back down the other side. The trail was cut into the hillside but the floor of the valley sloped upward to meet it, and near the bridge was a waterwheel and an old stone mill. The day was hot and the place deserted, so I bathed in the icy water and dried in the sun.

Late in the afternoon, I came to a high bluff, climbed it, and found a warren of rough stone houses huddled on top. The trail ran level for a mile beyond, and then the flat land ended in a long, grassy slope like a meadow gently tilted. The grass was damp, and gray clouds hung overhead like a low, fluffy ceiling. The hill and the path rose to meet them. There were a few houses scattered on the hillside; at the crest of the hill was the monastery of Dolangsa.

The lamasery was small and built in Tibetan style, with a flat roof, smooth white outer walls, heavy wooden doors, and inside them a dimly lit hall with ceiling and columns painted red and walls covered with visions of heaven and hell. Three red-robed monks sat in the center, singing sacred mantras. Their guttural chants sounded like the voice of creation, or like a baritone singing through a trumpet. The chants reached a crescendo, and then the monks blew real trumpets, long brass horns taller than a man. The service was over. I went outside. I asked one of the monks where I could sleep and he shrugged his shoulders in cosmic unconcern. I went back down the hill.

A few minutes later I reached the first of the houses. It was built in roughly the same fashion as those I had seen in the medieval hamlets

I had passed through earlier, but it looked trim and spruce and modern. The people of Dolangsa were Sherpas, a Tibetan people famous as traders and mountaineers, and they were evidently richer or more enterprising than their neighbors. A young man came out of the house and skipped down the steps to the path. He wore a windbreaker and chinos. He welcomed me and invited me to stay the night. I followed him up the stairs.

A large hall ran the length of the house. At one end was the kitchen, a small, wood-paneled alcove that dominated the room. Pots and pans and ewers, all of them lovingly burnished, hung from pegs, and a vast wood-burning oven was built under a platform at the center. The rest of the hall was cold and bare and seemed tacked on as an afterthought. An older woman dressed in black proudly sat between her stove and her pans. She presented us with cups of tea. The oven was warm and we all sat around it until it was time to sleep.

Early the next morning I headed downhill, back toward Budipa and Barabise. Somewhere near Budipa I came to a fork in the trail. The right-hand path I recognized; it snaked downhill toward Barabise and the highway. But the left-hand road was a mystery and an enticement. It curved south, wound its way around a hill, and after that was lost from view. I followed it. Why not? I had a day to spare.

After an hour's brisk walk, I came to the crest of a hill and found rice fields spread below, clinging to the curving hillside like sinuous ribbons of jade. I saw a bare-chested boy driving a water buffalo. Beyond the fields were houses. Most of them seemed deserted, but one was literally swarming with people. The yard around it was full, there were faces at the windows, and even the roof was alive with wriggling arms and legs. Curious, I went closer and soon found the explanation. The roof was being thatched and the whole village had joined in. Men and women carried sheaves of straw to the courtyard and dumped them in a heap. Others tossed the bales to the workers on the roof. Usually they caught the sheaves, but sometimes they missed and the straw rained back to earth. The people below shouted then, and the roofers shouted back. Both roofers and throwers made frequent trips to the large earthen jug of beer that stood in a corner of the yard. The owner of the house, a big white-haired man who reminded me of Hari Chander's father, was responsible for keeping the jug full. He spent the day shuttling between courtyard and kitchen, where he was preparing the feast that would be served when the work was done.

There were as many people around the jug as on the roof and I didn't think the work would ever get done. But everyone was having fun, so I put down my pack and joined them. I helped the men who were heaving sheaves to the roofers. My first throw missed and the bale broke, but after that my aim improved. By the end of the day, the roof was completed. Smoke and rain would soon blacken it, but it was clean now, and the fresh-cut straw gleamed like a wheat field hanging in the sky.

With the work over, the number of workers seemed to increase and all of them sat in the yard and waited for the feast to begin. The owner and his sons brought out the food. Smiling, the old man put a bowl before me, and for the first time since leaving Nagda I felt truly welcome.

An old wooden bowl filled to the brim with spicy stew, a house of earth and brand-new thatch, with barely enough room to hold us; I slept on the floor, wedged in between the old man and one of his sons. The next night I had a room to myself, in Kathmandu, and I ate on shining china. My next meal was wrapped in plastic, and eaten with plastic all around me and five miles of sky below; I was on my way to Bangkok.

✕◈✕

My plane landed and I took a bus into town. Bangkok, capital of Thailand, is as spread out as Los Angeles and for the next two hours I watched a slow-moving panorama of skyscrapers and shopping centers and vast, chaotic intersections where eight-lane highways met. I cringed. I hated the place on sight.

Later, I came to like Bangkok. I found quiet alleys, wooden houses, groves of palm trees, and countless monasteries, shrines, and temples. The people were quick to laugh but slow to anger, and no one screamed or shouted. To the devoutly Buddhist Thais, any display of selfish, jarring emotion is not only boorish but sinful. Everyone knows that greedy children and angry adults become hungry ghosts when they die.

On my first trip to Thailand in 1977, I, like most tourists, had gone north to see Chiang Mai and the hill tribes. This time I went northeast, to the land that Westerners know as the Korat Plateau, though it is not really a plateau at all, but a rolling, densely populated plain. The Thais call it Issan. It is the poorest, least developed part of Thailand, and the most traditional.

Thailand has good roads and comfortable buses with kamikaze drivers, so I was soon deep in Issan, closer as the crow flies to Vietnam than to Bangkok. I visited Nakhon Ratchasima and Khon Kaen and Nong Khai and Sakon Nakhon, towns whose long and for me unpronounceable names were the most exotic things about them. They were little Bangkoks all of them, cities of cars and concrete, whose builders had a penchant for avocado green and a shade of orange that reminded me of frozen concentrate. I viewed all this with mixed emotions; the towns were ugly, but the abundance of shops meant that even in the countryside many people had money to spare.

South of Sakon Nakhon, around the town of Roi Et, is the poorest part of Issan. Thirty miles north of Roi Et, my bus stopped at an unmarked junction. There was a side road running east, and another bus waiting by the curb. Why not, I thought, and I left my bus and boarded the other.

The bus drove east. The land was flat and dotted with villages. All of them were electrified, which amazed me. In all of Africa I had never seen a village with electricity, but here, even in the poorest part of the country, power pylons marched along beside the road.

Then the pylons stopped. I got off there, walked along the road until I found a track, and then followed that to a cluster of houses. At the nearest house, a wizened old farmer, startled, gestured to me to follow him. He led me across fields and ditches to a long, two-story building that housed the local high school.

Most of the teachers lived in a dormitory behind the school, but the headmaster had a house in the village, and it was there that I spent the night. The head, though quite young, was portly and had an air of authority about him, which he used to mask his natural shyness. He was a big man in the village, not only because of his position but also because his house, though only a small wooden cottage, had a battery-operated television set, the only one in the village. His friends would visit him to watch TV; he had an amazing number of friends and that evening the house was as crowded as a theater.

The next morning two of the teachers showed me around the village. It was large, a grid of unpaved lanes lined with rambling wooden houses set in exuberant gardens. Some of the houses were wooden shacks that seemed about to collapse, while others had bright factory-made siding, big glass windows, and aluminum deck chairs outside. Some farmers had prospered, others not. Beyond the houses was the village *wat*, or temple, an enormous white hall with a red-and-green tile roof. The yard was littered with poles and papier-mâché, which were being transformed into floats and costumes for an upcoming festival. Nearby, a wooden hall housed the monastery; I saw many young novices and a sprinkling of older monks. They were teachers, for the monastery, like the high school that lay at the opposite end of the village, was a place of learning.

Two days later I was back in Bangkok. From there I flew to Rangoon, capital of Burma. Burma welcomes tourists, provided they come by plane and leave within seven days. I found rooms in a lodging house near the gold-roofed Sule Pagoda. The train to Mandalay left at seven so I woke at five. It was not yet dawn, and I looked out the window at the damp velvet darkness of the equatorial night. A long line of monks, all in crimson togas, all with black lacquer bowls in hand, shuffled past in silence. They were the only traffic moving on the narrow rutted road that was the main street in Rangoon.

I walked through the sleeping city to the station. The train left more or less on time. I had a ticket from Rangoon to Mandalay but I got off somewhere in between, at a place called Thazi. Thazi was a row of wooden houses and a line of decrepit trucks that took passengers to Meiktila, the nearest town. My truck broke down and then it started to rain. The passengers huddled in the center of the leaking canopy as the driver tinkered with the engine. By the time we reached Meiktila, it was dark. I found a small hotel, with four rooms separated by flimsy partitions, a narrow hallway between them, and at the end of the hall a statue of Buddha festooned with bulbs like a Christmas tree. Then I went outside. It was eight o'clock and the town was shut up for the night. In an old sagging house on a street of old sagging houses, a twenty-five-watt bulb burned behind an open door. It was a restaurant, the only one open, so I ate and then went to bed.

The next morning I got a ride to a small town named Mahlaing. Mahlaing had a very large market, with row after row of stalls selling fruit and spices and lacquer bowls and thousands of things besides, all of them homemade or home-grown. On a side road near the market was the oldest bus I'd ever seen. "Is this bus going to a village?" I asked two men who stood nearby. "Yes, to a village," one of them answered, trying in vain to keep a straight face. "Thank you," I said, and got on the bus. A crowd of farmers got on behind: men and women with seamed and sun-browned faces, carrying the pots and pans and bolts of cloth they had bought and the rice and chickens they had failed to sell. We drove out of town and down an unpaved road that soon became a dusty track that wriggled its way across the dry and sandy plains of Upper Burma.

Three hours later we reached the village. It was large, as large as the one I had found in Thailand, with hundreds of houses spread out along a grid of dusty lanes. How can I ever find the headman, I wondered, but he soon found me. News of my arrival traveled fast. I was the first white man to come there in many, many years, perhaps the first since the British left; no one was quite sure.

The headman and I walked through the village to the fields beyond. He was a thin man, quite tall with short black hair and sharp features, and he seldom smiled. "Too dry, too dry," he said as we scuffed across the red, sandy fields. "The rains did not come." Then back to the village, past a boarded-up government shop, down lane after lane of old wooden houses, all large and lovingly built without benefit of plate-glass windows or plywood siding. We stopped at the temple, a long, wooden hall, its timbers richly carved and painted dark brown. An old monk sat on the veranda, his face benign as he watched a group of red-robed novices playing football in the yard.

Near the monastery was another, larger playing field, a long wooden hall with a thatched roof, and a tall wooden pole on which a hand-painted flag fluttered feebly; that was the village school. "They are teaching English now," the headman told me, and took me inside to see the new English textbook, already dogeared, just received from Rangoon.

"Now you must eat," said the headman, as we came to his own house, a large timbered cabin half hidden among trees and brightly colored flowers. We sat on the smooth planking of the veranda as a crowd of staring children filled the garden. The headman apologized for their rudeness; "They have never seen a man who is not Burmese," he explained. The children soon got bored and drifted off, and then the headman's wife emerged carrying trays of lacquer bowls. She walked toward us with the grace of a dancer, set the tray down, and went inside again. There were five different dishes; subtle curries flavored with lemon grass and coconut and cloves and coriander. It was the best food I'd eaten in weeks; she must have started cooking as soon as I arrived. "Has your wife been to cooking school in Rangoon?" I asked. She hadn't, of course, but I knew my question would please him and I was sure he would repeat it to her at the first opportunity.

After dinner, the headman took me to visit his neighbors, and I spent the rest of the evening answering questions about America. "How much money do your farmers make in a year?" one man asked. They all watched me intently; that was the thing that interested them the most. "Some people earn ten thousand dollars," I told them, "sixty thousand kyats." "Here we earn three hundred," one of them told me. "Believe me," I said, "we are not two hundred times as happy."

The next morning I took the bus back to Mahlaing. I would have stayed longer but someone had told me that even the slightest rain would turn the road into an impassable quagmire.

I had planned to stop in Mahlaing only long enough to change buses, but an elderly lady saw me and invited me to her house for refreshment. She was fluent in English, and spoke it with the easy authority of one born to wealth and power. She took me around the market and then to the town's monastery to meet a senior monk who was her spiritual adviser. After that, we went to her house, a cottage in the poorest part of town, tiny but very clean. She sat me down, gave me lemon squash, and showed me page after page of photographs pasted in albums tied together with faded ribbon, but none of them gave me a clue to her enigmatic past. We exchanged addresses and then she walked me to the station.

I took a bus to Meiktila and a battered old station wagon south to Pyinmana, a town halfway between Mandalay and Rangoon. It was a four-hour drive, and I watched dry savanna give way to lush green jungle. Pyinmana was quite a large town; it had two small hotels, both of them full, a big market, and three or four cafés with fluorescent lights and ceiling fans and young men wearing blue jeans. There were also two lovely temples and an artificial lake crossed by a causeway. The Mandalay-Rangoon express stopped at Pyinmana, and after a night in an old British rest house I caught the southbound train. I bought a ticket to Rangoon but on a whim I got off at a place called Pyu.

There are eight express stops between Rangoon and Mandalay and of those eight towns Pyu is by far the smallest. Half the trains simply skip it. There was a row of weatherbeaten storefronts and a restaurant called Bismillah's Hotel. It was early afternoon and the restaurant was empty, except for the owner and an Indian named Pandy who was evidently a permanent fixture. Pandy was a man of thirty-five, slight and voluble. He jumped up when he saw me. "Come," he said, "you must meet all my friends," and I barely had enough time to wriggle out of my pack before he rushed me out the door and down the road.

Pandy had a lot of friends, though most of them didn't value his company as highly as he would have wished them to. They viewed him, I think, as a sort of poor relation. But with me beside him, things were different. Most people who lived in Pyu never left it, and their only link with the outside world was the one or two foreigners who stopped there each year. My presence raised Pandy's status immensely.

Most of the people Pandy knew were Indian. Almost a million Indians came to Burma during the days of British rule. That was a period of prosperity in Burma, but not for everyone. Vast plantations grew rice for export and one-quarter of all Burmese lost their land. The Burmese blamed the Indian immigrants for much of the inequity and, in Pyu at least, Indians and Burmese still kept apart. They went to separate schools. The Indian school was a tiny shack that could have fit quite comfortably inside one of the Burmese school's many classrooms.

In a house near the Indian school lived two old men. They had come to Burma fifty years before and not been to India since. I asked them if they ever thought of returning. Why go back? said one. Too much money, said the other. India for them was only a vague and distant memory; Pyu was their home.

There was no hotel in Pyu but the police told me I could sleep at their station. I left my pack with them and went back to Bismillah's. Bismillah served me a huge dinner and would not let me pay for it. There was a play that night, so after dinner I followed the crowds through the town to the theater, a big old hall with metal chairs and an old red curtain. I expected to be bored to tears and I made up my mind to stay for half an hour only. The lights dimmed and the music began. There was a traditional Burmese orchestra on the left of the stage, and a rock band to the right. They both played together, and the liquid notes of the *kye-waing* (which sounds like a xylophone) were interwoven with the molten fire of an electric guitar. Then the curtain rose and a troupe of dancers came on stage. They gave a marvelous performance that blended Burmese dance and Chinese opera. That was only the curtain raiser. Skits, songs, and dances followed, then two stand-up comics, and then, starting around midnight, a full-length play, a long, involved melodrama about a group of Burmese soldiers. Like the music, the skits and the play were neither wholly traditional nor wholly modern, but a strange and glorious hybrid of the two. I assumed that the performers must be famed throughout Burma, and when I got to Rangoon I tried to track them down. No one had heard of them.

Pandy and I spent the next morning strolling. After that we went back to Bismillah's, and then it started to rain. Rain poured without pause for two hours, and Pandy pulled me into the worst of it to watch the northbound train arrive. Pandy lived for those six minutes a day when the expresses stopped at Pyu station and he never dreamed that I might not share his enthusiasm. We ran to the station, past a long line of women who were trudging through the rain with trays of fruit and candy balanced on their heads. The train arrived; the women held up their wares and hoped someone would buy them. Pandy ran from one car to another. In the last car he found a pair of tall, blond teenagers conversing in German. "Two Germans!" said Pandy, with all the excitement of an ornithologist sighting a Bahama yellowthroat in Central Park. Then, dripping wet, he ran back to town and burst into Bismillah's, eager to tell the world—*his* world—that two Europeans had just passed through it.

29

CHINA OFF THE BEATEN TRACK

Travel is addictive. No matter how far you've gone, there are always other lands beyond the horizon, hidden places each with their own peculiar secrets waiting to be revealed. And the very best of these, the places whose names have the power of talismans, are those that lie just beyond the borders of the attainable. For me, as for many of the travelers who crept along the underbelly of Asia in those years, that place was China. Almost every country in Asia had a Chinese border, but no one could cross it, and no one knew what lay beyond.

Red China, my high-school teachers called it, and its people were Blue Ants or Yellow Perils. They were inscrutable, the Chinese, infinitely patient and infinitely cunning. They were devious; they had agents in Chinese restaurants around the world ready, on Peking's command, to put plague germs into the eggrolls. Even worse, ten-foot-high platforms were secretly being built throughout China and, at a time secretly prearranged and synchronized to the tenth of a second, a billion Chinese would jump off these platforms, causing shock waves and earthquakes that would destroy the free world.

I heard that story in 1963; people believed it then. Later, fashions changed and another view of China became fashionable: a billion comrades resolutely marching toward utopia. Day-care centers, small-scale industry, holistic medicine, even buses run by biogas; all those were daydreams in America, but in China they were real. Or so people said; no one knew for sure because no one could go to China.

Often, during my years of travel, I thought of China. I saw landlords and landless, shantytowns and Mercedes-Benzes, people whose land was turned into somebody else's plantation, people who left their land to flock to noxious cities and ended up begging in the streets. I saw many things I would have preferred to forget, and sometimes I would think, "That wouldn't happen in China." Or would it? There seemed no way to find out, no way at all, until the day in August 1981 when I discovered the shop that sold visas to China.

It was a one-room office in Mongkok, in the British colony of Hong Kong, fairly near the snake-soup shops on Temple Street and a few blocks north of the big McDonald's on Nathan Road. It was a small room with plastic wallpaper designed to look like wood. There were no windows; if there had been, they might have yielded a glimpse of the bright blue harbor which lay two miles to the south, and the glass and shiny steel of the Hong Kong skyline, and beyond that the steep green hills that make Asia's most modern city one of its most beautiful as well. The proprietor was a portly, friendly man who always wore a suit and tie; he looked quite ordinary and no one knew how he managed to get visas from a country which had not allowed individual, unsupervised travel in over thirty years and which arguably has *never* allowed it, at least since the days of Marco Polo, except when forced to do so by the West.

Rumors of the shop reached Bangkok. I didn't quite believe them but I could not put them out of my mind and a few days later I flew to Hong Kong. I left my passport at the shop and after four days I had my visa. It was written entirely in Chinese and endorsed with the blood-red seal of the Guangdong Province Public Security Bureau. My passport had evidently been taken across the border and someone inside China—a cop on the take perhaps—had stamped it.

Now, with hindsight, I think the Chinese government very likely knew what was going on. They were letting in a trickle of travelers as a test, before deciding to open the floodgates, as they have since done. But I didn't know that then, and there appeared to be something illicit and almost supernatural about the way my visa was obtained. All during my first trip to China, it seemed I was there only through willing suspension of disbelief.

On the last day of August 1981, I took the slow train to China. It was an hour's ride from Kowloon station to the border post at Lo Wu. I walked past a line of Hong Kong constables, all shine and polish and razor-sharp trouser creases, and across an iron-girdered footbridge that spanned a sluggish, reed-choked stream. That stream was the border, and midway along the bridge stood an impassive young soldier dressed in the baggy green fatigues and red-starred cap of the People's Liberation Army. He waved at me to stop. I showed him my visa and he smiled and stepped aside.

On the other side of the bridge, right at the edge of China, was a huge concrete hall built like a mausoleum. I walked inside; it was empty. My footsteps echoed on polished flooring as I crossed to a row of overstuffed armchairs, their plush but faded upholstery protected by antimacassars from the imprint of alien heads. A young nurse, her nose and mouth hidden behind a gauze mask, entered the room, and I had to fill out a long questionnaire designed to ensure that I did not have, and had never had, any contagious or communicable diseases. Sterility, discipline, and big gloomy buildings. China was just like I expected.

I took a train to Canton, a three-hour ride through hills and paddies, a muted, delicate green-and-brown landscape that was uniquely Asian but could have been anywhere in Asia. Then, without warning, we rounded a grassy hill and pulled into Canton station. I walked down a ramp, through a gate, and into the open air. I was at one end of a large square, an expanse of asphalt so vast, so featureless that, despite the thousands of people swarming over its surface, it looked deserted. All around the plaza were bleak gray buildings whose fortresslike façades gave no clue what was inside and discouraged any attempt to find out.

Someone in Hong Kong had told me that I could find a hotel in Haizhu Square near the river. Take the number 5 bus, he had said, so I did. I got off when I saw the river, and followed it to Haizhu

Square and into the hotel. I had bought a phrasebook in Hong Kong, and I showed the man at the desk the phrase that read "Do you have a single room?" Blank stare. Silence. Total incomprehension. I didn't know how to respond to that, so I showed him the phrase again, and, when that didn't work, yet again. Finally he led me out the door.

The Chinese tacitly equate reason and civilization with language, and many of them, faced with someone who does not speak Chinese, suffer from paralysis tinged with panic. In restaurants, I tried to order food by pointing, which had worked in Thailand and Africa and everywhere else, but when I did it here the waitresses gaped in amazement. I could almost read their minds. "What is he doing with his finger?" they were thinking. For them, I was an alien, inscrutable, impossible to understand. But, unlike the waitresses, this clerk had good reason to be perplexed. I had been trying to get a room at the waterworks bureau; the hotel was across the street.

That hotel wouldn't take me, and by the time I found one that did it was too late to do anything but sleep. I was wakened the next morning by the light of the rising sun. My hotel, twenty-three stories high, was probably one of the five tallest buildings in China, and my twelfth-floor window had an unbroken view of sun and sky, with a maze of brown brick buildings far below. There was, in every hotel in China, a thermos of boiling water, so I brewed some tea, drank it, and ran outside to explore.

Just beyond the hotel threshold I was grabbed by a grimy child with a tin cup. A beggar! I was shocked and angry to find beggars in the People's Republic and I considered handing the urchin over to the nearest cop. Fortunately I didn't; I gave him a coin instead, and walked on, following Liberation Road north from the square. The street was narrower than I expected. Torrents of bicycles flowed down it, but they left the center lane free for trolleys and buses, which were green and battered and always full and cost two cents to ride.

I continued walking north, out of sight of the hotel, and it was like stepping back in time. The buildings here were five-story row houses, finished with stucco and stone, proud and flamboyant mansions in an era when a five-story building was something to be proud of. Down a side street now, and there was almost no traffic at all, just old white houses and thick green trees and silence. Then a small market, rudely dressed men with wind-chapped skin squatting by piles of fresh vegetables, shining silver fish and clucking, indignant chickens. Nearby, a restaurant, dimly lit, cavernous and crowded. It was hot inside, and many of the patrons took off their shirts and ate bare-chested. One of them called to me from a rickety wooden balcony, so I found my way upstairs and joined a group of farmers, all of them smiling, all amazed to see me. An old man ordered for me: sweet and sour pork which, as everyone in China knows, is what pale-skinned people like best.

A few blocks beyond the restaurant I found a school, and peeped through a fence at a yard full of shouting, laughing students at play. After that, I went back to the main road, then through a gap between the mansions and into a world of small whitewashed houses and cobbled lanes four feet wide, the world of alleys which lies behind any street in Canton. The lanes were too narrow for wheeled traffic, and the people of the neighborhood used them as a communal patio. They brought out stools and chairs and put them on the flagstones, and there they sat, washing clothes and plucking chickens and talking to pass the time.

I wandered through the maze of alleys and ended up back on Liberation Road. The row houses which lined it all had overhanging upper stories, so the whole street was a long and shady arcade. There were hundreds of tiny shops and restaurants, most of them collective enterprises run by the local neighborhood association (which keeps and distributes any profits), and scores of street vendors, who were in business on their own. Some had wooden pushcarts stocked with clothes and notions; others had stoves on their cart and set up tiny sidewalk cafés; one or two even sold incense and hell notes to burn for the dead. The hell notes are an ingenious device; seemingly ordinary pieces of paper, when burned they are credited to the ancestors' bank accounts in the spirit world. Why do they call China communist? I wondered at the end of my first day there. Even their heaven is organized along capitalist lines.

In the morning I took the bus to the station to buy a ticket to Wuhan. China made me greedy. I wanted to see all of it and didn't know where to start. Wuhan, a large city halfway to Peking, seemed as good a place as any. It was one of the few places listed on my travel permit, a four-page internal passport which all foreigners were required to carry. You could not visit a town unless it was listed on your permit and when I had applied for mine the day before at the police station I had asked for ten cities, including Wuhan, picked off a map more or less at random. Most towns were off-limits to foreigners, and the list of open places was, like most documents in China (including the Peking phone book and even the country's leading newspaper), classified and impossible to obtain. It was even possible that there was no such list at all. The Chinese bureaucracy often gives surprisingly wide latitude to administrative officials, who can, it is hoped, weigh the facts in a specific case far more fairly than the drafters of broad codes and regulations. Despite all that, the first English phrase many bureaucrats learn is, "It is clearly forbidden by our regulations." And one of the first Chinese words I came to recognize was *buxing*, which means forbidden.

There was a sellout crowd at the Canton ticket office. After three hours on line, which I spent rehearsing the words for "I want go Wuhan," my turn came, but I got the words wrong and the ticket seller, a shy young girl in pigtails, panicked and shut the window. The people behind me, who had also waited all morning, panicked too and tried to pull me away in the hope that, with me gone, the ticket window would reopen. I clung to the railing but in the end I was shoved away. I joined another line, and the people on it insisted that I go to the front. The clerk at that window made a phone call, an interpreter came, and I got my ticket.

My train left at 10:40 P.M., so I took the number 31 bus back into town, south along People's Road, past tall buildings of weathered gray stone with colonnades like Greek temples. Once the offices of European banks and corporations, they had long since been converted into shops, apartments, and warehouses. A short walk west and I found myself at the river, a narrow, quiet part of it with thick green trees, old stone bridges, and people fishing from the bank. I followed an alley and found a market hidden at the end of it. I squeezed past tables heaped high with herbs and spices. There were starfish and snakeskins and deer horns and other, stranger things I could not identify. Beyond the herbal medicines was a section that looked like a zoo, piles of wire cages stuffed with monkeys and owls and civets and pangolins. (Pangolins are strange little mammals which look like dwarf armadillos.) A young, ruddy-faced man was busily skinning a live pangolin, and an older man was heating a pan to fry it. I pushed my way through the crowds, wanting to leave that place as fast as I could, and I found myself in the section where dogs were butchered. An old man was dickering over the price of a freshly cut dog haunch. I ran down the first alley I saw, and I was surrounded by flowers. There were potted plants and goldfish and strangely shaped rocks, all for sale. Old men ate dogs but they also kept gardens and even those who had no yard to landscape could afford to keep a plant or fish or a singing cricket in a cage.

Night fell, and the dimly lit streets grew quiet. People strolled along the avenues; in the side streets, families sat outside their houses, the men in bright white undershirts, Mao jackets carefully set aside, everyone relaxing in the cool air of the night. I went back to the station. There was a separate waiting room for each train and I followed the signs to mine. At ten o'clock, a platoon of blue-suited guards checked each ticket, herded the huge crowd into two neat lines, and marched us off to the platform. There another troop of blue-suits split the lines into ten smaller lines, each positioned at the exact spot where one of the ten cars would stop. A loudspeaker played a stirring march and the long green train slowly glided in.

At the sight of the train, everyone dashed for the doors and the orderly lines dissolved into a mob. Everyone shoved everybody else; young men pushed their elders aside in the mad rush to be first on board. Some of the blue-suits shouted at the milling crowd, but most recognized the limits of their power and kept silent. I, like the rest, wormed my way on board and found myself in a new, brightly lit car with thinly padded wooden seats, each of them numbered. All of the tickets had seat numbers stamped on them, so there was no reason to shove at all.

I found my seat, martial music blasted from the station speakers, and the train pulled out. It was precisely 10:40 P.M. The music didn't stop; instead it grew louder and I realized there were speakers on the train. China probably has more loudspeakers than any other nation on earth. I saw them in village houses and tied to trees beside the rice fields. I heard their tinny bellow from behind brick walls, strident female voices shouting "One-Two-Three-Four" as the factory workers did calisthenics in unison. But the speakers on the train were the worst, because I could not walk away. I was a captive audience, forced to listen to a never-ending stream of marches, Chinese opera, comedy shows, and old American favorites like "Red River Valley" sung in Chinese. In "hard seat," which is what third class is called in a classless society, the speakers can't be turned off; in the two higher classes they can, but no one does. They are not viewed as an Orwellian intrusion but as a welcome relief from boredom.

Each train has its own disk jockey, who works in a cramped little studio in one of the carriages. That means that the speakers go off during the afternoon, because in those days every worker in China, including the D.J., was guaranteed a two-hour siesta. The right to an afternoon nap was written into the Chinese constitution, and it was one of the few constitutional provisions that was always scrupulously honored.

We stopped at stations during the night and I watched the people fight to get on. I saw wide-eyed panic in their faces, as if this were the last train to safety, the last lifeboat on a sinking ship, or the last food in a famine. At times I thought I was back in Karamoja. For thousands of years, the Chinese have learned to value order, politeness, and cooperation, but for thousands of years they have also known famine and privation, and in most of them (as in most of us) beneath a tranquil surface lurks the panic of a zero-sum world, a world in which only the shovers survive. I had always thought that the self-lessness and idealism preached by Mao and by Confucius before him were quintessentially Chinese, but I began to suspect that Mao sought, not to embody the Chinese world view, but to change it. He was more radical than I had known.

At one of the stations, a farmer threw his sack on top of my backpack, and then started shouting at me, evidently complaining that my pack had damaged his bag. Immediately everyone around me joined in, all taking my side and telling the farmer to mind his tongue. One must not be rude to a foreigner.

At five in the evening, we arrived in Wuhan. Sprawling, enormous Wuhan was once three separate cities and still has three train stations. I got off at the wrong one and found myself adrift in a city of three million, none of whom spoke English. My Chinese was improving; I could say "Where is cheap hotel?" and "I want single room." The first phrase got me to a barrackslike hall at the end of a wide, deserted road flanked by high walls and gray buildings. The second got me a room inside it. Two policemen visited me that evening. I later learned that tourists must stay in tourist hotels; cheap hotels are for Chinese only. The policemen tried to tell me that, but I could not understand a word they said, so after a while they shrugged their shoulders and left.

The part of town around my hostel was as bleak and depressing as a week of rain. The Yangtse River cuts Wuhan in half, and on the other side of it was Zhongshan Road, with grand old European buildings and block after block of shops and stores and theaters, every foot jammed with strollers from dawn to dusk, but even this, the liveliest part of town, seemed staid and dour after Canton. It was like being dumped in Zurich after a holiday in Rome.

Two days later I took a train to Zhengzhou, halfway between Wuhan and Peking. Most of Zhengzhou is a vast wasteland of brick and smokestacks and steel. China had more factories than any other country I had seen, except of course my own. Big and ugly, with tall, fat stacks belching noxious gases, they were a blight upon the land, but they spewed forth steel and concrete, trucks and tractors and TV sets. They made China well-nigh self-sufficient in products that other countries (even those that, like Thailand, seemed far more prosperous) were forced to import, at great cost, from the West. Most of the factories built dormitories for their workers, great and soulless brick beehives which lacked heat and even running water but which seemed like palaces when compared to the shanties of Bombay and Nairobi.

Many Chinese factories were incredibly inefficient and a few produced nothing at all. In those days, a factory's output was planned by the state and there was no incentive to increase it. Workers, no matter how lazy or incompetent, could never be fired; their jobs were guaranteed for life. A dreadful system, and it is being changed. Factories may now set their own output, keep their profits, and fire incompetent workers. It was indeed a dreadful system—except for the workers. I remembered the woman I had met in Calcutta. Her eyesight had failed and she had lost her job, and now she was a beggar. That could not happen in China. For a people scarred by the memory of starvation, a people who even now sometimes greet each other by asking "Have you eaten?" the lifetime meal ticket of a factory job is the most prized possession conceivable.

The streets of Zhengzhou form a grid. Each square has a factory. Each factory, each square, forms a unit. The unit is the most important organization in China, and every Chinese belongs to one, be it a factory, a retail store, or a department of a university. Each unit has a staff of supervisors, the most senior of whom are usually Party members. The unit distributes ration coupons for flour, rice, and clothing.

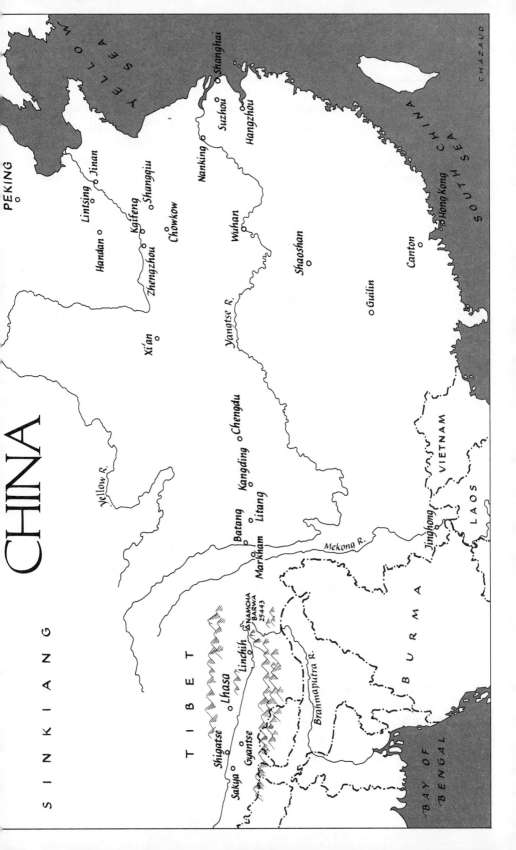

It determines who is criticized and who is promoted, who will be permitted to live in the factory's apartment blocks and who will be allowed to buy a bicycle. You can't change your job without the unit's permission, or marry or get a divorce or have a child. And often, at places like hotels and police stations, people ask your unit before they ask your name.

Zhengzhou is old, as old as China, and though most of the city is a checkerboard of concrete and brick, there is a part of town that lies beyond the grid, a neighborhood where parallel streets meet, narrow into alleys, and run off at crazy angles. There are old wooden houses and crowded open-air markets, and so many people throng the streets that every day seems like a holiday. This is the old city; the modern part of town did not obliterate it but grew up alongside it. I walked east along a street of ramshackle houses and just beyond the edge of town I found a tall mound of earth snaking through the cornfields. It was a fragment of the city wall, which was four miles long and was already quite old when Moses led his people out of Egypt.

Fifty miles east of Zhengzhou, at Kaifeng, are ramparts that are taller and more impressive. A thousand years ago Kaifeng was the capital of China. Here, in eleventh-century Kaifeng, scientists developed a creation theory of the universe remarkably similar to those propounded by modern physics, a creation theory with no Creator, and as a result of their speculation atheism became the state doctrine. At about the same time, a progressive prime minister instituted a broad-based program of economic reform, with price controls, credit agencies to aid poor farmers, and extensive irrigation projects.

In China, as in India, history moves in circles. During the past thirty years, China has undergone radical transformation, but all of China's changes find their roots in China's past. China has been cut off from the rest of the world for so long that even when its people are seeking to break with the past they turn to it for guidance.

China was less isolated a thousand years ago; ideas and peoples mixed more freely then and as a result Kaifeng even today has a Jewish neighborhood, a Moslem quarter, and a big stone church in between. Scattered about the town are temples and pagodas, some restored, most in ruins, and there are streets and streets of sagging old houses with carved wood paneling, rickety balconies, and elegantly latticed windows. History was everywhere; this was a part of China I wanted to explore.

There was a bus station near my hotel with a big map of the region, so I picked a tiny town named Chowkow more or less at random and bought a ticket there. A few minutes beyond the station, the countryside began, and rippling fields of wheat stretched unbroken to the horizon. The air was crisp, with a breath of chill; it was autumn, the wheat was golden, and soon the trees would turn to brown. I felt a fleeting touch of sadness; for almost five years I had moved through an endless summer, and the hint of winter in the wind was like a sudden reminder that nothing is eternal.

Once or twice we passed through tiny towns with crowded streets and low brick houses, and once we came to a crossroads with a thatch-roofed shelter where a wizened old man sold tea. There were no road signs; anyone who didn't know the way was probably not authorized to be there. We turned right, which meant we were heading south. The land was dotted with villages, huddles of houses with brown earth walls and roofs of red clay tile, the sort of cottages a Sung Dynasty artist might have painted to symbolize rustic man in harmony with nature. We drove quickly, too quickly, and all I could catch were fleeting glimpses of village life. I saw an old woman dressed in black sitting on the ground outside her house; I saw children playing with ducks beside a stream; I saw men and women in harness, pulling heavy carts and drawing plows.

That last sight astounded me. In all the rest of Asia, even in India (where sacred cows must work for a living), there are animals to pull the plow, but here, though I saw some draft animals, there was not enough food to keep as many as the people needed. I had not dreamed that China was so poor.

China is poor, unbelievably poor, poor in the one resource that matters: land. Most of China is barren. Only 15 percent of its area, or about 250 million acres, can be farmed; the United States, with one-fourth China's population, has 370 million acres of farmland and even India has more acreage per capita. As if that weren't enough, China is cursed with a climate so erratic and malign that it seems to give the lie to the thousand-year official policy of atheism. Every year, some of China's precious cropland is hit by drought or flood. Even as I rode through the fields around Kaifeng—which had themselves been devastated by drought the year before—much of Sichuan was under water and Peking was in the grip of a two-year dry spell.

Limited land and a large population make poverty and famine inevitable, and for thousands of years China's people lived on the brink of disaster. Even in the best of years, farmers grew barely enough to feed their families. In a year of drought or flood, the peasant would be forced to sell his land. He would then, if he were lucky, become someone else's tenant, forced to give up half his crop as rent and always at the mercy of landlords, moneylenders, and tax collectors. If unlucky, he would starve.

To the peasant, the right to own land, the right to sell land, meant in practice the right to lose it. When the Communists came to power, they eliminated private ownership and replaced it with a system of collective farming. Fields were communal and the whole village worked together. At harvest time the village sold the crop to the state and divided the proceeds among the villagers.

In the years between 1952 and 1977, grain production doubled. Some people still went hungry, but those terrible years of famine, when farmers were forced to sell their children or even to eat them, were things of the past. But in those years the population also doubled, eating up the increase. Hoping to spur production even more, China's leaders introduced a new method of land allotment. Under the new system, local officials assign a field to each household, which must turn over part of the harvest to the village. The family may keep the rest and may sell it on the open market.

Mao Tse-tung and his followers believed that China would prosper only when her people learned to be selfless. For the farmers, Mao prescribed cooperation and zeal, "plain living and hard struggle"—the same virtues that had helped his army win the civil war. To the Maoist, the very thought of people working for themselves and making a profit was the worst sort of heresy, but the new system has apparently worked wonders. Harvests have increased by 12 percent each year, making the People's Republic the largest wheat producer in the world. The scene at Canton train station was perhaps symbolic of larger truths.

As I rode through the countryside, I tried to pick out the villages that had gone over to the new system. Any field with a lot of people in it—and I saw quite a few—was still being worked communally. It was an exciting time to be in China, a time of change; the new method was being introduced and you could see both systems working side by side. All this lent drama to the panorama outside the window and I was almost disappointed when, after four hours, the bus reached its destination.

I walked down a street of brick walls and factories, which, though recently constructed, were the sort of rust-red buildings you'd expect to find in an old New England mill town. Chowkow was remote but not immune from change. Fluorescent-lit roadside stalls sold clothes and thermoses and carrying bags, and the street was quite crowded. I came to a row of dumpling houses; one had an outside patio so I ordered a meal and sat down. I watched the people strolling by and they in turn stopped to stare at me. Within minutes hundreds of people had assembled to watch me eat and the crowd was still growing. The proprietor pulled me inside, through a tiny kitchen and into a walled garden. There were gaps in the red brick wall, and eyes peered through them. From time to time heads popped over the wall and then fell back; the wall was ten feet high. The proprietor threw garbage through the cracks and hurled a brick whenever a head appeared. The heads ducked but invariably came back up again. This might be the only chance in their lifetime for these people to see a man who was not Chinese, and it was worth being hit by a brick to catch a glimpse of me.

A hard-faced young man appeared and started shouting at everyone, including me. He was apparently some sort of official. After a while, he left, and I walked off to find a hotel. Chowkow had a guesthouse for visiting officials, a large building, new but prematurely aged. The receptionist gave me a suite, two rooms of battered furniture and a toilet that didn't work. He wanted forty yuan (twenty dollars) but settled for ten.

The police came at ten thirty. There were ten of them, some in uniform (a Mao suit with red collar tabs) and some in plainclothes (a Mao suit without collar tabs). None spoke English, but all were softspoken and polite. They knew I should not be there but they didn't know what to do with me. Finally they left.

The next morning a young policeman appeared with a message. I was to take the next bus to Shangqiu. Shangqiu was a town on the main rail line, larger than Chowkow but also closed to foreigners. The bus left at two, which gave me four hours. I walked from one side of Chowkow to the other, looking for the older part of town, hoping to glimpse a carved wood façade, a roof with curling eaves, or maybe a ruined pagoda, the graceful ghosts of Imperial China, but all I found were red brick walls and harsh right angles.

The streets were even more crowded than the night before, filled with farmers from every village for miles around. They made the trip by bicycle or on foot for the chance to shop or stroll or simply loiter. All of them, shoppers and strollers alike, dropped whatever they were doing when they saw me, and I had soon collected a crowd of several hundred slack-jawed gawkers. When I stopped, they silently clustered around me, and when I moved, they followed. As I walked, more people joined the parade, and then still more, until those on the fringes had no hope of seeing me and might not have known what was going on at all. They blocked the street to traffic and spilled over onto the sidewalk. A squad of policemen in smart white Mao jackets came and ordered the silent, staring crowd to disperse but the people ignored them, paid them no more heed than they would a buzzing fly.

The policemen led me inside the bus station, and, eager to be free of the crowd, I followed. There were several buses leaving that afternoon, and at 2 P.M. precisely a spirited march came over the station speakers and a long line of battered buses rumbled out of the station in the vehicular equivalent of quick time.

Shangqiu, like Zhengzhou, is one of the oldest towns in China, but in the past thirty years it has been transformed into an array of six-story apartment blocks, a high-rise version of Chowkow. I arrived long past sunset, and moonlight and silence lent the stolid town an air of mystery. The streets were deserted, except for a tiny square where old men sat and a few children played. There was a hotel on one side of the square, and I rented a room for three yuan. I ate my dinner at a nearby dumpling stall run by an impassive old man who was too polite or too phlegmatic to notice I was not Chinese. When I got back to my room, the police were waiting.

There were two of them, an older man in a rumpled gray Mao suit and a younger one in a spotless white uniform. "Do not be afraid!" the younger man greeted me. "We are the police of the Chinese Communist Party." His words were not as reassuring as he had intended, but they were the first words of English I had heard since leaving Canton.

I showed the men my travel pass, and they noticed at once that the nearest cities listed on it were Zhengzhou and Nanking. I was several hundred miles off course, and I expected a scolding at the very least, but none came. Stay the night, they said, but leave tomorrow.

At seven in the morning, the younger policeman banged on my door. A jeep was waiting downstairs, and he drove me to the station. He helped me buy my ticket, and treated me to breakfast, a bowl of noodle soup. Shortly after eight, the Sinkiang-to-Shanghai express pulled in, the cars bright and shining despite their long and dusty journey across the Gobi. The policeman had a word with the conductor, and despite my hard-seat ticket (which would have meant hard-stand since all the third-class seats were taken) I was given a slightly softer seat in the next class up.

Twelve hours later I was walking along Zhongshan Road in Nanking wondering where I would spend the night. There were almost as many small hotels along Zhongshan as there were shops and neon-lit cafés, but none of them would let me stay. When I asked for a bed, the clerks all replied with that commonest and most frustrating of Chinese expressions, which is written *"meiyou"* but pronounced— or, more often, bleated—maayo. It means "there isn't any" but can also mean "I can't be bothered to give you any," and some sales-clerks say it almost by reflex. I've even come across one or two who brayed it out before I'd opened my mouth.

In any Chinese city, only one or two hotels are open to foreigners and the rest are off-limits to all but Chinese. A lot of tour groups visited Nanking, and the hotel owners all knew the rules. In the cities I had been to up to now, they hadn't and neither did I, so I had no idea why I was being turned away. After two hours of *meiyou*, I asked a traffic cop where to find a hotel; he told me to wait and telephoned for a taxi. Find me a cheap place to stay, I told the driver, and he drove me to a huge, modern tourist complex, a sort of Chinese motel, and had a very long talk with the clerk, and the upshot was that I paid eight yuan, about four dollars, and got a bed in a six-bed room in the same luxury wing where the hundred-dollar-a-day tour groups stayed. The driver took the fare, accepted my thanks but refused my tip, and left.

Thus was I introduced to the bewildering world of the Chinese tourist hotel, where every building has at least five grades of bed and every bed has at least seven different prices and getting one of the cheaper beds can take negotiations protracted enough to get you an oil concession in most other countries. "Wait till you get to Shang-

hai," one of my roommates told me. "They made me pay forty dollars there, and I'm Chinese."

I planned to go to Shanghai, but after hearing that I was in no
hurry to get there, and I spent the better part of a week in Suzhou,
an old and gracious city, a place of old stone houses, wood-trimmed
walls, and tile roofs, of sampans gliding on limpid canals, a town of
wood and stone and water, and of gardens.

One of my fantasies of life in China involved a garden. It was set
in a carved wood pavilion by a tranquil lake. In the pavilion sits a
scholar, his long robes ruffled by the autumn breeze. It is night and
the moon has risen. For a long, long time, the old scholar contem-
plates the golden harvest moon and its twin swimming in the rippling
waters. Then he picks up a brush, lights a lantern, and writes a poem
in a clear, flowing hand.

The gardens of Suzhou are filled with graceful wood pavilions, and
in the nearby city of Hangzhou is a teahouse named "Autumn Moon
on the Still Lake." But the scholars have gone and in their place I
found noisy young men in Mao suits and punk-style sunglasses.
There were also Chinese tourists, some from as far away as Urumchi
but most from Shanghai. They came in groups and families, never
alone, and instead of looking around preferred to spend their time
taking photographs. The father would leisurely adjust his ancient
camera as the rest of the family stood rigid as stone, holding a pose
intended to appear candid and casual.

In old China, taste and culture were the province not of the
masses, as in Africa, Thailand, and (to a much lesser extent) India
and Japan, but of the elite. Scholarship and learning were used to define that elite, and the all-powerful civil service was selected by examination. When the Communists came to power that elite was swept
away, and along with them went much of the politeness and aesthetic
sensibility that the West still regards as quintessentially Chinese.

The gardens of Suzhou, even the largest, are surrounded by brick
walls fifteen feet high. To the peasants of Imperial China, those walls
were insurmountable barriers. Now the gates are open and the gardens' charm is gone.

On to Shanghai. Thanks to a tip from a kindly receptionist, I went
to the Pujiang Hotel, where a bed cost not forty dollars but four. The
Pujiang, formerly the Astor House, had a wood-paneled lobby, wide
corridors, and ceilings twice as high as in any modern building. It

dated from the turn of the century and was built, staffed, and used by the Europeans who dominated Shanghai life until the Communists turned them out. The Astor House was conveniently located a short walk away from the British consulate, the Hong Kong and Shanghai Bank, and the Shanghai Club. Though the settlers have gone, the buildings remain; central Shanghai's granite skyscrapers were all built before 1940 and my first impression of Shanghai was of a city frozen in time.

But things had changed. The Shanghai Club was a Chinese-only hotel, and the waterfront parks, which once excluded dogs and Chinese, had been taken over by young, snuggling couples who could be alone nowhere else. That, too, was a change, a relaxation, although the young lovers were careful not to go too far; for those unmarried, sex was against the law.

Everything was crowded in Shanghai. The parks were teeming and the pavements were all but impassable. I went into a restaurant along Nanking Road and could not find a seat until a group of students called me over to their table. They had a banquet spread before them and I happily joined in. They spoke English and, though we talked for hours, politics was never mentioned.

Things had indeed changed. Fifteen years before, people like that would have talked politics and nothing else. Put politics in command, said Mao, and the students did, for in those days people believed that they could change the world. Attack the Establishment, said Mao, storm the citadel, and they did, but when the smoke of battle cleared the citadel remained unbreached and the young, idealistic students, including a million youths from Shanghai alone, found themselves exiled to remote villages thousands of miles from home.

Today, China is truly changing. It is at a turning point, a crossroads, but everyone is sick of politics. The old idealism is gone, though for many faith in Mao has been replaced by an equally naive faith in the West. Some youths, a very small but visible minority, wear blue jeans, gold crosses, and sunglasses from Taiwan. The students who entertained me did not dress like that, but they, like everyone else in Shanghai, were fascinated by America, so I invited them to join me at the Peace Hotel, whose downstairs bar had the only jazz band in China.

My invitation seemed to make them nervous. Two of them went with me, but the rest suddenly remembered urgent appointments and hurriedly took their leave. The three of us walked to the hotel and through its gloriously opulent Art Deco lobby and it was a miracle that we weren't stopped. China's top hotels are off-limits to Chinese.

We went to the bar and found a table. On the table was a neatly typed notice stating that citizens of the People's Republic were not allowed in the bar. That made my two friends very edgy indeed. Then the band came on. They were all middle-aged Shanghainese; they played the big-band numbers they had learned in the forties and they played them well. Perhaps those were the most modern tunes they knew. I ordered sodas for my friends; they gulped them down, listened to the first short number, and left. They felt as unwelcome in the bar as they would have fifty years before, when the Peace was named the Cathay and elegant Europeans in evening dress came there to dance the night away. The songs were the same then, and perhaps the band was too.

Now, of course, it was not the Europeans but the Chinese who put the Peace Hotel in quarantine. China, in 1981, viewed the West with all its traditional ambivalence. It wanted to import the latest Western technology but not the latest Western ways of thought. It wanted its factories to churn out a full range of consumer goods without creating a nation of consumers. It sought to open the floodgates and still remain in control of what came through them.

The government was, or tried to be, very selective. Marching music was good, and could be heard in every factory and train. Swing was not good; it had more than a hint of subversion and so was limited to places like the Peace Hotel. Disco dancing was very bad, and people were arrested for it. Westerners themselves were considered even more dangerous than their music. Students who talked to foreigners could be disciplined; workers who made European friends jeopardized their chances of promotion; people who invited Westerners into their houses were sometimes questioned by detectives the moment their visitors had gone.

In China at least, there is nothing new under the sun; everything has been tried before. *Modernization* is the current catchword; a century before, it was *self-strengthening*. The Imperial government planned for China to adopt Western know-how and technology but to keep her traditional culture intact. Their long-winded yet revealing slogan was "Learn the superior techniques of the barbarians to control the barbarians." A pleasant idea, satisfying reformers and conservative Confucian opponents alike, but a failure. Can it work today?

I left Shanghai and went on to Hangzhou and after a few days there I took a train north to Jinan. It was autumn in Hangzhou; the sun was warm and golden and the willows that grew around the lake still trailed leaves of green. Autumn in Hangzhou, but winter in Jinan, and after a nineteen-hour ride I stepped off the train and into an icy wind. As I crossed the huge and empty square outside the station, the wind followed me, swirling dead leaves in my wake.

There is a puritan, ascetic streak to Chinese Communism that reminded me of Buddhism at its most austere. To the radicals of the Cultural Revolution, beauty was a bourgeois indulgence, and happiness—except perhaps for the pleasant glow that comes with exceeding one's work quota—was positively subversive. This dour philosophy spawned the Mao suit, that drab, shapeless sack which negates the body as well as covers it. And it also gave rise to the buildings of Jinan.

Block after block of squat, thick-walled bunkers, and even the bustling crowds that filled the shops on Jingsi Road could not lighten the leaden pall that cloaked the town. Half the shops, it seemed, were liquor stores. People drink a lot in China, and the drinkers are always sullen and sad. Wait till dark and walk down any street in China and you'll see them, sitting on metal chairs in dimly lit cafés, staring at the dank concrete walls or playing drinking games (the kind where the loser must take another drink), with loud shouts and thinly veiled aggression.

The countryside west of Jinan was reputed to be crowded and undeveloped, one of China's many pockets of poverty. The newspapers claimed that the new agricultural reforms had worked wonders there, but since the area was off-limits to foreigners, no one, except the government, knew for sure. I decided to find out, so I bought a ticket to a town named Lintsing, a six-hour drive west of Jinan.

Just outside Jinan, the road ended at a river, and the driver carefully eased the bus onto a ferry. The river was muddy and not especially wide but the current was the fastest I'd ever seen and I was afraid it would sweep the boat away. Huang He, the other passengers said. The Yellow River.

The ferry fought its way across, and then we drove on. The land was rich and fertile, and the black earth was dotted with fluffy clouds of cotton. It was harvest time and groups of people were picking the cotton. All of them, men and women alike, wore brand-new shirts in the brightest possible colors. They must be well off, I thought, to wear good clothes in the fields. I saw a diesel-powered water pump, and a mile farther on we passed a big red tractor chugging along the road.

Lintsing was a market town and most of the business was done on the street. Farmers sold vegetables and sidewalk vendors sold shirts and coats and sweatsuits. The villagers were too well-mannered to gawk at me, or perhaps they found the pushcarts full of bright cotton shirts more alluring. A ramshackle old house had been converted into a restaurant, and an old man in a white apron served me a plate of meat cooked with green peppers. Some men from the town sat down with me. They seemed bemused and slightly stunned by my presence. "An American in Lintsing!" they kept repeating, as if to convince themselves that I was really there. After eating, I took a bus to Handan, a half day's drive farther west.

Tourists were allowed to visit Handan, but apparently none ever had, and the city authorities did not know what to do with me. My travel permit did not list Handan, but I was allowed to stay the night. The next day I was given a car and a driver and an interpreter and a banquet, all without charge but all compulsory. The guide was very friendly and polite, but he made sure I saw nothing of the city, except for a huge municipal park on the edge of town. The banquet was lavish and must have cost quite a lot, but the food was slippery and bland and all tasted the same. There were huge platters of such rare delicacies as canned mushrooms, which my two guardians ate with gusto. After that, they drove me to the station. We passed red brick houses, crowded plazas, tiny cafés filled with workers eating, and I had a fleeting glimpse of the city they had tried all day to hide. Then we reached the station, and they put me on a northbound train. It was the number 16 Canton-Peking fast express, the fastest train in the nation, and it did the trip from Handan to the capital in just under four hours.

China, in Chinese, means central nation. Maps printed in China use a reverse Mercator system that puts China at the center of things and consigns the rest of the world to the edges. To the Chinese, their nation is their universe, and in this, as in so many things, China reminded me of home. In Peking, as in Manhattan, I could sense an ambiance of quiet pride, a mixture of dignity, complacency, and sophistication. Everyone, even the stolid old farmers who drove donkey carts down Jianguo Road, knew that their city was the center of the world.

Apart from that, much of Peking appears pleasantly provincial. There are exceptions; Changan Avenue, as straight and wide and boring as an interstate highway, a scattering of massive monuments, one of which, the Great Hall of the People, is bigger than all the halls of the Imperial Palace combined, and a few formations of twelve-story apartment blocks along Jianguomen Avenue, all serve to remind the viewer of the power of the state that built them, but even in the midst of the vast expanse of gray that is Tienanmen Square you can look up and see kites flying.

On my first day in the capital, I walked south from Tienanmen, past Quianmen Gate, an ancient stone bastion as large as a Spanish castle, and along narrow, crowded Quianmen Road, the main street in that part of Peking. It was a bright, sunny day, warm and pleasant, and the streets were jammed. In another day or two, the cold would come and people would walk about hunched and swaddled. All of Peking was out today, trying to soak up sunshine the way a squirrel gathers acorns for the winter.

The vendors were out in force, young men for the most part, pushing carts laden with sweatsuits, long underwear, heavy woolens. Quianmen was lined with shops and restaurants; I had seen photographs of the street taken at the turn of the century and some of the buildings looked familiar. I went into one of the newer restaurants and found myself in a huge hall with shabby green walls, metal chairs, and big tables. There was a line of people waiting behind each chair, for this was the most famous duck restaurant in the world. After a long wait I got a seat and ordered a Peking duck, which cost the equivalent of three dollars. The other people at my table were visitors from the countryside; they, too, had ordered a duck but didn't know how to eat it. I showed them how to roll meat and skin and sauce together in a pancake. Then my duck came. The people of Peking are too blasé to stare at anything, but most of the diners glanced at me from time to time to see if I could finish the duck. I did, though I took care to leave some soup and pancakes for the many beggars who roamed the aisles, grabbing what they could from the tables.

It was evening by then, but Quianmen was still crowded. I turned down a side road and found myself alone. On either side were decrepit row houses that leaned against one another for support. That road led me into a maze of alleys, street after street of old stone walls, behind which lay—there was no way to tell. Those ancient walls guarded their secrets well. It was dark, that ghostly half dark of a starry night, but there were street lights at some of the intersections. People sat under the lamps, some sprawled on lawn chairs, others on low wooden stools, none of them alone, all of them part of a group. They played cards or chatted or sat in silence, as much at ease as villagers around a campfire.

Indian summer, warmth out of time, that shortest and most joyous of seasons, continued. At Badaling, where the Great Wall comes closest to the capital, the lush green hills looked like crumpled velvet and the wall was an ivory serpent meandering among the folds. Near the Ming Tombs, a wizened old woman sold persimmons, and the tree-clad hills in the distance had turned the color of ripe persimmons. It was a strange, illicit time; in the city, you could feel the summer sun and smell the smoke of roasting chestnuts and autumn leaves burning. And then the cold came, great icy gusts which swept down from Siberia, and I packed my bag like a refugee and took the first train south.

South, due south, and the wheels clacked and pounded as we sped across the Huang He, across the Yangtse, through golden wheat fields and later through shimmering fields of rice. This was a green land, the south, watered by lakes and rivers. Working in pairs, farmers pedaled huge wooden treadmills to pump water to the fields. They glanced up as we passed, but did not slacken speed.

I got off the train at Changsha, capital of Hunan Province, and hitched a ride on a tour bus going to Shaoshan. Of the hundred-odd places in China where tourists were allowed to go, all but a handful were cities. Shaoshan was a village, albeit the most famous village in China. Mao was born there, in a rambling old house built of mud bricks and tile. The homely cottage had become a shrine, and a long line of pilgrims waited to see it. Nearby, a more modern building held a Mao museum. All of Shaoshan would, I expected, be a museum, full of large, ultramodern buildings intended to show foreign visitors how much progress China had made since Mao's birth. A stage set, I thought, but I didn't mind. It was good to smell the earth around me, to feel it underfoot instead of seeing it through the sealed window of a speeding train. I spent the night in a guesthouse built like a country villa. I woke early; the air was crisp, a perfect day for walking.

The guesthouse was surrounded by gardens; beyond them was a plaza where three roads met. One led to Mao's house; another went to Changsha; I picked the third. The road was paved, but every mile or so dirt tributaries joined it, and after going several miles I turned down one of those side roads. It wound through the rice fields, past clusters of houses that looked a lot like Mao's, only smaller. Outside one was a baby, bundled into so many layers of clothing he looked like a plump teddy bear. He was sitting in a boxlike version of a baby carriage, made from wood and crudely fashioned, obviously by the parents themselves. Nearby was an old woman, the grandmother perhaps. She and Mao were contemporaries and might have known each other. She called to me, smiled, and brought me a cup of tea. The tea was hot water with a tiny shred of leaf floating in it, put in to show me she was not so poor and ill-mannered as to force a guest to drink plain water.

The woman was glad of my company; she was alone, for the rest of the village was working in the fields. It was harvest time. The villages around Shaoshan still retained the communal system of farming, and groups of twenty or thirty men and women worked together, reaping the stalks from one field and then moving on to the next. Another, smaller team collected the sheaves and dumped them in a threshing machine. The thresher, an oblong box three feet high, was powered by a foot pedal; it took strength to work it but compared to such methods as mortar and pestle it was a labor-saving device.

Each group of workers, or production team, had a leader. The leaders, at least in the Shaoshan area, wore white pith helmets as symbols of their authority. A mile or so beyond the old woman's farmhouse I passed a production team at work. The leader stood apart, barking out commands, and the farmers, seething with anger, shouted back at him. The leader had a row of ballpoint pens, the Chinese equivalent of a Brooks Brothers shirt, in his pocket; his feet were dry. No one noticed me, and I walked on.

A few minutes later, I saw another team. The leader was working as hard as anyone and his legs were spattered with mud. This was a happy team; the farmers laughed and joked and when they saw me everyone stopped working. They clustered around me, gave me tea, told me I should come to live with them. Did Communism work in China? I had often wondered, but now the answer seemed obvious. In some villages it worked ideally, in others it was a disaster, and in many, perhaps most, it was something in between.

Beyond the villages the plain ended, and the road skirted a range of high, rounded hills. Like most hills in overcrowded China, which has had a timber shortage for two thousand years, these were covered with grass and bushes but totally devoid of trees. A footpath led into the hills, and of course I followed it. The trail narrowed as it climbed and finally petered out altogether, leaving me at the bottom of a steep and bushy slope. I saw a girl herding goats. I tried to ask her if there were houses on the other side but she was not very helpful. She could not understand my rudimentary Mandarin, and she may have thought I was a ghost or a demon. Hoping to satisfy me, she shrugged and nodded and loped off down the hill. It was four o'clock; if I turned back now I would have to find my way to the hotel in the dark. I went on up the slope. It was not a long climb, but not an easy one. I fell and cut my hand. I rounded the crest and saw another valley below me.

I came to a footpath and then a house. It was surprisingly high, whitewashed, and far larger than the cottages across the hills, but like them it was built of dried earth, wood, and tile. A woman emerged; she had seen me climbing down the hill and she brought a wooden stool for me to sit on. I rested a while, and drank a big bowl of cool water with a tea leaf, token of hospitality, floating in it. Then I thanked her and continued into the valley.

Rice fields covered the valley floor, and there were houses on the slopes. Unlike most of China, the people here valued privacy and had the space to indulge their desire, and from most of the homesteads it was a five-minute walk to the nearest neighbor. None of them, of course, wanted too much privacy, so each home was within sight and shouting distance of all the others. The people of the valley formed a single team, and I saw them working together in the fields. There were no solar topees on this side of the hills, and I could not pick out the leader. The villagers seemed glad to see me; they let me run the thresher. It was just as well that they were friendly. The sun had set so I would have to stay the night.

The golden sheaves of grain seemed paler now, and the hills were tinged with purple. Soon it would be dark. I followed a path uphill to the nearest house. It was, like the others, built of earth, but this one had columns in front like an antebellum mansion. Near the pillars was a sack of cement and another of red ceramic tiles. A thin, middle-aged man was mixing a bowl of cement. He had already plastered half of one column and studded it with tiles. The new surface looked just like brick and mortar and soon no one would be able to tell that the columns were, like everything else in the valley, really built of mud.

Behind the columns, the door was open. I went through it and into the kitchen. Though the outside was painted white, inside the walls were bare, brown as the earth from which they were made. A large oven, built of sun-dried bricks, took up half the room. A fire burned inside, and a large pot of rice simmered on top. A woman came up the hill from the fields and entered the kitchen. She was stocky, middle-aged; I recognized her from the fields. As soon as she saw me, she gave me a bowl of rice, with two or three small pieces of vegetable on top. She served the same to the man outside, to a boy who ran in as we were eating, and to herself; this was the evening meal.

I ate and went outside. Twilight was fading into night. A few small children ran around the yard, chasing each other and giggling when someone was caught. Apart from their shrieks, the whole valley lay quiet, bathed in a silence as soothing as starlight, as deep and vast as the night.

The autumn air was chilly without the sun to warm it, and after a time I returned to the kitchen. The woman, seeing I was cold, threw a tangled ball of brambles into the fire. They blazed, warmed me for a minute, and then died down. She waited a while, and then threw another; firewood was rare here, even brambles. She asked where I had come from; I told her I had walked from Shaoshan. A group of men from the village came in without knocking and sat around the fire. They talked for over an hour, with the woman taking charge of the discussion. I couldn't understand a word of it, but the strident tone of their voices made it obvious that this was more than a casual chat. They could well have been fixing next year's quotas or the like, but I was certain they were talking about me.

By the time the visitors had left, I was sleepy. My hostess took me into the next room and proudly showed me my bed, a massive four-poster. It had a white cotton canopy, two warm quilts, and a wooden frame that gleamed with bright red lacquer. I had to share the bed with the woman's teenage son, but he was asleep already, as inert as the sack of cement on the patio, and he was still sleeping at three in the morning, when I was nudged awake.

Two men were waiting in the kitchen. They had come to take me back to Shaoshan. It was chilly in the kitchen, and I was tired. We'll leave at seven, I said, and went back to sleep. I had the bed to myself; the son was gone. I woke at dawn and found the men still there, sitting in the cold, dark kitchen. I recognized one of them; he was a clerk from the hotel. He smiled at me, a smile of pure delight, as if spending the night on a hard wooden chair was the most pleasant thing he could imagine. For him to have shown his true feelings would have been grossly impolite. I was sorry I had made him wait in the cold.

I followed the men down the hill and out of the valley. After half an hour the path joined a dirt road, where a jeep waited. Next to it stood the son; he had been sent out to guard the jeep. The men were silent during the ten-mile drive, and they left me in silence at the hotel, and my walk in the hills was never mentioned. There was no need; they had shown me that, however far from the beaten track I strayed, they could find me.

The next morning I was at Changsha station, elbowing my way aboard the night express to Canton. All the seats were taken, so I squatted in the corridor with a family of farmers. A young soldier offered me his seat. A few minutes later, the train stopped at Zhuzhou. A lot of people got off there, and after that there were seats for all. I curled up and slept as best I could. The following morning I got to talking with a student on his way to Canton. He spoke fluent English. The other passengers jammed the aisles around us, eager to see a Chinese who could talk a foreigner's language. They shouted questions for him to translate. The first question was, as it always is in China, "How old are you?" One man wanted to know how much money I made. "Tell him a lie," the student advised me. The question, polite in China but impolite in the West, posed a problem, and a falsehood, the student thought, was the perfect solution, which in China means the solution that gives the least offense. The questioner would receive an answer and be satisfied, while I would not have to reveal private information. But I couldn't bring myself to lie, and the man, realizing that his question had offended me, slunk back to his seat.

I arrived in Canton in time to catch the train to the frontier. I was glad to be in Hong Kong; it felt like coming home. Five years on the road, and I still could derive comfort from neon lights and fast-food franchises and signs in English. I wouldn't make a good Buddhist, I thought. Perhaps I was homesick; perhaps I had been gone too long.

I got another visa from the same little shop and went back to Canton, and it was as if a jackhammer pounding in the background had suddenly stopped. Tree-lined streets, soft lights, quiet nights, and I wondered how I had ever felt at home across the border.

I wanted to go to Guilin, two hundred miles northwest of Canton, but there was no direct train. I would have to go north, almost as far as Changsha, wait twelve hours at a junction, and then catch another train southwest. A traveler I had met who spoke fluent Chinese had told me that there were no long-distance buses in China, but one day while walking near the hotel, I stumbled upon a bus station. Only in China could a whole network of transport remain hidden, unknown to outsiders, even those who have lived in the country for years. One of the ticket windows had the Chinese characters for Guilin written above it. I knew enough Chinese by now to buy a bus ticket, and so I did. The young clerk was amused at my halting Chinese; I was apparently the first foreigner to visit the station.

A few hours outside Canton, the paving ended and the road climbed into the hills. From time to time we passed a village. The houses were made of earth and decorated with streamers painted with auspicious sayings. All the banners were red, not because red was the color of Communism but because it brought good fortune.

There was one other American on the bus. He had heard about the bus service from me and had rushed to buy a ticket. He spoke fluent Cantonese and chatted with the other passengers, who were farmers. He spent the rest of his time taking photographs, and there was quite a lot to photograph: those remote, ancient villages, isolated from change and time, crowded towns, views of hill and river. At one point the highway passed right through a huge market, or so it seemed, because the shoulder had been taken over by produce stalls and vendors and the customers used the road itself as a sidewalk. Hundreds of booths and thousands of faces, and the camera clicked like a gun on rapid fire.

We spent the night in a drafty big hotel in an old town by the river. The road was paved from there and by the second afternoon I saw the first of the limestone peaks for which Guilin is famous. Fifty miles before Guilin, the bus stopped in Yangshuo, a small town but open to tourists. I got off to stretch my legs, and found tiny white-washed houses dwarfed by brooding crags. I got my pack, found a hotel, and stayed for three days. The town was surrounded by green cliffs, tawny fields of grain, and collections of earthen houses huddled together. An old, bearded ferryman rowed me across the river. He had a hawklike face and a piercing gaze. On one side of the tiny wooden craft was a heap of bedding; his boat was also his home. I roamed the fields on the other side. In one field I found an ancient stele, in another a carved stone lion; history lay everywhere, like leaves on a forest floor.

After that, Guilin was a disappointment. Most of the city was de-signed by someone hopelessly infatuated with ferroconcrete. It took me six hours to get a hotel room. The clerk, polite, sympathetic, unctuous as an undertaker, regretted to inform me that all of the rooms were full, except the most expensive. I suspected that was not true, but if I had said so he would have responded with polite but righteous indignation. So I waited, and waited, asking each hour, and eventually (without anyone checking out) a four-dollar room sud-denly became vacant.

I encountered many hotel clerks like that, masters of deception. In China, deceit and politeness are often intertwined. Someone who of-fered me his seat on a bus or train would pretend, very convincingly, that he wanted to stand; that way I would not feel I had taken his seat. Lying is not considered an absolute evil, and, possibly as a re-sult, some Chinese are able to lie with a clear conscience. Many of them become hotel receptionists.

A day in Guilin made me yearn for the countryside beyond. The hotel had a train schedule, and tucked in among the fast expresses was a listing for a local train that went to a place I had never heard of. It left in the morning and I could take it both ways and be back by dusk.

The first stop after Guilin was Guilin North, and the next was a dull industrial suburb. Then came a town, a village, and a stop with nothing at all, not even a station, only a siding and tall green hills. I got off; I had five hours to explore before the train returned.

I followed a paved road and then a dirt road. It led through the fields to a village. I walked past squealing pigs, adobe houses, and a brand-new tractor. The road became a footpath that followed the crest of the hill; below me was a wide, majestic river with a range of rounded hills in the distance. I scrambled down the slope to the bank of the river and was rowed across it in an old wooden ferry. On the other side were rice fields and a cobbled path running through them.

Suddenly I heard music. Cymbals clashed; drums pounded. It was loud, discordant, and joyous, and its soaring exuberance embodied all that cities like Jinan lacked. Long before the band came into view, I knew I was about to join a festival.

Behind the musicians, a group of people carried a sort of open palanquin heaped high with gifts: new shoes and shining metal thermoses and quilts of red brocade. The litter was heavy but the people walked quite fast, eager to get to wherever they were going. After them came a ragtag train of small boys and idle adults who had run from fields and houses to watch the parade. They swirled around me like a stream, and I yielded to the current and followed.

Soon the fields gave way to open ground, and after that the path, still narrow, still cobbled, became the main street of a village. *Bong, clang, tsing-boom!* The band played even louder now, and the marchers moved faster; I followed, though I wanted to slow down. The village deserved far more than a passing glance. Its houses were built of hand-hewn blocks of stone. They had latticework windows, carved wood doorframes, and soaring roofs that curved like dragons' backs. They were centuries old, those houses, and would last for centuries to come.

At the far end of the village, one house stood apart from the rest. As we approached it, people rushed out to welcome us. Someone lit a string of firecrackers. We marched through a gate and into an already crowded courtyard. Around the cobbled court were the wings of a mansion, low, airy pavilions with large latticed windows. A swift, purling stream ran through the yard. The musicians sat down beside it, lit cigarettes, and relaxed. Their work was over. Someone brought them tea and bowls of pork and rice.

Over them, over all the large and happy crowd, hundreds of bright red streamers danced in the wind. Red was an auspicious color, the color of life and of marriage, and this was indeed a wedding. The procession had escorted the bride-to-be from her parents' house to that of her husband, but the girl had trailed behind, lost among the marchers. She was not the star attraction. The center of attention was the presents her parents had sent. In China, as in Kenya, a man must buy his bride, but the bride's family must supply furnishings for the new household. The gifts were displayed in one of the rooms adjoining the yard; it was a small room and people went in groups of two or three to inspect the presents. I saw them whispering together, evaluating the gifts, trying to guess how much they cost.

Food was served, large platters of fat, crispy pork, enough for everyone. Most people squatted in the yard to eat but a table was spread for a select few, and I was invited to join them. I ate a few pieces of pork and then I left; I did not want to miss the train. One of the men took me as far as the river and then ran back to catch the end of the feast.

As I waited for the ferry I could see the tile roofs of the village behind me; in front was the wide and lazy river and a clump of bamboo that swayed in the wind. The strongest gale could not break it. Everything in sight, and everything I had seen that day, belonged to a world I thought had vanished long ago. Fishermen glided by on bamboo rafts two feet wide; they trusted the river and let its currents guide them. The fishermen were old; they had seen war and liberation, Great Leap Forward and Cultural Revolution, and had weathered them all. From where I stood, between the village and the water, those great campaigns seemed like storms at sea, which ruffle the surface of the ocean but leave the sea bed undisturbed.

30

TIBET:1982

I first saw Tibet in the spring of 1982, from a train and from a distance. I was on my way to Turfan, a sleepy oasis town in the deserts of Sinkiang. The train was the number 171 slow express from Zhengzhou to Urumchi and it was the third day of the journey. It was an old train, but the conductors kept it spotless. They washed the floors every hour. Each evening the train leader would inspect the train and award a red banner (red not for happiness but for Communism) to the crew of the cleanest car. On the first night, my car won the banner, and all the next day passengers as well as conductors pitched in to clean our car and keep the flag. I helped with the work, and even gave my seat to an old lady, for which I was rewarded by a letter of commendation from the leader. It was, I thought, the cleanest, and the pleasantest, train in China, and it helped me understand how trains and factories ran in the days when workers had no material incentive to keep them running.

It was two thousand miles from Zhengzhou to Turfan, and we stopped each hour to take on coal and water. A long ride, but I had plenty to do. I spent the days taking notes and revising manuscripts.

After Guilin, I had made a vast, three-month loop around southwest China. Back in Hong Kong, I met, more or less by chance, a publisher named Magnus Bartlett who had realized that independent China travel was the coming thing and wanted someone to write a guidebook about it. I took the job, spent the next few months writing, and then went back into China to visit a few of the places I hadn't been to already.

On that third morning, I was reading what I had written about Jinghong, a tiny town near the Laotian border. I had been held prisoner at gunpoint in a village in the hills beyond the town, and I relived the moments of sheer terror I had felt when, having escaped my captors just before dawn, I ran and ran through swirling mist but could not find my way out of the village. And then, with half my mind in Jinghong and the other half gathering up the resolve to help mop down the train, I looked out the window and saw Tibet.

We were crossing the Gansu Corridor, a narrow strip of fertile land south of the Gobi Desert. There were green fields and camels and clusters of brown, flat-roofed houses, and far, far away and high above them snow-capped peaks sparkled in the sun. Those were the Qilian mountains, and they stood on the edge of Tibet.

White is the color of snow, of innocence, and (on maps that are honest) of lands unknown. Perhaps because they were snow seen from a desert, or perhaps because they were a part of the Tibet-Qinghai plateau, those peaks, burning with white fire and impossibly far away, seemed the purest thing I had ever seen.

Beware the sight of innocence, for it leads to obsession. The next day the train reached Turfan. I found myself in a world of mosques and markets, earth-brick houses, rich red carpets, and righteous-faced old men with long wispy beards and prayer caps. For a few weeks, I forgot Tibet. But the seed had been planted, and it grew.

Tibet was closed to foreigners, except for a few, carefully selected groups. Diplomats posted in Peking fought among themselves for the privilege of going there. Independent travel was forbidden, but there were rumors, whisperings, that people had sneaked in. I could try, I thought. I could hitch south from the rail line. But I was in China to write about places tourists could go, not regions where they couldn't. And so I went east, to Xi'an, that fabled ancient city that was once a rival to Baghdad, Constantinople, and Rome. (And which, in the year 763, was sacked by Tibetan armies.) I found restaurants full of ragged beggars; I found old abandoned temples hidden behind factories. Farther east, to Luoyang and Tientsin and the industrial wasteland of Manchuria, and then south and back to Hong Kong.

In a Kowloon bar called Ned Kelly's, I met two travelers who had been to Tibet. They seemed like gods to me. I was ablaze with envy and admiration and, at the same time, I wondered how I could be so naive. They told me how much the hotels cost in Lhasa but they said very little about what they had seen. I imagined a land of cold, thin air and brilliant sunlight, a place where, if only I could get there, I would see clearly for the first time.

I finished writing my guidebook in Hong Kong on my thirtieth birthday in August, and a few days later I went back into China. I had made up my mind to go to Tibet. On the night before I left I had a strange but comforting dream. I was on board a plane landing at Lhasa Airport. The laws of gravity had been suspended to allow us to hover between earth and heaven. Slowly, slowly, we floated down, as gently as an autumn leaf. We glided in stately silence toward the runway, and outside I could see people waving, smiling in welcome.

The next day, in Canton, I got a travel permit and a ticket to a city where tourists never went. The police of any town in China may add cities to a tourist's travel permit. Tibet is an exception—permission to go there can come only from Peking—but I hoped to find a town whose police did not know this. The permit they gave me would not be valid, but it would have an official seal, and in China such seals are rarely questioned. Many travelers, including the two I had met in Ned Kelly's, had tried this trick before me, provoking a blizzard of memoranda from Peking, so I doubted that there was an official left in China who did not know that Tibet was a forbidden zone. But if there was, I would probably find him in the region I was about to visit. Few if any tourists had been there before.

The first city I tried was the capital of the province. I went to the police station and found the foreign affairs office. The woman in charge seemed a kindly sort, but when I asked for Lhasa she glared at me as if she'd caught me selling dirty pictures. I left as soon as I could.

At the next town I came to, the young uniformed policeman on duty spoke only Chinese. I asked for permission to visit four cities; three were nearby and one was Lhasa. He took my permit and wrote in the three towns I didn't want. "You can apply for Lhasa in

Chengdu," he told me. (Chengdu is the capital of Sichuan, which borders Tibet, and the police station there was adorned with type-written notices that read "Permits to La-sa not allowed.") "I don't want to go to Chengdu," I improvised. "I want to fly directly from Chungking." "Apply in Chungking." "That will take a day," I said. "It will save me a day if you give me Lhasa now."

He picked up his pen, held it an inch above my permit, and stared into space. He stayed in that position, frozen, for about a minute, a very long minute, and I tried to keep my face impassive. Then the pen swooped and wrote *Lhasa*.

There were no more trains that day, so I made my way back to my hotel, shivering with shock and elation. The policeman is bound to tell his boss, I decided, if only to make conversation. ("There was an American here today! You'll never guess what he wanted.") At any moment I expected a knock on the door, but none came.

That was the beginning of a long and nervous journey. I had to get to Chengdu to catch the Lhasa plane, and that meant traveling halfway across China. If I stayed at a hotel, the police would check my permit, so I spent the next three nights on riverboats and trains. I had met quite a few travelers who had had their permits endorsed for Lhasa in one town and confiscated in the next.

On the second day I changed trains in Wuhan. I had breakfast in a hotel near the station. The hotel served ham and eggs and the wood-paneled dining room was full of tourists. Things had changed since the year before, when I'd stayed three days in Wuhan and not seen any travelers at all. I ate my eggs alone. I was bursting to talk about Tibet, but anyone I told would ask me where I had gotten my permit, and if the news spread, if a horde of travelers descended on that remote town and all of them asked for Lhasa, the policeman's superiors would inevitably find out and he would be in serious trouble. I promised myself I would never divulge the name of the town, and I never did.

The airline office in Chengdu was a dingy concrete building hidden in an alley near East Wind Road. Tickets for the Lhasa flight went on sale the morning before departure. The hotel had let me keep my travel permit, so I took it to the office and stood in line behind two Nepali traders. My turn came and the ticket clerk took my permit and called another man over. I wondered if they would phone the police; sometimes they did, or so I had been told, but this time they didn't. "Three hundred twenty-two yuan," the clerk said. I pushed a huge wad of bills across the counter and got, in exchange, a ticket to Tibet.

Ticket in hand, I walked through crowded cobbled streets of half-timbered Tudor-style houses, pushing my way past bicycle rickshaws and hand-pulled wooden carts loaded with cabbages, past sellers and gawkers and passersby until, at the intersection of West Jade Dragon Street and People's Road, the streets widened and the crowds thinned. Down People's Road I went, past the Exhibition Center built to replace the wondrous old palaces that were destroyed during the Cultural Revolution, until I came to the huge Mao statue. Mao was facing south, staring down People's Road, and his gaze followed me as I walked back to the hotel.

Mammoth monolithic exhibition halls, wide half-deserted boulevards and squares, and tall all-seeing statues; all of modern Chengdu glorified the power of the state. I had always assumed that the Communist Party was run like the cities it built—after all, Stalin is still a hero in China—but the past few days had made me wonder. In a government run by fear, a prudent functionary takes no action at all without permission from above; even an application to visit Canton would be viewed with suspicion. But in some towns in China the police happily doled out permits to go wherever you liked—and Peking couldn't stop them! Each town had its own policy and each jealously guarded its prerogatives. Some cities continued to issue Lhasa permits even after being told to stop. More and more, the system seemed to resemble the older part of town, an uncharted maze of crooked, nameless alleys.

Flights to Lhasa leave at dawn and it was still dark when I got to the airport. The terminal had not yet opened and groups of passengers huddled outside, vague shadows in the night. The sky lightened, the doors opened, a sleepy-eyed stewardess checked me in. Soon it was time to board. The tiny turboprop looked like the doomed plane in *Lost Horizon*. The engines roared, the plane taxied to takeoff. It broke through the clouds and climbed toward the sun.

We landed at Lhasa three hours later, gliding in a lazy arc around the airfield, gently descending with all the slowness of a dream. Through the window I saw herds of yaks and watching herdsmen and the bluest sky in the world. The airport was fifty miles from the city, and the road passed through a wild, rugged land of rocks and rushing rivers, barren plains and tussocks of grass. I watched it all, trying to imprint every detail in my mind, thinking that even if the police in Lhasa sent me back that day, I would have a memory of Tibet that no one could take away.

I spent my first hour in Lhasa in the lobby of the Number One Guesthouse, a damp, chilly room with dirty white walls with slogans painted on them. The longest wall read SERVE THE PEOPLE! Several people from the plane waited to be served; it was just past midday and the receptionists were taking their constitutionally guaranteed naps. One man, a college graduate, spoke English. University graduates do not choose their jobs in China; the state tells them where to work and the state had sent this one to Tibet. He sat on the steps—there were no chairs—and stared at the dingy hall that might be his home for years to come. I tried to reassure him, tell him he might be assigned an easy job as a tour guide, but he could not believe that tourists would pay to come to Lhasa. To most Chinese, a posting in Tibet is the worst thing short of prison.

A young Englishman walked into the lobby. "There's one bed free in my room," he said, and I followed him up the stairs. His room had four beds, a wooden table littered with the remains of yesterday's meal, and, hanging everywhere, pencil sketches he had drawn of Tibet. Paul, the Englishman, had gotten his permit in the same town as the people I had met in Hong Kong and had spent the past two months in Lhasa; one of the other travelers who shared the room had been there for three. Most hotel rooms in China are compulsively tidy, and the cheerful clutter my new roommates lived in made me think of the Oriental Lodge and Freak Street and my first sight of the pagodas of Kathmandu, made me remember those far-off days when my world was filled with magic and nearly everything I saw seemed wondrous and strange.

"You can have the bed by the window," Paul told me. Through the window I saw a muddy yard, a few concrete outbuildings, the brick wall of the compound. Behind and above rose the Potala, the palace of the Dalai Lama. It dwarfed all this flotsam of modern China the way towering cliffs so often dwarf the tiny people painted below them in ancient Chinese paintings. Built high on a hill, the age-old palace had stark white walls that, thanks to the use of slant and set-back, managed to seem at once massive and graceful. It soared above the town like a god-king's sky ship come to rest atop a mountain. I stared as if it were a vision. Paul, in turn, stared at me; he had been in town so long he hardly noticed the view. Since he was English and I American, he expected me to say, "Oh, wow!" at any moment, but I didn't give him the satisfaction. "I'm going into town," I said instead.

Lhasa is twelve thousand feet above sea level and climbing a flight of stairs was an effort. I knew I should spend my first day resting, but I couldn't, not with Lhasa just outside the door.

Outside the hotel gate, as it happened, was a row of concrete buildings that contained a food store, a book store, and a department store. The food store stocked cans of Flying Wheel brand peanuts and Ma Ling mandarin orange segments from Shanghai; this was the Chinese part of town. It was not an unattractive neighborhood; the buildings were whitewashed, the road narrow and lined with shady trees. No one had the gall, or the energy, to build an eight-lane People's Highway here.

Paul had told me to turn left at the gate, so I did, and after half a mile I came to a junction. A huge billboard stood beyond, with a painting of the Potala encircled by ten-lane highways, all of them full of cars. Behind this vision of a brave new Lhasa were muddy streets and flimsy houses. The billboard was a border, the last outpost of modern China. I walked on past it and entered a foreign land.

Two or three blocks of jerry-built shacks housed small shops and cafés, and beyond those were buildings unlike any I had ever seen: flat-roofed row houses, with rough stone walls as thick as battlements. The walls were shining white, except for the part that framed the windows, which was painted black. The windows were large and oblong, and some had little wooden planters and flowers basking in the sun.

The street ended at a courtyard, a portico of pillars, and a gateway painted red. People filled the yard, most of them women, their hair in braids, their rough homespun *chubas* (the traditional Tibetan sleeveless dress) worn and faded. The women knelt, threw themselves flat on the ground, got up, and knelt again. And again, and again. Some had their knees tied together for support; some wore gloves to protect their hands. They moved slowly, but they moaned and muttered as they made the prostrations, and I felt in them a strange, barely suppressed frenzy that was at once alien and thrilling. One or two had the glazed, wide-eyed stare of cattle who, after days of thirst, suddenly see a lake just ahead. Just beyond the gate, the women knew, was the holiest shrine in the world. The Jokhang Temple had been founded a thousand years before, and the once-rough stones that paved the courtyard were worn as smooth as pebbles in a river.

The Tibetan Autonomous Region, like every province in the People's Republic, ran on Peking time. The sun rose after eight, reached its zenith at two in the afternoon, and blessed Lhasa with long and radiant evenings that made me feel as if I were cheating time. The streets around the Jokhang were never empty—even at the hottest part of the day there would always be someone shuffling around the bazaar—but as evening approached they came alive. The shrines and monasteries of Lhasa attracted pilgrims from all over Tibet. They came from the farthest reaches of the vast plateau, most by truck but some on foot, for a year spent walking was a small price to pay for salvation.

Day after day I was drawn to the Jokhang to watch the crowds. Their costumes all looked the same at first, but after a few days I learned to tell them apart. There were black-robed women from Qinghai, who wore their waist-length hair in a hundred tiny braids. There were men from Kham, with daggers at their waists and ribbons in their hair. There were nomads from the north with ragged yakskins thrown over bare shoulders. Lamas trailed yellow robes, vendors sold yogurt and yak meat and pictures of the Dalai Lama, and countless beggars, stray dogs, and children searched for scraps and handouts. And the whole vast, motley crowd was in constant motion, surging through the streets in a continuous parade. The streets form a circle around the Jokhang and, since it brings good luck to walk around a temple, provided of course you do it clockwise, everyone marched in orbits of devotion until, sometime after eight, darkness fell and ended the procession.

The bookstore near the guesthouse sold bright, colorful posters, mass-produced art for the masses. I bought several and hung them on the walls of my room. I wanted to make it homelike; I wanted to stay as long as I could. Paul and I and all the other travelers in town took our breakfasts at a teahouse near the Potala, and we made great communal feasts of yogurt and fresh tomatoes and Ma Ling canned sardines. The yogurt was sold by an old woman who could usually be found sitting on the sidewalk near the guesthouse; it was the only decent food in Lhasa. There were teahouses scattered throughout the town. Most of them were dimly lit and crowded, and had wooden tables and low, smoke-stained ceilings with wooden beams. One, just behind the mosque, had a garden, where we usually met for tea in the late afternoon. And after tea it was time to join the parade.

I felt at home in Lhasa but I wanted to see the rest of Tibet, to visit the places whence those pilgrims came. I started making short trips out of town. First I went to Sera, a monastery three miles north of the guesthouse. Those three miles were filled with concrete sheds and barracks and compounds with blank walls around them. Loud-speakers blared "One! Two! Three! Four!" It was calisthenics time. And then I saw the white-walled halls of Sera, rising above the factories like a pristine Aegean island above the wine-dark sea.

Thirty years ago, before the Chinese came, there were twenty-five hundred monasteries in Tibet, and Sera, which stood in the midst of verdant countryside, had almost ten thousand monks and was still not the largest. Today there are fewer than twenty monasteries; the rest are closed, and most are in ruins. The big red pagodas of the Xiao-zhao temple, which lies between Sera and the Jokhang, were gutted sometime in the sixties. Squatters have moved in, though the main hall lies empty, stripped bare except for a huge painting of Chairman Mao. The great monastery of Ganden was razed to the ground though Paul, who visited it, told me it was being rebuilt, lovingly but slowly, by teams of pious Tibetans. Sera has fared far better than most. It has two hundred monks, and the buildings remain. There are streets and streets of whitewashed houses; with ten thousand monks Sera was a city in itself. Now it is a ghost town.

Two hundred monks were enough to keep the main temples open. There was a service in one of them: rows and rows of red-robed lamas chanting prayers in a low, hypnotic drone that echoed through the dimly lit hall, ricocheting off the low red ceiling, resonating in niches filled with beatific Buddha statues and bouncing off walls covered with blue-and-orange monsters who wore garlands of severed heads around their massive necks. The oil lamps flickered; the chanting slowed. A young man in a windbreaker stepped forward. He was a Nepali merchant and the sponsor of this service. Carrying a huge wad of bills, he walked down the aisle, leaving money in front of each monk.

A few days later I hitchhiked to Drepung, which had once been the largest monastery in the world. Not all its monks had been scholars; quite a few (who were called *dob-dobs*) joined street gangs and earned a living as hired muscle. But those who studied took their studies seriously, and a doctorate from Drepung took twenty years of arduous study to obtain. Drepung, Sera, and two or three other lamaseries were the last repositories of a two-thousand-year tradition of scholarship and learning. Tibet, once a nation of warriors as fearsome as the Huns, had, by the year 900, become a land of monks and scholars. They crossed the Himalayas to attend the great Buddhist universities of Bihar; they immersed themselves in science and metaphysics and carried those heady doctrines back to Tibet, where a millennium of monks elaborated and refined them.

I found libraries in Drepung, stacked floor to ceiling with manuscripts, all covered with the dust of long disuse. There were three hundred monks at the monastery, all of them quite old. Soon the species will be extinct, I thought, but then I saw a young novice helping to light a prayer lamp. Later, while walking between two temples, I heard young voices chanting. Schoolboys in a classroom; I was sure of it. I searched for the school but could not find it; the chant went on for quite a while but I could not pinpoint the direction. It seemed to come from everywhere at once.

Drepung was six miles west of Lhasa. I wanted to go farther, but that was strictly forbidden. The police allowed travelers with Tibet permits to stay in Lhasa but not to leave it—except to go to the airport. Quite a few travelers tried to visit other Tibetan towns, and the lanky, deceptively boyish-looking head of the foreign affairs branch had become expert in tracking them down. He knew that anyone leaving town would check out of the hotel and would check back in on returning, so each day he leafed through the hotel register trying (and probably hoping) to spot the same name twice. Other, less subtle measures were taken. Drivers were warned not to pick up hitchhikers, and it was rumored that there were police checkpoints on the roads leading out of town.

Toward the end of September, two French travelers, Babette and Arlette, arrived in Lhasa. Babette had spent a lot of time with Tibetan refugees and expected to witness an atrocity on every street corner. She was surprised to find that the quarter million Chinese soldiers in Tibet kept to their bases, except for the one day a week when the army went shopping. On that day, the streets were filled with soldiers, gawky boys most of them, dressed in baggy uniforms several sizes too large.

Two hundred miles west of Lhasa was an old market town named Gyantse. There was a monastery there, and a ruined castle perched high on a hill. Babette, Arlette, and I decided to go there together; there was comfort, if not safety, in numbers. We checked out of the hotel in the evening (*alea iacta est*, I thought) and at half past six the next morning we tiptoed through dark and silent corridors to the hotel gate which happily had not been locked that night. A month or two before, we could have stood outside the hotel and flagged down the first truck that came, but drivers didn't stop for hitchhikers anymore and our only chance of a ride was the passenger trucks that left from the Jokhang. I hoped there was a truck that day.

It was still night and the streets were deserted. We got to the old city by seven. A five-ton flatbed truck was parked near that huge painting of cars and highways that we travelers called the Lhasa 2000 sign. The back was full of passengers. "Where are you going?" I asked them. Most Tibetans speak a few words of Chinese though many are reluctant to admit it. "Shigatse," an old man replied. The road to Shigatse passed through Gyantse, so we climbed in the truck and waited.

More passengers came, and then still more, and then the driver showed up and took our fares. By the time it left the truck was as full as a Freetown *poda poda* and the three of us had somehow ended up in the back, which is the part that takes the bumps. There was a junction ten miles west of town that would have been an excellent place to set up a roadblock, and we three kept our heads between our knees until we had passed it.

The paving ended and the bumps began. The road crossed the Brahmaputra River and headed into the hills. The hills became mountains and the passengers started to say their prayers. They prayed in a low droning murmur which sounded like an anguished wind. The road was a narrow ledge cut into the mountainside, and prayer seemed a reasonable way to pass the time. Ahead of us steep brown hills rose like a wall, their summits hidden from view. At the top of the hills was a pass between the mountains. The road curved like a serpent gone berserk, a series of switchbacks slowly rising. Three miles above sea level, and the road was still climbing. Suddenly, almost without warning, we crested the pass, and everyone on the truck shrieked with relief and exultation. A forest of prayer flags fluttered above us, there were snow-capped mountains on the far horizon, and spread below us were the brilliant blue waters of a vast inland sea.

It was called Yamdrok Tso, which means Turquoise Lake, and for the next hour we skirted its shores. Villages fringed the lake, and I saw rough stone houses, wooden fishing boats, one red tractor, and sturdy women in homespun dresses. After the lake came a range of hills and valleys, a barren, windswept plateau covered with half-dead grass, and, in the middle of the plateau, a concrete hangar where surly men in white aprons served up bowls of rice and grease: a truck stop, Chinese-style. We parked outside it and the Tibetans stopped praying. One man amused himself by trying on Arlette's sunglasses. An hour for lunch, and then another climb to another pass. Just beyond the pass was a glacier, a sheet of dirty ice. The road wound through a narrow valley, and I saw black hairy dots high on the hills around us. The dots moved and I realized they were yaks grazing. The valley widened, and I saw a few stone houses clinging to the steep brown hills. After this valley came another, this one far wider. Suddenly there were trees and walls and houses. The truck stopped then, and the driver said "Gyantse."

We stayed a week in Gyantse. I had seen a photograph of the town taken in the 1930s, and, despite a disastrous flood in the early fifties, the town had, in outward appearance at least, changed but little. There were two high hills and a straggle of low stone houses spread between them. At the foot of one of the hills was the monastery; atop the other was an ancient castle. Between the two ran a cobbled street lined with old row houses whose stone walls were roughly plastered with earth. There were shops and stalls and vendors; this street was the town's marketplace. Farmers sold fresh butter and very stale cheese. One of them gave me a pat of yak butter. It tasted like Roquefort cheese.

At the end of the street loomed the high brown walls of the monastery. Outside the main hall sat a circle of older men, with a half-completed sculpture in the middle. The men were making gods from clay and their hands were muddy. Much of the building had been damaged during the sixties; now it was being restored. Many of the original frescoes remained intact, and, crossing an inner courtyard and climbing a rickety ladder, I found a huge chapel whose walls were covered with superb mandalas. Two monks sat by a window. They were reading a book whose pages were two inches high and a foot wide. "Dalai Lama foto," one of them called to me. I had bought a wallet-sized photograph of the Dalai Lama in the Lhasa market, so I pulled it out and gave it to him. He smiled, touched it to his forehead, and handed it back. He was not, as I had thought he was, trying to beg a photograph. Like every Tibetan, he already had one of his own. He simply wanted to see which side I was on.

Outside, a caravan of yaks, their horns adorned with red ribbons, plodded between the main hall and the five-hundred-year-old Golden Temple. The hall, long, low and oblong, looked like any other temple in Tibet, but the Golden Temple was unique. Like St. Basil's in Moscow, it is hard to say whether it was the work of a madman or a genius. Five whitewashed stories rise like steps, and concealed within each story are twenty chapels, windowless, every inch covered with frescoes as vivid as nightmare visions. Atop the hundred chapels is a huge white cylinder; on top of that, another square, with eyes painted on the outer walls; and above that is a delicate bronze pagoda, covered with gilt filigree and several stories high.

Behind the Golden Temple was a hill, and halfway up was a ruined pavilion. Its steps were level with the golden crown of the Golden Temple, and far below were tiny mud-brown houses, a muddy river, a dusty cobbled road. The town was like an island, and all around it, stretching as far as I could see, shimmered a sea of golden barley as big and bright as Yamdrok Tso. It was a long, hard climb to the pavilion, but something about the scene—the silence perhaps, or the perspective, or the way the barley rippled in the wind—something, in any case, that I could never define drew me there again and again. I felt that something most toward sunset, when the vast and silent valley seemed enchanted, asleep and wrapped in a spell. Nothing moved at all except the wind.

Those fields of grain were a sure sign that villages lay beyond. Early one morning Babette and I set off down the road, through the fields, and across the river. We found another road and followed it past mud-brick houses and, an hour outside town, a schoolhouse. Wide-eyed village children sat in rows as the teacher wrote a sentence in Tibetan on a blackboard. We saw hills in the distance, and the road, by now little more than a footpath, went to join them. "Let's see where it goes," I said, and we did.

Before the Chinese occupation, the monasteries and nobles owned huge estates and most Tibetans farmed someone else's land. The Chinese broke up the estates but forced the Tibetans to farm communally and to plant wheat instead of barley. Wheat cannot grow in Tibet, and the people were, according to refugees, reduced to starvation. Later, reforms were made and beginning in 1980 farmers were allowed to grow what they liked and sell their produce in the markets.

Disaster, famine, and then reform; that was Tibet's recent past as we knew it. But no outsiders had visited a Tibetan village in thirty years, so all our knowledge was based on hearsay, on the reports of witnesses all of whom were biased. Babette and I hoped to find a village and see conditions for ourselves.

A few miles beyond the school, the fields ended. Beyond was a flat and arid wasteland of stony, sunbaked soil. Somewhere in the middle of it the road petered out, as if dried up by the fierce heat of the sun. By now the fields had shrunk to a line on the horizon, a vague mirage in a world of sun and glare and rock. I saw something far ahead of us; it looked manmade so we went on. After an hour, we reached it, stared, and walked around it, trying to guess who had put it there and why. It was a huge excavation lined with brick and surrounded by earthworks, seemingly without purpose and utterly alien. From the shape of the corners, we deduced that it was a five-pointed star. Perhaps it was meant to be seen from space, a road sign for galactic hitchhikers, or a signal to other planets that Communism prevailed in Tibet.

Whatever the star's purpose, it made a good vantage point, but even from the top of the earthworks there was no life in sight. We were lost on the baking sands of Tibet, which should have been amusing, since Tibet is not known for its hot climate, but wasn't. I was already covered with chalky white dust.

We could have gone back but then we would have walked all day for nothing, and neither of us wanted that. We decided to go just a little farther—as dangerous a decision as a gambler vowing to play just one more hand. The odds were against us. The population density of Tibet is about one-hundredth that of Nepal, and I was very nearly lost in Nepal.

The hills around us shone like beaten bronze. We walked on. It was almost time to turn back. Far ahead and to the right we saw the silhouette of a man. He was coming toward us. We waved and shouted but he didn't answer. He passed within fifty yards of us and never said a word. The desert had taught him not to chase mirages.

We decided to continue. The man must have come from somewhere. There had been hills to the right of us since the wasteland began, but we finally came to the end of the range. We turned right, into a hidden valley. I saw dots and lines, far in the distance. Another star, I thought; I was beginning to get discouraged. Half an hour more, and the dots became goats and cows. There must be herders nearby, I said, and ten minutes later we saw them. They were children.

They left their goats and bounded toward us. They were happy and excited and made little goatlike leaps as they ran. There were seven of them—eight, if you counted the baby one of the girls carried on her back. The boys wore Tibetan shirts and baggy trousers; one had a green army cap and a red sleeveless sweater. The girls had on black homespun *chubas* and factory-made blouses; they wore pink plastic bangles and ribbons in their hair. All of them were covered with dust and mud. I sat down and the children sat around, giggling, touching each other for reassurance, very excited and slightly afraid.

I looked behind them and there was the village: low adobe houses, flat roofs shaggy with sheaves of barley, mud-brick walls concealing hidden gardens. The pale brown houses harmonized with the hills beyond. Everything, in fact, seemed to blend together—the houses, the tawny stubble of the pastures, the strangely purple hills, the pale blue sky—all washed and united by the clear, liquid light of the high plateau. Sunlight does strange things at that altitude. We had been climbing ever since leaving Gyantse and by now we had reached fourteen thousand feet, which is roughly halfway to the stratosphere. This hidden valley at the top of the world seemed the prettiest spot I had ever seen.

Of course it wasn't. Its natural charm was embellished, made irresistible simply because it was hidden, hard to get to, and in Tibet. And we had to leave. If we stayed more than half an hour, we would have to cross the river in the dark.

But now the men were coming. They had seen the children abandon their flocks and ran out to see why. One was wearing a black *chuba* and red felt boots. Another had an old shirt, trousers, and a black cotton sweater. He drove up in a horse-drawn wagon; the Chinese had brought the wheel to Tibet. Next came a gray-haired woman. She had a mud-stained *chuba*, turquoise and coral earrings, and a face that time and the weather had wrinkled into sagacity. The men stepped aside to let her pass. She led us through a gate and a garden and into her house. A large crowd—the entire village probably—soon filled the garden. They stared at us through the windows. The windows were made of glass and set in wooden frames so new I could almost smell the resin. The whole room looked fresh and clean; it was either newly built or newly renovated. The house next door, just visible over the garden wall, was having a new wing added, and the yard was littered with planks and boards.

The woman poured us tea from a thermos. Then she rummaged in a big wooden chest, the kind that pirates used to bury treasure. With the triumphant grin of a magician who produces a unicorn when you expected a rabbit, she pulled out a handful of tiny potatoes. Food was scarce here, it seemed, but the village was more prosperous than many I had seen across the border in Nepal. Hanging from a peg on the wall was a transistor radio in a leather case. Next to it, in a gilded frame, was a photograph of the Dalai Lama.

Soon, far too soon, it was time to leave. We tried, as best we could, to thank the woman, hoping she would not be offended that we expressed our gratitude in Chinese. I walked around the village, looking over walls and into gardens. Some of the older houses were built of large, rough blocks of stone that looked scavenged rather than hewn. Two of the houses had tall stone towers, but there was no time to visit them. One last lingering stare and then we left without looking back.

Babette, who never liked to use the same road twice, said there was probably a shortcut through the hills. Instead of turning where we had turned before, she said, we should go straight. We did, and found a line of rounded knolls covered with short green grass. We kept the hills on our left and reached the Gyantse rest house just before sunset.

The next evening Babette and Arlette got a ride on a jeep going back to Lhasa. I stayed another day in Gyantse, walked across the hill behind the Golden Temple, and found a small village, a rushing stream, and a Chinese-built hydroelectric power station. In the morning I took a bus to Shigatse, which lay forty miles west of Gyantse, across a copper-colored plain. Shigatse was the second largest town in Tibet—tiny Gyantse, barely more than a village, was third—and its lamasery was reputed to have more monks than any other.

Shigatse's other claim to fame was its police. It was harder to spend one night there undetected than to stay a month anywhere else in Tibet. Don't even walk past the police station, one traveler told me, or they'll catch you and send you back to Lhasa. But I had timed my arrival for the first day of October; it was a national holiday and as I had expected the station was closed. I had three days before it opened.

The Shigatse guesthouse had rows of low prefabricated barracks separated by courtyards of flayed earth. Most of Shigatse looked like that. A town renowned for its beauty had been transformed into one of the ugliest places I could remember.

The Tashilumpo, Shigatse's lamasery, was cloistered from the town by a high stone wall. The only gap in the ramparts was the front gate, and the gatekeeper would not let me in. *"Buxing,"* he said. Forbidden. And he shrugged his shoulders to show he was only obeying orders. The monks or, more likely, the police, had decided to place Tashilumpo off-limits.

The monasteries in Lhasa had become moribund; Tashilumpo, it was rumored, was still alive. I spent the next few days trying to wangle my way in. I sat outside the gate until nightfall. Tibetans were allowed to enter and hundreds did, older people mostly, their heads bowed and hands holding offerings to place before the many shrines. I sat by the gate, watching them, watching the deep blue sky. Magnus, my publisher, had told me the trouble he had getting his photo essay on Tibet printed. Make the sky bluer, he would tell the printers, put more blue in, and they would reply that no sky on earth could possibly be that blue. Late in the afternoon, a long line of lamas passed through the gate. They carried hoes and spades and were on their way to the fields. The government required all monks to perform "useful labor." One of them dropped a biscuit in my lap.

With the monks gone, I took time off for tea. It was a holiday and there was only one teahouse open. Most of Shigatse was busy setting off firecrackers. Inside the tea shop sat Joe and Molly, two teachers from Colorado. They had worked in China, spoke fluent Chinese, and had been in Tibet longer than any other travelers I met. They had just come from a village called Sakya which, they thought, was the prettiest place in Tibet. It was a hundred miles west of Shigatse and fifteen miles south of the main road. "You might get a lift to the junction," Joe told me, "but you should count on walking from there."

I finished my tea and ordered another. We talked about travel, Tibet, and the police. This was inevitable; travelers in Tibet spent most of their waking hours thinking about the police. Joe told me about a Frenchman who had hitchhiked from Peking without any travel permit at all. One of Joe's friends had met him in a remote part of southern Tibet. The Frenchman hadn't seen a European in weeks, Joe said, hadn't spoken anything but Chinese in all that time, and the first thing he said was, "The police. I think they're after me." They finally caught him in Shigatse.

A string of firecrackers went off outside, loud as gunshots. "Looks like they just caught another tourist," I said.

The next day I found a drainpipe under the wall and wriggled through it into the monastery. I made it as far as the first chapel. The guards found me there five minutes later, dragged me out, and pushed me through the gate. I went back to town, found a government official, and had him write a note authorizing me to enter the monastery. The next morning I presented it with a flourish to the guard at the gate. "Wait here," he said, and took it inside. A few minutes later, a lama came to find me. Fat and impressive and robed in gold brocade, he handed me my letter and told me to go away. Outside the gate, a truck was parked. A group of pilgrims from Qinghai sat beside it. They had built a fire and were brewing tea. "You go where?" I asked. "Sakya," a man said.

I found the driver, who told me they were leaving right away. I told him to wait for me, I'd be back in five minutes, and ran the mile back to the hotel, packed and paid the bill, and dashed back to where the truck had been. It was gone. Then I saw it, coming toward me. The driver had gone to meet me at the hotel.

It was nearly six o'clock when we reached the junction. We turned south, and, after five or six miles of twists and turns, we entered a broad valley. Far, far in the distance I could see a huge black wall. An army base, I decided, or perhaps a factory. It was too big to be Tibetan, I thought, forgetting that the Potala was taller than any building in Peking. An hour later, we parked beside the wall. There was a gate and I could see temples inside. This was Sakya monastery; the temples, the wall, and everything inside it had been built in the thirteenth century, in the days when Sakya was the most powerful lamasery in Tibet.

Next to the monastery was an inn and next to the inn was Paul. "You got any food?" he shouted. He and Richard, an American, had been in Sakya for three days with nothing to eat but a plate of stale buns. "A can of ham," I said, and he dragged me upstairs. The tiny inn had been built in Tibetan style, and the long hall that was their room could have been a temple. It had crimson pillars and ceiling beams painted with clouds and flowers. Also five rumpled beds and a heap of garbage in a corner.

They left the next morning. Fifteen miles to the main road; they could walk it by noon and, with luck, hitch a ride by one or two. If not, they would walk; they were bound for Nepal and expected to walk most of the way. "See you at Studio 54," said Richard, as he and Paul headed out the door and into the cobbled lane that skirted the monastery wall.

They were painting the wall that morning in red and black stripes. A man stood on top of the ramparts, a hundred feet at least above the ground, and poured paint over the side. Mornings were cold in Sakya, and just beyond the dripping paint were sheets of ice where dew had frozen. A train of donkeys, bells jangling, filed over the icy cobbles. Inside the seven-hundred-year-old temple, monks were chanting; outside it, on a flat terrace below the wall, women threshed grain. They pounded the stalks with flails, drove cattle over them, and winnowed the fallen seed in the wind. As they worked, they sang, slow, happy songs, high-pitched and melodic. Their voices light as air, they sang to the wind, calling it to blow the chaff away.

On the other side of the monastery, and, like the temples, pro-tected by a wall, was a Chinese-style compound, with dormitories, meeting hall, and communal canteen. According to Paul, the canteen, which had been closed for the holiday, usually turned tourists away. That afternoon, a truck was parked outside it and workers were un-loading cabbages. I helped them carry the cabbages into the kitchen. The canteen manager saw me hard at work; stay and eat with us, he said, and I did.

Down the road from the compound were two small shops, usually closed and stocked with such surprising items as candy from Shang-hai. Behind the stores was a river. On the other side, the bank rose sharply. Tall stone houses, some of them quite large, clung to the hillside. In the evening, the steep and narrow lanes that ran between them were full of cattle being driven home. They spent the day grazing and slept on the ground floor of the houses. Those houses looked a thousand years old, especially toward sunset, and some of them might have been.

On the other side of the monastery—the side where black-robed women threshed and sang—was a range of low, grassy hills. That was where the cows were pastured. Beyond the hills was a narrow valley, ruined temples with prayer flags flying above them, three or four big old farmhouses, whitewashed and half-timbered. A young girl drove a flock of goats up a hillside; an old man plowed a field. The plow was pulled by a *dzo*, a cross between cow and yak.

At the head of the valley was another range of hills, and one day I climbed them. The high pastures lay beyond. They were used in summer, and I found a cluster of crude stone shelters where the herd-ers camped. Nearby was a large stone-walled corral where the ani-mals spent the night. It was the second week of October and the pens were empty. The flocks had been driven back to Sakya, where they would stay until next summer. Silent, windswept, deserted, the hills waited for winter.

Across a rounded knoll and down into another valley. A few goats grazed on the lower slopes. There was a lean-to at the foot of the hills, and inside, by a fire, sat a boy of fifteen. He was the goatherd and, having decided that his goats knew how to graze on their own, he had gone into the shelter for a tea break. I drank a mug of tea, and then went back across those wild, empty hills to Sakya.

That night I paid my hotel bill—five days, five dollars—and the next morning I left, on foot but hoping for a ride. It was early; the air was brisk and my breath made clouds. Noisy, slow-moving herds of goats and *dzos* blocked the road, forced me to wait until they had crossed it. There were no trucks that morning, only goats; the main road was fifteen miles away. The track was flat, fairly easy going, and the land beside it was dotted with fields and houses. After I had walked about halfway, a passing jeep took me to the junction.

I stood by the road, trying to flag a lift to Lhasa. Convoys of khaki-colored trucks, en route to the capital from the void of western

Tibet, rumbled past without stopping. Their drivers had been warned not to pick up hitchhikers. Six hours passed, and I began to look for a place to spend the night. I saw a village in the distance and started to walk toward it. I had one last, desperate idea. The drivers might think I was a freeloader, so I got out a handful of bills and waved them. Five minutes later I had a ride to Shigatse. I offered to pay the driver but he took me for nothing.

At six the next morning, I was back on the road, hoping to catch the first passenger truck to Lhasa. There were four that day; two wouldn't take me, one broke down, and I got on the last. It left at eleven, and I was sure that we'd have to navigate those hairpin curves beyond the lake in the dark. We drove fast and reached the high pass by sunset. Twenty miles of cliffhanging curves below us, all downhill, so the driver turned off his engine, the Tibetans started praying, and the truck coasted down, slowly at first but quite fast toward the end.

Lhasa had changed. It was colder now, chilly even at noon, and the hills around the city were covered with snow. In the morning the sky was steely gray; sometimes there were storms. One night, the Lhasa 2000 billboard blew down; the next morning, it was covered with laughing children who were jumping all over those ten-lane highways, using that proud painting of a space-age Lhasa as a trampoline.

Most of the travelers had left, and none came to take their place. Mine had been the last Lhasa permit issued. A group of Chinese athletes arrived; they had bicycled from Shanghai. Since my Chinese was limited, so was our conversation. I walked around the Jokhang but after Gyantse and Sakya the people, like the weather, seemed colder, and I realized that in three weeks in Lhasa I had not made a single friend. Some travelers had made acquaintances in town, and they told me that the people appeared unfriendly because they were afraid of the police. Still, the people (except for the pilgrims) did seem a bit dour. One night I heard roars of laughter in the street. I followed the sound to find a huge crowd gathered. In the center was a dwarf, and half of Lhasa, it seemed, had turned out to bait him.

Each day was colder than the one before; flakes of snow swirled around the Jokhang. Winter was coming. It was time to leave. I wanted to go by road and the first heavy snowfall would close the roads until next year. I heard stories about trucks caught by snow in the passes, the passengers trapped without food or heat or shelter; the army usually found their bodies in the spring.

Two roads led out of Tibet. One went north, through the bleak wastes of the Changthang to the dreary Siberia of Qinghai. The other ran east to Chengdu. Both were unpaved. The northern route was the easier of the two; the Chengdu road was over a thousand miles long and though far more scenic than the other route it took up to three weeks to travel. It passed through Kham, a region in eastern Tibet. People from Kham are called Khambas; the other Tibetans fear them and *khamba* has become the Tibetan word for bandit.

I fell into the habit of looking at license plates. A truck's plates could tell you where it came from; the first two digits told the province, and the third and fourth the town. Most of the trucks had 230 plates, which meant they came from Lhasa. I spotted the occasional 2312 from Shigatse, and a few 26s from Qinghai. One morning I saw a 233 parked near the Jokhang. 233 meant Kham. I kept my eye on that truck, and two days later I saw it being loaded. The driver was there. A big man, bluff and hearty, he looked the sort who would drink a lot and would be fun to be with, drunk or sober. He was leaving the next morning, he said, for Chamdo. Chamdo was the largest town in Kham. Yes, he would take me there. The price was thirty-five yuan. I was to meet him at eight at the house where he was staying.

I woke up at three in the morning. I was convinced that I would arrive at his house to find the truck already gone. By leaving before I came, the driver would be spared the unpleasantness of telling me he could not take me. And he must refuse, I thought, must surely know that the eastern road through sensitive, restive Kham was completely off-limits to outsiders.

I decided not to spare him. I crept out of the hotel, walked into town, and found the truck. It was a flatbed, and the back was open to the wind. I climbed inside. There were people there already, wrapped in thick yakskin cloaks. It was freezing. I lay on the floor of the truck, between two snoring Tibetans, half-awake and half-dreaming until dawn.

The driver showed up at eight-thirty, looked at me strangely, and started the engine. He had probably waited for me at his house. Before we left, he asked to see my travel permit. It listed Chengdu, and that was where I was going, so he was satisfied.

East of Lhasa the hills were brown and barren. We crossed a stream, and I noticed a few red bushes on the cliffs above me. Then the road started climbing. A few hours out of Lhasa, we crossed the first pass. It was under fifteen thousand feet, the lowest of four passes we had to get across, but it was covered with snow. A bad sign. But in the valley beyond it had not yet snowed. We came down off the icy, barren pass and found ourselves in virgin forest. Nothing, nothing, not even fiery dragons and horses with wings, could have surprised me more. I had thought Tibet was a desert and I knew that trees could not survive at such a height, well over fourteen thousand feet, and yet all around us were spruce and fir and tall shaggy pines, sumac and oak and maple. It was autumn here, and the sumac had begun to turn. The sumac grew in patches, splashes of red and yellow amidst the omnipresent green. Below the road rushed a river clear as crystal, its water so pure I could see right through it to smooth, rounded pebbles that shone like precious stones.

Late in the day, we turned off the road. The truck stopped and the driver got down from the cab. "This is my village," he announced. It didn't look like a village. There were rows of neat semidetached houses, their white concrete walls gleaming; off to one side stood a communal mess hall. "Come," said the driver, and he pulled me into one of the houses, leaving the other passengers to fend for themselves. Inside, a tiny room, factory-made chairs and table, photographs of family members hanging on the whitewashed wall but none of the Dalai Lama. A stout Tibetan woman in a Mao suit shook my hand. She had short iron-gray hair. "My mother," said the driver. We sat down and his mother brought us bowls of food and glasses of whiskey that looked and smelled like kerosene. "Drink," the driver urged. "Is good." I took a sip and succeeded in getting it down. More men in Mao suits arrived—uncles and cousins, come to welcome their long-lost relation—and they all drank together. Then they laughed, patted each other on the back, told funny stories, and drank some more. I managed to finish my glass.

I rented a room in the village guesthouse; rooms cost one yuan, or half a dollar, and the other passengers chose to save the money and sleep outside. I woke at seven and ran out, afraid the truck had gone without me, but an hour passed and then another and the driver had still not showed up. I went to his parents' house and found him in bed. "Ohhhh," he moaned. He put his hand over his forehead, tried to get up, and couldn't. "I'm sick," he said. "We stay here today, leave tomorrow." I had a bottle of aspirin in my bag, so I gave him three tablets. Half an hour later, he was out of bed, smiling, calling to the passengers to get on board, we leave right away. The passengers, who had resigned themselves to a day's delay, were amazed, and quite a few of them wanted aspirins for themselves. They were all in good health but a pill whose magic was as strong as that might—who could tell?—ward off hangovers for years to come. Not for the last time, I was reminded of the Karamojong.

"Aspirin, isn't it?" one of the passengers said as we bumped along the one-lane dirt highway. He had a white jacket and a superior smirk; a paramedic trained in Lhasa, he was going to his village a half day down the road. The other people on the truck—eight men, three women, a boy, and a girl—were Khambas. The younger of the men (who were the same age as Karamojong warriors) wore their hair long and tied it in raffish braids with bright red yarn. Some wore earrings and all wore daggers; they looked like pirates. They were loud and coarse, rude but honest. There was no spite or malice in them, none at all, but they would not tell a lie to avoid giving offense. I liked them.

There were times, though, when I hated them. The seat of my pants had torn on the way back from Shigatse, and the Khambas spent hours pretending to peer through the hole, speculating on the dimensions of what lay inside, telling me (using graphic, unmistakable gestures) how a man like me could enjoy himself with the three women on the truck. The ladies in question buried their faces in their hands and started praying; they tried to look scandalized but I think they were more amused than offended.

A few hours later we stopped at a grassy meadow by a stream. Tea time. I ran off to gather firewood. The other passengers had brought along supplies of tea and *tsampa*. You can buy food along the way, people in Lhasa had told me. No need to carry any, they said, so I hadn't. One of the Khambas gave me a bowl of buttered tea; another poured in a handful of *tsampa*. Tibetans drink their tea with yak butter, which is quite palatable, provided you think of it as soup and not as tea. When mixed with *tsampa*, which is white barley flour, the tea turns into porridge, edible plain but delicious with a spoon of sugar stirred in—and sure enough, another Khamba passed me a bag of sugar.

We drove through a town of concrete and tile and then the road started climbing, winding its way through high humpback hills covered with yellow-leaved trees. An hour into the hills, we stopped. A woman sat beside the road, calmly knitting. She spoke to the driver and pointed at the hills. I heard an angry rumble like a speeding train. An avalanche. The passengers jumped down. Half of them ducked under the truck and the rest pressed against the hill. I chose the truck. But what if it's buried, I thought, and ran to the hillside. But what if a rock hits me, I thought, and raced back to the truck. The Khambas doubled over with laughter.

The avalanche fell several hundred feet behind us. It was the first of four; we didn't even stop for the others. In the evening, after we had parked for the night outside a cluster of wood cabins, I saw half a hill slide down, a brief and roaring river of trees and mud.

The government had built rest houses every hundred miles or so where a driver could find a bed and a bowl of rice. This was one of them. I shared a room with a group of men in sweat suits who were going to Chengdu. The truck left at seven, and daybreak found us in a small but appalling town that bristled with ugly buildings. Sleepy-faced men in Mao suits stumbled through the streets; loudspeakers blared the morning news. An hour later, we crossed a long bridge and passed through a town named Linchih, where we stopped for breakfast in a restaurant that looked like a factory. Beyond Linchih, the forest closed in again and we had our tea in a wooded glen with a sparkling white peak at the head of it: a solitary spire, snowy and slender and framed with green. The driver had chosen the spot well; beyond it, the road made a curve and the mountain was gone.

We reached the next rest house after dark. I got a bed and everyone else slept in the truck. Some of the men built a fire in the parking lot and brewed a pot of tea. "Remember, we leave at five," the driver warned me when I left to go to sleep. That was a problem. I had no alarm and I couldn't even see my watch because the generator went off at midnight. I slept, woke up, dozed again, went to find a fire to see the time. Five-ten. I ran to the truck. Everyone was fast asleep, snoring, untroubled, oblivious to the time. Caa-ca-CAAA! I said. I had had my sleep cut short by chickens in a thousand towns from Bali to Timbuctu; now it was my turn. The Khambas sprang up, startled; then they laughed, grumbled, and headed for the truck.

We left at five thirty. It was freezing and two hours before dawn.

Dim shadows loomed above us in the starlight. Shivering in the back of the truck, I watched the snowy peaks take shape as the night parted, saw them turn pink, then gold, then white. Later we passed beside a frozen lake. Around us were bare branches covered with ice; above us, like points on a compass, four jagged, snow-capped mountains.

Later that afternoon, quite without warning, the forest ended. The land beyond, like most of Tibet, was cold, hilly desert. The hills were bare and rocky, but there were a few green spots in the valleys, and we stopped for tea in a grassy meadow where yaks were grazing. "Tonight no hotel," the driver said. "Sleep in truck." "Good, very good," I answered, but for the next few hours I thought about the cold, sleepless night to come. The others slept outside each night, but they had yakskins to keep them warm. As I worried, the road forked and we turned off the highway to park in the yard of a rest house. The driver jumped down from the cab; he was wearing a grin a mile wide.

The first thing I did, just to be sure, was to find the office and rent a bed. Then I bought dinner for myself and the two sooty-faced children, who had eaten nothing but tea and *tsampa* since leaving Lhasa. There was still an hour of daylight remaining, so I went out walking. The road ran along a bluff, past workshops and official-looking compounds. Behind and below the buildings ran a river; on the other side was a jumble of mud-walled houses. I scrambled down the bank and across a wooden footbridge.

Children surrounded me, children wearing khaki Mao suits and army caps, children with runny noses and slingshots in their pockets. I walked through the village (mud walls, glass windows, prayer flags flying) and they trooped along behind me. One boy wanted me to visit his house, another wanted me to go to his; they couldn't agree where to take me so in the end I went to none. Instead, they led me to a cairn, a heap of sacred stones each carved with Buddhist mantras, and then back to the bridge.

That night they showed a movie in one of the compounds near the rest house. Most of the village was there. It was one of the recent breed of Chinese films, a love story set in Imperial Peking. I watched until the poor but honest scholar won the lady, and then I went to bed.

The next morning everyone was excited. They would be home in

Chamdo by nightfall. Chamdo is a hundred miles north of the road to Sichuan, so when we reached the Chamdo turnoff I told the driver to leave me there. I had spent five days with him and his crew of Khambas, and I wished it could have been longer. They were the only friends I had made in seven weeks in Tibet.

Everything was hot and brown: the road, the plain, the distant hills. I sat in the dust with a family of dusty Tibetans on their way west. They built a fire, brewed a pot of tea, and shared it with me. Near the junction was a big brown rest house for people who were stranded overnight. Sometime around noon, three trucks came from the west and stopped at the rest house. They were big, half-empty flatbeds with plenty of room in back. The drivers had gone off somewhere but one of the passengers told me to jump on, so I did.

There were five or six people in back already: some wiry old men in homespun *chubas*, a few women, and an obnoxious young man of twenty. He wore a sport shirt and khaki trousers and as we bounced along the narrow dirt track he favored us with his singing. He sang loudly and off-key; he knew we others wanted him to stop and that, for him, was part of the fun. The road was a ten-foot strip of dirt with rock on one side and a long drop on the other, and at least his singing took my mind off that. The drop was on our right, so if a truck came from the other direction we would be on the outside when it passed.

The road became level; there were fields and flat-topped houses. The truck stopped, and one of the women got off and trudged off toward her village. I found a long rubber hose on the floor of the truck, put one end near one of the Tibetans and said *Ooooooo* into the other. Everyone wanted to try the tube after that; it was more fun than a radio.

Late that afternoon, we reached a range of barren hills, a dry, rocky wasteland with not a speck of green. That night we stopped at a concrete rest house that seemed to have sprouted from the rock. As soon as we parked, I went off to find a toilet—or privy, to be precise, since outside of Lhasa there are no flush toilets in Tibet. I went the wrong way and wandered into a schoolyard, but I saw what I was looking for and went in. There were, as usual in China, no partitions, and a group of schoolboys came to watch. Then, shouting came from outside. The teacher had come. He spoke in Chinese. "You boys, get out of there!" "Teacher, teacher, there's a white man in the toilet!"

"A white man? Nonsense." And the teacher came in, stayed and stared, wide-eyed and amazed.

There was a restaurant at the rest house and when I walked in the three drivers were already eating. They were sad-faced short-haired Tibetans who wore flowery shirts and leather jackets. They called me over and insisted on buying me dinner. One of them had a cassette player, and after eating they listened to mournful Tibetan music as they passed a bottle around.

I left them drinking and went to sleep. Slept and woke, and we drove off with the stars still shining. Still in darkness, we crossed a bridge that spanned a high-walled canyon. Far below us, the Mekong River rushed toward the torrid zone, carrying meltwater from the glaciers of Tibet to water palm trees by the China Sea.

Two hours later, we reached a town that seemed to have been built of clay: a red town, a mud town, streets and walls and houses done in matching shades of ocher. The houses were thick-walled, flat-roofed fortresses, most of them several stories high; there was probably a wood framework and possibly a layer of stone under the mud. The name of the town was Markham. It was smaller than many villages, but most maps show it. Names and dots look better than blank space.

We parked on the main and only street, just beyond a mud-plastered arch with a Chinese sign on top. I thought that we would be there for only a few minutes, so I jogged up and down the road, made a quick foray into a side alley, hoping to see as much of the town as I could. Those mud castles were, to me, far more exciting than the brick-and-concrete warrens into which all the towns east of Lhasa had been transformed.

I got back to find the other passengers lazily climbing down from the truck. The obnoxious young man had changed into a red robe; he was, I realized, a monk. He went into a nearby house. Through the doorway I saw him embracing an older woman, probably his mother: the pious, dutiful son returning home. He saw me out of the corner of his eye and waved for me to go away.

Several other passengers went into the house next door. I followed them and found myself in an inside courtyard. One side was open; two horses were tethered there. The other side was a crudely roofed arcade with a wooden ladder leading to an upper story. Straw was scattered on the floor, as in a barnyard. Two men, Khambas, dressed in black with red felt boots and daggers gleaming, came down the ladder and welcomed the visitors. One of the Khambas carried a sack of large white pellets. The passengers examined them and then started to dicker over price. I left before the deal was completed so I never found out what they were buying.

I went back to the truck and spent the next hour watching the crowds of children who had come to look at me. A few of the boldest climbed onto the truck for a better view. One of the other passengers passed by. I asked him where the drivers had gone and he pointed toward an alley. I walked down the alley, across a courtyard, past a cow, through a door, and up a flight of stairs, and I found myself in one of those large but cozy Himalayan kitchens: mud walls, big hearth, low ceiling, wooden cupboards full of copper pots, all of them polished. The drivers were there, seated by the fire, and a white-haired woman was doing her best to brew tea, cook dumplings, and carry on two or three conversations, all at the same time. When the tea was ready, she poured it into a long wooden churn and sloshed it around to blend the butter in. I helped to churn the tea—it has to be done vigorously or the butter won't homogenize—and I helped to eat the dumplings and then it was time to leave.

An hour later and we had reached the Yangtse. The Chinese call it the Long River—and indeed no river in Asia is longer—but to the people who live on its upper reaches it is known as the river of gold. It didn't look golden to me, but light greeny-blue and very fast and surprisingly wide. The river forms the border between Sichuan and Tibet, though until the eighteenth century the border was hundreds of miles father east and even today most of the people in western Sichuan are Tibetan.

The bridge that spanned the river had an army checkpoint on either side. As soon as it came into view, I stretched out on the floor of the truck for a nap. The other passengers, guessing the reason for my sudden snooze, threw their coats over me until I looked like a heap of baggage. Drive, stop. First checkpoint. Drive, stop. Second checkpoint. The truck started again and I opened my eyes.

We stopped in a village with a tiny shop where the driver bought cookies and a hairbrush. Then the road ran through a range of rolling hills and down into a wooded valley. I saw fields and orchards, red clay houses, and a town with tree-lined streets. The town was named Batang. For centuries, it had been a staging post on the caravan route to China; now it was a place where truck drivers stopped for lunch. There was a small but crowded restaurant and a row of stucco storefronts painted blue and green. One of the shops had a patio where old men sat in the shade. It was a pleasant town, the first I'd seen since leaving Lhasa, and also the first where anyone had bothered to plant trees. I had spent the past week on trucks, getting up at dawn, riding in back half-frozen, being bumped and jostled until sundown. I should have been exhausted; instead I was exhilarated, but the week's ride made those few shade trees seem like a lush oasis.

I found the driver in the café and told him I was staying. The old, rambling building next door was an inn. Rooms were big and bare, with planks for flooring and more planks, on trestles, for beds. The rent was thirty cents a night. The police came within an hour, as I had expected they would. In the 1950s, Batang had been a center of Tibetan resistance; after years of brutal fighting, the Chinese army finally crushed the revolt but Khambas, like Afghans, are slow to forget. The presence of a foreigner in such a sensitive area was bound to cause suspicion. But the policeman who knocked at the door did not seem overly suspicious. I told him I was on my way from Lhasa to Chengdu. An old man, stoop-shouldered and soft-spoken, he carefully examined my travel permit, saw that both Chengdu and Lhasa were on it, and was satisfied. "But this room is not very good," he said, making a sweeping gesture that took in the dingy walls, the warped planking, the bare light bulb dangling from a wire. "I will find you better," he told me, but I assured him that the inn was good enough for me. He warned me not to walk outside the town. "It isn't safe," he cautioned me, but he didn't say why.

It was evening, twilight, and I heard water rushing over stones, a sharp, clear sound as crisp as mountain air. It came from behind the inn. I followed the sound but didn't find it; I found instead an old and winding road paved with flagstones and lined on either side with tall, clay-faced houses. Behind its one street of trees and stucco, Batang, like Markham, was a terra-cotta town. The lane was very narrow and the buildings on either side joined together to form a solid wall, a wall that looked natural and not manmade, eroded rather than built, like the banks of a river with a few windows stuck in. As I walked, a few lights winked on in the houses. As day faded, the walls seemed even taller; moonlight cloaked them in silver and mystery, and behind them I heard the sound of flowing water, the ghost perhaps of the long-dead river that made them.

Beyond those ancient houses were wheat fields, and in the midst of the fields, about a mile from the town, stood a lamasery. I set off in search of it the next morning and, after getting directions from a puzzled farmer, I found a mud-walled building two stories high. The monastery had once been much grander. It had been razed by Chinese armies in 1905, rebuilt, bombed in 1956, rebuilt, and then demolished once more during the Cultural Revolution. Now it was being restored yet again. In the main temple, a large, bare hall on the ground floor, there was scaffolding everywhere and workers plastering the walls. The caretaker, an old Tibetan, showed me around. "Yes, there are lamas," he said, "two of them, very holy men. They are not here today; they have gone to Chengdu." Before leaving Lhasa, I had bought two photographs of the Dalai Lama, so I gave one to him. At the sight of the photo, desire overcame politeness; he snatched it, put it on the cloth-covered table that was serving as temporary altar, and asked for another. "The first was for the temple," he said; "this one will be for me."

Back in town, I went down a side alley, past more clay houses, to an enormous stone tower with houses built on top: the town gate, sole remnant of a city wall torn down long ago. Beyond the gate, slippery steps led to the river's edge. It was little more than a playful stream, easy to cross, its banks a tangle of exuberant shrubs and drooping willows. On the other side a path led uphill, past fields, fruit trees, and large farmhouses. I had now gone beyond the edge of town, a region where, according to the policeman, unknown dangers lurked. I kept a lookout for thugs and bandits, but the only living things I saw were a flock of goats and a boy running behind them.

I ate at the café and then went to find a tailor. I was tired of Khambas laughing at the hole in my pants and this was my first chance to have it mended. I stopped passersby, made sewing gestures, and was taken to a house in the old quarter. Inside was a large workroom with rows of tables and sewing machines. There were quite a few people at work, with a young woman in charge. She loaned me a robe and took my jeans, and all the tailors gathered round to examine the hole and discuss how it should be mended. It took a long time. I went up to the roof, which had a view of flat brown rooftops, willows, and the narrow chasm of the street. I came down to find the seat of my pants entirely replaced, tough new fabric expertly sewn in with French seams. I took out money to pay the tailors, but they waved it away. As I was leaving, the woman in charge took me aside, pulled out her wallet, and gave me a handful of ration coupons. It was quite a big handful, perhaps a year's supply. "For new trousers," she said, and she was hurt when I didn't take them. I went to the biggest shop in town and bought a poster of woods in autumn. Then I gave it to the tailors and helped them hang it on the wall of their dim and windowless workroom.

Dinner at the café, and then to bed. That café was a hitchhiker's dream. It had the only decent food in five hundred miles, so every truck that passed it stopped. Or so I thought. Early the following morning, I stood outside the café, waiting for the trucks to come. The sun rose, the day dragged on, the peak lunch trade came and went, and I still hadn't moved. All the loafers who sat outside the store, plus a hundred-odd assorted passersby, had gathered to watch me hitch. They cheered when they sighted a truck, loudly debated whether it would stop and pick me up, and booed when it didn't. Never had a hitcher had such a large and appreciative audience. At first, I enjoyed my brief instant of stardom, but as that instant lengthened into hours the crowd began to get on my nerves.

Everyone I had met had assumed that my travel permit, which listed Lhasa and Chengdu, was valid for all points in between, and by now I had come to believe it myself. But my permit would expire in five days and I had to be in Chengdu before then to renew it. Permit in hand, I went to the local government offices. They were housed in a gray concrete hall, its inside a warren of cubbyholes and bureaucrats at work. I asked for a ride on any truck headed east. A polite young woman told me no, that wasn't possible, there were no government trucks at all that day.

Late in the afternoon, a convoy of jeeps parked outside the restaurant. One of the passengers stayed to watch the jeeps, while the rest of them eagerly ran into the café. I started a conversation with the one who had stayed outside. He was shy, bespectacled, intelligent. He always paused to think before he spoke. He and the others were engineers on their way back to Shanghai after several months' work in Tibet. "Can I ride with you?" I asked, and the young engineer took me to meet the convoy leader. He scrutinized my permit and told me please to come back later, they would discuss the matter and let me know their decision.

I passed the time walking. A block beyond the municipal offices, a driveway to a warehouse had been turned into an open-air theater. There were rows of benches, a podium, and on the podium was a television—which meant that my quaint town of mud and willows had a TV transmitter hidden somewhere in it. Twenty or thirty people, mostly men, had come to watch TV; the rest of Batang, it seemed, still preferred to stay at home, spend the night in sleep or quiet conversation, or walk the moon-spattered paths by the river's edge.

The engineers left Batang the next morning. There were three jeeps, all fully loaded with crates and cardboard boxes, but they made a place for me in one of them between the driver and the engineer I had met outside the restaurant the afternoon before. Batang, altitude eight thousand feet, was on the floor of a long valley. The road followed a stream that meandered across the valley and then, leaving the stream, wriggled over a low range of hills into another valley, this one narrow and rocky. This valley, too, had its river, and I could see clusters of solidly built stone houses clinging to the cliffs on the other side. What little level land there was was strewn with pebbles; only stones could grow here and I wondered how any one could live here and survive.

We had been climbing since leaving Batang. We had to cross a pass that day, and then a high plateau. The road went through a part of the plateau that was white on my map, which meant that it was higher than five thousand meters, or sixteen thousand four hundred feet, above sea level. We stopped for lunch at an army camp. Wide-eyed privates hurriedly set up a table and brought us cabbage and rice in metal bowls, with little plates of peanuts and sour pickles, luxuries both, on the side.

After lunch came the final climb to the pass, and we rose above the snow line and entered a frozen land of white and gray, a world without color. Beyond the pass stretched the plateau, flat, windswept, and carpeted with short brown grass. All around us, yaks were grazing; scattered here and there were the tents of the nomads who owned them. The tents were black and billowy, like sails tethered in the wind.

The Drokbas, the nomads of Tibet, are an aloof, reclusive people who look down on those of fixed abode, even Khambas, and think of Lhasa as a lowland. They came to Lhasa sometimes, to sell and trade and worship at the shrines. They would set up camp behind the Potala, in traffic circles, wherever they could find a patch of open ground. Their ragged black tents seemed forlorn and out of place in the city, and they left as soon as they could.

Here, on the high plateau, those same tents were beautiful, as sleek and full of grace as a ship in full rigging or a falcon on the wing. This land of thin air and far horizons was the nomad's domain.

The road was straight and level and the tents were far away. A quick glimpse from a distance, and then they were gone. We passed another camp, and then another. "Let's stop at the next one," I said, "and take a look around." (What I actually said was, "I want look round that place.") As far as I knew, most Chinese thought of Tibetans as savages, and I met a few in Lhasa who had never set foot in the old city. "Visit the Jokhang," I told them. "It's not safe," they replied. And so I expected my suggestion to visit the nearest camps to be, if not refused outright, quietly ignored and politely forgotten. And if it were accepted, what would the nomads think to see a convoy of khaki-colored jeeps come tearing off the road to surround their encampment? Would they flee or fight?

The next camp we saw was a small one, three tents a quarter mile away. We turned off the road and headed for the tents. The camp seemed deserted. There was no sign of life at all. I ran to the nearest tent, pulled a flap of cloth aside, stooped, and went in.

It was light inside the tent; that was the first surprise. The yaks-wool walls were gossamer thin, and sunlight sparkled through a thousand tiny gaps in the fabric, turning the everyday objects inside to gold. There were sheepskin pallets on the ground, stacks of chests and boxes, woven blankets and wicker baskets, a wooden churn, metal pots and pans black with soot. I barely noticed the furnishings at first, and for the first few seconds paid scant attention to the man who rose to greet me. Something else caught my eye. The tent was very large, its ceiling too high to touch, and hanging from the center tentpole, impaled by an especially bright shaft of light from a large hole in the ceiling, was the flayed and bloody carcass of a yak.

He was a tall man, and he stood erect. His black handwoven *chuba* was patched and frayed, but the dagger in his belt had just been polished. He cared about his appearance. He had braided his hair, tied the braid with yarn, and pulled it through a ring of bone or ivory. He had a high, aquiline nose, skin like burnished copper, and piercing eyes that glowed with the fiery pride shared by nomads all over the world. There was no fear in those eyes, or surprise either. We were guests who had to be properly welcomed.

There was a pot of tea on the fire, bowls and glasses and a china cup. He gave me the cup, and then poured a glass for the engineer, who had come in behind me. From his trouser pocket, the engineer pulled out the only pack of cigarettes within a hundred miles. He offered it to our host. The nomad took one and lit it. Take the whole packet, the engineer gestured, but the man refused. A cigarette for a cup of tea was a fair exchange of gifts, but only a beggar would take a whole pack.

I heard tires crunching over stony ground. One of the other jeeps had turned off the road to see why we had stopped. There was another sound as well, a strange drumming noise I couldn't place. I left the tent. Behind it was another, which, like the first, was black and drab and big enough to hold a hundred men. I stepped inside.

And into an explosion of color and sound. Ribbons of yellow and pink, pennants of orange and blue, fabulous long *tankas* writhing with gods and demons hung from the ridge pole in a forest of festoons. Below was an altar, and a long low table covered with orange cloth. There were two lamas robed in red; they were chanting, and a short-haired youth in a yellow *chuba* was banging on a huge drum. The drum, like the banners, hung from the ceiling, and the tent was filled with booming and singing and swirling ribbons. An old man draped in a sheepskin sat and swayed and chanted under his breath. He wasn't a monk but he knew the prayers. He was beaming, and the boy smiled as he banged the drum. Even the monks looked happy.

I had seen services in Sakya and Sera, and though they were quite impressive it seemed as if some vital thing was lacking. The monks would go through the liturgy as fast as they could, as if they had more important things to do afterward. Here the monks savored every word and the boy in the yellow shirt drummed with all his might. He stopped when he saw me and got up to pour me tea. Then, his duty done, he went back to his drum.

By now there were two other strangers in the tent—the engineer and the convoy leader, who had come in the second jeep five minutes before and now wanted to leave. As we were walking to the jeeps, our host from the other tent ran out to say good-bye. I had one Dalai Lama photo remaining and when the engineers weren't looking I gave it to him. He took my hand, pressed it, then slowly walked away.

It had snowed on the far side of the plateau, and the eastern hills looked like wavelets on a white and stormy sea. Beyond, rising from that inland ocean, were the snow-capped peaks of yet another mountain range. The road zigzagged down from the plateau, through the foothills and toward the mountains, and all the way it was coated with ice. In a week or two, it would be impassable. It was dangerous even now, slippery and frozen, with a thousand-foot drop waiting if we slipped too far.

Slowly but safely, we came down from the plateau. After the plateau, all else was anticlimax. There were no more nomads or high passes. The weather turned cloudy and I never saw the mountains again. We passed through a town called Litang (altitude fifteen thousand four hundred feet), all mud walls and markets, and spent the night at a dreary place named Yakiang. Yakiang was brick and slate and smoke-stained concrete, satanic mills and factories and people with the grimy, hardened look of refugees. The town was built on a hill and all the windows faced inward, and it wasn't until I walked to the hotel's outhouse that I saw the rugged beauty that the town had turned its back on: a steep and rocky limestone canyon and, at the bottom, the flashing turquoise serpent of the Yalung River.

The next day we had a banquet at a tiny roadside restaurant. The food was Sichuanese and remarkably good. That afternoon, we reached Kangding (altitude eight thousand feet), the first large town I'd seen since Lhasa. The engineers planned to spend three or four days there, but I had to get to Chengdu sooner than that, so they helped me find the station and buy a ticket for the two-day ride.

Kangding was the last town before the plains. My hotel was pink and built of concrete; nearby was a crumbling stone wall and an abandoned lamasery, Chinese shops and a Tibetan market, crooked streets and wooden houses and a river that ran right through town. It was a wide, fast, and noisy river and it cooled the air around it with icy water from Tibet. The town was neat and tame but the river was wild.

That night a policeman came to my room. To go to Lhasa, he said, is forbidden. I've come from Lhasa, I said. I showed him my permit and my bus ticket to Chengdu. The Kangding police had been ordered to prevent foreigners from hitchhiking to Tibet but since I had already made the journey there was nothing they could do. He apologized for disturbing me and left.

The bus was due to leave at six thirty. Guided by the sound of rushing water, I followed the river through the dark and sleeping town to the station. The old red bus left on time. The route to Chengdu led through scruffy forests to a pass that was low only in comparison with those that went before. The one-lane dirt road was crowded and we had to stop quite often for trucks going the other way. On the other side of the pass was Luding. We stopped for breakfast there. We had our choice of three restaurants and innumerable outdoor stalls but I chose instead to walk up a hill to see the wide gray Dadu River. Three bridges spanned it side by side: a centuries-old wooden footbridge supported by nine iron chains, a newer one with black steel girders, and a larger bridge, even more modern, supported by wide concrete pylons. During the Long March, Mao's Red Army captured and crossed the footbridge; the other two had not yet been built. On either end of the wooden bridge were stone towers crowned by pagodas. Behind them were concrete office blocks.

Late that afternoon we reached Ya'an, where we were to spend the night. It was a large and busy town, with one very long street of shops and wooden houses and sidewalk cafés. Ramshackle half-timbered houses, their tile eaves sagging, teahouses crowded with farmers in Mao suits, the sound of people coughing and spitting in the street, a thousand things reminded me I was back in China again.

I missed Tibet, as I always miss those places to which I can never return. It was not the pure and perfect land of my dreams, but, as I should have learned long before, my dreams do not create the world.

For six years, the world had created my dreams. I did not travel to find myself, but to find my fellow man, to learn other ways of life and perhaps, as an added bonus, to improve my own. But Tibet had been an obsession.

I had been chasing an image of Tibet. The image had long since shattered, and it was Tibet itself that I now loved.

Rice fields and wooden houses, the road to Chengdu was flat and paved and easy. Just outside the city we crossed a railroad line and saw a locomotive scooting along. It was only a tiny engine, the kind used for shunting freight, but I heard gasps from the Tibetans on the bus. They had never seen a train before.

You could go by train from Chengdu to Hong Kong, and in a few days I would. After that, Pan Am to Japan and then the long flight over the pole and into a New York winter. But after the plateau, all else was anticlimax.

AFTERWORD

The world of the village seems timeless, but it is not immune to change. Deserts grow and forests are cut down. I left Mboma, the forest village in Zaire, in early 1979; since then, the world has lost between three and five hundred thousand square miles of rain forest—an area almost twice the size of Texas.

In 1984, drought and famine swept across Africa, turning much of the continent into a large-scale Karamoja. Meanwhile, birth rates soar, cities grow, and the modern world becomes ever larger. There is television now in New Guinea's Baliem Valley, and video game parlors in Ladakh. But modernization, for the most part, is confined to towns and cities, and most of the villages I described have, I suspect, changed very little, if at all, since I visited them.

There are exceptions. The Russian occupation of Afghanistan left no village untouched. The Russian army, a hundred thousand strong, invaded the country in the final days of 1979, and in the years of bitter fighting that followed four and a half million Afghans became refugees. Most of them settled in the tribal area of Pakistan's North-West Frontier. Today, over half a decade later, the Russians are still there, unable to subdue the poorly armed guerrilla bands who oppose them. The Afghans, as I had guessed they would, proved to be the toughest people on earth.

In Iran, the shah, whose throne had seemed unshakable when I visited Teheran in late 1978, was overthrown a few months later. He was replaced by the Ayatollah Khomeini, and the nation which had struck me as too flashy and modern became a Moslem theocracy.

China, too, is fast changing—in the opposite direction, moving from theocratic to flashy and modern. Or is it? Even the Chinese find it hard to tell. In 1982, disco dancing was strictly illegal. By 1985, it had apparently won Party approval, and some work units made disco lessons compulsory. The government, it seems, promotes development provided it can be controlled. But development can rarely if ever be controlled by the developers.

There have been forcible, and for the most part bloodless, changes of government in several of the countries I visited in Africa. Emperor Bokassa I, the Central African autocrat, was overthrown in 1979 with the aid of a thousand French paratroopers, and Bokassa's Central African Empire was renamed the Central African Republic. One year later, in Liberia, a small band of soldiers led by Sgt. Samuel Doe attacked the presidential palace and killed the president. So ended the long rule of the Americo-Liberians. For the first time in 150 years, the 97 percent of the population who were not descended from freed American slaves were given a voice in the government—though the voice was that of the new leader, President Samuel Doe.

On the last day of 1983, the army seized power in Nigeria. The country had been under military rule in early 1979, when I made my second trip to Kano, but a few months later elections were held and a civilian government took over. In the years that followed, the demand for oil declined, Nigeria's oil exports were halved, and economic boom gave way to recession. The soldiers blamed the civilians; they promised to manage the economy better. They didn't, and in August 1985, the new leaders were themselves overthrown in another coup.

In 1984, Sékou Touré of Guinea died; the revolution was over. A group of army officers seized control of the government and denounced Touré for systematic violations of human rights. The next year, another group of soldiers tried to overthrow the new government—and failed. Guinea's rulers announced that those responsible had been arrested and would be shot after a fair trial.

The next year, 1985, saw coups d'état in Uganda and the Sudan. Two years before, Gaafar Nimeiry, the Sudanese president, had imposed Islamic law upon the entire country, including the non-Moslem south. Nimeiry then divided the autonomous Southern Region into three provinces; the result was civil war. By 1985, well-organized guerrilla armies based in Ethiopia were attacking towns and army bases throughout the southern Sudan. Nimeiry's popularity waned in the north as well, and in April of 1985 a series of demonstrations and riots in Khartoum prompted the army to seize power. The war, however, still continues.

In Uganda, the UPC won the 1980 elections and Obote became president. Those few optimists left in the country hoped that some measure of stability would follow. It didn't. Most people felt the elections were rigged and one of the defeated candidates formed a guerrilla army to challenge Obote's rule.

Tens and possibly hundreds of thousands of innocent civilians died as government troops attacked real and imagined enemies. Obote was ousted in a military coup in July 1985, and replaced by a broadly based government that included some of his supporters and most of his opponents, but the fighting continued and in early 1986 the guerrilla army captured Kampala.

Coups and wars and mass starvation; the Third World presents a grim picture when viewed from afar. But I am sure that if only I could return to the villages, things would seem different, and most of the unpleasant happenings that inspire front-page headlines here would, in the quieter world of the village, be perceived as nothing more than tinny voices on the radio.

INDEX